STRUCTURED COMPUTER ORGANIZATION

SECOND EDITION

ANDREW S. TANENBAUM

Vrije Universiteit
Amsterdam, The Netherlands

PRENTICE-HALL, INC.

ENGLEWOOD CLIFFS, NEW JERSEY 07632

Library of Congress Cataloging in Publication Data

Tanenbaum, Andrew, S. (date)
   Structured Computer Organization

   Includes index.
     1. Electronic digital computers—Programming.
I. Title
QA76.6.T38 1984   001.64′2   83-2916
ISBN 0-13-854489-1

To Suzanne, Barbara, Marvin and the memory of Sweetie π

Production/editorial supervision: Nancy Milnamow
Manufacturing buyer: Gordon Osbourne

10 9 8 7 6 5

Printed in the United States of America

ISBN 0-13-854489-1

PRENTICE-HALL INTERNATIONAL, INC., *London*
PRENTICE-HALL OF AUSTRALIA PTY. LTD., *Sydney*
EDITORA PRENTICE-HALL DO BRASIL, LTDA., *Rio de Janeiro*
PRENTICE-HALL OF CANADA, LTD., *Toronto*
PRENTICE-HALL OF INDIA PRIVATE LTD., *New Delhi*
PRENTICE-HALL OF JAPAN, INC., *Tokyo*
PRENTICE-HALL OF SOUTHEAST ASIA PTE. LTD., *Singapore*
WHITEHALL BOOKS LTD., *Wellington, New Zealand*

CONTENTS

APPENDIXES

Karnough maps
Simulation program (usefulness)

PREFACE

The first edition of this book was based on the idea that a computer can be regarded as a hierarchy of levels, each one performing some well-defined function. This fundamental concept has proven its worth many times over in the intervening years, so it has been retained and even strengthed in this second edition. In the first edition, four levels—the microprogramming level, the conventional machine level, the operating system machine level, and the assembly language—were discussed in detail. In the second edition, all four are still treated, and a new level, the digital logic level, which is below the microprogramming level, has been added.

I have made this addition because the advent of inexpensive microcomputers has made some knowledge of computer hardware in general, and digital electronics in particular, much more important than it formerly was. In the past, the typical computer user got no closer to the machine than the counter where card decks were placed for input. The user did not need to know anything about computer hardware because the computer center had a large staff of experts who took care of such matters. In the future, many (probably most) users will have a computer on their desks at work and another in their living room at home. Furthermore, advances in VLSI technology are turning many programmers into chip designers, thus further blurring the distinction between hardware and software. Since the user has much more contact with the hardware under these circumstance, it is correspondingly more important to have at least some basic knowledge about how computers really work. The new material (Chapter 3) attempts to provide this background.

The addition of Chapter 3 is by no means the only change, however. In this edition I have placed more emphasis on smaller machines and less on larger ones, in keeping with the changes that are ocurring in the computer industry as a whole. In the first edition, the IBM 370, CDC Cyber, and DEC PDP-11 were used as running examples throughout the text. In the second edition, the Cyber has been dropped and replaced by two popular micros: the Zilog Z80 and the Motorola MC68000. The former is an 8-bit machine, whereas the latter is a 16/32-bit machine, depending on one's perspective. The 370 architecture is still extremely widespread, being used not only in the IBM 370 series itself, but also in the IBM 43xx and 303x machines, Amdahl computers, and others as well. Similarly, the PDP-11 is still very popular, so it too has been retained in the second edition.

Another important change is the use of Pascal to describe algorithms instead of PL/1. Pascal is not only much simpler and more elegant, but compilers for it are also available for a far greater range of machines than for PL/1.

Numerous sections of the book have been completely rewritten or brought up to date. To give an idea of the scope of the changes, of the 236 figures present in this edition, 132 were not present in the original one. A brief chapter-by-chapter rundown will give some idea of what has been modified.

Chapter 1 introduces the basic idea of a multilevel machine. It has stood up well and is substantially the same as it was before.

Chapter 2 now contains considerably more material about computer networks (both local and long-haul) and distributed systems than it did before. Other than some changes in the order of presentation, the rest of the chapter is largely intact.

Chapter 3 is completely new. It treats a level, the digital logic level, ignored in the first edition. It starts with the fundamental building blocks of all computers, the gates, proceeds through combinational circuits, memories, and buses, and winds up presenting a simple, but complete computer (Fig. 3-39) that even someone with no previous knowledge of electronics should be able to understand thoroughly after having read the chapter.

Chapter 4 (the microprogramming level) has been moved before the conventional machine level, so as to present the levels in a more logical order, from bottom to top. Except for a brief discussion of the IBM 370/125's microprogramming level, this chapter is also completely new. It is now based on a microarchitecture that is more realistic than its predecessor (it is loosely based on the AMD 2903 bit slice), yet it is still simple enough for beginners to understand. The rather long discussion of multiplication and division has been eliminated, and the PDP-11/60 has replaced the PDP-11/40 as a detailed example. The chapter begins with a brief review of Chap. 3, making it possible to omit Chap. 3 in a course and still be able to study Chap. 4.

Chapter 5 (the conventional machine level) contains considerable new material about the Z80 and 68000. To make room for it, the section on data structures has been dropped. Several people have pointed out that it did not really belong in a book on computer organization in the first place.

Chapter 6 (the operating system machine level) has several important changes. The most important of these is the addition of two new examples: the UNIX* operating system and CP/M†. They are both widely used, but quite different in almost

---

*UNIX is a trademark of Bell Laboratories.

†CP/M is a trademark of Digital Research, Inc.

every way. The last section, on job control languages, has been rewritten, with the CDC version being replaced by the UNIX shell.

Chapter 7 (the assembly language level) has been shortened by removing nearly all the material on searching and sorting. These properly belong in other courses and other books.

Chapter 8 (multilevel machines) has been heavily modified, reflecting, among other things, the reincarnation of UNCOL in recent years.

Chapter 9 (suggested readings and bibliography) has been rewritten from scratch to bring it up to date.

Appendices A (binary numbers) and B (floating-point numbers) are essentially the same, but Appendix C has been expanded and incorporated into Chapter 3.

One last change that is not visible, but nevertheless is of considerable importance, is the existence of a problem solutions manual. Several people have pointed out how useful it can be when using the book as a text for a course, so I have provided one. It can be obtained from Prentice-Hall. Many of the problems themselves are also new.

Again I have been fortunate in having expert assistance in preparing the manuscript. I especially want to thank Raphael Finkel for his extremely detailed reading of the manuscript. He made so many suggestions for improvement that it would take hours just to count, let alone mention, them, but using statistical techniques I estimate the number at 2600. My wife thanks him for trying to remove all my sexist assumptions (e.g., "he" for the programmer). Unfortunately, the English language lacks neuter third-person-singular pronouns for people, so the remaining occurrences of "he" should be read as "he or she."

Wiebren de Jonge went over part of the manuscript in his inimitable way, improving the contents, accuracy, style, grammar, spelling, and punctuation in many places, and generally keeping me on my toes, lest I incur his wrath. Numerous other people have also helped in ways large and small. I would especially like to single out Ed Keizer, Jim van Keulen, Jan Looyen, John van Meurs, Sape Mullender, Hans van Staveren, and Johan Stevenson for their suggestions. I am indebted to them all.

My students have served as generally enthusiastic guinea pigs. In particular, Sander Advocaat, Inge Bonninga, Nick de Bray, Wim de Schipper, Sjoerd Mullender, Sylvia van Egmond, Alexander van Gent, Peter van Leeuwen, Robbert van Renesse, and Martin Waage each earned one or more *kwartjes* for their help.

The second edition was prepared using the UNIX system's excellent text processing tools instead of the CDC Cyber. Having both lowercase and uppercase letters makes life an awful lot easier. The book was typeset by the Information Sciences Corporation using *troff*. I would like to thank Marc Nodell for his help in this regard.

Several companies have generously permitted me to adapt information from their copyrighted publications about their products as follows: Digital Equipment Corporation— *PDP-11 Processor Handbook*, and *PDP-11/60 Microprogramming Specification*; Digital Research—information about the internal workings of CP/M; IBM—*IBM System 370 Principles of Operation Manual* and engineering drawings for the IBM 3125 CPU; Motorola—information about the MC68000 taken from the user's manual; Texas Instruments—pin layouts from *The TTL Data Book for Design Engineers*; and Zilog—a description of the Z80 microprocessor taken from the data sheet. Any errors in the descriptions of these computers are my responsibility.

Finally, I once again want to thank Suzanne for her patience and *sinaasappels,* and Barbara and Marvin for executing a *sleep* primitive within an hour or so of the appointed time, thus giving me the opportunity to "play with the computer" every evening.

ANDREW S. TANENBAUM

1

INTRODUCTION

A digital computer is a machine that can solve problems for people by carrying out instructions given to it. A sequence of instructions describing how to perform a certain task is called a **program**. The electronic circuits of each computer can recognize and directly execute a limited set of simple instructions into which all its programs must be converted before they can be executed. These basic instructions are rarely much more complicated than:

Add 2 numbers.

Check a number to see if it is zero.

Move a piece of data from one part of the computer's memory to another.

Together, a computer's primitive instructions form a language in which it is possible for people to communicate with the computer. Such a language is called a **machine language**.

The people designing a new computer must decide what instructions to include in its machine language. Usually they try to make the primitive instructions as simple as possible, consistent with the computer's intended use and performance requirements, in order to reduce the complexity and cost of the electronics needed. Because most machine languages are so simple, it is difficult and tedious for people to use them.

This problem can be attacked in two principal ways: both involve designing a new set of instructions that is more convenient for people to use than the set of built-in machine instructions. Taken together, these new instructions also form a language, which we will call L2, just as the built-in machine instructions form a language, which we will call L1. The two approaches differ in the way programs written in L2 are executed by the computer, which, after all, can only execute programs written in its machine language, L1.

One method of executing a program written in L2 is first to replace each instruction in it by an equivalent sequence of instructions in L1. The resulting program consists entirely of L1 instructions. The computer then executes the new L1 program instead of the old L2 program. This technique is called **translation**.

The other technique is to write a program in L1 that takes programs in L2 as input data and carries them out by examining each instruction in turn and executing the equivalent sequence of L1 instructions directly. This technique does not require first generating a new program in L1. It is called **interpretation** and the program that carries it out is called an **interpreter**.

Translation and interpretation are similar. In both methods instructions in L2 are ultimately carried out by executing equivalent sequences of instructions in L1. The difference is that, in translation, the entire L2 program is first converted to an L1 program, the L2 program is thrown away, and then the new L1 program is executed. In interpretation, after each L2 instruction is examined and decoded, it is carried out immediately. No translated program is generated. Both methods are widely used.

Rather than thinking in terms of translation or interpretation, it is often more convenient to imagine the existence of a hypothetical computer or **virtual machine** whose machine language is L2. If such a machine could be constructed cheaply enough, there would be no need for having L1 or a machine that executed programs in L1 at all. People could simply write their programs in L2 and have the computer execute them directly. Even though the virtual machine whose language is L2 is too expensive to construct out of electronic circuits, people can still write programs for it. These programs can either be interpreted or translated by a program written in L1 that itself can be directly executed by the existing computer. In other words, people can write programs for virtual machines, just as though they really existed.

To make translation or interpretation practical, the languages L1 and L2 must not be "too" different. This constraint often means that L2, although better than L1, will still be far from ideal for most applications. That L2 should be far from ideal is perhaps discouraging in light of the original purpose for creating it—namely, to relieve the programmer of the burden of having to express algorithms in a language more suited to machines than people. However, the situation is far from hopeless.

The obvious approach is to invent still another set of instructions that is more people-oriented and less machine-oriented than those of L2. This third set also forms a language, which we will call L3. People can write programs in L3 just as though a virtual machine with L3 as its machine language really existed. Such programs can either be translated to L2 or executed by an interpreter written in L2.

The invention of a whole series of languages, each one more convenient than its predecessors, can go on indefinitely until a suitable one is finally achieved. Each language uses its predecessor as a basis, so we may view a computer using this technique as a series of **layers** or **levels**, one on top of another, as shown in Fig. 1-1. The bottom-most language or level is the simplest and the highest language or level is the most sophisticated.

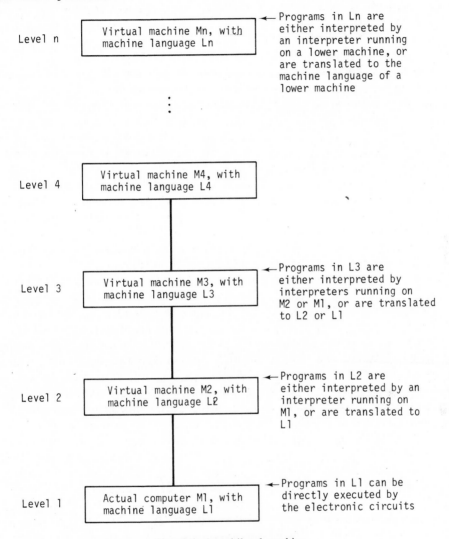

Fig. 1-1. A multilevel machine.

1.1. LANGUAGES, LEVELS, AND VIRTUAL MACHINES

There is an important relation between a language and a virtual machine. Each machine has some machine language, consisting of all the instructions that the machine can execute. In effect, a machine defines a language. Similarly, a language defines a machine—namely, the machine that can execute all programs written in the language. Of course, the machine defined by a certain language may be enormously complicated and expensive to construct directly out of electronic circuits but we can imagine it nevertheless. A machine with Ada*, Pascal, or COBOL as its machine language would be a complex beast indeed but it is certainly conceivable, and perhaps in a few years such a machine will be considered trivial to build.

A computer with n levels can be regarded as n different virtual machines, each with a different machine language. We will use the terms "level" and "virtual machine" interchangeably. Only programs written in language L1 can be directly carried out by the electronic circuits, without the need for intervening translation or interpretation. Programs written in L2, L3, ..., Ln must either be interpreted by an interpreter running on a lower level or translated to another language corresponding to a lower level.

A person whose job it is to write programs for the level n virtual machine need not be aware of the underlying interpreters and translators. The machine structure ensures that these programs will somehow be executed. It is of little interest whether they are carried out step by step by an interpreter which, in turn, is also carried out by another interpreter, or whether they are carried out directly by the electronics. The same result appears in both cases: the programs are executed.

Most programmers using an n-level machine are only interested in the top level, the one least resembling the machine language at the very bottom. However, people interested in understanding how a computer really works must study all the levels. People interested in designing new computers or designing new levels (i.e., new virtual machines) must also be familiar with levels other than the top one. The concepts and techniques of constructing machines as a series of levels and the details of some important levels themselves form the main subject of this book. The title *Structured Computer Organization* comes from the fact that viewing a computer as a hierarchy of levels provides a good structure or framework for understanding how computers are organized. Furthermore, designing a computer system as a series of levels helps to ensure that the resulting product will be well structured.

1.2. CONTEMPORARY MULTILEVEL MACHINES

Most modern computers consist of two or more levels. Six-level machines are not at all unusual, as shown in Fig. 1-2. Level 0, at the bottom, is the machine's true hardware. Its circuits carry out the machine language programs of level 1. For the sake of completeness, we should mention the existence of yet another level below our level 0. This level, not shown in Fig. 1-2, because it falls within the realm of electrical engineering (and is thus outside the scope of this book) is called the **device level**. At this level, the designer sees individual transistors, which are the lowest-level

---

*Ada is a trademark of the U.S. Department of Defense.

primitives for computer designers. (Of course, one can also ask how transistors work inside but that gets into solid-state physics.)

L6 Software packages

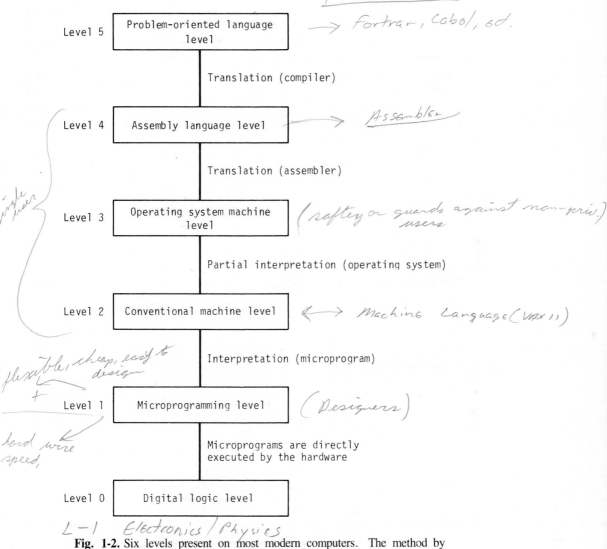

Level 5 — Problem-oriented language level → Fortran, Cobol, ed.

Translation (compiler)

Level 4 — Assembly language level → Assembler

Translation (assembler)

Level 3 — Operating system machine level (safety or guards against non-priv.) users

Partial interpretation (operating system)

Level 2 — Conventional machine level ← → Machine Language (VAX 11)

Interpretation (microprogram)

flexible, cheap, easy to design +

Level 1 — Microprogramming level (Designers)

hard wire speed,

Microprograms are directly executed by the hardware

Level 0 — Digital logic level

L−1 Electronics / Physics

Fig. 1-2. Six levels present on most modern computers. The method by which each level is supported is indicated below it, along with the name of the supporting program in parentheses.

At the lowest level that we will study, the **digital logic level**, the interesting objects are called **gates**. These gates are digital, unlike transistors, which are analog. Each gate has one or more digital inputs (signals representing 0 or 1) and computes as output some simple function of these inputs, such as AND or OR. Each gate is built up of at most a handful of transistors. We will examine the digital logic level in detail in Chap. 3. Although knowledge of the device level is something of a specialty, with the advent of microprocessors and microcomputers, more and more people are coming in contact with the digital logic level. For this reason we have included the latter in our model and devoted an entire chapter of the book to it.

The next level up is level 1, which is the true machine language level. In contrast to level 0, where there is no concept of a program as a sequence of instructions to be carried out, in level 1 there is definitely a program, called a **microprogram**, whose job it is to interpret the instructions of level 2. We will call level 1 the **microprogramming level**. Although it is true that no two computers have identical microprogramming levels, enough similarities exist to allow us to abstract out the essential features of the level and discuss it as though it were well defined. For example, few machines have more than 20 instructions at this level and most of these instructions involve moving data from one part of the machine to another, or making some simple tests.

Each level 1 machine has one or more microprograms that can run on it. Each microprogram implicitly defines a level 2 language (and a virtual machine, whose machine language is that language). These level 2 machines also have much in common. Even level 2 machines from different manufacturers have more similarities than differences. In this book we will call this level the **conventional machine level**, for lack of a generally agreed-upon name.

Every computer manufacturer publishes a manual for each of the computers it sells, entitled "Machine Language Reference Manual" or "Principles of Operation of the Western Wombat Model 100X Computer" or something similar. These manuals are really about the level 2 virtual machine, not the level 1 actual machine. When they describe the machine's instruction set, they are in fact describing the instructions carried out interpretively by the microprogram, not the hardware instructions themselves. If a computer manufacturer provided two interpreters for one of its machines, interpreting two different level 2 machine languages, it would need to provide two "machine language" reference manuals, one for each interpreter.

It should be mentioned that some computers, particularly older ones, do not have a microprogramming level. On these machines the conventional machine level instructions are carried out directly by the electronic circuits (level 0), without any level 1 intervening interpreter. As a result, level 1 and not level 2 is the conventional machine level. Nevertheless, we will continue to call the conventional machine level "level 2," despite these exceptions.

The third level is usually a hybrid level. Most of the instructions in its language are also in the level 2 language. (There is no reason why an instruction appearing at one level cannot be present at other levels as well.) In addition, there is a set of new instructions, a different memory organization, the ability to run two or more programs in parallel, and various other features. More variation exists between level 3 machines than between either level 1 machines or level 2 machines.

The new facilities added at level 3 are carried out by an interpreter running at level 2, which, historically, has been called an **operating system**. Those level 3 instructions identical to level 2's are carried out directly by the microprogram, not by the operating system. In other words, some of the level 3 instructions are interpreted by the operating system and some of the level 3 instructions are interpreted directly by the microprogram. This is what we mean by "hybrid." We will call this level the **operating system machine level**.

There is a fundamental break between levels 3 and 4. The lowest three levels are not designed for direct use by the average garden-variety programmer. They are intended primarily for running the interpreters and translators needed to support the higher levels. These interpreters and translators are written by people called **systems programmers** who specialize in designing and implementing new virtual machines. Levels 4 and above are intended for the applications programmer with a problem to solve.

Another change occurring at level 4 is the method by which the higher levels are supported. Levels 2 and 3 are always interpreted. Levels 4, 5, and above are usually, although not always, supported by translation.

Yet another difference between levels 1, 2, and 3, on the one hand, and levels 4, 5, and higher, on the other, is the nature of the language provided. The machine languages of levels 1, 2, and 3 are numeric. Programs in them consist of long series of numbers, which are fine for machines but bad for people. Starting at level 4, the languages contain words and abbreviations meaningful to people.

Level 4, the assembly language level, is really a symbolic form for one of the underlying languages. This level provides a method for people to write programs for levels 1, 2, and 3 in a form that is not as unpleasant as the virtual machine languages themselves. Programs in assembly language are first translated to level 1, 2, or 3 language and then interpreted by the appropriate virtual or actual machine. The program that performs the translation is called an **assembler**. Assembly language once was important but it is becoming less important as time goes on.

Level 5 consists of languages designed to be used by applications programmers with problems to solve. Such languages are called by many names, including **high-level languages** and **problem-oriented languages**. Literally hundreds of different ones exist. A few of the better known ones are Ada, ALGOL 68, APL, BASIC, C, COBOL, FORTRAN, LISP, Pascal, and PL/1. Programs written in these languages are generally translated to level 3 or level 4 by translators known as **compilers**, although occasionally they are interpreted instead.

Levels 6 and above consist of collections of programs designed to create machines specifically tailored to certain applications. They contain large amounts of information about that application. It is possible to imagine virtual machines intended for applications in administration, education, computer design, and so on. These levels are an area of current research.

In summary, the key thing to remember is that computers are designed as a series of levels, each one built on its predecessor. Each level represents a distinct abstraction, with different objects and operations present. By designing and analyzing computers in this fashion, we are temporarily able to suppress irrelevant details and thus reduce a complex subject to something easier to understand.

1.3. HISTORICAL EVOLUTION OF MULTILEVEL MACHINES

To provide some perspective on multilevel machines, we will briefly examine their historical development. The first digital computers, back in the 1940s, had only two levels: the conventional machine level, in which all the programming was done, and the digital logic level, which executed these programs. The digital logic level's circuits were complicated, difficult to understand and build, and unreliable.

In 1951, M. V. Wilkes, in England, suggested the idea of designing a three-level computer in order to drastically simplify the hardware. This machine was to have a built-in, unchangeable interpreter, whose function was to execute conventional machine language programs interpretively. Because the hardware would now only have to execute microprograms, which have a limited instruction repertoire, instead of conventional machine language programs, which have a much larger instruction repertoire, fewer electronic circuits would be needed. Because electronic circuits were made from vacuum tubes at the time, such simplification promised to reduce tube count and hence enhance reliability. A few of these three-level machines were constructed during the 1950s. More were constructed during the 1960s. By 1970 the idea of having the conventional machine level be interpreted by a microprogram, instead of directly by the electronics, was widespread.

Assemblers and compilers were developed during the 1950s to ease the programmer's task. In those days most computers were "open shop," which meant that the programmer had to operate the machine personally. Next to each machine was a sign-up sheet. A programmer wanting to run a program signed up for a block of time, say Wednesday morning 3 to 5 A.M. (many programmers liked to work when it was quiet in the machine room). When the time arrived, the programmer headed for the machine room with a deck of cards in one hand and a sharpened pencil in the other. Upon arriving in the computer room, he gently nudged the previous programmer toward the door and took over the computer.

If he wanted to run a FORTRAN program, he went through the following steps:

1. He went over to the cabinet where the program library was kept, took out the big green deck labeled FORTRAN compiler, put it in the card reader, and pushed the start button.

2. He put his FORTRAN program in the card reader and pushed the continue button. The program was read in.

3. When the computer stopped, he read his FORTRAN program in a second time. Although some compilers only required one pass over the input, many required two or more.

4. Finally, the translation neared completion. The programmer often became nervous near the end because if the compiler found an error in his program, he had to correct it and start all over again. If there were no errors, the compiler punched out the translated machine language program on cards.

5. The programmer then put the machine language program in the card reader along with the subroutine library deck and read them both in.

6. The program began executing. More often than not it did not work and unexpectedly stopped in the middle. Generally, the programmer fiddled with the console switches and looked at the console lights for a little while. If lucky, he figured out the problem, corrected the error, and went back to the cabinet containing the big green FORTRAN compiler to start all over again. If less fortunate, he made a printout of memory and took it home to study.

This procedure, with minor variations, was normal at many computer centers for years. It forced the programmers to learn how to operate the machine and to know what to do when it broke down, which was often. The machine was frequently idle while people were carrying cards around the room or scratching their heads trying to find out why their programs were not behaving the way they were supposed to.

Around 1960 people tried to reduce the amount of wasted time by automating the operator's job. A program called an **operating system** was kept in the computer at all times. The programmer provided certain control cards along with the program that were read and carried out by the operating system. Figure 1-3 shows a sample deck for one of the first widespread operating systems, FMS (FORTRAN Monitor System), on the IBM 709.

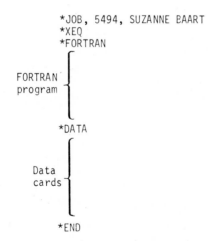

Fig. 1-3. A sample job for the FMS operating system.

The operating system read the ∗JOB card and used the information on it for accounting purposes. (The asterisk was used to identify control cards.) Later, it read the ∗FORTRAN card, which was an instruction to load the FORTRAN compiler from a magnetic tape. When the compiler finished, it returned control back to the operating system, which then read the *DATA card. This was an instruction to execute the translated program, using the cards following the *DATA card as the data.

Although the operating system was designed to automate the operator's job (hence the name), it was also the first step in the development of a new virtual machine. The *FORTRAN card could be viewed as a virtual "compile program" instruction. Similarly, the *DATA card could be regarded as a virtual "execute program" instruction. A level with only two instructions was not much of a level, but it was a start in that direction.

In subsequent years, operating systems became more and more sophisticated. New instructions, facilities, and features were added to the conventional machine level until it began to take on the appearance of a new level. Some of this new level's instructions were identical to the conventional machine level instructions, but others, particularly input/output instructions, were completely different. The new instructions were often known as "operating system macros" or "supervisor calls" and the terms still linger on.

Operating systems developed in other ways as well. The early ones read card decks and printed output on the line printer. This organization was known as a **batch system**. Usually there was a wait of several hours between the time a program was submitted and the time the results were ready.

In the early 1960s researchers at Dartmouth College, MIT, and elsewhere developed operating systems that allowed programmers to communicate directly with the computer. In these systems, remote terminals were connected to the central computer via telephone lines. A programmer could type in a program and get the results typed back almost immediately, right in his own office, or in his garage at home, or wherever he kept his terminal. These systems were, and still are, called **time-sharing systems**.

Our interest in operating systems is in those parts that interpret the instructions and features present in level 3 and not present in level 2 rather than in the time-sharing aspects. Although we will not emphasize it, you should keep in mind that operating systems do more than just interpret parts of level 3 programs.

1.4. HARDWARE, SOFTWARE, AND MULTILEVEL MACHINES

Programs written in a computer's machine language (level 1) can be directly executed by the computer's electronic circuits (level 0), without any intervening interpreters or translators. These electronic circuits, along with the memory and input/output devices, form the computer's **hardware**. Hardware consists of tangible objects—integrated circuits, printed circuit boards, cables, power supplies, memories, card readers, line printers, and terminals—rather than abstract ideas, algorithms, or instructions.

Software, in contrast, consists of **algorithms** (detailed instructions telling how to do something) and their computer representations—namely, programs. Programs can be represented on punched cards, magnetic tape, photographic film, and other media but the essence of software is the set of instructions that makes up the programs, not the physical media on which they are recorded.

An intermediate form between hardware and software is **firmware**, which consists of software embedded in electronic devices during their manufacture. Firmware is used when the programs are rarely or never expected to be changed, for example, in toys or appliances. Firmware is also used when the programs must not be lost when the power is off (e.g., when the doll's battery runs down). In many computers, the microprogram is in firmware.

A central theme of this book that will occur over and over again is:

Hardware and software are logically equivalent.

Any operation performed by software can also be built directly into the hardware and any instruction executed by the hardware can also be simulated in software. The decision to put certain functions in hardware and others in software is based on such factors as cost, speed, reliability, and frequency of expected changes. There are no hard and fast rules to the effect that X must go into the hardware and Y must be programmed explicitly. Designers with different goals may, and often do, make different decisions.

On the very first computers, the distinction between hardware and software was clear. The hardware carried out a few simple instructions, such as ADD and JUMP, and everything else was programmed explicitly. If a program needed to multiply two numbers, the programmer had to write his own multiplication procedure or borrow one from the library. As time progressed, it became obvious to hardware designers that certain operations were being performed frequently enough to justify constructing special hardware circuits to execute them directly (to make them faster). The result was a trend toward moving operations downward, to a lower level. What had previously been programmed explicitly at the conventional machine level was later found below it in the hardware.

With the coming of age of microprogramming and multilevel computers, the reverse trend also became apparent. On the earliest computers there was no doubt that the ADD instruction was carried out directly by the hardware. On a microprogrammed computer, the conventional machine level's ADD instruction was interpreted by a microprogram running at the bottom level and was carried out as a series of small steps: fetch the instruction, determine its type, locate the data to be added, fetch the data from memory, perform the addition, and store the result. This was an example of a function that moved upward, from the hardware level to the microprogram. Once again we emphasize: There are no hard and fast rules about what must be in hardware and what must be in software.

When developing a multilevel machine, the designers must decide what to put in each level. This is a generalization of the problem mentioned earlier, of deciding what to put in the hardware and what to put in the software, the hardware merely being the lowest level. It is interesting to note some of the features of some modern computers that are now performed by the hardware or microprogram but that originally were explicitly programmed at the conventional machine level. They include:

1. Instructions for integer multiplication and division.

2. Floating-point arithmetic instructions (see Appendix B).

3. Double-precision arithmetic instructions (arithmetic on numbers with twice as many significant figures as usual).

4. Instructions for calling and returning from procedures.

5. Instructions for speeding up looping.

6. Instructions for counting (adding 1 to a variable).

7. Instructions for handling character strings.

8. Features to speed up computations involving arrays (indexing and indirect addressing).

9. Features to permit programs to be moved in memory after they have started running (relocation facilities).

10. Clocks for timing programs.

11. Interrupt systems that signal the computer as soon as an input or output operation is completed.

12. The ability to stop one program and start another in a small number of instructions (process switching).

The point of this discussion is to show that the boundary between hardware and software is arbitrary and constantly changing. Today's software is tomorrow's hardware, and vice versa. Furthermore, the boundaries between the various levels are also fluid. From the programmer's point of view, how an instruction is actually implemented is unimportant (except perhaps for its speed). A person programming at the conventional machine level can use its multiply instruction as though it were a hardware instruction without having to worry about it, or even be aware of whether it really is a hardware instruction or not. One person's hardware is another person's software.

The fact that a programmer need not be aware of how the level he is using is implemented leads to the idea of structured machine design. A level is often called a virtual machine because the programmer thinks of it as a real physical machine, even though it does not actually exist. By structuring a machine as a series of levels, programmers working on level n need not be aware of all the messy details of the underlying levels. This structuring enormously simplifies the production of complex (virtual) machines.

1.5. PROCESSES

A fundamental concept in computer organization is the **process**. A **process** (sometimes called a **sequential process**) is basically a program in execution. It is an active entity, capable of causing events to happen. A process (i.e., a running program) may draw Chinese characters on the pen-and-ink plotter, or it may play chess with a human being sitting at a terminal, or it may regulate production in an automated factory, among innumerable many other activities. A process is in contrast to a program, which is a passive entity. A program lying on someone's desk cannot do anything by itself.

One can draw an analogy between a process and a living animal. Both are capable of doing things. Both are capable of changing their environment in certain ways. On the other hand, both a program and a dead animal or model of an animal are passive and cannot cause events to happen. This discussion is certainly not meant to suggest that a process is alive but merely to point out that the difference between a process and a program has a certain similarity to the difference between a living and a nonliving animal.

At any instant of time, a process is in a certain state. The state of a process tells how far the process is in its computation. It contains all the information needed to stop the process and then restart it later. The process state consists of (at least) the following information:

1. The program.

2. An indication of which instruction is to be executed next.

3. The values of all the program's variables and data.

4. The status and position of all input/output devices being used.

As a process progresses in time, its state changes. Different instructions in turn become "the next instruction to be executed." The variables take on successive values. Although it is also possible for a process to modify its program during execution, doing so is considered poor programming practice. We will assume that the program is not changed by the process. It is often convenient to group all the changeable parts of a process's state together under the heading **state vector**. We can now regard a process as consisting of two parts: a program (which does not change) and a state vector (which does change). The program consists of instructions for changing the state vector.

As an example of a process moving from one state to another, consider the Pascal program of Fig. 1-4.

The state of this program during execution can be characterized by three items of information: i, j, and the instruction to be executed next. The set of successive state vectors for a process executing this program is shown in Fig. 1-5.

A process passes through a time-ordered sequence of states. In order for a

```
program simple;
label 1, 2, 3, 4, 5, 6;
var i, j: integer;
begin
  1: i := 0;
  2: j := 1;
  3: i := i + 2;
  4: j := i + j;
  5: i := i * j + 4;
  6: j := i * i
end.
```

Fig. 1-4. A sample Pascal program.

program to be able to execute, that is, become a process, it must have a computer or **processor** to run on. The function of the processor is to advance the process from one state to the next. In other words, all a processor does is make changes in a process's state vector.

A process has two important properties:

1. The effect of a process is independent of its execution speed.

2. If a process executes again with the same data, it goes through precisely the same sequence of states and gives the same result.

These properties emphasize the sequential nature of a process. A sequential process is defined by *what* happens, not *how fast* it happens.

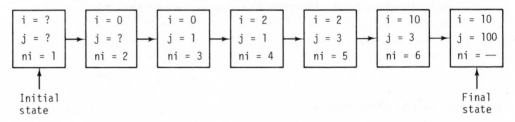

Fig. 1-5. The state vector for a process executing the program *simple* changes in time, where *ni* is the label of the next instruction to be executed.

The processor that moves a process from one state to the next state need not be a hardware machine. It could equally well be another process. When one process, P1, advances another process, P2, by changing P2's state vector, P1 is, in fact, interpreting P2's program. This means that P1 is a running interpreter.

The process concept provides another way of characterizing an interpreter. An interpreter is a program that, when executed, pushes the state vector of some process,

P, through the sequence of states required by P's program. This activity amounts to executing P and is precisely the same thing a hardware processor would do. Figure 1-6 shows a three-level computer on which level 3 is supported by an interpreter running on level 2, and on which level 2 is supported by an interpreter running at level 1. At each level are a program and a state vector. The hardware fetches instructions from P1 and changes SV1 appropriately after each instruction in order to execute P1. This level 1 process fetches the instructions of P2 and makes the corresponding changes to SV2 needed to execute P2. In other words, P1 interprets P2.

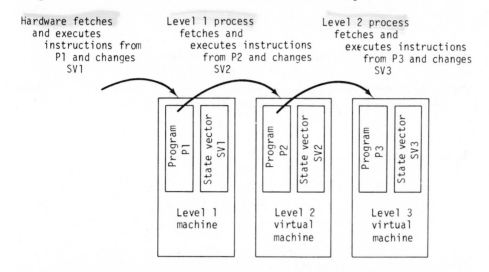

Fig. 1-6. A three-level system with interpreters supporting levels 2 and 3.

Just as P1 interprets P2, P2 interprets P3. The program P3 might either be yet another interpreter or an applications program that solved some problem for one of the computer center's clients. This three-level construction has three programs and three state vectors. At each level there is a "next instruction to be executed."

1.6. OUTLINE OF THIS BOOK

This book is about multilevel computers (which includes nearly all modern computers) and how they are organized. We will examine five levels in considerable detail—namely, the digital logic level, the microprogramming level, the conventional machine level, the operating system machine level, and the assembly language level. Some of the basic issues to be examined are:

1. The overall design of the level (and why it was designed that way).

2. The kinds of instructions available.

3. The kinds of data used.

4. The mechanisms available for altering the flow of control.

5. The memory organization and addressing.

6. The relationship between instruction set and memory organization.

7. The method by which the level is implemented.

These topics are sometimes loosely grouped together under the imprecise labels of **computer organization** or **computer architecture**. The two terms are widely used as synonyms.

We are primarily concerned with concepts rather than details or formal mathematics. For that reason, some of the examples given will be highly simplified, to emphasize the central ideas and not the details.

To provide some insight into how the ideas presented in this book can be, and are, applied in practice, we will examine four well-known computers in some detail. These four are the IBM 370, the DEC PDP-11, the Motorola 68000, and the Zilog Z80. These four have been chosen for several reasons. First, all are widely used and the reader is likely to have access to at least one of them. Second, each one has its own unique architecture, which provides a basis for comparison and encourages a "what are the alternatives?" attitude. Books dealing with only one machine often leave the reader with a "true machine design revealed" feeling, which is absurd in light of the many compromises and arbitrary decisions that designers are forced to make. You are encouraged to study these and all other computers with a critical eye and to try to understand why things are the way they are, as well as how they could have been done differently rather than simply accepting them as given.

It should be made clear from the beginning that this is not a book about how to program the IBM 370, PDP-11, Motorola 68000, or Zilog Z80. These machines will be used for illustrative purposes where appropriate but we make no pretense of being complete. Readers wishing a thorough introduction to one of them should consult the manufacturer's publications.

Chapter 2 is an introduction to the basic components of a computer—processors, memories, and input/output equipment—and the techniques used to interconnect them and transmit information among them. This material has relevance to more than one level and often to all levels of a multilevel system. It is intended to provide an overview of the system architecture.

Chapters 3, 4, 5, 6, and 7 each deal with one specific level shown in Fig. 1-2. Our treatment is bottom-up, because machines have traditionally been designed that way. The design of level k is largely determined by the properties of level $k - 1$, so it is hard to understand any level unless you already have a good grasp of the underlying level that motivated its design. Also, it is pedagogically sound to proceed from the simpler lower levels to the more complex higher levels rather than vice versa.

Chapter 3 is about the digital logic level, the machine's true hardware. It discusses what gates are and how they can be combined into useful circuits. Boolean algebra, a tool for analyzing digital circuits, is also introduced. The chapter culminates in the design for a simple, but complete, microcomputer system.

Chapter 4 introduces the concepts of microprogramming and the architecture of the microprogramming level, plus its relation to the conventional machine that it supports. A major part of the chapter consists of a simple example machine worked out in detail. The chapter also contains discussions of the microprogramming level of some real machines.

Chapter 5 discusses the conventional machine level, the one most computer vendors advertise as the machine language. First, we will examine the level in the abstract and then we look at our example machines in detail.

Chapter 6 covers some of the instructions, memory organization, and control mechanisms present at the operating system machine level.

Chapter 7 introduces the assembly language level. Because the assembly language level, unlike the levels below it, is usually implemented by translation instead of interpretation, the emphasis here is on the translation process rather than the details of any specific assembly languages. The related topics of macros (which is itself a translation technique) and linking (which is really the last phase of the translation process) are also covered.

Chapter 8 takes a more global view of multilevel machines and investigates a variety of topics related to multilevel machines as a whole.

Chapter 9 contains an annotated list of suggested readings, arranged by subject, and an alphabetical list of literature citations. It is the most important chapter in the book. Use it.

The appendices contain brief introductions to finite-precision arithmetic, including binary numbers, and floating-point numbers.

PROBLEMS

1. Explain each of the following terms in your own words.
   a. Translator.
   b. Interpreter.
   c. Virtual machine.
   d. State vector.

2. What is the difference between interpretation and translation?

3. Can the sequence of states through which a process passes be affected by the input data? Explain.

4. Is it conceivable for a compiler to generate output for level 1 instead of level 2? Discuss the pros and cons of this proposal.

5. Can you imagine any multilevel computer in which the device level and digital logic levels were not the lowest levels? Explain.

6. Show all the states that a process executing the following program would have during its execution, assuming that each line is a single, indivisible instruction.

program *diet* ;
label 1, 2, 3, 4, 5;
var *weight, reasonable: integer*;
begin
  1: *reasonable* := 160;
  2: *weight* := 200;
  3: **while** *weight* > *reasonable* **do**
  4:   *weight* := *weight* − 10
  5:
end.

7. If the programs P1 and P2 of Fig. 1-6 are identical, what is the relationship between the machine languages of virtual machines 2 and 3?

8. Consider a computer with identical interpreters at levels 1, 2, and 3. It takes an interpreter n instructions to fetch, examine, and execute one instruction. A level 1 instruction takes k nanoseconds to execute. How long does it take for an instruction at levels 2, 3, and 4?

9. Consider a multilevel computer in which all the levels are different. Each level has instructions that are m times as powerful as those of the level below it; that is, one level r instruction can do the work of m level $r - 1$ instructions. If a level 1 program requires k seconds to run, how long would equivalent programs take at levels 2, 3 and 4, assuming n level r instructions are required to interpret a single $r + 1$ instruction?

10. Some instructions at the operating system machine level are identical to conventional machine language instructions. These instructions are carried out directly by the microprogram rather than by the operating system. In light of your answer to the preceding problem, why do you think this is the case?

11. In what sense are hardware and software equivalent? Not equivalent?

12. How many levels of Fig. 1-2 does your computer have? Which level does your reference manual describe?

2

COMPUTER SYSTEMS ORGANIZATION

A digital computer consists of an interconnected system of processors, memories, and input/output devices. This chapter is an introduction to these three components and to the methods by which computers are interconnected. The purpose of the chapter is to provide an overview of how computers are organized, as background for the detailed examination of specific levels in the five succeeding chapters.

2.1. PROCESSORS

The organization of a simple computer is shown in Fig. 2-1. The **central processing unit** (CPU) is the "brain" of the computer. Its function is to execute programs stored in the main memory by fetching their instructions, examining them, and then executing them one after another. The CPU is composed of several distinct parts. The control unit is responsible for fetching instructions from main memory and determining their type. The arithmetic and logical unit performs operations such as addition and Boolean AND needed to carry out the instructions.

The CPU also contains a small, high-speed memory used to store temporary results and certain control information. This memory consists of a number of **registers**, each of which has a certain function. The most important register is the **program counter** (PC), which points to the next instruction to be executed. The name "program counter" is somewhat misleading because it has nothing to do with *counting* anything, but the term is universally used. Also important is the **instruction**

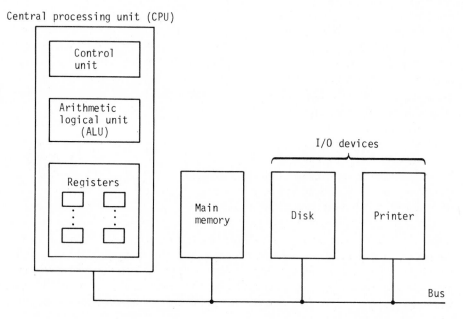

Fig. 2-1. The organization of a simple computer with one CPU and two I/O devices.

register (IR), which holds the instruction currently being executed. Most computers have other registers as well, some of them available to the level 2 and 3 programmers for storing intermediate results.

2.1.1. Instruction Execution

The CPU executes each instruction in a series of small steps:

1. Fetch the next instruction from memory into the instruction register.

2. Change the program counter so that it points to the following instruction.

3. Determine the type of instruction just fetched.

4. If the instruction uses data in memory, determine where they are.

5. Fetch the data, if any, into internal CPU registers.

6. Execute the instruction.

7. Store the results in the proper place.

8. Go to step 1 to begin executing the following instruction.

This description of how a CPU works closely resembles a program written in English. Figure 2-2 shows this informal program rewritten as a Pascal procedure. The very fact that it is possible to write a program that can imitate the function of a CPU shows that a program need not be executed by a "hardware" CPU consisting of a box full of electronics. Instead, a program can be carried out by having another program fetch, examine, and execute its instructions. A program (such as Fig. 2-2) that fetches, examines, and executes the instructions of another program is called an interpreter, as mentioned in Chap. 1.

This equivalence between hardware processors and interpreters has important implications for computer organization. After having specified the machine language, L, for a new computer, the design group can decide whether they want to build a hardware processor to execute programs in L directly or whether they want to write an interpreter instead. If they choose to write an interpreter, they must also provide some machine to run the interpreter.

Because an interpreter breaks the instructions of its target machine into small steps, the machine on which the interpreter runs can often be much simpler, and therefore less expensive than a hardware processor for the target machine would be. For economic as well as other reasons, programs at the conventional machine level of most modern computers are carried out by an interpreter running on a totally different and much more primitive level 1 machine that we have called the microprogramming level.

The collection of all instructions available to the programmer at a level is called the **instruction set** of that level. The number of instructions in the instruction set varies from machine to machine and from level to level. For the conventional machine level, for example, the size of the instruction set is typically in the range 20 to 300. A large instruction set is not necessarily better than a small one. In fact, the opposite tends to be true. A large instruction set often means that the instructions are not very general. Compilers for high-level languages, such as Ada, FORTRAN, Pascal, and PL/1, generally perform better on machines with small, well-chosen instruction sets than on machines with large, unwieldy ones.

Be sure you realize that the instruction set and organization of the microprogramming level is, in fact, the instruction set and organization of the hardware (CPU). The instruction set and organization of the conventional machine level, in contrast, is determined by the microprogram, and not by the hardware.

Not all processors are general-purpose CPUs. Computers often contain one or more processors with a specific function that requires a limited, specially designed instruction set. Such special-purpose processors are widely used to perform input/output. As an example, consider a graphics terminal, a device with a screen similar to that of a television set, on which the computer can display drawings of electrical circuits, blueprints of buildings, maps, graphs of data, and many other kinds of useful information.

A graphics terminal normally contains a highly specialized processor and a memory. The graphics processor may have instructions to plot points in several intensities and colors; draw solid, dotted, and dashed lines; display characters; and produce

```
type word = ... ;
     address = ... ;
     mem = array[0 .. 4095] of word ;
procedure interpreter (memory : mem ; ac : word ;  StartingAddress : address )
```

(This procedure interprets programs for a simple machine with 1
instruction per word . The memory consists of a sequence of words
numbered 0, 1, ..., 4095. The machine has a processor register
called the *ac*, used for arithmetic . The ADD instruction adds a
word to the *ac*, for example . The interpreter keeps running until
the run bit is turned off by a HALT instruction . The state of a
process running on this machine consists of memory, the program
counter, the run bit, and the *ac*. The initial state is passed
in via the parameters .)

```
var ProgramCounter, DataLocation : address ;
    InstrRegister, data : word ;
    DataNeeded : boolean ;
    InstrType : integer ;
    RunBit : 0..1;

begin
    ProgramCounter := StartingAddress ;
    RunBit := 1;
    while RunBit = 1 do
      begin
        {Fetch next instruction into the instruction register}
        InstrRegister := memory [ProgramCounter ];

        {Advance the program counter to point to the next instruction}
        ProgramCounter := ProgramCounter + 1;

        {Decode the instruction and record its type}
        DetermineInstrType (InstrRegister, InstrType );

        {Locate data used by instruction.}
        FindData (InstrType, InstrRegister, DataLocation, DataNeeded );

        {Fetch data from memory if need be}
        if DataNeeded then data := memory [DataLocation ];

        {Advance the process by executing the instruction}
        execute (InstrType, data, memory, ac, ProgramCounter, RunBit )
      end
end;
```

Fig. 2-2. An interpreter for a simple computer.

geometric figures such as squares, circles, and triangles. Such an instruction set is obviously different from what a general-purpose CPU needs.

2.1.2. Parallel Instruction Execution

Although early computers had a single CPU that executed instructions one at a time, certain more advanced designs increase the effective computing speed by allowing several instructions to be executed at the same time. The simplest method is to have two or more independent CPUs sharing a common memory, as shown in Fig. 2-3(a). Usually, each CPU has its own program to run, with no interaction between the CPUs. A computer with multiple processors that share a common main memory is called a **multiprocessor**.

Some problems require carrying out the same computation on many sets of data. For example, a weather prediction program might read hourly temperature measurements taken from 1000 weather stations and then compute the daily average at each station by performing exactly the same computation on each set of 24 hourly readings. For each station's data, it would load the first value into a register, then add the second value, then the third, and so on. Finally, it would divide the sum by 24. Because the same program is used on each data set, a processor with one program counter and one instruction decoder but n arithmetic units and n register sets could carry out computations on n data sets simultaneously.

This configuration, which is shown in Fig. 2-3(b), is sometimes called a single-instruction-stream multiple-data-stream processor, or an **array processor**. An example of this type of organization is the ILLIAC IV, designed at the University of Illinois and constructed by the Burroughs Corporation. The ILLIAC IV consists of four control units, each of which operates on 64 data sets simultaneously. The ILLIAC IV can perform four different computations at the same time, each computation being carried out on 64 sets of data, making a total of 256 calculations in parallel.

The CDC 6600 and some of the CDC Cybers use yet another form of parallel instruction execution. These machines have separate arithmetic units for addition, multiplication, division, and other operations, for a total of 10 separate units (including two of some units). Each one has a single control unit that fetches and decodes instructions. As soon as the type of an instruction is known, it is sent to the appropriate unit (e.g., multiplication), and the fetching and decoding of the next instruction begins, concurrently with the execution of the first instruction. A well-tuned program may have up to 10 instructions being executed simultaneously. This scheme only makes sense if the time needed to fetch and decode an instruction is small compared to the time needed to carry it out, which is the case on the CDC machines. Figure 2-3(c) illustrates this concept.

A related processor organization is the **pipeline** machine, shown in Fig. 2-3(d). In this design, each of the steps in executing an instruction (e.g., fetch instruction into the instruction register, determine instruction type, locate the data) has a separate unit within the CPU to perform it. When the machine starts, the initial instruction is fetched by the first unit. Then the second unit begins decoding the initial instruction

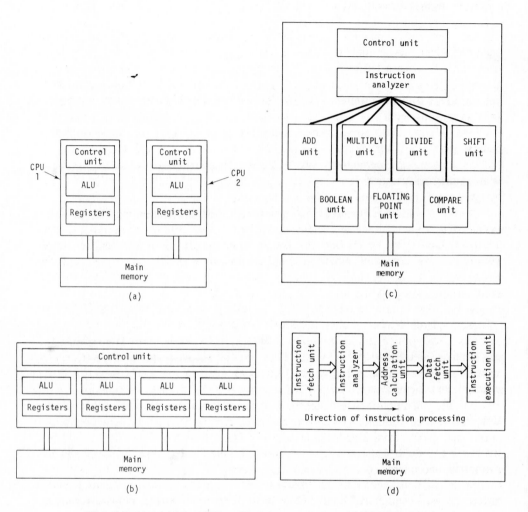

Fig. 2-3. (a) Multiple CPUs. (b) Array processor. (c) Multiple functional units. (d) Pipelining.

while the first unit is busy fetching the second instruction. A little later the third unit is busy examining the initial instruction to see if it needs data from memory, while the second unit is decoding the second instruction and the first unit is busy fetching the next instruction. The IBM 360/195, CDC STAR, and University of Manchester MU5 use sophisticated forms of pipelining.

A pipeline machine can be compared to an automobile assembly line: at each position along the (dis)assembly line the same function is performed on the stream of instructions that come by. The ones near the end of the pipeline are nearly completed; and the ones near the beginning of the pipeline are barely started.

2.1.3. Processor Classification

Judging by the amount of attention microprocessors and microcomputers get in both the popular press and in technical journals, one might assume that everybody knew what they were talking about. Nothing could be further from the truth. If you ask n different computer scientists to define "microprocessor" or "microcomputer" you are likely to get n different answers. To see how this has come about, we need a little ancient history.

Until about 1960, all computers were big: they occupied hundreds of square meters, gave off enough heat to warm whole buildings, cost a small fortune, and had staffs of dozens of programmers, operators, and technicians to keep them contented. With minor modifications, this model still holds for most computer centers. These behemoths are called **mainframes**.

Around 1961, DEC (Digital Equipment Corporation) introduced the PDP-1, which occupied less than 10 square meters, could barely heat its own room, cost a mere $120,000, and could be managed by two or three people. This was the first **minicomputer**. By 1965 minicomputers could be had for $20,000 and were selling like hotcakes. At this price a department of a company or university could buy its own computer, and thousands did.

In 1972 Intel introduced the first CPU contained on a single chip, the 4004. By current standards it was a primitive machine but it was an instant success and within a few years had given birth to an entire industry. Because the term "minicomputer" was already in use for something much larger, these single-chip CPUs were called **microprocessors**. A computer system using a microprocessor as CPU was obviously called a **microcomputer**.

At first, mainframes, minicomputers, and microcomputers had clear technical differences. For example, mainframes had word lengths of at least 32 bits, minicomputers had 16-bit word lengths, and microcomputers had 8-bit word lengths. Also, mainframes could handle large memories, minis could handle medium-sized memories, and micros could have only small memories.

As a result of enormous improvements in integrated circuit technology, these differences no longer exist. Some micros have 32-bit word lengths and can address as much memory as a mainframe. It is therefore meaningless to try to make a distinction based on technical characteristics.

What is still (more-or-less) meaningful is a distinction made on typical usage. A mainframe is a big machine operated by a computer center for the benefit of a large community of often unrelated users. When used for time sharing, a mainframe is normally equipped with many megabytes of main memory, thousands of megabytes of disk memory, and can support 100 or so interactive users.

A minicomputer is a smaller machine typically owned and operated by a single department or project. As a time-sharing machine, it might have at most a few megabytes of main memory, a few hundred megabytes of disk memory, and the ability to support a few dozen terminals. With the arrival of the "superminis" (e.g., DEC VAX 11/780) in the late 1970s, the distinction between a mini and a mainframe was blurred even more, because the superminis can be configured to have the computing power of small mainframes.

A microcomputer, in contrast, is typically not thought of as a computer at all, but is embedded inside a piece of equipment such as a car or television. In this configuration it has little memory and no disks. The confusion arises because it is possible to equip the larger microcomputers with a megabyte of memory and several disks, in effect using them as minicomputers or even small mainframes.

The conclusion of this discussion is that no conceptual difference exists between mainframes, minicomputers, and microcomputers. They are simply rough names for various overlapping parts of a continuous spectrum of processor power. Furthermore, future developments in technology are likely to make these names even less meaningful than they are already.

2.2. MEMORY

The **memory** is that part of the computer where programs and data are stored. Some computer scientists use the term **store** or **storage** rather than memory. Without a memory from which the processors can read and write information, there would be no stored-program digital computers as we know them.

2.2.1. Bits

The basic unit of memory is the binary digit, called a **bit**. A bit may contain a 0 or a 1. It is the simplest possible unit. (A device capable of storing only zeros could hardly form the basis of a memory system.)

People often say that computers use binary arithmetic because it is "efficient." What they mean (although they rarely realize it) is that digital information can be stored by distinguishing between different values of some continuous physical quantity, such as voltage or current. The more values that must be distinguished, the less separation between adjacent values, and the less reliable the memory. The binary number system requires only two values to be distinguished. Consequently, it is the most reliable method for encoding digital information. If you are unfamiliar with binary numbers, see Appendix A.

Some computers are advertised as having decimal rather than binary arithmetic. This trick is accomplished by using 4 bits to store one decimal digit. Four bits provide 16 combinations, used for the 10 digits 0 through 9, with six combinations not used. The number 1944 is shown below encoded in decimal and in pure binary, using 16 bits in each example:

decimal: 0001 1001 0100 0100   binary: 0000011110011000

Sixteen bits in the decimal format can store the numbers from 0 to 9999, giving only 10,000 combinations, whereas a 16-bit pure binary number can store 65536 different combinations. For this reason, people say that binary is more efficient.

However, consider what would happen if some brilliant young electrical engineer invented a highly reliable electronic device that could directly store the digits 0 to 9 by dividing the region from 0 to 10 volts into 10 parts. Four of these devices could store any decimal number from 0 to 9999. Four such devices would provide 10,000 combinations. They could also be used to store binary numbers, by only using 0 and 1, in which case, four of them could only store 16 combinations. With such devices, the decimal system is obviously more efficient.

2.2.2. Memory Addresses

Memories consist of a number of **cells** (or **locations**) each of which can store a piece of information. Each cell has a number, called its **address**, by which programs can refer to it. If a memory has n cells, they will have addresses 0 to $n - 1$. All cells in a memory contain the same number of bits. If a cell consists of k bits, it can hold any one of 2^k different bit combinations. Figure 2-4 shows three different organizations for a 96-bit memory. Note that adjacent cells have consecutive addresses (by definition).

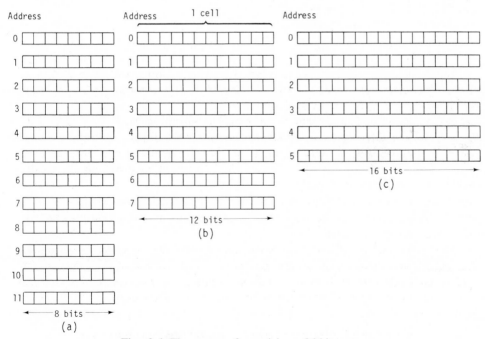

Fig. 2-4. Three ways of organizing a 96-bit memory.

Computers that use the binary number system (including octal and hexadecimal notation for binary numbers) also express memory addresses as binary numbers. If an address has m bits, the maximum number of cells directly addressable is 2^m. For example, an address used to reference the memory of Fig. 2-4(a) would need at least 4 bits in order to express all the numbers from 0 to 11. A 3-bit address would be sufficient for Fig. 2-4(b) and (c), however. The number of bits in the address is related to the maximum number of directly addressable cells in the memory and is independent of the number of bits per cell. A memory with 2^{12} cells of 8 bits each and a memory with 2^{12} cells of 60 bits each would each need 12-bit addresses.

The number of bits per cell for some computers that have been sold commercially follows.

Burroughs B1700:	1 bit per cell
IBM 370:	8 bits per cell
DEC PDP-8:	12 bits per cell
DEC ~~IBM 1130:~~	16 bits per cell
DEC PDP-15:	18 bits per cell
XDS 940:	24 bits per cell
Electrologica X8:	27 bits per cell
XDS Sigma 9:	32 bits per cell
Honeywell 6180:	36 bits per cell
CDC 3600:	48 bits per cell
CDC Cyber	60 bits per cell

On some machines the term **word** is used in place of cell. On other machines, especially machines with 8 bits per cell, the term **byte** is used instead of cell, and the term "word" is reserved for 2 bytes, or 4 bytes, depending on the machine. This situation, unfortunately, can lead to much confusion.

The significance of a cell is that it is the smallest addressable unit. Each cell has a unique address; consecutive cells have addresses differing by 1. The significance of a word is that, at level 2, registers that can hold one word are usually available for temporary storage. Furthermore, there are instructions to fetch and store an entire word in one operation. Following popular usage, we will use the term "word" rather than "cell" to indicate the basic information unit of memory, except where the distinction is significant. Keep in mind that the relation between words and cells depends on the machine in question.

The CPU communicates with the main memory using two registers—the **memory address register** (MAR) and the **memory buffer register** (MBR). When the CPU needs to read a word from memory, either an instruction or data, it loads the address of the word it wants into the MAR and sends a read signal to the memory. The memory begins operating; after one memory cycle it puts the desired word in the MBR, where the CPU can take it out and use it. To write a word into memory, the CPU puts the address to be stored into the MAR and the word to be stored in the MBR. Then it signals the memory to begin a store operation. Except on a few computers, the MAR and MBR are not directly accessible to level 2 programs, although they are always accessible to level 1 programs.

2.2.3. Metabits

Although main memory is used to store both programs and data, the processor generally has no way of telling whether a particular cell contains an instruction or data. A common programming error is for a program to jump into the data accidentally and try to execute them. Inadvertent attempts to execute data (or to multiply one machine instruction by another) could be caught immediately by the processor if each cell (or word) had an extra bit associated with it, containing a 0 for instructions and a 1 for data, as shown in Fig. 2-5.

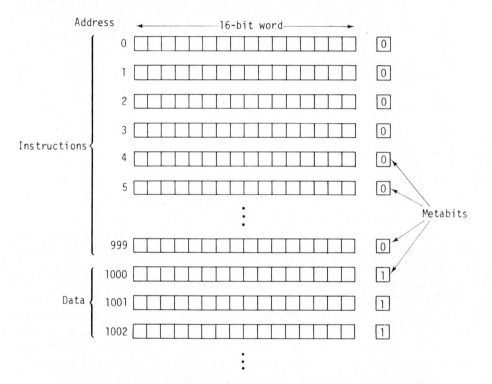

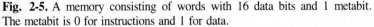

Fig. 2-5. A memory consisting of words with 16 data bits and 1 metabit. The metabit is 0 for instructions and 1 for data.

An extra bit associated with each cell (or word) used to indicate its contents is called a **metabit** or **tag bit**. The following method shows how the metabits of Fig. 2-5 could be used to detect some programming errors. When the processor fetches a cell (or word) from memory, either data or instruction, the metabit associated with that memory word would be loaded into a special metabit register within the processor. If the metabit register contains a 1 after an instruction fetch or a 0 after a data fetch, the processor would stop execution and print an error message.

Metabits can be used for other purposes as well. For example, if each cell (or word) had several metabits instead of just one, the metabits could not only distinguish between instructions and data but for the latter could also specify the type of data. Characters, integers, floating-point numbers (see Appendix B), decimal numbers, and other data types could each be uniquely indicated by the metabits. Doing so would eliminate the need for different instructions for integer addition, floating-point addition, and decimal addition. There could be a single addition instruction and the processor would examine the metabits to see which kind was needed. A further extension would provide metabits (a) to indicate integer arrays, floating-point arrays, and decimal arrays as well as other data types, and (b) to allow the addition instruction to operate on whole one-, two-, and three-dimensional arrays as well as individual numbers.

2.2.4. Secondary Memory

Because every word in main memory is directly accessible in a very short time, main memory is relatively expensive. Consequently, most computers have slower, cheaper, and usually much larger secondary memories as well. Secondary memories are used to hold large sets of data.

Magnetic Tapes

Historically, **magnetic tape** was the first kind of secondary memory. A computer tape drive is analogous to a home tape recorder: a 2400-ft-long tape is wound from the feed reel past a recording head to the take-up reel. By varying the current in the recording head, the computer can write information on the tape in the form of little magnetized spots.

Figure 2-6 shows how information is organized on a magnetic tape. On a computer with 8-bit bytes, each frame contains 1 byte, plus an extra, redundant bit, called a parity bit, to improve reliability. Typical recording density is 1600 frames (bytes) per inch (noted as 1600 bpi), which means that the distance between frames is less than 1/1000 of an inch. Other common densities are 800 bpi and 6250 bpi. After a tape drive has finished writing a record, it leaves a gap on the tape while slowing down. If the program writes short physical records on the tape, most of the space will be wasted in the gaps. By writing physical records that are much longer than the gap, the tape utilization can be kept high.

Magnetic tapes are sequential-access devices. If the tape is positioned at the beginning, to read physical record n, it is first necessary to read physical records 1 through $n - 1$, one at a time. If the information desired is near the end of the tape, the program will have to read almost the entire tape, which may take several minutes. Forcing a CPU that can execute millions of instructions per second to wait 200 sec while a tape is advanced is wasteful. Tapes are most appropriate when the data must be accessed sequentially.

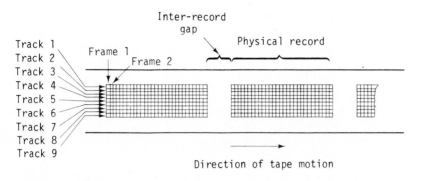

Fig. 2-6. Information on a magnetic tape is recorded as a sequence of rectangular bit matrices.

Magnetic Disks

A **disk** is a piece of metal, about the size and shape of an LP phonograph record, to which a magnetizable coating has been applied at the factory, generally on both sides. Information is recorded on a number of concentric circles, called **tracks** (see Fig. 2-7). Disks typically have a few hundred tracks per surface. Each drive has a movable head that can be moved closer to, or farther from, the center. The head is wide enough to read or write information from exactly one track. A disk drive often has several disks stacked vertically about an inch apart. In such a configuration the arm will have one head next to each surface, all of which move in and out together. The radial position of the heads (distance from the spindle) is called the **cylinder address**. A disk drive with n platters will have $2n$ surfaces, hence $2n$ tracks per cylinder.

Tracks are divided into **sectors**, normally between 10 and 100 sectors per track. A sector consists of a certain number of machine words, typically 32 to 256. On some disks the number of sectors per track can be set by the program.

Each disk drive has a small special-purpose computer associated with it, called the disk **controller**. The controller helps to transfer information between main memory and the disk. To specify a transfer, the program must provide the following information: the cylinder and surface, which together specify a unique track, the sector number where the information starts, the number of words to be transmitted, the main memory address where the information comes from or goes to, and whether information is to be read from the disk or written onto it. Disk transfers always start at the beginning of a sector, never in the middle. If a multisector transfer crosses a track boundary within a cylinder, no time is lost, but if it crosses a cylinder boundary, (at least) one rotation time is lost on account of the seek.

If the head happens to be positioned over the wrong cylinder, it must first be moved. This motion is called a **seek**. A seek typically takes 5 msec between adjacent tracks and 50 msec to go from the innermost cylinder to the outermost cylinder.

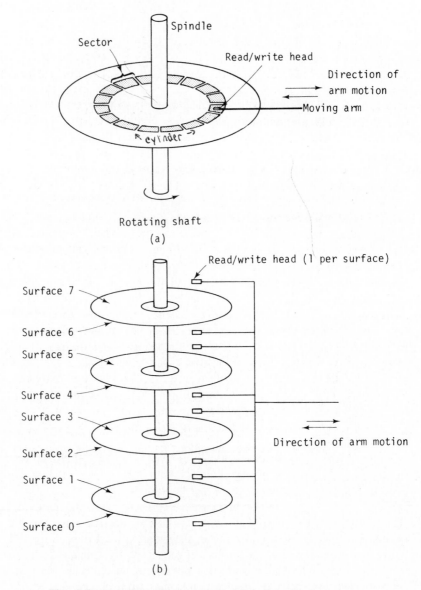

Fig. 2-7. (a) A disk with one platter. (b) A disk with four platters.

Once the head is positioned properly, the controller must wait until the first sector has rotated under the head before beginning the transfer. The time wasted waiting for the right sector varies from 0, if the program is lucky, to the complete rotation time if it just missed. This waiting time is called the **rotational latency**. Most disks rotate at 3600 rotations/min, giving a maximum latency of 16.67 msec. The total access time is the seek time plus the rotational latency. The information is transferred at a rate of one track per rotation period.

Some disk drives are constructed so that the disks themselves can be removed and brought to another computer, or stored, just like a tape. On larger machines, removable disk packs (storage modules) typically have capacities in the range 40 megabytes to several hundred megabytes. On microcomputers, however, the most common removable disks are the **floppy disks**, so called because they are physically flexible. A floppy disk looks like a 45-rpm record encased in a square jacket and can hold anywhere from a few tenths of a megabyte to several megabytes.

Some microcomputers also use hard (i.e., nonflexible) **winchester** disks, with capacities in the tens of megabytes. Larger winchester disks, with capacities up to about 1000 megabytes or more are also available for minis and mainframes. Winchester disks are characterized by having hermetically sealed disk packs, with each pack having a head assembly inside it. This arrangement is more expensive than the open storage module packs, because each pack has a built-in head assembly, but it is also better protected against dust, hence more reliable. On the least expensive winchester drives, the packs are not removable; on the more expensive ones they sometimes are.

Magnetic Drums

A variation on the disk is the **drum**, a cylinder on which information can be recorded magnetically (see Fig. 2-8). Along the length of the drum are many fixed read/write heads. Each head can read or write one track. The tracks are again divided into sectors. Because the heads do not move, there is no seek time. Furthermore, several heads may be reading or writing in parallel. Drums have a smaller capacity than disks but access is much faster because there is no seek time. Some drums have two or more sets of heads, spaced uniformly around the circumference of the drum. With two sets of heads, a given sector will always appear under one set of heads or the other within at most one-half of the rotation period. **Fixed-head disks** are logically similar to drums in that the heads do not move but have the physical appearance of a disk. Do not confuse fixed-head disks with "fixed disks," which are merely disks whose recording medium cannot be removed from the drive. Fixed disks are often combined with removable ones, the fixed disk for normal use and the removable one for making backups. Drums are never combined with anything else in one device.

Optical Memories

In recent years, optical (as opposed to magnetic) memories have become available. They have much higher recording densities than conventional magnetic media. For example, a strip of ordinary 35-mm black-and-white film 3 ft long can hold more information than a 2400-ft magnetic tape.

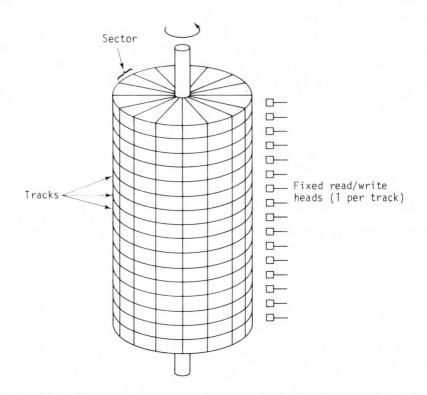

Fig. 2-8. A drum.

An especially interesting optical memory is the **video disk**. Although these disks were originally developed for recording television programs, they can be put to more esthetic use as computer storage devices. The disks are inherently digital, with the information recorded as a sequence of pits burned into the surface by an electron beam or laser. Television has a bandwidth of 6 MHz, so a 1-hour disk has a capacity of about 20 gigabits, depending on the recording details. Not only are video disks huge but both the drives and the disks themselves are dirt cheap compared to magnetic disks of comparable performance. One characteristic, however, that limits their application is that once a video disk has been written, it cannot be erased as a magnetic disk can be.

2.3. INPUT/OUTPUT

Before a computer can get to work solving a problem, it must be given the program, plus the data if there are any. After it has found the solution, the computer must communicate this solution to the human beings who posed the problem in the first place. The topic of getting information into and out of computers is called input/output, or usually just **I/O**.

Not all input comes from people and not all output is intended for people. A computer-operated solar telescope may get its input data directly from instruments observing the sun. A computer controlling an automated chemical plant may direct its output to machines throughout the plant that regulate the chemicals being produced.

2.3.1. I/O Devices

Hundreds of kinds of I/O devices are available today and the number is growing rapidly. A few of the more common ones are listed below.

Cathode ray tube (CRT) terminals

Modified electric typewriters (teletypewriters)

Card readers

Card punches

High-speed line printers

Optical readers that read printed matter, such as books

Mark sensors that can read cards marked with a special pencil

Pen and ink plotters that draw graphs

Paper tape readers

Paper tape punches

Magnetic ink readers that read bank checks

Experimental equipment such as cyclotrons or telescopes

Rats and other laboratory animals used in psychology experiments

2.3.2. I/O Processors

Some I/O devices can transmit a large amount of data in a short time. If the CPU had to process every character separately, much CPU time would be wasted. To avoid tying up the CPU for long periods of time on I/O, most medium-size and large computers have one or more specialized, low-cost I/O processors. Because the I/O is performed by these special processors, the CPU is available to spend most of its time on more difficult computations. The I/O processors can run in parallel with the CPU. In other words, while the CPU is busy computing, the I/O processors can be doing I/O.

2.3.3. Character Codes

Each computer has a set of characters that it can input and output. As a bare minimum, this set includes the 26 capital letters, the 10 digits 0 through 9, and a few punctuation marks, such as space, period, minus sign, comma, and carriage return. More sophisticated character sets include both capital letters and small letters, the 10 digits, a wide assortment of punctuation marks, a collection of special characters useful in mathematics and business, and sometimes even Greek letters.

In order to transfer these characters into the computer, each one is assigned a number: for example, a = 1, b = 2, ..., z = 26, + = 27, − = 28. The mapping of characters onto integers is called a **character code**. Present-day computers use either a 6-, 7-, 8- or 9-bit code. A 6-bit code allows only $2^6 = 64$ characters—namely, 26 letters, 10 digits, and 28 other characters, mostly punctuation marks and mathematical symbols.

For many applications 64 characters are not enough, in which case a 7- or 8-bit character code must be used. A 7-bit character code allows up to 128 characters. One widely used 7-bit code is called ASCII (American Standard Code for Information Interchange). Figure 2-9 shows the ASCII code. Codes 1 to 37 (octal) are control characters and do not print. The most widely used 8-bit character code is the IBM EBCDIC code.

2.3.4. Error-Correcting Codes

Computers, like human beings, are inclined to make errors occasionally. In particular, CPUs and main memory do not have any moving parts and thus are highly reliable but I/O devices usually involve physical motion and are consequently less reliable. Errors can be caused by specks of dust on the reading heads of a paper tape reader, card reader, magnetic tape drive, or disk. They can also be caused by attempting to read old, dirty or warped cards, not to mention cards that have been bent, folded, spindled, or mutilated (unintentionally or otherwise). Data transmitted over a telephone line may be received incorrectly if the line is noisy. Electrical power surges can cause errors. In short, when characters or other data must be input, output, or transmitted from one place to another, errors can occur. In this section we will investigate character codes that allow errors to be detected, and in some cases, even corrected.

A simple but widely used method for detecting single errors, that is, one bit changed from a 0 to a 1 or a 1 to a 0, is to add a **parity bit** to each character. In an odd-parity code, the parity bit is chosen so that the number of 1 bits in the character, including the parity bit, is an odd number. In an even-parity code, the parity bit is chosen so that the number of 1s in the character, including the parity bit, is an even number. Figure 2-10 illustrates the creation of an 8-bit even-parity code from 7-bit ASCII characters. If one bit is changed during transmission, the number of 1s in the received character will have the wrong parity, and the receiver will know an error has occurred.

Control characters

0	NUL	Null	20	DLE	Data link escape
1	SOH	Start of heading	21	DC1	Device control 1
2	STX	Start of text	22	DC2	Device control 2
3	ETX	End of text	23	DC3	Device control 3
4	EOT	End of transmission	24	DC4	Device control 4
5	ENQ	Enquiry	25	NAK	Negative acknowledge
6	ACK	Acknowledge	26	SYN	Synchronous idle
7	BEL	Bell	27	ETB	End of transmission block
10	BS	Backspace	30	CAN	Cancel
11	HT	Horizontal tab	31	EM	End of medium
12	LF	Line feed	32	SUB	Substitute
13	VT	Vertical tab	33	ESC	Escape
14	FF	Form feed	34	FS	File separator
15	CR	Carriage return	35	GS	Group separator
16	SO	Shift out	36	RS	Record separator
17	SI	Shift in	37	US	Unit separator

40	(Space)	60	0	100	@	120	P	140	`	160	p
41	!	61	1	101	A	121	Q	141	a	161	q
42	"	62	2	102	B	122	R	142	b	162	r
43	#	63	3	103	C	123	S	143	c	163	s
44	$	64	4	104	D	124	T	144	d	164	t
45	%	65	5	105	E	125	U	145	e	165	u
46	&	66	6	106	F	126	V	146	f	166	v
47	'	67	7	107	G	127	W	147	g	167	w
50	(	70	8	110	H	130	X	150	h	170	x
51	)	71	9	111	I	131	Y	151	i	171	y
52	*	72	:	112	J	132	Z	152	j	172	z
53	+	73	;	113	K	133	[	153	k	173	{
54	,	74	<	114	L	134	\	154	l	174	|
55	-	75	=	115	M	135	]	155	m	175	}
56	.	76	>	116	N	136	^	156	n	176	~
57	/	77	?	117	O	137	_	157	o	177	(Delete)

Fig. 2-9. The ASCII character code (octal).

A method for not only detecting errors but for correcting them as well was devised by Richard Hamming (1950) and is known as a **Hamming code**. In a Hamming code, k parity bits are added to an n-bit character, forming a new character of length $n + k$ bits. The bits are numbered starting at 1, not 0, with bit 1 the leftmost (high-order) bit. All bits whose bit number is a power of 2 are parity bits; the rest are used for data. For a 7-bit ASCII character, 4 parity bits are added. Bits 1, 2, 4, and 8 are parity bits, and bits 3, 5, 6, 7, 9, 10, and 11 are the 7 data bits. A Hamming code can be used on characters or messages of any length, although we will illustrate its use with 7-bit ASCII characters (and even parity).

Each parity bit checks specific bit positions; the parity bit is set so that the total

Bit position

P	2^6	2^5	2^4	2^3	2^2	2^1	2^0		
1	1	1	0	0	0	0	1	a	(4 1's)
1	1	1	0	0	0	1	0	b	(4 1's)
0	1	1	0	0	0	1	1	c	(4 1's)
1	1	1	1	1	0	1	0	z	(6 1's)
0	1	0	0	0	0	0	1	A	(2 1's)

Parity bit   7 bit ASCII character code   Character

Fig. 2-10. A parity bit can be added to a 7-bit ASCII character to ensure that every character contains an even number of 1s.

number of 1s in the checked positions is even. The bit positions checked by the parity bits are:

Bit 1 checks bits 1, 3, 5, 7, 9, 11.

Bit 2 checks bits 2, 3, 6, 7, 10, 11.

Bit 4 checks bits 4, 5, 6, 7.

Bit 8 checks bits 8, 9, 10, 11.

In general, bit n is checked by those bits b_1, b_2, $\cdots$, b_j such that $b_1 + b_2 + \cdots + b_j = n$. For example, bit 5 is checked by bits 1 and 4 because $1 + 4 = 5$. Bit 6 is checked by bits 2 and 4 because $2 + 4 = 6$. Figure 2-11 shows construction of a Hamming code for the character "b."

The ASCII character "b" is represented by the binary number 1100010. The Hamming code for b in binary is 00111001010. Consider what would happen if the leftmost bit were changed during transmission. The received character would be 10111001010 instead of 00111001010. The 4 parity bits will be checked by the receiver, with the following results:

Parity bit 1 incorrect (bits 1, 3, 5, 7, 9, and 11 contain three 1s).

Parity bit 2 correct (bits 2, 3, 6, 7, 10, and 11 contain two 1s).

Parity bit 4 correct (bits 4, 5, 6, and 7 contain two 1s).

Parity bit 8 correct (bits 8, 9, 10, and 11 contain two 1s).

The total number of 1s in bits 1, 3, 5, 7, 9, and 11 should be an even number because even parity is being used. The incorrect bit must be one of the bits checked by parity bit 1—namely, bit 1, 3, 5, 7, 9, or 11. Because parity bit 2 is correct, we know that bits 2, 3, 6, 7, 10, and 11 are correct, so the error was not in bits 3, 7, or 11. That leaves 1, 5, and 9. Parity bit 4 is correct, meaning that bits 4, 5, 6, and 7 contain no errors. That narrows the choice down to 1 or 9. Parity bit 8 is also correct, so bit 9 is correct. Consequently, the incorrect bit must be bit 1. Because it was received as a 1, it must have been transmitted as a 0. In this manner, errors can be corrected.

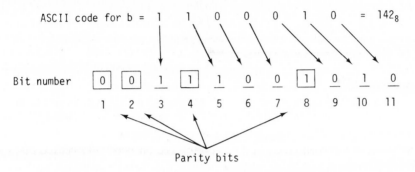

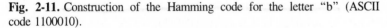

Fig. 2-11. Construction of the Hamming code for the letter "b" (ASCII code 1100010).

A simple method for finding the incorrect bit is first to compute all the parity bits in the received character. If all are correct, there was no error (or more than one). Then add up all the incorrect parity bits, counting 1 for bit 1, 2 for bit 2, 4 for bit 4, and so on. The resulting sum is the position of the incorrect bit. For example, if parity bits 1 and 8 are correct but 2 and 4 are incorrect, bit 6 (2 + 4) has been inverted.

We will now briefly consider the problem of multiple errors. A character code is a list of all the characters producible by a certain device and their mappings onto the binary integers of a certain number of bits. Consider a pair of characters taken from some character code. For this and every other pair of characters, one can ask the question: How many bits must be changed in character 1 to produce character 2? If the two characters have the same bit pattern except for one bit, then only one bit must be changed in order to produce one from the other. If one consists of n ones and the other consists of n zeros, n bits must be changed to produce one from the other. The minimum number of changes that can produce one character from the other is called the **Hamming distance** between the characters. A character code in which at least one pair of characters has a distance d, but no pair has a distance less than d, is called a distance d code.

If every possible combination of n bits is used in a certain code, it is a distance 1 code, because changing one bit in any character will still produce a valid character. A code that uses n data bits and 1 parity bit to encode 2^n characters is a distance 2 code, because making one change to any character will give a parity error (i.e., a combination that is not a valid character), but making a second change will restore the correct parity. In general, a distance d code will detect up to $d - 1$ errors, because, by definition, it takes at least d changes to produce a valid character from another valid character. It is not possible to change a valid character into another valid character with only $d - 1$ changes.

2.3.5. Frequency-Dependent Codes

When large amounts of text are stored or transmitted, it frequently pays to look for ways to compress the text into a smaller number of bits. The time needed to transmit a certain message is proportional to the number of bits in the message. By compacting the data to be sent, transmission times can be reduced. Furthermore, compacted data require fewer bits to store.

One way of doing so is to eliminate the restriction that all character codes must be the same length. If the codes for common letters such as "e" and "t" were shorter than the codes for rare letters such as "q" and "x," the total number of bits needed to store or transmit the text would be decreased. Such a coding scheme is called a frequency-dependent code or **Huffman code** (Huffman, 1952).

This method can only be used if the probability of occurrence of each character is known at the time the code is designed. A code based on the probabilities for English text may not be optimum for Pascal programs and will be far from optimum for transmitting messages in Hungarian or Polish. Figure 2-12 gives a frequency distribution for English text.

A	6.22	J	0.06		S	5.81
B	1.32	K	0.31		T	7.68
C	3.11	L	3.07		U	2.27
D	2.97	M	2.48		V	0.70
E	10.53	N	5.73		W	1.13
F	1.68	O	6.06		X	0.25
G	1.65	P	1.89		Y	1.07
H	3.63	Q	0.10		Z	0.06
I	6.14	R	5.87	space	18.21

Fig. 2-12. Percent distribution of letters and space for English text. Sample based on the first edition of this book (669,701 characters).

As an example, we will construct a Huffman code for the digits 0, 1, 2, ..., 9, based on the following probabilities.

Digit	0	1	2	3	4	5	6	7	8	9
Frequency	.20	.25	.15	.08	.07	.06	.05	.05	.05	.04

It should be emphasized that in order to use this encoding method for a particular application, the a priori frequencies of use for each character must be known. The code to be developed as an example is appropriate only for those transmissions where 0s represent about 20% of the characters, 1s 25%, and so on.

The first step in constructing the code is to write down the probability of each character under the character, as above. The order in which the characters are listed is unimportant and may be changed during the construction. Next, the two smallest probabilities are found and a new probability equal to the sum of the two smallest ones is added to the table. The two smallest probabilities are then marked with an asterisk so they will not be used again, and lines are drawn between the old and new ones. This process is shown in Fig. 2-13(a).

The process of finding the two smallest unmarked probabilities and creating a new one is then repeated. In Fig. 2-13(b), .05 and .05 are the two smallest. In Fig. 2-13(c), .06 and .07 are the two smallest. In Fig. 2-13(d), .08 and .09 are the two smallest. The fact that .08 is one of the original probabilities and .09 was generated from .04 and .05 is unimportant. In this step, .08 and .09 makes .17.

Figure 2-13(e) shows the complete tree built up by repetition of this process until only one unmarked probability, whose value is 1.00, remains. The characters have been rearranged for readability. To derive the code for a character, start at the root of the tree (1.00) and follow the path to the character, writing down a 0 for every left branch taken and a 1 for every right branch. For example, to get from the root to the character 6, first go left to .43 (i.e., do not go right to .57) and write down 0. Then go right to .23 and write down a 1, giving 01 so far. Then go right again, giving 011. Finally, go left, giving 0110. The complete code is shown in Fig. 2-13(f).

The shortest codes, 00 and 10, are assigned to the two most common characters, whereas the two longest codes are assigned to relatively infrequently occurring characters. This situation, of course, is to be contrasted with the one where each character is assigned a 4-bit code.

Characters 0, 1, and 2 together account for 60% of the characters to be transmitted and all three are shorter than 4 bits. If this character code is used for encoding numbers having the preceding distribution, 45% of the characters will require 2 bits, 15% will require 3 bits, 31% will require 4 bits, and 9% will require 5 bits. This averages to 3.04 bits per character. A list of 1,000,000 numbers would require only 3,040,000 bits using this code, whereas 4,000,000 would be needed using a 4-bit code.

The character code generated by this algorithm is not unique. By interchanging the positions of 8 and 9 in Fig. 2-13(e), for example, we get 11111 for 8 and 11110 for 9, instead of the other way around. Furthermore, replacing all the 1s by 0s, and vice versa, also produces a new code. However, none of these transformations affects the information density of the code, because the only thing that matters is how many bits each character is assigned, not the particular value of the code.

The decoding process for a Huffman-coded message received one bit at a time consists of examining the first bit to see if it is a valid code. If it is not, the first 2 bits are examined to see if they constitute a valid code. If not, the first 3 bits are checked, and so on. Eventually, a character is recognized and the process is repeated, beginning with the first bit following the character.

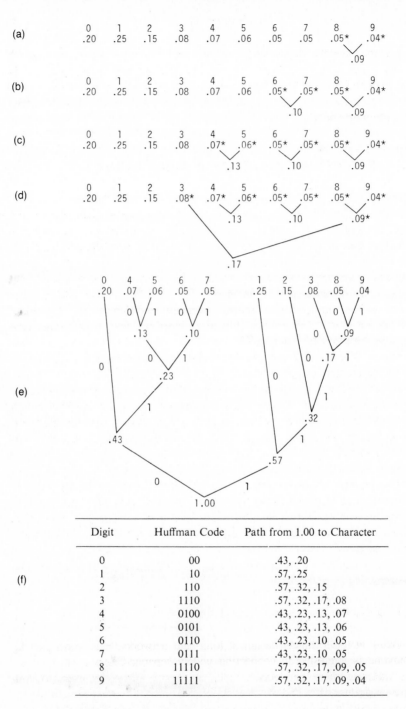

Fig. 2-13. (a)-(d) Construction of a Huffman code for the digits 0 to 9 based on the a priori relative frequencies given in the text. (e) The final Huffman tree. (f) The Huffman code.

42

Huffman codes have the disadvantage of being especially sensitive to error. If one bit is received wrong, the receiving program will lose track of the character boundaries and become hopelessly lost. To improve the reliability, the Huffman-coded message could be divided into groups of n bits, with each group of n bits then encoded in a Hamming code.

2.4. COMPUTER NETWORKS AND DISTRIBUTED SYSTEMS

Many years ago, a computer consisted of a single machine built up from the components discussed earlier: processors, memories, and I/O devices. Nowadays many computers are interconnected to form networks and distributed systems. In the remainder of this chapter we will look at various aspects of these decentralized systems.

Networks and distributed systems can be roughly classified by two independent parameters: physical distance and coherence. The first parameter distinguishes between systems whose computers are far apart, typically in different cities, and those whose computers are close together, typically in a single building. The former type are known as **long-haul** systems and have a moderate (e.g., 2.4 to 64 kbps) data rate between computers. The latter type are known as **local** systems and have a high (e.g., 1 to 10 Mbps) data rate between computers.

The coherence parameter distinguishes systems that attempt to act like a single coherent entity to their users from those that simply provide communication among otherwise independent computers. We will call a coherent system a **distributed system** and a collection of independent computers a **computer network**. Thus the difference between a distributed system and a network is how the software is organized, not what communication channels are available or how fast they are. If the users are unaware of the individual computers and can log onto the system as a whole, the system is a distributed one. If, however, they are aware of the component computers (e.g., need a separate account on each one), the system is a network. By this definition, a distributed system is a special case of a network, one that looks like a single machine to its clients.

In the following sections, we will look at long-haul networks, local networks, and distributed systems.

2.4.1. Long-Haul Networks

Before looking at the technical design of long-haul networks, it is worth pausing to see why anyone is interested in connecting widely separated computers together. Several goals motivate these networks. First, a network allows its users to conveniently share programs, data, documents, and ideas. Using the network file-transfer facility, people at different sites can easily collaborate on projects such as the development of software or writing reports, articles, or books. All the information is kept on-line, so every project participant can inspect the latest version of the common files at any instant. Electronic mail, which can be delivered in a fraction of a minute, also plays an important role in bringing widely separated users into close contact. In effect, the network can end the "tyranny of geography."

Second, a long-haul network allows people to take advantage of unusual computers or other facilities located at a great distance. Scientists all over the United States could take advantage of the enormous computing power of the ILLIAC IV located in California, by accessing it over the U.S. Department of Defense's ARPANET. Other resources that can be used via a network are large data bases (e.g., a computerized medical library) and unusual I/O devices.

Third, the overall reliability of the network can be much higher than the reliability of any of its components. The ARPANET, which has dozens of nodes across the United States and Europe, has PDP-10s at MIT, the University of Utah, and Stanford, among other places. If the University of Utah PDP-10 is out of service for repairs one day, Utah programmers with the appropriate authorization can nevertheless work at MIT or Stanford. The network allows programmers to continue their work as usual, even though their local machine is not available.

Fourth, if the work load at one node becomes more than that node can handle, some of it can be farmed out to another node with a lighter work load. Load sharing is particularly beneficial if the network spans several time zones. At 10 A.M. Eastern Standard Time many of the programmers working at MIT have arrived at work and are busy using the local computers. At that moment it is only 7 A.M. in California, and probably there is little or no work to be done at Stanford. Similarly, at 4 P.M. Pacific Standard Time, there is a lot of activity at Stanford but most of the programmers at MIT have long since gone home. A network allows programmers at one computer center to take advantage of unused computer facilities at another computer center, thus making more economical use of the system. From this point of view, an international network spanning all 24 time zones would be ideal.

Figure 2-14 shows two alternative network topologies. Each circle represents one node. In the star configuration, Fig. 2-14(a), any node can communicate with any other node by sending a message to the central node, D. The message is then sent to the destination. The star configuration has the disadvantage that if the central node is out of service, the network ceases to function.

An alternative topology is the distributed network, an example of which is shown in Fig. 2-14(b). In a distributed network, there is no central node to which all the nodes are connected. The decision as to which nodes should be connected to which other nodes is based on such factors as distance between the nodes, amount of message traffic expected between the nodes, and existence of appropriate communication facilities between the nodes. In a distributed network, alternate paths from every node to every other node can be, and usually are, provided. For example, if a power failure at H completely removes it from the network, G can still communicate with I via the path G-E-J-I. If neither H nor E is functioning, G can use the path G-C-D-F-J-I to communicate with I.

The ARPA network is a highly sophisticated network, with nodes at many universities and research institutes. Each node of the ARPA network consists of a

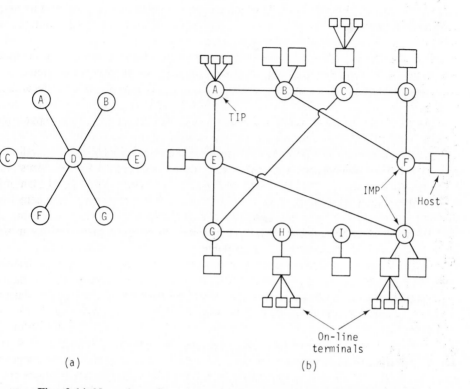

(a)   (b)

Fig. 2-14. Network configurations. (a) Star network. (b) Distributed network.

minicomputer to which may be connected one or more other large computers, called **hosts**. The minicomputers are called **IMPs** (Interface Message Processors), and **TIPs** (Terminal IMPs) and are responsible for the communication aspect of the network. The TIPs are parasite nodes. They allow on-line terminals to connect directly to the network without using a host computer. Information is moved around the network from node to node in messages of up to about 8000 bits. Each message contains a code specifying its destination.

An on-line user at node H in Fig. 2-14(b) who wants to communicate with the host computer at node D types a message into the main computer at H. The message is then passed to the IMP at H. The IMP puts the message into a queue in its own memory. A little later, the message is retrieved and sent to the IMP at G. The IMP at G examines the message to see if it is intended for one of its hosts, and upon discovering that the message is for D, queues the message, and continues whatever it was doing when the message arrived. When the message gets to the head of the queue, it will be sent to IMP C. Finally, it will be sent to the IMP at D, which will recognize that the message is for one of its own hosts, and give it to the host.

The ARPA network is an example of a **store-and-forward** network, so named because messages are stored at each node along the route and forwarded to the next node at a later time. In general, messages cannot be forwarded immediately because the needed transmission line may be in use forwarding another message. Furthermore, there may already be several other messages in the queue patiently waiting for their turns to be forwarded along that same transmission line.

Networks are a new and evolving field of research with many unsolved problems. One problem is how to permit different kinds of computers in the network in such a way as to allow programs written for one kind to be run on another kind. Still another problem involves the sharing of data between computers with different data formats, character codes, and so on. A further problem concerns determining how to route messages to their destination most efficiently. For example, in Fig. 2-14(b) the route from A to C via A -B -C may look shorter than A -E -J -F -D -C, but if the queue at B is full and the queues at E, J, F, and D are all empty, the latter route may be faster.

Yet another problem is deciding how to share the work load among the nodes. For example, if someone at E has a large program to be run using a large data base at D as input, should the data be sent to E or should the program be sent to D? Perhaps both program and data should be sent to F if there is a light work load there.

Another problem involves accounting. If a user at H has a program at E and a file at D sent to F for some computing, how do you keep track of who pays for what?

2.4.2. Telecommunication

In a local network, it is feasible to connect the computers and terminals by simply stringing wires or coaxial cables between them. In a long-haul network, however, the cost of doing so is almost always prohibitive. Moreover, in countries where the telephone company or PTT (Postal, Telephone, and Telegraph administration) enjoys a monopoly, it is also illegal. As a result, it is usually necessary to use the existing telephone network for communication purposes. This situation is perhaps unfortunate in that telephone networks were designed for transmitting the human voice in more-or-less recognizable form, not digital data, but they can be used to transmit digital data if the number of bits per second is sufficiently low.

The maximum number of bits per second that can be transmitted over a given channel (telephone line, radio transmission, etc.) is a characteristic of the channel. The limitation is imposed by the noise level of the channel. If an attempt is made to transmit more bits per second than the channel is capable of transmitting, some information will be lost; that is, errors will occur. No channel has a precise maximum bit rate in the sense that messages transmitted at, say, 1,204,364 bps (bits per second) will be received without error and messages transmitted at 1,204,365 bps will be hopelessly garbled. What happens is that as the bit rate increases, the error rate also increases. Above a certain error rate, a channel may be unacceptable. Telephone lines are rarely used at bit rates exceeding 9600 bps. In contrast, most tape drives can transmit information to main memory at a rate exceeding 1,000,000 bps. A computer with a 16-bit word and a memory cycle time of 1 μsec can transfer information to or from the memory at 16,000,000 bps.

To transmit digital information over an analog line, each second is divided into n indivisible time intervals. During each interval, one or more bits can be transmitted. For example, if the computer could set the line to 1, 2, 3, or 4 volts during any time interval, those four voltages could be used to represent 00,01,10, or 11, thus allowing 2 bits to be sent per time interval. An n-**baud** line is one in which the signal can change n times per second (i.e., n intervals per second). If each change has four possibilities, as in the preceding example, the transmission is called **dibit**, and the bit rate is twice the baud rate.

Modulation

Information entering or leaving a digital computer is in binary form. The voltage on an input line takes on only two values, as shown in Fig. 2-15(a). Two-level signals suffer considerable distortion when transmitted over a voice-grade telephone line, thereby leading to transmission errors. A pure sine wave signal at a frequency of 1000 to 2000 Hz, called a **carrier**, can be transmitted with relatively little distortion, however, and this fact is exploited as the basis of most telecommunication systems.

Because the pulsations of a sine wave are completely predictable, a pure sine wave transmits no information at all. However, by varying the amplitude, frequency, or phase, a sequence of 1s and 0s can be transmitted, as shown in Fig. 2-15. This process is called **modulation**. In amplitude modulation [see Fig. 2-15(b)], two different voltage levels are used, for 0 and 1, respectively. A person listening to digital data transmitted at a very low data rate would hear a loud noise for a 1 and no noise for a 0.

In frequency modulation [see Fig. 2-15(c)], the voltage level is constant but the carrier frequency is different for 1 and 0. A person listening to frequency modulated digital data would hear two tones, corresponding to 0 and 1. Frequency modulation is often referred to as **frequency shift keying.** It is employed in the 300-bps modems used to connect terminals to computers over dial-up lines.

In simple phase modulation [see Fig. 2-15(d)], the amplitude and frequency do not change, but the phase of the carrier is reversed 180 degrees when the data switches from 0 to 1 or 1 to 0. In more sophisticated phase-modulated systems, at the start of each indivisible time interval, the phase of the carrier is abruptly shifted by 45, 135, 225, or 315 degrees, to allow 2 bits per time interval. Dibit phase encoding is one of the most commonly used methods at speeds above 300 bps, for reasons of cost and reliability.

If the data to be transmitted consist of a series of 8-bit characters, it would be desirable to have a connection capable of transmitting 8 bits simultaneously—that is, eight pairs of wires. Because voice-grade telephone lines provide only one channel, the bits must be sent serially, one after another (or in groups of two if dibit modulation is being used). A device that accepts characters from a computer in the form of two-level signals, one bit at a time, and transmits the bits in groups of one or two, in

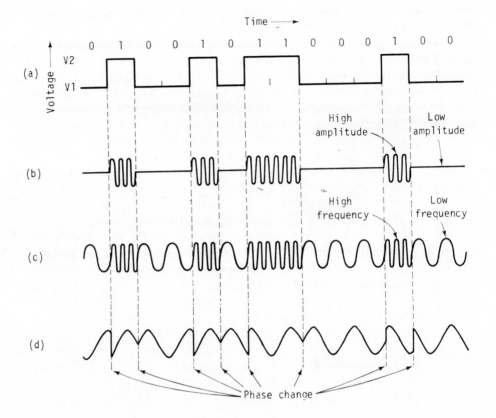

Fig. 2-15. Transmission of the binary number 01001011000100 over a telephone line bit by bit. (a) Two-level signal. (b) Amplitude modulation.
(c) Frequency modulation. (d) Phase modulation.

amplitude-, frequency-, or phase-modulated form, is usually called a **modem**
(**mo**dulator-**dem**odulator).

The transmitting modem sends the individual bits within one character at regularly
spaced time intervals. For example, 1200 baud implies one signal change every 833
μsec. A second modem at the receiving end is used to convert a modulated carrier to
a binary number. Because the bits arrive at the receiver at regularly spaced intervals,
once the receiving modem has determined the start of the character, its clock tells it
when to sample the line to read the values of the individual bits.

Asynchronous and Synchronous Transmission

Two different methods are used for transmitting characters. In **asynchronous**
transmission, the time interval between two characters is not fixed, although the time
interval between two consecutive bits within a character is fixed. For example, a

person typing at a time-sharing terminal will not type at uniform speed, so the time interval between two successive characters will not be constant.

This speed variation raises the problem of how the receiver can recognize the first bit of a character. If the modulation methods of Fig. 2-15 are used, there is no way to distinguish between no data and a 0 bit. A character consisting entirely of 0s would be completely invisible. Furthermore, a character consisting of a 1 followed by seven 0s could not be distinguished from a character consisting of 7 0s followed by a 1, because the receiver would have no way of recognizing the start of the character.

In order to permit the receiver to recognize the start of a character, a start bit is transmitted directly before each character. To improve reliability, 1 or 2 stop bits are transmitted directly after each character. Normally, the line is kept in the 1 state while no data are being transmitted to allow a broken circuit to be detected, so the start bit is 0. The stop bits are then 1, to distinguish them from start bits. Between the start and stop bits, the data bits are transmitted at uniformly spaced time intervals. A timer in the receiving modem is started when the start bit arrives, allowing the modem to tell which bit is which. Asynchronous communication is illustrated in Fig. 2-16(a).

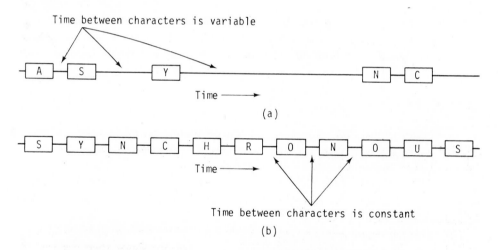

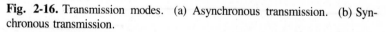

Fig. 2-16. Transmission modes. (a) Asynchronous transmission. (b) Synchronous transmission.

The most common bit rates used for asynchronous transmission are 110, 300, 600, 1200, and 2400 bps. At 110 bps, two stops are used, so a 7-bit ASCII character plus parity bit plus 1 start bit plus 2 stop bits gives 11 bits per character. Therefore, 110 bps corresponds to 10 characters/sec. The higher rates use only 1 stop bit.

In **synchronous** transmission, the need for non-information-carrying start and stop bits is eliminated. The result is to speed up data transmission. Synchronous communication often proceeds at bit rates of 4800 bps, 9600 bps, or even higher. In this method, once the modems have synchronized, they continue to send characters in order to remain in synchronization, even if there are no data to transmit. A special "idle" character is sent when there are no data. In ASCII, SYN is generally used. In synchronous transmission, unlike asynchronous transmission, the interval between two characters is always exactly the same.

Synchronous transmission requires that the clocks in the transmitter and receiver remain synchronized for long periods of time, whereas asynchronous transmission does not, because the start of each character is explicitly indicated by a start bit. The length of time a transmission can be carried on without resynchronizing the receiver to the phase of the transmitter depends on the stability of the clocks. Typically, the clocks are stable enough to allow blocks of thousands of characters to be sent without having to resynchronize. These blocks sometimes use Hamming codes or other techniques to detect and correct transmission errors. Synchronous transmission is illustrated in Fig. 2-16(b).

Simplex, Half-Duplex, and Full-Duplex Transmission

Three modes of transmission are used for communication purposes: simplex, half-duplex, and full-duplex. A **simplex** line is capable of transmitting data in only one direction. The reason is not due to any property of the wires themselves but simply because one end has only a transmitter and the other end has only a receiver. This configuration is rarely used by computers because it provides no way for the receiver to transmit an acknowledgment signal to the sender, indicating that the message was received correctly. Radio and television broadcasting are examples of simplex transmission.

A **half-duplex** line can send and receive data in both directions but not simultaneously. During any transmission, one modem is the transmitter and the other is the receiver. A common situation is for device A, acting as the transmitter, to send a series of characters to device B, acting as the receiver. Then A and B simultaneously switch roles and B sends a message back to A specifying whether the characters were received without error or not. If there were no transmission errors, A and B switch roles again and A sends the next message to B. If there were errors, A retransmits the garbled message again. The "conversation" between the transmitter and the receiver about what to do next is called the **protocol**. The time required to switch a half-duplex line from one direction to the other may be many character times. A railroad track is an example of a half-duplex channel, because it can handle traffic going either way but not at the same time.

A **full-duplex** line can, in contrast, send and receive data in both directions simultaneously. Conceptually, a full-duplex line is equivalent to two simplex lines, one in each direction. Because two transmissions may be proceeding in parallel, one in each direction, a full-duplex line can transmit more information than a half-duplex line of the same data rate. Furthermore, full-duplex lines do not waste any time switching directions.

2.4.3. Local Networks

Although long-haul networks are forced by economics or law to use the public telephone network for their transmission lines, the situation with local networks is different. When the computers are physically located within about 1 km of each other and all on private property, it is often feasible to run a coaxial cable or twisted wire pair around the site. All the computers can then just tap onto this common transmission facility, which typically can provide a data rate of 10 Mbps. Several different local network architectures are in widespread use. We will now look at two examples.

Ethernet

One of the best known local network types is based on the Ethernet* Network (Metcalfe and Boggs, 1976). The Ethernet uses a single coaxial cable called the **ether**, named after the *luminiferous ether* through which electromagnetic radiation was once alleged to propagate. The ether is a broadcast medium; that is, each message sent on it is received at each computer on the network. It is up to each host interface to select out those that are actually intended for it. An eight-host Ethernet is shown in Fig. 2-17(a).

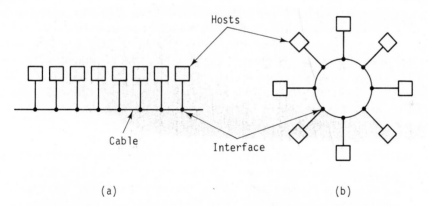

(a)   (b)

Fig. 2-17. Two kinds of local networks. (a) An Ethernet network. (b) A ring network.

When a host has a message to send, it passes the message to its interface for transmission. The interface then listens to the ether to hear if it is currently in use by another host. If so, the interface waits until the present message is finished, and then starts sending itself. If the ether is not in use, the interface begins transmitting immediately.

---

*Ethernet is a trademark of Xerox Corporation.

A problem occurs when two or more hosts become ready to transmit during the transmission of a third host. According to the algorithm above, both must wait until the third-party transmission terminates, then both may start. Unfortunately, they will interfere with each other, so each one is required to monitor the cable to see if the signal on it is the same as the one it is broadcasting. If an interface detects a difference (i.e., a collision), it broadcasts a noise burst to alert all other interfaces to the collision, terminates its own transmission, waits a random time, and then tries again later. If the collision repeats again, the next random waiting time is chosen from a longer interval to reduce the chance of yet another collision.

Ring Networks

A completely different approach to local networking is the ring network, depicted in Fig. 2-17(b). Although various types of rings have been proposed and built (Clark et al., 1978; Farber and Larson, 1972; Liu, 1978; Needham, 1979), we will focus on one of the more popular organizations, the **token ring**. In this type of local network, each interface contains a 1-bit buffer. The collection of these buffers in all the interfaces together forms a giant shift register. At any moment, each interface can read or write the bit in its buffer.

When the network is brought up, a special bit pattern called the **token** is inserted into the giant shift register by the network controller. To send a message, an interface must first capture and remove the token, something it does by inverting the last bit as the token is shifted through its buffer. Having mutilated the token, the potential sender knows that no other interface will be able to find the token, let alone capture it, so it is now free to put its message onto the ring without fear of interference. When the sender is finished, it flips the last bit of the token back again to give someone else the chance to capture it.

2.4.4. Distributed Systems

As we mentioned earlier, a distributed system is a collection of computers that acts like a single machine to its users. In other words, the users are not aware of the existence of multiple independent machines. The organization and software for such systems is a subject of intense research at present and our ideas about them are in a state of constant flux. As an introduction to this subject, below we will briefly look at one kind of distributed system.

The distributed system of Fig. 2-18 consists of machines used in two ways: as dedicated processors and as pool processors. Each dedicated processor or **server** performs a specific function, for example, managing a class of I/O device such as disks, terminals, line printers, or phototypesetters. Other servers are specialized to run specific programs such as compilers, assemblers, data-base systems, fast Fourier transforms, and so on. Some of these servers may have specialized instruction sets or hardware to make them more efficient than general-purpose processors.

The **pool processors** do not have specifically assigned tasks. Instead, when a

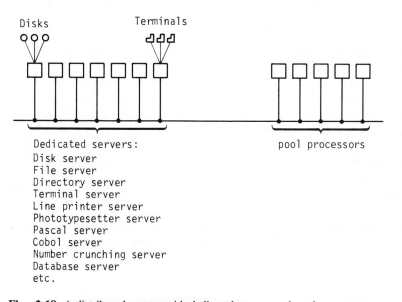

Fig. 2-18. A distributed system with dedicated servers and pool processors.

user needs to run a program for which no server exists, one or more processors from the pool are temporarily assigned. When the job is finished, the processors are returned to the pool to wait for reassignment. In this scheme, it is advantageous to design programs as a collection of cooperating processes, to allow each process to run on a separate CPU, and thus be faster than having them all share a single machine.

It is interesting to note the similarity between the systems of Fig. 2-18 and Fig. 2-3(c). In both cases dedicated processors exist for specific tasks. The difference is that in Fig. 2-18 the tasks are "large," such as a compilation, whereas in Fig. 2-3(c) they are "small," such as a single multiplication. In the future these two systems may grow toward each other, with systems having a multitude of specialized processors for jobs both small and large. Some existing distributed systems are discussed by Birrell et al. (1982), Jones et al. (1977), and Wittie (1979)

2.5. SUMMARY

Computer systems are built up from three types of components: processors, memories, and I/O devices. The task of a processor is to fetch instructions one at a time from a memory, decode them, and carry them out. The fetch-execute cycle can always be described as an algorithm and, in fact, is often carried out by a software interpreter running at a lower level.

Memories can be categorized as primary or secondary. The primary memory is used to hold the program currently being executed. Its access time is short—a few hundred nanoseconds at most—and independent of the address being accessed. Secondary memories, in contrast, have access times that are much longer (milliseconds or more) and dependent on the location of the data being read or written. Tapes and disks are the most common secondary memories.

I/O devices are used to transfer information into and out of the computer. Examples are terminals, card readers, and printers. Most I/O devices use either the ASCII or EBCDIC character codes. When data must be transmitted over an unreliable channel, parity bits and Hamming codes can be used to increase reliability. When data compression rather than error correction is required, Huffman codes can be used.

It is becoming increasingly common to have computers connected together to form networks, either long-haul or local. Communication in a long-haul network is typically accomplished by sending an amplitude-, frequency-, or phase-modulated carrier over a telephone line or satellite channel. At low speeds, transmission is usually asynchronous, but at high speeds it is nearly always synchronous.

Local networks can be based on contention for a common channel, as in the Ethernet, or token passing on a ring, among other possibilities. Local networks are sometimes used as the hardware base for building distributed systems.

PROBLEMS

Thur 25

1. What is the purpose of step 2 in the list of Sec. 2.1.1? What would happen if this step were omitted?

2. A certain computation is highly sequential—that is, each step depends on the one preceding it. Would an array processor or a pipeline processor be more appropriate for this computation? Explain.

3. To compete with the newly invented printing press, a certain medieval monastery decided to mass produce handwritten paperback books by assembling a vast number of scribes in a huge hall. The head monk would then call out the first word of the book to be produced and all the scribes would copy it down. Then the head monk would call out the second word and all the scribes would copy it down. This process was repeated until the entire book had been read aloud and copied. Which of the parallel processor systems of Fig. 2-3 does this system most resemble?

4. A standard punched card has 80 columns of 12 positions. How large a character set can be used if it is required that every character be represented by a single column with at most three holes?

5. Estimate how many characters, including spaces, a typical book contains. How many bits are needed to encode a book in ASCII with parity? How many 1600-bpi tapes are needed to store a library of 10^6 books?

6. Estimate the maximum storage capacity of the human brain using the following assumptions. All memory is coded as DNA molecules. A DNA molecule is a linear sequence of the four basic nucleotides: A, C, G, and T. From the average weight of a nucleotide,

roughly 10^{-20} gram, and an average brain weight of 1500 grams, deduce the bit capacity of the brain for this encoding form. *Note*: This calculation is only an upper limit, because the brain contains many cells that perform functions other than memory.

7. Which of the following memories are possible? Which are reasonable? Explain.

    a.   10-Bit MAR, 1024 cells,   8-bit cell size
    b.   10-Bit MAR, 1024 cells,   12-bit cell size
    c.   9-Bit MAR, 1024 cells,   10-bit cell size
    d.   11-Bit MAR, 1024 cells,   10-bit cell size
    e.   10-Bit MAR,   10 cells, 1024-bit cell size
    f. 1024-Bit MAR,   10 cells,   10-bit cell size

8. Sociologists can get three possible answers to a typical survey question such as "Do you believe in the tooth fairy?" —namely, yes, no, and no opinion. With this in mind, the Sociomagnetic Computer Company has decided to build a computer to process survey data. This computer has a trinary memory—that is, each byte (tryte?) consists of 8 trits, with a trit holding a 0, 1, or 2. How many trits are needed to hold a 6-bit number? Give an expression for the number of trits needed to hold n bits.

9. A certain computer can be equipped with 262,144 bytes of memory. Why would a manufacturer choose such a peculiar number, instead of an easy-to-remember number like 250,000?

10. Consider a computer memory consisting of 2^{20} 64-bit words. Four numeric types exist: binary integers, binary floating-point numbers, decimal integers, and decimal floating-point numbers. The CPU has only one ADD instruction and uses the memory's metabits to determine the type of addition needed. How many metabits are needed per word? How many bits are needed for the entire memory, data plus metabits?

11. The transfer rate between a CPU and its associated memory is orders of magnitude higher than the mechanical I/O transfer rate. How can this imbalance cause inefficiencies?

12. Measure your own reading speed. How does your data rate compare to that of a 300-bps telephone line?

13. Compute the data rate of the human eye using the following information. The visual field consists of about 10^6 elements (pixels). Each pixel can be reduced to a superposition of the three primary colors, each of which has 64 intensities. The time resolution is 100 msec.

14. How long does it take to read a disk with 800 cylinders, each containing five tracks of 32 sectors? First, all the sectors of track 0 are to be read starting at sector 0, then all the sectors of track 1 starting at sector 0, and so on. The rotation time is 20 msec, and a seek takes 10 msec between adjacent cylinders and 50 msec for the worst case. Switching between tracks of a cylinder can be done instantaneously.

15. The director of your local computer center has just decided that the appropriate place for all its card punches, card readers, and similar equipment is the Smithsonian Institution. However, just to be on the safe side, it has also been decided to save all existing card decks on magnetic tape. If the interrecord gap on the 1600-bpi tapes used is 0.25 inch, and fifteen 80-column cards are written per physical tape record, how many 2000-card boxes will fit on a 2400-ft tape?

16. Decode the following binary ASCII text: 1001001 0100000 1001100 1001111 1010110 1000101 0100000 1011001 1001111 1010101 0101110.

17. Devise an even-parity Hamming code for the digits 0 to 9.

18. Devise a code for the digits 0 to 9 whose Hamming distance is 2.

19. In a Hamming code, some bits are "wasted" in the sense that they are used for checking and not information. What is the percentage of wasted bits for messages whose total length (data + check bits) is $2^n - 1$?. Evaluate this expression numerically for values of n from 3 to 10.

20. Transmission errors on telephone lines often occur in bursts rather than individually. Because the basic Hamming code can only correct single errors within a character, it is of no use if a noise burst garbles n consecutive bits. Devise a method of transmitting ASCII text over a line where noise bursts may garble as many as 100 consecutive bits. Assume that the minimum interval between two noise bursts is thousands of characters. *Hint:* Think carefully about the order of bit transmission.

21. Four symbols S_1, S_2, S_3, and S_4, with occurrence probabilities $P_1 > P_2 > P_3 > P_4$, respectively, are to be Huffman encoded. What is the mean number of bits per symbol? If it is necessary to distinguish various cases, answer the question for each case.

22. Decode the following Huffman-coded text using the code of Fig. 2-13: 110100011001111110.

23. What information *must* be present in the packets sent in a computer network? What information *might* be present as well?

24. Two computer science students are having an argument about long-haul networks. The first student claims that if message traffic increases beyond a certain amount, the IMPs should be provided with more memory. The second student claims that the IMPs should be replaced with faster IMPs. Under what circumstances is each proposal reasonable?

25. When even-parity ASCII text is transmitted asynchronously at a rate of 10 characters/sec over a 110-bps line, what percentage of the received bits actually contain data (as opposed to overhead)?

26. A certain asynchronous ASCII terminal does parity checking and prints at 60 characters/sec. Which speed should it use: 110, 300, 600, or 1200 bps?

27. The Hi-Fi Modem Company has just designed a new frequency-modulation modem that uses 16 frequencies instead of just 2. Each second is divided into n equal time intervals, each of which contains one of the 16 possible tones. How many bits per second can this modem transmit, using synchronous transmission?

28. How many characters/sec (7 bits + parity) can be transmitted over a 2400-bps line in each of the following modes?

    a. Synchronous
    b. Asynchronous (1 start bit and 1 stop bit)

29. To model channel access on the Ethernet, imagine that time is slotted into discrete 1-μsec time slots. After a collision, each computer randomly chooses one of the two following slots to use. If both computers choose the same slot, a collision occurs and a new interval

of length four slots is used on the next round, with each computer choosing one of the four slots. If another collision occurs, eight slots are used next time, and so on. Give an expression for the mean number of rounds required to resolve an initial collision.

30. Write a procedure *hamming* (*ascii, encoded*) that converts the low-order 7 bits of *ascii* into an 11-bit integer stored in *encoded*.

31. Write a function *distance* (*code, n, k*) that takes an array *code*, of *n* characters of *k* bits each as input, and returns the distance of the character set as output.

3

THE DIGITAL LOGIC LEVEL

At the bottom of the hierarchy of Fig. 1-2 we find the digital logic level, the computer's real hardware. In this chapter, we will examine many aspects of digital logic, as a building block for the study of higher levels in subsequent chapters. Our study will emphasize microcomputers over larger machines not only because they are simpler (and thus easier to study) but also because they are becoming increasingly important compared to larger machines.

The basic elements from which all digital computers are constructed are amazingly simple. We will begin our study by looking at these basic elements and also at the special two-valued algebra (Boolean algebra) used to analyze them. Next we will examine some fundamental circuits that can be built using gates in simple combinations, including circuits for doing arithmetic. The following topic is how gates can be combined to store information, that is, how memories are organized. After that, we come to the subject of CPUs and especially how single chip CPUs interface with memory and peripheral devices.

3.1. GATES AND BOOLEAN ALGEBRA

Digital circuits can be constructed from a small number of primitive elements by combining them in innumerable ways. In the following sections we will describe these primitive elements, show how they can be combined, and introduce a powerful tool for analyzing their behavior.

3.1.1. Gates

A digital circuit is one in which only two logical values are present. Typically, a signal between 0 and 1 volt represents one value (e.g., binary 0) and a signal between 2 and 5 volts represents the other value (e.g., binary 1). Voltages outside these two ranges are not permitted. Tiny electronic devices, called **gates**, can compute various functions of these two-valued signals. These gates form the hardware basis on which all digital computers are built.

Although the details of how gates work inside is really beyond the scope of this book, belonging to a level below our level 0, the **device level**, we will now digress ever so briefly to take a quick look at the basic idea, which is really quite simple. All modern digital logic ultimately rests on the fact that a transistor can be made to operate as a very fast binary switch. In Fig. 3-1(a) we have shown a single bipolar transistor (the circle) embedded in a simple circuit. This transistor has three connections to the outside world: the **collector**, the **base**, and the **emitter**. When the input voltage, V_{in} is below a certain critical value, the transistor turns off and acts like an infinite resistance, causing the output of the circuit, V_{out}, to take on a value close to V_{cc}. When V_{in} exceeds the critical value, the transistor switches on and acts like a perfect conductor, causing V_{out} to be pulled down to ground (by convention, 0 volts).

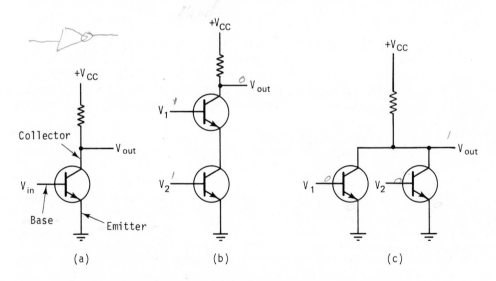

Fig. 3-1. (a) A transistor inverter. (b) A NAND gate. (c) A NOR gate.

The important thing to notice is that when V_{in} is low, V_{out} is high, and vice versa. This circuit is thus an inverter, converting a logical 0 to a logical 1, and a logical 1 to a logical 0. The resistor is needed to limit the amount of current drawn by the transistor. The time required to switch from one state to the other is typically a few nanoseconds.

In Fig. 3-1(b) two transistors are cascaded in series. If both V_1 and V_2 are high, both transistors will conduct and V_{out} will be pulled low. If either input is low, the corresponding transistor will turn off, and the output will be high. In other words, V_{out} will be low if and only if both V_1 and V_2 are high.

In Fig. 3-1(c) the two transistors are wired in parallel instead of in series. In this configuration, if either input is high, the corresponding transistor will turn on and pull the output down to ground. If both inputs are low, the output will remain high.

These three circuits, or their equivalents, form the three simplest gates. They are called NOT, NAND, and NOR gates, respectively. NOT gates are often called **inverters**; we will use the two terms interchangeably. If we now adopt the convention that "high" (V_{cc} volts) is a logical 1, and that "low" (ground) is a logical 0, we can express the output value as a function of the input values. The conventional symbols used to depict these three gates are shown in Fig. 3-2(a)-(c), along with the functional behavior for each circuit.

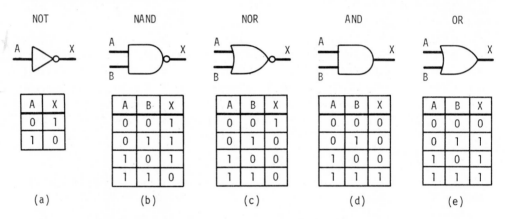

Fig. 3-2. The symbols and functional behavior for the five basic gates.

If the output signal of Fig. 3-1(b) is fed into an inverter circuit, we get another circuit with precisely the inverse of the NAND gate—namely, a circuit whose output is 1 if and only if both inputs are 1. Such a circuit is called an AND gate; its symbol and functional description are given in Fig. 3-2(d). Similarly, the NOR gate can be connected to an inverter to yield a circuit whose output is 1 if either or both inputs is a 1 but 0 if both inputs are 0. The symbol and functional description of this circuit, called an OR gate, are given in Fig. 3-2(e). The small circles used as part of the symbols for the inverter, NAND gate, and NOR gate are called **inversion bubbles**. They are often used in other contexts as well to indicate an inverted signal.

The five gates of Fig. 3-2 are the principal building blocks of the digital logic level. From the foregoing discussion, it should be clear that the NAND and NOR gates require two transistors each, whereas the AND and OR gates require three each. For this reason, many computers are based on NAND and NOR gates rather than the more familiar AND and OR gates. (In practice, all the gates are implemented somewhat differently, but NAND and NOR are still simpler than AND and OR.) In passing it is worth noting that gates may have more than two inputs. In principle, a NAND gate, for example, may have arbitrarily many inputs, but in practice more than eight inputs is unusual.

Although the subject of how gates are constructed belongs to the device level, we would like to mention the major families of manufacturing technology because they are referred to frequently. The two major technologies are **bipolar** and **MOS** (Metal Oxide Semiconductor). The major bipolar types are **TTL** (Transistor-Transistor Logic), which has been the workhorse of digital electronics for years, and **ECL** (Emitter-Coupled Logic), which is used when very high-speed operation is required.

MOS gates are 10 times slower than TTL and 100 times slower than ECL but require almost no power and almost no space, so large numbers of them can be packed together tightly. MOS comes in many varieties, including PMOS, NMOS, and CMOS, with new varieties continually appearing.

3.1.2. Boolean Algebra

To describe the circuits that can be built by combining gates, a new type of algebra is needed, one in which variables and functions can take on only the values 0 and 1. Such an algebra is called a **Boolean algebra**, after its discoverer, the English mathematician George Boole (1815-1864). Strictly speaking, we are really referring to a specific type of Boolean algebra, a **switching algebra**, but the term "Boolean algebra" is so widely used to mean "switching algebra" that we will not make the distinction.

Just as there are functions in "ordinary" (i.e, secondary-school) algebra, so are there functions in Boolean algebra. A Boolean function has one or more input variables and yields a result that depends only on the values of these variables. A simple function, f, can be defined by saying that $f(A)$ is 1 if A is 0 and $f(A)$ is 0 if A is 1. This function is the NOT function of Fig. 3-2(a).

Because a Boolean function of n variables has only 2^n possible sets of input values, the function can be completely described by giving a table with 2^n rows, each row telling the value of the function for a different combination of input values. Such a table is called a **truth table**. The tables of Fig. 3-2 are examples of truth tables. If we agree to always list the rows of a truth table in numerical order (base 2), that is, for two variables in the order 00, 01, 10, and 11, the function can be completely described by the 2^n−bit binary number obtained by reading the result column of the truth table vertically. Thus NAND is 1110, NOR is 1000, AND is 0001, and OR is 0111. Obviously, only 16 Boolean functions of two variables exist, corresponding to the 16 possible 4-bit result strings. In contrast, ordinary (i.e., high school) algebra has an infinite number of functions of two variables, none of which can be described by giving a table of outputs for all possible inputs because each variable can take on any one of an infinite number of possible values. Clearly, finiteness has its virtues.

Figure 3-3(a) shows the truth table for a Boolean function of three variables: $M = f(A, B, C)$. This function is the majority logic function, that is, it is 0 if a majority of its inputs are 0, and 1 if a majority of its inputs are 1. Although any Boolean function can be fully specified by giving its truth table, as the number of variables increases, this notation becomes increasingly cumbersome. Instead, another notation is frequently used.

To see how this other notation comes about, note that any Boolean function can be specified by telling which combinations of input variables give an output value of 1. For the function of Fig. 3-3(a) there are four combinations of input variables that make M 1. By convention, we will place a bar over an input variable to indicate that its value is inverted. The absence of a bar means that it is not inverted. Furthermore, we will use implied multiplication or a dot to mean AND and + to mean OR. Thus, for example, $A\bar{B}C$ means $A = 1$ and $B = 0$ and $C = 1$. Also, $A\bar{B} + B\bar{C}$ means ($A = 1$ and $B = 0$) or ($B = 1$ and $C = 0$). The four rows of Fig. 3-3(a) producing 1 bits in the output are: $\bar{A}BC$, $A\bar{B}C$, $AB\bar{C}$, and ABC. The function, M, is true if any one of these four conditions is true; hence we can write.

$$M = \bar{A}BC + A\bar{B}C + AB\bar{C} + ABC$$

as a compact way of giving the truth table. A function of n variables can thus be described by giving a "sum" of at most 2^n n-variable "product" terms. This formulation is especially important, as we will see shortly, because it leads directly to an implementation of the function using standard gates.

3.1.3. Implementation of Boolean Functions

As mentioned above, the formulation of a Boolean function as a sum of up to 2^n product terms leads directly to a possible implementation. Using Fig. 3-3 as an example, we can see how this implementation is accomplished. In Fig. 3-3(b), the inputs, A, B, and C, are shown at the left edge and the output function, M, is shown at the right edge. Because complements of the input variables are needed, they are generated by tapping the inputs and passing them through the inverters labeled 1, 2, and 3. To keep the figure from becoming cluttered, we have drawn in six vertical lines, three of which are connected to the input variables, and three of which are connected to their complements. These lines provide a convenient source for the inputs to subsequent gates. For example, gates 5, 6, and 7 all use A as an input. In an actual circuit these gates would probably be wired directly to A without using any intermediate "vertical" wires.

The circuit contains four AND gates, one for each term in the equation for M (i.e., one for each row in the truth table having a 1 bit in the result column). Each AND gate computes one row of the truth table, as indicated. Finally, all the product terms are ORed together to get the final result.

The circuit of Fig. 3-3(b) uses a convention that we will need repeatedly throughout this book: when two lines cross, no connection is implied unless a heavy dot is present at the intersection. For example, the output of gate 3 crosses all six vertical lines but it is connected only to $\bar{C}$. Be warned that some authors use other conventions.

A	B	C	M
0	0	0	0
0	0	1	0
0	1	0	0
0	1	1	1
1	0	0	0
1	0	1	1
1	1	0	1
1	1	1	1

(a)

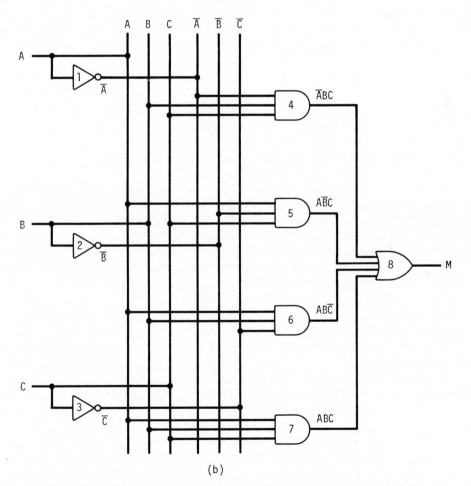

(b)

Fig. 3-3. (a) The truth table for the majority function of three variables. (b) A circuit for (a).

From the example of Fig. 3-3 it should be clear how to implement a circuit for any Boolean function:

1. Write down the truth table for the function.

2. Provide inverters to generate the complement of each input.

3. Draw an AND gate for each term with a 1 in the result column.

4. Wire the AND gates to the appropriate inputs.

5. Feed the output of all the AND gates into an OR gate.

Although we have shown how any Boolean function can be implemented using NOT, AND, and OR gates, it is often convenient to implement circuits using only a single type of gate. Fortunately, it is straightforward to convert circuits generated by the preceding algorithm to pure NAND or pure NOR form. To make such a conversion, all we need is a way to implement NOT, AND, and OR using a single gate type. The top row of Fig. 3-4 shows how all three of these can be implemented using only NAND gates; the bottom row shows how it can be done using only NOR gates. In both cases a value can be inverted using a single gate, whereas both AND and OR require three gates each. Thus to implement a Boolean function using only NAND or only NOR gates, first follow the procedure given above for constructing it with NOT, AND, and OR. Then replace the multi-input gates with equivalent circuits using two-input gates. For example, $A + B + C + D$ can be computed as $(A + B) + (C + D)$, using three two-input OR gates. Finally, the NOT, AND, and OR gates are replaced by the circuits of Fig. 3-4.

Although this procedure does not lead to the optimal circuits, in the sense of the minimum number of gates, it does show that a solution is always feasible. Both NAND and NOR gates are said to be **complete**, because any Boolean function can be computed using either of them. No other gate has this property, which is another reason they are often preferred for the building blocks of circuits.

3.1.4. Circuit Equivalence

Circuit designers naturally try to reduce the number of gates in their products to reduce component cost, printed circuit board space, power consumption, and so on. To reduce the complexity of a circuit, the designer must find another circuit that computes the same function as the original but does so with fewer gates (or perhaps with simpler gates, for example, two-input gates instead of four-input gates). In the search for equivalent circuits, Boolean algebra can be a valuable tool.

As an example of how Boolean algebra can be used, consider the circuit and truth table for $AB + AC$ shown in Fig. 3-5(a). Although we have not discussed them yet, many of the rules of ordinary algebra also hold for Boolean algebra. In particular, $AB + AC$ can be factored into $A(B + C)$ using the distributive law. Figure 3-5(b) shows the circuit and truth table for $A(B + C)$. Because two functions are

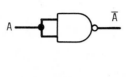

(a)

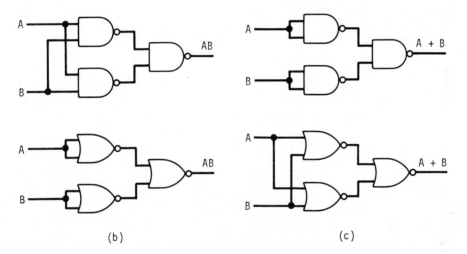

(b)   (c)

Fig. 3-4. Construction of (a) NOT, (b) AND, and (c) OR gates using only
NAND gates or only NOR gates.

equivalent if and only if they have the same output for all possible inputs, it is easy to
see from the truth tables of Fig. 3-5 that $A(B + C)$ is equivalent to $AB + AC$.
Despite this equivalence, the circuit of Fig. 3-5(b) is clearly better than that of
Fig. 3-5(a) because it contains fewer gates.

In general, a circuit designer can represent a circuit as a Boolean function and
then apply the laws of Boolean algebra to this representation in an attempt to find a
simpler but equivalent one. From the final representation, a new circuit can be constructed.

To use this approach, we need some identities from Boolean algebra. Figure 3-6
shows some of the major ones. It is interesting to note that each law has two forms
that are **duals** of each other. By interchanging AND and OR and also 0 and 1, either
form can be produced from the other one. All the laws can be easily proven by

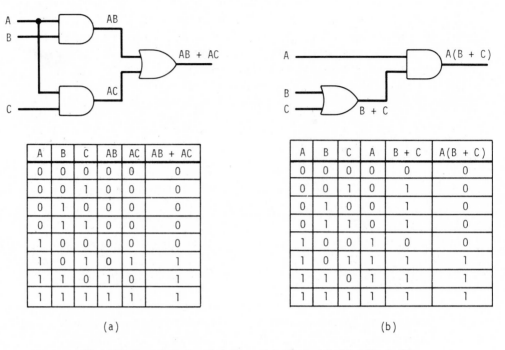

Fig. 3-5. Two equivalent functions. (a) $AB + AC$. (b) $A(B + C)$.

constructing their truth tables. Except for de Morgan's law, the absorption law, and the AND form of the distributive law, the results are reasonably intuitive. De Morgan's law can be extended to more variables, for example, $\overline{ABC} = \overline{A} + \overline{B} + \overline{C}$.

Name	AND form	OR form
Identity law	$1A = A$	$0 + A = A$
Null law	$0A = 0$	$1 + A = 1$
Idempotent law	$AA = A$	$A + A = A$
Inverse law	$A\overline{A} = 0$	$A + \overline{A} = 1$
Commutative law	$AB = BA$	$A + B = B + A$
Associative law	$(AB)C = A(BC)$	$(A + B) + C = A + (B + C)$
Distributive law	$A + BC = (A + B)(A + C)$	$A(B + C) = AB + AC$
Absorption law	$A(A + B) = A$	$A + AB = A$
De Morgan's law	$\overline{AB} = \overline{A} + \overline{B}$	$\overline{A + B} = \overline{A}\overline{B}$

Fig. 3-6. Some identities of Boolean algebra.

De Morgan's law suggests an alternative notation. In Fig. 3-7(a) the AND form is shown with negation indicated by inversion bubbles, both for input and output. Thus an OR gate with inverted inputs is equivalent to a NAND gate. From Fig. 3-7(b), the dual form of de Morgan's law, it is clear that a NOR gate can be drawn as an AND gate with negated inputs. By negating both forms of de Morgan's law, we arrive at Fig. 3-7(c) and (d), which show equivalent representations of the AND and OR gates. Analogous symbols exist for the multiple variable forms of de Morgan's law (e.g., an *n* input NAND gate becomes an OR gate with *n* inverted inputs).

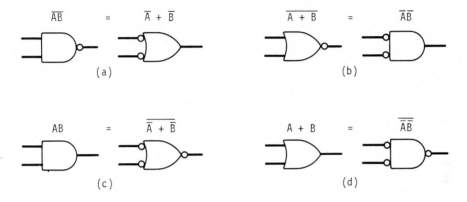

Fig. 3-7. Alternative symbols for some gates: (a) NAND. (b) NOR. (c) AND. (d) OR.

Using the identities of Fig. 3-7 and the analogous ones for multi-input gates, it becomes much easier to convert the sum-of-products representation of a truth table to pure NAND or pure NOR form. As an example, consider the XOR (exclusive or) function of Fig. 3-8(a). The standard sum-of-products circuit is shown in Fig. 3-8(b). To convert to NAND form, the lines connecting the output of the AND gates to the input of the OR gate should be redrawn with two inversion bubbles, as shown in Fig. 3-8(c). Finally, using Fig. 3-7(a), we arrive at Fig. 3-8(d). The variables $\overline{A}$ and $\overline{B}$ can be generated from A and B using NAND or NOR gates with their inputs tied together. Note that inversion bubbles can be moved along a line at will, for example, from the outputs of the input gates in Fig. 3-8(d) to the inputs of the output gate.

As a final note on circuit equivalence, we will now demonstrate the surprising result that the same physical gate can compute different functions, depending on the conventions used. In Fig. 3-9(a) we show the output of a certain gate, *F*, for different input combinations. Both inputs and outputs are shown in volts. If we adopt the convention that 0 volts is logical 0 and 5 volts is logical 1, called **positive logic**, we get the truth table of Fig. 3-9(b), the AND function. If, however, we adopt **negative logic**, which has 0 volts as logical 1 and 5 volts as logical 0, we get the truth table of Fig. 3-9(c), the OR function.

Thus the convention chosen to map voltages onto logical values is of great importance. Except where otherwise specified, we will henceforth use positive logic, so the terms logical 1, true, and high are synonyms, as are logical 0, false, and low.

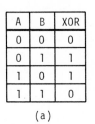

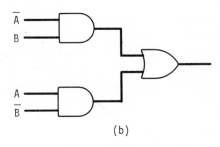

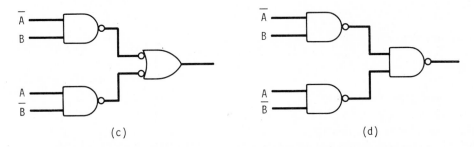

Fig. 3-8. (a) Truth table for EXCLUSIVE OR. (b)-(d) Three circuits for computing it.

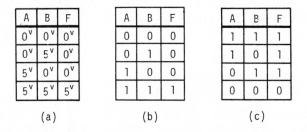

Fig. 3-9. (a) Electrical characteristics of a device. (b) Positive logic. (c) Negative logic.

3.2. BASIC DIGITAL LOGIC CIRCUITS

In the previous sections we saw how to implement truth tables and other simple circuits using individual gates. In practice, few circuits are actually constructed gate-by-gate anymore, although this once was common. Nowadays, the usual building blocks are modules containing a number of gates. In the following sections we will examine these building blocks more closely and see how they are used and how they can be constructed from individual gates.

3.2.1. Integrated Circuits

Gates are not manufactured or sold individually but rather in units called **integrated circuits**, often called **ICs** or **chips**. An IC is a square piece of silicon about 5×5 mm on which some gates have been deposited. ICs are usually mounted in rectangular plastic or ceramic packages measuring 5 to 15 mm wide and 20 to 50 mm long. Along the long edges are two parallel rows of pins about 5 mm long that can be inserted in sockets or soldered to printed circuit boards. Each pin connects to the input or output of some gate on the chip or to power or to ground. The packages with two rows of pins outside and ICs inside are technically known as **dual inline packages** or **DIPs**, but everyone calls them chips, thus blurring the distinction between the piece of silicon and its package. The most common packages have 14, 16, 18, 20, 22, 24, 28, 40, 64, or 68 pins. For some special applications square packages with pins on all four sides are sometimes used.

Chips can be divided into rough classes based on the number of gates they contain:

SSI (Small Scale Integrated) circuit: 1 to 10 gates
MSI (Medium Scale Integrated) circuit: 10 to 100 gates
LSI (Large Scale Integrated) circuit: 100 to 100,000 gates
VLSI (Very Large Scale Integrated) circuit: >100,000 gates

These classes have different properties and are used in different ways.

An SSI chip typically contains two to six independent gates, each of which can be used individually, in the style of the previous sections. Figure 3-10 illustrates a schematic drawing of a common SSI chip containing four NAND gates. Each of these gates has two inputs and one output, requiring a total of 12 pins for the four gates. In addition, the chip needs power (typically about 5 volts, denoted by V_{cc}), and ground (GND), which are shared by all gates. The package generally has a notch near pin 1 to identify the orientation. To avoid clutter in circuit diagrams, neither power, nor ground, nor unused gates are conventionally shown.

Figure 3-11 shows some other common SSI chips. These chips belong to the 7400 TTL series developed by Texas Instruments and now produced by many semiconductor manufacturers. They are most appropriate for simple circuits that cannot be realized any other way. The circuit of Fig. 3-3(b) could be constructed from one 7404, two 7411s, and one 7432. No four-input OR gate is available in the 7400 series, but the same function can be computed by ORing pairs of inputs and then ORing the results together. Symbolically, this can be represented as $A + B + C + D = (A + B) + (C + D)$, that is, A and B are ORed together as are C and D, with these two sums then being ORed. If the circuit of Fig. 3-3(b) were actually constructed this way, the printed circuit board on which they were mounted would contain conducting wire-like tracks to connect the appropriate pins. Some of the gates would not be used. The 7486 chip contains a gate we have not shown before, the EXCLUSIVE OR gate, which is a one-gate equivalent to the circuit of Fig. 3-8.

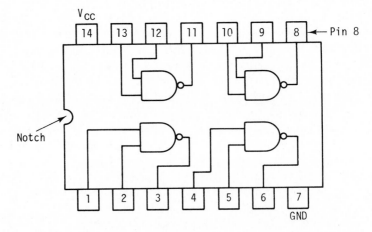

Fig. 3-10. An SSI chip containing four gates.

For our purposes, all gates are ideal in the sense that the output appears as soon as the input is applied. In reality, chips have a finite **gate delay**, which is the time it takes for the signal to propagate from the input to the output. Typical delays are 1 to 20 nsec. In schematics one often sees numbers like 74S00, 74L00, 74H00, and 74LS00. These represent functionally equivalent chips with different delay/power/price trade-offs. The 74C00 series consists of CMOS chips that are functionally identical to the corresponding 7400 TTL ones.

It is within the current state of the art to put nearly a million gates on a single chip. Because any circuit can be built up from NAND gates, you might think that a manufacturer could make a very general chip containing the equivalent of 250,000 chips like the 7400. Unfortunately, such a chip would need 3,000,002 pins. With the standard pin spacing of 0.1 inch, the chip would be over 2 miles long, which might have a negative effect on sales. Clearly, the only way to take advantage of the technology is to design circuits with a high gate/pin ratio. In the following sections we will look at simple MSI circuits that combine a number of gates internally to provide a useful function requiring only a limited number of external connections (pins). After that we will examine two applications requiring thousands of gates (LSI) yet only 20 to 40 pins—namely, memory chips and microprocessor chips. The dividing line between LSI and VLSI is vague, but a typical VLSI chip might have a large microprocessor *and* considerable memory on the same chip.

3.2.2. Combinational Circuits

Many applications of digital logic require a circuit with multiple inputs and multiple outputs in which the outputs are uniquely determined by the current inputs. Such a circuit is called a **combinational circuit**. Not all circuits have this property. For example, a circuit containing memory elements may generate outputs that depend on

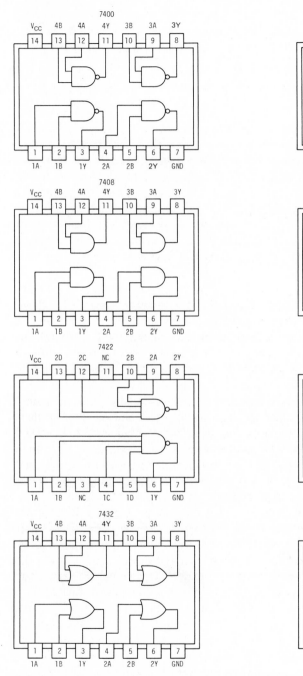
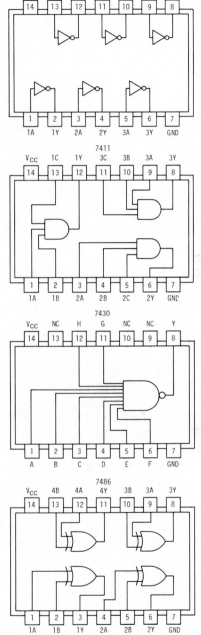

Fig. 3-11. Some SSI chips. Pin layouts from *The TTL Data Book for Design Engineers*, copyright © 1976 Texas Instruments Incorporated.

the stored values as well as the input variables. A circuit implementing a truth table, such as that of Fig. 3-3(a), is a typical example of a combinational circuit. In this section we will examine some frequently used combinational circuits, as examples of MSI chips.

Multiplexers

At the digital logic level, a **multiplexer** is a circuit with 2^n data inputs, one data output, and n control inputs that select one of the data inputs. The selected data input is "gated" (i.e., routed) to the output. Figure 3-12 is a schematic diagram for an eight-input multiplexer. The three control lines, A, B, and C, encode a 3-bit number that specifies which of the eight input lines is gated to the OR gate and thence to the output. No matter what value is on the control lines, seven of the AND gates will always output 0; the other one may output either 0 or 1, depending on the value of the selected input line. Each AND gate is enabled by a different combination of the control inputs.

The circuit of Fig. 3-12 is an ideal candidate for implementation as an MSI chip, as illustrated in Fig.3-13(a). Such a chip has eight data inputs, three control inputs, and one output. When power and ground are included, the chip could be implemented in a 14-pin package. Using this MSI multiplexer chip, we can implement the circuit of Fig. 3-3(b) on a single chip, as shown in Fig. 3-13(b). For each combination of A, B, and C, one of the data input lines is selected. Each input is wired to either V_{cc} (logical 1) or ground (logical 0). The algorithm for wiring the inputs is simple: input D_i is the same as the value in row i of the truth table. In Fig. 3-3(a), rows 0, 1, 2, and 4 are 0, so the corresponding inputs are grounded; the remaining rows are 1, so they are wired to logical 1. In this manner any truth table of three variables can be implemented using the chip of Fig. 3-13(a).

We have already seen how a multiplexer chip can be used to select one of several inputs and how it can implement a truth table. Another of its applications is as a parallel-to-serial data converter. By putting 8 bits of data on the input lines and then stepping the control lines sequentially from 000 to 111 (binary), the 8 bits are put onto the output line in series. A typical use for parallel-to-serial conversion is in a keyboard, where each keystroke implicitly defines a 7- or 8-bit number that must be output serially over a telephone line.

The MSI chip of Fig. 3-13(a) has eight data inputs. Chips similar to it are commercially available, as are multiplexer chips with 16 data inputs. Furthermore, chips with two independent four-input multiplexers exist, as do chips with four independent two-input multiplexers. Some of these chips provide both the selected output and its complement, and some have an additional input line that forces the output to 0, independent of the inputs (i.e., a chip enable/disable pin).

The inverse of a multiplexer is a **demultiplexer**, which routes its single input signal to one of 2^n outputs, depending on the values of the n control lines. If the binary value on the control lines is k, output k is selected.

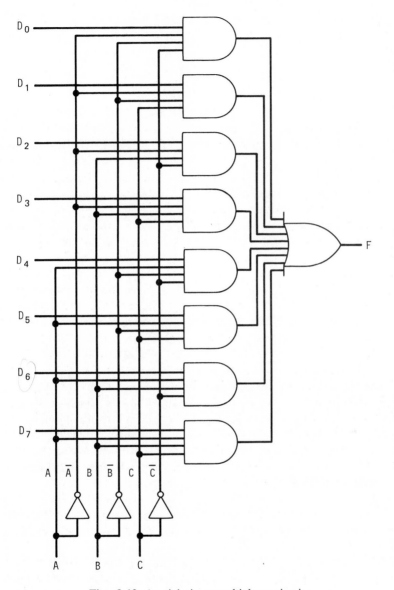

Fig. 3-12. An eight-input multiplexer circuit.

Decoders

As a second example of an MSI chip, we will now look at a circuit that takes an
n-bit number as input and uses it to select (i.e., set to 1) exactly one of the 2^n output
lines. Such a circuit, illustrated for $n = 3$ in Fig. 3-14, is called a **decoder**.

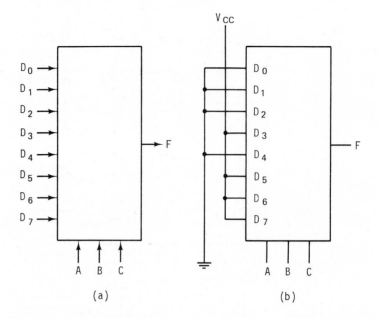

Fig. 3-13. (a) An MSI multiplexer chip. (b) The same chip wired to compute the majority function.

To see where a decoder might be useful, imagine a memory consisting of eight chips, each containing 8K bytes. Chip 0 has addresses 0 to 8191, chip 1 has addresses 8192 to 16383, and so on. When an address is presented to the memory, the high-order 3 bits are used to select one of the eight chips. Using the circuit of Fig. 3-14, these 3 bits are the three inputs, A, B, and C. Depending on the inputs, exactly one of the eight output lines, D_0, ..., D_7, is 1; the rest are 0. Each output line enables one of the eight memory chips. Because only one output line is set to 1, only one chip is enabled.

The operation of the circuit of Fig. 3-14 is straightforward. Each AND gate has three inputs, of which the first is either A or $\bar{A}$, the second is either B or $\bar{B}$, and the third is either C or $\bar{C}$. Each gate is enabled by a different combination of inputs: D_0 by $\bar{A}\,\bar{B}\,\bar{C}$, D_1 by $\bar{A}\,\bar{B}\,C$, and so on.

Commercially available MSI decoder chips include 4-to-16, 3-to-8 and dual 2-to-4 (i.e, two 2-to-4 decoders packaged together in a single chip). Furthermore, 4-to-10 decoders for decoding binary-coded decimal numbers are also common.

Comparators

Another useful MSI chip is the **comparator**, which compares two input words. The simple comparator of Fig. 3-15 takes two inputs, A, and B, each of length 4 bits, and produces 1 if they are equal and a 0 if they are not equal. The circuit is based on

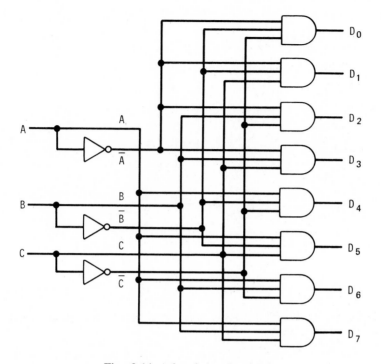

Fig. 3-14. A 3-to-8 decoder circuit.

the EXCLUSIVE OR gate, which puts out a 0 if its inputs are equal and a 1 if they are unequal. If the two input words are equal, all four of the EXCLUSIVE OR gates must output 0. These four signals can then be ORed together; if the result is 0, the input words are equal, otherwise not. In our example we have used a NOR gate as the final stage to reverse the sense of the test: 1 means equal, 0 means unequal. Commercially available MSI comparator chips not only have a pin for $A = B$, but also pins for $A < B$ and $A > B$.

Programmed Logic Arrays

We saw earlier that arbitrary functions (truth tables) can be constructed by computing product terms with AND gates and then ORing the products together. A very general chip for forming sums of products is the **programmed logic array** or **PLA**, which is shown in Fig. 3-16. This chip, the 74S330, has input lines for 12 variables. The complement of each input is generated internally, making 24 input signals in all. The heart of the circuit is an array of 50 AND gates, each of which can potentially have any subset of the 24 input signals as an input. Which input signal goes to which AND gate is determined by a 24 × 50 bit matrix supplied by the user. Each input line to the 50 AND gates contains a fuse. When shipped from the factory, all 1200 fuses

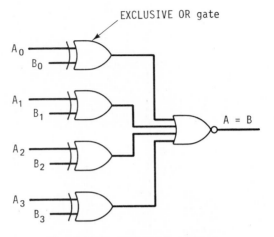

Fig. 3-15. A simple 4-bit comparator.

are intact. To program the matrix the user burns out selected fuses by applying a high voltage to the chip.

The output part of the circuit consists of six OR gates, each of which has up to 50 inputs, corresponding to the 50 outputs of the AND gates. Again here, a user-supplied (50 × 6) matrix tells which of the potential connections actually exist. The chip has 12 input pins, 6 output pins, power, and ground, and comes in a 20-pin package.

As an example of how a PLA can be used, let us reconsider the circuit of Fig. 3-3(b) once more. It has three inputs, four AND gates, one OR gate, and three inverters. With the appropriate internal connections made, our PLA can compute this function using three of its 12 inputs, four of its 50 AND gates, and one of its six OR gates. (The four AND gates should compute $\overline{A}BC$, $A\overline{B}C$, $AB\overline{C}$, and ABC, respectively; the OR gate takes these four product terms as input.) In fact, the same PLA could be wired up to compute simultaneously a total of four functions of similar complexity. For these simple functions the number of input variables is the limiting factor; for more complicated ones it might be the AND or OR gates.

We can now compare the three different ways we have discussed for implementing the truth table of Fig. 3-3(a). Using SSI components, we need four chips. Alternatively, we could suffice with one MSI multiplexer chip , as shown in Fig. 3-13(b). Finally, we could use a quarter of one PLA chip. Obviously, if many functions are needed, the PLA is more efficient than the other two methods.

3.2.3. Arithmetic Circuits

It is now time to move on from the general-purpose MSI circuits discussed above to MSI combinational circuits used for doing arithmetic. We will begin with a simple 8-bit shifter, then look at how adders are constructed, and finally examine arithmetic logical units, which play a central role in any computer.

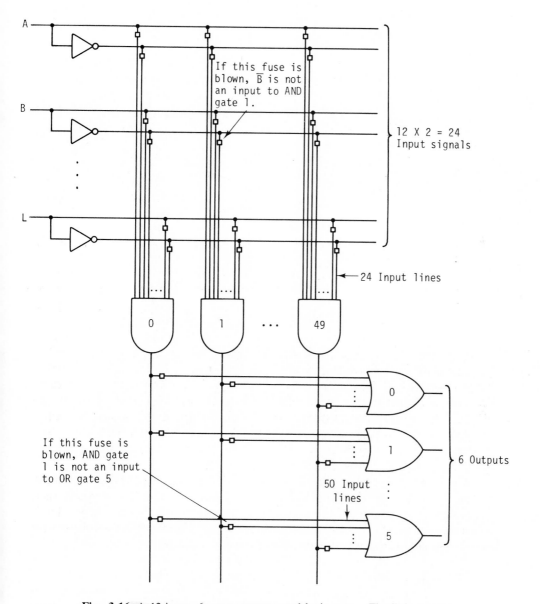

Fig. 3-16. A 12-input, 6-output programmed logic array. The little squares represent fuses that can be burned out to determine the function to be computed. The fuses are arranged in two matrices: the upper one for the AND gates and the lower one for the OR gates.

Shifters

Our first arithmetic MSI circuit is an eight-input, eight-output shifter (see Fig. 3-17). Eight bits of input are presented on lines D_0, ..., D_7. The output, which is just the input shifted one bit, is available on lines S_0, ..., S_7. The control line, C, determines the direction of the shift, 0 for left and 1 for right.

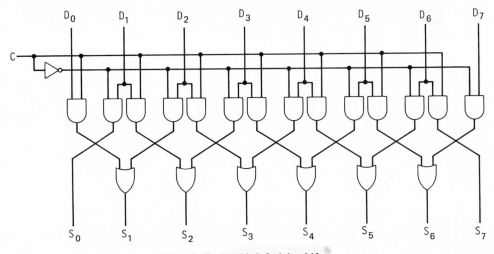

Fig. 3-17. A 1-bit left/right shifter.

To see how the circuit works, notice the pairs of AND gates for all the bits except the gates on the end. When $C = 1$, the right member of each pair is turned on, passing the corresponding input bit to output. Because the right AND gate is wired to the input of the OR gate to its right, a right shift is performed. When $C = 0$, it is the left member of the AND gate pair that turns on, effecting a left shift.

Adders

A computer that cannot add integers is unthinkable. Consequently, circuits for performing addition are an essential part of every CPU. The truth table for 1-bit addition is shown in Fig. 3-18(a). Two outputs are present, the sum of the inputs, A and B, and the carry to the next (leftward) position. A circuit for computing both the sum and the carry is given in Fig. 3-18(b). This circuit is known as a **half adder**.

Although a half adder is adequate for summing the low-order bits of two multibit input words, it will not do for a bit position in the middle of the word because it does not handle the carry into the position from the right. Instead, the **full adder** of Fig. 3-19 is needed. From inspection of the circuit it should be clear that a full adder is built up from two half adders. The *Sum* output line is 1 if an odd number of A, B, and the *Carry in* are 1. The *Carry out* is 1 if either A and B are both 1 (left input to the OR gate) or exactly one of them is 1 and the *Carry in* bit is also 1.

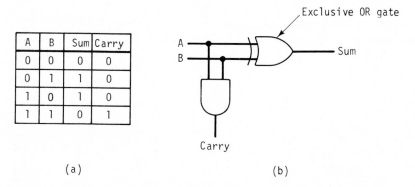

A	B	Sum	Carry
0	0	0	0
0	1	1	0
1	0	1	0
1	1	0	1

(a)   (b)

Fig. 3-18. (a) Truth table for 1-bit addition. (b) A circuit for a half adder.

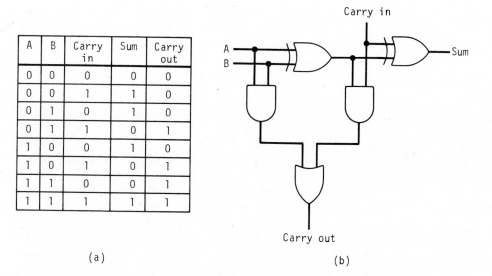

A	B	Carry in	Sum	Carry out
0	0	0	0	0
0	0	1	1	0
0	1	0	1	0
0	1	1	0	1
1	0	0	1	0
1	0	1	0	1
1	1	0	0	1
1	1	1	1	1

(a)   (b)

Fig. 3-19. (a) Truth table for full adder. (b) Circuit for a full adder.

To build an adder for, say, two 16-bit words, one just replicates the circuit of Fig. 3-19(b) 16 times. The carry out of a bit is used as the carry into its left neighbor. The carry into the rightmost bit is wired to 0. This type of adder is called a **ripple carry adder**, because in the worst case, adding 1 to 111...111 (binary), the addition cannot complete until the carry has rippled all the way from the rightmost bit to the leftmost bit. Adders that do not have this delay, and hence are faster, also exist (Blaauw, 1976).

Arithmetic Logical Units

Most computers contain a single circuit for performing at least the basic operations of AND, OR, and sum of two machine words. Typically, such a circuit for n-bit words is built up of n identical circuits for the individual bit positions. Figure 3-20 is a simple example of such a circuit, called an **arithmetic logical unit** or **ALU**. It can compute any one of four functions—namely, A AND B, A OR B, $\bar{B}$, or $A + B$, depending on whether the function-select input lines F_0 and F_1 contain 00, 01, 10, or 11 (binary), respectively.

The lower left-hand corner of our ALU contains a 2-bit decoder to generate enable lines for the four operations, based on F_0 and F_1. The upper left-hand corner has the logic to compute A AND B, A OR B, and $\bar{B}$, but at most one of these results is passed onto the final OR gate, depending on the enable lines coming out of the decoder. Because exactly one of the decoder outputs will be 1, exactly one of the four AND gates driving the OR gate will be enabled; the other three will output 0, independent of A and B.

The lower right-hand corner of the ALU contains a full adder for computing the sum of A and B, including handling the carries, because it is likely that several of these circuits will eventually be wired in parallel to perform full-word operations. Chips like Fig. 3-20 are actually available and are known as **bit slices**. They allow the computer designer to build an ALU of any desired width. Chips containing four or eight slices on one chip are also available to simplify the design and reduce chip count.

3.2.4. Clocks

In many digital circuits the order in which events happen is critical. Sometimes one event must precede another, sometimes two events must occur simultaneously. To allow designers to achieve the required timing relations, many digital circuits use clocks to provide synchronization. A **clock** in this context is a circuit that emits a series of pulses with a precise pulse width and precise interval between consecutive pulses. The interval between corresponding edges of two consecutive pulses is called the **clock cycle time**. Pulse frequencies are commonly between 1 and 100 MHz, corresponding to clock cycles of 1000 nsec to 10 nsec. To achieve high accuracy, the clock frequency is usually controlled by a crystal oscillator.

In a computer, many events may happen during a single clock cycle. If these events must occur in a specific order, the clock cycle must be divided into subcycles. A common way of providing finer resolution than the basic clock is to tap the primary clock line and insert a circuit with a known delay in it, thus generating a secondary clock signal that is phase-shifted from the primary, as shown in Fig. 3-21(a). The timing diagram of Fig. 3-21(b) provides four time references for discrete events:

1. Rising edge of C1

2. Falling edge of C1

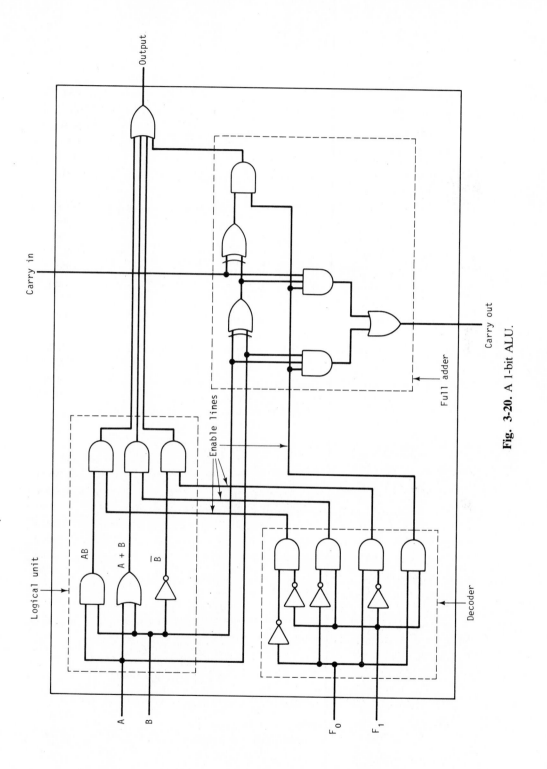

Fig. 3-20. A 1-bit ALU.

3. Rising edge of C2

4. Falling edge of C2

By tying different events to the various edges, the required sequencing can be achieved. If more than four time references are needed within a clock cycle, more secondary lines can be tapped from the primary, with different delays.

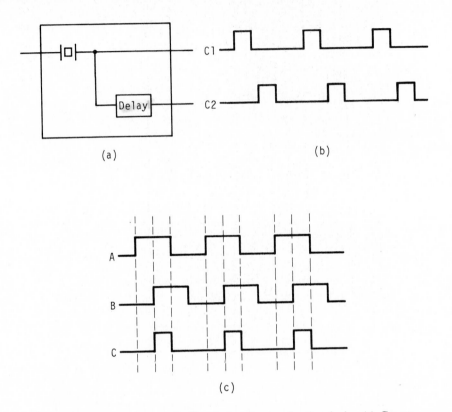

(a)   (b)

(c)

Fig. 3-21. (a) A clock. (b) The timing diagram for the clock. (c) Generation of an asymmetric clock.

In some circuits it is necessary to divide time into intervals rather than define points in time. This effect can be easily achieved by causing some events to happen when C1 is high and other events to happen when C2 is high. If more than two intervals are needed, more clock lines can be provided or the high states of the two clocks can be made to overlap partially in time. In the latter case four intervals can be distinguished: $\overline{C1}$ AND $\overline{C2}$, $\overline{C1}$ AND C2, C1 AND $\overline{C2}$, and C1 AND C2.

As an aside, it probably should be pointed out that Fig. 3-21(a)-(b) is really something of a simplification. Real clocks are symmetric, with time spent in the high state equal to the time spent in the low state, as shown by A in Fig. 3-21(c). To generate an asymmetric pulse train, the basic clock is shifted using a delay circuit, as shown by B in Fig. 3-21(c). Finally, these two are ANDed together, to get C in Fig. 3-21(c). It is this signal that is shown as C1 in Fig. 3-21(b). C2 can be generated by delaying C1.

3.3. MEMORY

An essential component of every computer is its memory. Without memory there could be no computers as we now know them. Memory is used for storing both instructions to be executed and data. In the following sections we will examine the basic components of a memory system starting at the gate level to see how they work and how they are combined to produce large memories.

3.3.1. Latches

To create a 1-bit memory, we need a circuit that somehow "remembers" previous input values. Such a circuit can be constructed from two NOR gates, as illustrated in Fig. 3-22(a). Analogous circuits can be built from NAND gates. We will not mention these further, however, because they are conceptually identical to the NOR versions.

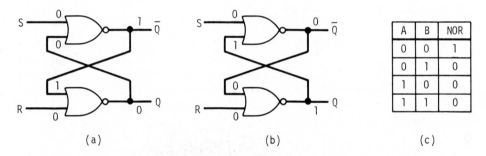

Fig. 3-22. (a) A NOR latch in state 0. (b) A NOR latch in state 1. (c) Truth table for NOR.

The circuit of Fig. 3-22(a) is called an **SR latch**. It has two inputs, S, for Setting the latch, and R, for Resetting (i.e., clearing) it. It also has two outputs, Q and $\overline{Q}$, which are complementary, as we will see shortly. Unlike a combinational circuit, the outputs of the latch are not uniquely determined by the current inputs.

To see how this comes about, let us assume that both S and R are 0, which they are most of the time. For argument's sake, let us further assume that $Q = 0$. Because Q is fed back into the upper NOR gate, both of its inputs are 0, so its output, $\overline{Q}$, is 1. The 1 is fed back into the lower gate, which then has inputs 1 and 0, yielding $Q = 0$. This state is at least consistent and is depicted in Fig. 3-22(a).

Now let us imagine that Q is not 0 but 1, with R and S still 0. The upper gate has inputs of 0 and 1, and an output, $\overline{Q}$, of 0, which is fed back to the lower gate.

This state, shown in Fig. 3-22(b), is also consistent. A state with both outputs equal to 0 is inconsistent, because it forces both gates to have two 0s as input, which, if true, would produce 1, not 0, as output. Similarly, it is impossible to have both outputs equal to 1, because that would force the inputs to 0 and 1, which yields 0, not 1. Our conclusion is simple: For $R = S = 0$, the latch has two stable states, which we will refer to as 0 and 1, depending on Q.

Now let us examine the effect of the inputs on the state of the latch. Suppose that S becomes 1 while $Q = 0$. The inputs to the upper gate are then 1 and 0, forcing the output to 0. This change makes both inputs to the lower gate 0, forcing the output to 1. Thus setting S (i.e., making it 1) switches the state from 0 to 1. Setting R in state 0 has no effect because the output of the lower gate is the same for inputs of 10 and 11.

Using similar reasoning, it is easy to see that setting S in state 1 has no effect but that setting R drives the latch to state 0. In summary, when S is turned on momentarily, the latch ends up in state 1, regardless of what state it was previously in. Likewise, setting R forces the latch to state 0. The circuit "remembers" whether S or R was last on. Using this property we can build computer memories.

Clocked SR Latches

It is often convenient to prevent the latch from changing state except at certain specified times. To achieve this goal, we modify the basic circuit slightly, as shown in Fig. 3-23, to get a **clocked SR latch**. This circuit has an additional input, the clock, which is normally 0. With the clock 0, both AND gates output 0, independent of S and R, and the latch does not change state. When the clock is 1, the effect of the AND gates vanishes and the latch becomes sensitive to S and R. Despite its name, the clock signal need not be driven by a clock. The terms **enable** and **strobe** are also widely used to mean that the clock input is 1; that is, the circuit is sensitive to the state of S and R.

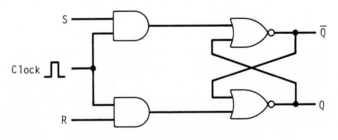

Fig. 3-23. A clocked SR latch.

Up until now we have carefully swept the problem of what happens when both S and R are 1 under the rug. And for good reason: the circuit becomes nondeterministic when both R and S finally return to 0. The only consistent state for $S = R = 1$ is

$Q = \bar{Q} = 0$, but as soon as both inputs return to 0, the latch must jump to one of its two stable states. If either input drops back to 0 before the other, the one remaining 1 longest wins, because when just one input is 1, it forces the state. If both inputs return to 0 simultaneously (which is very unlikely), the latch jumps to one of its stable states at random.

Clocked JK Latches

To prevent this ambiguity, we can modify the circuit again to get the **clocked JK latch** of Fig. 3-24. Here the outputs have been fed back into the AND gates. Because one of the outputs is always 0, setting both inputs to 1 only causes one of the AND gates to put out a 1—namely, the one attached to the output in 1 state. Let us consider the effect of $J = K = 1$ on each of the stable states. In state 0, the upper gate will be enabled and the lower one disabled, causing the latch to go to state 1. In state 1, the lower gate will be enabled and the upper one disabled, causing the latch to go to state 0. In both cases the latch switches state. The ambiguity has been removed. The letters J and K are universally used to distinguish JK latches from SR latches but they do not stand for anything in particular.

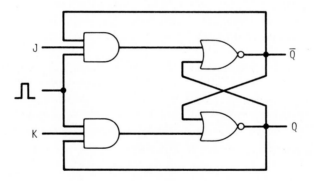

Fig. 3-24. A clocked JK latch.

Clocked D Latches

Another way to resolve the SR latch's ambiguity is to make sure that it cannot occur. Figure 3-25 gives a latch circuit with only one input, D. Because the input to the lower AND gate is always the complement of the input to the upper one, the problem of both inputs being 1 never arises. When $D = 1$ and the clock is 1, the latch is driven into state logical 1. When $D = 0$ and the clock is 1, the latch is driven into state logical 0. Put in other terms, when the clock is 1, the current value of D is sampled and stored in the latch. This circuit, called a **clocked D latch**, is a true 1-bit memory. The value stored is always available at Q. To load the current value of D into the memory, a positive pulse is put on the clock line.

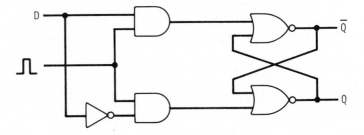

Fig. 3-25. A clocked D latch.

3.3.2. Flip-Flops and Registers

In many circuits it is necessary to sample the value on a certain line at a particular instant in time and store it. In principle, one way to achieve this goal is to use a clocked D latch with a very short pulse on the clock line around the time the sample is to be made. In practice, generating very short pulses can be difficult, so a variation on the latch circuit has been developed. In this variant, called a **flip-flop**, the state transition does not occur when the clock is 1 but during the clock transition from 0 to 1 or from 1 to 0 instead. Thus the length of the clock pulse is unimportant, as long as the transitions occur fast.

For emphasis, we will repeat the difference between a flip-flop and a latch. A flip-flop is **edge triggered**, whereas a latch is **level triggered**. Be warned, however, that in the literature these terms are often confused. Many authors use "flip-flop" when they are referring to a latch, and vice versa.

The standard symbols for latches and flip-flops are shown in Fig. 3-26. Figure 3-26(a) is a latch whose state is loaded when the clock, CK, is 1, in contrast to Fig. 3-26(b) which is a latch whose clock is normally 1 but which drops to 0 momentarily to load the state from D. Figure 3-26(c) and (d) are flip-flops rather than latches, which is indicated by the pointy symbol on the clock inputs. Figure 3-26(c) changes state on the rising edge of the clock pulse (0 to 1 transition), whereas Fig. 3-26(d) changes state on the falling edge (1 to 0 transition). Many, but not all, latches and flip-flops also have $\overline{Q}$ as an output, and some have two additional inputs *Set* or *Preset* (force state to logical 1) and *Reset* or *Clear* (force state to logical 0). In addition to D flip-flops, JK flip-flops are also available.

Registers

Flip-flops are available in a variety of configurations. A simple one, containing two independent D flip-flops with clear and preset signals, is illustrated in Fig. 3-27(a). Although packaged together in the same 14-pin chip, the two flip-flops are unrelated. A quite different arrangement is the octal flip-flop of Fig. 3-27(b). Here the eight (hence the term "octal") D flip-flops are not only missing the $\overline{Q}$ and preset

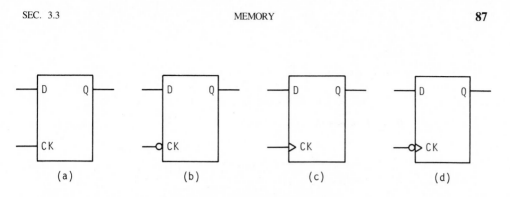

Fig. 3-26. D latches and flip-flops.

lines, but all the clock lines are ganged together and driven by pin 11. The flip-flops themselves are of the Fig. 3-26(d) type, but the inversion bubbles on the flip-flops are canceled by the inverter tied to pin 11, so the flip-flops are loaded on the rising transition. All eight clear signals are also ganged, so when pin 1 goes to 0, all the flip-flops are forced to their 0 state. In case you are wondering why pin 11 is inverted at the input and then inverted again at each CK signal, an input signal may not have enough current to drive all eight flip-flops; the input inverter is really being used as an amplifier.

While the obvious reason for ganging the clock and clear lines of Fig. 3-27(b) is to save pins, in this configuration the chip is used in a different way from eight unrelated flip-flops. It is used as a single 8-bit register. Alternatively, two such chips can be used in parallel to form a 16-bit register by tying their respective pins 1 and 11 together. We will look at registers and their uses more closely in Chap. 4.

For the time being, the interesting thing to note is how the scarcity of pins drives chip design inexorably toward circuits with higher and higher gate-to-pin ratios. The simple D latch of Fig. 3-25 requires five gates, so an octal latch chip analogous to Fig. 3-27(b) needs 57 gates, including the eight inverters for CK and the eight inverters for CLR. An edge-triggered flip-flop is more complex than a latch internally, so Fig. 3-27(b) represents the equivalent of something like 100 gates, a far cry from the simple SSI chips of Fig. 3-11. In the next section we will study a different internal organization for memory chips, which allows a much higher gate-to-pin ratio.

3.3.3. Memory Organization

Although we have now progressed from the simple 1-bit memory of Fig. 3-25 to the 8-bit memory of Fig. 3-27(b) we cannot continue this way due to lack of pins on the chip. Each flip-flop requires two pins, D, and Q, in addition to the control pins shared by all the flip-flops. To build large memories a different organization is required.

What we need is a design in which the number of pins grows logarithmically rather than linearly with the memory capacity. A widely used memory organization that meets this criterion is shown in Fig. 3-28. This example illustrates a memory

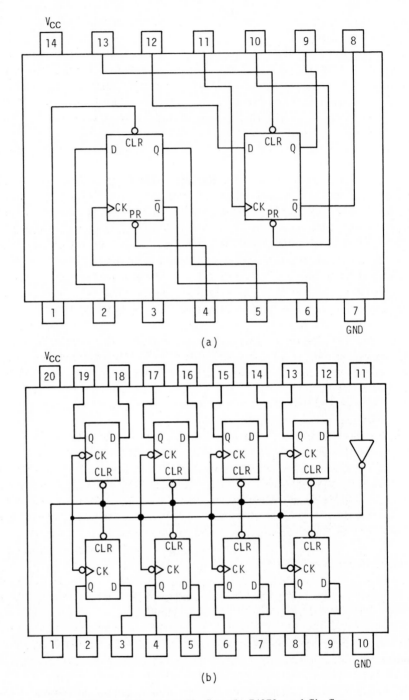

Fig. 3-27. (a) 7474 dual D flip-flop. (b) 74273 octal flip-flop.

with four 3-bit words. Each operation reads or writes a full 3-bit word. While the total memory capacity of 12 bits is hardly more than our octal flip-flop, it requires fewer pins and most important, the design extends easily to large memories.

While the memory of Fig. 3-28 may look complicated at first, it is really quite simple due to its regular structure. It has eight input lines and three output lines. Three inputs are data: I_0, I_1, and I_2; two are for the address: A_0 and A_1; and three are for control: CS for Chip Select, RD for distinguishing between read and write, and OE for Output Enable. The three outputs are for data: D_0, D_1, and D_2. In principle this memory could be put into a 14-pin package, including power and ground versus 20 pins for the octal flip-flop.

To select this memory chip, external logic must set CS high and also set RD high (logical 1) for read and low (logical 0) for write. The two address lines must be set to indicate which of the four 3-bit words is to be read or written. For a read operation, the data input lines are not used, but the word selected is placed on the data output lines. For a write operation, the bits present on the data input lines are loaded into the selected memory word; the data output lines are not used.

Now let us look at Fig. 3-28 closely to see how it works. The four word-select AND gates at the left of the memory form a decoder. The input inverters have been placed so that each gate is enabled (output is high) by a different address. Each gate drives a word select line, from top to bottom for words 0, 1, 2, and 3. When the chip has been selected for a write, the vertical line labeled CS $\cdot$ $\overline{\text{RD}}$ will be high, enabling one of the four write gates, depending on which word select line is high. The output of the write gate drives all the CK signals for the selected word, loading the input data into the flip-flops for that word. A write is only done if CS is high and RD is low and even then only the word selected by A_0 and A_1 is written; the other words are not changed.

Read is similar to write. The address decoding is exactly the same as for write. But now the CS $\cdot$ $\overline{\text{RD}}$ line is low, so all the write gates are disabled and none of the flip-flops are modified. Instead, the word select line that is chosen enables the AND gates tied to the Q bits of the selected word. Thus one word outputs its data into the four-input OR gates at the bottom of the figure, while the other three words output 0. Consequently, the output of the OR gates is identical to the value stored in the word selected. The three words not selected make no contribution to the output.

Although we could have designed a circuit in which the three OR gates were just fed into the three output data lines, doing so sometimes causes problems. In particular, we have shown the data input lines and the data output lines as being different, but in actual memories the same lines are used. If we had tied the OR gates to the data output lines, the chip would try to output data, that is, force each line to a specific value, even on writes, thus interfering with the input data. For this reason, it is desirable to have a way to connect the OR gates to the data output lines on reads but disconnect them completely on writes. What we need is an electronic switch that can make or break a connection in a few nanoseconds.

Fortunately, such switches exist. Figure 3-29(a) shows the symbol for what is called a **noninverting buffer**. It has a data input, a data output, and a control input.

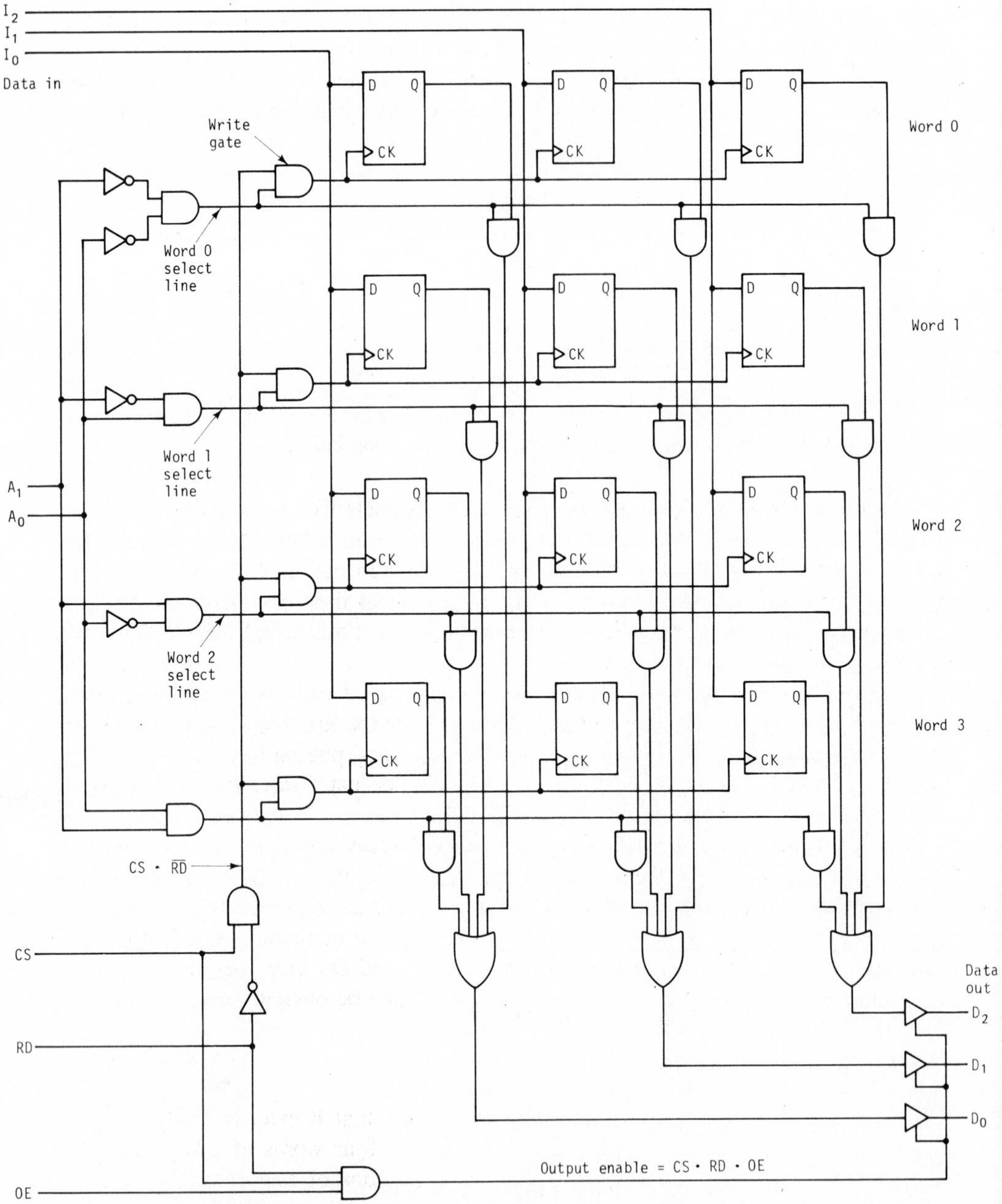

Fig. 3-28. Logic diagram for a 4 × 3 memory. Each row is one of the four 3-bit words. A read or write operation always reads or writes a complete word.

When the control input is high, the buffer acts like a wire, as shown in Fig. 3-29(b). When the control input is low, the buffer acts like an open circuit, as shown in Fig. 3-29(c); it is as though someone detached the data output from the rest of the circuit with a wirecutter. However, in contrast to the wirecutter approach, the connection can be subsequently restored in a few nanoseconds by just making the control signal high again.

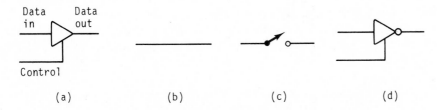

Fig. 3-29. (a) A noninverting buffer. (b) Effect of (a) when control is high. (c) Effect of (a) when control is low. (d) An inverting buffer.

Figure 3-29(d) shows an **inverting buffer**, which acts like a normal inverter when control is high and disconnects the output from the circuit when control is low. Both kinds of buffers are **tri-state devices**, because they can output 0, 1, or none of the above (open circuit). Buffers also amplify signals, so they can drive many inputs simultaneously. They are sometimes used in circuits for this reason, even when their switching properties are not needed.

Getting back to the memory circuit, it should now be clear what the three noninverting buffers on the data output lines are for. When CS, RD, and OE are all high, the output enable signal is also high enabling the buffers and putting a word onto the output lines. When any one of CS, RD, or OE is low, the data outputs are disconnected from the rest of the circuit.

As an aside, in Chap. 2 we discussed how a memory appears from the outside—namely, an MAR for the memory address and an MBR for the data. From Fig. 3-28 it is apparent that A_0 and A_1 are taken from a 2-bit MAR, while the three data inputs and three data outputs correspond to the MBR. Because memories usually have only one MBR, the importance of disconnecting D_0, D_1, and D_2 from the MBR on writes to memory to avoid interfering with I_0, I_1, and I_2 should be obvious now.

3.3.4. Memory Properties

The nice thing about the memory of Fig. 3-28 is that it extends easily to larger sizes. As we drew it, the memory is 4×3, that is, four words of 3 bits each. To extend it to 4×8 we need only add five more columns of four flip-flops each, as well as five more input lines and five more output lines. To go from 4×3 to 8×3 we must add four more rows of three flip-flops each, as well as an address line A_2. With this kind of structure, the number of words in the memory should be a power of 2 for maximum efficiency, but the number of bits in a word can be anything.

Because integrated circuit technology is well suited to making chips whose internal structure is a repetitive two-dimensional pattern, memory chips are an ideal application for it. As the technology improves, the number of bits that can be put on a chip keeps increasing, typically by a factor of 4 every 3 or 4 years. In the early 1970s, chips had 1K bits; in later years, they had 4K, 16K, 64K, 256K, and so on. By 1990, chips with millions of bits may be commonplace. The larger chips do not always render the smaller ones obsolete due to different trade-offs in capacity, speed, power, price, and interfacing convenience.

For any given memory size, there are various ways of organizing the chip. Figure 3-30 shows two possible organizations for a 16K-bit chip, 2K $\times$ 8 and 16K $\times$ 1. In the former, 11 address lines are needed to address the selected *byte*, and eight data lines are needed for loading and storing data. In the latter, 14 address lines are needed to address the selected *bit*, but only one line is needed for data in and one for data out. In both cases lines are needed for distinguishing reads from writes and for chip select. The $\overline{\text{OE}}$ line is Output Enable; when it is 0 the output is present, when it is 1 it is not present (i.e., the chip output is disconnected from the circuit). The $\overline{\text{WE}}$ line is for Write Enable. The bars over $\overline{\text{OE}}$, $\overline{\text{WE}}$, and $\overline{\text{CS}}$ mean that the signal is enabled in the low voltage state (logical 0) rather than the high-voltage state (logical 1). This convention will be discussed in more detail later.

Note that building a memory with a 16-bit MBR from 16K $\times$ 1 chips requires 16 chips in parallel and gives a total capacity of at least 32K bytes, whereas using 2K $\times$ 8 chips requires only two chips in parallel and allows memories as small as 4K bytes.

The memories we have studied so far can all be read and written. Such memories are called **RAMs** (Random Access Memories), which is a misnomer because all memory chips are randomly accessible, but the term is well established. RAMs come in two varieties, static and dynamic. **Static RAMs** are constructed internally using circuits similar to our basic D latch. These memories have the property that their contents are retained as long as the power is kept on: seconds, minutes, hours, even days.

Dynamic RAMs, in contrast, do not use latch-like circuits. Instead, a dynamic RAM is an array of tiny capacitors, each of which can be charged or discharged, allowing 0 and 1 to be stored. Because the electric charge tends to leak out, each bit in a dynamic RAM must be **refreshed** every few milliseconds to prevent the data from leaking away. Because external logic must take care of the refreshing, dynamic RAMs require more complex interfacing than static ones, although in many applications this disadvantage is compensated for by their larger capacities. Some dynamic RAMs have on-chip refresh logic, providing both high capacity and simple interfacing. Such chips are said to be **quasi-static**.

RAMs are not the only kind of memory chips. In many applications, such as toys, appliances, and cars, the program and some of the data must remain stored even when the power is turned off. Furthermore, once installed, neither the program nor the data are ever changed. These requirements have led to the development of **ROMs** (Read-Only Memories), which cannot be changed or erased, intentionally or otherwise. The data in a ROM are inserted during its manufacture, essentially by exposing

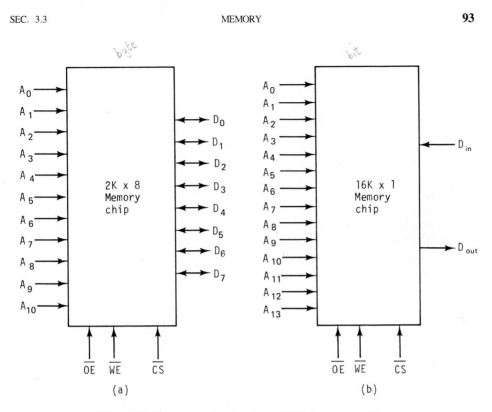

Fig. 3-30. Two ways of organizing a 16K-bit memory chip.

a photosensitive material through a mask containing the desired bit pattern and then etching away the exposed (or unexposed) surface. The only way to change the program in a ROM is to replace the entire chip.

ROMs are much cheaper than RAMs when ordered in large volumes to defray the cost of making the mask. However, they are inflexible, because they cannot be changed after manufacture and the turnaround time between placing an order and receiving the ROMs may be many weeks. To make it easier for companies to develop new ROM-based products, the **PROM** (Programmable ROM) was invented. This chip is like a ROM, except that it can be programmed (once) in the field, greatly reducing turnaround time.

The next development in this line was the **EPROM** (Erasable PROM), which can not only be field-programmed but also field-erased. When the quartz window in an EPROM is exposed to a strong ultraviolet light for 15 minutes, all the bits are set to 1. If many changes are expected during the design cycle, EPROMs are far more economical than PROMs because they can be reused.

Even better than the EPROM is the **EEPROM** (Electrically Erasable PROM), also called an **EAROM** (Electrically Alterable ROM), which can be erased by applying pulses to it instead of requiring it to put in a special chamber for exposure to ultraviolet light. EEPROMs differ from RAMs in that both writing a byte and erasing a byte take thousands of times longer, although access times for reading ROMs, PROMs, EPROMs, EEPROMs, and RAMs are comparable (a few hundred nanoseconds at most).

3.4. MICROPROCESSORS AND MICROCOMPUTERS

Armed with information about SSI chips, MSI chips, and LSI memory chips, we can now tackle the main topic of this chapter—microprocessors and microcomputers. First, we will look at some general aspects of microprocessors as viewed from the digital logic level, including **pinout** (what the signals on the various pins mean) and buses. Then we will examine two popular microprocessors, the Zilog Z80 and the Motorola MC68000 in considerable detail.

3.4.1. Microprocessor Chips

For the purposes of this book we will use the term "microprocessor" to mean any CPU that is contained on a single chip and "microcomputer" to mean a system containing a microprocessor, memory, and some I/O equipment. With this definition it is clear that some microcomputers are more powerful than some minicomputers. Our definition is based on packaging, which makes it appropriate for the digital logic level we are now studying.

We have chosen to focus on CPUs contained on a single chip for a good reason: their interface with the rest of the system is well defined. A typical microprocessor chip has 40, 48, or 64 pins, through which all its communication with the outside world must take place. By understanding the function of all the pins, we can learn how the CPU interacts with the memory and I/O devices at the digital logic level. Although the following material specifically relates to microprocessors, the basic ideas, for example, how CPUs reference memory, how I/O devices are interfaced, and so on, also hold for minicomputers and to some extent for mainframes, albeit in slightly different form.

The pins on a microprocessor chip can be divided into three types: address, data, and control. Every CPU has an address space that it can read and write, commonly bytes numbered 0 to $2^n - 1$. Such a microprocessor needs n pins on which to transmit addresses to memory.

It also needs some pins to send data to memory and receive data from memory. Normally, the microprocessor will have as many data pins as it has bits in its word, in order to read or write a word in one memory cycle. Thus a microprocessor with an 8-bit word, 8-bit registers, and so on, will need eight data pins, whereas a microprocessor with a 16-bit word, 16-bit registers, and so on, usually has 16 data pins. Although it makes little sense to have more data pins than the word length, some microprocessors have only half as many pins as there are bits in a word. Consequently, they need two memory cycles to read or write a word. Although this slows down the machine, it also saves pins and makes the machine cheaper.

The control pins regulate the flow and timing of data to and from the microprocessor and have other miscellaneous uses. Their number and function vary considerably among microprocessors. Some pins regulate memory access, others deal with I/O, and some are needed for power, ground, and clock signals. We will describe the control pins in more detail below, after having described how the various components of a microcomputer are interconnected.

3.4.2. Microcomputer Buses

The components of a microcomputer, the microprocessor, memory, and I/O controller chips, are connected by a collection of parallel wires called a **bus**. The lines (wires) in the bus can be classified as address, data, or control. They correspond closely but not exactly, to the microprocessor's pins. Several buses have been standardized by IEEE and other organizations to facilitate interconnection of processors, memories, and other devices from different vendors (Boberg, 1980; Burr et al., 1979; Elmquist et al., 1979; Gilbert, 1982).

Figure 3-31 illustrates a simple microcomputer with a 2K × 8 EPROM for the program, a 2K × 8 RAM for data, and an I/O chip. In this figure, the 16 address lines (called the **address bus**), the 8 data lines (called the **data bus**), and the (unspecified number of) control lines (called the **control bus**) are shaded to indicate that more than one line is present.

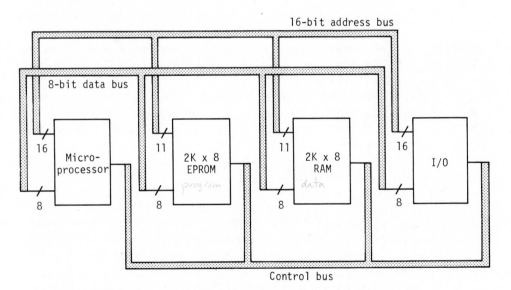

Fig. 3-31. A microcomputer with EPROM, RAM, and an I/O chip.

Another convention used in the figure is the short diagonal line with a number, telling how many bits are meant. For example, the microprocessor is connected to all

16 address lines, but the 2K EPROM only has 2048 bytes, so it only connects to 11 address lines, because $2048 = 2^{11}$. Which of the 16 lines are used and how the various chips are selected will be discussed later.

Communication between chips exhibits a master/slave relationship. One chip, the master, initiates a request to the other, the slave. Sometimes the slave replies, sometimes it just carries out the request silently. At any instant, at most one chip can be master, although many can be slaves. A typical bus transaction is the microprocessor, as master, requesting a byte from the RAM, as slave.

When a device is neither master nor slave, it must not interfere with transactions using the bus. In Fig. 3-28 we saw how using tri-state buffers on output lines could allow the chip to detach itself when not selected. In general, each chip in Fig. 3-31 that can output a signal onto a bus line will have an internal tri-state buffer to release the line when it is not being used, in order to allow other devices to use it. This process is called **floating** the bus. If one device tries to output 0 onto a bus line and another device tries to output a 1, one of the devices will burn out. Chips that OR their values onto the bus rather than trying to force the bus to their values do exist (open collector chips) but they have some drawbacks and are rarely used for microcomputer buses. Note that only *output* lines need be tristatable; a chip is free to look at its inputs all the time without causing conflicts. In Fig. 3-28, for example, the memory may read the address lines even when it is not selected, because it does no harm.

Just for the sake of completeness, we note that even if a device only reads a bus line, it does have an effect because it draws some current from the line. The chip driving the bus can output only a limited amount, which means that its **fanout** (the number of chips that can simultaneously read the output) is limited. For 74xx series TTL chips, the fanout is 10; for 74LSxx series it is 40; for MOS devices, such as microprocessor chips, there may be enough current to drive several other MOS chips but not enough to drive more than one or two standard 74xx TTL chips. High fanout can be achieved by putting tri-state buffers on the output lines, because they not only disconnect the chip when disabled but they normally provide enough current to drive 10 standard TTL chips when enabled.

Control Lines

When the microcomputer of Fig. 3-31 wants to read a byte from memory, it must output some information onto the buses. It puts the address it needs on the address bus and releases the data bus (using its tri-state buffers), but it must also indicate somehow that it is requesting a memory read. How it makes this request depends on the control lines available. One common arrangement is to have two control lines READ and WRITE. By setting the appropriate line to 1, it can tell the memory what to do.

Although we will study memory interfacing in detail later, for the time being we just note that normally a microcomputer has a combinational circuit attached to the address bus to determine which memory chip to select, based on the current address.

For example, if the EPROM is positioned from 0 to 2K in the address space, addresses containing all zeros in the high-order 5 bits should select the EPROM.

Many memory chips react when chip select is low rather than when it is high. To indicate that a signal is active (i.e., enabled) low instead of high, by convention a bar is drawn over its name. Thus a signal called READ is normally low (e.g., 0 to 1 volts), and goes high (e.g., 2 to 5 volts) to indicate that a read cycle is required. In contrast, a signal called $\overline{\text{READ}}$ would normally be high, and would be driven low by the microprocessor to initiate a read cycle. The choice between active high and active low is made by the designers of the microprocessor.

To avoid confusion, we will often use the term **asserted** to mean that a signal is in its active state, whatever that may be. Similarly, **negated** means that the signal is in its inactive (normal) state. Thus for a microprocessor with a pin called READ we would say: READ is asserted to start a memory cycle. For a different microprocessor with a pin called $\overline{\text{READ}}$, we would say: $\overline{\text{READ}}$ is asserted to start a memory cycle. For the former machine, asserted means set high; for the latter it means set low.

An alternative design to having signals (i.e, microprocessor pins and bus lines) called READ and WRITE is to have signals MEMREQ and R/W. The former is asserted when memory request is needed, and the latter is used to distinguish reads from writes.

Numerous other control lines are conceivable. Rather than trying to enumerate them in some abstract way, we have chosen to present two popular microprocessors, the Zilog Z80 and the Motorola MC68000, in some detail. These machines differ in many ways, and by the end of the discussion of both of them you should have a much better idea of what control lines are needed in a bus and why.

3.4.3. The Z80 Microprocessor

The Z80 is a complete 8-bit CPU in a 40-pin package. It has 158 instructions and can address 64K of memory. Its instructions are a superset of the Intel 8080 microprocessor, but the two chips are not pin compatible. We have chosen the Z80 as our first example because it is simple, powerful, and widely used in innumerable applications and products. Throughout our discussion we will use the term "Z80" to mean not only the original Z80 but also the Z80A, Z80B, and so on, which are functionally identical but faster.

Z80 Pinout

The Z80 has 16 address lines, 8 data lines, 13 control lines, power, ground, and clock input, as shown in Fig. 3-32. Both the address lines and the data lines are asserted high , but all the control signals are asserted low, as indicated by the bars. All the address and data lines and some of the control lines can be floated to allow other devices to become bus master. Figure 3-32 is a logical rather than a physical pinout; the actual signals are not grouped together so conveniently.

The $\overline{\text{MREQ}}$, $\overline{\text{IORQ}}$, $\overline{\text{RD}}$, $\overline{\text{WR}}$, and $\overline{\text{WAIT}}$ lines are for reading and writing memory and

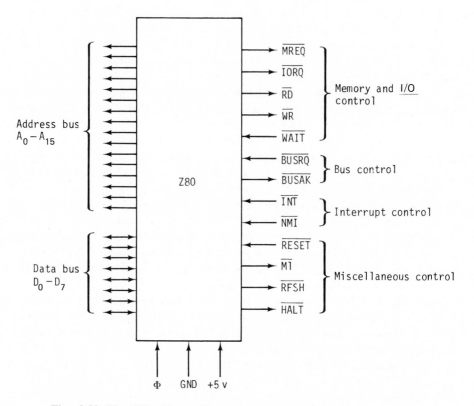

Fig. 3-32. The Z80 address, data, and control signals. The arrows designate input, output, and bidirectional lines.

I/O devices. To read from memory, the Z80 puts the desired address on the address lines and then asserts both $\overline{\text{MREQ}}$ and $\overline{\text{RD}}$. After waiting a certain period of time for the memory to respond, the Z80 then strobes (loads) the byte in from the data lines. A write consists of setting up both the address and data lines, then asserting both $\overline{\text{MREQ}}$ and $\overline{\text{WR}}$.

To read or write an I/O device, the same procedure is followed, except that $\overline{\text{IORQ}}$ is used instead of $\overline{\text{MREQ}}$. Thus memory and the I/O devices occupy two distinct address spaces, with the choice between $\overline{\text{MREQ}}$ and $\overline{\text{IORQ}}$ indicating which one is being referenced. Most memory chips have a chip select line that is asserted low, so $\overline{\text{MREQ}}$ can be used to drive it, possibly ANDed with the output of an address comparator. By wiring $\overline{\text{MREQ}}$ to the chip select lines of the memory chips and $\overline{\text{IORQ}}$ to the chip select lines of the I/O chips, no conflict arises when the same address corresponds to both memory and an I/O device.

The Z80 expects the memory to put the requested byte on the data lines within a certain fixed time. However, the Z80 designers made a provision to allow the use of memories too slow to meet the basic requirements. These slow memories assert $\overline{\text{WAIT}}$ after being selected and keep it asserted until they have placed the data on the bus. The assertion of this signal tells the Z80 to just wait until it is negated.

In many microcomputers I/O devices can also become bus master. When a device other than the CPU is bus master, the CPU must refrain from using the bus—in effect do nothing—until the other device is finished. To achieve the necessary synchronization, the signals $\overline{\text{BUSRQ}}$ and $\overline{\text{BUSAK}}$ are provided. To request permission to become bus master, an I/O device asserts $\overline{\text{BUSRQ}}$. When the CPU is finished with its current cycle, it floats the address lines, data lines, and those control lines that an I/O device might need ($\overline{\text{MREQ}}$, $\overline{\text{IORQ}}$, $\overline{\text{RD}}$, and $\overline{\text{WR}}$) and then asserts $\overline{\text{BUSAK}}$ to grant permission to use the bus. Recognition and response to $\overline{\text{BUSRQ}}$ is done entirely in hardware; the Z80 programmer is completely unaware of it. If multiple I/O devices are competing for the bus, external arbitration logic is needed.

An I/O device may need to signal the CPU, for example, to announce that a data transfer has been completed. To do this, it only needs to assert $\overline{\text{INT}}$, which causes a program interrupt at the end of the current instruction, if interrupts are currently enabled. $\overline{\text{NMI}}$ (NonMaskable Interrupt) can also be used for causing interrupts. However, unlike $\overline{\text{INT}}$, it cannot be disabled in software. It is therefore typically used to report errors or potentially disastrous external conditions.

$\overline{\text{RESET}}$ is an external signal used to reset the internal status of the CPU and make it jump to location 0. It is normally used to start the microcomputer after the power has come on, or to reboot after a crash. Typically, $\overline{\text{RESET}}$ is just connected to a button on the front panel.

$\overline{\text{MI}}$ is output by the Z80 at the start of each instruction read. It is provided for compatibility with the 8080, where it plays an important role, and to allow other chips to distinguish between opcode reads and data reads, which have different properties. (The opcode is the first byte of the instruction; it identifies the operation to be performed.) In particular, opcode reads are longer than data reads to allow time for dynamic memories to be refreshed. During the second half of an opcode read cycle, the Z80 asserts $\overline{\text{RFSH}}$ and puts a 7-bit counter on the address lines to help keep track of which part of the memory is due for refreshing.

Because the Z80 plays an important role in refreshing the dynamic RAMs, it never stops, not even after a HALT instruction. Instead, it just keeps asserting $\overline{\text{RFSH}}$ while waiting for an interrupt. After a HALT instruction has been executed, however, the $\overline{\text{HALT}}$ line is asserted to tell the rest of the system that the CPU is "stopped" waiting for an interrupt.

The three remaining lines are power, ground, and clock (Φ). The Z80 is powered by a single 5-volt supply, and draws 1.5 watts. The clock is a 5-volt square wave at any frequency up to some maximum (2.5, 4, or 6 MHz) depending on the chip version. Because each instruction takes a specific number of clock cycles, the CPU speed is directly proportional to the clock frequency. Unlike many microprocessors, the Z80 has no lower limit on the clock frequency. Furthermore, successive clock periods need not be equally long. The Φ input can even be driven by a toggle switch to allow a system designer to step through a program bus cycle by bus cycle.

Z80 Memory Request Timing

When the Z80 needs to read a byte from memory, it puts the address of the byte on the address lines and then asserts $\overline{MREQ}$ and $\overline{RD}$, as mentioned above. In this section we are going to look at the precise timing of the various signals in detail because being able to read timing diagrams is essential to understanding how memory chips and I/O chips are interfaced to microprocessors.

A typical Z80 instruction is LD A,7, which loads the constant 7 into a Z80 register, the accumulator. The instruction occupies two bytes in memory, one for the opcode and one for the constant (7) to be loaded. Figure 3-33 shows the basic timing for this instruction. The instruction requires two machine cycles for its execution: one to read the opcode byte and one to read the operand byte. The opcode read takes four clock periods (which includes asserting signals for refreshing dynamic RAMs) and the operand read takes three clock periods. If the clock frequency is, say, 4 MHz, each clock period will be 250 nsec, so the full instruction execution will take 1750 nsec. Note that the rising and falling edges of the clock have not been drawn straight up and down, because no electrical signal can change in zero time.

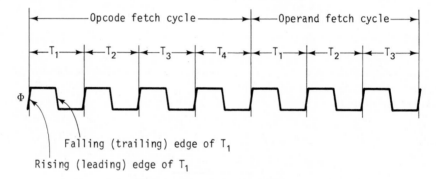

Fig. 3-33. Timing for LD A,7.

Figure 3-34(a) shows the operand read cycle of the load instruction in more detail, although slightly simplified from that of a real Z80. The clock, address, data, $\overline{MREQ}$, and $\overline{RD}$ lines are all shown on the same time scale. The start of T_1 is defined by the rising edge of the clock. Part way through T_1 the Z80 puts the address of the byte it wants on the address lines, A_0 to A_{15}. Because the address is not a single value, like the clock, we cannot show it as a single line in the figure; instead, it is shown as two lines, with a crossing at the time that the address changes. Furthermore, the shading prior to the crossing indicates that the shaded value is not important. Using the same shading convention, we see that the contents of the data lines are not significant until well into T_3.

After the address lines have had a chance to settle down to their new values, $\overline{MREQ}$ and $\overline{RD}$ are asserted. Nothing happens during T_2, to give the memory time to decode the address and put the data on the bus. At the falling edge of T_3 the Z80

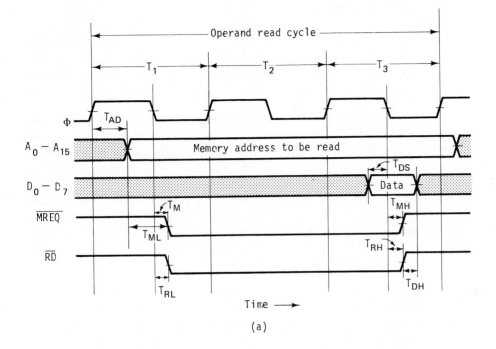

(a)

Symbol	Parameter	Min	Max	Unit
T_{AD}	Address output delay		110	n sec
T_{ML}	Address stable prior to $\overline{MREQ}$	60		n sec
T_M	$\overline{MREQ}$ delay from falling edge of Φ in T_1		85	n sec
T_{RL}	RD delay from falling edge of Φ in T_1		85	n sec
T_{DS}	Data setup time prior to falling edge of Φ	50		n sec
T_{MH}	$\overline{MREQ}$ delay from falling edge of Φ in T_3		85	n sec
T_{RH}	$\overline{RD}$ delay from falling edge of Φ in T_3		85	n sec
T_{DH}	Data hold time from negation of $\overline{RD}$	0		n sec

(b)

Fig. 3-34. (a) Z80 operand read timing. (b) Specification of some critical times.

strobes the data lines, latching (i.e., storing) the value in an internal register. Having read the data, the Z80 negates $\overline{MREQ}$ and $\overline{RD}$. If need be, another memory cycle can begin at the next rising edge of the clock.

In the timing specification of Fig. 3-34(b), eight symbols that occur in the timing diagram are further clarified. T_{AD}, for example, is the time interval between the rising edge of the T_1 clock and the address lines being set. According to the timing specification, $T_{AD} \leq 110$ nsec. (For this example we assume a 250 nsec clock period, with 10 nsec rise and fall times.) This means that the chip manufacturer guarantees that during any operand read cycle, the Z80 will output the address to be read within 110 nsec of the T_1 rising clock.

The timing specifications also require that the data be available on the data lines at least 50 nsec before the falling edge of T_3, to give it time to settle down before the Z80 strobes (i.e., reads) it in. The combination of the constraints on T_{AD} and T_{DS} means that in the worst case, the memory will have only 250 + 250 + 125 - 110 - 50 = 465 nsec from the time the address appears until it must produce the data. If memory cannot respond fast enough, it must assert $\overline{\text{WAIT}}$ prior to the falling edge of T_2 when $\overline{\text{WAIT}}$ is strobed.

The timing specification further guarantees that the address will be set up at least 60 nsec prior to $\overline{\text{MREQ}}$ being asserted. This time can be important if $\overline{\text{MREQ}}$ drives chip select on the memory chip because some memories require an address setup time prior to chip select. Clearly, the microcomputer designer should not choose a memory chip with a 75-nsec setup time.

The constraint on T_M and T_{RL} mean that $\overline{\text{MREQ}}$ and $\overline{\text{RD}}$ will both be asserted within 85 nsec from the T_1 falling clock. In the worst case, the memory chip will have only 250 + 250 - 85 - 50 = 365 nsec after the assertion of $\overline{\text{MREQ}}$ and $\overline{\text{RD}}$ to get its data onto the bus. This constraint is in addition to the address constraint.

T_{MH} and T_{RH} tell how long it takes $\overline{\text{MREQ}}$ and $\overline{\text{RD}}$ to be negated after the data have been strobed in. Finally, T_{DH} tells how long the memory must hold the data on the bus after $\overline{\text{RD}}$ has been negated. As far as the Z80 is concerned, the memory can remove the data from the bus as soon as $\overline{\text{RD}}$ has been negated; on some other microprocessors, the data must be kept stable for a little while after a request.

We would like to point out that Fig. 3-34 is a simplified version of the true Z80 timing. In reality, 49 different critical times are specified (not just for read, however). Nevertheless, Fig. 3-34 gives a good flavor for microprocessor timing requirements. Figures like this one are part of every microprocessor product specification and that of other chips as well.

3.4.4. The 68000 Microprocessor

As a second example of a microprocessor chip, we will now look at the Motorola MC68000 (Stritter and Gunter, 1979), or just 68000 for short. By any measure, the 68000 is more powerful (and more expensive) than the Z80. It can address 16M bytes of memory (versus 64K for the Z80), read and write data 16 bits at a time (versus 8 for the Z80) and is much faster. It also has many instructions that operate on 8-, 16-, or 32-bit quantities (versus mostly 8-bit and a few 16-bit instructions for the Z80). The 68000 is really a family of CPUs including the 68010, 68020, and so on, but the differences between the members will not concern us here.

In fact, from the programmer's point of view, it can be argued that the 68000 is a 32-bit word machine because it has 32-bit registers and so many instructions to use them. However, as seen from the digital logic level, it appears to be a 16-bit word machine because it reads and writes memory in 16-bit units. (A good way to see if a computer scientist is a hardware or software person is to ask if the 68000 is a 16-bit machine or a 32-bit machine.) If one were to categorize machines as micros, minis, or mainframes based on their architecture, the 68000 would be a large mini or a small mainframe.

68000 Pinout

The 68000 has 23 address lines, 16 data lines, 20 control lines, power ($2 \times$), ground ($2 \times$), and clock, as shown in Fig. 3-35. Addresses are actually 24 bits but because word addresses must be even, bit A_0 is always 0, and is not output. The 16 data lines are normally used to read or write 16-bit words but provision has also been made for reading and writing bytes. Reading and writing 32-bit quantities requires two memory cycles.

Memory reads and writes are done differently on the 68000 than on the Z80. To read a word, the 68000 puts the address on the bus, sets R/$\overline{\text{W}}$ (high for a read and low for a write), and then asserts $\overline{\text{AS}}$ (Address Strobe). This scheme is more efficient than the Z80's, because only two lines are needed ($\overline{\text{AS}}$, and R/$\overline{\text{W}}$), instead of three ($\overline{\text{MREQ}}$, $\overline{\text{RD}}$, and $\overline{\text{WR}}$). Unlike the Z80, the 68000 does not have a separate address space for I/O devices, so there is no signal analogous to $\overline{\text{IORQ}}$.

The $\overline{\text{UDS}}$ (Upper Data Strobe) and $\overline{\text{LDS}}$ (Lower Data Strobe) signals distinguish byte operations from word operations. If only one of them is asserted, only the corresponding byte is read or written. If both are asserted, both bytes (i.e., a full 16-bit word) are read or written.

In addition to the differences with the Z80 just described, there is also a more fundamental difference. On a read, the Z80 expects the memory to put the data on the bus 50 nsec before the falling edge of T_3, or failing to do so, to assert $\overline{\text{WAIT}}$ during T_2. Because memory transfers are closely tied to the clock they are called **synchronous**. The 68000 has no such expectations. The memory can take as long as it wants to. When it is finished, the memory just asserts $\overline{\text{DTACK}}$ to say it is done. Similarly, on a write, the memory just asserts $\overline{\text{DTACK}}$ when it has latched the data. The 68000 is **asynchronous**. A system like the 68000 that asserts a signal and then waits for another signal to be asserted as a reply is said to use **handshaking**.

The $\overline{\text{BR}}$ (Bus Request) line is used by I/O devices to request the bus. The $\overline{\text{BG}}$ (Bus Grant) line is asserted by the 68000 to announce that the bus has indeed been floated. This protocol is the same as on the Z80. A difference with the Z80, however, is the presence of the $\overline{\text{BGACK}}$ line, which is asserted by the requesting device after it sees the bus grant. In principle, a device could request and be granted the bus and then assert $\overline{\text{BGACK}}$. At this point $\overline{\text{BR}}$ and $\overline{\text{BG}}$ are available for another device to request and be granted the bus while the previous device was still using it for transferring data. The second device could not, of course, actually start using the bus until the first one indi-

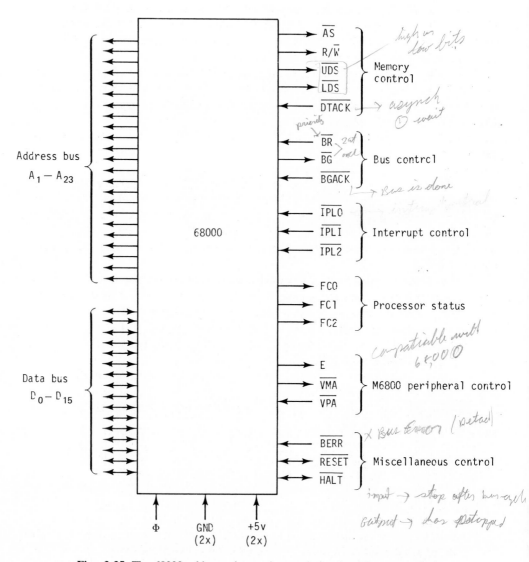

Fig. 3-35. The 68000 address, data and control signals. The arrows designate input, output, and bidirectional lines.

cated that it was finished by negating $\overline{\text{BGACK}}$. By allowing the bus grant protocol to run in parallel with data transfer, bus cycles are saved.

The three $\overline{\text{IPL}}$ pins are used to encode the priority of an I/O device requesting an interrupt. If the device has a higher priority than the CPU currently has, the interrupt occurs; otherwise, it must wait. This technique is more flexible than on the Z80, where interrupts are either enabled or disabled.

The three $\overline{FC}$ lines are used by the 68000 to output certain status information. E, $\overline{VMA}$, and $\overline{VPA}$ are signals present on the M6800 microprocessor chip (a predecessor of the 68000), and are provided here to allow the 68000 to use peripheral chips designed for the M6800, which is synchronous, like the Z80.

$\overline{BERR}$ (Bus ERRor) is used to inform the 68000 that something is wrong, for example, a device does not respond. If no such signal was available, an attempt to read from nonexistent memory would cause the 68000 to hang forever waiting for $\overline{DTACK}$. Typically, an external timer asserts $\overline{BERR}$ if no response to a read or write request is forthcoming within a reasonable interval. The Z80 does not need such protection because an attempt to read nonexistent memory will just cause it to strobe in nonexistent data in T_3 but not to hang.

$\overline{RESET}$ can be used to reset the CPU, as on the Z80 but it can also be asserted under program control to reset I/O devices. $\overline{HALT}$ is also a bidirectional line. As an output, it indicates that the 68000 has stopped, just as on the Z80. As an input, it causes the CPU to stop after the current bus cycle, to allow programs to be run one bus cycle at a time. On the Z80 single cycling is accomplished by slowing down the clock, something the 68000 cannot tolerate.

Power, ground, and the clock serve the same function as on the Z80. The only difference is that power and ground are each needed on two pins. If future versions of the chip need two more pins, these two can always be reclaimed later.

3.5. INTERFACING

A microcomputer system consists of a microprocessor, some memory chips, and some I/O chips connected in such a way that they work together. We have already studied memories and microprocessors in some detail. After a brief introduction to I/O chips, we will see how the pieces can be put together, concluding with an examination of a small but complete microcomputer.

3.5.1. I/O Chips

Numerous I/O chips are already available and new ones are being introduced all the time. Common chips include UARTs, USARTs, CRT controllers, floppy disk controllers, and PIOs. A **UART** (Universal Asynchronous Receiver Transmitter) is a chip that can read a byte from the data bus and output it a bit at a time on a serial line for a terminal, or input data from a terminal. UARTs usually allow speeds from 50 bps to 19.2 kbps; character widths from 5 to 8 bits; 1, 1.5, or 2 stop bits; and provide even, odd, or no parity, all under program control. **USART**s (Universal Synchronous Asynchronous Receiver Transmitters) can handle synchronous transmission using a variety of protocols as well as performing all the UART functions. As an example of how I/O chips work and are interfaced, we will now look in some detail at parallel I/O.

PIO Chips

A typical **PIO** (Parallel Input/Output) chip is the Intel 8255A, shown in Fig. 3-36. It has 24 I/O lines that can interface to any TTL-compatible device, for example, keyboards, switches, lights, printers, disk controllers, or paper tape readers. In a nutshell, the CPU program can write a 0 or 1 to any line, or read the input status of any line, providing great flexibility. A small microprocessor-based system using a PIO can often replace a complete board full of SSI or MSI chips.

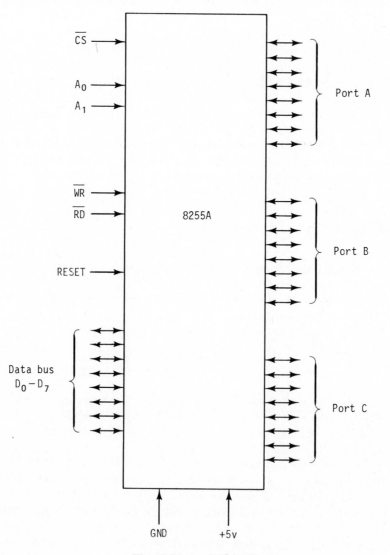

Fig. 3-36. An 8255A PIO chip.

Although the CPU can configure the 8255A in many ways by loading status registers within the chip, we will concentrate on some of the simpler modes of operation. The simplest way of using the 8255A is as three independent 8-bit ports, A, B, and C. Associated with each port is an 8-bit latch register. To set the lines on a port, the CPU just writes an 8-bit number into the corresponding register, and the 8-bit number appears on the output lines and stays there until the register is rewritten. To use a port for input, the CPU just reads the corresponding register.

Other operating modes provide for handshaking with external devices. For example, to output to a device that is not always ready to accept data, the 8255A can present data on an output port and wait for the device to send a pulse back saying that it has accepted the data and wants more. The necessary logic for latching such pulses and making them available to the CPU is included in the 8255A but we will not consider it further.

From the functional diagram of the 8255A we can see that in addition to 24 pins for the three ports, it has eight lines that connect directly to the data bus, a chip select line, read and write lines (that correspond exactly to the signals of the same name on the Intel 8080 and Zilog Z80), two address lines, and a line for resetting the chip. The two address lines select one of the four internal registers, corresponding to ports A, B, C, and the status register, which has bits determining which ports are for input and which for output, and other functions. Normally, the two address lines are connected to the low-order bits of the address bus.

3.5.2. Address Decoding

Up until now we have been deliberately vague about how chip select is asserted on the memory and I/O chips we have looked at. It is now time to look more carefully at how this is done. Let us consider a simple microcomputer consisting of a Z80 CPU, a 2K × 8 EPROM for the program, a 2K × 8 RAM for the data, and a PIO. This four-chip (so far) system might be used as a prototype for the brain of a toy or appliance. Once it went into production, the EPROM would normally be replaced by a ROM.

The PIO can be selected in one of two ways, as a true I/O device or as part of memory. If we choose to use it as an I/O device, then we must select it using $\overline{\text{IORQ}}$. If we use the other approach, **memory-mapped I/O**, then we must assign it four bytes of the address space for the three ports and the control register. The choice is somewhat arbitrary. We will choose memory-mapped I/O because it illustrates some issues in address decoding.

The EPROM needs 2K of address space, the RAM also needs 2K of address space, and the PIO needs 4 bytes. Because the Z80 address space is 64K, we must make a choice about where to put the three devices. One possible choice is shown in Fig. 3-37. The EPROM occupies addresses 000000 to 003777, the RAM occupies addresses 100000 to 103777, and the PIO occupies the highest four bytes of the address space, 177774 to 177777 (all addresses are in octal). From the programmer's point of view, it makes no difference which addresses are used; however, for interfacing it does matter. If we had chosen to address the PIO via the I/O space, it would not need any memory addresses (but it would need four I/O space addresses).

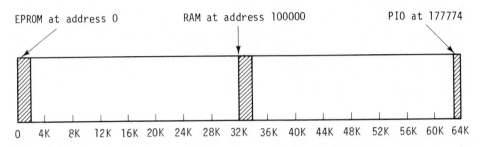

Fig. 3-37. Location of the EPROM, RAM, and PIO in the Z80's 64K address space. The upper addresses are in octal, the lower ones are in decimal.

With the address assignments of Fig. 3-37, the EPROM should be selected by any 16-bit memory address of the form 00000xxxxxxxxxxx. In other words, any address whose 5 high-order bits are all 0s falls in the bottom 2K of memory, hence in the EPROM. Thus the EPROM's chip select could be wired to a 5-bit comparator one of whose inputs was permanently wired to 00000.

A better way to achieve the same effect is to use a five-input OR gate, with the five inputs attached to address lines A_{11} to A_{15}. If and only if all five lines are 0 will the output be 0, thus asserting $\overline{CS}$ (which is asserted low). Unfortunately, no five-input OR gate exists in the standard SSI series. The closest we can come is an eight-input NOR gate. By grounding three inputs and inverting the output we can nevertheless produce the correct signal, as shown in Fig. 3-38(a). By convention, unused inputs are not shown in circuit diagrams.

The same principle can be used for the RAM. However, the RAM should respond to binary addresses of the form 10000xxxxxxxxxxx, so an additional inverter is needed as shown in the figure. The PIO address decoding is more complicated, because it is selected by the four addresses of the form 11111111111111xx. A possible circuit that asserts $\overline{CS}$ only when the correct address appears on the address bus is shown in the figure. It uses two eight-input NAND gates to feed an OR gate. To build the address decoding logic of Fig. 3-38(a) using SSI requires six chips—the four eight-input chips, an OR gate, and a chip with three inverters. The address decoding requires more chips than the CPU, memory, and I/O device combined!

However, if the computer really consists of only the CPU, two memory chips, and the PIO, we can use a trick to simplify greatly the address decoding. The trick is based on the fact that all EPROM addresses, and only EPROM addresses, have a 0 in the high-order bit, A_{15}. Therefore, we can just wire $\overline{CS}$ to A_{15} directly, as shown in Fig. 3-38(b) At this point the decision to put the RAM at 100000 (octal) may seem much less arbitrary. The RAM decoding can be done by noting that the only valid addresses of the form 10xxxxxxxxxxxxxx are in the RAM, so 2 bits of decoding is

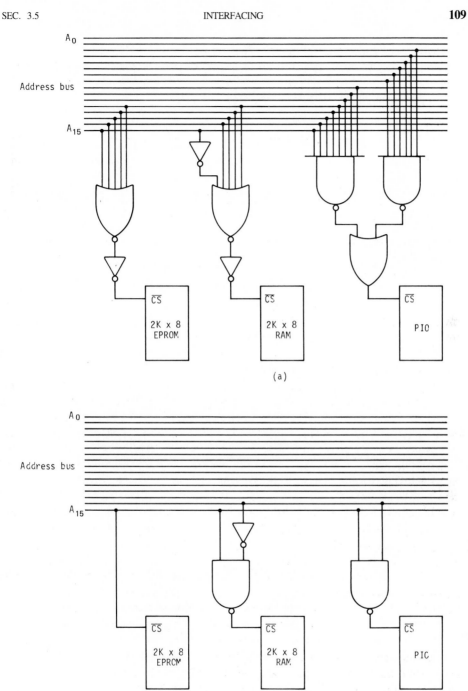

Fig. 3-38. (a) Full address decoding. (b) Partial address decoding.

sufficient. Similarly, any address starting with 11 must be a PIO address. The complete decoding logic is now two NAND gates and an inverter. Because an inverter can be made from a NAND gate by just tying the two inputs together, a single quad NAND chip is now more than sufficient.

The address decoding logic of Fig. 3-38(b) is called **partial address decoding**, because the full addresses are not used. It has the property that a read from addresses 004000, 010000, or 014000 will give the same result. In fact, every address in the bottom half of the address space will select the EPROM. Because the extra addresses are not used, no harm is done, but if one is designing a computer that may be expanded in the future (an unlikely occurrence in a toy), partial decoding should be avoided because it ties up too much address space.

Another common address decoding technique is to use a decoder chip, such as that shown in Fig. 3-14. By connecting the three inputs to the three high-order address lines, we get eight outputs, corresponding to addresses in the first 8K, second 8K, and so on. For a computer with eight RAMs, each 8K $\times$ 8, one such chip provides the complete decoding. For a computer with eight 2K $\times$ 8 memory chips, a single decoder is also sufficient, provided that the memory chips are each located in distinct 8K chunks of address space. (Remember our earlier remark that the position of the memory and I/O chips within the address space matters.)

3.5.3. An Example Microcomputer

As the culmination of our study of the digital logic level, we will now combine all the pieces to get a small but complete microcomputer. Our six-chip system is shown in Fig. 3-39. It consists of a Z80 CPU, a 2K $\times$ 8 EPROM, a 2K $\times$ 8 static RAM, a PIO chip, a quad NAND gate chip for partial address decoding, the same as in Fig. 3-38(b), and a three-input NAND gate for driving the PIO's chip select pin. We have already studied the Z80 (Fig. 3-32), the memory chips [Fig. 3-30(a)], and the PIO (Fig. 3-36). All that is left to do is look at the interconnection. In fact, we have even seen an outline of that in Fig. 3-31. (A slightly simpler version of the computer using the I/O space instead of memory mapping for the PIO is the subject of Prob. 26.)

Let us first look at the CPU. The eight data lines are fed to the other three LSI chips in a straightforward way via the data bus, so we have not shown the detail here. Thirteen of the address lines are also used. The other three lines, A_{11} to A_{13}, are not used. Similarly, $\overline{MI}$, $\overline{IORQ}$, $\overline{RFSH}$, $\overline{HALT}$, and $\overline{BUSAK}$ are all output signals that are not used, so no connection to them is needed. The four input signals that are not used, $\overline{INT}$, $\overline{NMI}$, $\overline{WAIT}$, and $\overline{BUSRQ}$ are wired high to keep them negated.

$\overline{MREQ}$ is used to enable the output lines on both memory chips. Note that the two memory chips only generate output when both $\overline{CS}$ and $\overline{OE}$ are asserted. $\overline{WR}$ and $\overline{RD}$ are needed for the corresponding PIO signals, and $\overline{WR}$ is also needed for the RAM. Because the EPROM cannot be written into while sitting in the computer, it does not need a signal to distinguish read from write.

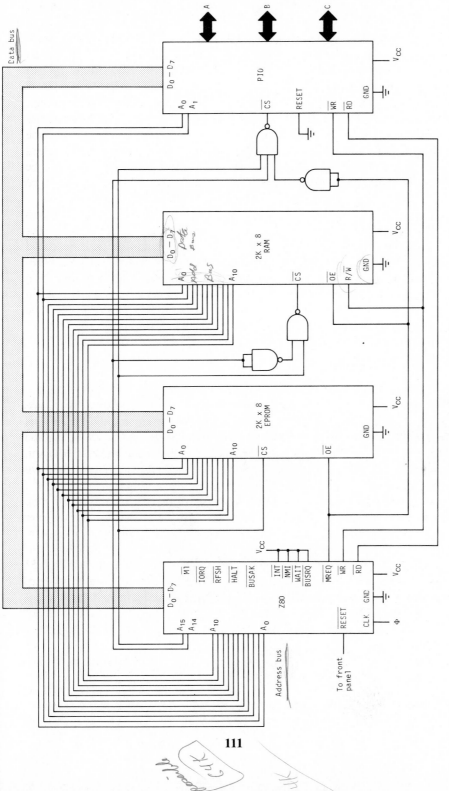

Fig. 3-39. A Z80-based microcomputer.

111

The $\overline{\text{RESET}}$ signal is wired to a button on the front panel to allow the microcomputer to be reset manually.

To make our microcomputer actually work, two more items are needed: a power supply and a clock. Depending on the specific chips chosen, the microcomputer will consume about 3.5 watts of power. For the clock, any square wave source up to the maximum frequency of the Z80 chip chosen will do.

We have come a long way from the basic transistor inverter to a complete computer system. Hopefully it is clear by now that there is nothing mysterious about how a computer works. We have described the operation of static RAMs down to the gate level. In the next chapter we will examine CPUs down to the gate level as well.

3.6. SUMMARY

Computers are constructed from integrated circuit chips containing tiny switching elements called gates. The most common gates are AND, OR, NAND, NOR, and NOT. Simple circuits can be built up by directly combining individual gates using SSI chips.

More complex circuits are constructed using standard MSI components such as multiplexers, demultiplexers, encoders, decoders, shifters, and ALUs. Arbitrary Boolean functions can be programmed using a PLA. If many Boolean functions are needed, PLAs are much more efficient (i.e., require fewer chips), than using SSI chips.

The components of (static) memories are latches and flip-flops, each of which can store 1-bit of information. These can be combined linearly into octal latches and flip-flops or logarithmically into full-scale word-oriented memories. Memories are available as RAM, ROM, PROM, EPROM, and EEPROM. Static memories need not be refreshed; they keep their values as long as the power remains on. Dynamic memories, on the other hand, must be refreshed periodically to compensate for leakage from the little capacitors on the chip.

The components of a computer system are connected by buses. Most of the pins on a typical microprocessor chip directly drive one bus line. The bus lines can be divided into address, data, and control lines. The Z80 and 68000 were discussed as examples, and a small but complete, Z80 system was given as an example and described in detail. The Z80 system contained the microprocessor chip, an EPROM chip for the program, a RAM chip for the data, and a PIO chip for interfacing with the outside world. In addition, two SSI chips were needed for address decoding.

PROBLEMS

1. A logician drives into a drive-in restaurant and says, "I want a hamburger or a hot dog and french fries." The cook flunked out of sixth grade and doesn't know (or care) whether "and" has precedence over "or." As far as he is concerned, one interpretation is as good

as the other. Which of the following cases are valid interpretations of the order? (Note that in English "or" means "exclusive or.")

    a. Just a hamburger.
    b. Just a hot dog.
    c. Just french fries.
    d. A hot dog and french fries.
    e. A hamburger and french fries.
    f. A hot dog and a hamburger.
    g. All three.
    h. Nothing—the logician goes hungry for being a wiseguy.

2. A missionary lost in Southern California stops at a fork in the road. He knows that two motorcycle gangs inhabit the area, one of which always tells the truth and one of which always lies. He wants to know which road leads to Disneyland. What question should he ask?

3. There exist four Boolean functions of a single variable and 16 functions of two variables. How many functions of three variables are there? Of n variables?

4. Use a truth table to show that $P = (P$ AND $Q)$ OR $(P$ AND NOT $Q)$.

5. Use de Morgan's law to find the complement of $A\bar{B}$.

6. Using the three-variable multiplexer chip of Fig. 3-13, implement a function whose output is the parity of the inputs, that is, the output is 1 if and only if an odd number of inputs are 1.

7. Put on your thinking cap. The three-variable multiplexer chip of Fig. 3-13 is actually capable of computing an arbitrary function of *four* Boolean variables. Describe how, and as an example, draw the logic diagram for the function that is 0 if the English word for the truth table row has an even number of letters, 1 if it has an odd number of letters (e.g., 0000 = zero = four letters → 0; 0111 = seven = five letters → 1; 1101 = thirteen = eight letters → 0). *Hint*: If we call the fourth input variable D, the eight input lines may be wired to V_{cc}, ground, D, or $\bar{D}$.

8. Draw the logic diagram of a 2-bit demultiplexer, a circuit whose single input line is steered to one of the four output lines depending on the state of the two control lines.

9. Draw the logic diagram of a 2-bit encoder, a circuit with four input lines, exactly one of which is high at any instant, and two output lines whose 2-bit binary value tells which input is high.

10. Redraw the PLA of Fig. 3-16 in enough detail to show how the majority logic function of Fig. 3-3 can be implemented. In particular, be sure to show which connections are present in both matrices.

11. What does this circuit do?

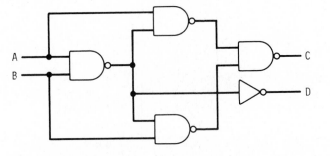

12. A common MSI chip is a 4-bit adder. Four of these chips can be hooked up to form a 16-bit adder. How many pins would you expect the 4-bit adder chip to have? Why?

13. An n-bit adder can be constructed by cascading n full adders in series, with the carry into stage i, C_i, coming from the output of stage $i - 1$. The carry into stage 0, C_0, is 0. If each stage takes T nsec to produce its sum and carry, the carry into stage i will not be valid until iT nsec after the start of the addition. For large n the time required for the carry to ripple through to the high-order stage may be unacceptably long. Design an adder that works faster. *Hint*: Each C_i can be expressed in terms of the operand bits A_{i-1} and B_{i-1} as well as the carry C_{i-1}. Using this relation it is possible to express C_i as a function of the inputs to stages 0 to $i - 1$, so all the carries can be generated simultaneously.

14. If all the gates in Fig. 3-20 have a propagation delay of 10 nsec, and all other delays can be ignored, what is the earliest time a circuit using this design can be sure of having a valid output bit?

15. What is the quiescent state of the S and R inputs to an SR latch built of two NAND gates?

16. Given a JK flip-flop packaged in a chip, is it possible to convert it to a D flip-flop using external logic? If so, how? If not, why not? What about the reverse, that is, converting a D flip-flop into a JK one?

17. To help meet the payments on your new personal computer, you have taken up consulting for fledgling SSI chip manufacturers. One of your clients is thinking about putting out a chip containing four D flip-flops, each containing both Q and $\overline{Q}$, on request of a potentially important customer. The proposed design has all four clock signals ganged together, also on request. Neither preset nor clear is present. Your assignment is to give a professional evaluation of the design.

18. The circuit depicted below consists of four JK flip-flops, each triggered by the 1-to-0 transition on its clock input. None of the J or K inputs are connected, which means that they are all logical 1. The value stored in the circuit can be seen as a 4-bit number, $ABCD$. The input line consists of rectangular pulses 1 msec wide, spaced 100 msec apart. If $ABCD$ is initially 0000, what will it be after 13 input pulses?

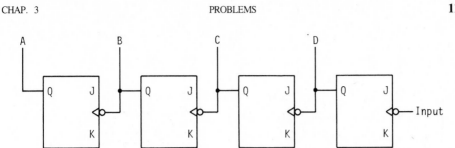

19. The 4 × 3 memory of Fig. 3-28 uses 22 AND gates and three OR gates. If the circuit were to be expanded to 256 × 8, how many of each would be needed?

20. As more and more memory is squeezed onto a single chip, the number of pins needed to address it also increases. It is often inconvenient to have large numbers of address pins on a chip. Devise a way to address 2^n words of memory using fewer than n pins.

21. A finite-state machine has 2^n possible states. At each clock pulse, it reads in a k-bit symbol, emits a k-bit output symbol, and switches to a new state. The symbol emitted and the new state depend on the current state and the input symbol. Describe how the machine can be implemented using a ROM, and tell how big the ROM must be.

22. A computer with a 32-bit wide data bus uses 4K × 8 static RAM memory chips. What is the smallest memory (in bytes) that this computer can have?

23. Referring to the timing diagram of Fig. 3-34, suppose that you slowed the clock down to a period of 400 nsec instead of 250 nsec as shown but the timing constraints remained unchanged. How much time would the memory have to get the data onto the bus after $\overline{\text{MREQ}}$ was asserted, in the worst case?

24. The Z80's jump instruction occupies 3 bytes, one for the opcode and two for the address. If the internal processing time within the CPU chip were zero, how long would the instruction take on a system with a 2.5-MHz clock?

25. In Fig. 3-31(b), T_{ML} is specified to be at least 60 nsec. Can you envision a chip in which it is negative? In other words, could the CPU assert $\overline{\text{MREQ}}$ before the address was stable? Why or why not?

26. What changes must be made to the circuit of Fig. 3-39 to have the PIO selected as input/output ports 0 to 3, instead of as memory addresses in the top quadrant of memory?

27. Imagine that you have built the system of Fig. 3-39, programmed it to play tic-tac-toe and lose, and have started selling it in volume to the incoming computer science freshman class as an ego booster. Suddenly your marketing manager comes running in waving a computer printout claiming that it is time to bring out a new version. You are too lazy to change the hardware, so you decide the simplest change is to move the RAM within the address space. To what address(es), if any, can you move it without invalidating the program?

28. Write a program to simulate the behavior of an $m \times n$ array of two-input NAND gates. This circuit, contained on a chip, has j input pins and k output pins. The values of j, k, m, and n are compile-time parameters of the simulation. The program should start off by reading in a "wiring list," each wire of which specifies an input and an output. An input is either one of the j input pins or the output of some NAND gate. An output is either one of the k output pins or an input to some NAND gate. Unused inputs are logical 1. After reading in the wiring list, the program should print the output for each of the 2^j possible inputs. Gate array chips like this one are widely used for putting custom circuits on a chip because most of the work (depositing the gate array on the chip) is independent of the circuit to be implemented. Only the wiring is specific to each design.

29. Write a program to read in two arbitrary Boolean expressions and see if they represent the same function.

30. Write a program to read in a collection of Boolean expressions and compute the 24×50 and 50×6 matrices needed to implement them with the PLA of Fig. 3-16. Print the matrices on the line printer.

4

THE MICROPROGRAMMING LEVEL

The boundary between hardware and software is not well defined and, further-more, is constantly shifting. Early computers had instructions for arithmetic, Boolean operations, shifting, comparing, looping, and so on, that were all directly executed by the hardware. For each instruction, a specific hardware circuit was present to carry it out. One could unscrew the back panel and point to the electronic components used by the division instruction, at least in principle.

On a modern multilevel computer, it is no longer possible to isolate the division circuits because there are no division circuits. All the instructions available at the conventional machine level (e.g., instructions for arithmetic, Boolean, shifting, com-paring, and looping) are carried out one step at a time by an interpreter running at the microprogramming level. The modern-day equivalent of looking for the division cir-cuits is to get out a list of the microprogram and looking for that portion of it which interprets division instructions.

Although programs at any level may be carried out by a software interpreter, and although this interpreter itself may also be executed by another interpreter, this hierar-chy cannot go on indefinitely. At the bottom level, there must be a physical hardware machine, with integrated circuits, power supplies, and similar "hard" objects. These items were the subject of the preceding chapter. In this chapter we will study how the hardware components are controlled by the microprogram and how the microprogram interprets the conventional machine level.

Because the architecture of the microprogramming level, called the **microarchi-tecture**, is defined by the hardware, it is usually primitive and awkward to program.

Timing considerations are frequently important, for example. These considerations led Rosin (1974) to define microprogramming as "the implementation of hopefully reasonable systems through interpretation on unreasonable machines."

The microprogramming level has a specific function: to execute interpreters for other (hopefully, more reasonable) virtual machines. This design goal naturally leads to an organization highly optimized toward fetching, examining, and executing conventional machine instructions, and, in some cases, more sophisticated instructions. The issues and trade-offs involved in the organization and design for this level will be examined in this chapter.

We will begin our study of the microprogramming level by briefly reviewing the basic building blocks discussed in Chap. 3, because they are part of the architecture of the microprogramming level, hence of concern to the microprogrammer. (A "microprogrammer" is someone who writes microprograms, not a small programmer.) Next, we come to the heart of the subject, how more complex instructions can be built up from sequences of primitive instructions. This topic will be discussed in detail and illustrated by an extensive example. Afterward we will examine the various factors that must be considered when designing a computer's microprogramming level, in order to better understand why it is the way it is. Finally, we will examine the microprogramming level of two commercially available computers.

4.1. REVIEW OF THE DIGITAL LOGIC LEVEL

The microprogrammer's job is to write a program to control the machine's registers, buses, ALUs, memories, and other hardware components. We have studied these devices in the preceding chapter; now we will just review them briefly to put them in perspective. After the review, we will also say a little about the different conceptual ways of packaging the components.

4.1.1. Registers

A register is a device capable of storing information. The microprogramming level always has some registers available to hold information needed for the processing of the instruction currently being interpreted. Conceptually, registers are the same as main memory, the difference being that the registers are physically located within the processor itself, so they can be read from and stored into faster than words in main memory, which is usually off-chip. Larger and more expensive machines usually have more registers than smaller and cheaper ones, which have to use main memory for storing intermediate results. On some computers a group of registers numbered 0, 1, 2, ..., $n - 1$, is available at the microprogramming level, and is called **local storage** or **scratchpad storage**.

A register can be characterized by a single number: how many bits it can hold. Figure 4-1 shows a 16-bit register with the bit-numbering convention used in this book. Information placed in a register remains there until some other information

Bit number   15 14 13 12 11 10 9 8 7 6 5 4 3 2 1 0

| 0 | 0 | 0 | 0 | 1 | 1 | 0 | 0 | 1 | 0 | 1 | 1 | 0 | 0 | 1 | 0 |

Fig. 4-1. A 16-bit register can hold 16 bits of information.

replaces it. The process of reading information out of a register does not affect the contents of the register. In other words, when a register is read, a copy is made of its contents and the original is left undisturbed in the register.

4.1.2. Buses

A bus is a collection of wires used to transmit signals in parallel. Typically, buses are used to allow the contents of one register to be copied to another one. If both the source and destination registers are n bits wide, then the bus will need n lines (wires) for data, and possibly a few additional ones for synchronization and control as well. Buses are used because parallel transfer of all the bits at once is much faster than serial transmission a bit at a time.

A bus may be unidirectional or bidirectional. A unidirectional bus can only transfer data in one direction, whereas a bidirectional bus can transfer data in either direction but not both simultaneously. Unidirectional buses are typically used to connect two registers, one of which is always the source and the other of which is always the destination. Bidirectional buses are typically used when any of a collection of registers can be the source and any other one can be the destination.

Many devices have the ability to connect and disconnect themselves electrically from the buses to which they are physically attached. These connections can be made or broken in nanoseconds. A bus whose devices have this property is called a **tri-state** bus, because each line can be 0, 1, or disconnected. Tri-state buses are commonly used when a bus has many devices attached to it, all of which can potentially put information onto the bus.

In most microarchitectures, some registers are connected to one or more input buses and one or more output buses. Figure 4-2(a) depicts an 8-bit register connected to an input bus and to an output bus. The register consists of eight D-type flip-flops, each connected to the output bus via a noninverting buffer. Each one holds 1 bit. The register has two control signals, CK (ClocK, which really means "load register"), and OE (Output Enable), both of which are connected to all the flip-flops. Normally, both signals are in their quiescent state but occasionally they may be **asserted**, causing some action to happen. (We will use the term "asserted" instead of "set high" or "set low" to avoid having to specify which condition makes the signal active, and also to avoid the issue of whether actions happen when a control signal has a certain value, or whether they are triggered by transitions from one state to another, either high to low or low to high.) The opposite of asserted is **negated**.

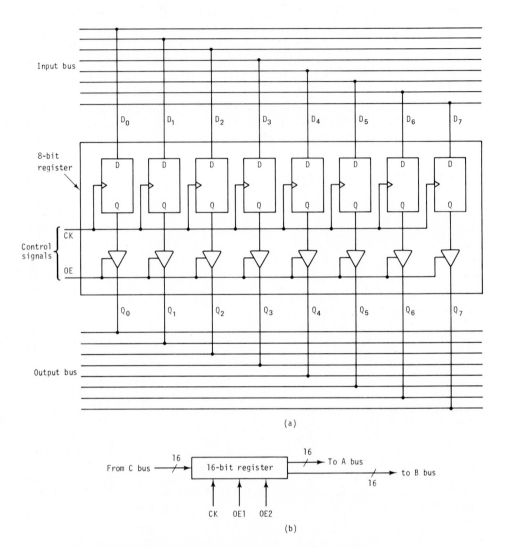

Fig. 4-2. (a) Detail of an 8-bit register connected to an input bus and an output bus. (b) Symbolic representation of a 16-bit register with one input bus and two output buses.

When CK is negated, the contents of the register are not affected by the signals on the bus. When CK is asserted, the register is loaded from the input bus. When OE is negated, the register is disconnected from the output bus, and effectively ceases to exist as far as other registers on the bus are concerned. When OE is asserted, the contents of the register are put onto the output bus.

If another register, R, has its input connected to this register's output bus, it may be possible to transfer information from this register to R. To do so, OE must be asserted and kept asserted long enough for the output on the bus to become stable. Then register R's CK line must be asserted, loading R from the bus. (Here we have sort of let the cat out of the bag—clearly, OE must be asserted by a high or low value rather than a transition, so it can be kept asserted long enough to make the output stable and give R a chance to read it in.) The operation of gating a register onto a bus so another register can load the value in occurs often at the microprogramming level, as we will see shortly. As a second example of registers and buses, Figure 4-2(b) shows a 16-bit register with two output buses, each controlled by a different OE signal.

4.1.3. Multiplexers and Decoders

Circuits that have one or more input lines and compute one or more output values that are uniquely determined by the present inputs are called **combinational circuits**. Two of the most important ones are multiplexers and decoders. A **multiplexer** has 2^n data inputs (individual lines or buses), one data output of the same width as the inputs, and an n-bit control input that selects one of the inputs and routes it to the output. Figure 4-3(a) shows a multiplexer with two buses as input. The 1-bit control signal selects A or B as the output. Figure 3-12 shows the circuit for an 8-input multiplexer.

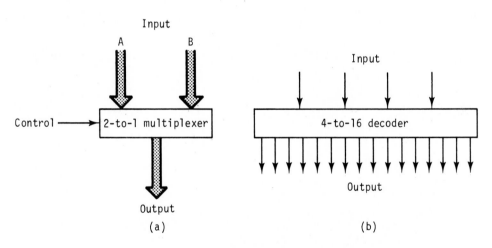

Input

A   B

Control ⟶ 2-to-1 multiplexer

Output

(a)

Input

4-to-16 decoder

Output

(b)

Fig. 4-3. (a) A 2-to-1 multiplexer. (b) A 4-to-16 decoder.

The inverse of a multiplexer is a **demultiplexer**, which routes its single input to one of its 2^n outputs, depending on the value of the n control lines.

Another important combinational circuit is the **decoder** which has n input lines and 2^n output lines, numbered 0 to $2^n - 1$. If the binary number on the input lines is k, then output line k will be 1 and all the other output lines will be 0. A decoder always has exactly one output line set to 1, with the rest 0. Figure 4-3(b) symbolically illustrates a 4-to-16 decoder; Fig. 3-14 shows the circuit for a 3-to-8 decoder.

The inverse of a decoder is an **encoder**, which has 2^n inputs and n outputs. Only one input line may be 1, and its number, in binary, is presented as the output.

4.1.4. ALUs and Shifters

Every computer needs some way to do arithmetic. The simplest circuit is just an adder, which takes two n-bit inputs and produces their sum as output. A more general arithmetic circuit is the **ALU** or **Arithmetic Logical Unit**. It also has two data inputs and one data output, but it also has some control inputs and outputs. The ALU of Fig. 4-4(a) has two function bits, F_0 and F_1, that determine which function the ALU is to perform. The ALU we will use in our example can compute $A + B$, A AND B, A as well as $\bar{A}$. The first two of these are self-explanatory; the third function just copies A to the output; the fourth one outputs the inverse of A. The third function may seem pointless but later we will see what it is used for. Figure 3-20 shows a four-function ALU that operates on one data bit. By replicating this circuit n times and feeding the carry from bit i into bit $i + 1$, we can make an n-bit wide ALU that performs AND, OR, NOT, and addition.

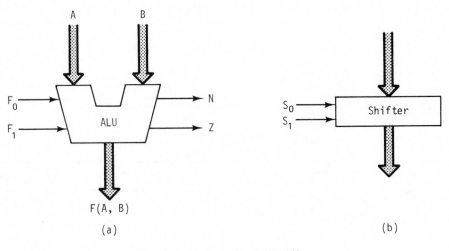

Fig. 4-4. (a) An ALU. (b) A shifter.

An ALU may also have control outputs. Typical outputs are lines that are 1 when the ALU output is negative, when it is zero, when there is a carry out of the highest bit, or when an overflow occurred. The example of Fig. 4-4(a) has two control outputs, N, which indicates that the ALU output is negative, and Z, which indicates that the ALU output is zero. The N bit is just a copy of the high-order output bit. The Z bit is the NOR of all the ALU output bits.

Although some ALUs can also perform shift operations, most of the time it is necessary to have a separate shift unit. This circuit can shift a multibit input 1 bit left or right, or perform no shift at all. Figure 4-4(b) is the symbol we will use for a shifter; a circuit can be found in Fig. 3-17.

4.1.5. Clocks

Computer circuits are normally driven by a **clock,** a device that emits a periodic sequence of pulses. These pulses define machine cycles. During each machine cycle, some basic activity occurs, such as the execution of a microinstruction. It is frequently useful to divide a cycle into subcycles, so different parts of the microinstruction can be performed in a well-defined order. For example, the inputs to the ALU must be made available and allowed to become stable before the output can be stored.

Figure 4-5(a) shows a symbolic clock with four outputs. The top one is the primary output; the other three are derived from it by inserting various length delays into the output lines. The primary clock shown in Fig. 4-5(b) (top line) has a pulse width equal to one-fourth of the cycle time. The other three outputs are shown for delays of one, two, and three times the pulse width. The result is a circuit that divides each cycle into four equally long subcycles. For more detail, see Fig. 3-21.

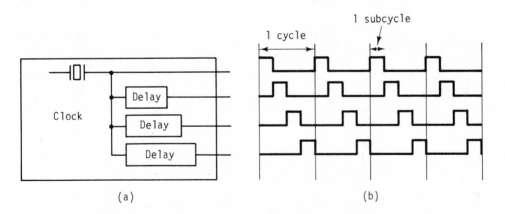

Fig. 4-5. (a) A clock with four outputs. (b) The output timing diagram.

To cause four different transitions that must occur in one cycle to happen in a certain order, the computer designer could AND the enabling signal for each with a different clock line: The transition tied to the primary clock line would happen first, the transition tied to the clock line with the shortest delay would happen second, and so forth.

4.1.6. Main Memory

Processors need to be able to read data from memory and write data to memory. Most computers have an address bus, a data bus, and a control bus for communication between the CPU and memory. To read from memory, the CPU puts a memory address on the address bus and sets the control signals appropriately, for example, by asserting RD (READ). The memory then puts the requested item on the data bus. In some computers memory read/write is synchronous, that is, the memory must respond within a fixed time. On others, the memory may take as long as it wants, signaling the presence of data using a control line when it is finished.

Writes to memory are done similarly. The CPU puts the data to be written on the data bus and the address to be stored into on the address bus and then it asserts WR (WRITE). (An alternative to having RD and WR is to have MREQ, which indicates that a memory request is desired, and RW, which distinguishes read from write.)

A memory access is nearly always considerably longer than the time required to execute a single microinstruction. Consequently, the microprogram must keep the correct values on the address and data buses for several microinstructions. To simplify this task, it is often convenient to have two registers, the **MAR** (Memory Address Register) and the **MBR** (Memory Buffer Register) that drive the address and data buses, respectively. For our purposes it will be convenient to arrange the buses as indicated in Fig. 4-6. Both registers sit between the CPU and the system bus. The address bus is unidirectional on both sides and is loaded from the CPU side when the control line is asserted. The output to the system address lines is always enabled [or possibly only during reads and writes, which requires an output enable line driven by the OR of RD and WR (not shown)]. The MBR control line causes data to be loaded from the "Data in" bus on the CPU side. The "Data out" line is always enabled. The system data bus is bidirectional, outputting MBR when WR is asserted and loading MBR when RD is asserted.

4.1.7. Component Packaging

In the previous sections we have reviewed various circuits that can be combined to form a computer. These circuits are commercially available in several conceptually different forms. The most straightforward way is in MSI (Medium Scale Integration) packages, with each chip containing one component: for example, a register, an ALU, or a shifter. This approach is illustrated in Fig. 4-7(a). The components are then wired together to form the computer. Because a wide variety of high-speed, low-cost MSI chips are available, many computers have been built this way.

The main drawback to building a computer from MSI parts is the large number of chips required, which occupy many boards, consume much power, and dissipate significant heat. Another technique is to use **bit-slice** chips. Each bit-slice chip has, for example, 1 bit of the registers, ALU, and other components. Figure 3-20 shows what a 1-bit ALU slice looks like inside. We could easily extend that design to add, for example, sixteen 1-bit registers, a 1-bit shifter, and other 1-bit wide components. By

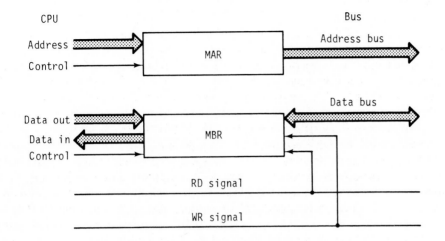

Fig. 4-6. The registers used to drive the address and data buses.

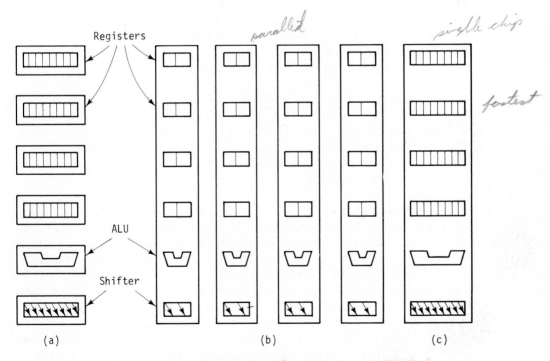

Fig. 4-7. Three ways of building a computer. (a) MSI chips. (b) Bit slice. (c) LSI chip.

taking, say, 32 such chips and putting them side by side, we would have a machine with sixteen 32-bit registers, a 32-bit ALU, a 32-bit shifter, and so on.

Alternatively, with only 16 chips we could build a 16-bit machine. Bit slices give the designer the ability to put together a machine of any word length easily. Bit slices with 2 or even 4 bits per slice are also widely available. Figure 4-7(b) depicts an 8-bit wide machine built out of four 2-bit slices. In general, the bit-slice approach requires fewer chips and much less design time than the MSI approach but usually produces slower machines.

A third approach to combining the components is to put the complete processor on a single chip [see Fig. 4-7(c)]. While this obviously reduces chip count dramatically (to one chip), it also has some disadvantages. To start with, the technology required to pack large numbers of components on a chip is a different one than is used for MSI or bit-slice chips, and it usually produces slower machines. Furthermore, both the design and manufacturing technologies are exceedingly complicated and expensive. In contrast, just about any competent electrical engineer can design a simple computer from MSI or bit-slice chips without too much trouble. From the point of view of a computer manufacturer who expects to be building computers for years, it is probably worth the trouble to master the technologies needed for making single-chip processors; for a company that just needs one special-purpose machine, it is probably not. The choices then become: use a commercially available processor, contract out to have someone else design and manufacture a special-purpose chip, or build it from MSI or bit-slice components.

4.2. AN EXAMPLE MICROARCHITECTURE

Now that we have reviewed all the basic components from which the microprogramming level is constructed, it is time to see how they are connected. Because general principles are few and far between in this area, we will introduce the subject by means of a detailed example.

4.2.1. The Data Path

The **data path** of our example microarchitecture is shown in Fig. 4-8. (The data path is that part of the CPU containing the ALU, its inputs, and its outputs.) It contains 16 identical 16-bit registers, labeled PC, AC, SP, and so on, that form a scratchpad memory accessible only to the microprogramming level. The registers labeled 0, +1, and −1 will be used to hold the indicated constants; the meaning of the other register names will be explained later. (Actually, 0 is never used in our simple examples but it probably would be needed in a more complicated machine, so we have included it because we have more registers than we can use anyway.) Each register can output its contents onto one or both of two internal buses, the A bus and the B bus, and each can be loaded from a third internal bus, the C bus, as shown in the figure.

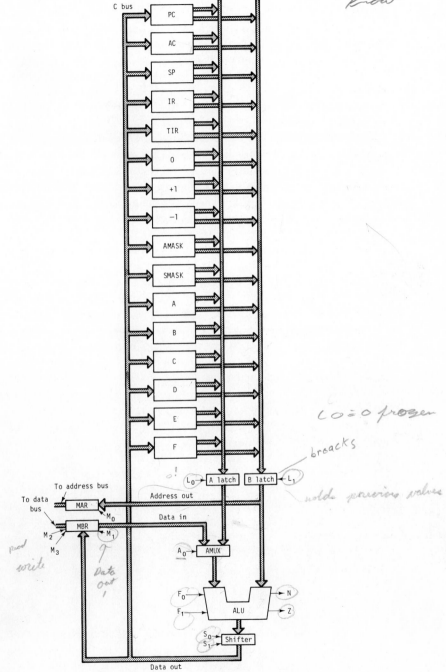

Fig. 4-8. The data path of the example microarchitecture used in this chapter.

The A and B buses feed into a 16-bit-wide ALU that can perform four functions: A + B, A AND B, A, and NOT A. The function to be performed is specified by the two ALU control lines, F_0 and F_1. The ALU generates two status bits based on the current ALU output: N, which is set when the ALU output is negative, and Z, which is set when the ALU output is zero.

The ALU output goes into a shifter, which can shift it 1 bit in either direction, or not at all. It is possible to perform a 2-bit left shift of a register, R, by computing R + R in the ALU (which is a 1-bit left shift), and then shifting the sum another bit left using the shifter.

Neither the A bus nor the B bus feeds the ALU directly. Instead, each one feeds a latch (i.e., a register) that in turn feeds the ALU. The latches are needed because the ALU is a combinational circuit—it continuously computes the output for the current input and function code. This organization can cause problems when computing, for example, A := A + B. As A is being stored into, the value on the A bus begins to change, which causes the ALU output and thus the C bus to change as well. Consequently, the wrong value may be stored into A. Put in other words, in the assignment A := A + B, the A on the right-hand side is the original A value, not some peculiar bit-by-bit mixture of the old and new values. By inserting latches in the A and B buses, we can freeze the original A and B values there early in the cycle, so the ALU is shielded from changes on the buses as a new value is being stored in the scratchpad. The loading of the latches is controlled by L_0 and L_1.

To communicate with memory, we have included an MAR and an MBR in the microarchitecture. The MAR can be loaded from the B latch, in parallel with an ALU operation. The M_0 line controls loading of MAR. On writes, the MBR can be loaded with the shifter output, in parallel with, or instead of, a store back into the scratchpad. M_1 controls loading MBR from the shifter output. On reads, the data read from memory can be presented to the left input of the ALU via the A multiplexer, indicated by Amux in Fig. 4-8. A control line, A_0, determines whether the A latch or the MBR is fed into the ALU.

The microarchitecture of Fig. 4-8 is similar to that of a commercially available bit slice, the 2903, made by Advanced Micro Devices. The 2903 is a 4-bit slice, so our machine would be built by wiring four 2903s in parallel. The principal difference between our microarchitecture and the 2903 is our omission (for reasons of simplicity) of the Q register and its associated shifter and multiplexers. The Q register is used for interpreting multiplication and division instructions, subjects not covered in this book. The 2903 also has a more extensive repertoire of ALU and shifter functions and ALU output signals.

4.2.2. Microinstructions

To control the data path of Fig. 4-8 we need 61 signals, as follows:

16 signals to control loading the A bus from the scratchpad

16 signals to control loading the B bus from the scratchpad

16 signals to control loading the scratchpad from the C bus

2 signals to control the A and B latches

2 signals to control the ALU function

2 signals to control the shifter

4 signals to control the MAR and MBR

2 signals to indicate memory read and memory write

1 signal to control the Amux

Given the values of the 61 signals, we can perform one cycle of the data path. A cycle consists of gating values onto the A and B buses, latching them in the two bus latches, running the values through the ALU and shifter, and finally storing the results in the scratchpad and/or MBR. In addition, the MAR can also be loaded, and a memory cycle initiated. As a first approximation, we could have a 61-bit control register, with one bit for each control signal. A 1 bit means that the signal is asserted and a 0 means that it is negated.

However, at the price of a small increase in circuitry, we can greatly reduce the number of bits needed to control the data path. To begin with, we have 16 bits for controlling input to the A bus, which allows 2^{16} combinations of source registers. Unfortunately, only 16 of these combinations are permitted—namely, each of the 16 registers all by itself. Therefore, we can encode the A bus information in 4 bits and use a decoder to actually generate the 16 control signals. The same holds for the B bus.

The situation is slightly different for the C bus. In principle, multiple simultaneous stores into the scratchpad are feasible, but in practice this feature is virtually never useful and most hardware does not provide for it. Therefore, we will also encode the C bus control in 4 bits. Having saved $3 \times 12 = 36$ bits, we now need 25 control bits to drive the data path. L_0 and L_1 are always needed at a certain point in time, so they will be supplied by the clock, leaving us with 23 control bits. One additional signal that is not strictly required, but is often useful, is one to enable/disable storing the C bus in the scratchpad. In some situations one merely wishes to perform an ALU operation to generate the N and Z signals but does not wish to store the result. With this extra bit, which we will call ENC (ENable C), we can indicate that the C bus is to be stored (ENC = 1) or not (ENC = 0).

At this point we can control the data path with a 24-bit number. Now we note that RD and WR can be used to control latching MBR from the system data bus and enabling MBR onto it, respectively. This observation reduces the number of independent control signals to 22.

The next step in the design of the microarchitecture is to invent a microinstruction format containing 22 bits. Figure 4-9 shows such a format, with two additional fields COND and ADDR, which will be described shortly. The microinstruction contains 13 fields, 11 of which are as follows:

AMUX   —controls left ALU input: 0 = A latch, 1 = MBR

ALU   —ALU function: 0 = A + B, 1 = A AND B, 2 = A, 3 = $\overline{A}$

SH   —shifter function: 0 = no shift, 1 = right, 2 = left

MBR   —load MBR from shifter: 0 = don't load MBR, 1 = load MBR

MAR   —load MAR from B latch: 0 = don't load MAR, 1 = load MAR

RD   —requests memory read: 0 = no read, 1 = load MBR from memory

WR   —requests memory write: 0 = no write, 1 = write MBR to memory

ENC   —controls storing into scratchpad: 0 = don't store, 1 = store

C   —selects register for storing into if ENC = 1: 0 = PC, 1 = AC, etc.

B   —selects B bus source: 0 = PC, 1 = AC, etc.

A   —selects A bus source: 0 = PC, 1 = AC, etc.

The ordering of the fields is completely arbitrary. This ordering has been chosen to minimize line crossings in a subsequent figure. (Actually, this criterion is not as crazy as it sounds; line crossings in figures usually correspond to wire crossings on printed circuit boards or on chips, which causes trouble in two-dimensional designs.)

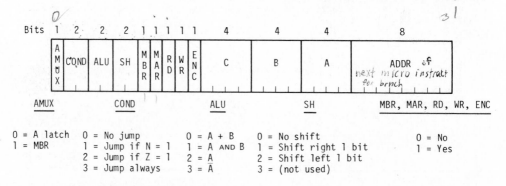

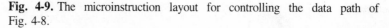

Fig. 4-9. The microinstruction layout for controlling the data path of Fig. 4-8.

4.2.3. Microinstruction Timing

Although our discussion of how a microinstruction can control the data path during one cycle is almost complete, we have neglected one issue up until now: timing. A basic ALU cycle consists of setting up the A and B latches, giving the ALU and shifter time to do their work, and storing the results. It is obvious that these events must happen in that sequence. If we try to store the C bus into the scratchpad before the A and B latches have been loaded, garbage will be stored instead of useful data. To achieve the correct event sequencing, we now introduce a four-phase clock, that is, a clock with four subcycles, like that of Fig. 4-5. The key events during each of the four subcycles are as follows:

1. Load the next microinstruction to be executed into a register called **MIR**, the MicroInstruction Register.

2. Gate registers onto the A and B buses and capture them in the A and B latches.

3. Now that the inputs are stable, give the ALU and shifter time to produce a stable output and load the MAR if required.

4. Now that the shifter output is stable, store the C bus in the scratchpad and load the MBR, if either is required.

Figure 4-10 is a detailed block diagram of the complete microarchitecture of our example machine. It may look imposing initially but it is worth studying carefully. When you fully understand every box and every line on it, you will be well on your way to understanding the microprogramming level. The block diagram has two parts, the data path, on the left, which we have already discussed in detail, and the control section, on the right, which we will now look at.

The largest and most important item in the control portion of the machine is the **control store**. This is where the microinstructions are kept. On some machines it is read-only memory; on others it is read/write memory. In our example, microinstructions will be 32 bits wide and the microinstruction address space will consist of 256 words, so the control store will occupy a maximum of $256 \times 32 = 8192$ bits.

Like any other memory, the control store needs an MAR and an MBR. We will call the MAR the **MPC** (MicroProgram Counter), because its only function is to point to the next microinstruction to be executed. The MBR is just the **MIR** as mentioned above. Be sure you realize that the control store and main memory are completely different, the former holding the microprogram and the latter the conventional machine language program.

From Fig. 4-10 it is clear that the control store continuously tries to copy the microinstruction addressed by the MPC into the MIR. However, the MIR is only loaded during subcycle 1, as indicated by the dashed line from the clock to it. During the other three subcycles it is not affected, no matter what happens to MPC.

During subcycle 2, the MIR is stable, and the various fields begin controlling the data path. In particular, A and B cause data to be gated onto the A and B buses. The A decoder and B decoder boxes in the block diagram provide for the 4-to-16 decoding of each field necessary to drive the OE1 and OE2 lines in the registers [see Fig. 4-2(b)]. The clock activates the A and B latches during this subcycle, providing stable ALU inputs for the rest of the cycle. While data are being gated onto the A and B buses, the Increment unit in the control section of the machine computes MPC + 1, in preparation for loading the next sequential microinstruction during the next cycle.

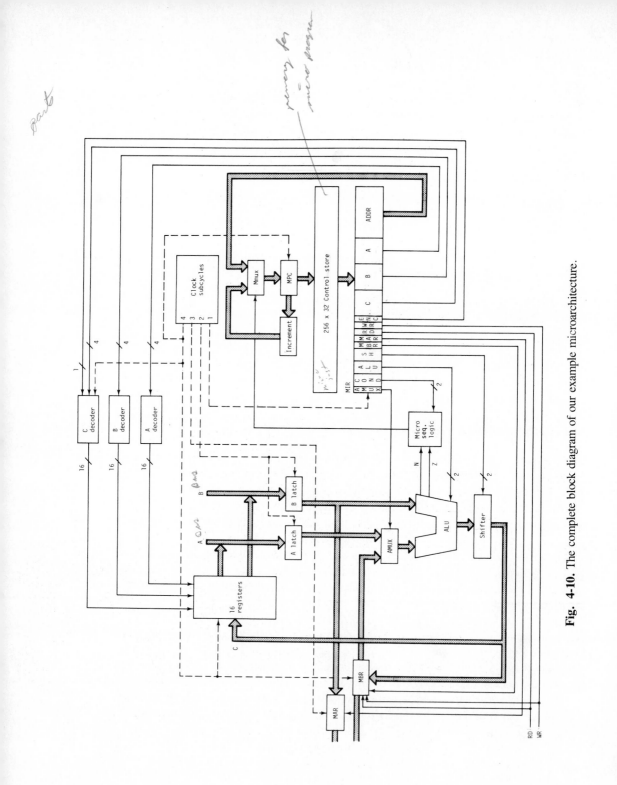

Fig. 4-10. The complete block diagram of our example microarchitecture.

132

In the third subcycle, the ALU and shifter are given time to produce valid results. The AMUX microinstruction field determines the left input to the ALU; the right input is always the B latch. Although the ALU is a combinational circuit, the time it takes to compute a sum is determined by the carry-propagation time, not the normal gate delay. While the ALU and shifter are computing, the MAR is loaded from the B bus if the MAR field in the microinstruction is 1.

During the fourth and final subcycle, the C bus may be stored back into the scratchpad and MBR, depending on ENC and MBR. The box labeled "C decoder" takes ENC, the fourth clock line, and the C field from the microinstruction as inputs, and generates the 16 control signals. Internally it performs a 4-to-16 decode of the C field, and then ANDs each of these with a signal derived from ANDing the subcycle 4 line with ENC. Thus a scratchpad register is only loaded if three conditions prevail:

1. ENC = 1.

2. It is subcycle 4.

3. The register has been selected by the C field.

The MBR is also loaded during subcycle 4 if MBR = 1.

The two signals that control memory, RD and WR are asserted as long as they are present in MIR. In effect, the corresponding MIR fields act like latches.

4.2.4. Microinstruction Sequencing

The only remaining issue is how the next microinstruction is chosen. Although some of the time it is sufficient just to fetch the next microinstruction in sequence, some mechanism is needed to allow conditional jumps in the microprogram in order to enable it to make decisions. For this reason we have provided two fields in each microinstruction: ADDR, which is the address of a potential successor to the current microinstruction, and COND, which determines whether the next microinstruction is fetched from MPC + 1 or ADDR. Every microinstruction potentially contains a conditional jump. This decision was made because conditional jumps are very common in microprograms and allowing every microinstruction to have two possible successors makes them run faster than the alternative of setting up some condition in one microinstruction and then testing it in the next. Most existing microarchitectures use our strategy in one form or another.

The choice of the next microinstruction is determined by the box labeled "Micro sequencing logic" during subcycle 4, when the ALU output signals N and Z are valid. The output of this box controls the M multiplexer (Mmux), which routes either MPC + 1 or ADDR to MPC, where it will direct the fetching of the next microinstruction. We have provided the microprogrammer with four choices concerning the next microinstruction. The choice is indicated by setting COND as follows:

0 = Do not jump; next microinstruction is taken from MPC + 1

1 = Jump to ADDR if N = 1

2 = Jump to ADDR if Z = 1

3 = Jump to ADDR unconditionally

The Micro sequencing logic combines the two ALU bits, N and Z, and the two COND bits, call them L and R for Left and Right, to generate an output. The correct signal is

$$Mmux = \bar{L}RN + L\bar{R}Z + LR = RN + LZ + LR$$

where + means INCLUSIVE OR. In words, the control signal to Mmux is 1 (routing ADDR to MPC) if LR is 01_2 and N = 1, or LR is 10_2 and Z = 1 or LR is 11_2. Otherwise, it is 0 and the next microinstruction in sequence is fetched. The circuit to compute the Mmux signal can be built from SSI components, as in Fig. 3-3(b), or be part of a PLA, as in Fig. 3-16.

To make our example machine slightly realistic, we will assume that a main memory cycle takes longer than a microinstruction. In particular, if a microinstruction starts a main memory read, by setting RD to 1, it must also have RD = 1 in the next microinstruction executed (which may or may not be located at the next control store address). The data become available two microinstructions after the read was initiated. If the microprogram has nothing else useful to do in the microinstruction following the one that initiated a memory read, the microinstruction just has RD = 1 and is effectively wasted. In the same way, a memory write also takes two microinstruction times to complete. This timing is somewhat better than that of the Z80 (see Fig. 3-33), because although the Z80 also needs only about two clock cycles for a read, from the middle of T_1 until the middle of T_3, it cannot begin a new memory read until T_4, whereas we will assume that the next read or write can be started in T_3.

For the sake of completeness, we would like to point out that the control portion of Fig. 4-10 is not included in the AMD 2903 chip, except for the 4-to-16 decoding logic. However, other bit-slice chips are available for the control portion, although not as simple as in our example.

4.3. AN EXAMPLE MACROARCHITECTURE

To continue our microprogramming level example, we now switch to the architecture of the conventional machine level to be supported by the interpreter running on the machine of Fig. 4-10. For convenience, we will call the architecture of the level 2 or 3 machine the **macroarchitecture**, to contrast it with level 1, the microarchitecture. (For the purposes of this chapter we will ignore level 3 because its instructions are largely those of level 2 and the differences are not important here.) Similarly, the level 2 instructions will be called **macroinstructions**. Thus for the duration of this chapter, the normal ADD, MOVE, and other instructions of the conventional machine level will be called macroinstructions. (The point of repeating this remark is that some assemblers have a facility to define assembly-time "macros," which are in no way related to what we mean by macroinstructions.) We will sometimes refer to our example level 1 machine as Mic-1 and the level 2 machine as Mac-1. Before we describe Mac-1, however, we will digress slightly to motivate its design.

4.3.1. Stacks

A modern macroarchitecture should be designed with the needs of high-level languages in mind. One of the most important design issues is addressing. To illustrate the problem that must be solved, consider the Pascal program of Fig. 4-11(a). The main program initializes two vectors, x and y, with values such that $x_k = k$ and $y_k = 2k + 1$. Then it computes the inner product (also called a dot product) of the two vectors. Whenever it needs to multiply two small positive integers, it calls the function *pmul*. (Imagine that the compiler is for a microcomputer and only implements a subset of Pascal, not including the multiplication operator.)

Block-structured languages like Pascal are normally implemented in such a way that when a procedure or function is exited, the storage it had been using for local variables is released. The easiest way to achieve this goal is by using a data structure called a stack. A **stack** is a contiguous block of memory containing some data and a **stack pointer** (SP) telling where the top of the stack is. The bottom of the stack is at a fixed address and will not concern us further. Figure 4-12(a) depicts a stack occupying six words of memory. The bottom of the stack is at 4020 and the top of the stack, where SP points, is at 4015. Our stacks will grow from high memory addresses to low ones but the opposite choice is equally good.

Several operations are defined on stacks. Two of the most important are PUSH X and POP Y. PUSH advances the stack pointer (by decrementing it in our example) and then puts X into memory at the location now pointed to by SP. PUSH increases the stack size by one item. POP Y, in contrast, reduces the stack size by storing the top item on the stack in Y, and then removing it by incrementing the stack pointer by the size of the item popped. Figure 4-12(b) shows how the stack of Fig. 4-12(a) looks after a 16-bit word containing 5 has been pushed on the stack.

Another operation that can be performed on a stack is advancing the stack pointer without actually pushing any data. This is normally done when a procedure or function is entered, to reserve space for local variables. Figure 4-13(a) shows how memory might be allocated during the execution of the main program of Fig. 4-11. We have arbitrarily assumed that the memory consists of 4096 16-bit words, and that the words 4021 to 4095 are used by the operating system, and hence not available for storing variables. The Pascal variable k is stored at address 4020. (Addresses are given in decimal.) The array x requires 20 words, from 4000 to 4019. The array y starts at 3980 for $y[1]$ and extends to 3999 for $y[20]$. While the main program is executing outside *pmul*, SP has the value 3980, indicating that the top of the stack is at 3980.

```
program InnerProduct (output );

{This program initializes two vectors, x and y, of 20 elements each,
 then computes their inner product :
       x[1] * y[1] + x[2] * y[2] + ... + x[20] * y[20] }

const max = 20;                                     {size of the vectors}

type SmallInt = 0..100;
     vec = array[1..max ] of SmallInt ;

var k : integer ;
    x , y : vec ;


function pmul (a , b : SmallInt ): integer ;
{This function multiplies its two parameters together and returns the product.
 It performs the multiplication by repeated addition .}
var p , j : integer ;
begin                                               {0: reserve stack space for p and j}
  if (a = 0) or (b = 0) then                         {1: if either one is 0, result is 0}
    pmul := 0                                        {2: function returns 0}
  else
    begin
      p := 0;                                        {3: initialize p}
      for j := 1 to a do                              {4: add b to p a times}
        p := p + b;                                  {5: do the addition}
      pmul := p                                      {6: assign result to function}
    end
end; {pmul}                                          {7: remove locals and return value}


procedure inner (var v : vec ; var ans : integer );
{Compute the inner product of v and x and return it in ans.}
var sum , i : integer ;
begin                                               {8: reserve stack space for sum and i}
  sum := 0;                                          {9: sum will accumulate inner product}
  for i := 1 to max do                               {10: loop through all the elements}
    sum := sum + pmul (x [i ], v [i ]);              {11: accumulate one term}
  ans := sum                                         {12: copy result to ans}
end; {inner}                                         {13: remove sum and i and return}


begin                                               {14: reserve space for k, x, and y}
  for k := 1 to max do                               {15: initialization loop}
    begin
      x [k ] := k ;                                  {16: initialize x}
      y [k ] := pmul (2, k ) + 1;                    {17: initialize y}
    end;
  inner (y , k );                                    {18: call inner}
  writeln (k )                                       {19: print results}
end.
```

Fig. 4-11(a). A Pascal program to compute an inner product.

```
K = 4020        /DEFINE SOME SYMBOLS
X = 4000
Y = 3980
A = 4
B = 3
P = 1
J = 0
V = 4
ANS = 3
SUM = 1
I = 0


        JUMP  MAIN    /START AT MAIN PROGRAM
PMUL:   DESP  2       /0
        LODL  A       /1
        JNZE  ANOTZ   /JUMP IF A <> 0
        LOCO  0       /2
        JUMP  DONE    /RETURN 0
ANOTZ:  LODL  B       /AC := B
        JNZE  BNOTZ   /JUMP IF B <> 0
        LOCO  0       /2
        JUMP  DONE    /RETURN 0
BNOTZ:  LOCO  0       /3
        STOL  P       /P := 0
        LOCO  1       /4
        STOL  J       /J := 1
        LODL  A       /CAN LOOP BE EXECUTED?
        JNEG  L2      /A < 0, DO NOT LOOP
        JZER  L2      /A = 0, DO NOT LOOP
L1:     LODL  P       /5
        ADDL  B       /AC := P + B
        STOL  P       /P := P + B
        LOCO  1       /TEST AT END OF LOOP
        ADDL  J       /AC := J + 1
        STOL  J       /J := J + 1
        SUBL  A       /AC := J - A
        JNEG  L1      /JUMP IF J < A
        JZER  L1      /JUMP IF J = A
L2:     LODL  P       /6
DONE:   INSP  2       /7
        RETN          /RETURN


INNER:  DESP  2       /8
        LOCO  0       /9
        STOL  SUM     /SUM := 0
        LOCO  1       /10
        STOL  I       /I := 1
L3:     LOCO  X-1     /11
        ADDL  I       /AC := X + I - 1
        PSHI          /PUSH X[I]
        LODL  V       /AC := ADDRESS OF VECTOR
        ADDL  I       /AC := V + I
        SUBD  C1      /V BEGINS AT 1, NOT 0
        PSHI          /PUSH V[I]
        CALL  PMUL    /PMUL(X[I],V[I])


        INSP  2       /REMOVE PARAMS
        ADDL  SUM     /AC := SUM + PMUL(...)
        STOL  SUM     /SUM := SUM + PMUL(...)
        LOCO  1       /TEST AT END OF LOOP
        ADDL  I       /AC := I + 1
        STOL  I       /I := I + 1
        SUBD  C20     /AC := I - MAX
        JNEG  L3      /JUMP IF I < MAX
        JZER  L3      /JUMP IF I = MAX
        LODL  SUM     /12
        PUSH          /PUSH SUM
        LODL  ANS     /AC := ADDRESS OF ANS
        POPI          /ANS := SUM
        INSP  2       /13
        RETN          /RETURN
MAIN:   DESP  41      /14
        LOCO  1       /15
        STOD  K       /K IS NOT A LOCAL
L4:     LODD  K       /16
        PUSH          /PUSH K ONTO STACK
        LOCO  X-1     /AC := (ADDRESS OF X[1])-1
        ADDD  K       /AC := X + K - 1
        POPI          /X[K] := K
        LOCO  2       /17
        PUSH          /PREPARE PMUL(2,...)
        LODD  K       /PREPARE PMUL(2,K)
        PUSH          /BOTH PARAMS PUSHED
        CALL  PMUL    /PMUL(2,K)
        INSP  2       /REMOVE PARAMETERS
        ADDD  C1      /AC := 2*K + 1
        PUSH          /PREPARE Y[K] := 2*K+1
        LOCO  Y-1     /AC := (ADDRESS OF Y[1])-1
        ADDD  K       /AC := Y + K
        POPI          /Y[K] := 2*K+1
        LOCO  1       /TEST AT END OF LOOP
        ADDD  K       /AC := K + 1
        STOD  K       /K := K + 1
        SUBD  C20     /AC := K - MAX
        JNEG  L4      /JUMP IF K < 0
        JZER  L4      /JUMP IF K = MAX
        LOCO  Y       /18
        PUSH          /PUSH ADDRESS OF Y
        LOCO  K       /AC := ADDRESS OF K
        PUSH          /PUSH IT ALSO
        CALL  INNER   /PROCEDURE CALL
        INSP  2       /REMOVE PARAMS
        LODD  K       /19
        PUSH          /PREPARE WRITELN(K)
        CALL  OUTNUM1 /LIBRARY ROUTINE
        INSP  1       /REMOVE PARAM
        CALL  STOP    /END OF JOB
C1:     1             /CONSTANT 1
C20:    20            /CONSTANT 20
```

Fig. 4-11(b). *InnerProduct* in assembly language.

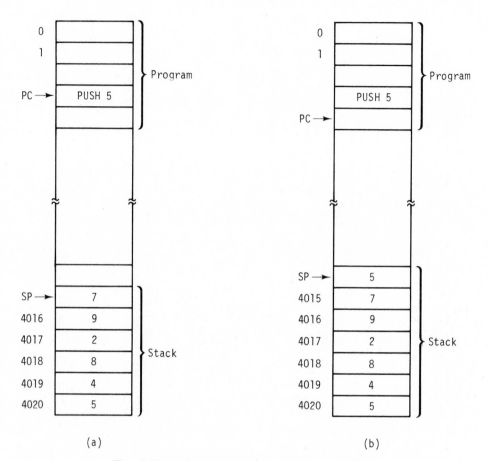

Fig. 4-12. (a) A stack. (b) The stack after pushing 5.

When the main program wants to call *pmul*, it first pushes the parameters of the call, 2 and *k*, onto the stack, and then executes the call instruction, which pushes the return address onto the stack so that *pmul* will know where to return when it is finished. When *pmul* begins executing, SP is 3977. The first thing it does is advance the stack pointer by 2, to reserve two words for its own local variables, *p* and *j*. At this point SP is 3975, as shown in Fig. 4-13(b). The top five words on the stack constitute the stack frame used by *pmul*; they will be released when it is finished. The words 3979 and 3978 are labeled *a* and *b* because these are the names of *pmul*'s formal parameters but, of course, they contain 2 and *k*, respectively.

When *pmul* has returned and *inner* has been called, the stack configuration is as shown in Fig. 4-13(c). When *inner* calls *pmul*, the stack is as shown in Fig. 4-13(d). Now comes the problem. What code should the compiler generate to access *pmul*'s parameters and locals? If it tries to read *p* using an instruction like MOVE 3976,SOMEWHERE *pmul* will

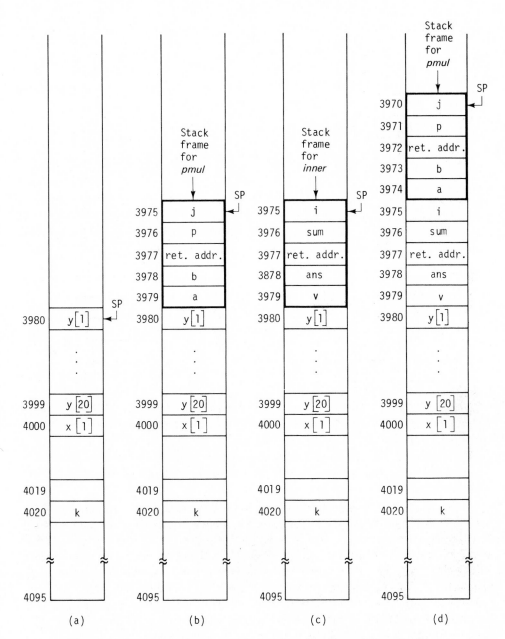

Fig. 4-13. Snapshots of memory during the execution of *InnerProduct.*
(a) Stack during execution of the main program. (b) Stack during execution
of *pmul*. (c) Stack during execution of *inner*. (d) Stack during execution of
pmul when called from *inner*.

work when called from the main program but not when called from *inner*. Similarly, MOVE 3971,SOMEWHERE will work when called from *inner*, but not when called from the main program. What is really needed is a way to say "fetch the word 1 higher than the current stack pointer." In other words, the Mac-1 needs an addressing mode that fetches or stores a word at a known distance relative to the stack pointer (or some equivalent addressing mode).

4.3.2. The Macroinstruction Set

With this addressing mode in mind, we are now ready to look at the Mac-1's architecture. Basically, it consists of a memory with 4096 16-bit words, and three registers visible to the level 2 programmer. The registers are the program counter, PC, the stack pointer, SP, and the accumulator, AC, which is used for moving data around, for arithmetic, and for other purposes. Three addressing modes are provided: direct, indirect, and local. Instructions using direct addressing contain a 12-bit absolute memory address in the low-order 12-bits. Such instructions are useful for accessing global variables, such as x in Fig. 4-11. Indirect addressing allows the programmer to compute a memory address, put it in AC, and then read or write the word addressed. This form of addressing is very general and is used for accessing array elements, among other things. Local addressing specifies an offset from SP and is used to access local variables, as we have just seen. Together, these three modes provide a simple but adequate addressing system.

The Mac-1 instruction set is shown in Fig. 4-14. The first column gives the binary encoding of the instruction. The second gives its assembly language mnemonic. The third gives its name and the fourth describes what it does by giving a Pascal fragment. In these fragments, $m[x]$ refers to memory word x. Thus LODD loads the accumulator from the memory word specified in its low-order 12-bits. LODD is thus direct addressing, whereas LODL loads the accumulator from the word at a distance x above SP, hence is local addressing. LODD, STOD, ADDD, and SUBD perform four basic functions using direct addressing, and LODL, STOL, ADDL, and SUBL perform the same functions using local addressing.

Five jump instructions are provided, one unconditional jump (JUMP) and four conditional ones (JPOS, JZER, JNEG, and JNZE). JUMP always copies its low-order 12 bits into the program counter, whereas the other four only do so if the specified condition is met.

LOCO loads a 12-bit constant in the range 0 to 4095 (inclusive) into AC. PSHI pushes onto the stack the word whose address is present in AC. The inverse operation is POPI, which pops a word from the stack and stores it in the memory word addressed by AC. PUSH and POP are useful for manipulating the stack in a variety of ways. SWAP exchanges the contents of AC and SP, which is useful when SP must be increased or decreased by an amount not known at compile time. INSP and DESP are used to change SP by amounts known at compile time. Because of the lack of encoding space, the offsets here have been limited to 8 bits. Finally, CALL calls a procedure, *write an assembly* / *assembly → machine*

Binary	Mnemonic	Instruction	Meaning
0000xxxxxxxxxxxx	LODD	Load direct	$ac := m[x]$
0001xxxxxxxxxxxx	STOD	Store direct	$m[x] := ac$
0010xxxxxxxxxxxx	ADDD	Add direct	$ac := ac + m[x]$
0011xxxxxxxxxxxx	SUBD	Subtract direct	$ac := ac - m[x]$
0100xxxxxxxxxxxx	JPOS	Jump positive	if $ac \geq 0$ then $pc := x$
0101xxxxxxxxxxxx	JZER	Jump zero	if $ac = 0$ then $pc := x$
0110xxxxxxxxxxxx	JUMP	Jump	$pc := x$
0111xxxxxxxxxxxx	LOCO	Load constant	$ac := x$ $(0 \leq x \leq 4095)$
1000xxxxxxxxxxxx	LODL	Load local	$ac := m[sp + x]$
1001xxxxxxxxxxxx	STOL	Store local	$m[x + sp] := ac$
1010xxxxxxxxxxxx	ADDL	Add local	$ac := ac + m[sp + x]$
1011xxxxxxxxxxxx	SUBL	Subtract local	$ac := ac - m[sp + x]$
1100xxxxxxxxxxxx	JNEG	Jump negative	if $ac < 0$ then $pc := x$
1101xxxxxxxxxxxx	JNZE	Jump nonzero	if $ac \neq 0$ then $pc := x$
1110xxxxxxxxxxxx	CALL	Call procedure	$sp := sp - 1; m[sp] := pc; pc := x$
1111000000000000	PSHI	Push indirect	$sp := sp - 1; m[sp] := m[ac]$
1111001000000000	POPI	Pop indirect	$m[ac] := m[sp]; sp := sp + 1$
1111010000000000	PUSH	Push onto stack	$sp := sp - 1; m[sp] := ac$
1111011000000000	POP	Pop from stack	$ac := m[sp]; sp := sp + 1$
1111100000000000	RETN	Return	$pc := m[sp]; sp := sp + 1$
1111101000000000	SWAP	Swap ac, sp	$tmp := ac; ac := sp; sp := tmp$
11111100yyyyyyyy	INSP	Increment sp	$sp := sp + y$ $(0 \leq y \leq 255)$
11111110yyyyyyyy	DESP	Decrement sp	$sp := sp - y$ $(0 \leq y \leq 255)$

xxxxxxxxxxxx is a 12-bit machine address; in column 4 it is called x.
yyyyyyyy is an 8-bit constant; in column 4 it is called y.

Fig. 4-14. The Mac-1 instruction set.

saving the return address on the stack, and RETN returns from a procedure, by popping the return address and putting it into PC.

So far, our machine does not have any input/output instructions. Nor are we about to add any now. Instead, the machine will use memory-mapped I/O. A read from address 4092 will yield a 16-bit word with the next ASCII character from the standard input device in the low-order 7 bits and zeros in the high-order 9 bits. When a character is available in 4092, the high-order bit of the input status register, 4093, will be set. Reading 4092 clears 4093. The input routine will normally sit in a tight loop waiting for 4093 to go negative. When it does, the input routine will load AC from 4092 and return.

Output will be done using a similar scheme. A write to address 4094 will take the low-order 7 bits of the word written and copy them to the standard output device. The high-order bit of the output status register, word 4095, will then be cleared, coming back on again when the output device is ready to accept a new character. Standard input and output may be a terminal keyboard and visual display, or a card reader and printer or some other combination.

As an example of how one programs using this instruction set, see Fig. 4-11(b), which is the program of Fig. 4-11(a) compiled to assembly language by a compiler that does no optimization at all. (Optimized code would make the example hard to follow.) The numbers 0 to 19 in the comments, indicated by a slash in the assembly language, are intended to make it easier to link up the two halves of the figure. OUTNUM1 and STOP are library routines that perform the obvious functions.

4.4. AN EXAMPLE MICROPROGRAM

Having specified both the microarchitecture and the macroarchitecture in detail, the remaining issue is the implementation: What does a program running on the former and interpreting the latter look like, and how does it work? Before we can answer these questions, we must carefully consider in what language we want to do our microprogramming.

4.4.1. The Micro Assembly Language

In principle, we could write microprograms in binary, 32 bits per microinstruction. Masochistic programmers might even enjoy that; certainly nobody else would. Therefore, we need a symbolic language in which to express microprograms. One possible notation is to have the microprogrammer specify one microinstruction per line, naming each nonzero field and its value. For example, to add AC to A and store the result in AC, we could write

$$\text{ENC} = 1, \text{C} = 1, \text{B} = 1, \text{A} = 10$$

Many microprogramming languages look like this. Nevertheless, this notation is awful and so are they.

A much better idea is to use a high-level language notation, while retaining the basic concept of one source line per microinstruction. Conceivably, one could write microprograms in an ordinary high-level language but because efficiency is crucial in microprograms, we will stick to assembly language, which we define as a symbolic language that has a one-to-one mapping onto machine instructions. Remember that a

25% inefficiency in the microprogram slows the entire machine down by 25%. Let us call our high-level Micro Assembly Language "MAL," which is French for "sick," something you become if you are forced to write too many intricate microprograms for idiosyncratic machines. In MAL, stores into the 16 scratchpad registers or MAR and MBR are denoted by assignment statements. Thus the example in MAL above becomes $ac := a + ac$. (Because our intention is to make MAL Pascal-like, we will adopt the usual Pascal convention of lowercase italic names for identifiers.)

To indicate the use of the ALU functions 0, 1, 2, and 3, we can write: for example,

$$ac := a, \quad a := band(ir, smask), \quad \text{and } a := inv(a), \quad ac := a + ac,$$

respectively, where *band* stands for "Boolean and" and *inv* stands for invert. Shifts can be denoted by the functions *lshift* for left shifts and *rshift* for right shifts, as in

$$tir := lshift(tir + tir)$$

which puts *tir* on both the A and B buses, performs an addition, and left shifts the sum 1 bit left before storing it back in *tir*.

Unconditional jumps can be handled with **goto** statements; conditional jumps can test *n* or *z*: for example,

if *n* **then goto** 27

Assignments and jumps can be combined on the same line. However, a slight problem arises if we wish to test a register but not make a store. How do we specify which register is to be tested? To solve this problem we introduce the pseudo variable *alu*, which can be assigned a value just to indicate the ALU contents. For example,

$alu := tir;$ **if** *n* **then goto** 27;

means *tir* is to be run through the ALU (ALU code = 2) so its high-order bit can be tested. Note that the use of *alu* means that ENC = 0.

To indicate memory reads and writes, we will just put *rd* and *wr* in the source program. The order of the various parts of the source statement is, in principle, arbitrary but to enhance readability we will try to arrange them in the order that they are carried out. Figure 4-15 gives a few examples of MAL statements along with the corresponding microinstructions.

4.4.2. The Example Microprogram

We have finally reached the point where we can put all the pieces together. Figure 4-16 is the microprogram that runs on Mic-1 and interprets Mac-1. It is a surprisingly short program—only 79 lines. By now the choice of names for the scratchpad registers in Fig. 4-8 is obvious: PC, AC, and SP are used to hold the three Mac-1 registers . IR is the instruction register and holds the macroinstruction currently being

	A M U X	C O N D	A L U	S H	M B R	M A R	R D	W D	E N C	C	B	A	ADDR
mar := pc; rd;	0	0	2	0	0	1	1	0	0	0	0	0	00
rd;	0	0	2	0	0	0	1	0	0	0	0	0	00
ir := mbr	1	0	2	0	0	0	0	0	1	3	0	0	00
pc : = pc + 1	0	0	0	0	0	0	0	0	1	0	6	0	00
mar := ir; mbr := ac; wr;	0	0	?	0	1	1	0	1	0	0	3	1	00
alu := tir; if *n* **then goto** 15;	0	1	2	0	0	0	0	0	0	0	0	4	15
ac := inv (mbr);	1	0	3	0	0	0	0	0	1	1	0	0	00
tir : = l shift (tir); **if** *n* **then goto** 25;	0	1	2	2	0	0	0	0	1	4	0	4	25
alu := ac; **if** *z* **then goto** 22;	0	2	2	0	0	0	0	0	0	0	0	1	22
ac := band (ir, amask); **goto** 0	0	3	1	0	0	0	0	0	1	1	8	3	00
sp := sp + (−1); rd;	0	0	0	0	0	0	1	0	1	2	?	7	00
tir : = l shift (ir + ir); **if** *n* **then goto** 69	0	1	0	2	0	0	0	0	1	4	3	3	69

Fig. 4-15. Some MAL statements and the corresponding microinstructions.

executed. TIR is a temporary copy of IR, used for decoding the opcode. The next three registers hold the indicated constants. AMASK is the address mask, 007777 (octal), and is used to separate out opcode and address bits. SMASK is the stack mask, 000377 (octal), and is used in the INSP and DESP instructions to isolate the 8-bit offset. The remaining six registers have no assigned function and can be used as the microprogrammer wishes.

Like all interpreters, the microprogram of Fig. 4-16 has a main loop that fetches, decodes, and executes instructions from the program being interpreted, in this case, level 2 instructions. Its main loop begins on line 0, where it begins fetching the macroinstruction at PC. While waiting for the instruction to arrive, the microprogram increments PC and continues to assert the RD bus signal. When it arrives, in line 2, it is stored in IR and simultaneously the high-order bit (bit 15) is tested. If bit 15 is a 1, decoding proceeds at line 28, otherwise it continues on line 3. Assuming for the moment that the instruction is a LODD, bit 14 is tested on line 3, and TIR is loaded with the original instruction shifted left 2 bits, one using the adder and one using the shifter. Note that the ALU status bit N is determined by the ALU output, in which bit 14 is the high-order bit, because IR + IR shifts IR left 1 bit. The shifter output does not affect the ALU status bits.

All instructions having 00 in their two high-order bits eventually come to line 4 to have bit 13 tested, with the instructions beginning with 000 going to line 5 and those beginning with 001 going to line 11. Line 5 is an example of a microinstruction with ENC = 0; it just tests TIR but does not change it. Depending on the outcome of this test, the code for LODD or STOD is selected.

For LODD, the microcode must first fetch the word directly addressed by loading the low-order 12 bits of IR into MAR. In this case the high-order 4 bits are all zero but for STOD and other instructions they are not. However, because MAR is only 12 bits wide, the opcode bits do not affect the choice of word read. In line 7, the microprogram has nothing to do, so it just waits. When the word arrives, it is copied to AC and the microprogram jumps to the top of the loop. STOD, ADDD, and SUBD are similar. The only noteworthy point concerning them is how subtraction is done. It uses the fact that

$$x - y = x + (-y) = x + (\bar{y} + 1) = x + 1 + \bar{y}$$

in two's complement. The addition of 1 to AC is done on line 16, which would otherwise be wasted like line 13.

The microcode for JPOS begins on line 21. If AC < 0, the branch fails and the JPOS is terminated immediately by jumping back to the main loop. If, however, AC ≥ 0, the low-order 12 bits of IR are extracted by ANDing them with the 007777 mask and storing the result in PC. It does not cost anything extra to remove the opcode bits here, so we might as well do it. If it had cost an extra microinstruction, however, we would have had to look very carefully to see if having garbage in the high-order 4 bits of PC could cause trouble later.

In a certain sense, JZER (line 23) works the opposite of JPOS. With JPOS, if the condition is met, the jump fails and control returns to the main loop. With JZER, if the condition is met, the jump is taken. Because the code for performing the jump is the same for all the jump instructions, we can save microcode by just going to line 22 whenever feasible. This style of programming would generally be considered uncouth in an application program but in a microprogram, no holds are barred. Performance is everything.

JUMP and LOCO are straightforward, so the next interesting execution routine is for LODL. First, the absolute memory address to be referenced is computed by adding the offset contained in the instruction to SP. Then the memory read is initiated. Because the rest of the code is the same for LODL and LODD, we might as well use lines 7 and 8 for both of them. Not only does this save control store with no loss of execution speed but it also means fewer routines to debug. Analogous code is used for STOL, ADDL, and SUBL. The code for JNEG and JNZE is similar to JZER and JPOS, respectively (not the other way around). CALL first decrements SP, then pushes the return address onto the stack, and finally jumps to the procedure. Line 49 is almost identical to line 22; if it had been exactly the same, we could have eliminated 49 by putting an unconditional jump to 22 in 48. Unfortunately, we must continue to assert WR for another microinstruction.

The rest of the macroinstructions all have 1111 as the high-order 4 bits, so decoding of the address bits is required to tell them apart. The actual execution routines are straightforward so we will not comment on them further.

```
   0: mar := pc ; rd ;                                    {main loop}
   1: pc := pc + 1; rd ;                                  {increment pc}
   2: ir := mbr ; if n then goto 28;                      {save, decode mbr}
   3: tir := lshift (ir + ir ); if n then goto 19;
   4: tir := lshift (tir ); if n then goto 11;            {000x or 001x?}
   5: alu := tir ; if n then goto 9;                      {0000 or 0001?}

   6: mar := ir ; rd ;                                    {0000 = LODD}
   7: rd ;
   8: ac := mbr ; goto 0;

   9: mar := ir ; mbr := ac ; wr ;                        {0001 = STOD}
  10: wr ; goto 0;

  11: alu := tir ; if n then goto 15;                     {0010 or 0011?}

  12: mar := ir ; rd ;                                    {0010 = ADDD}
  13: rd ;
  14: ac := mbr + ac ; goto 0;

  15: mar := ir ; rd ;                                    {0011 = SUBD}
  16: ac := ac + 1; rd ;                                  {Note: x − y = x + 1 + not y}
  17: a := inv (mbr );
  18: ac := ac + a ; goto 0;

  19: tir := lshift (tir ); if n then goto 25;            {010x or 011x?}
  20: alu := tir ; if n then goto 23;                     {0100 or 0101?}

  21: alu := ac ; if n then goto 0;                       {0100 = JPOS}
  22: pc := band (ir , amask ); goto 0;                   {perform the jump}

  23: alu := ac ; if z then goto 22;                      {0101 = JZER}
  24: goto 0;                                             {jump failed}

  25: alu := tir ; if n then goto 27;                     {0110 or 0111?}
  26: pc := band (ir , amask ); goto 0;                   {0110 = JUMP}

  27: ac := band (ir , amask ); goto 0;                   {0111 = LOCO}

  28: tir := lshift (ir + ir ); if n then goto 40;        {10xx or 11xx?}
  29: tir := lshift (tir ); if n then goto 35;            {100x or 101x?}
  30: alu := tir ; if n then goto 33;                     {1000 or 1001?}

  31: a := ir + sp ;                                      {1000 = LODL}
  32: mar := a ; rd ; goto 7;

  33: a := ir + sp ;                                      {1001 = STOL}
  34: mar := a ; mbr := ac ; wr ; goto 10;

  35: alu := tir ; if n then goto 38;                     {010 or 1011?}

  36: a := ir + sp ;                                      {1010 = ADDL}
  37: mar := a ; rd ; goto 13;

  38: a := ir + sp ;                                      {1011 = SUBL}
  39: mar := a ; rd ; goto 16;
```

Fig. 4-16.   The microprogram.

40: *tir* := *lshift* (*tir*); **if** *n* **then goto** 46;   {110x or 111x?}
41: *alu* := *tir* ; **if** *n* **then goto** 44;   {1100 or 1101?}

42: *alu* := *ac* ; **if** *n* **then goto** 22;   {1100 = JNEG}
43: **goto** 0;

44: *alu* := *ac* ; **if** *z* **then goto** 0;   {1101 = JNZE}
45: *pc* := *band* (*ir* , *amask*); **goto** 0;

46: *tir* := *lshift* (*tir*); **if** *n* **then goto** 50;

47: *sp* := *sp* + (−1);   {1110 = CALL}
48: *mar* := *sp* ; *mbr* := *pc* ; *wr* ;
49: *pc* := *band* (*ir* , *amask*); *wr* ; **goto** 0;

50: *tir* := *lshift* (*tir*); **if** *n* **then goto** 65;   {1111, examine addr}
51: *tir* := *lshift* (*tir*); **if** *n* **then goto** 59;
52: *alu* := *tir* ; **if** *n* **then goto** 56;

53: *mar* := *ac* ; *rd* ;   {1111000 = PSHI}
54: *sp* := *sp* + (−1); *rd* ;
55: *mar* := *sp* ; *wr* ; **goto** 10;

56: *mar* := *sp* ; *sp* := *sp* + 1; *rd* ;   {1111001 = POPI}
57: *rd* ;
58: *mar* := *ac* ; *wr* ; **goto** 10;

59: *alu* := *tir* ; **if** *n* **then goto** 62;

60: *sp* := *sp* + (−1);   {1111010 = PUSH}
61: *mar* := *sp* ; *mbr* := *ac* ; *wr* ; **goto** 10;

62: *mar* := *sp* ; *sp* := *sp* + 1; *rd* ;   {1111011 = POP}
63: *rd* ;
64: *ac* := *mbr* ; **goto** 0;

65: *tir* := *lshift* (*tir*); **if** *n* **then goto** 73;
66: *alu* := *tir* ; **if** *n* **then goto** 70;

67: *mar* := *sp* ; *sp* := *sp* + 1; *rd* ;   {1111100 = RETN}
68: *rd* ;
69: *pc* := *mbr* ; **goto** 0;

70: *a* := *ac* ;   {1111101 = SWAP}
71: *ac* := *sp* ;
72: *sp* := *a* ; **goto** 0;

73: *alu* := *tir* ; **if** *n* **then goto** 76;

74: *a* := *band* (*ir* , *smask*);   {1111110 = INSP}
75: *sp* := *sp* + *a* ; **goto** 0;

76: *a* := *band* (*ir* , *smask*);   {1111111 = DESP}
77: *a* := *inv* (*a*);
78: *a* := *a* + 1; **goto** 75;

Fig. 4-16. (cont.).

4.4.3. Remarks about the Microprogram

Although we have discussed the microprogram in considerable detail, a few more points are worth making. In Fig. 4-16 we increment PC in line 1. It could equally well have been done in line 0, thus freeing line 1 for something else while waiting. In this machine there is nothing else to do but in a real machine the microprogram might use this opportunity to check for I/O devices awaiting service, refresh dynamic RAM, or something else.

If we leave line 1 the way it is, however, we can speed up the machine by modifying line 8 to read

$$mar := pc;\ ac := mbr;\ rd;\ \textbf{goto}\ 1;$$

In other words, we can start fetching the next instruction before we have really finished with the current one. This ability provides a primitive form of instruction pipelining [see Fig. 2-3(d)]. The same trick can be applied to other execution routines as well.

It is clear that a substantial amount of the execution time of each macroinstruction is devoted to decoding it bit by bit. This observation suggests that it might be useful to be able to load MPC under microprogram control. On many existing computers the microarchitecture has hardware support for extracting macroinstruction opcodes and stuffing them directly into MPC to effect a multiway branch. If, for example, we could shift the IR 9 bits to the right, clear the upper 9 bits, and put the resulting number into MPC, we would have a 128-way branch to locations 0 to 127. Each of these words would contain the first microinstruction for the corresponding macroinstruction. Although this approach wastes control store, it speeds up the machine greatly, so something like it is nearly always used in practice.

We have not said a word about how I/O is implemented. Nor do we have to. By using memory mapping, the CPU is not aware of the difference between true memory addresses and I/O device registers (see Fig. 3-39). The microprogram handles reads and writes to the top four words of the address space the same way it handles any other reads and writes.

4.4.4. Perspective

The time seems appropriate to stop for a minute and reflect on what microprogramming is all about. The basic idea is to start out with a simple hardware machine. In our example, it consists of little more than 22 registers, a small ROM for the control store, a glorified adder, an incrementer, a shifter, and some combinational circuitry for multiplexing, decoding, and sequencing. Using this hardware we were able to construct a software interpreter for carrying out the instructions of a level 2 machine. With the aid of a compiler, we can translate high-level language programs to level 2 instructions and then interpret these instructions one at a time.

Thus to run a program written in a high-level language, we must first translate it to level 2, and then interpret the resulting instructions. Level 2 effectively serves as an interface between the compiler and the interpreter. Although in principle the compiler could generate microcode directly, doing so is complicated and wasteful of space. Each of our macroinstructions occupies one 16-bit word, whereas the corresponding microcode, excluding the instruction decoding logic, requires about four 32-bit microinstructions, on the average. If we were to compile directly to level 1, the total storage needed would increase about eightfold. Furthermore, the increased storage needed is writable control store, which is far more expensive due to its high speed. Using main memory for microcode is not desirable because it results in a slow machine.

In light of these concrete examples, it should be clear why machines are now normally designed as a series of levels. It is done for efficiency and simplicity, because each level deals with another level of abstraction. The level 0 designer worries about how to squeeze the last few nanoseconds out of the ALU by using some spiffy new algorithm to reduce carry-propagation time. The microprogrammer worries about how to get the most mileage out of each microinstruction, typically by exploiting as much of the hardware's inherent parallelism as possible. The macroinstruction set designer worries about how to provide an interface that both the compiler writer and microprogrammer can learn to love, and be efficient at the same time. Clearly, each level has different goals, problems, techniques, and, in general, a different way of looking at the machine. By splitting the total machine design problem into several subproblems, we can attempt to master the inherent complexity in designing a modern computer.

4.5. DESIGN OF THE MICROPROGRAMMING LEVEL

Like just about everything else in computer science, the design of the microarchitecture is full of trade-offs. In the following sections we will look at some of the design issues and the corresponding trade-offs.

4.5.1. Horizontal versus Vertical Microprogramming

Probably the key trade-off is how much encoding should the microinstructions contain. If one were to build the Mic-1 on a single VLSI chip, one could ignore the abstractions such as registers, ALU, and so on, and just look at all the gates. To make the machine run, certain signals are needed, such as the 16 OE signals to gate the registers onto the A bus and the signals that control the ALU function. When we look inside the ALU, we see that the internal circuitry is actually driven by four lines, not two, because in the lower left-hand corner of Fig. 3-20 we find a 2-to-4 decoder circuit. In short, for each machine some set of n control signals applied at the appropriate places can make the machine run, without any decoding.

This point of view leads to a different microinstruction format: just make it n bits wide, one bit per control signal. Microinstructions designed according to this principle are called **horizontal** and represent one extreme of a spectrum of possibilities. At the other end of the spectrum are microinstructions with a small number of highly encoded fields. These are said to be **vertical**. The names come from how an artist might sketch their respective control stores: horizontal designs have a relatively small number of wide microinstructions; vertical ones have many narrow microinstructions.

Between these two extremes lie many mixed designs. Our microinstructions, for example, have a number of bits, such as MAR, MBR, RD, WR, and AMUX, that directly control hardware functions. On the other hand, the A, B, C, and ALU fields require some decoding logic before they can be applied to the individual gates. An extreme vertical microinstruction might just have an opcode, which is merely a generalization of our ALU field, and some operands, such as our A, B, and C fields. In such an organization, opcodes would be needed for reading and writing main memory, making microjumps, and so on, because the fields that control these functions in our machine would no longer be present.

To make the distinction between horizontal and vertical microinstructions clearer, let us now redesign our example microarchitecture to use vertical microinstructions. Each microinstruction will now contain three 4-bit fields, for a total of 12 bits, versus 32 in the original version. The first field is the opcode, OP, which tells what the microinstruction does. The next two fields are two registers, R1 and R2. For jumping they are combined to form a single 8-bit field, R. A typical microinstruction is ADD SP,AC, which means that AC is added to SP.

The complete list of microinstruction opcodes for this new machine, the Mic-2, is given in Fig. 4-17. From the list it is clear that each microinstruction performs only one function: if it performs an addition, it cannot also shift, load the MAR, or even keep RD asserted. With only 12 bits in the microinstruction there is only room to specify one operation.

Now we must redo Fig. 4-10 to reflect the new microinstructions. The new block diagram is shown in Fig. 4-18. The data path portion, on the left, is identical to the old one. Most of the control portion, on the right will also remain the same. In particular, we still need MIR and a control store (although the new ones are 12 bits wide instead of 32 bits wide). The sizes and functions of MPC, Mmux, the incrementer, the clock, and the micro sequencing logic are all identical to those in the horizontal design. Furthermore, we need 4-to-16 decoders for the R1 and R2 fields, analogous to those for A, B, and C in Fig. 4-10.

Three main differences between Fig. 4-10 and Fig. 4-18 are the boxes labeled AND, NZ, and OP decode. AND is needed because the R1 field now drives both the A bus and C bus. A problem arises because the A bus is loaded during subcycle 2 but the C bus may not be loaded into the scratchpad until the A and B latches are stable, in subcycle 3. The AND box ANDs the 16 decoded signals with both the subcycle 4 line from the clock and a signal coming from OP decode, which is equivalent to the old ENC signal. The result is that the 16 signals that load data into the scratchpad are asserted under the same conditions as before.

The NZ box is a 2-bit register that can be commanded to store the N and Z ALU signals. We need this facility because in the new design the ALU will do work in one microinstruction but the status bits will not be tested until the next one. Because the

Binary	Mnemonic	Instruction	Meaning
0000	ADD	Addition	$r1 := r1 + r2$
0001	AND	Boolean AND	$r1 := r1 \text{ AND } r2$
0010	MOVE	Move register	$r1 := r2$
0011	COMPL	Complement	$r1 := inv(r2)$
0100	LSHIFT	Left shift	$r1 := lshift(r2)$
0101	RSHIFT	Right shift	$r1 := rshift(r2)$
0110	GETMBR	Store MBR in register	$r1 := mbr$
0111	TEST	Test register	**if** $r2 < 0$ **then** $n := true$; **if** $r2 = 0$ **then** $z := true$
1000	BEGRD	Begin read	$mar := r1; rd$
1001	BEGWR	Begin write	$mar := r1; mbr := r2; wr$
1010	CONRD	Continue read	rd
1011	CONWR	Continue write	wr
1100		(not used)	
1101	NJUMP	Jump if N = 1	**if** n **then goto** r
1110	ZJUMP	Jump if Z = 1	**if** z **then goto** r
1111	UJUMP	Unconditional jump	**goto** r

$r = 16 * r1 + r2$

Fig. 4-17. The Mic-2 opcodes.

ALU has no internal storage and N and Z are derived from the current output, N being the high-order bit and Z being the OR of all the output bits, both status signals would be lost after a microinstruction if they were not latched somewhere.

The key element in the new microarchitecture is the OP decoder. This box takes the 4-bit OPCODE field and produces signals that drive the AND box, micro sequencing logic, NZ, Amux, ALU, shifter, MBR, MAR, RD and WR. The micro sequencing logic, ALU, and shifter each require two signals, which are identical to what they were in the previous design. In all, the OP decoder generates 13 distinct signals based on the current microinstruction's high-order 4 bits.

For each of the 16 possible microinstruction opcodes, the machine designer must determine which of the 13 signals emanating from the OP decoder are asserted and which are negated. In effect, a 16×13 binary matrix giving the value of each control line for each opcode must be generated. The matrix for the Mic-2 is given in Fig. 4-19. The columns are labeled with the signal names. The suffixes L and H stand for Low and High, respectively, and apply only to the devices with two control lines: the ALU, shifter, and micro sequencing logic.

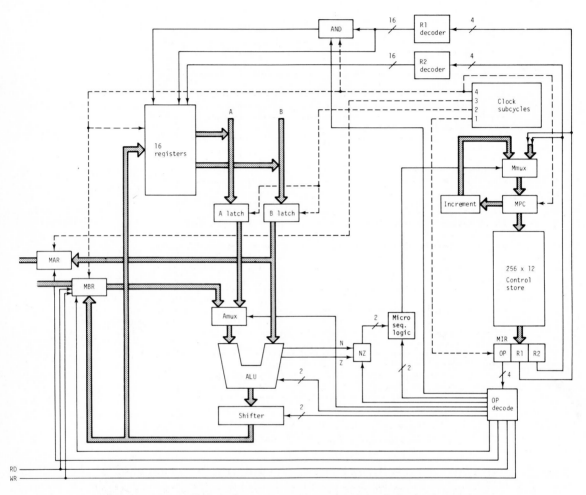

Fig. 4-18. A microarchitecture with vertical microinstructions.

As an example of a microinstruction opcode, consider BEGRD, which initiates a memory read. It uses ALU function 2 (select A bus), so ALUH = 1 and ALUL = 0. It also latches MAR and asserts RD. All the other control signals are negated. Now consider the jumps. Because we have decided to be compatible with the old micro sequencing logic, we need the MSLH MSLL pair to be 00 for no jump, 01 for jump on N, 10 for jump on Z, and 11 for unconditional jump. (Compatibility has reached such epidemic proportions in the computer industry that even hypothetical machines in textbooks are now compatible with their predecessors.) NJUMP generates 01, ZJUMP generates 10, and UJUMP generates 11. All the other opcodes generate 00.

Now comes the interesting part. How do we build a circuit with four input lines (the 4 opcode bits) and 13 output lines (the 13 control signals) that computes the

Cortrol lines

Microinstruction opcode		ALUH	ALUL	SHH	SHL	NZ	AMUX	AND	MAR	MBR	RD	WR	MSLH	MSLL
0	ADD					+		+						
1	AND		+			+		+						
2	MOVE	+				+		+						
3	COMPL	+	+			+		+						
4	LSHIFT	+		+		+		+						
5	RSHIFT	+			+	+		+						
6	GETMBR	+				+	+	+						
7	TEST	+				+								
8	BEGRD	+							+		+			
9	BEGWR	+							+	+		+		
10	CONRD	+									+			
11	CONWR	+										+		
12														
13	NJUMP	+												+
14	ZJUMP	+											+	
15	UJUMP	+											+	+

Fig. 4-19. The control signals for each microinstruction opcode. A plus means the signal is asserted; a blank means it is negated.

function of Fig. 4-19? Answer: Use one or more PLAs (or ROMs). Figure 4-19 is actually a slightly peculiar way to represent 13 four-variable truth tables, one per column, with the row number implicitly defining the values of the four variables. Hence the question of how to build the circuit reduces to the question of how one implements a truth table. The best way is with a four-input, 13-output PLA. If that is not available, three 74S330 12-input, six-output PLAs can also be used. If we label the four opcode bits A to D, high to low, then some outputs are:

$$\text{ALUL} = \quad \overline{A}\overline{B}\overline{C}D + \overline{A}\overline{B}CD = \overline{A}\overline{B}D$$

$$\text{SHH} = \quad \overline{A}B\overline{C}\overline{D}$$

$$\text{MAR} = \quad A\overline{B}\overline{C}\overline{D} + A\overline{B}\overline{C}D = A\overline{B}\overline{C}$$

$$\text{MSLH} = \quad ABC\overline{D} + ABCD = ABC$$

```
 0:  mar := pc ; rd ;
 1:  rd ;
     pc := pc + 1;
 2:  ir := mbr ;
     tir := lshift (ir );
     if n then goto 28;
 3:  tir := lshift (tir );
     if n then goto 19;
 4:  tir := lshift (tir );
     if n then goto 11;
 5:  alu := tir ;
     if n then goto 09;

 6:  mar := ir ; rd ; {LODD}
 7:  rd ;
 8:  ac := mbr ;
     goto 0;

 9:  mar := ir ; mbr := ac ; wr ; {STOD}
10:  wr ;
     goto 0;

11:  alu := tir ;
     if n then goto 15;

12:  mar := ir ; rd ; {ADDD}
13:  rd ;
14:  a := mbr ;
     ac := ac + a ;
     goto 0;

15:  mar := ir ; rd ; {SUBD}
16:  rd ;
99:  ac := ac + 1;
17:  a := mbr ;
     a := inv (a );
18:  ac := ac + a ;
     goto 0;

19:  tir := lshift (tir );
     if n then goto 25;
20:  alu := tir ;
     if n then goto 23;

21:  alu := ac ; {JPOS}
     if n then goto 0;
22:  pc := ir ;
     pc := band (pc , amask );
     goto 0;
```

```
23:  alu := ac ; {JZER}
     if z then goto 22;
24:  goto 0;

25:  alu := tir ;
     if n then goto 27;
26:  pc := ir ; {JUMP}
     pc := band (pc , amask );
     goto 0;

27:  ac := ir ; {LOCO}
     ac := band (ac , amask );
     goto 0;

28:  tir := lshift (tir );
     if n then goto 40;
29:  tir := lshift (tir );
     if n then goto 35;
30:  alu := tir ;
     if n then goto 33;

31:  a := ir ; {LODL}
     a := a + sp ;
32:  mar := a ; rd ;
     rd ;
     ac := mbr ;
     goto 0;

33:  a := ir ; {STOL}
     a := a + sp ;
34:  mar := a ; mbr := ac ; wr ;
     wr ;
     goto 0;

35:  alu := tir ;
     if n then goto 38;

36:  a := ir ; {ADDL}
     a := a + sp ;
37:  mar := a ; rd ;
     rd ;
     a := mbr ;
     ac := ac + a ;
     goto 0;
```

Fig. 4-20. The microprogram for Mic-2.

38: $a := ir$; {SUBL}
    $a := a + sp$;
39: $mar := a$; rd ;
    rd ;
    goto 99;

40: $tir := lshift (tir)$;
    if n **then goto** 46;
41: $alu := tir$;
    if n **then goto** 44;

42: $alu := ac$; {JNEG}
    if n **then goto** 22;
43: **goto** 0;

44: $alu := ac$; {JNZE}
    if z **then goto** 0;
45: $pc := ir$;
    $pc := band (pc , amask)$;
    goto 0;

46: $tir := lshift (tir)$;
    if n **then goto** 50;

47: $sp := sp + (-)$; {CALL}
48: $mar := sp$; $mbr := pc$; wr ;
    wr ;
49: $pc := ir$;
    $pc := band (pc , amask)$;
    goto 0;

50: $tir := lshift (tir)$;
    if n **then goto** 65;
51: $tir := lshift (tir)$;
    if n **then goto** 59;
52: $alu := tir$;
    if n **then goto** 56;

53: $mar := ac$; rd ; {PSHI}
    rd ;
54: $sp := sp + (-)$;
55: $a := mbr$;
    $mar := sp$; $mbr := a$; wr ;
    wr ;
    goto 0;

56: $mar := sp$; rd ; {POPI}
57: rd ;
    $sp := sp + 1$;

58: $a := mbr$;
    $mar := ac$; $mbr := a$; wr ;
    wr ;
    goto 0;
59: $alu := tir$;
    if n **then goto** 62;

60: $sp := sp + (-)$; {PUSH}
61: $mar := sp$; $mbr := ac$; wr ;
    wr ;
    goto 0;

62: $mar := sp$; rd ; {POP}
63: rd ;
    $sp := sp + 1$;
64: $ac := mbr$;
    goto 0;

65: $tir := lshift (tir)$;
    if n **then goto** 73;
66: $alu := tir$;
    if n **then goto** 70;
67: $mar := sp$; rd ; {RETN}
68: rd ;
    $sp := sp + 1$;
69: $pc := mbr$;
    goto 0;

70: $a := ac$; {SWAP}
71: $ac := sp$;
72: $sp := a$;
    goto 0;

73: $alu := tir$;
    if n **then goto** 76;

74: $a := ir$; {INSP}
    $a := band (a , smask)$;
75: $sp := sp + a$;
    goto 0;

76: $a := ir$; {DESP}
    $a := band (a , smask)$;
77: $a := inv (a)$;
78: $a := a + 1$;
    $sp := sp + a$;
    goto 0;

Fig. 4-20. (cont.).

Only 15 of the product terms must be generated internally, because $AB\overline{C}\overline{D}$ does not occur.

With the redesigned hardware now complete, we now need to rewrite the microprogram. It is given in Fig. 4-20. The labels have been kept the same to make comparison of the two microprograms easier. So has the syntax. We could have written it using typical assembly language notation (e.g., the opcodes of Fig. 4-17) but instead we have used MAL again because that is much easier to read. Note that MAL statements of the form *alu = reg* use the TEST microinstruction to set the N and Z bits. Be sure that you understand the difference between the microprogram in binary, as it is loaded into the control store, and the assembly language version given in the text.

By and large, this microprogram is simpler than the first one because each line only does one operation. As a consequence, many of the lines in the original one have had to be split up into two, three, or even four lines in this one. Another feature of the vertical design that increases the number of microinstructions is the lack of three-address instructions. See, for example, lines 22 and 27 in the first microprogram.

The original microprogram uses seventy-nine 32-bit words for a total of 2528 bits of control store. The second one uses one hundred sixty 12-bit words, for a total of 1920 bits. This difference represents a saving of 24% in control store. For a single-chip computer, it also represents a 24% saving in the chip area needed for the control store, which makes it easier and cheaper to manufacture. The penalty paid for the smaller control store is more microinstructions have to be executed per macroinstruction. Usually, this makes the machine slower. Consequently, fast, expensive machines tend to be horizontal, and slower, cheaper machines tend to be vertical.

The existence of highly encoded microinstructions, as in the Mic-2, raises some serious philosophical questions about what microprogramming is. The microinstruction set of Fig. 4-17 could almost pass for the *conventional machine language* instruction set of a very simple mini- or microcomputer. The PDP-8, for example, is a minicomputer with a 12-bit word whose instructions are not a whole lot more powerful than these. Considering that the "meaning" of the instructions is largely embedded in hardware (the OP decode PLA or circuit), one might well argue that the Mic-2 is really a nonmicroprogrammed machine that happens to have a software interpreter running on it for yet another machine. If the microprogram for the vertical machine were stored in main memory (as on the IBM 370/145, for example) then the distinction between a highly vertical microprogrammed machine and a hardwired one becomes even less clear. For a more thorough treatment of encoding and parallelism in microcode, see Dasgupta (1979).

4.5.2. Nanoprogramming

The designs discussed so far have had two memories: the main memory (used to hold the level 2 program) and the control store (used to hold the microprogram). A third memory, the **nanostore**, makes interesting trade-offs between horizontal and vertical microprogramming possible. Nanoprogramming is appropriate when many microinstructions occur several times. The microprogram of Fig. 4-16 does not have this property. The most commonly occurring microinstruction is the one containing just *rd*, and it occurs only five times.

Figure 4-21 illustrates the concept of nanoprogramming. In part (a), a microprogram of n microinstructions each w bits wide is shown. A total of nw bits of control store is needed to store the microprogram. Suppose that a careful study of the microprogram revealed that only m different microinstructions of the 2^w possibilities were actually used, with $m \ll n$. A special m-word w-bit nanostore could be used to store each unique microinstruction. Each microinstruction in the original program could then be replaced by the address of the nanostore word containing that microinstruction. Because there are only m words in the nanostore, the control store need only be $\log_2 m$ (rounded up to an integer) bits wide as shown in Fig. 4-21(b).

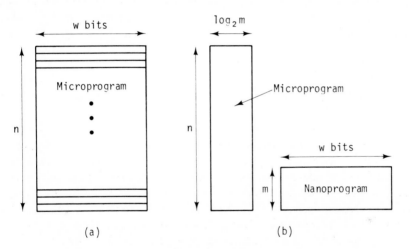

Fig. 4-21. (a) A conventional microprogram. (b) The corresponding nanoprogram if only m unique microinstructions occur in the microprogram.

The microprogram is executed as follows. The first word is fetched from the control store. It is then used to select a nanostore word, which is fetched and placed in the microinstruction register. The bits of this register are then used to control the gates for one cycle. At the end of the cycle, the next word is fetched from the control store and the process is repeated.

As an example, suppose that the original microprogram is 4096 × 100 bits but only 128 different microinstructions occur. A 128 × 100 bit nanostore will suffice to hold all the microinstructions needed. The control store then becomes 4096 × 7 bits, each word pointing to a nanoinstruction. The memory saving in this example is given by:

$$\text{saving} = 4096 \times 100 - 4096 \times 7 - 128 \times 100 = 368{,}128 \text{ bits}$$

The price that must be paid for saving control store is slower execution. The machine with the two-level control store will run slower than the original one because the fetch cycle now requires two memory references, one to the control store and one to the nanostore.

Nanoprogramming is most effective when the same microinstructions are heavily used. If two microinstructions that were almost the same could be counted as really being the same, the microprogram would contain fewer distinct microinstructions, each with a higher usage frequency. A variation on the basic idea allows precisely this. Words in the nanostore may be parameterized. For example, two microinstructions may differ only in field telling which register is to be gated onto some bus. By putting the register number in the control store instead of in the nanostore (i.e., putting zeros in the register field in the nanoinstructions) the two microinstructions can both point to the same nanoword. When the word is fetched and put into the microinstruction register, the register field is taken from the control store instead of the nanostore. Building up the microinstruction register partly from the control store and partly from the nanostore obviously requires special hardware, but it is not especially complex. Of course, using this approach increases the width of the control store, which may more than offset the gain made by having a smaller nanostore.

4.5.3. Improving Performance

Although the goal of nanoprogramming is to reduce the size of the control store, even at the price of slower execution, a fair amount of time and effort has also gone in the reverse direction: trying to speed up execution, even at the price of more control store. These two seemingly incompatible design goals relate to different marketing goals—producing inexpensive machines and producing fast machines. In this section we will look at some of the ways the straightforward microarchitecture of our examples can be souped up to make the machines run faster.

Up until now we have tacitly assumed that all four subcycles are equally long. While this approach is simple, it rarely results in optimum performance because invariably one of the four inherently takes more time than the other three. Having all subcycles be as long as the worst case slows the machine down. The way to fix this problem is to allow each subcycle to have a duration independent of the other ones. That way the length of each subcycle can be set to the amount of time needed to do the work, and no longer.

Although this is a step in the right direction, it is still too conservative because the length of each subcycle is still determined by the worst case for that subcycle. Consider, for example, subcycle 3 in our examples. If the ALU operation is an addition, the ALU probably needs more time (due to carry-propagation delays) than if the operation is merely select A. If the time devoted to subcycle 3 is a constant determined when the machine is designed, it has to be the time for addition, not for select A. An alternative strategy, however, is to let the subcycle time be determined by the specific operation to be performed, so it can be set as short as possible.

Once we decide to allow each subcycle to depend on the operation, we must find a way to implement this strategy. Slowing the clock down or speeding it up is technically difficult, so instead a master clock with a period much shorter than the subcycle time is used. Each subcycle then lasts a certain number of pulses. For example, if the ALU time can vary from 75 to 150 nsec, a master clock with a 25-nsec period can be used, with the subcycle taking between three and six periods.

Another question is: How does the machine know how long the subcycle should be? One of two approaches can be used here to tell it. In the first, the microinstruction itself contains one or more fields that explicitly give the timing. The other is to derive the timing based on the operation fields (using a PLA), the same way all the other control signals were generated for the vertical machine. The first approach costs control store bits and the second costs decoding logic and time.

Another way to get more horsepower out of the machine is to increase the flexibility of conditional microjumps. As an example of a problem that can occur, consider how to write the microcode for a macroinstruction SKIP LESS that compares AC to a specific memory word and skips over the next macroinstruction if AC is numerically less than memory. First, the microprogram must fetch the memory word, which then must be subtracted from AC (or a copy of AC). The trouble occurs because the subtraction of two valid 16-bit two's complement numbers can result in an overflow. Consequently, we cannot tell which number is smaller by just looking at the sign bit of the result. Some examples of subtraction are given in Fig. 4-22. In the fourth example, AC is less than memory but AC − memory is positive. The correct condition to be tested is N EXCLUSIVE OR V, where V indicates the presence or absence of overflow. (The hardware sets the V bit whenever the carry *into* the sign bit differs from the carry *out of* the sign bit.)

Fortunately, most ALUs generate not only N and Z but also V and C (carry) as well. However, if only four conditional jumps are available to the microprogrammer, one for each of NZVC, the SKIP LESS macroinstruction will require many microinstructions. To provide more flexibility, many machines do not have the ability to test individual ALU status bits. Instead, a single microinstruction bit causes NZVC to be ORed with the 4 low-order bits of the ADDR field, and the jump taken. Some examples are given in Fig. 4-23. If the 4 low-order bits are all 0, this becomes a 16-way jump. If they are all 1, the jump becomes an unconditional one to a specific address in 1111.

With this facility the SKIP LESS instruction becomes much easier to interpret. We choose the ADDR field ending in 0101, for example, 10000101 (binary), and perform the

AC	000100	000100	077777	100001	000010
Mem	000050	170000	177775	000010	100001
	000030	010100	100002	077771	100007
	N = 0	N = 0	N = 1	N = 0	N = 1
	V = 0	V = 0	V = 1	V = 1	V = 1

Fig. 4-22. Some examples of 16-bit two's complement subtraction in octal. The N and V bits for each result are also shown.

ADDR field	NZVC	Address jumped to
10000000	1001	10001001
10001000	1001	10001001
10001011	1001	10001011
10001011	1000	10001011
10001011	0000	10001011
10001111	0000	10001111
10001111	1100	10001111
10000000	1100	10001100

Fig. 4-23. Some examples of multiway jumping based on NZVC.

jump. The microinstructions at 10001101 and 10000111 deal with skips that succeed and those at 10000101 and 10001111 deal with skips that fail. No further decoding is needed. We could also have used a base address ending in 0000 instead of 0101 but these are enormously valuable, because they are the only ones available for 16-way jumps. Hence, they should not be chosen lightly.

It should be clear that with this kind of microinstruction sequence control, the placement of microinstructions in the control store can become a real headache. The first microinstruction executed following a 16-way jump must itself contain an unconditional jump because the word following it (except for the last one) is already in use as a possible jump destination. Where should each microinstruction jump to? Certainly not an address of the form xxxx0000, because they are too valuable, but all other addresses, except for those of the form xxxx1111, may also be needed sooner or later. The decision must be made carefully, to avoid running out of some kind of address. Once all the even addresses are gone, for example, it is no longer possible to test the C bit.

Yet another way to speed up the machine is to overlap the fetching of the next microinstruction with the execution of the current one (pipelining). In Fig. 4-10, for example, if the next microinstruction could somehow be fetched during subcycle 4, subcycle 1 would no longer be needed, and the clock could just generate pulses for subcycles 234234234.... The principal problem occurs in handling conditional jump microinstructions: if the machine waits until the ALU status lines are available before starting to fetch the next microinstruction, it is too late: the cycle is practically over and little overlap can be achieved. On some machines the problem is solved by just using the ALU status lines from the previous cycle, which, of course, have to be latched to keep them from vanishing. These values are available at the start of each microinstruction, so the next fetch can start as soon as the current fetch is finished, long before the execution of the current microinstruction has completed. Needless to say, this way of doing business greatly complicates life for the microprogrammer.

Technically, it is possible to write microprograms for such a machine in a reasonable way. For example, to test some word in the scratchpad and branch if it is negative, the microprogram can run the word through the ALU in a microinstruction *not* containing a jump. The next microinstruction is a no-op with conditional jump; that is, it does nothing except test the latched ALU status bits and jump. The price to be paid for programming in a rational way is doubling the jump time, an undesirable proposition.

The only solution is to get out a jar of aspirins and try to make the best of the situation. For example, the microprogrammer could make a guess which way the conditional jump will usually go, and use the second microinstruction to start doing the work that will probably be needed. Unfortunately, if the jump goes the other way, it may be necessary to undo some or all of it.

As a simple example, let us rewrite lines 11 to 18 of Fig. 4-16 for a machine with overlapped microinstruction fetching and execution. The results are shown in Fig. 4-24(a). In this example we are lucky because upon executing line 11 we know that the code for either ADDD or SUBD will follow, and both begin with the same microinstruction. Therefore, we just put the common microinstruction in line 12 to keep the machine busy while the jump is being carried out.

11: *alu* := *tir*;	52: *alu* := *tir*;
12: *mar* := *ir*; *rd*; **if** *n* **then goto** 16;	53: *mar* := *ac*; *rd*; **if** *n* **then goto** 56;
13: *rd*;	54: *sp* := *sp* + (−1); *rd*;
14: *ac* := *mbr* + *ac*; **goto** 0;	55: *mar* := *sp*; *wr*; **goto** 10;
	56: *rd*;
16: *ac* := *ac* + 1; *rd*;	57: *mar* := *sp*; *sp* := *sp* + 1; *rd*;
17: *a* := *inv*(*mbr*);	58: *rd*;
18: *ac* := *ac* + *a*; **goto** 0;	59: *mar* := *ac*; *wr*; **goto** 10;
(a)	*(b)*

Fig. 4-24. Two examples involving overlapped microinstruction fetching and execution.

A slightly less pleasant example is shown in Fig. 4-24(b). At line 52 we know that either PSHI or POPI will follow but unfortunately these two routines do not have the same first microinstruction. Suppose, however, that a statistical analysis of Mac-1 programs has shown PSHI to be far more common than POPI. Then we could proceed as shown in Fig. 4-24(b). For PSHI everything is fine but for POPI, by the time line 56 is reached, a memory read for the wrong word has already been initiated. Depending on the exact details of the hardware, it may or may not be possible to abort a memory read halfway through without gumming up the works. If we cannot abort it, we just finish it off and then start the correct read. In this example POPI takes 15 microinstructions instead of 13 as in Fig. 4-16. Nevertheless, if the use of overlapping has reduced the basic microinstruction time by even 15%, even POPI will be faster now than before.

If multiway jumps formed by ORing NZVC into the low-order bits of ADDR are used instead of individual bit tests, the situation becomes much more complicated. Furthermore, on many machines the overlapping of fetching and executing microinstructions is done in such a way that early during the execution of microinstruction n the choice of microinstruction $n + 1$ has to be made using the ALU status bits previously latched during microinstruction $n - 1$. We will not pursue the matter further here but at the very least the motivation for Rosin's definition of microprogramming may be clearer now.

4.6. THE IBM 370/125 MICROPROGRAMMING LEVEL

We have now finished our abstract discussion of microprogramming. It is time to see how the principles we have studied have been applied in practice. In the following sections we will examine the microprogramming levels of two commercially available machines: the IBM 370/125 and the PDP-11/60. We have not included the Z80 in this chapter because it is not microprogrammed. The Motorola 68000 *is* microprogrammed, but due to the highly competitive nature of the microcomputer business, Motorola has decided not to divulge any details of the microarchitecture. Other than a few remarks in a paper by Stritter and Tredennick (1978), nothing about it has been published.

The IBM 370 model 125 is one of the smaller models of the 370 series and is widely used for business and administrative applications. A 370/125 consists of not just one but at least three processors, and possibly more, depending on the number of I/O channels.

Each 370/125 has one processor that serves as the CPU, fetching, examining, and executing 370 programs stored in main storage. The IBM designation for the processors used as CPUs on the 370 series is the model number plus 3000; the IBM 3125 processor is used as the CPU on the model 125. Each 370/125 also has a processor called the "service processor" or SVP. The SVP has three basic functions:

1. Loading programs into itself and all the other processors from a special disk drive.

2. Handling communication with the console operator.

3. Detecting hardware malfunctions in the other processors and keeping a record of them for the maintenance personnel.

Every 370/125 also has one or more processors called **IOPs** (Input-Output Processors) that perform all the I/O for the 370/125. Because the 370/125 is commonly used in applications requiring substantial I/O, the machine may be equipped with several

IOPs. In addition to these three kinds of processors, the 370/125 has a hardwired (i.e., not microprogrammed) unit called the **main storage controller** (MSC), which coordinates all requests from the CPU, SVP, and IOPs for reading or writing main storage.

4.6.1. The IBM 370/125 Microarchitecture

Figure 4-25 is a simplified diagram of the components and data paths in the CPU, as well as portions of the main storage controller.

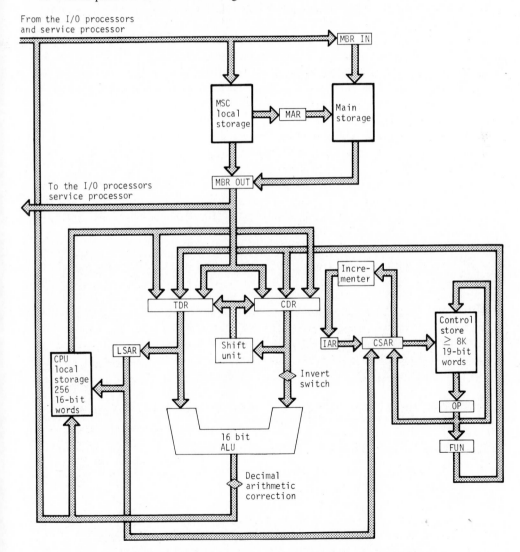

Fig. 4-25. Simplified diagram of the IBM 3125's microarchitecture.

Figure 4-26 summarizes the properties of these memories, registers, and functional units. The TDR, CDR, ALU inputs and outputs, shift unit, and CPU local storage are all 16 bits wide. Because the 370 conventional machine level general registers and data paths are 32 bits wide, the 370 general registers must be stored in two pieces and operations carried out separately on each piece. Thus the 3125 is both ·slower and cheaper than the larger models that have 32-bit registers and data paths.

Four separate memories are listed in Fig. 4-26, each with its own purpose. The main storage, control store, and CPU local storage hold the 370 program, microprogram, and microprogram variables (including the conventional machine level registers), respectively. The main storage controller also has a small memory of its own, to which the CPU, SVP, and IOPs have access. Each processor has an area of this memory assigned to it. The 3125 microinstructions reference main memory by specifying one of four possible words within the MSC local storage. The selected MSC word is used as the main storage address and gated into the MAR. This addressing method requires only 2 bits in the microinstruction for main memory addressing. The four words include:

1. The 370 level 2 IAR (program counter), used to fetch level 2 instructions.

2. Two operand addresses (level 2 instructions can have at most two operands in memory).

3. A communication word common to all the processors, which is used primarily for passing I/O instructions from the CPU to the IOPs for execution.

Associated with each operand address is a length field, giving the length of the operand.

The box labeled LSAR consists of four registers of 4 bits each rather than a single 16-bit register. The four registers, LSAR0, LSAR1, LSAR2, and LSAR3 can be used to form the 8-bit addresses needed to address the CPU local storage (locations 160 to 191 are optional, and locations 192 to 255 are reserved for possible future expansion). CPU local storage addresses can be formed in three ways:

1. All 8 bits are contained within the microinstruction (direct addressing).

2. The leftmost 4 bits are contained within the microinstruction and the rightmost 4 bits are taken from one of the LSARs.

3. The leftmost 4 bits come from LSAR0, and the rightmost 4 bits come from any one of the LSARs.

The first form is useful for accessing variables and counters. The second and third forms are useful for accessing the 370's level 2 registers. The high-order parts of the 16 general registers are kept at CPU local storage addresses 40 to 4F

MEMORIES

Name	Use	Cell size	Number of cells
Main storage	Holds the IBM 370 level 2 programs and data; this is the only memory the level 2 programmer is aware of	8	98K-128K
MSC local storage	Holds the program counter and other main storage addresses	23	32
CPU local storage	Holds the microprogram variables and the level 2 machine's registers	16	160-192
Control store	Holds the microprogram	19	8K-20K

REGISTERS

Name	Width	Use
TDR	16	Left input to ALU (true data register)
CDR	16	Right input to ALU (complement data register)
MBR IN	16	Halfwords to be stored in main storage are loaded here
MBR OUT	16	Halfwords read from main storage arrive here
CSAR	15	MAR (control storage address register)
OP	19	MBR (for reading and writing)
FUN	19	Holds microinstruction while it is being executed
LSAR	4 x 4	Used to address CPU local storage (local storage address registers)
IAR	3 x 15	Micro program counters (IAR0, IAR1, IAR2)

Notes: LSAR is 4 registers of 4 bits each
       IAR is 3 register of 15 bits each

FUNCTIONAL UNITS

Name	Output width	Use
ALU	16	Binary addition, AND, OR, and EXCLUSIVE OR
Shift unit	16	Shifts 0-15 bits left or right with zero fill
Incrementer	15	Increments current micro program counter (IAR) by 1
Invert switch	16	Controls ALU right input: CDR, 1's complement of CDR, 16 ones or 16 zeroes
Decimal arithmetic correction	16	Performs correction needed to convert binary addition to decimal addition

Fig. 4-26. Summary of the components of the IBM 3125's microprogramming level.

(hexadecimal), and the low-order parts are kept at addresses 50 to 5F. Access to the level 2 registers is easily performed by first loading the register number, 0 to F (hexadecimal) into an LSAR. CPU local storage addresses are then formed from the hex digits 4 or 5 (contained within the microinstruction itself) concatenated with the register number (from an LSAR).

A one-to-one correspondence exists between the 16 LSAR bits and the 16 TDR bits. Bits in the microinstructions enable gating all or part of the TDR into the four LSARs. In this way, the register numbers can be loaded into the LSARs.

The 3125 has three microprogram counters (labeled IAR in Fig. 4-26). At any instant, one of them is the "current" one and is used for fetching microinstructions from the control store. When the main microprogram is running, IAR0 is used. When the microprogram calls a microprocedure, the return address is put in IAR0, the procedure's starting address is put in IAR1, and IAR1 becomes the current microprogram counter.

A return from a procedure simply makes IAR0 the current microprogram counter again. In essence, IAR0 and IAR1 form a two word stack. A procedure in the microprogram may not call another procedure. IAR2 is loaded and becomes current only when an interrupt occurs. The incrementer adds 1 to the current IAR after each microinstruction is fetched.

The invert switch controls the right ALU input. Its four positions correspond to:

1. CDR

2. One's complement of CDR

3. Sixteen 1 bits (-1 in twos complement)

4. Sixteen 0 bits

Once set by a microinstruction, it remains set until explicitly changed by another microinstruction.

4.6.2. IBM 3125 Microinstructions

The IBM 3125 microinstructions are neither purely horizontal nor purely vertical but a mixture of both organizations. Opcodes range from 2 to 6 bits. The remainder of the 19-bit microinstruction is divided into fields whose number, size, and function are different for each of the 13 opcodes. Furthermore, some microinstructions have several minor variations, with the actual format being determined by certain bits within the microinstruction.

Figure 4-27 lists the primary function of each microinstruction. In addition, some microinstructions have fields for performing additional functions, which may be unrelated to the primary function. They include:

1. Return from procedure.

2. Set invert switch for use in subsequent ALU operations.

3. Copy left byte and/or right byte of TDR into corresponding LSARs.

4. Increment or decrement an MSC local storage address by 1 or 2 bytes.

Load TDR or CDR

1. Load 1 byte of TDR or CDR with immediate data. Zero or retain other byte.
2. Load 16-bit halfword into TDR or CDR from CPU local storage.
3. Load byte or halfword into TDR or CDR from main storage.
4. Load leftmost 7 bits or rightmost 16 bits of MSC local storage in TDR or CDR.

ALU operation (ADD, AND, OR, or EXCLUSIVE OR)

5. ALU operation. Store result in CPU local storage.
6. ALU operation. Store result in main storage.
7. ALU operation. Store result in MSC local storage.

Test and conditional branch

8. Test for presence or absence of one out of 48 conditions.
9. Branch on test. Conditional branch on outcome of previous test.
10. Conditional branch on 1 of 10 conditions irrespective of previous test.

Miscellaneous

11. Shift CDR left or right 0-15 bits with zero fill. Store result in CDR or TDR.
12. Sense and control. Read or set timers, clocks and other system devices.
13. Table look up. Used to examine level 2 machine opcodes and branch to microprogram address to start interpretation of the instruction.

Fig. 4-27. Principal functions of the IBM 3125 microinstructions. Each microinstruction has several secondary functions which are not shown.

Other fields provide addresses and other information needed to perform the primary function, such as:

1. ALU function (ADD, AND, OR, EXCLUSIVE OR).

2. Destination register for output from local or main storage (CDR or TDR).

3. Specification of CPU local storage addresses (immediate bits and LSAR numbers).

4. Determination of ALU output width (8 or 16 bits).

5. Immediate data (for loading either byte of CDR or TDR).

6. Enable or disable decimal arithmetic correction.

7. Handle carry bits for multiple-precision arithmetic.

8. Handle condition codes for multiple-precision arithmetic.

9. Specification of condition to be tested.

10. Branch address (partial or complete).

11. Enable or disable virtual memory (see Sec. 5.5).

Of course, not every one of the preceding 15 fields is present in every microinstruction.

The TEST microinstruction can test for the presence or absence of 48 different conditions or bits. They include the 16 TDR bits, various bits in the LSARs, certain hardware errors, certain exceptional conditions such as floating-point overflow, interrupt signals from the other processors, the ALU carry bit, and the condition code.

The BRANCH ON TEST microinstruction uses the result of the most recent TEST to branch to a new microprogram location (14 address bits are provided). In addition, a 2-bit field provides for optional procedure call or return (i.e., switching IARs).

In contrast, the CONDITIONAL BRANCH microinstruction can specify any one of 10 conditions to be both tested and branched on in a single microinstruction. These conditions include specific LSAR and TDR bits, ALU output zero or nonzero, and ALU carry bit set.

The SENSE AND CONTROL microinstruction can read the status of various timers, clocks, and exceptional conditions into CDR or TDR and can also set these devices and registers from CDR or TDR.

As an example of a microinstruction, the meanings of the fields in READ FROM MAIN STORAGE INTO TDR OR CDR are given in Fig. 4-28. The bits here are numbered from 0 (leftmost) to 18 (rightmost).

The time required to execute a microinstruction is 480 nsec. The execution time of a 370 conventional machine level instruction depends on the number of microinstructions needed. A few sample 370/125 instruction execution times (in nsec) follow:

LR	3840	(8 microinstructions)
AR	4800	(10 microinstructions)
L	6720	(14 microinstructions)
ST	7200	(15 microinstructions)
MR	$123360 + 2880N$	$(257 + 6N$ microinstructions) where N = number of 1 bits in the multiplier

Bits	Meaning
0–4	The opcode for this microinstruction is 11111 (binary)
5	1 = leave procedure
6	0 = read into CDR; 1 = read into TDR
7	1 = copy (new) TDR bits 0 to 3 to LSAR0 and TDR bits 4 to 7 to LSAR1
8	1 = copy (new) TDR bits 8 to 11 to LSAR2 and TDR bits 12 to 15 to LSAR3
9–10	set invert switch: 0 = 1's complement; 1 = no change; 2 = all 1's; 3 = all 0's
11	1 = check for exceptional conditions and trap if present
12	0 = read byte (8 bits); 1 = read half word (16 bits)
13	1 = increment selected MSC local storage register by byte or half word
14	1 = decrement selected MSC local storage register by byte or half word
15–16	MSC local storage address: 0 = IAR; 1 = operand 1; 2 = operand 2; 3 = i/o common register
17	0 = update MSC address; 1 = update MSC length
18	0 = disable virtual memory address translation; 1 = enable it

Fig. 4-28. Load TDR or CDR data register.

4.7. THE PDP-11/60 MICROPROGRAMMING LEVEL

Like the 370 series, no two models of the PDP-11 series have the same hardware (level 0) or microarchitecture (level 1). In the following sections we will briefly examine the microprogramming level of one of the larger PDP-11s, the PDP-11/60. This model is particularly appropriate to study because it is the only PDP-11 designed for customer microprogramming. Of its 4K control store, 3K is read-only memory but 1K is read/write memory, so users can add their own microcode to provide for new conventional machine level instructions.

4.7.1. The PDP-11/60 Microarchitecture

The most important part of the PDP-11/60 microarchitecture is the data path, a simplified diagram of which is shown in Fig. 4-29. In addition to the data path, the PDP-11/60 processor has a control section, a cache and a memory management unit (subjects to be covered in Chap. 6), and a writable control store section. These sections are connected by internal buses, which are not shown in Fig. 4-29.

The heart of the data path is the ALU, which consists of four garden-variety, off-the-shelf 74S181 chips cascaded to form a 16-bit-wide data path. The ALU is fed by two buses, A (right input) and B (left input), following DEC's naming convention. Each bus has four possible input devices, including five scratchpads and two multiplexers. The ALU output can be loaded into either or both of two registers, D and SR. The D register is the more important of the two, because it drives the shift tree, and provides the data to be rewritten into the scratchpads, as well as the Unibus data. SR, the shift register, which is primarily used in shift instructions, can shift right 1 or

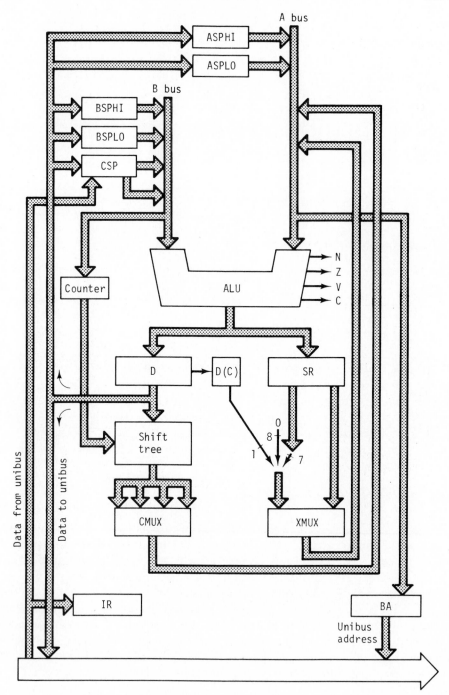

Fig. 4-29. Simplified diagram of the PDP-11/60's data path.

2 bits or left 1 bit in a cycle. The shift tree, in contrast, can shift 1 bit left or 1 to 14 bits right. However, the shift tree is pure combinational circuitry, so it, unlike SR, does not retain a value from one microinstruction to the next. The remaining components of the data path are IR, which holds the current macroinstruction, BA, which is the MAR, and an 8-bit counter used for microprogram loops. A summary of the major components of the data path is given in Fig. 4-30.

MEMORIES

Name	Use	Cell size	Number of cells
Main memory	Holds level 2 programs	8	248K
ASPHI	Corsole, control and floating point registers	16	16
ASPLO	Level 2 general registers + floating point	16	16
BSPHI	Miscellaneous and floating point registers	16	16
BSPLO	Level 2 general registers + floating point	16	16
CSP	Miscellanous constants and variables	16	16

REGISTERS

Name	Width	Use
D	16	ALU latch. Provides output to scratchpads and Unibus
SR	16	Shift register. Right 1 or 2, left 1 bit/cycle
IR	16	Instruction register. Holds current macroinsturction
BA	18	Bus address. Tells Unibus where to read or write
Counter	8	Counter. Holds iteration count for shifting, etc.
D(C)	1	Carry latch. Can be loaded from various sources

FUNCTIONAL UNITS

Name	Width	Use
ALU	16	Performs any one of 16 arithmetic/logical functions
Shift tree	16	1-bit left or 1-14 bit right shift, byte swap, sign extend
CMUX	16	Last stage of the shift tree
XMUX	16	Selects SR or word with D(C) + 8 zeroes + 7 bits of SR

Fig. 4-30. Summary of the components of the PDP-11/60 data path.

The PDP-11/60 has five distinct scratchpad memories: ASPHI, ASPLO, BSPHI, BSPLO, and CSP. Each consists of sixteen 16-bit registers. The first eight words of ASPLO and BSPLO hold identical copies of the eight general registers visible to the

PDP-11 conventional machine level programmer. The registers are replicated to allow two of them to be read out in parallel, one per scratchpad, for speed. The six 8-byte level 2 floating-point registers are also kept in the A and B scratchpads, with a quarter of each register in each of ASPLO, ASPHI, BSPLO, and BSPHI. The remaining words in A and B are control registers, the console registers, and miscellaneous constants.

The CSP scratchpad contains a collection of miscellaneous constants and variables but differs from the other four scratchpads in the way it is addressed. It has two addressing modes. In the first one, the microprogrammer can specify any of the 16 registers in a 4-bit microinstruction field. In the other one, only the last four words can be addressed. These words contain the constants 0, 1, 2, and the memory buffer register, MBR in CSP[13] (13 is decimal here, as are all numbers in this section unless otherwise noted).

The data path interfaces with the rest of the processor and the Unibus devices (including memory) via the D register, the BA register, and the MBR (CSP[13]). To read a memory word, the microprogrammer loads the memory address to be read into BA via the A bus and specifies the bus function code in a microinstruction field. Near the end of the *following* microinstruction the Unibus data are available in CSP[13]. On the way in, they can be copied into IR as well, under microprogram control. Memory writes are done in a similar way, with the data to be written coming from D.

The basic 170-nsec microinstruction cycle is divided into four subcycles by clock pulses. During subcycle 0, data are gated onto the A and B buses, and the ALU performs its computation. The ALU output can be loaded into D or SR or both either during subcycle 1 or 2, under microprogram control. If the result is to be rewritten into a scratchpad, D must be loaded during subcycle 1 to provide enough time for the rewrite. However, if one of the ALU operands is CSP[13], that is, a memory word read by the previous microinstruction, the ALU output is not stable until subcycle 2, so D cannot be loaded in time to permit rewriting the scratchpad. The fetching of the next microinstruction is initiated during subcycle 3. This overlap complicates the semantics of conditional jumps enormously, as we will see later. Please note that the description above is highly simplified, because some actions are triggered by rising or falling clock pulses and others are level-triggered.

4.7.2. The PDP-11/60 Microinstructions

PDP-11/60 microinstructions are highly horizontal, with about 20 fields in a typical one. Most of these fields are present in nearly all microinstructions but some fields have different functions in different microinstructions. Figure 4-31 shows the basic structure of the PDP-11/60 microinstruction, including some of the variations. Bits 36 and 37, for example, contain the ASEL, CMUX, or XMUX field depending on the value of AEN. The technique of having the meaning of one field be determined by the setting of another field is called **bit steering**.

47 46 45 44 43 42 41 40 39 38 37 36 35 34 33

ALU	BEN	BSEL	AEN	ASEL / CMUX / XMUX	RIF

```
0   A̅                 0  BSPLO      BEN ≠ 3       0  XMUX     ASEL        3-bit constant
1   A + B + PS(C)      1  BSPHI                    1  CMUX     0  Imm0     used in
2   A̅B̅                 2  CSP         0  DF        2  ASPLO    1  Imm1     conjunction
3   0                  3  Consts      1  SF        3  ASPHI    2  DF       with ASEL
4   A + B + D(C)                      2  Imm0                  3  SF       and BSEL
5   A + B + D(C)                      3  Imm1                               to address
6   A_XOR B                                                    CMUX        scratchpad
7   A̅B                                BEN = 3                  0  Left 1
8   A + B                                                      1  No shift
9   A + B                            0  CSP [15]               2  Right 1
10  B                                1  CSP [14]               3  Right 2
11  AB                               2  CSP [13]
12  A + B + 1                        3  CSP [12]               XMUX
13  A − B
14  A OR B                                                     0,2  SR
15  A                                                          1,3  D(C),0,SR
```

32 31 30 29 28 27 26 25 24 23 22 21 20 19 18 17

COUT	WHEN	CLKD	CLKSR	CLKBA	SCC	BGB	CSP ADDRESS / BB BUS CODE / BMUX AMUX	WR CSP	hI LO	WRSEL

```
0  CIN        When      ⌐————————————⌐    1  Bus    Address  CSP          ⌐————————⌐
1  PS(C)      to        Control          0  No     Control  shift tree   Control
2  ALU0       load      loading                    Control  Unibus       rewriting
3  ALU7       D         of D, SR, BA                                      of
4  ALU15      and/or                     Set                              scratchpads
5  COUT7      SR                         condition
6  COUT15                                codes
7  D(C)
```

16 15 14 13 12 11 10 9 8 7 6 5 4 3 2 1 0

WRSP	MOD	UBF	UPF

```
Rewrite              Micro      Base address of next
0  None   0 Rewrite  branch     microinstruction
1  ASP    1 RES,counter control
2  BSP
3  Both
```

Fig. 4-31. The principal fields of the PDP-11/60 microinstructions.

Let us now examine the microinstruction of Fig. 4-31 field by field to see how it controls the data path. The high-order 4 bits comprise the ALU field, which determines which of the 16 possible ALU functions is to be performed. Most of the functions listed in Fig. 4-31 are self-explanatory, although a brief remark may be helpful for three codes. Code 1 adds A and B and the carry bit stored in the program status word. (The program status word is a 16-bit register that holds certain processor status information, including the four ALU status signals, NZVC.) Code 3 generates 16 zeros. Code 8 does an addition or subtraction depending on the value of the 1-bit wide D(C) register. Not all 16 functions are used in the PDP-11/60 but remember that the ALU is based on an off-the-shelf chip that was designed years ago, certainly not with the PDP-11/60 in mind.

As an aside, it is interesting to note that machine designers are constantly faced with the decision whether their company should design and manufacture some chip itself or whether it should buy a standard chip from one of the semiconductor vendors. An MSI chip like the 74S181 costs about a dollar, so if sales projections indicate that x chips will be needed, the question becomes: "Can we design and manufacture x of these chips for less than x dollars?" If the answer is no, which it will be unless a huge volume is needed, the designers will normally choose to use standard chips. This reasoning shows why so many computers have been built from standard TTL MSI and bit-slice chips in the past.

The inputs to the A and B buses are determined by the BEN (B ENable), BSEL (B SELect), AEN (A ENable), ASEL (A SELect), and RIF (Register Immediate Field) fields. Each of the two ALU input buses has four possible sources, so BEN and AEN, which enable the bus inputs, are each 2 bits wide. In a perfect world, two 5-bit microinstruction fields would be provided for specifying which of the 32 ASP scratchpad registers and which of the 32 BSP scratchpad registers were to be selected. Unfortunately, the goal of simple scratchpad addressing conflicted with the goal of a microinstruction that fit in 48 bits (three PDP-11 words), so a somewhat peculiar scratchpad addressing system was devised.

When BEN is 0 or 1, BSPLO or BSPHI, respectively, is enabled as input to the B bus, with BSEL selecting the specific register. BSEL = 0 means that IR bits 0 to 2 select one of the first eight registers. BSEL = 1 means that IR bits 6 to 8 provide the register number. ASEL = 2 or 3 work the same way. These two IR fields are the destination and source registers for the PDP-11 level 2 instructions, respectively. When the level 2 instruction is, for example, MOV R2,X, the microprogram can use these scratchpad addressing forms to select the proper register without having to isolate the register field within the macroinstruction.

When BEN = 2, the CSP scratchpad is gated onto the B bus, with the CSP ADDRESS field (bits 20 to 23) specifying the register. When BEN = 3, one of the four registers CSP[12-15] is the B bus input, with BSEL telling which of the four it is to be. The latter addressing mode is like bit steering, because it allows bits 20-23 to be used for something else while making the four most important CSP registers still available.

In many circumstances, the microprogrammer wants to address a specific BSP scratchpad register, independent of the current contents of IR. This address requires 5 bits. One of these bits is provided by BEN, which selects either BSPLO or BSPHI. Another bit is provided by using values 2 or 3 in BSEL. ("Imm" in Fig. 4-31 stands for "Immediate," which means a literal value—more about this in Chap. 5.) The 3 remaining bits come from RIF.

The A bus is enabled in a similar way; however, a complication arises due to the presence of only one RIF field. If AEN is 2 or 3 and ASEL is 0 or 1, the RIF field determines the A input. It is possible to select ASP via AEN and BSP via BEN, with immediate addressing chosen for both (BSEL = 2 or 3 and ASEL = 0 or 1), in which case RIF forms part of the address for both inputs. In effect, 10 bits of information are squeezed into 7 bits, putting certain unnatural constraints on which pairs of registers may be selected simultaneously. As if this were not enough, in positions 20 to 23 and 35 a 1 means 0 and a 0 means 1. (Nobody ever said that microprogramming was for 100-pound weaklings.)

When AEN is 0 or 1, one of the multiplexers provides the A bus source. As mentioned earlier, both the shift tree and CMUX in Fig. 4-29 are combinational circuits (no storage), so when the CMUX is selected, the CMUX, BMUX, and AMUX microinstruction fields determine how D, the previous ALU output, is shifted to generate the A bus input. The AMUX and BMUX fields control multiplexers internal to the shift tree. Their organization and interaction with the CMUX are sufficiently esoteric that the less said here the better. When AEN = 0, words derived from SR can be used as input to the A bus.

Having discussed how the ALU function and inputs are selected, it is now time to see what happens to the ALU output. COUT provides eight ways of loading D(C), mostly from specific ALU bits, carries into or out of specific ALU bit positions, or the previous D(C). CLKD and CLKSR tell whether D and/or SR are to be "clocked" (engineering jargon for loaded) during the current microinstruction. If either one or both is loaded, WHEN tells whether this happens during subcycle 1 or 2. CLKBA is similar to CLKD and CLKSR, except that it controls loading BA from the A bus. If BA is loaded, it happens during subcycle 0, independent of WHEN. If SCC is set, the 4 ALU status bits, NZVC, are saved in the program status word for use in a subsequent microinstruction. For example, COUT = 1 copies the saved carry bit to D(C) and ALU = 1 adds A and B and the saved carry bit.

The microprogrammer can control the Unibus by setting the BGB (BeGin Bus cycle), BB (Bus Box), and BUS CODE fields of the microinstruction. If a bus cycle is to be initiated, BGB = 1; otherwise, it is 0. BB tells whether the Unibus or the internal bus connecting the various sections of the processor is to be used. For a Unibus cycle, BUS CODE specifies read versus write, byte versus word, whether IR is to be loaded, and various other specialized functions. Because the bus control fields overlap CSP ADDRESS and the fields that control the shift tree, a microinstruction initiating a bus cycle cannot use the shift tree or address CSP[0-11], although CSP[12-15] can be addressed using BEN = 3.

Bits 14 to 19 control rewriting of the ALU output into the scratchpads. It is possible to input two values to the ALU, compute some function of them, and store the result back in a scratchpad register, all in a single cycle. MOD is a steering bit that enables rewriting if 0, disables it if 1. MOD = 1 affects the 8-bit counter register and a residual control register used to set up intraprocessor communication paths, among other things. WRSP enables rewriting of ASP or BSP or both. When WRSEL = 0 the register addressed by the ASP fields is rewritten; otherwise, the register addressed by the BSP fields is rewritten. The HILO bit determines whether the low (0) or high (1) scratchpad is to be rewritten. Because of the way the addressing is done, it is possible to rewrite a register that was not used as an ALU input. For example, if WRSP = 2, BEN = 0, WRSEL = 1, and HILO = 1, data come from BSPLO but go back into BSPHI. However, the register rewritten, 0 to 15, has the same address as the source. Setting WRCSP to 1 enables writing the Unibus data to CSP.

As is usually the case on horizontally microprogrammed machines designed for high performance, microinstruction sequencing on the PDP-11/60 is a trifle bizarre. The control store address space of 4096 words is divided into eight 512-word pages. No microprogram counter is present. Instead, the address of the next microinstruction is computed during subcycle 3 as follows. The low-order 9 bits consist of a number formed by ORing one of 32 possible functions of the machine state with UPF. The function to be used is determined by UBF.

Many of the functions, all of which are computed by hardware, return a few bits of IR in the low-order bits and zeros in the high-order bits of the 9-bit number. For example, UBF = 1 returns IR bits 12 to 15 in the low-order 4 bits. Thus if IR = 020104 (octal) and UPF = 310 (octal), the next microinstruction will be fetched from 002 OR 310 = 312. The upper 4 bits of PDP-11 level 2 instructions determine the primary opcode group, so UBF = 1 provides a fast 16-way jump for instruction decoding. In addition to testing certain predefined fields in IR, UBF values can select certain bits in D, SR, BA, and other registers.

Some of the UBF codes test bits such as D(C) that may be changed on every microinstruction. Because of the partial overlap of microinstruction fetching and execution, the UBF and UPF fields in microinstruction k determine the address of microinstruction $k + 1$ by using the conditions set up in microinstruction $k - 1$. Thus the microprogrammer wishing to test some condition must arrange for the test to be performed and the result to be kept stable until the succeeding microinstruction, where UBF specifies that it is to be tested. The trick to writing an efficient microprogram is to arrange for the succeeding microinstruction to do useful work without interfering with the condition to be tested.

Six of the UBF codes are special, and are used for their side effects, not their values. For example, there exist UBF codes to load a special hardware return register with either D or a field from the microinstruction that overlaps the ALU input fields. Another UBF code takes the next microinstruction address from this return register instead of making the usual computation. Together, these two codes provide a facility for microprogram subroutines. Because the return register (which is in the control section of the processor) can be routed into the data path, it can be stored in a scratchpad to allow nested microprocedure calls.

So far we have only discussed the low-order 9 bits of the next microinstruction address. The high-order 3 bits, which determine the page of the microinstruction, come from a 3-bit page register that can be loaded in several ways, among them, from a constant in a microinstruction and from the (12 bit-wide) return register.

Although the treatment described may seem somewhat complicated and detailed, be assured that it has been *greatly* simplified for pedagogical reasons. A substantial portion of the hardware is outside the data path and has been ignored here. Even within the data path we have intentionally glossed over many subtle issues. Nevertheless, the general picture that emerged is faithful to the spirit of the PDP-11/60 (and the other large PDP-11s as well).

4.8. SUMMARY

At the microprogramming level, the CPU consists of two principal components: the data path and the control section. The data path consists primarily of a scratchpad memory and an ALU/shifter portion. A cycle consists of extracting some operands from the scratchpad, running them through the ALU/shifter, and possibly storing the results back in the scratchpad.

The control section consists primarily of the control store, where the microprogram is kept. Each microinstruction in the control store controls the gates in the data path during one microcycle. In the example given, the microcycles were divided into subcycles controlled by a clock. During the first subcycle, the microinstruction is fetched from the control store and put into an internal register. In the second subcycle, the ALU inputs are latched to keep them stable throughout the microinstruction. In the third subcycle, the ALU and shifter perform their work. Finally, in the fourth subcycle, the result may be stored back in the scratchpad if it is needed for use in a subsequent microinstruction.

Microinstruction sequencing can best be described as bizarre. Few machines have an explicit program counter at the microprogramming level. Instead, microinstructions generally contain the base address of their successors. This base address is typically ORed with a few status bits to produce the final address. On many machines, the base address from one microinstruction is combined with status bits resulting from the previous one to produce a jump address that does not take effect until one instruction later.

Microinstructions can be organized horizontally, with one bit per gate, vertically, with a few fields requiring complex decoding, or something in between. Horizontal organization leads to long words and fast, highly parallel machines. Vertical organization leads to slower machines but usually to more efficient use of the control store.

Performance can be improved using techniques such as nanoprogramming, variable cycle times, pipelining, and multiway branching. Each technique brings with it some increased complexity, however. The microarchitectures of two commercially available machines were examined in some detail.

PROBLEMS

1. Translate the following Pascal function to Mac-1 assembly language.

   function *min(i, j, k: SmallInt): SmallInt;*
   var *m: SmallInt;*
   begin
       if *i < j* **then** *m := i* **else** *m := j;*
       if *k < m* **then** *m := k;*
       min := m
   end;

   The type *SmallInt* is the same subrange as in the text.

2. Translate the Pascal statement

   if *i < j* **then goto** 100;

   to Mac-1 assembly language. Both *i* and *j* are 16-bit two's complement integers. Be careful: If *i* = 32767 and *j* = −10, a subtraction will give an undetected overflow.

3. In Fig. 4-11(b) we reload K in the line labeled L4. The two preceding statements ensure that K is in AC after all. Why bother loading it again?

4. Compute the execution time in microinstructions for each Mac-1 instruction running on Mic-1.

5. Repeat the preceding problem but now for Mic-2.

6. Try to compile the Pascal statement

   n := a[i]

   directly to Mic-1 instructions, bypassing the Mac-1 level altogether. Discuss your attempt.

7. Consider a possible revision of Mic-1 in which the two sequencing fields COND and ADDR are removed, giving 22-bit microinstructions. Microjumps are now handled by distinct 22-bit microinstructions. The ALU N and Z bits are also latched, to make them available to a subsequent microjump. Compare the size of the original Mic-1 program with the one needed for this new design.

8. Do the following two Mic-1 statements perform exactly the same function? Explain.

   a := a + a; **if** *n* **then goto** 0;
   a := lshift(a); **if** *n* **then goto** 0;

9. Your only listing of a key Mic-1 microprogram was accidentally put into the automatic document feeder for the paper shredder instead of the photocopier next to it. You will now have to reconstruct the source program from a core dump. In the course of the disassembly you come across the binary number
   1100 1000000 1 0001 1001 00000000 1000
   Rewrite it in assembly language.

10. How many bit patterns are there for the following Mic-1 instruction?

   ac := mbr + a; **if** *n* **then goto** 100;

11. Imagine that you work for a company that is selling a machine with Mic-1 as level 1 and Mac-1 as level 2. The semiconductor vendor that normally supplies your chips has just announced a big clearance sale on one's complement ALUs. Your purchasing department jumped at the chance and bought a whole carload of them. Will the microprogram of Fig. 4-16 continue to work with a one's complement ALU instead of the original two's complement one? In the new machine negative numbers are to be represented in one's complement, of course.

12. If main memory reads and writes took three microinstructions instead of two on Mic-1, would the microprogram size be affected, and if so, by how much?

13. The COND field in the Mic-1 word is 2 bits, which gives four distinct codes. If one of these codes were needed for something else, for example, testing a newly implementing ALU overflow status bit, which of the existing four codes would you recommend sacrificing?

14. Propose adding a simple facility to Mic-1 for calling micro-level procedures. Some way must be found to both call and return from microprocedures, which may not be nested (i.e., a microprocedure may not call another microprocedure). You may modify the Mic-1 architecture but try to minimize the changes needed and restrictions introduced.

15. Microarchitects are constantly faced with trade-offs between elegance (i.e., orthogonality of fields) and control store size. Suppose that you had the job of modifying Mic-1 to add a bit to COND or ADDR and take a bit away from one of the other 11 fields. Make a suggestion of where to find the bit without impairing the functionality of Mic-1 too much.

16. Computer design is driven to a significant degree by technology. Microprogramming is attractive because fast, cheap ROMs exist for use as control store. Consider what changes would occur if developments in PLA technology suddenly made even very large PLAs much faster, cheaper, and easier to produce than ROMs. Discuss how Mac-1 could be implemented directly in hardware with a PLA and no microprogram at all.

17. Are there places in the microprogram for Mic-2 where the microprogrammer was forced to choose between time versus memory in a way not required in the microprogram for Mic-1? If so, give an example.

18. The microinstructions of Mic-2 are much more compact than those of Mic-1 (12 bits versus 32 bits). Can you envision a Mic-3 with still shorter microinstructions? Discuss.

19. The president of the Nano-Micro-Milli Memory Corporation has been so impressed by the sales of their nanostores that he has considered adding a picostore to the product line. The picostore would be referenced by the nanostore, the same way the nanostore is referenced by the control store; that is, each nanoword would contain the address of a picoinstruction just as the control store contains nanoinstruction addresses. You are the Vice-President in Charge of Getting Rid of Stupid Ideas. What do you think of this proposal?

20. If we were to implement the program of Fig. 4-16 using nanoprogramming, how many bits would the control store plus nanostore require together? Compare this to the number of control store bits in the original design.

21. On the IBM 370/125 the level 2 multiplication instruction execution time depends on the number of 1 bits in the multiplier. Give a plausible explanation.

22. How many PDP-11/60 microinstructions are needed to gate D into BA? Into SR?

23. Write a Mac-1 assembly language procedure to multiply two signed integers whose product fits in 16 bits.

24. Write a test program in Mac-1 assembly language to verify that the microprogram is correctly functioning. Check out each instruction with a series of known operands to see if the known result occurs. Such programs are widely used by computer repairmen to try to pinpoint hardware failures.

25. The manufacturer of the Mac-1 has just received a telegram from its most important customer. The telegram reads: "Must have new instruction to shift AC left n bits, where n is low-order 4 bits of instruction. Need tomorrow morning 8 A.M. Send new microprogram by telegram. Hurry." Your job is to implement the microcode for the shift.

26. Write a Mic-1 simulator in your favorite assembly language. The simulator should read in the microprogram as a series of 32-character (0 and 1) input lines, followed by a blank line. Then it reads in the Mac-1 program, 16 bits per line, also terminated by a blank line. Each program is loaded at address 0 of its memory and the simulation begins with microinstruction 0 and macroinstruction 0.

5

THE CONVENTIONAL MACHINE LEVEL

This chapter introduces the conventional machine level (level 2) and discusses many aspects of its architecture. Historically, level 2 was developed before any of the other levels, and it is still widely (and incorrectly) regarded as "the" machine language. This situation has come about because on many machines the microprogram is in a read-only memory, which means that users (as opposed to the machine's manufacturer) cannot write programs for level 1. Furthermore, even on machines that are user microprogrammable, the enormous complexity of the level 1 architecture is enough to scare off all but the most stouthearted programmers. In addition, because no machines have protection hardware at level 1, it is not possible to allow one person to debug new microprograms while anyone else is using the machine. This characteristic further inhibits user microprogramming.

5.1. EXAMPLES OF THE CONVENTIONAL MACHINE LEVEL

Rather than attempt to define rigorously what the conventional machine level is (which is probably impossible anyway), we will introduce this level by means of four examples. The next four sections are devoted to examining the conventional machine level of four families of well-known, commercially available computers: the IBM 370, the DEC PDP-11, the Motorola MC68000, and the Zilog Z80. The purpose of choosing four existing computers to study is to show how the ideas discussed here can be applied to the "real world." These machines will be compared and contrasted in many ways and they will continue to serve as running examples in succeeding chapters, as they have in past ones.

You should not draw the conclusion that the remainder of the book is about programming the 370, PDP-11, 68000 or Z80. These machines will be used to illustrate the idea of designing a computer as a series of levels. Various features of their respective organizations will be examined and some information about programming them will be introduced where necessary. Early in the chapter, the complete instruction sets for all four machines will be presented in tables. You are not expected to fully understand them initially, although going through each list and making educated guesses about what the instructions probably do is certainly instructive. Many of the instructions will be discussed in more detail later in the chapter.

Nevertheless, you should keep in mind the central, unifying idea that computers can be designed in a structured way. The technique of building a computer as a series of levels is a powerful structuring technique. An understanding of some of the details and idiosyncrasies of the four machines is necessary to understand the various levels but try to relate the details to the overall structure and do not wallow in them.

5.1.1. IBM System/370

In 1964 IBM introduced the System/360, a family of computers with identical level 2 architectures and instruction sets but spanning a wide range of performance and price. The idea behind the 360 was to allow customers to buy whichever model was appropriate at the time of purchase and later be able to upgrade to a larger model as the work increased, without having to rewrite any programs. In the early 1970s, IBM brought out various models of the System/370 series as successors to the 360 series using more modern technology. The level 2 architecture of the 370 series is a minor extension of the 360 series. In subsequent years IBM marketed the 43xx series (4331, 4341, etc.), 30xx series (3031, 3032, 3033, etc.) and other computers whose level 2 architectures are practically identical to that of the 370. For the sake of simplicity, we have chosen to refer to these machines collectively as the 370, but you should be aware that minor architectural differences exist among the various series, and even between models of one series. Thus at level 2, all the machines are nearly identical but at level 0 and level 1 they are all completely different.

An IBM 370 consists of one or more CPUs, one or more I/O processors, a main memory, and various I/O devices, as shown in Fig. 5-1. Three kinds of I/O processors exist, called **multiplexer channels**, **block multiplexer channels**, and **selector channels**, the first type being used with low-speed I/O devices, such as card readers, printers, and card punches, and the other two being used with high-speed I/O devices, such as disks, drums, and tapes. All the processors in the computer have access to main memory for reading and writing. The channels have a few internal registers but no main memory of their own.

The smallest addressable unit in the main memory is the byte, consisting of 8 bits. Each byte has a unique address, numbered 0, 1, 2, 3, 4, ..., $n - 1$, where n is the number of bytes of memory, up to a maximum of $n = 2^{24}$. Two consecutive

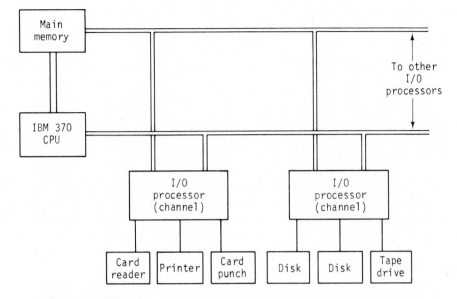

Fig. 5-1. Organization of an IBM 370 computer with one CPU and two I/O processors (channels).

bytes form a half word, 4 consecutive bytes form a word, and 8 consecutive bytes form a double word. Words are more important than half words or double words, so the 370 is often regarded as having a 32-bit word. The address of a half word, word, or double word is the address of its lowest-numbered byte, which, on some older models, must be an integral multiple of 2, 4, or 8, respectively. Figure 5-2 illustrates the addressing structure of the 370 memory. Each byte is part of a half word, a word, and a double word. For example, byte 7 is the low-order (rightmost) byte of the half word at 6, the word at 4, and the double word at 0. The CPU has instructions for fetching bytes, half words, words, and double words.

The 370 has a special format for storing packed decimal numbers. Four bits are needed to represent a digit in the range 0 to 9, so two decimal digits can be packed into one 8-bit byte. In this format, a byte may contain any number from 0 to 99. If used to store numbers in pure binary form, a byte can hold any number between 0 and 255, and 7 bits are sufficient to hold all the numbers from 0 to 99. The packed decimal format does not use memory optimally.

Packed decimal numbers do have certain advantages over binary numbers, however. Data input to the computer or output from the computer are in decimal notation, because people use decimal numbers. When binary numbers are used internally, the input must be converted from decimal to binary, processed in binary, and then reconverted from binary to decimal. If the amount of computation is small, the CPU may spend most of its time performing conversions. If the amount of computation is

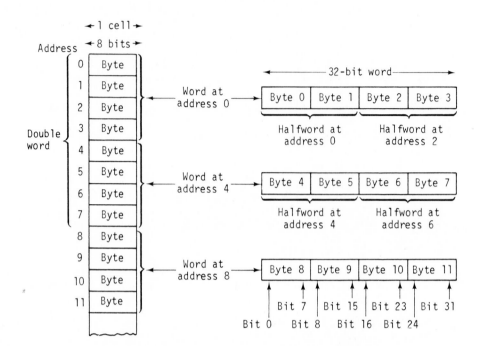

Fig. 5-2. Addressing structure of the IBM 370's main memory.

large, the faster speed of the binary arithmetic instructions makes the conversions worthwhile. Packed decimal numbers are widely used in business applications.

A program at the conventional machine level on a 370 has access to 20 high-speed CPU registers used for performing arithmetic and logical operations, as well as for storing intermediate results. Sixteen of these are general-purpose registers of length 32 bits, numbered from 0 to 15. The other four registers, numbered 0, 2, 4, and 6, are 64 bits long and are used for floating-point arithmetic. The 370 hardware also contains a number of other registers, such as an instruction register, program status word, MAR, and MBR but they are only accessible at the microprogramming level. Figure 5-3 illustrates the registers used by conventional-machine-level programs. The 370 also has 16 control registers, but these are used only by the operating system and will not concern us further.

The 370 level 2 instructions are either 16, 32, or 48 bits in length and may be located at any even address. Nearly all instructions contain an 8-bit operation code, specifying which operation is to be carried out. The remaining bits are used to specify where the data for the instruction is located—in registers, memory, or both. The 370 has some general-purpose instructions used in almost all programs, some instructions intended primarily for scientific calculations, and some instructions primarily useful for commercial applications. The level 2 instruction set contains about 200 instructions. A list of most of these instructions is given in Fig. 5-4.

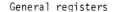

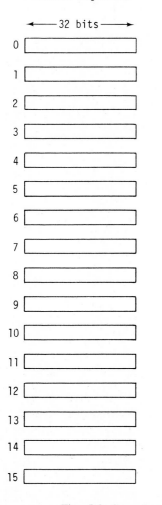

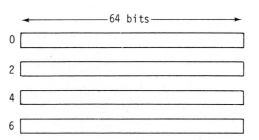

Fig. 5-3. General registers and floating-point registers on the 370.

5.1.2. DEC PDP-11

The DEC PDP-11 series consists of a number of small to medium-sized computers. Due to their short (16-bit) word length, they are often called **minicomputers**, although, as we mentioned earlier, the boundaries between mainframes, minicomputers, and microcomputers are highly elusive. The PDP-11s are widely used in such applications as data communication, industrial process control, scientific experiment monitoring and data collection, interactive computer graphics, and education.

A PDP-11 consists of a CPU, a main memory, and various I/O devices, as

RR format

xxxx	Branching and status switching 0000xxxx		Fixed-point fullword and logical 0001xxxx		Floating-point long 0010xxxx		Floating-point short 0011xxxx	
0000			LPR	Load positive	LPDR	Load positive	LPER	Load positive
0001			LNR	Load negative	LNDR	Load negative	LNER	Load negative
0010			LTR	Load and test	LTDR	Load and test	LTER	Load and test
0011			LCR	Load complement	LCDR	Load complement	LCER	Load complement
0100	SPM	Set program mask	NR	And	HDR	Halve	HER	Halve
0101	BALR	Branch and link	CLR	Compare logical	LRDR	Load rounded (E to L)	LRER	Load rounded (L to SH)
0110	BCTR	Branch on count	OR	Or	MXR	Multiply (E)	AXR	Add normalized (E)
0111	BCR	Branch/condition	XR	Exclusive or	MXDR	Multiply (L to E)	SXR	Subtract normalized (E)
1000	SSK	Set storage key	LR	Load	LDR	Load	LER	Load
1001	ISK	Insert key	CR	Compare	CDR	Compare	CER	Compare
1010	SVC	Supervisor call	AR	Add	ADR	Add N	AER	Add N
1011			SR	Subtract	SDR	Subtract N	SER	Subtract N
1100			MR	Multiply	MDR	Multiply	MER	Multiply
1101			DR	Divide	DDR	Divide	DER	Divide
1110	MVCL	Move long	ALR	Add logical	AWR	Add U	AUR	Add U
1111	CLCL	Compare logical long	SLR	Subtract logical	SWR	Subtract U	SUR	Subtract U

RX format

xxxx	Fixed-point halfword and branching 0100xxxx		Fixed-point fullword and logical 0101xxxx		Floating-point long 0110xxxx		Floating-point short 0111xxxx	
0000	STH	Store	ST	Store	STD	Store	STE	Store
0001	LA	Load address						
0010	STC	Store character						
0011	IC	Insert character						
0100	EX	Execute	N	And				
0101	BAL	Branch and link	CL	Compare logical				
0110	BCT	Branch on count	O	Or	MXD	Multiply (L to E)		
0111	BC	Branch/condition	X	Exclusive or				
1000	LH	Load	L	Load	LD	Load	LE	Load
1001	CH	Compare	C	Compare	CD	Compare	CE	Compare
1010	AH	Add	A	Add	AD	Add N	AE	Add N
1011	SH	Subtract	S	Subtract	SD	Subtract N	SE	Subtract N
1100	MH	Multiply	M	Multiply	MD	Multiply	ME	Multiply
1101			D	Divide	DD	Divide	DE	Divide
1110	CVD	Convert-decimal	AL	Add logical	AW	Add U	AU	Add U
1111	CVB	Convert-binary	SL	Subtract logical	SW	Subtract U	SU	Subtract U

Fig. 5-4. The IBM 370 Instruction set. The instructions marked with an asterisk are actually groups of instructions with a 16-bit opcode. The abbreviation for each instruction is given before the name.

RS, SI, S format

	Branching status switching and shifting 1000xxxx	Fixed-point logical and input/output 1001xxxx	1010xxxx	1011xxxx
xxxx				
0000	SSM Set system mask	STM Store multiple		
0001	LPSW Load PSW	TM Test under mask		LRA Load real address
0010	diagnose	MVI Move		(15 instructions)*
0011	WRD Write direct	TS Test and set		
0100	RDD Read direct	NI And		
0101	BXH Branch/high	CLI Compare logical		
0110	BXLE Branch/low-equal	OI Or		STCTL Store control
0111	SRL Shift right SL	XI Exclusive or		LCTL Load control
1000	SLL Shift left SL	LM Load multiple		
1001	SRA Shift right single			
1010	SLA Shift left single			CS Compare and swap
1011	SRDL Shift right DL			CDS Compare D and swap
1100	SLDL Shift left DL	SIO Start I/O *	STNSM Store then and mask	
1101	SRDA Shift right double	TIO Test I/O *	STOSM Store then or mask	CLM Comp chars masked
1110	SLDA Shift left double	HIO Halt I/O *	SIGP Signal processor	STCM Store chars masked
1111		TCH Test channel	MC Monitor call	ICM Insert chars masked

SS format

	1100xxxx	Logical 1101xxxx	1110xxxx	Decimal 1111xxxx
xxxx				
0000				SRP Shift and round
0001		MVN Move numerics		MVO Move with offset
0010		MVC Move		PACK Pack
0011		MVZ Move zones		UNPK Unpack
0100		NC And		
0101		CLC Compare logical		
0110		OC Or		
0111		XC Exclusive or		
1000				ZAP Zero and add
1001				CP Compare
1010				AP Add
1011				SP Subtract
1100		TR Translate		MP Multiply
1101		TRT Translate and test		DP Divide
1110		ED Edit		
1111		EDMK Edit and mark		

Note: N = Normalized   DL = Double logical   E = Extended
SL = Single Logical   U = Unnormalized   L = Long
    SH = Short

187

illustrated in Fig. 5-5. Unlike the larger and more expensive 370, the PDP-11 has no I/O processors. All components of the PDP-11 are connected by a single bus called the **UNIBUS**. The UNIBUS is used for transmitting information from one component to another. For example, the CPU can read information from memory, the disk can store information into memory, or a CRT display can refresh its screen directly from the disk. At any instant in time only one transfer may be proceeding, although the UNIBUS can be switched from one pair of devices to another in about 400 nsec.

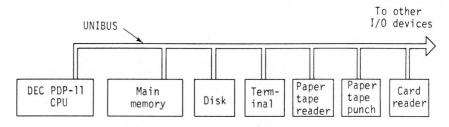

Fig. 5-5. Organization of a PDP-11 computer.

The presence of only one communication path in the computer, although conceptually simple and inexpensive, has some disadvantages. Consider, for example, the situation where the CPU is running while information is being read into the memory from the disk at a rate of one word per n CPU instructions. Most of the time the UNIBUS will be used to transmit information from the memory to the CPU, as shown in Fig. 5-6(a); about once every n instructions the UNIBUS will be needed to transfer a word from the disk to memory, as shown in Fig. 5-6(b). When this situation occurs, the UNIBUS will be taken away from the CPU, and the disk-to-memory transfer will proceed. The CPU simply waits until the word has been transferred and the UNIBUS is then available again.

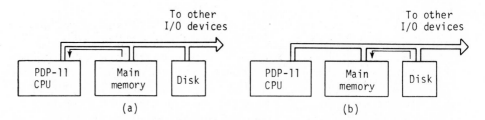

Fig. 5-6. (a) The UNIBUS being used to transfer data from main memory to the CPU. (b) The UNIBUS being used to transfer data from the disk to main memory.

This technique, called **cycle stealing**, slows the CPU down a little because the CPU is idle while the disk is using the UNIBUS to communicate with the memory. Associated with each device is a priority. When two or more devices request use of the UNIBUS simultaneously, the one with the highest priority gets it and the other devices must wait.

The smallest addressable unit in the PDP-11s memory is a byte, consisting of 8 bits. Two bytes make a 16-bit word. Although the basic addressable unit (cell) on the PDP-11 is the same as on the 370, the PDP-11 word length is half that of the 370. The PDP-11 memory is illustrated in Fig. 5-7.

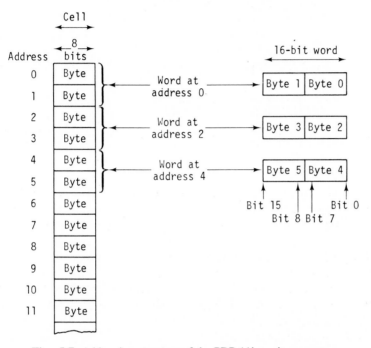

Fig. 5-7. Addressing structure of the PDP-11's main memory.

The PDP-11 level 2 machine has eight 16-bit general-purpose registers and (optionally) six 64-bit floating-point registers. The registers are illustrated in Fig. 5-8. General registers 0 to 5 are used for a variety of purposes, but registers 6 and 7 have specific functions. Register 6 is a stack pointer (to be explained in Sec. 5.3.7). Register 7 is the program counter. It always contains the address of the next instruction word to be fetched. Each time an instruction word is fetched from memory, the program counter is automatically incremented by two. The increment is two instead of one because a word contains two bytes and consecutive words have addresses differing by two. For example, 100 and 102 are addresses of consecutive memory words. Word addresses are always even.

Instructions are 16, 32, and 48 bits, although the formats are completely different from the 370's instructions. Figure 5-9 shows the conventional machine level instructions for the PDP-11/44. The instruction sets on some of the other models are slightly different.

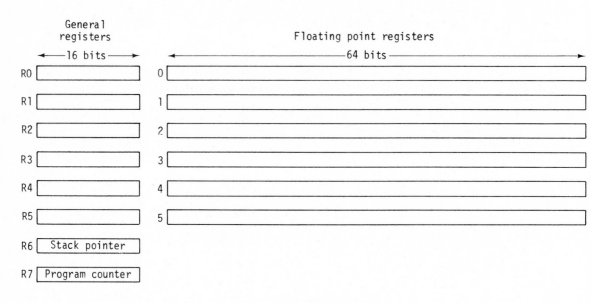

Fig. 5-8. PDP-11 registers.

5.1.3. Motorola MC68000

The Motorola MC68000 (68000 for short) represents the third generation of Motorola microprocessors. The first generation was the 6800, an 8-bit machine. The second generation was the 6809, which has some 8- and some 16-bit characteristics. The 68000 is a 16- or 32-bit microprocessor, depending on one's perspective. Seen from level 0, it looks like a 16-bit machine because it has a 16-bit data bus. However, seen from level 2, it looks like a 32-bit machine because it has 32-bit registers and can manipulate 32-bit quantities in a single instruction. Either way, it is one of the largest and most powerful microprocessors yet devised. All three processors have completely different architectures at all levels.

The 68000 is the newest of our four example machines and incorporates a number of modern ideas not present in the other machines. In particular, it was clearly designed with the needs of modern high-level languages in mind rather than the needs of the assembly language programmer. It also makes much better use of statistical information about programs than do the other three. For example, it is well known (Knuth, 1971; Tanenbaum, 1978; Wortman, 1972) that small constants occur much more frequently than large ones, so the 68000 has a special (short) instruction to move an 8-bit constant to a register, and other special instructions to add and subtract the constants 1 to 8. Special instructions are also provided for making efficient procedure calls.

Like the 370 and PDP-11, the 68000 cell size is 8 bits. Addresses are 32 bits, so the architecture provides for up to 2^{32} bytes of memory, which is far larger than the 2^{24} bytes of the 370 and 2^{17} bytes available to the user of the largest PDP-11 model.

Group 1, 4-bit opcodes. Format: xxxxsssssddddd

xxxx		
0000	---	See groups 2 and 3
0001	MOV	Move
0010	CMP	Compare
0011	BIT	Bit test
0100	BIC	Bit clear
0101	BIS	Bit set
0110	ADD	Add
0111	---	See group 10
1000	---	See groups 11, 13 and 14
1001	MOVB	Move byte
1010	CMPB	Compare byte
1011	BITB	Bit test byte
1100	BICB	Bit clear byte
1101	BISB	Bit set byte
1110	SUB	Subtract
1111	---	(Floating point instructions)

Group 2, 8-bit opcodes. Format: 00000xxxkkkkkkkk

xxx		
000	---	See group 4
001	BR	Branch
010	BNE	Branch not equal
011	BEQ	Branch equal
100	BGE	Branch greater than or equal
101	BLT	Branch less than
110	BGT	Branch greater than
111	BLE	Branch less than or equal

Group 3, 7-bit opcodes. Format: 00001xxrrrddddd

xx		
00	JSR	Jump to subroutine
01	---	See group 5
10	---	See group 6
11	(CSM)	Call supervisor mode

Group 4, 10-bit opcodes. Format: 00000000xxddddd

xx		
00	---	See group 7
01	JMP	Jump
10	---	See group 8
11	SWAB	Swap bytes

Group 5, 10-bit opcodes. Format: 0000101xxxddddd

xxx		
000	CLR	Clear
001	COM	Complement (1's complement)
010	INC	Increment
011	DEC	Decrement
100	NEG	Negate (2's complement)
101	ADC	Add carry
110	SBC	Subtract carry
111	TST	Test

Group 6, 10-bit opcodes. Format: 0000110xxxddddd

xxx		
000	ROR	Rotate right 1 bit
001	ROL	Rotate left 1 bit
010	ASR	Arithmetic shift right 1 bit
011	ASL	Arithmetic shift left 1 bit
100	(MARK)	Clean up stack. dddddd = count
101	(MFPI)	Move from previous instruction space
110	(MTPI)	Move to previous instruction space
111	(SXT)	Sign extend

Notes: sssss specifies a source;
      dddddd specifies a destination;
      rrr specifies a register;

Group 7, 12-bit opcodes. Format: 0000000000xxcccc

xx		
00	---	See group 9
01	---	Spare
10	CCC	Clear condition codes
11	SCC	Set condition codes

Group 8, 13-bit opcodes. Format: 0000000010xxxrrr

xxx		
000	RTS	Return from subroutine
011	(SPL)	Set priority level

Group 9, 16-bit opcodes. Format: 0000000000000xxx

xxx		
000	HALT	Halt
001	WAIT	Wait
010	RTI	Return from interrupt
011	BPT	Breakpoint
100	IOT	I/O trap
101	RESET	Reset
110	(RTT)	Return from trap
111	(MFPT)	

Group 10, 7-bit opcodes. Format: 0111xxxrrrddddd

xxx		
000	(MUL)	Multiply
001	(DIV)	Divide
010	(ASH)	Arithmetic shift
011	(ASHC)	Arithmetic shift combined
100	(XOR)	Exclusive or
111	(SOB)	Subtract one and branch

Group 11, 8-bit opcodes. Format: 10000xxxkkkkkkkk

xxx		
000	BPL	Branch on plus
001	BMI	Branch on minus
010	BHI	Branch higher
011	BLOS	Branch lower or same
100	BVC	Branch on overflow clear
101	BVS	Branch on overflow set
110	BCC	Branch on carry clear
111	BCS	Branch on carry set

Group 12, 8-bit opcodes. Format: 1000100xkkkkkkkk

x		
0	EMT	Emulator trap
1	TRAP	Trap

Group 12, 10-bit opcodes. Format: 1000101xxxddddd

xxx		
000	CLRB	Clear byte
001	COMB	Complement byte
010	INCB	Increment byte
011	DECB	Decrement byte
100	NEGB	Negate byte
101	ADCB	Add carry byte
110	SBCB	Subtract carry byte
111	TSTB	Test byte

Group 14, 10-bit opcodes. Format: 1000110xxxddddd

xxx		
000	RORB	Rotate byte right 1 bit
001	ROLB	Rotate byte left 1 bit
010	ASRB	Shift byte right 1 bit
011	ASLB	Shift byte left 1 bit
100	----	Spare
101	(MFPD)	Move from previous data space
110	(MTPD)	Move to previous data space
111	----	Spare

x specifies opcode bits;
kkkkkkkk specifies an offset or constant;
cccc specifies condition code bits

Fig. 5-9. The PDP-11 instruction set. The optional floating-point instructions are not shown.

Memory addressing is a clear example of where the terms "mainframe," "minicomputer," and "microcomputer" have lost all meaning—the microcomputer in this case beats the mainframe by a factor of more than 200 and the mini by a factor of more than 30,000. The 68000's memory architecture is shown in Fig. 5-10. In this book we will follow Motorola's terminology of calling a 16-bit quantity a word and a 32-bit quantity a long word (instead of calling them halfwords and words, respectively).

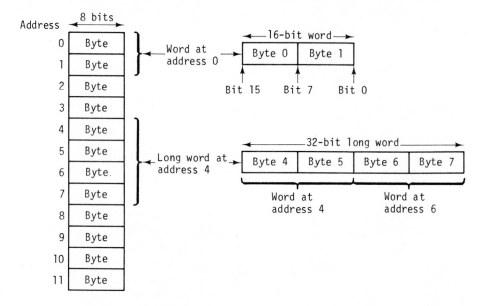

Fig. 5-10. Addressing structure of the 68000's main memory.

Like the 370, the 68000 has sixteen 32-bit registers but unlike the 370, they are not all general purpose. Eight of them, A0 to A7, are address registers and normally hold addresses of variables and data structures located in main memory. A0 to A6 have no dedicated function, but A7 is the stack pointer. The other eight registers, D0 to D7, are general-purpose data registers. Most calculations take place in them. The 68000 CPU does not have floating-point instructions, so it does not have any floating-point registers. If floating-point calculations are needed, a separate floating-point processor chip must be included in the system. The registers are shown in Fig. 5-11.

To avoid confusion later, take a good look at the bit and byte numbering conventions used by IBM, DEC, and Motorola. IBM numbers both its bits and its bytes from left to right. Bit 0 is to the left of bit 1 and byte 0 is to the left of byte 1 (low-order byte of a word is odd). DEC, in contrast, numbers its bits and bytes from right to left, so bit 0 is to the right of bit 1 and byte 0 is also to the right of byte 1 (low-order byte of a word is even). Motorola uses neither scheme. Instead, it numbers the

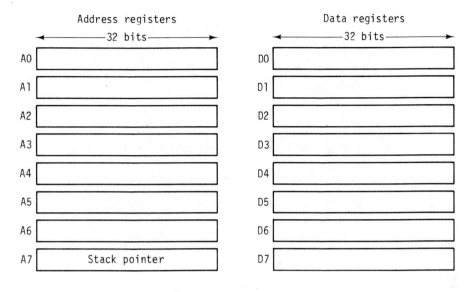

Fig. 5-11. 68000 registers.

bits right to left (like DEC) and the bytes left to right (like IBM). For a delightful commentary on the standardization of numbering systems, see (Cohen, 1981).

In keeping with the idea of producing a machine well suited to high-level languages, the 68000 designers outfitted the CPU with a small but powerful, instruction set. It is shown in Fig. 5-12. The numerical opcodes are not given for the 68000 because they do not group together in a coherent way. The terms SRC and DST in the figure refer to the source and destination, respectively. Unfortunately, the 68000 is not entirely regular on this point, and the set of allowed operands allowed as source and destination varies irregularly from instruction to instruction. Except for the MOVE instruction, at least one of the operands of two-operand instructions must be a register. In this respect the PDP-11 is much more regular, because the rules for source and destination are the same for almost every instruction, and there is no restriction that one operand must be a register, except MUL and DIV.

Nearly all 68000 instructions contain a field telling whether the operands are bytes, words, or long words. ADD, for example, can add two bytes, two words, or two long words, depending on this field. Two notable exceptions to this rule are multiply and divide, the former only working on 16-bit words, and the latter only working on 32-bit dividends and 16-bit divisors. Several of the instructions listed in Fig. 5-12 have a number of variations, including special forms for constant operands of various lengths, as mentioned above.

In addition to the usual collection of instructions operating on binary numbers, the 68000 also has three instructions for doing binary-coded decimal arithmetic, and four instructions for manipulating individual bits. It also has a flexible set of instructions for jumping, calling, and returning from procedures, and conditional trapping. Like

BIT MANIPULATION INSTRUCTIONS

BTST	BIT,DST	- Test the indicated bit and set Z condition code
BSET	BIT,DST	- Test the indicated bit and then set it to 1
BCLR	BIT,DST	- Test the indicated bit and then clear it to 0
BCHG	BIT,DST	- Test the indicated bit and then invert it

COMPARE AND TEST INSTRUCTIONS

CMP	SRC,DST	- Compare SRC to DST and set condition codes
TAS	DST	- Test and set DST in one indivisible cycle
TST	SRC	- Compare SRC to 0 and set condition codes
S_{CC}	DST	- Set DST to all 0s or all 1s depending on condition

TRANSFER INSTRUCTIONS

BRA	DST	- Unconditional branch relative to current instruction
B_{CC}	DST	- Conditional branch relative to current instruction
JMP	DST	- Unconditional jump using general addressing modes
BSR	DST	- Branch to subroutine relative to current instruction
JSR	DST	- Jump to subroutine using general addressing modes
RTS		- Return from subroutine (just pop return address)
RTR		- Return from subroutine and restore condition codes
RTE		- Return from exception (pop status register and return address)
DB_{CC}	Dn,DST	- Loop instruction using both count and condition

MISCELLANEOUS INSTRUCTIONS

LEA	SRC,An	- Compute the effective address and load it into An
PEA	SRC	- Compute the effective address and push it onto the stack
LINK	An,N	- Used for procedure entry
UNLK	An	- Used for procedure exit
TRAP	SRC	- Initiate exception processing via one of 16 vectors
TRAPV		- Trap if overflow bit set
CHK	SRC,Dn	- Check range of Dn and trap if invalid
NOP		- No operation
RESET		- Reset the bus
STOP		- Stop the machine

Fig. 5-12. Summary of the Motorola 68000 instruction set.

DATA MOVEMENT INSTRUCTIONS

MOVE	SRC,DST	- Move the source to the destination
MOVEM	SRC,DST	- Move up to 16 registers to or from memory
MOVEP	SRC,DST	- Move data from a D register to alternate memory bytes
EXG	SRC,DST	- Exchange two registers
SWAP	Dn	- Exchange low-order and high-order words of a D register

BINARY ARITHMETIC INSTRUCTIONS

ADD	SRC,DST	- Add SRC to DST
SUB	SRC,DST	- Subtract SRC from DST
MULS	SRC,Dn	- Signed 16-bit multiply of SRC by Dn
MULU	SRC,Dn	- Unsigned 16-bit multiply of SRC by Dn
DIVS	SRC,Dn	- Divide signed 16-bit SRC into signed 32-bit Dn
DIVU	SRC,Dn	- Divide unsigned 16-bit SRC into unsigned 32-bit Dn
NEG	DST	- Negate DST (2's complement)
EXT	Dn	- Sign-extend byte to word, or word to long word
CLR	DST	- Clear DST (set it to zero)

SHIFT/ROTATE INSTRUCTIONS

ASL	CNT,DST	- Shift DST arithmetically left by CNT bits
ASR	CNT,DST	- Shift DST arithmetically right by CNT bits
LSL	CNT,DST	- Shift DST logically left by CNT bits
LSR	CNT,DST	- Shift DST logically right by CNT bits
ROL	CNT,DST	- Rotate DST left by CNT bits
ROR	CNT,DST	- Rotate DST right by CNT bits
ROXL	CNT,DST	- Rotate DST and extend bit left by CNT bits
ROXR	CNT,DST	- Rotate DST and extend bit right by CNT bits

BINARY CODED DECIMAL ARITHMETIC INSTRUCTIONS

ABCD	SRC,DST	- Add SRC to DST using BCD arithmetic
SBCD	SRC,DST	- Subtract SRC from DST using BCD arithmetic
NBCD	DST	- Negate DST using BCD arithmetic

BOOLEAN INSTRUCTIONS

AND	SRC,DST	- Boolean AND of SRC and DST
OR	SRC,DST	- Boolean INCLUSIVE OR of SRC and DST
EOR	SRC,DST	- Boolean EXCLUSIVE OR of SRC and DST
NOT	DST	- Boolean NOT of DST (1's complement)

Fig. 5-12. (cont.).

the PDP-11, the 68000 uses memory-mapped input/output, and therefore has no specific I/O instructions.

It is a little difficult to say anything about the system architecture and bus structure of the 68000 because it can be, and is, used with many different buses. Nevertheless, it is safe to say that virtually all 68000-based computer systems use a single bus architecture and cycle stealing, the same as the PDP-11. Furthermore, most of them do not have anything resembling the 370's I/O channels. In these respects the 68000 is similar to traditional minicomputers like the PDP-11, even though its address space, register width, and computational power actually make it more like a small mainframe.

5.1.4. Zilog Z80

The Zilog Z80 is an 8-bit CPU, although it has a few instructions that also manipulate 16-bit quantities. The architecture is compatible with that of the Intel 8080 and its instruction set contains the 8080's as a subset. It was clearly designed to take advantage of the 8080's enormous popularity and existing software, yet provide a competitive advantage by using modern technology (e.g., it needs only one power supply, versus three for the 8080) and architectural extensions (e.g., more registers and a more powerful instruction set). Despite the arrival of the 16- and 32-bit microprocessors such as the Intel 8086, Zilog Z8000, and Motorola 68000, the Z80 has remained popular due to its extremely low price and large existing software base.

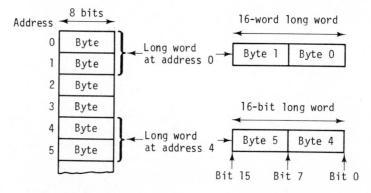

Fig. 5-13. Addressing structure of the Z80's main memory.

The Z80 memory is organized as a sequence of 8-bit bytes. Because most instructions deal with 8-bit quantities, the term "word" is often used to refer to bytes on the Z80. We will call 16-bit quantities "long words." The Z80 memory structure is shown in Fig. 5-13. Both bits and bytes are numbered from right to left, the same as on the PDP-11, and opposite from the 370. A long word can begin at either an even or an odd address, but the low-order byte always has an address one less than the high-order byte. Maximum addressable memory is 2^{16} bytes.

The Z80 has 22 registers logically divided into three groups (see Fig. 5-14). The main register group has seven general-purpose 8-bit registers: A, B, C, D, E, H, and L. A is the accumulator and is used for doing 8-bit arithmetic. B, C, D, and E are used primarily for holding variables, intermediate results, and the like. H and L can be used for holding temporary results but more important, can also be used as a long word to hold a 16-bit memory address. The Z80 has instructions to load a byte into a register from the memory location addressed by HL and store a register into the memory location addressed by HL. The HL register pair is present in the Z80 because it is present in the 8080, which needed it for compatibility with *its* predecessor, the Intel 8008. BC and DE also function as 16-bit register pairs in some instructions but not for memory addressing like HL. The F register holds various flags such as the condition code bits set by compare instructions and then tested by subsequent conditional jump instructions.

```
     Main register set          Alternate register set

     ◄8 bits►◄8 bits►              ◄8 bits►◄8 bits►

     ┌────────┬────────┐          ┌────────┬────────┐
     │   A    │   F    │          │   A'   │   F'   │
     ├────────┼────────┤          ├────────┼────────┤
     │   B    │   C    │          │   B'   │   C'   │
     ├────────┼────────┤          ├────────┼────────┤
     │   D    │   E    │          │   D'   │   E'   │
     ├────────┼────────┤          ├────────┼────────┤
     │   H    │   L    │          │   H'   │   L'   │
     └────────┴────────┘          └────────┴────────┘


              ┌────────┬────────┐
              │   I    │   R    │
              ├────────┴────────┤
           IX │ (Index register x)│
              ├─────────────────┤
           IY │ (Index register y)│
              ├─────────────────┤
           SP │ (Stack pointer)  │
              ├─────────────────┤
           PC │ (Program counter)│
              └─────────────────┘
```

Fig. 5-14. Z80 registers.

The second register set (not present in the 8080) is identical to the first one. Its primary use is in interrupt handling. When an I/O device completes, the hardware can be requested to cause an interrupt, temporarily transferring control to an interrupt handling routine. This routine can then finish off the current I/O operation and perhaps start the next one. To do its work, it also needs registers. On the 8080 the interrupt routine must first save all the registers it needs; when it is done it must restore them, so as not to affect the running program. On the Z80, the interrupt routine need only switch to the alternate register set on entry and the main register set on exit, which is much faster. Some models of the PDP-11 also have two register sets.

8-BIT LOADS
LD	R,SRC	- Load register with register, constant, or memory
LD	DST,R	- Store the register at the destination
LD	DST,N	- Store an 8-bit number in memory
LD	A,SRC	- Load A from a register or memory
LD	DST,A	- Store A in a register or memory

16-BIT LOADS
LD	RR,NN	- Load BC, DE, HL, SP, IX, or IY with constant NN
LD	RR,SRC	- Load BC, DE, HL, SP, IX, or IY with 2 bytes from memory
LD	DST,RR	- Store BC, DE, HL, SP, IX, or IY in memory
LD	SP,RR	- Load SP from HL, IX, or IY
PUSH	RR	- Push BC, DE, HL, AF, IX, or IY onto the stack
POP	RR	- Pop BC, DE, HL, AF, IX, or IY from the stack

EXCHANGES
EX	DE,HL	- Exchange DE and HL
EX	AF,AF′	- Exchange AF with corresponding alternate set registers
EXX		- Exchange BC, DE, and HL with corresponding alternate registers
EX	(SP),RR	- Exchange 2 bytes on top of stack with HL, IX, or IY

MEMORY BLOCK MOVES
LDI	- Move (HL) to (DE), increment HL and DE, decrement BC
LDIR	- Same as LDI, but repeat until BC = 0
LDD	- Move (HL) to (DE), decrement HL and DE, decrement BC
LDDR	- same as LDD, but repeat until BC = 0

MEMORY BLOCK SEARCHES
CPI	- Compare A to (HL), increment HL, decrement BC
CPIR	- Same as CPI, but repeat until A = (HL) or BC = 0
CPD	- Compare A to (HL), decrement HL, decrement BC
CPDR	- Same as CPD, but repeat until A = (HL) or BC = 0

8-BIT ARITHMETIC
ADD	SRC	- Add register, constant, or memory byte to A
ADC	SRC	- Add register, constant, or memory byte and carry bit to A
SUB	SRC	- Subtract register, constant, or memory byte from A
SBC	SRC	- Subtract register, constant, or memory byte and carry from A
AND	SRC	- Boolean AND of register, constant, or memory byte with A
OR	SRC	- Boolean OR of register, constant, or memory byte with A
XOR	SRC	- Boolean XOR of register, constant, or memory byte with A
CP	SRC	- Compare register, constant, or memory byte to A and set flags
INC	DST	- Add 1 to register or memory byte
DEC	DST	- Subtract 1 from register or memory byte

16-BIT ARITHMETIC
ADD	HL,RR	- Add BC, DE, HL, or SP to HL
ADC	HL,RR	- Add carry bit and BC, DE, HL, or SP to HL
SBC	HL,RR	- Subtract carry bit and BC, DE, HL, or SP from HL
ADD	IX,RR	- Add BC, DE, IX, or SP to IX
ADD	IY,RR	- Add BC, DE, IY, or SP to IY
INC	RR	- Add 1 to BC, DE, HL, SP, IX, or IY
DEC	RR	- Subtract 1 from BC, DE, HL, SP, IX, or IY

ROTATES AND SHIFTS
RLC	SRC	- Rotate reg/mem left; bit 7 goes to carry and bit 0
RL	SRC	- Rotate reg/mem left; bit 7 goes to carry, old carry to bit 0
RRC	SRC	- Rotate reg/mem right; bit 0 goes to carry and bit 7
RR	SRC	- Rotate reg/mem right; bit 0 goes to carry, old carry to bit 7
SLA	SRC	- Shift reg/mem left; bit 0 filled with 0
SRA	SRC	- Shift reg/mem right with sign extension; bit 0 goes to carry
SRL	SRC	- Shift reg/mem right; bit 7 filled with 0, bit 0 to carry
RLD		- Rotate decimal; three half bytes rotated left
RRD		- Rotate decimal; three half bytes rotated right

Fig. 5-15. Z80 instruction set.

BIT OPERATIONS
BIT	K,SRC	- Test bit K of register or memory byte
SET	K,SRC	- Set bit K of register or memory byte to 1
RES	K,SRC	- Reset (set to zero) bit K of register or memory byte

MISCELLANEOUS
DAA		- Converts A into packed binary coded decimal after addition
CPL		- Set A to its one's complement
NEG		- Set A to its two's complement
CCF		- Complement the carry flag
SCF		- Set the carry flag to 1
NOP		- No operation
HALT		- Halt CPU
DI		- Disable interrupts
EI		- Enable Interrupts
IM	N	- Set interrupt mode to 1, 2, or 3

JUMPS
JP	DST	- Unconditional jump to DST
JP	CC,DST	- Conditional jump to DST if indicated condition is true
JR	OFF	- Relative jump; OFF tells distance from current PC
JR	CC,OFF	- Conditional relative jump
JP	(RR)	- Unconditional jump to address in HL, IX, or IY
DJNZ	OFF	- Decrement B; jump to DST unless B = 0

CALL, RETURN, AND RESTART
CALL	DST	- Call procedure at DST; push return address onto the stack
CALL	CC,DST	- Call procedure at DST if condition is met, otherwise NOP
RET		- Pop return address from stack to PC
RET	CC	- Return from procedure if condition met
RETI		- Return from interrupt
RETN		- Return from nonmaskable interrupt
RST	L	- Push PC onto the stack and jump to address 8*L (L < 9)

INPUT/OUTPUT
IN	A,(N)	- Input a byte to A from I/O port N
IN	R,(C)	- Input a byte to R from port specified in C register
INI		- Input a byte from port in C to (HL); increment HL, decrement B
INIR		- Same as INI, but repeat until B = 0
IND		- Input a byte from port in C to (HL); decrement HL, decrement B
INDR		- Same as IND, but repeat until B = 0
OUT	(N),A	- Output a byte from A to port N
OUT	(C),R	- Output a byte from R to port specified in C
OUTI		- Output byte (HL) to port in C; increment HL, decrement B
OTIR		- Same as OUTI, but repeat until B = 0
OUTD		- Output byte (HL) to port in C; decrement HL, decrement B
OTDR		- Same as OUTD, but repeat until B = 0

Notes:
   A, B, C, D, E, H, and L are 8-bit registers
   AF, BC, DE, HL, IX, and IY are 16-bit registers or register pairs
   SRC is a source; the exact list of legal sources is instruction dependent
   DST is a destination; the list of legal destinations is instruction dependent
   OFF is a signed, relative, 1-byte displacement for short distance jumps
   R is an 8-bit register: A, B, C, D, E, F, H, L
   RR is an instruction-dependent 16-bit register or register pair
   N is an 8-bit constant
   NN is a 16-bit constant
   CC is a condition: zero, nonzero, carry, no carry; in some instructions, others
   Parentheses mean "the contents of," e.g. (HL) means memory byte addressed by HL

Fig. 5-15   (cont.).

The IX and IY **index registers** are both 16 bits and are used to hold memory addresses. They are used to point to 256-byte blocks of memory that are being heavily used. A byte in either of these two blocks can be accessed efficiently by specifying the appropriate index register and the location of the byte relative to the index register (-128 to $+127$). The index registers are another feature not present in the 8080.

The four remaining registers are the stack pointer, program counter, I register, and R register. The stack pointer and program counter point to the top of the stack and the next instruction byte to be fetched, respectively. The I register holds the high-order 8 bits of the memory address at which the interrupt handling routine is located. The low-order 8 bits are provided by the interrupting device itself. The R register is used keeping track of which block of dynamic RAM memory must be refreshed next. It is automatically incremented after every instruction fetch and output onto the address bus during the second half of each instruction fetch cycle. It is of no interest to the level 2 programmer so we will not mention it further.

As 8-bit machines go, the Z80's instruction set is quite powerful. It has instructions to load and store both 8-bit registers and 16-bit registers (IX, IY, SP) and register pairs (BC, DE, HL), instructions to do 8-bit arithmetic on the accumulator and 16-bit arithmetic on HL, a wide selection of shifts and rotates, block moves and compares, as well as jumps, calls, and returns, both conditional and unconditional. The problem with the Z80 is that its instruction set and addressing are somewhat irregular. For example, it has instructions to add a register pair to HL with or without the carry bit, and there is an instruction to subtract a register pair and the carry bit from HL but no instruction to subtract a register pair from HL without also subtracting the carry bit. The table in Fig. 5-15 gives a summary of the Z80 instruction set, but be warned that the rules for what is allowed as a source and what is allowed as a destination are different for almost every instruction.

5.2. INSTRUCTION FORMATS

A program consists of a sequence of instructions, each one specifying some particular action. Part of the instruction, called the operation code, or **opcode** for short, tells what action is to be performed. Many instructions contain or specify the location of data used by the instruction. For example, an instruction that compares two characters to see if they are the same must specify which characters are to be compared. The general subject of specifying where the operands are (i.e., their addresses) is called **addressing** and is discussed in Sec. 5.3.

Figure 5-16 shows several typical formats for level 2 instructions. On some level 2 machines, all instructions have the same length; on others there may be two or three lengths. Moreover, instructions may be shorter, the same length as, or longer than the word length.

Some possible relations between instruction length and word length are shown in Fig. 5-17.

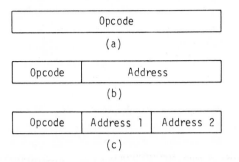

Fig. 5-16. Three typical instruction formats: (a) zero-address instruction. (b) one-address instruction. (c) two-address instruction.

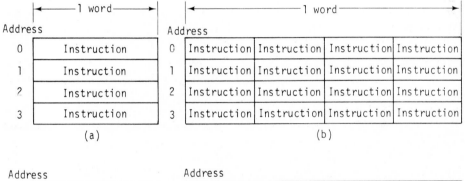

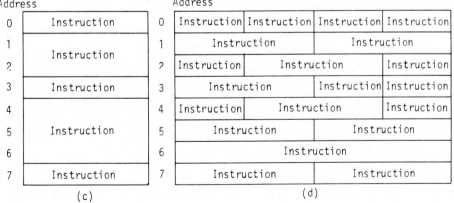

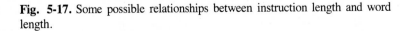

Fig. 5-17. Some possible relationships between instruction length and word length.

5.2.1. Design Criteria for Instruction Formats

When a computer design team has to choose an instruction format (or formats) for their machine, they must consider a number of factors. First, and most important, short instructions are better than long ones. A program consisting of n 16-bit instructions takes up only half as much memory space as n 32-bit instructions. Memory is not free after all, so designers do not like to waste it.

A second reason is that each memory has a particular transfer rate that is determined by the technology and engineering design of the memory. The transfer rate of a memory is the number of bits per second that can be read out of the memory. A fast memory can give a processor (or an I/O device) more bits per second than a slow memory.

If the transfer rate of a particular memory is t bps and the average instruction length is r bits, the memory can deliver at most t/r instructions per second. Therefore, the rate at which instructions are executed (i.e., the processor speed) depends on the instruction length. Shorter instructions mean a faster processor. If the time required to execute an instruction is long compared to the time required to fetch it from memory, the instruction fetch time will not be so important. However, with fast CPUs, the memory is often the bottleneck. Increasing the number of instructions fetched per second is therefore an important design criterion.

Sufficient room in the instruction to express all the operations desired is a second design criterion for instruction formats. A machine with 2^n operations and an instruction smaller than n bits is impossible. There simply will not be enough room in the opcode.

A third design criterion is that it is highly desirable that the machine's word length be an integral multiple of its character length. If the character code has k bits, the word length should be k, $2k$, $3k$, $4k$, $5k$, . . . ; otherwise, space will be wasted when characters are stored. Of course, it is possible to store 3.5 characters per word, but doing so causes severe inefficiencies in accessing the characters. The restrictions placed on the word length by the character code affect the instruction length, because either an instruction should occupy an integral number of bytes or words, or an integral number of instructions should fit in a word. A design with a 9-bit character, a 12-bit instruction, and a 31-bit word would be a catastrophe.

A fourth criterion concerns the number of bits in an address field. Consider the design of a machine with an 8-bit character (possibly 7 bits plus parity) and a main memory that must hold 2^{16} characters. The designers could choose to assign consecutive addresses to units of 8, 16, 24, or 32 bits, as well as other possibilities.

Imagine what would happen if the design team degenerated into two warring factions, one advocating making the 8-bit byte the basic unit of memory, and the other advocating the 32-bit word as the basic unit of memory. The former group would propose a memory of 2^{16} bytes, numbered 0, 1, 2, 3, ..., 65535. The latter group would propose a memory of 2^{14} words numbered 0, 1, 2, 3, ..., 16383. Both memory organizations have the same bit capacity.

The first group would point out that in order to compare two characters in the 32-bit word organization, the program would not only have to fetch the words containing the characters but would also have to extract each character from its word in order to compare them. Doing so costs extra instructions and therefore wastes space. The 8-bit organization, on the other hand, provides an address for every character, thus making the comparison much easier.

The 32-bit word supporters would retaliate by pointing out that their proposal requires only 2^{14} separate addresses, giving an address length of only 14 bits, whereas the 8-bit byte proposal requires 16 bits to address the same memory. A shorter address means a shorter instruction, which not only takes up less space but also requires less time to fetch. Alternatively, they could retain the 16-bit address to reference a memory four times as large as the 8-bit organization allows.

This example demonstrates that in order to gain a finer memory resolution, one must pay the price of longer addresses, which, in general, means longer instructions. The ultimate in resolution is a memory organization in which every bit is directly addressable (e.g., the Burroughs B1700). At the other extreme is a memory consisting of very long words (e.g., the CDC Cyber series has 60-bit words).

5.2.2. Expanding Opcodes

In the preceding section we saw how short addresses and good memory resolution could be traded off against each other. In this section we will examine trade-offs involving both opcodes and addresses. Consider an $n + k$ bit instruction with a k-bit opcode and a single n-bit address. This instruction allows 2^k different operations and 2^n addressable memory cells. Alternatively, the same $n + k$ bits could be broken up into a $(k - 1)$ bit opcode, and an $(n + 1)$ bit address, meaning only half as many instructions but either twice as much memory addressable, or the same amount of memory but with twice the resolution. A $(k + 1)$ bit opcode and an $(n - 1)$ bit address gives more operations, but the price is either a smaller number of cells addressable, or poorer resolution and the same amount of memory addressable. Quite sophisticated trade-offs are possible between opcode bits and address bits as well as the simpler ones just described. The scheme discussed in the following paragraphs is called an **expanding opcode.**

The concept of an expanding opcode can be most clearly seen by an example. Consider a machine in which instructions are 16 bits long and addresses are 4 bits long, as shown in Fig. 5-18. This situation might be reasonable for a machine that has 16 registers (hence a 4-bit register address) on which all arithmetic operations take place. One design would be a 4-bit opcode and three addresses in each instruction, giving 16 three-address instructions.

However, if the designers need 15 three-address instructions, 14 two-address instructions, 31 one-address instructions, and 16 instructions with no address at all, they can use opcodes 0 to 14 as three-address instructions but interpret opcode 15 differently (see Fig. 5-19).

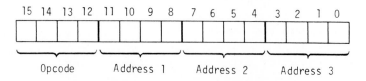

Fig. 5-18. An instruction with a 4-bit opcode and three 4-bit address fields.

Opcode 15 means that the opcode is contained in bits 8 to 15 instead of 12 to 15. Bits 0 to 3 and 4 to 7 form two addresses, as usual. The 14 two-address instructions all have 1111 in the leftmost 4 bits, and numbers from 0000 to 1101 in bits 8 to 11. Instructions with 1111 in the leftmost 4 bits and either 1110 or 1111 in bits 8 to 11 will be treated specially. They will be treated as though their opcodes were in bits 4 to 15. The result is 32 new opcodes. Because only 31 are needed, opcode 111111111111 is interpreted to mean that the real opcode is in bits 0 to 15, giving 16 instructions with no address.

As we proceeded through this discussion, the opcode kept getting longer and longer; that is, the three-address instructions have a 4-bit opcode, the two-address instructions have an 8-bit opcode, the one-address instructions have a 12-bit opcode, and the zero-address instructions have a 16-bit opcode. Figure 5-9 illustrates how the PDP-11's expanding opcodes are organized.

Computer designers frequently leave room in the instruction set for new instructions to be added in the future. In a well-designed computer, an instruction with an unimplemented opcode should be treated as an error and some appropriate action taken.

A variation on the expanding-opcode idea is to have some part of the opcode specify the instruction format and length. For example, the 2 leftmost bits might indicate instruction lengths of 8, 16, 32, or 64 bits, depending on which of the four values 00, 01, 10, and 11 they contain. In this case, there is no trade-off between opcode and address. Instructions that need a long address part simply take up more space than instructions that need a short address part.

5.2.3. Examples of Instruction Formats

In this section we will examine the instruction formats of the 370, PDP-11, 68000, and Z80 conventional machine levels. The 370 level 2 machine has five major instruction formats, illustrated in Fig. 5-20, as well as one other format that is not important for our purposes (S format). The RR format is 16 bits, the RS, RX, and SI formats are 32 bits, and the SS format is 48 bits. In this context, R stands for register, S for storage, X for index, and I for immediate. The length of an instruction is related to the number of memory addresses it uses. The basic instruction length is 16 bits, with an additional 16 bits for each memory address specified. The opcode is

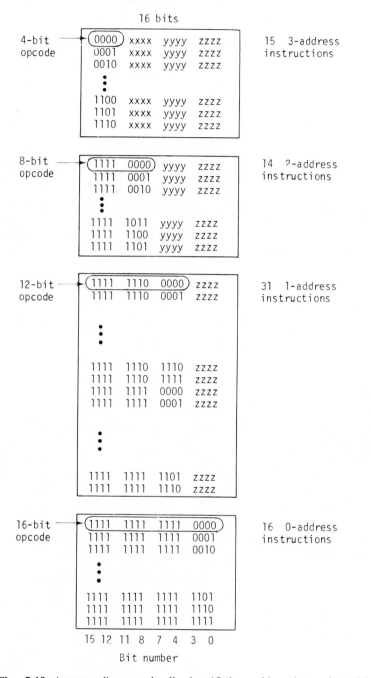

Fig. 5-19. An expanding opcode allowing 15 three-address instructions, 14 two-address instructions, 31 one-address instructions, and 16 zero-address instructions. The fields marked xxxx, yyyy, and zzzz are 4-bit address fields.

exactly 8 bits long for all these instructions, with the leftmost 2 bits specifying the instruction length and formats as follows:

00 = RR format

01 = RX format

10 = RS or SI format

11 = SS format

The 6 remaining opcode bits are used to distinguish among the various instructions of each type. Six bits means a maximum of 64 instructions in each of the four classes listed above.

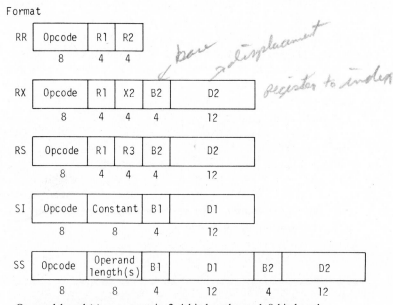

Operand length(s) may contain 2 4-bit lengths or 1 8-bit length;
R1, R2, R3 specify registers for operands and results;
B1, B2 specify base registers used in addressing;
D1, D2 are positive displacements from 0 to 4095 used for
  addressing memory in conjunction with a base register
X2 specifies an index register

Fig. 5-20. Principal instruction formats used on the 370. The numbers indicate the lengths of the fields.

The second byte of the 370 instructions consists either of two 4-bit fields specifying registers or operand lengths, or one 8-bit field specifying a constant or an operand length. The second and third halfwords always contain the specification of a memory address, using a 4-bit field for a base register and a 12-bit field for a displacement (discussed in Sec. 5.3).

Although the PDP-11 is a minicomputer, its instruction formats and addressing techniques are highly sophisticated. Figure 5-21 shows the major PDP-11 instruction formats in a way comparable to those of the IBM 370. However, from a narrow technical perspective, all instructions are actually 16 bits, and what appear to be 32- or 48-bit instructions are really 16-bit instructions followed by one or two data words. This point will be discussed in detail in Sec. 5.3.8.

The PDP-11 uses an expanding opcode scheme. If bits 12 to 14 contain 1 to 6, the instruction is a double-operand instruction; otherwise, the leftmost 7, 8, or 10 bits are used for the opcode. The fields marked "Source" and "Dest" in Fig. 5-21 each contain two 3-bit fields, one specifying the addressing mode (to be discussed in Sec. 5.3.8) and the other specifying one of the eight general registers. As a sneak preview, 0 means register mode, with the operand in the specified register, and 1 means register indirect, with the address of the operand in the register.

The 68000's instruction encoding presents an interesting contrast to that of the PDP-11. It is clear that in regard to the instruction set and addressing modes, the 68000 designers were considerably influenced by the PDP-11 but in regard to bit encoding, they went a different route. The basic philosophy behind the PDP-11 instruction encoding is **orthogonality** of opcodes and operands—in other words, an instruction should consist of an opcode field and zero, one, or two operand fields, with all operand fields encoded the same way. Although Fig. 5-21 has 13 formats, if we only look at the first word, which is the crucial one, only eight formats are used, including one for floating-point. The key two-operand instructions—MOV, CMP, BIT, BIC, BIS, ADD, MOVB, CMPB, BITB, BICB, BISB, and SUB—use format 1 (or 9 or 13, depending on the addressing mode). They all use the same 6-bit encoding both for source and for destination. To a considerable extent the one-operand instructions are similarly consistent using format 5.

With the 68000, the situation is quite different. The 68000 has more instructions than the PDP-11, and three data lengths (byte, word, long) instead of two (byte, word), so the designers could not afford the luxury of orthogonal, or even regular, instruction encoding. Squeezing all the instructions into 16 bits was clearly a struggle, so no bit combinations could be wasted. The result was at least 18 formats (excluding floating-point), depending slightly on precisely where one draws the line between variations of one instruction and two different instructions. The first word of each of these instruction formats is shown in Fig. 5-22. Like the PDP-11, many instructions have additional words following the instruction to provide constants and memory addresses.

Rather than aim for orthogonality, the 68000 designers tried to allocate more opcode space to important (i.e., frequently used) instructions and less opcode space to unimportant ones. In general, this approach leads to more efficient object programs but more complicated compilers. MOVE is unquestionably the most important instruction in any program and is encoded using format 1, with a size field (1 = byte,

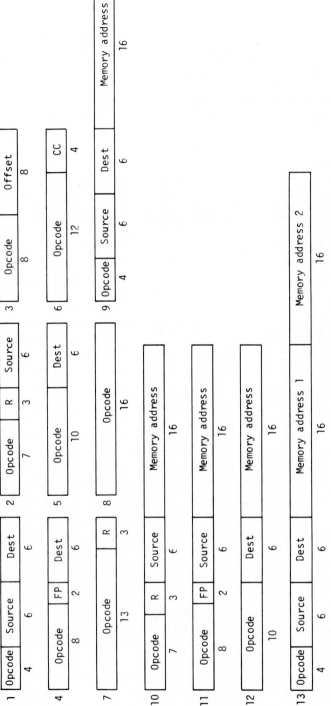

Fig. 5-21. Instruction formats used on the PDP-11. The numbers indicate the field lengths.

Source and dest each contain a 3-bit addressing mode field and a 3-bit register number;
FP is 1 of the floating point registers 0, 1, 2, or 3;
R is 1 of the general registers;
CC is the condition code field

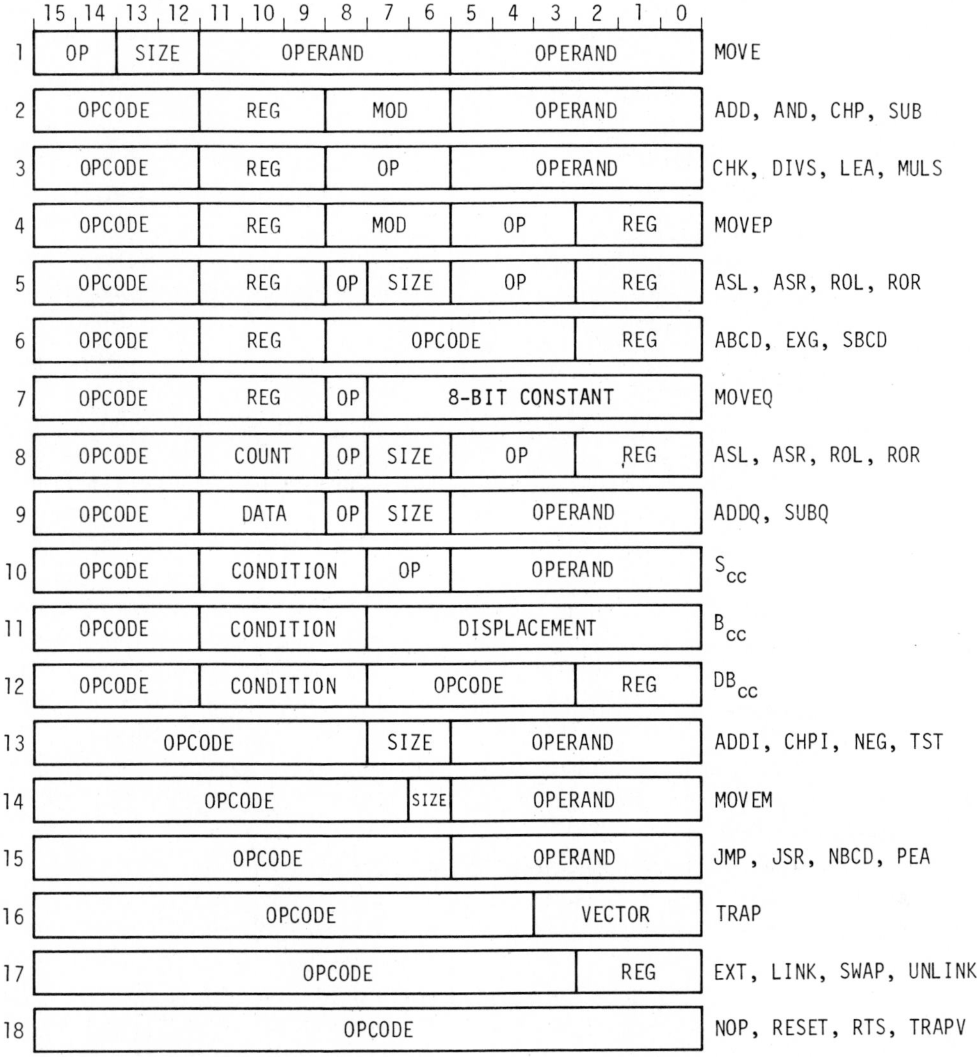

	15	14	13	12	11	10	9	8	7	6	5	4	3	2	1	0	
1	OP		SIZE		OPERAND					OPERAND							MOVE
2	OPCODE			REG			MOD			OPERAND							ADD, AND, CHP, SUB
3	OPCODE			REG			OP			OPERAND							CHK, DIVS, LEA, MULS
4	OPCODE			REG			MOD			OP			REG				MOVEP
5	OPCODE			REG		OP	SIZE		OP			REG					ASL, ASR, ROL, ROR
6	OPCODE			REG			OPCODE					REG					ABCD, EXG, SBCD
7	OPCODE			REG		OP	8-BIT CONSTANT										MOVEQ
8	OPCODE			COUNT		OP	SIZE		OP			REG					ASL, ASR, ROL, ROR
9	OPCODE			DATA		OP	SIZE		OPERAND								ADDQ, SUBQ
10	OPCODE			CONDITION			OP			OPERAND							S_{cc}
11	OPCODE			CONDITION			DISPLACEMENT										B_{cc}
12	OPCODE			CONDITION			OPCODE					REG					DB_{cc}
13	OPCODE						SIZE		OPERAND								ADDI, CHPI, NEG, TST
14	OPCODE							SIZE	OPERAND								MOVEM
15	OPCODE								OPERAND								JMP, JSR, NBCD, PEA
16	OPCODE									VECTOR							TRAP
17	OPCODE									REG							EXT, LINK, SWAP, UNLINK
18	OPCODE																NOP, RESET, RTS, TRAPV

```
OPCODE, OP determine instruction
OPERAND determines data operated on
REG selects a register
SIZE chooses byte, word, long
MOD determines if OPERAND is source or destination, and length
COUNT, DATA are constants in the range 1-8
CONDITION specifies one of 16 possible conditions to test
DISPLACEMENT is signed offset for branches
VECTOR specifies where to trap
```

Fig. 5-22. Instruction formats used on the 68000 (first word only).

2 = long, 3 = word) and two 6-bit operand fields. Each operand field has a 3-bit mode and a 3-bit register field, like the PDP-11, although the set of modes available is somewhat different. The 68000 has 16 registers, not 8, so not every mode can be used with every register; the mode implicitly specifies either an A register or a D register. If bits had not been so tight, the 68000 designers might just have let a MOVE with SIZE = 0 be an illegal instruction for the sake of opcode decoding simplicity. That not being the case, they used SIZE = 0 to encode a variety of instructions in several different formats.

Having allocated nearly a quarter (3/16) of the entire opcode space to one instruction, MOVE, providing two 6-bit operand fields for all the other two-operand instructions was out of the question. Instead, most of the two-operand instructions have one fully general 6-bit operand field (OPERAND) and one 3-bit register field (REG), using formats 2 or 3. This means that the 68000 can add a register to a register, memory to a register, or a register to memory but not memory to memory, as the PDP-11 can. The MOD field in format 2 distinguishes among byte, word, and long, and also whether the OPERAND field refers to the source or destination. Because $3 \times 2 = 6$ and 3 bits yield eight possibilities, the other two MOD values are used to indicate completely different instructions.

Some instructions have multiple formats. The shift and rotate instructions, for example, have one variant, format 8, with a constant shift count (COUNT) as part of the instruction, and another variant, format 5, where the count is taken from a specified register. Formats 7 and 9 exist because numerous studies have shown that most constants appearing in programs are small. Format 7 allows an 8-bit constant to be loaded into a register in a single 16-bit instruction. Format 9 allows a number in the range 1 to 8 to be added or subtracted from an operand efficiently. To add 9 to a register, the ADDI instruction (format 13) is needed, with an extra 16-bit word required to store the constant 9.

At first glance it might appear logical that bits 12 to 15 should determine the format, but that is not done because not all formats have equally many instructions. To statically divide the opcode space into 16 equally large groups (which is more or less what the PDP-11 does) would waste too much valuable encoding space. Instead, it is sometimes necessary to examine all 16 bits to separate two unrelated instructions.

An extreme example of this effect is the way S_{CC} (format 10) and DB_{CC} (format 12) are distinguished from ADDQ and SUBQ (format 9). All four instructions have a 5 in the upper four bits, as shown in Fig. 5-23. The latter two are easily differentiated from the former two by the presence of the illegal SIZE = 3 field (the encoding of the lengths is instruction dependent for some peculiar reason; for ADDQ and SUBQ, in contrast to MOVE, 0 = byte, 1 = word, 2 = long, 3 = illegal). Separating S_{CC} from DB_{CC} is tricky because all 16 conditions are legal in both. The solution chosen is to forbid MODE = 1 in S_{CC}. Although not especially elegant, it works, and in any event illustrates the problems that can arise when one tries to pack a lot of information in a limited number of bits.

The encoding problem on the Z80 is even worse due to the design decision to make the Z80 bit-compatible with the 8080, which itself was designed as a more-or-

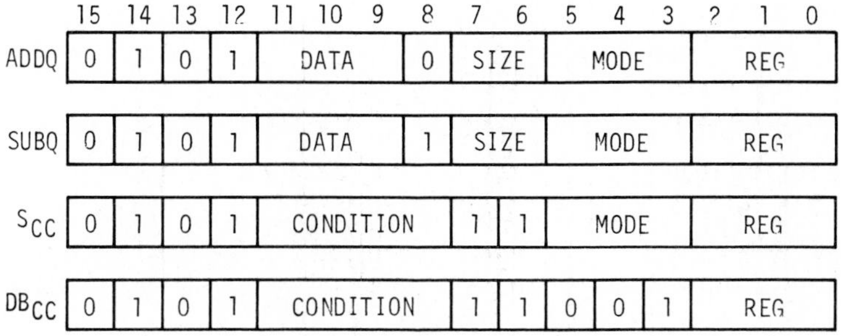

	15	14	13	12	11	10	9	8	7	6	5	4	3	2	1	0
ADDQ	0	1	0	1	DATA			0	SIZE		MODE			REG		
SUBQ	0	1	0	1	DATA			1	SIZE		MODE			REG		
S$_{CC}$	0	1	0	1	CONDITION			1	1		MODE			REG		
DB$_{CC}$	0	1	0	1	CONDITION			1	1	0	0	1		REG		

Fig. 5-23. Four 68000 instructions.

less compatible extension of the earlier 8008, which was an 8-bit version of the 4-bit 4004. This design decision meant that all existing 8080 (conventional machine level) programs had to work on the Z80 without modification. Consequently, the Z80 designers were not permitted to change any of the 8080 instructions. All the new instructions had to use opcodes not used in the 8080. This process led to a more complex instruction encoding than a complete redesign from the ground up would have yielded. The Z80 instruction formats are shown in Fig. 5-24.

Although it is not our purpose to describe the Z80 instructions in detail here, a few words may be helpful. To start with, the field labeled RR in Fig. 5-24 is a 2-bit field specifying one of the 16-bit registers or register pairs. Because there are six of them, each instruction can only access four of the six. The four available varies from instruction to instruction and is implicit in the opcode. Generally speaking, the most useful registers have been chosen for each instruction.

In Zilog's assembly language notation, the destination comes before the source, like IBM's but unlike DEC's and Motorola's. Thus LD A,(HL) means load the memory byte addressed by HL into A, and *not* store A in the memory byte addressed by HL. The latter is LD (HL),A.

Although we will discuss indexed addressing in detail shortly, for the time being just note that LD (IX+DISP),N means load the 8-bit constant N into the memory location whose address is equal to the sum of the index register IX and an 8-bit displacement, DISP.

More than on most machines, instruction length on the Z80 correlates with frequency of usage. A substantial number of instructions are only 8 bits (versus a minimum of 16 on the 370, PDP-11, and 68000). Included among these is an instruction to move any 8-bit register to any other 8-bit register (format 3). Similar to the 68000, this one instruction occupies one-fourth of the (1-byte) opcode space. The decision to have frequent instructions be short and less frequent ones be long is reminiscent of a Huffman code. It saves space but tends to slow down instruction decoding. Wilner (1972) discusses in detail the use of frequency-dependent instruction encoding on the Burroughs B1700.

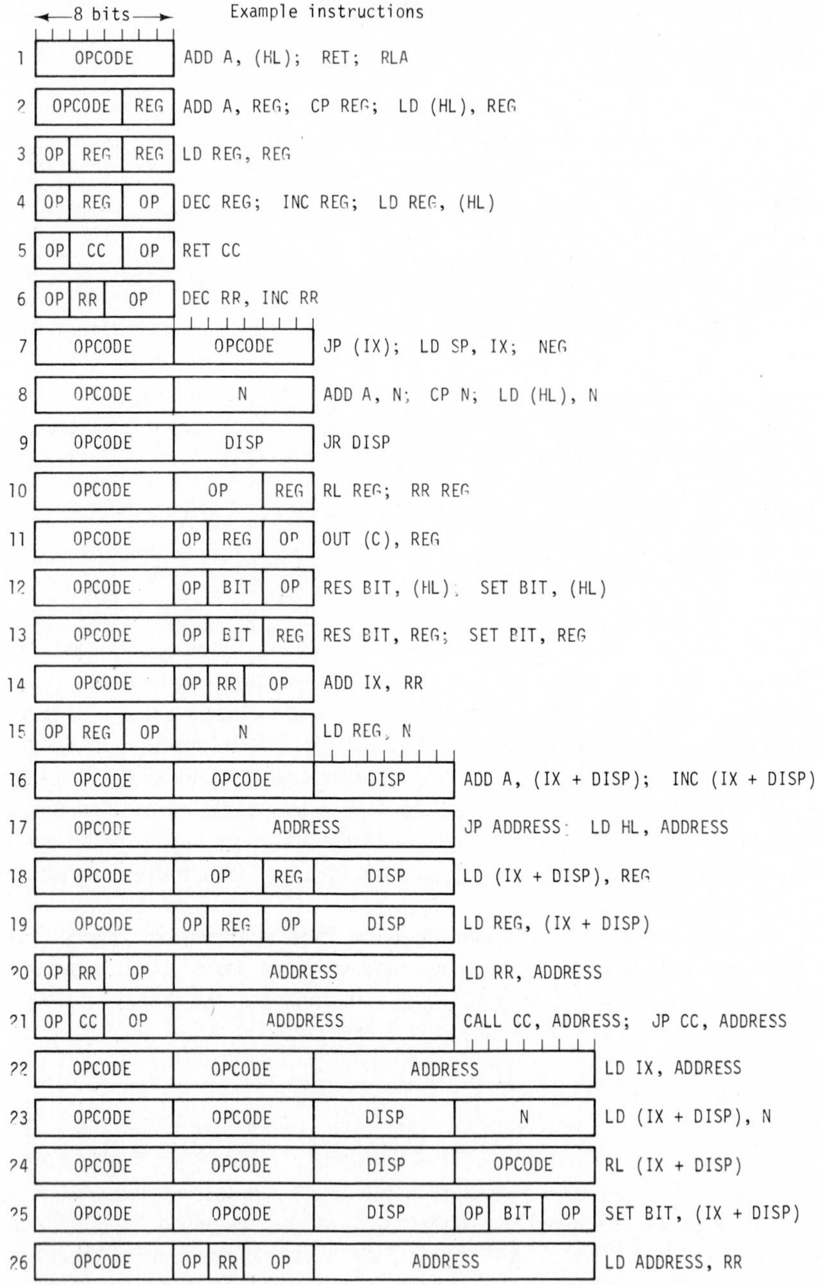

```
      ◄──8 bits──►        Example instructions

1   │   OPCODE    │        ADD A, (HL);  RET;  RLA

2   │ OPCODE │ REG │       ADD A, REG;  CP REG;  LD (HL), REG

3   │OP│ REG │ REG │       LD REG, REG

4   │OP│ REG │ OP │        DEC REG;  INC REG;  LD REG, (HL)

5   │OP│ CC │ OP │         RET CC

6   │OP│RR│ OP │           DEC RR, INC RR

7   │   OPCODE   │   OPCODE   │   JP (IX);  LD SP, IX;  NEG

8   │   OPCODE   │     N      │   ADD A, N;  CP N;  LD (HL), N

9   │   OPCODE   │    DISP    │   JR DISP

10  │   OPCODE   │  OP  │ REG │   RL REG;  RR REG

11  │   OPCODE   │ OP│ REG │ OP │  OUT (C), REG

12  │   OPCODE   │ OP│ BIT │ OP │  RES BIT, (HL);  SET BIT, (HL)

13  │   OPCODE   │ OP│ BIT │ REG │ RES BIT, REG;  SET BIT, REG

14  │   OPCODE   │ OP│RR│ OP │    ADD IX, RR

15  │OP│ REG │ OP │      N      │  LD REG, N

16  │   OPCODE   │   OPCODE   │   DISP   │  ADD A, (IX + DISP);  INC (IX + DISP)

17  │   OPCODE   │      ADDRESS      │   JP ADDRESS;  LD HL, ADDRESS

18  │   OPCODE   │ OP │ REG │  DISP  │   LD (IX + DISP), REG

19  │   OPCODE   │OP│ REG │ OP │  DISP  │  LD REG, (IX + DISP)

20  │OP│RR│ OP │      ADDRESS      │   LD RR, ADDRESS

21  │OP│CC│ OP │      ADDDRESS     │   CALL CC, ADDRESS;  JP CC, ADDRESS

22  │   OPCODE   │   OPCODE   │     ADDRESS     │  LD IX, ADDRESS

23  │   OPCODE   │   OPCODE   │  DISP  │    N    │  LD (IX + DISP), N

24  │   OPCODE   │   OPCODE   │  DISP  │  OPCODE  │  RL (IX + DISP)

25  │   OPCODE   │   OPCODE   │  DISP  │OP│ BIT │ OP │  SET BIT, (IX + DISP)

26  │   OPCODE   │OP│RR│ OP │     ADDRESS     │  LD ADDRESS, RR
```

OPCODE, OP determine instruction
REG is an 8-bit register (A, B, C, D, E, F, H, L)
RR is a 16-bit register (IX, IY, SP) or register pair (BC, DE, HL)
N is an unsigned constant
DISP is a signed constant
ADDRESS is a memory address
BIT is a bit number (0-7)
CC is a condition to be tested

Fig. 5-24. The Z80 instruction formats.

5.3. ADDRESSING

Instructions can be classified according to the number of addresses they use. It should be kept in mind that a collection of numbered CPU registers, in effect, forms a high-speed memory and defines an address space. An instruction that adds register 1 to register 2 should be classified as having two addresses because the instruction must specify which registers are to be added, just as an instruction that adds two memory words must specify which words.

Instructions specifying one, two, and three addresses are all common. On many machines that do arithmetic with only one address, a special register called the **accumulator** provides one of the operands. On these machines, the address is usually the address of a memory word m, in which the operand is located. The instruction for addition specifying the address m has the effect

$$accumulator := accumulator + memory[m]$$

Two-address add instructions use one address as the source and the other as the destination. The source is then added to the destination:

$$destination := destination + source$$

On the 370 this is written as ADD DESTINATION,SOURCE, whereas on the PDP-11 and 68000 it is written as ADD SOURCE,DESTINATION. Clearly, their respective designers had different taste in operand ordering, just as they did in bit numbering. The Z80 has only one-address arithmetic instructions, with the A register used as the accumulator.

Three-address instructions specify two sources and a destination. The two sources are added and stored at the destination.

Up to this point we have paid relatively little attention to how the bits of an address field are interpreted to find the operand. One possibility is that they contain the memory address of the operand. Other possibilities also exist, however, and in the following sections we will explore some of them.

5.3.1. Immediate Addressing

The simplest way for an instruction to specify an operand is for the address part of the instruction actually to contain the operand itself rather than an address or other information describing where the operand is. Such an operand is called an **immediate operand** because it is automatically fetched from memory at the same time the instruction itself is fetched; hence it is immediately available for use.

Immediate addressing has the virtue of not requiring an extra memory reference to fetch the operand. It has the disadvantage of restricting the operand to a number that can fit in an address field. In an instruction with a 3-bit address (e.g., register field), the operands would be restricted to 3 bits, which rather limits their usefulness.

The IBM 370 conventional machine level has MOVE, COMPARE, and three

Boolean instructions (AND, OR, and EXCLUSIVE OR) as well as several other instructions that contain a 1-byte immediate operand.

The PDP-11, with its more general addressing, can have an immediate operand anywhere it makes sense. These instructions use formats 9, 10, and 13 in Fig. 5-21, with a 16-bit two's complement constant in place of one of the addresses.

The 68000 also allows immediate operands in contexts where that is reasonable, extending the basic 16-bit instruction with one word for byte or word constants and two words for long constants. With byte constants, one of the bytes in the extra word is not used. In addition to the immediate instructions ADDI, CMPI, etc. (see Fig. 5-22, format 13), it has the "Quick" instructions ADDQ, SUBQ, and MOVEQ, for small constants (format 9).

The Z80 has instructions to load 8- and 16-bit constants into registers and memory, and instructions with immediate operands that use the A register. These instructions use formats 8, 15, and 23 in Fig. 5-24.

5.3.2. Direct Addressing

Another simple method for specifying an operand is to give the address of the memory word where the operand is contained. This form is called **direct addressing**. The details of how the computer knows which addresses are immediate and which are direct will be discussed later. On some machines, the opcodes for ADD IMMEDIATE and ADD DIRECT are different.

The 370 does not have direct addressing.

The PDP-11 not only has direct address instructions with one address but it also has a series of instructions that have two direct addresses. These instructions use format 13 in Fig. 5-21 and include instructions for adding one memory word to another, comparing two memory words, and so on.

The 68000 has two forms of direct addressing, one with a 16-bit address and one with a 32-bit address. Addresses in the first 64K of memory can be referenced with the short form, whereas addresses above 64K need the long form. These two forms are indicated by values in the 3-bit MOD field, and thus apply to all instructions with one or more OPERAND fields in Fig. 5-22.

5.3.3. Register Addressing

Register addressing is conceptually the same as direct addressing. In this form of addressing, the address field contains the number of the register in which the operand is stored. A machine with 16 registers and 65536 memory words really has two address spaces. One might think of an address on such a machine as having two parts: (a) one bit telling whether a register or a memory word is desired and (b) an address field telling which register or memory word is desired. Because there are fewer registers than memory words, a smaller address is needed, and thus different format instructions are often used for register operands and memory operands.

If there were a corresponding register instruction for every instruction which addressed memory, half the opcodes would be for memory operands and half for register operands. One bit would be needed in the opcode to designate which address space was to be used. If this bit were then removed from the opcode field and placed in the address field, the fact that two address spaces were being used would be clearer.

Machines are designed with registers for two reasons: (a) registers are faster than main memory and (b) because there are so few of them, only a few bits are needed to address them. Unfortunately, having 8 or 16 registers also greatly complicates programming because decisions must be made as to which operands and which intermediate results are to be kept in the limited number of registers, and which are to be kept in main memory. W. L. van der Poel (1968) has astutely remarked that computers ought to be provided with either 0, 1, or an infinite number of each feature (infinite meaning sufficiently many that the programmer need not have to waste any time thinking about what to do if something runs out).

The 370, PDP-11, 68000, and Z80 all have a wide repertoire of instructions that take their operands from registers and leave their results in a register. A typical instruction is ADD. On the 370, register-to-register ADD uses RR format; on the PDP-11 it uses format 1; on the 68000 it uses format 2; on the Z80 it also uses format 2 but unlike the 370 and PDP-11, where any register can be the destination, and the 68000, where any D register can be the destination, the Z80 destination register must be A for 8-bit additions and HL for 16-bit additions. All four machines can add memory to at least one register.

5.3.4. Indirect Addressing

Direct addressing is a scheme in which the address specifies which memory word or register contains the operand. Indirect addressing is a scheme in which the address specifies which memory word or register contains not the operand but the address of the operand. As an example, consider the PDP-11 instruction to load register R1 indirectly from memory location 1000, where location 1000 contains 1510, as shown in Fig. 5-25(b).

First, the contents of location 1000 are fetched into an internal CPU register. This 16-bit number (1510) is not put in R. If it were, as in Fig. 5-25(a), we would have a direct address instruction. Instead, the contents of location 1510 are fetched and put into R1. The number at location 1000 is not the operand but instead it "points to" the operand. For this reason, it is called a **pointer**. The 370, 68000, and Z80 do not have indirect addressing using a pointer in memory, but the 68000 and Z80 can address indirectly through a pointer in a register (an A register on the 68000; BC, DE, or HL on the Z80).

Some machines, although none of our four examples, have multiple-level indirect addressing. If the word containing the actual address also has the indirect bit on, the address it contains is used as a pointer to still another word. This process goes on indefinitely, until a word without the indirect bit is found.

Immediate, direct, indirect, and multiple-level indirect addressing exhibit a certain

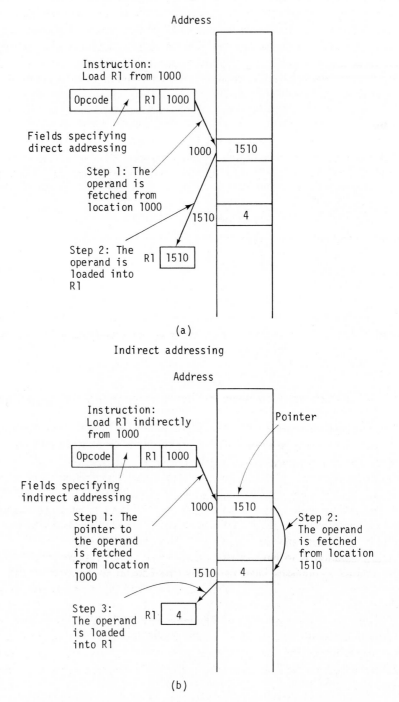

Fig. 5-25. Comparison of direct and indirect addressing. (a) Direct addressing. (b) Indirect addressing. The instruction format is the PDP-11's.

progression. Immediate addressing requires zero memory references, because the operand was fetched along with the instruction, which we will not count here. Direct addressing requires one memory reference, to fetch the operand. Indirect addressing requires two memory references, one for the pointer and one for the operand. Multiple-level indirect addressing requires at least three memory references, two or more for pointers and one for the operand. Memory references in this context include register references.

5.3.5. Indexing

Many algorithms require performing some operation on a sequence of data structures stored in consecutive memory locations. For example, consider a block of n machine words occupying locations

$A, A + 1, A + 2, \cdots, A + n - 1$

which must be moved to locations

$B, B + 1, B + 2, \cdots, B + n - 1$

Assuming that the machine has an instruction

MOVE A,B

that moves the contents of location A to location B, one could execute this instruction, modify the instruction itself to read

MOVE A+1,B+1

execute it again, then modify it again and repeat the cycle until all n words had been copied.

Although programs that modify themselves were once popular, they are now considered bad programming practice. They are difficult to debug and they make sharing of a program among several users of a time-sharing system difficult.

The copying problem can also be solved by indirect addressing. One register or memory word is loaded with the address A; a second one is loaded with B. The MOVE instructions uses these two as pointers. After each word has copied, the pointers are each to be increased by one. The pointers are part of the data, not part of the program, of course, and are not shared by simultaneous users.

Another solution is to have one or more registers, called **index registers**, which work as follows. Addresses have two parts: the number of an index register and a constant. The address of the operand is the sum of the constant and the contents of the index register. In the example above, if both addresses are indexed using an index register containing the integer k, the instruction MOVE A, B will move the contents of memory location $A + k$ to $B + k$. By initializing the index register to 0 and incrementing it by the word size after each word is copied, only one register is needed for the copy loop. Furthermore, incrementing a register is faster than incrementing a memory location.

Indexing is also commonly used to address a field at a known offset from the start of a given structure.

The IBM 370 RX instructions can use any of the general registers except 0 as an index register. The instructions that perform arithmetic or Boolean operations using a register and a memory location may have indexing specified for the memory location. The index register to be used is specified in the X2 field of the RX instruction. If the X2 field contains a 0, no indexing is performed. After the address and contents of the index register are added, only the low-order 24 bits are used as the address.

All the PDP-11 instructions that contain a memory address can have that address indexed, using any of the eight general registers. Moreover, instructions with two memory addresses may specify a different index register for each address, unlike the IBM 370 SS format instructions, which may not be indexed at all.

The 68000 allows indexing off an A register with a (signed) 16-bit displacement. It also has an addressing mode that computes the sum of an A register, a second register (either A or D), and a signed 8-bit displacement, and fetches or stores the operand in the location so addressed.

The Z80 does not really have addressing modes like the PDP-11 and 68000 but it does have instructions that can specify an operand as the byte located at a distance k from the byte pointed to by IX or IY, where k is a signed 8-bit displacement contained in the instruction (Z80 formats 16, 18, 19, 23, 24, and 25).

In the example given above it was necessary to explicitly increment the index register by the word size after each use of it. The need to increment or decrement an index register just before or after it is used is so common that some computers provide special instructions or addressing modes, or even special index registers that automatically increment or decrement themselves. Automatic modification of an index register is called **autoindexing**. The PDP-11 can use any of its general registers for autoindexing. The 68000 can autoindex using any of the A registers. The 370 and Z80 do not have autoindexing.

5.3.6. Base-Register Addressing

The distribution of memory references made by most programs is highly nonuniform. Most fetches and stores come from a few data areas. Explicit references to the program itself (except for jumps) are rare. The 370 and some other machines exploit this nonuniformity to reduce the number of bits in the addresses.

The address length can be reduced by having a number of **base registers**, each containing a pointer to some memory location. Addresses consist of two parts: a base register number and an integer called the **displacement**. The addressing computation adds the displacement to the contents of the selected base register to produce the address of the operand. A base register must contain sufficiently many bits to allow it to point to any memory address. If a machine has n base registers, and the displacement contains k bits, the programmer will be able to choose any n regions of 2^k addresses each to be accessible at any one instant.

Figure 5-26 illustrates this situation for the case of four base registers e.g., 32 bits each and a 12-bit displacement. The address in this example is actually 14 bits—2 bits to specify a base register and 12 bits to specify a displacement. A 14-bit address can specify 2^{14} memory locations. In Fig. 5-26 four regions of 2^{12} addresses each are accessible, making 2^{14} in all. The shaded areas can be accessed but the areas between them are impossible to access. If the program needs data from one of them, it must first change a base register to point to some address not more than 4095 addresses before the desired location.

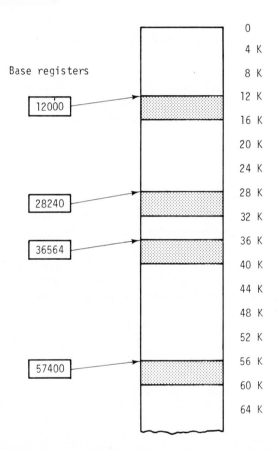

Fig. 5-26. Base-register addressing using four base registers and a 12-bit positive displacement. The shaded regions are accessible without changing a base register.

You may have noticed that in both indexing and base-register addressing, the contents of the selected register are added to a constant contained in the instruction itself to produce the address of the operand. Thus there appears to be no difference between the two modes of addressing. This observation is, in fact, true. Traditional usage is that when the displacement has enough bits to address the entire memory itself, the scheme is called indexing. Otherwise, it is called base-register addressing. Furthermore, base-register addressing schemes usually allow two registers to be specified, the operand address being the sum of both registers and the displacement. One of the registers can then be used for indexing through memory as in the example of copying a block of words from A to B.

The IBM 370 computers use base-register addressing, with 16 registers and a 12-bit displacement. The addressable unit is the byte, so a maximum of 2^{16} bytes may be addressable at one time, unless both a base register *and* an index register are specified. In practice, some of the general registers are normally needed for index registers, procedure calls, and other purposes, so they are not available as base registers. Furthermore, when used as a base register, register 0 behaves as though it contained a zero, no matter what its actual contents are. Consequently, not all 16 are available for use as base registers. The total address space consists of 2^{24} bytes; therefore less than 1% of the address space is available at any one instant. However, if the program avoids spreading its data over too wide a range of addresses, this 1% may be more than adequate. A 4-bit base-register field and a 12-bit displacement field save 8 bits compared to a 24-bit direct address.

5.3.7. Stack Addressing

We have already noted that having machine instructions be as short as possible is highly desirable for saving both CPU time and memory. The ultimate limit in reducing address lengths would be to have instructions with no addresses at all, just opcodes. Surprisingly enough, this situation is possible. It is accomplished by organizing the machine around a data structure called a stack.

A **stack** consists of data items (words, characters, bits, etc.) stored in consecutive order in the memory. The first item pushed onto the stack is said to be at the bottom of the stack. The item most recently pushed onto the stack is said to be on the top of the stack. Associated with each stack is a register or memory word that contains the address of the top of the stack. It is called the **stack pointer**.

Although we have discussed stacks in Chap. 4, we will review that material briefly here because using stacks for arithmetic is quite different from using stacks for holding local variables (both uses can be combined, of course). Figure 5-27 illustrates the operation of a stack. In Fig. 5-27(a) two items are already on the stack. The bottom of the stack is at memory location 1000 and the top of the stack is at memory location 1001. The stack pointer contains the address of the item on the top of the stack, namely, 1001; that is, it "points" to the top of the stack. In Fig. 5-27(b), 6 has been pushed onto the stack and the stack pointer indicates 1002 as the new top of the stack. In Fig. 5-27(c), 75 has been pushed onto the stack, raising the stack pointer to 1003. In Fig. 5-27(d), 75 has been popped off the stack.

Computers that are stack-oriented have an instruction to push the contents of a memory location or a register onto the stack. Such an instruction must both copy the item and increment the stack pointer. Similarly, an instruction to pop the top of the stack into a register or memory location must make a new copy in the proper place

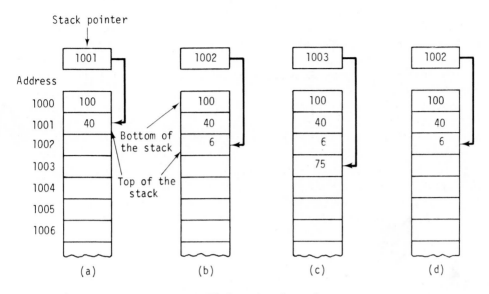

Stack pointer

Address

Fig. 5-27. Operation of a stack.

and decrement the stack pointer. Some computers have their stacks upside down, with new items being pushed into consecutively lower numbered memory locations rather than consecutively higher numbered locations, as in Fig. 5-27.

Instructions with no addresses are used in conjunction with a stack. This form of addressing specifies that the two operands are to be popped off the stack, one after another, the operation performed (e.g., multiplication or AND) and the result pushed back onto the stack. Figure 5-28(a) shows a stack containing four items. A multiply instruction has the effect of popping the 5 and the 6 off the stack, temporarily resetting the stack pointer 1001, and then pushing the result, 30, onto the stack, as shown in Fig. 5-28(b). If an addition is then performed, the result will be as shown in Fig. 5-28(c).

Reverse Polish

It is a long-standing tradition in mathematics to write the operator between the operands, as in $x + y$ rather than after the operands, as in $x \ y \ +$. The form with the operator "in" between the operands is called **infix** notation. The form with the operator after the operands is called **postfix** or **reverse Polish**, after the Polish logician J. Lukasiewicz (1958), who investigated the properties of this notation.

Reverse Polish has a number of advantages over infix for expressing algebraic formulas. First, any formula can be expressed without parentheses. Second, it is convenient for evaluating formulas on computers with stacks. Third, infix operators have precedence, which is arbitrary and undesirable. For example we know that

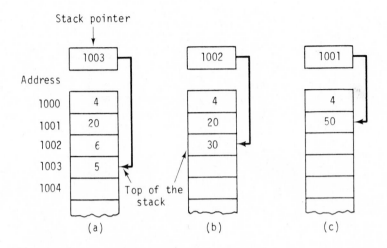

Fig. 5-28. Using a stack for arithmetic. (a) Initial configuration. (b) After a multiplication. (c) After an addition.

$a \times b + c$ means $(a \times b) + c$ and not $a \times (b + c)$ because multiplication has been arbitrarily defined to have precedence over addition. Reverse Polish eliminates this nuisance.

Several algorithms for converting infix formulas into reverse Polish exist. The one given below is an adaptation of an idea due to E. W. Dijkstra. Assume that a formula is composed of the following symbols: variables, the dyadic (two-operand) operators $+ - */$. and left and right parentheses. To mark the ends of a formula, we will insert the symbol $\perp$ after the last symbol and before the first symbol.

Figure 5-29 shows a railroad track from New York to California, with a spur in the middle that heads off toward Texas. Each symbol in the formula is represented by one railroad car. The train moves westward (to the left). When each car arrives at the switch, it must stop and ask if it should go to California directly or take a side trip to Texas. Cars containing variables always go directly to California and never to Texas. Cars containing other symbols must inquire about the contents of the nearest car on the Texas line before entering the switch.

Figure 5-30 shows what happens, depending on the contents of the nearest car on the Texas line and the car at the switch. The first $\perp$ always goes to Texas. The numbers refer to the following situations:

1. The car at the switch heads toward Texas.

2. The most recent car on the Texas line turns around and goes to California.

3. Both the car at the switch and the most recent car on the Texas line are hijacked and disappear (i.e., both are deleted).

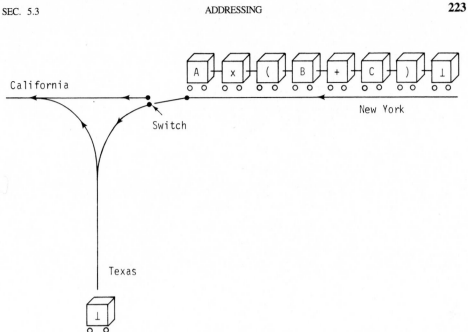

Fig. 5-29. Each railroad car represents one symbol in the formula to be converted from infix to reverse Polish.

4. Stop. The symbols now in California represent the reverse Polish formula when read from left to right.

5. Stop. An error has occurred. The original formula was not correctly balanced.

Car at the switch

		⊥	+	−	×	/	(	)
	⊥	4	1	1	1	1	1	5
	+	?	2	2	1	1	1	?
Most recently arrived car on the Texas line	−	2	2	2	1	1	1	2
	×	?	?	?	?	?	1	2
	/	?	2	?	?	?	1	?
	(	5	1	1	1	1	1	3

Fig. 5-30. Decision table used by the infix to reverse Polish algorithm.

After each action is taken, a new comparison is made between the car at the switch, which may be the same car as in the previous comparison or it may be the next car, and the car that is now the last one on the Texas line. The process continues until step 4 is reached. Notice that the Texas line is being used as a stack, with routing a car to Texas being a push operation, and turning a car already on the Texas line around and sending it to California being a pop operation.

The order of the variables is the same in infix and reverse Polish. Figure 5-31 gives examples of infix formulas and their reverse Polish equivalents.

Infix	Reverse Polish
A + B x C	ABC x +
A x B + C	AB x C +
A x B + C x D	AB x CD x +
(A + B)/(C - D)	AB + CD - /
A x B/C	AB x C /
((A + B) x C + D)/(E + F + G)	AB + C x D + EF + G + /

Fig. 5-31. Examples of infix formulas and their reverse Polish equivalents.

Evaluation of Reverse Polish Formulas

The following algorithm evaluates a reverse Polish formula.

ALGORITHM

1. Examine each symbol in the reverse Polish formula, starting at the extreme left until you come to an operator.

2. Write down the operator and the two operands immediately to its left on a piece of scratch paper.

3. Erase the operator and the operands from the formula, creating a hole.

4. Perform the operation on the operands and write the result in the hole.

5. If the formula now consists of one value, that is the answer and the algorithm is finished; otherwise, go to step 1.

Figure 5-32 depicts the evaluation of a reverse Polish formula. The order of the operators is the order in which they are actually evaluated.

Reverse Polish is the ideal notation for evaluating formulas on a computer with a stack. The formula consists of n symbols, each one either a variable (i.e., something with a value), or an operator. The algorithm for evaluating a reverse Polish formula using a stack is as follows.

Infix formula (8 + 2 x 5)/(1 + 3 x 2 - 4)

Reverse Polish formula 8 2 5 x + 1 3 2 x + 4 - /

Step	Formula to be evaluated	Leftmost operator	Left operand	Right operand	Result	New formula after performing operation
1	8 2 5 x + 1 3 2 x + 4 - /	x	2	5	10	8 10 + 1 3 2 x + 4 - /
2	8 10 + 1 3 2 x + 4 - /	+	8	10	18	18 1 3 2 x + 4 - /
3	18 1 3 2 x + 4 - /	x	3	2	6	18 1 6 + 4 - /
4	18 1 6 + 4 - /	+	1	6	7	18 7 4 - /
5	18 7 4 - /	-	7	4	3	18 3 /
6	18 3 /	/	18	3	6	6

Fig. 5-32. Evaluation of the formula $(8 + 2 \times 5)/(1 + 3 \times 2 - 4)$ by converting it to reverse Polish and then evaluating the reverse Polish.

ALGORITHM

1. Set k to 1.

2. Examine the kth symbol. If it is a variable, push it onto the stack. If it is an operator, pop the top two items off the stack, perform the operation, and push the result back onto the stack.

3. If $k = n$, the algorithm terminates and the answer is on the stack; otherwise, add 1 to k and go to step 2.

Figure 5-33 shows the evaluation of the same formula as in Fig. 5-32 but using a stack this time. The number on top of the stack is the right operand, not the left operand.

A computer organized around a stack offers several advantages compared to multiregister machines, such as the 370, PDP-11, 68000, and Z80:

1. Short instructions because many instructions have no addresses.

2. Formulas are easy to evaluate.

3. Complicated algorithms to optimize register use are not needed.

Although none of our four example machines has stack arithmetic instructions, some

Infix formula (8 + 2 x 5)/(1 + 3 x 2 - 4)

Reverse Polish formula 8 2 5 x + 1 3 2 x + 4 - /

Step

1	8 2 5 x + 1 3 2 x + 4 - /	Push 8
2	2 5 x + 1 3 2 x + 4 - /	Push 2
3	5 x + 1 3 2 x + 4 - /	Push 5
4	x + 1 3 2 x + 4 - /	Multiply 2 x 5
5	+ 1 3 2 x + 4 - /	Add 8 + 10
6	1 3 2 x + 4 - /	Push 1
7	3 2 x + 4 - /	Push 3
8	2 x + 4 - /	Push 2
9	x + 4 - /	Multiply 3 x 2
10	+ 4 - /	Add 1 + 6
11	4 - /	Push 4
12	- /	Subtract 7 - 4
13	/	Divide 18/3

(a)

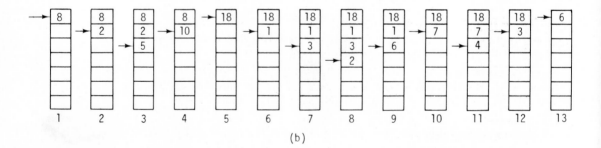

1   2   3   4   5   6   7   8   9   10   11   12   13

(b)

Fig. 5-33. Use of a stack to evaluate a reverse Polish formula. (a) Steps in the evaluation process. (b) The stack after the corresponding step in (a). The arrow is stack pointer.

compilers for these machines use the registers to simulate a stack in software, at a certain cost in performance compared to having level 2 instructions to perform stack arithmetic directly.

The PDP-11 and 68000 do not have stack arithmetic instructions but they do have stack addressing. The instructions to push a word onto a stack and pop a word off a stack use autoindexing. Both machines have addressing modes for predecrement and postincrement. In predecrement mode the stack pointer (a register) is first decremented and then the register is used as a pointer. In postincrement mode the indirection is first done, and then the register is incremented. If stacks grow from high addresses to low addresses and the stack pointer always points to the top of the stack (lowest numerical address containing a stack item), predecrement mode can be used for push and postincrement mode can be used for pop. Alternatively, if stacks grow from low addresses to high ones and by convention the stack pointer points to the first empty cell on the stack instead of the last full one, postincrement can be used for push and predecrement for pop.

5.3.8. Addressing on the PDP-11 and the 68000

The previous sections discussed a number of different addressing modes—immediate addressing, direct addressing, indirect addressing, indexing, and so on. There still remains the question of how the hardware or level 1 interpreter knows whether an address is immediate, direct, indirect, and so on. One solution is to have a separate opcode for each addressing mode—that is, separate opcodes for ADD IMMEDIATE, ADD DIRECT, ADD INDIRECT, and so on. Another way is to make the mode part of the address. Each instruction could contain a few bits per address specifying which form of addressing was desired.

The PDP-11 has a large number of addressing modes and is therefore worth examining in detail. The 68000 is similar and will be summarized afterward. Figure 5-34(a) shows the format of the two-operand instructions, such as MOVE, ADD, COMPARE, and INCLUSIVE OR. Each operand has a 3-bit addressing mode and a 3-bit register field. The meaning of the modes is given in Fig. 5-34(b). Remember that register 7 is the program counter and that it is advanced by 2 immediately after an instruction word is fetched (before the instruction is executed).

All PDP-11 instructions are actually only 16 bits, but, in some cases one or two extra words directly following the instruction are used by the instruction and can be considered part of it. Mode 6 and mode 7 addressing require a 16-bit constant for indexing. Furthermore, if either mode 2 or mode 3 is specified with register 7 (the program counter), the following sequence of steps occurs.

First, the instruction is fetched and register 7 is increased by 2 (a word is 2 bytes). Then register 7 is used as a pointer to the data (mode 2) or the address of the data (mode 3). In both cases, the word pointed to by R7 is the word following the instruction. After this word is fetched, the autoincrementing of register 7 takes place, increasing register 7 by 2. Autoincrement addressing that specifies the program counter is a clever trick allowing the word following the instruction to be used as data. In mode 2 this word is the operand, yielding immediate addressing. In mode 3 this word is the address of the operand, yielding direct addressing. If both source and destination require an extra word, the first one is for the source.

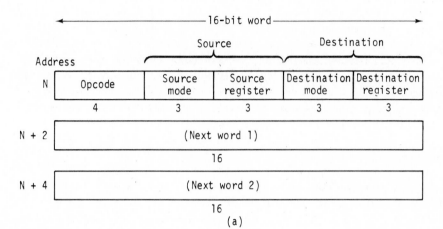

(a)

Mode	Name	How the operand is located
0	Register addressing	The operand is in R.
1	Register indirect	R contains a pointer to the operand.
2	Autoincrement	The content of R is fetched and used as a pointer to the operand. After this step, but before the instruction is executed, R is incremented by 1 (byte instructions) or 2 (word instructions).
3	Autoincrement indirect	The address of a memory word containing a pointer to the operand is fetched from R. Then R is incremented by 1 or 2 before the instruction is executed.
4	Autodecrement	R is first decremented by 1 or 2. The new value of R is then used as a pointer to the operand.
5	Autodecrement indirect	R is first decremented by 1 or 2. The new value of R is then used as the address of a memory location containing a pointer to the operand.
6	Indexing	The operand is at the address equal to the sum of R (the index register) and the 16 bit 2's complement offset in the next word. In modes 6 and 7, the program counter (R7) is incremented by 2 immediately after the next word is fetched.
7	Indexing + indirect addressing	The memory location containing a pointer to the operand is found by adding the contents of R and the next word. In modes 6 and 7, the program counter (R7) is incremented by 2 immediately after the next word is fetched.

(b)

Fig. 5-34. (a) Format of a PDP-11 two-address instruction. (b) Description of the PDP-11 addressing modes. R is the register specified along with the mode.

The PDP-11 has an interesting form of addressing called **self-relative** or **position-independent** addressing. When mode 6 and register 7 are specified, the operand address is found by forming the sum of the index word following the instruction and the program counter. In effect, the index word gives the operand address by specifying how far away it is from the instruction itself, either in front or behind.

If all memory references use this form of addressing instead of direct addressing (mode 3 with register 7), a program can be loaded anywhere in memory and it will run correctly. In addition, it can also be moved after being loaded, because although the absolute addresses of the needed operands change, their distance from the instructions referencing them remains fixed. However, if any return addresses from procedure calls are on the stack, moving the program is impossible because these addresses are absolute.

As an example of the power of the PDP-11 addressing mechanism, consider the MOV instruction of Fig. 5-35(a). This instruction moves the source operand to register 4. Figure 5-35(b) shows all the different variations of this instruction for different source modes and registers.

Because both the source addressing mode and the destination addressing mode can be independently specified, a single opcode yields a large number of different instructions. For example, the ADD instruction can be used to:

Add a register to another register (0, 0).

Add a register to a memory word (0, 6).

Add a memory word to a register (6, 0).

Add a memory word to another memory word (6, 6).

Pop a word from a stack and add it to a register (2, 0).

Pop a word from a stack and add it to a memory word (2, 6).

Add an immediate operand to a register (2, 0).

Add an immediate operand to a memory word (2, 6).

Add an immediate operand to the top word on the stack (2, 1).

Add a register to the top word on the stack (0, 1).

Add a memory word to the top word on the stack (6, 1).

Add a memory word to an indirectly specified address (6, 7).

Add a register to an indirectly specified address (0, 7).

Add an immediate operand to an indirectly specified address (2, 7).

There are many other possibilities as well. The numbers in parentheses in the list above are the source and destination modes. Note that mode 6 with R7 can always be replaced by mode 3 with R7 (i.e., memory can be addressed self-relative or directly).

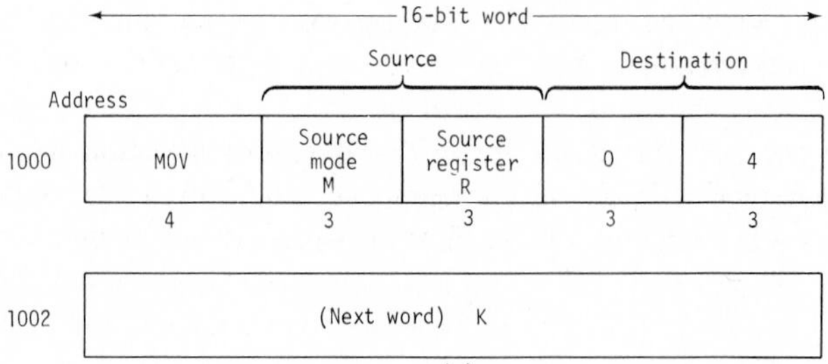

(a)

Source register

Source mode M	R = 0 - 5	R = 6	R = 7
0	Move R to R4 (register - register) Example: MOV R3, R4	Move stack pointer to R4 Example: MOV SP, R4	Move program counter to R4 Example: MOV PC, R4
1	Move memory word pointed to by R to R4 Example: MOV *R3, R4	Move top of the stack to R4, but do not remove it from the stack Example: MOV *SP, R4	Move K to R4; program counter is not incremented again so K will be executed as the next instruction Example: MOV *PC, R4
2	Move memory word pointed to by R to R4 and add 2 to R Example: MOV (R3)+, R4	Remove a word from the stack and put it in R4 (pop instruction) Example: MOV (SP)+, R4	Move K to R4 (immediate) addressing) Example: MOV $24, R4
3	Move to R4 the memory word addressed by the word R points to, and add 2 to R Example: MOV *(R3)+, R4	Pop the address of the source operand from the stack, and move the source operand itself to R4 Example MOV * (SP) +, R4	Load R4 from memory address K (direct addressing) Example: MOV *$24, R4
4	Decrement R by 2 and then load R4 from the address R points to Example: MOV -(R3), R4	M = 4 and R = 6 is not useful as a source; however it is used as a destination in push instructions Example of push: MOV $6, -(SP)	Not used (causes an infinite loop)
5	Decrement R by 2 and then load R4 indirectly from the address R points to Example: MOV *-(R3), R4	Not used	Not used (causes an infinite loop)
6	Load R4 with the memory word at C(R) + K (indexing) Example: MOV 24(R3), R4	Load R4 with the word K/2 words below the top of the stack Example: MOV 24(SP), R4	Load R4 with the word K/2 words from this instruction (self relative addressing) Example: MOV X, R4 Note: The assembler computes the appropriate constant to address X
7	Load R4 with the memory word pointed to by C(R) + K (indexing + indirect addressing) Example: MOV *24(R3), R4	Load R4 from the word whose address is K/2 words below the top of the stack Example: MOV *24(SP), R4	Load R4 with the word pointed to by the word K bytes from this instruction (indirect addressing) Example: MOV *X, R4 Note: The assembler computes the appropriate constant to address X

(b)

Fig. 5-35. (a) A PDP-11 instruction that moves a word to register R4. (b) Different variations for different source modes and registers. R is the register and C(R) is its contents. The dollar sign indicates an immediate operand and the asterisk indicates indirection (UNIX assembler notation).

Also, note that mode 1 with register 6 uses the top word of the stack as a source or destination but does not remove it from the stack, whereas mode 2 with register 6 does remove it.

Although only one opcode is used, the PDP-11 ADD instruction has dozens of distinct and useful variations. If all the variations of all 12 two-address instructions were counted as separate instructions, the PDP-11 would have hundreds of instructions. Because of the extreme flexibility of its addressing modes, the PDP-11 has a far more powerful and useful instruction set than the instruction list might indicate at first glance.

The 68000's addressing modes are similar to those of the PDP-11. They are summarized in Fig. 5-36. On both machines an operand is specified by a 6-bit field consisting of a 3-bit mode and a 3-bit register. The 68000 program counter is not a general register, so the trick used on the PDP-11 for achieving immediate addressing and direct addressing by autoincrementing the program counter does not apply. Instead, explicit addressing modes are provided. The stack pointer is addressable, however (as A7), so all the stack addressing modes do apply to the 68000.

Mode	Reg	Extra words	Description
0	D	0	Operand in register D
1	A	0	Operand in register A
2	A	0	Pointer to operand in register A
3	A	0	Pointer in A; autoincrement A after use
4	A	0	Autodecrement A; then use as pointer
5	A	1	Indexed mode with 16-bit displacement
6	A	1	A + index register + 8-bit displacement yields address
7	0	1	Direct addressing with 16-bit address
7	1	2	Direct addressing with 32-bit address
7	2	1	Operand address is PC + 16-bit displacement
7	3	1	Operand address is PC + index + 8-bit displacement
7	4	1 or 2	Immediate data

Fig. 5-36. Addressing modes on the 68000.

5.3.9. Discussion of Addressing Modes

PDP-11 addressing modes 0, 1, and 2 (including immediate addressing), mode 3 register 7 (direct addressing), and modes 4 and 6 are available on the 68000 in essentially the same form. Modes 3 (except for direct addressing), 5, and 7 are not available. On the other hand, the two 68000 modes that use an index register (A or D) are not present on the PDP-11. Because the modes that both machines have are far more important than the other ones, the addressing power of the two machines can be said to be essentially equal.

On the other hand, neither the 370 nor the Z80 has addressing anywhere nearly as sophisticated as these two. The 370 lacks indirect addressing, autoindexing, and stack addressing. Furthermore, the addressing modes of its operands are not independently specifiable. For example, the 370 has different opcodes for add memory to register and add register to register, and no instructions to add a register to a memory word or one memory word to another. (It does have an instruction to add two numbers in memory in decimal format, however.)

The freedom of a computer designer to include or exclude certain types of addressing from a new machine is severely constrained by the number of bits available for encoding the addressing information.

As an example, consider the possibility of adding eight more general registers to the PDP-11, so that it would have 16, just as the 370 does. Having 16 registers would have required a 4-bit field to specify a register instead of a 3-bit field, assuming that all registers were equivalent and not arbitrarily divided into two classes as on the 68000. The result would have increased the two-operand instructions to 18 bits and the one operand instructions to 17 bits, awkward numbers considering the byte/word organization of the PDP-11.

The eight additional registers could have been accommodated by reducing the 3-bit field specifying the addressing mode to 2 bits, at the cost of eliminating several types of addressing. For example, the four allowed types could be register, indexing, autoincrement (which becomes immediate when the program counter is specified as the register), and autodecrement. Direct and indirect addressing would have been eliminated. Alternatively, they could have been included and the two autoindexing forms deleted, eliminating the stack addressing and immediate instructions. No matter what choice was made, the addressing power of the PDP-11 would have been severely weakened.

Another solution would be to do what Motorola did—partition the registers into two groups and, in effect, use only eight of the registers for addressing. The price Motorola paid, of course, is a less symmetric machine than the PDP-11. Yet another solution was used on the DEC VAX series—simply use more bits. The VAX has a 4-bit mode field and a 4-bit register field, requiring an additional byte per operand above and beyond the address or offset itself.

We have now completed our examination of the various trade-offs possible between opcodes and addresses, and various forms of addressing. When approaching a new computer, you should examine the instruction set and addressing possibilities not only to see which ones are available but also to understand why those choices were made and what the consequences of alternative choices would have been.

5.4. INSTRUCTION TYPES

Conventional machine level instructions can be approximately separated into two groups: general-purpose instructions and special-purpose instructions. The general-purpose instructions have wide application. For example, the ability to move data around in the machine is something that is needed by almost every application. The special-purpose instructions have much narrower applications. For example, the 68000 MOVEP instruction takes the contents of a D register and stores it in memory in alternate bytes, with an unused byte between the data bytes. Few applications can make effective use of this instruction and no compiler will ever generate it. (It was included to simplify communication with older, 8-bit-wide peripheral chips.) In the following sections we will discuss the major groups of general-purpose instructions.

Every instruction changes the state vector of the process that executed it. Even a NO OPERATION instruction changes the state vector because the program counter has a different value after it than before it. One can regard each instruction as a rule for transforming the old state vector into a new state vector. Some instructions change the value of one or more memory words or registers. Other instructions merely change the program counter. In the following discussion of specific instructions, keep in mind the fact that each instruction represents an algorithm for changing the old state vector into a new one.

As an aside, it is interesting to note that computer manufacturers seem to think the larger a machine's instruction set, the better. Nevertheless, good arguments exist for keeping instruction sets as small as possible (Patterson and Séquin, 1981; Fairclough, 1982; Patterson and Piepho, 1982).

5.4.1. Data Movement Instructions

Copying data from one place to another is the most fundamental of all operations. By copying we mean the creating of a new object, with the identical bit pattern as the original. This use of the word "movement" is somewhat different from its normal usage in English. When we say that Marvin Mongoose has moved from New York to California, we do not mean that an identical copy of Mr. Mongoose was created in California and that the original is still in New York. When we say that the contents of memory location 2000 have been moved to some register, we almost always mean that an identical copy has been created there and that the original is still undisturbed in location 2000. Data movement instructions would better be called "data duplication" instructions, but the term "data movement" is already established.

Data can be stored in several places, differing in the way the words are accessed. Three common places are in a particular memory word, in a register, or on the stack. The stack is kept either in special registers or in memory but the way it is accessed is different from standard memory accesses. A memory access requires an address, whereas pushing an item onto the stack does not explicitly address the stack. Data movement instructions require that both the source of the information (i.e., the original) and the destination (i.e., where the copy is to be placed) be specified either explicitly or implicitly.

Data movement instructions must somehow indicate the amount of data to be moved. Instructions exist to move quantities of data ranging from 1 bit to the entire memory. On fixed word length machines, the number of words to be moved is usually specified by the instruction—for example, separate instructions for move a word and move a halfword. Variable-word-length machines often have instructions specifying only the source and destination addresses but not the amount. The move continues until an end of data field mark is found in the data itself.

The 370 has over 20 distinct instructions for moving data, the exact number depending on whether such instructions as LOAD POSITIVE (LPR) are counted or not. Instructions are provided for moving data in units of 1, 2, 3, 4, and 8 bytes, as well as variable length data of any length.

These instructions fall into four general groups: loading registers from memory, storing registers into memory, register-to-register transfer, and memory-to-memory moves. In addition, separate instructions are provided for transfers involving general registers, 32-bit floating-point numbers, and 64-bit floating-point numbers. Also, certain instructions not only move data but set the condition code (a 2-bit register that the program can test), depending on whether the item moved is negative, positive, or zero. Such a large number of distinct instructions leads to a somewhat cumbersome instruction set.

When trying to understand why certain decisions were made, it is often helpful to examine the alternative choices. An alternative design (not chosen by IBM) would have been to have a single, general-purpose move instruction. Such an instruction would have to specify the source of the data (general register, floating-point register, memory, or immediate operand), the destination of the data (general register, floating-point register, or memory), the number of bytes to be moved, and a bit telling whether the condition code was to be set or left unchanged.

As mentioned earlier, an instruction of this kind is called **orthogonal** because each parameter is independent of the others. In addition to being simpler to use, such an instruction would be more general. For example, by specifying a move from memory to floating-point register 0 and a length of 32 bytes, all four floating-point registers could be loaded in one instruction. A single general-purpose move instruction, although easier to use, would have had the disadvantage of increasing the average instruction length, thereby using more memory and slowing down the machine. Machine designers are constantly forced to make compromises, carefully trying to balance all the relevant factors.

The PDP-11 has six data movement instructions. MOV and MOVB are orthogonal instructions that can move words and bytes respectively from general registers, memory, stacks, or immediate data to any of the above. The opcodes for MOV and MOVB differ only in one bit, bit 15, which can be regarded as the "length bit," specifying whether one or two bytes are to be moved. This orthogonal design was not carried over into the floating-point instructions (for lack of encoding room in the address specification field), and separate instructions are provided for loading and storing 32- and 64-bit floating-point numbers.

The 68000 has a MOVE instruction, that, like the PDP-11's, is completely general and orthogonal and can move data from register, memory, or stack to any one of these using arbitrary addressing modes for both source and destination. In addition, it has the MOVEQ instruction for fast moves of small numbers and MOVEM to save or restore any or all of the 16 general registers in a single instruction.

Although the Zilog assembly language uses LD for all moves, the Z80 actually has a large number of different instructions for different sources and destinations. With regard to lack of uniformity, it resembles the 370.

5.4.2. Dyadic Operations

Dyadic operations are those that combine two operands to produce a result. Just about all level 2 machines have instructions to perform addition and subtraction on integers. Except for the 8-bit microcomputers, multiplication and division of integers are standard as well. It is presumably unnecessary to explain why computers are equipped with arithmetic instructions.

Another group of dyadic operations includes the Boolean instructions. Although 16 Boolean functions of two variables exist, few, if any, level 2 machines have instructions for all 16. For example, the function that *computes* TRUE, independent of the arguments, is useless. If the bit pattern for TRUE is needed somewhere in the machine, it can simply be moved there rather than be computed. Similar arguments suggest that an instruction to implement $f(P, Q) = P$ would be rather useless.

Three instructions present in many machines are AND, OR, and EXCLUSIVE OR. On fixed-word-length machines, AND computes the bit-by-bit Boolean product of two one-word arguments, the result of which is also a word. Sometimes there exist instructions for half words and/or double words as well. Similar remarks apply to the other Boolean operations.

An important use of AND is for extracting bits from words. Consider, for example, a 32-bit-word-length machine in which four 8-bit characters are stored per word. Suppose that it is necessary to separate the second character from the other three in order to print it; that is, it is necessary to create a word which contains that character in the rightmost 8 bits, referred to as **right justified** with zeros in the leftmost 24 bits.

To extract the character, the word containing the character is ANDed with a constant, called a **mask**. The result of this operation is that the unwanted bits are all changed into zeros—that is, masked out—as shown below.

```
10110111 10111100 11011011 10001011  A
00000000 11111111 00000000 00000000  B (mask)
00000000 10111100 00000000 00000000  A AND B
```

The result would then be shifted 16 bits to the right to isolate the character at the right end of the word.

An important use of OR is to pack bits into a word, packing being the inverse of extracting. To change the rightmost 8 bits of a 32-bit word without disturbing the other 24 bits, first the unwanted 8 bits are masked out and then the new character is ORed in, as shown below.

```
10110111 10111100 11011011 10001011  A
11111111 11111111 11111111 00000000  B (mask)
10110111 10111100 11011011 00000000  A AND B
00000000 00000000 00000000 01010111  C
10110111 10111100 11011011 01010111  (A AND B) OR C
```

The AND operation tends to remove 1s, because there are never more 1s in the result than in either of the operands. The OR operation tends to insert 1s, because there are always at least as many 1s in the result as in the operand with the most 1s. The EXCLUSIVE OR operation, on the other hand, is symmetric, tending, on the average, neither to insert or remove 1s. This symmetry with respect to 1s and 0s is occasionally useful—for example, in generating "random numbers."

Early computers performed floating-point arithmetic by calling software procedures but today many computers, especially those intended for scientific work, have floating-point instructions at level 2 for reasons of speed. Some machines provide several lengths of floating-point numbers, the shorter ones for speed and the longer ones for occasions when many digits of accuracy are needed. Floating-point numbers are discussed in Appendix B.

5.4.3. Monadic Operations

Monadic operations have one operand and produce one result. Because one fewer address has to be specified than with dyadic operations, the instructions are sometimes shorter.

Instructions to shift or rotate the contents of a word or byte are quite useful and are often provided in several different variations. Shifts are operations in which the bits are moved to the left or right, with bits shifted off the end of the word being lost. Rotates are shifts in which bits pushed off one end reappear on the other end. The difference between a shift and a rotate is illustrated below.

00000000 00000000 00000000 01110011 A
00000000 00000000 00000000 00011100 A shifted right 2 bits
11000000 00000000 00000000 00011100 A rotated right 2 bits

Both left and right shifts and rotates are useful. If an n-bit word is left rotated k bits, the result is the same as if it had been right rotated $n - k$ bits.

Right shifts are often performed with sign extension. This means that positions vacated on the left end of the word are filled up with the original sign bit, 0 or 1. It is as though the sign bit were dragged along to the right. Among other things, it means that a negative number will remain negative. This situation is illustrated below for 2-bit right shifts.

11111111 11111111 11111111 11110000 A
00111111 11111111 11111111 11111100 A shifted without sign extension
11111111 11111111 11111111 11111100 A shifted with sign extension

An important use of shifting is multiplication and division by powers of 2. If a positive integer is left shifted k bits, the result, barring overflow, is the original number multiplied by 2^k. If a positive integer is right shifted k bits, the result is the original number divided by 2^k.

Shifting can be used to speed up certain arithmetic operations. Consider, for example, computing $18 \times n$ for some positive integer n. Because $18 \times n = 16 \times n + 2 \times n$, $16 \times n$ can be obtained by shifting a copy of n 4 bits to the left. $2 \times n$ can be obtained by shifting n 1 bit to the left. The sum of these two numbers is $18 \times n$. The multiplication has been accomplished by a move, two shifts and an addition, which is often faster than a multiplication.

Shifting negative numbers, even with sign extension, gives quite different results, however. Consider for example the one's complement number, -1. Shifted 1 bit to the left it yields -3. Another 1 bit shift to the left yields -7:

```
11111111 11111111 11111111 11111110   −1 in one's complement
11111111 11111111 11111111 11111100   −1 shifted left 1 bit = −3
11111111 11111111 11111111 11111000   −1 shifted left 2 bits = −7
```

Left shifting one's complement negative numbers does not multiply by 2. Right shifting does simulate division correctly however.

Now consider a two's complement representation of -1. Right shifted 6 bits with sign extension, it yields -1, whereas the integral part of $-1/64$ should be 0:

```
11111111 11111111 11111111 11111111   −1 in two's complement
11111111 11111111 11111111 11111111   −1 shifted right 6 bits = −1
```

Left shifting does, however, simulate multiplication by 2.

Rotate operations are useful for packing and unpacking bit sequences from words. If it is desired to test all the bits in a word, rotating the word 1 bit at a time either way successively puts each bit in the sign bit, where it can be easily tested, and also restores the word to its original value when all bits have been tested.

The 370 has eight instructions for shifting data in registers. Two lengths are provided—32 bits and 64 bits—the latter consisting of two consecutive registers, which are treated as a unit. Both left and right shifts are provided. Shifts can be categorized as arithmetic or logical. In the arithmetic shifts, the sign bit is unchanged and sign extension takes place for right shifts. In the logical shifts, all 32 or 64 bits are shifted, the sign bit may be changed, and no sign extension takes place. Shifts up to 64 bits may be specified for all eight shifts. The 370 does not have any rotate instructions.

The PDP-11 has 10 shift and rotate instructions, eight of which form a group of 1-bit shift and rotate instructions. Separate instructions are provided for word and byte, left and right, and shift and rotate. The other two (which are absent on some of the smaller models) act on 16- or 32-bit data and can perform shifts or rotates of more than one bit. Unlike the 370, the PDP-11 has a carry bit that participates in most shift and rotate instructions. The carry bit is conceptually to the left of sign bit. A right rotate of 1 bit will move the carry bit into the sign bit and load the carry bit from the rightmost bit of the word or byte being rotated. This step facilitates multiple-precision arithmetic.

The 68000 has four shift and four rotate instructions. Two shifts, ASL and ASR, are arithmetic and perform sign extension on right shifts. The other two are logical and do not sign extend. The rotates involve both the carry bit and the extend bit in various ways. The extend bit is set the same as the carry bit by arithmetic operations but is not affected by moves, Boolean instructions and certain other instructions. The Z80 has a surprisingly complete and symmetric set of shift and rotate instructions.

Both arithmetic and logical shifts in both directions are provided, as well as rotates in both directions with and without the carry bit.

Certain dyadic operations occur so frequently with particular operands that level 2 machines sometimes have monadic instructions to accomplish them quickly. Moving zero to a memory word or register is extremely common when initializing a calculation. Moving zero is, of course, a special case of the general move data instructions. For efficiency, a CLEAR operation, with only one address, the location to be cleared (i.e.; set to zero), is often provided.

Adding 1 to a register or memory word is also commonly used for counting. A monadic form of the add instruction is the increment operation, which adds 1. The negate operation is another example. Negating X is really computing $0 - X$, a dyadic subtraction but again, for efficiency, a separate NEGATE instruction is sometimes provided.

The PDP-11 and 68000 have instructions to add 1 to a word or byte, subtract 1 from a word or byte, negate a word or byte, clear a word or byte, and compare a word or byte to 0, all unnecessary in the sense that a dyadic instruction could be used but provided for reasons of efficiency.

5.4.4. Comparisons and Conditional Jumps

Nearly all programs need the ability to test their data and alter the sequence of instructions to be executed based on the results. A simple example is the square root function, $\sqrt{x}$. If x is negative the procedure gives an error message; otherwise, it computes the square root. A function *sqrt* has to test x and then jump, depending on whether it is negative or not.

A common method for doing so is to provide conditional jump (often called conditional branch) instructions that test some condition and jump to a particular memory address if the condition is met. Sometimes a bit in the instruction can be set to 1 or 0, meaning that the jump is to occur if the condition is met or the condition is not met, respectively.

The most common condition to be tested is whether a particular bit in the machine is 0 or not. If an instruction tests the sign bit of a two's complement number and jumps to LABEL if it is 1, the statements beginning at LABEL will be executed if the number was negative, and the statements following the conditional jump will be executed if it was 0 or positive. The same test made on a one's complement number will always jump to LABEL if the tested number is less than or equal to -1, and it will never jump to LABEL if the tested number is greater than or equal to 1. If the number is 0, the jump may happen or not, depending on whether it is $+0$ or -0. That is obviously rather unpleasant, because mathematically $+0 = -0$, and is, in fact, one of the strongest arguments against one's complement arithmetic and in favor of two's complement arithmetic.

Many machines have bits that are used to indicate specific conditions. For example, there may be an overflow bit that is set to 1 whenever an arithmetic operation gives an incorrect result. By testing this bit one checks for overflow on the previous arithmetic operation, so that if an overflow occurred, a jump can be made to an error routine. The 68000 even has a special, short instruction, TRAPV, which traps if the overflow bit is on. Similarly, some processors have a carry bit that is set when a carry occurs from the leftmost bit, for example, if two negative numbers are added. A carry from the leftmost bit is quite normal and should not be confused with an overflow. Testing of the carry bit is needed for multiple-precision arithmetic.

Some machines have an instruction to test the rightmost bit of a word. It allows the program to test if a (positive) number is odd or even in one instruction.

Testing for zero is important for loops and many other purposes. If all the conditional jump instructions tested only one bit, to test a particular word for 0, one would need a separate test for each bit, to ensure that none was a 1. To avoid this situation, many machines have an instruction to test a word and jump if it is zero. Of course, this solution merely passes the buck to level 1. In practice, the hardware usually contains a register, all of whose bits are ORed together, to give a single bit telling whether the register contains any 1 bits.

Comparing two words or characters to see if they are equal or, if not, which one is greater is also important, in sorting for example. To perform this test, three addresses are needed, two for the data items, and one for the address to jump to if the condition is true. Computers whose instruction format allows three addresses per instruction have no trouble but those that do not must do something to get around this problem.

One common solution is to provide an instruction that performs a comparison and sets one or more condition bits to record the result. A subsequent instruction can test the condition bits and jump if the two compared values were equal, or unequal, or if the first was greater, and so on. All four of our example machines use this approach. To compare a register to a memory word, for example, the 370 has the C instruction, the PDP-11 and 68000 the CMP instruction, and the Z80 the CP instruction. All four machines have a set of conditional jumps to test the condition code bits.

Some subtle points are involved in comparing two numbers. First, on one's complement machines $+0$ and -0 are different, for example, on a 32-bit machine,

00000000 00000000 00000000 00000000 $+0$ in one's complement
11111111 11111111 11111111 11111111 -0 in one's complement

A decision has to be made by the designers whether $+0$ and -0 are equal and, if not, which is larger. No matter which way it is decided, there are convincing arguments that the wrong decision was made. If the designers make $+0 = -0$, then the fact that a comparison yields equal does not mean that the bit patterns of the compared data items are the same. Consider a machine with a 32-bit word in which four 8-bit characters are stored. If four characters whose code is 0 are stored in a word, the word will contain 32 zeros. If four characters whose code is 255 are stored in a word, the word will contain 32 ones. If these two words compare as equal because $+0 = -0$, a text processing program may mistakenly conclude that the two words contain the same four characters.

If, on the other hand, the hardware treats -0 and $+0$ as unequal, the result of adding -1 to $+1$ and comparing the result to $+0$ may well be that they are unequal, because -1 added to $+1$ may give -0 as the result. Needless to say, this situation is highly undesirable. Two's complement machines, including all four of our examples, do not have problems with $+0$ and -0, but one's complement machines do have these troubles. The word is gradually getting out to machine architects and as a result, one's complement machines are slowly dying out.

Another subtle point relating to comparing numbers is deciding whether or not the numbers should be considered signed or not. Three-bit binary numbers can be ordered in one of two ways. From smallest to largest:

Unsigned	Signed	
000	100	(smallest)
001	101	
010	110	
011	111	
100	000	
101	001	
110	010	
111	011	(largest)

The column on the left shows the positive integers 0 to 7 in increasing order. The column on the right shows the twos complement signed integers -4 to $+3$. The answer to the question "Is 011 greater than 100?" depends on whether or not the numbers are regarded as being signed. Most machines have jump instructions for both orderings.

Machines with fewer than three addresses per instruction sometimes handle conditional jumping with an instruction that skips the next sequential instruction if the condition is met. That instruction will frequently be a jump instruction. On some machines several instructions may be skipped, instead of just one, the number to be skipped being specified in the instruction itself. The PDP-11, for example, can skip up to 127 words forward or 128 words backward. Whether one considers this a glorified skip instruction or an emaciated conditional jump instruction is a matter of taste. The 68000 B_{CC} instruction has two variants, one with an 8-bit displacement like the PDP-11, and one with a 16-bit displacement. A 4-bit field within the instruction (see format 11 in Fig. 5-22) specifies the condition to be tested.

The unconditional jump is a special case of the conditional jump in which the condition is always met.

5.4.5. Procedure Call Instructions

A procedure is a group of instructions that performs some task and that can be invoked (called) from several places in the program. The term **subroutine** is often used instead of procedure, especially when referring to assembly language programs.

When the procedure has finished its task, it must return to the statement after the call. Therefore, the return address must be transmitted to the procedure so that it knows where to return.

The return address may be placed in any of three places: memory, a register, or the stack. Far and away the worst solution is putting it in a single, fixed memory location. In this scheme, if the procedure called another procedure, the second call would cause the return address from the first one to be lost.

A slight improvement is having the procedure call instruction store the return address in the first word of the procedure, with the first executable instruction being in the second word. The procedure can then return by jumping indirectly to the first word or, if the hardware puts the opcode for jump in the first word along with the return address, jumping directly to it. The procedure may call other procedures, because each procedure has space for one return address. If the procedure calls itself, this scheme fails, because the first return address will be destroyed by the second call. The ability for a procedure to call itself, called **recursion**, is exceedingly important both for theorists and practical programmers. Furthermore, if procedure A calls procedure B, and procedure B calls procedure C, and procedure C calls procedure A (indirect recursion), this scheme also fails.

A bigger improvement is to have the procedure call instruction put the return address in a register, leaving the responsibility for storing it in a safe place to the procedure. If the procedure is recursive, it will have to put the return address in a different place each time it is called. The 370 uses this method.

The best thing for the procedure call instruction to do with the return address is to push it onto a stack. When the procedure has finished, it pops the return address off the stack and stuffs it into the program counter. If this form of procedure call is available, recursion does not cause any special problems; the return address will automatically be saved in such a way as to avoid destroying previous return addresses. The PDP-11, 68000, and Z80 all use this method. Alone among the four, the Z80 also has instructions for conditional call and conditional return, depending on condition code bits.

5.4.6. Loop Control

The need to execute a group of instructions a fixed number of times occurs frequently and thus some machines have instructions to facilitate doing this. All the schemes involve a counter that is increased or decreased by some constant once each time through the loop. The counter is also tested once each time through the loop. If a certain condition holds, the loop is terminated.

One method initializes a counter outside the loop and then immediately begins executing the loop code. The last instruction of the loop updates the counter and, if the termination condition is not yet satisfied, jumps back to the first instruction of the loop. Otherwise, the loop is finished and it falls through, executing the first instruction beyond the loop. This form of looping is characterized as test-at-the-end type looping, and is illustrated in Fig. 5-37(a).

```
                                               i := 1;

              i : = 1;
                                       1:      if i > n then goto 2;
   1:         {first statement}                {first statement}
              {second statement}               {second statement}
               .                                .
               .                                .
               .                                .
              {last statement}                 {last statement}
              i := i + 1;                       i := i + 1;
              if i <= n then goto 1;            goto 1;

   2:         {first statement after loop}  2: {first statement after loop}

                   (a)                                (b)
```

Fig. 5-37. (a) Test-at-the-end loop. (b) Test-at-the-beginning loop.

Test-at-the-end looping has the property that the loop will always be executed at least once, even if n is less than or equal to 0. Consider, as an example, a program that maintains personnel records for a company. At a certain point in the program, it is reading information about a particular employee. It reads in n, the number of children the employee has, and executes a loop n times, once per child, reading the child's name, sex, and birthday, so that the company can send him or her a birthday present, one of the company's fringe benefits. If the employee does not have any children, n will be 0 but the loop will still be executed once sending presents and giving erroneous results.

Figure 5-37(b) shows another way of performing the test that works properly even for n less than or equal to 0. Notice that the testing is different in the two cases, so that if a single level 2 instruction does both the increment and the test, the designers are forced to choose one method or the other.

Consider the code that should be produced for the Pascal statement

for $i := 1$ **to** n **do begin** ... **end**

If the compiler does not have any information about n, it must use the approach of Fig. 5-37(b) to correctly handle the case of $n \leq 0$. If, however, it can determine that $n > 0$, for example, by seeing where n is assigned, it may use the better code of Fig. 5-37(a). The FORTRAN standard formerly stated that all loops were to be executed once, to allow the more efficient code of Fig. 5-37(a) to be generated all the time. In 1977, that defect was corrected when even the FORTRAN community began to realize that having a loop statement with outlandish semantics was not a good idea, even if it did save one jump instruction per loop.

The PDP-11 has an instruction, SOB, which subtracts 1 from a counter and jumps if the result is nonzero. Although this instruction is useful for loops that count downward, it is not useful for the more common situation of counting upward. The 370 has a more general loop instruction that can add or subtract an arbitrary constant instead of only subtracting 1. The 68000 instruction DB_{CC} is roughly similar to SOB, except that it tests not only a register but also a condition specified by a 4-bit field within the instruction (format 12 in Fig. 5-22).

Although the Z80 has no general looping primitives, it does have block move (LDIR and LDDR) instructions that constitute a complete copy loop by themselves. It also has single instruction loops for searching (CPIR and CPDR), input (INIR and INDR) and output (OTIR and OTDR).

5.4.7. Input/Output

No other group of instructions exhibits as much variety from machine to machine as the I/O instructions. A basic distinction can be made between level 2 machines that have explicit I/O instructions and those that do not.

The simplest possible I/O method is the one used in some microcomputers. These microcomputers have a single input instruction and a single output instruction that selects one of the I/O devices. A single character is transferred between a fixed register in the processor and the selected I/O device. The processor must execute an explicit instruction for each and every character read or written.

The next step upward is a computer in which the CPU specifies the device, the memory address where the data are or is to be put, and the number of words or characters to be transmitted. Such a condition allows one instruction per block of data. I/O devices that transfer blocks of data to or from memory by themselves (without requiring the CPU) are called **direct memory access** devices or more commonly **DMA** devices.

The 370 is an example of a computer with a simple I/O processor, which IBM calls a channel. The IBM channel is a special-purpose computer with a limited instruction set consisting of read, write, read backward, control (e.g., rewind a tape, skip a line on the printer), sense (provides status information), and jump. The CPU performs I/O by first creating a channel program and storing it in main memory, assuming that the channel program was not already there. Then it puts the address of the channel program in the word at main memory location 72. Finally, the CPU executes a START I/O instruction whose address field specifies the channel and I/O device to be started. The channel then fetches the address of its program from memory location 72, puts that address in its program counter, and begins executing its channel program. The various memory words involved are illustrated in Fig. 5-38.

A channel program consists of one or more 64-bit instructions for the channel. Each instruction contains an 8-bit opcode telling which operation is to be performed (e.g., READ, WRITE, JUMP); a 24-bit main memory address, telling where the data are to be read from or written into; and a count, telling how many bytes are to be transferred. In addition, some miscellaneous bits specify such items as no data transmission (good for skipping a record on a tape) and "stop the channel after this instruction is complete." Once the START I/O instruction has been executed, the CPU is free to continue computing in parallel with the channel.

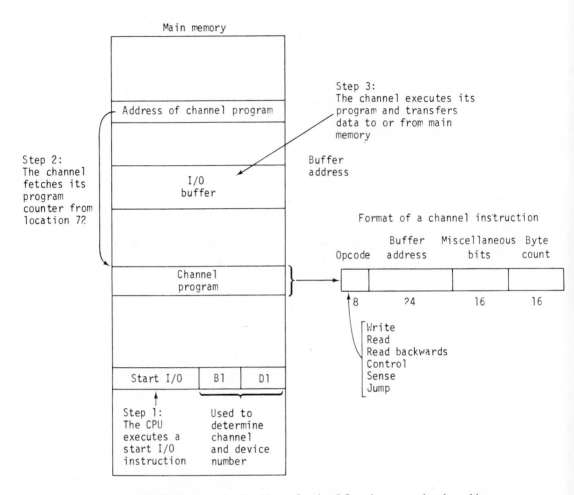

Fig. 5-38. The steps involved in performing I/O at the conventional machine level on the IBM 370.

In addition to the START I/O instruction, the 370 CPU has a few other I/O instructions. The HALT I/O instruction forcibly stops all activity in the selected channel. The TEST I/O and TEST CHANNEL instructions are used to determine the current status of I/O activity.

Level 2 machines that have no explicit I/O instructions generally use memory-mapped I/O. When this technique is used, as on the PDP-11 and 68000, for example, certain memory addresses are allocated as device control, status, and buffer registers. Each device register has a unique address. To perform I/O, the CPU writes control information into these registers. Each device constantly monitors its control registers and when it sees that the CPU has written a command to it, decodes and carries the command out. The advantage of memory-mapped I/O is that no special I/O instructions are needed: the full power of the instruction set and all the addressing modes can be used to access the device registers. The disadvantage is that it wastes a little bit of address space.

As an example of the operation of the PDP-11 I/O system, consider the standard line printer, which is probably the simplest PDP-11 peripheral. Associated with the printer are two registers: the status register, at address 777514 (octal), and the buffer register, at address 777516 (octal). These registers are shown in Fig. 5-39(a). Three of the bits in the status register are used; the other 13 are ignored. When bit 7 is a 1, the printer is ready to receive a character. The program provides the character to be printed by moving it to the low-order half of the buffer register using an ordinary MOVE or MOVB instruction. As long as the READY bit stays on, the program can continue moving characters to the buffer register. When the READY bit goes off, the program must cease feeding data to the printer to give it time to print what it has already received. Bit 6 can be set by the program to request an interrupt when the READY bit comes on again, so the program need not keep inspecting it. Bit 15 is set by the hardware when something is wrong, such as no power or no paper.

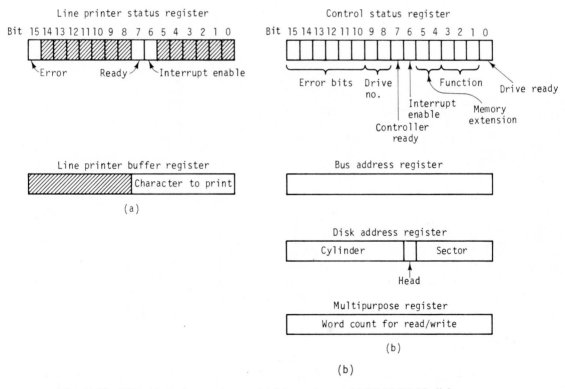

Fig. 5-39. PDP-11 device registers. (a) Line printer. (b) RL01/RL02 disk.

More complicated I/O devices require more status registers. The RL01/RL02 disk, for example, uses a total of four registers containing a variety of fields, as shown in Fig. 5-39(b). Each register has a unique memory address by which the program can read it or store into it. More sophisticated disks can have more than a dozen device registers with more than 100 fields. The RL01/RL02 control register provides status about the controller and drives, including error reporting. It also has a field which the program loads with a function code to indicate the operation desired. The meaning of the other three registers depends on the function code loaded. For READ and WRITE, the other three contain the memory address to read into or write from, the disk address, and the word count. For SEEK, WRITE CHECK, and other operations, they have somewhat different meanings.

The Z80 has explicit I/O instructions, although system designers are free to do I/O with memory mapping if they choose, as we did in Chap. 3. When memory mapping is not used, the Z80 still has (8-bit-wide) device registers, only now they are not part of the memory address space. Instead, each device register has a number from 0 to 255, called an **I/O port**.

The simplest I/O instructions are IN A,(N), which copies one byte from port N to the A register, and OUT (N),A, which copies one byte from the A register to port N. The byte transferred may be either data, control information, or status information, depending on the port selected. Slightly more complex are IN R,(C) and OUT (C),R, which take the port number from the C register. The next step up are INI, IND, OUTI, and OUTD. All these instructions expect a memory address in HL, a count in B, and a port number in C. First, a normal IN or OUT is done, copying a byte to or from the memory location pointed to by HL. Then HL is incremented or decremented by 1 and B is decremented by 1. The final I/O instructions are INIR, INDR, OTIR, and OTDR, which are the same as the previous four, except that they keep going until B = 0. In effect, each one does a block transfer to or from memory. This transfer is not DMA, however, because the CPU is occupied the entire time. Nevertheless, it is faster and takes up less space in memory than an explicitly programmed loop to do the same job.

5.5. FLOW OF CONTROL

Flow of control refers to the sequence in which instructions are executed. In general, successively executed instructions are fetched from consecutive memory locations. Procedure calls cause the flow of control to be altered, stopping the procedure currently executing and starting the called procedure. Coroutines are related to procedures and cause similar alterations in the flow of control. Traps and interrupts also cause the flow of control to be altered when special conditions occur. All these topics will be discussed in the following sections.

5.5.1. Sequential Flow of Control and Jumps

Most instructions do not alter the flow of control. After an instruction is executed, the one following it in memory is fetched and executed. After each instruction, the program counter is increased by the number of memory locations in that instruction. If observed over an interval of time that is long compared to the average instruction time, the program counter is approximately a linear function of time, increasing by the average instruction length per average instruction time. Stated another way, the dynamic order in which the processor actually executes the instructions is the same as the order in which they appear on the program listing.

If a program contains jumps, this simple relation between the order in which instructions appear in memory and the order in which they are executed is no longer true. When jumps are present, the program counter is no longer a monotonically increasing function of time, as shown in Fig. 5-40(b). As a result, it becomes difficult to visualize the instruction execution sequence from the program listing. When programmers have trouble keeping track of the sequence in which the processor will execute the instructions, they are prone to make errors. This observation led Dijkstra (1968a) to write a then controversial letter entitled "GO TO Statement Considered Harmful," in which he suggested avoiding GO TO statements. Since that time languages without GO TO statements have become popular. Of course, these programs compile down to level 2 programs that may contain many jumps, because the implementation of IF, WHILE, and other high-level control structures require jumping around.

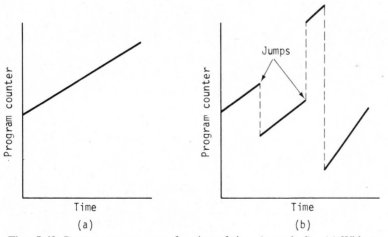

Fig. 5-40. Program counter as a function of time (smoothed). (a) Without jumps. (b) With jumps.

Jumps are frequently difficult to avoid when programming in a language lacking structuring statements such as IF ... THEN ... ELSE and WHILE ... DO .... Relying on jumps as the primary method of controlling the flow of execution makes it difficult, if not impossible, to write error-free, well-structured programs. For this and other reasons, programming at the conventional machine level is becoming obsolete.

5.5.2. Procedures

The most important technique for structuring programs is the procedure. From one point of view, a procedure call alters the flow of control just as a jump does, but unlike the jump, when finished performing its task, it returns control to the statement or instruction following the call.

However, from another point of view, a procedure body can be regarded as defining a new instruction on a higher level. From this standpoint, a procedure call can be thought of as a single instruction, even though the procedure may be quite complicated. Similarly, a person programming at level 2 can certainly regard the multiplication instruction as a single instruction, even though it is carried out by an interpreter running at level 1 as a large number of successive steps.

By writing a collection of procedures, a programmer can define a new level with a new, larger, and more convenient instruction set. Programs for this new level consist of sequences of instructions, some of which are procedure calls and some of which are the original level 2 instructions. Associated with the execution of a program at this new level is a "virtual program counter," which points to the current instruction (counting a procedure execution as a single instruction) and increases monotonically in time. The direct correspondence between the execution sequence and the listing sequence makes it easy to understand what the program does.

In Sec. 5.4.5, we mentioned recursive procedures—that is, procedures that call themselves. Now we will give an example of one. The "Towers of Hanoi" is an ancient problem that has a simple solution involving recursion. The problem requires three pegs, on the first of which sit a series of n concentric disks, each of which is smaller in diameter than the disk directly below it. The second and third pegs are initially empty. The object is to transfer all the disks to peg 3, one disk at a time, but at no time may a larger disk rest on a smaller one. Figure 5-41 shows the initial configuration for $n = 5$ disks.

The solution of moving n disks from peg 1 to peg 3 consists first of moving $n - 1$ disks from peg 1 to peg 2, then moving 1 disk from peg 1 to peg 3, then moving $n - 1$ disks from peg 2 to peg 3 (see Fig. 5-42). To solve the problem we need a procedure to move k disks from peg i to peg j. Whenever this procedure is called, by

$$towers\,(n,\ i,\ j\,)$$

the solution is printed out. The procedure first tests to see if $n = 1$. If so, the solution is trivial, just move the one disk from i to j. If $n \neq 1$, the solution consists of three parts as discussed above, each being a recursive procedure call.

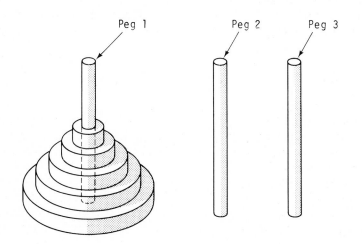

Fig. 5-41. Initial configuration for the Towers of Hanoi problem for five disks.

The complete solution is shown in Fig. 5-43. The call

$$towers\,(3,\ 1,\ 3)$$

to solve the problem of Fig. 5-42 will generate three more calls because n is not 1, namely

$$towers\,(2,\ 1,\ 2)$$
$$towers\,(1,\ 1,\ 3)$$
$$towers\,(2,\ 2,\ 3)$$

The first and third will, in turn, also generate three more calls, making seven generated calls in all.

In order to have recursive procedures, we need a stack to store the parameters. Each time a procedure is called, a block of memory called a **stack frame** is reserved on the stack for the parameters, return address, and local variables, if any. The frame most recently created is the current frame. In our examples, the stack always grows downward, from high memory addresses to low ones. We have chosen this convention because the PDP-11, 68000, and Z80 all use it; the 370 is neutral. A push, therefore, decreases the stack pointer by the word size. On the PDP-11, 68000, and Z80, the hardware stack pointer can be used directly. On the 370, one of the base registers must be chosen as stack pointer. For our examples, we will use general register 6.

In addition to the stack pointer, which points to the top of the stack (lowest numerical address), it is often convenient to have a local base pointer, LB, which points to a fixed location within the frame. Figure 5-44 shows the stack frame for machine with a 16-bit word such as the PDP-11. The stack begins at 1000 and grows downward toward address 0. The original call to *towers* pushes n, i, and j, onto the

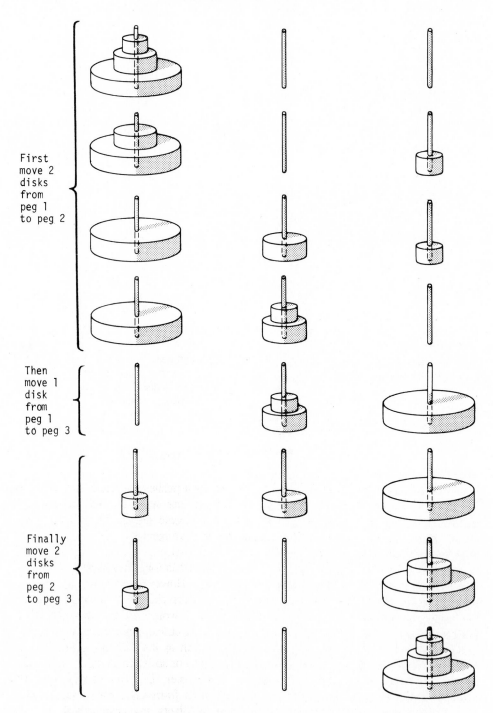

Fig. 5-42. The seven steps required to solve the Towers of Hanoi for three disks.

procedure *towers* (*n*, *i*, *j* : *integer*);
{ Towers of Hanoi:

n is the number of disks
i is the starting peg
j is the goal peg
$k = 6 - i - j$ is the other peg

To move the *n* disks from *i* to *j* first check to see if *n* is 1.
If so, the solution is just one move . If not, decompose the problem
into three subproblems and solve them in sequence :

   1. Move $n - 1$ disks from *i* to *k*
   2. Move 1 disk from *i* to *j*
   3. Move $n - 1$ disks from *k* to *j* }

var *k* : *integer* ;

begin
  if $n = 1$
    then *writeln* ('*Move a disk from peg*', i, ' *to peg* ', j)
    else
      begin
        $k := 6 - i - j$;   {compute the number of the third peg}
        towers ($n-1$, *i*, *k*);   {move $n - 1$ disks from *i* to *k*}
        towers (1, *i*, *j*);   {move 1 disk from *i* to *j*}
        towers ($n-1$, *k*, *j*)   {move $n - 1$ disks from *k* to *j*}
      end
end; { towers }

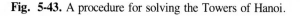

Fig. 5-43. A procedure for solving the Towers of Hanoi.

stack, and then executes a JSR (CALL) instruction that pushes the return address onto
the stack, at address 994. On entry, the called procedure stores the old value of LB
on the stack, and then advances the stack pointer to allocate storage for the local variables. With only one 16-bit local variable, SP is decremented by 2. The situation
after these things have been done is shown in Fig. 5-44(a).

    With this background, we can now explain what LB is for. In principle, variables
could be referenced by giving their offsets from SP. However, as words are pushed
onto the stack and popped from the stack, these offsets change. Although in some
cases the compiler can keep track of the number of words on the stack and thus
correct the offsets, in some cases it cannot, and in all cases considerable administration is required. Furthermore, on some machines, such as the Z80, accessing a variable at a known distance from SP requires a half dozen or so instructions.

    Consequently, many compilers use a second register, LB, for referencing both
local variables and parameters because their distances from LB do not change with
pushes and pops. Actual parameters have positive offsets and local variables have

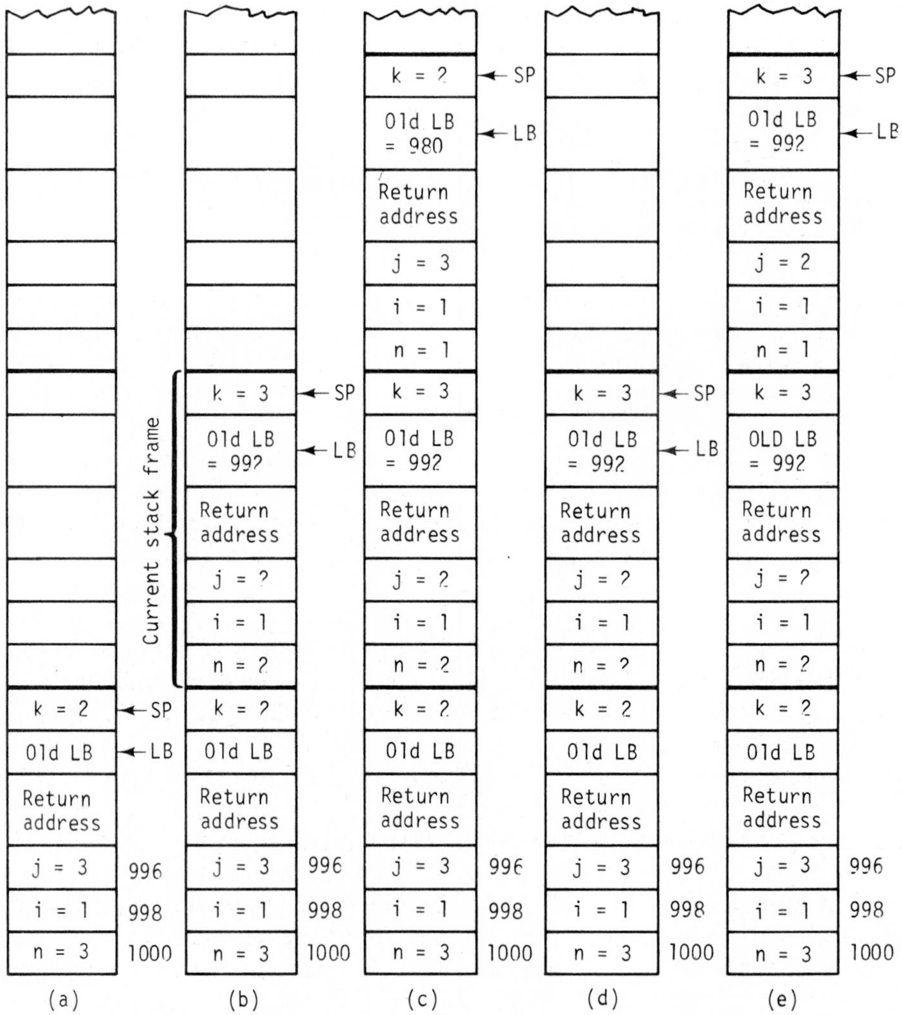

Fig. 5-44. The stack at several points during the execution of Fig. 5-43.

negative offsets from LB. The first thing a procedure must do when called is save the previous LB (so it can be restored at procedure exit), copy SP into LB to create the new LB, and advance SP to reserve space for the local variables. This code is called the **procedure prolog**. One of the most important characteristics of any computer is how short and fast it can make the prolog and the analogous code for returning. If the prolog is long and slow, procedure calls will be expensive. Programmers who worship at the altar of efficiency will learn to avoid writing many short procedures and write large, monolithic, unstructured programs instead.

Now let us get back to the Towers of Hanoi problem. Each procedure call adds a new frame to the stack and each procedure return removes a frame from the stack. In order to illustrate the use of a stack in implementing recursive procedures, we will trace the calls starting with

$$towers\,(3,\ 1,\ 3)$$

Figure 5-44(a) shows the stack just after this call has been made. The procedure first tests to see if $n = 1$, and on discovering that $n = 3$, makes the call

$$towers\,(2,\ 1,\ 2)$$

After this call is completed the stack is as shown in Fig. 5-44(b), and the procedure starts again at the beginning (a called procedure always starts at the beginning). This time the test for $n = 1$ fails again and the call

$$towers\,(1,\ 1,\ 3)$$

is made. The stack then is as shown in Fig. 5-44(c) and the program counter points to the start of the procedure. This time the test succeeds and a line is printed. Next, the procedure returns by removing one stack frame, resetting LB and SP to Fig. 5-44(d). It then continues executing at the return address, which is the second call:

$$towers\,(1,\ 1,\ 2)$$

This adds a new frame to the stack as shown in Fig. 5-44(e). Another line is printed; after the return a frame is removed from the stack. The procedure calls continue in this way until original call completes execution and the frame of Fig. 5-44(a) is removed from the stack.

Several ways exist for a procedure to pass parameters to a procedure it calls. One way is to put them in the registers. This idea is fine provided that there are enough registers and provided that the called procedure copies the parameters to the stack before beginning execution. A simpler method is to have the calling procedure put the parameters on the stack itself in the first place. The instructions required to call a procedure and pass it parameters are known as the **calling sequence**.

Figure 5-45 shows the program of Fig. 5-43 "hand compiled" to the assembly language of the 370, PDP-11, 68000, and Z80. An attempt has been made to have the assembly correspond closely to the Pascal text rather than optimize it. The four example procedures should be studied in the order Z80 first, then 370, PDP-11 and finally 68000 to see why compiler writers often have such strong opinions about machine architectures. The Z80 code is not very elegant or efficient and the 370 code is not much better, although in fairness to the 370, if we ran the stack from low addresses to high ones and did some optimizing it would improve. The PDP-11 code is much more pleasant, because a register, constant, local variable or parameter can be pushed onto the stack in a single instruction. The 68000 is pure luxury; not only does it have the excellent stack instructions of the PDP-11 but it even has a single instruction (LINK) that carries out the entire prolog and special instructions for moving small constants about.

A few comments about Fig. 5-45 may be helpful at this point. We have chosen to use 16-bit words for the Z80 and PDP-11 and 32-bit words for the 370 and 68000. The Z80 version really uses only 8-bit numbers for i, j, and n, but stores them as 16-bit numbers on the stack because the Z80's push and pop instructions push and pop 16-bit quantities. In any event, i and j are certainly less than 256, and running *towers* with $n > 255$ requires more machine time than most readers can afford anyway.

A pleasant feature of the Z80 is its PUSH and POP instructions, which are only 1 byte long. A much less pleasant feature is its lack of an instruction to increment SP after a procedure call to remove the parameters. One way to add k to SP is to execute k INC SP instructions. Another way is to pop $k/2$ words to a scratch register (assuming that k is even). For large k neither of these is attractive and a much more complicated instruction sequence is required. Fortunately, for us, for our program $k \leq 6$, we will just use POP DE to remove the parameters.

The 370 version has a few noteworthy features, the most important of which comes from the 370's inability to have negative offsets from a base register. If we were to use the model of Fig. 5-44(a), it would not be possible to access the local variable because it is below LB. We solve this problem by having LB point to the last local instead of the first one. With LB in register 13 and a 32-bit word, n is loaded into register 1 using L 1,20(19) because n is five words above LB. Another point about the 370 version is the lack of a PUSH instruction. Instead, we simulate PUSH by decrementing SP (register 14) by 4 and then indirecting through it. If the stack ran upward instead of downward and the compiler kept track of a simulated SP, it would not be necessary to change SP until the last parameter had been pushed.

The PDP-11 and 68000 versions are similar and fairly straightforward and require little comment.

The secret of the stack's success is a procedure's ability to automatically access a different set of parameters, local variables (if any), and a return address every time it is called, even if previous calls are not yet finished. If fixed memory locations are used to store a procedure's parameters, local variables, and return address, the procedure cannot be called recursively.

Recursion has many applications in computer science, one of the most important being in compiler writing. A large number of compilers use recursion heavily. For example, some compilers have a procedure for processing each construction in the language they compile, such as declarations, expressions, variables, assignment statements and IF statements. An expression is made up of a series of terms, such as

$$a*b*c, \quad y/z, \quad \text{or} \quad r*s/t$$

separated by addition and subtraction operators. The procedure *expression* may call the procedure *term* to help it. An element of a term may be a parenthesized expression, as in $a + 3*(b + c + d)$, therefore, the procedure *expression* may call the procedure *term* which may then call *expression*. This situation is clearly recursive and it is quite common.

5.5.3. Coroutines

In the usual calling sequence, there is a clear distinction between the calling procedure and called procedure. Consider a procedure A, which calls a procedure B. Procedure B computes for a while and then returns to A. At first sight you might consider this situation symmetric, because neither A nor B is a main program, both being procedures. (Procedure A may have been called by the main program but that is irrelevant.) Furthermore, first control is transferred from A to B —the call—and later control is transferred from B to A —the return.

The asymmetry arises from the fact that when control passes from A to B, procedure B begins executing at the beginning; when B returns to A, execution starts not at the beginning of A but at the statement following the call. If A runs for a while and calls B again, execution starts at the beginning of B again, not the statement following the previous return. If, in the course of running, A calls B many times, B starts at the beginning all over again each and every time, whereas A never starts over again, as illustrated in Fig. 5-46.

This difference is reflected in the method by which control is passed between A and B. When A calls B, it uses the procedure call instruction, which puts the return address (i.e., the address of the statement following the call) somewhere useful, for example, on top of the stack. It then puts the address of B into the program counter to complete the call. When B returns, it does not use the call instruction but instead it uses the return instruction, which simply pops the return address from the stack and puts it into the program counter.

Sometimes it is useful to have two procedures A and B, each of which calls the other as a procedure. When B returns to A, it jumps to the statement following the call to B, as above. When A transfers control to B, it goes not to the beginning (except the first time) but to the statement following the most recent "return," that is, the most recent call of A, as shown in Fig. 5-47. Two procedures, each of which regards the other as a procedure (in the sense that it is called, performs some work, and then returns to the statement following the call), are called **coroutines**.

Neither the usual call nor the usual return instruction will suffice to call coroutines, because the address to jump to comes from the stack like a return, but unlike a return, the coroutine call itself puts a return address somewhere for the subsequent return to it. It would be nice if there were an instruction to exchange the top of the stack with the program counter. In detail, this instruction would first pop the old return address off the stack into a temporary internal register, then push the program counter onto the stack, and finally, transfer the contents of the temporary register into the program counter. Because one word is popped off the stack and one word is pushed onto the stack, the stack pointer does not change. A coroutine calling sequence would be first initialized by pushing the address of one of the coroutines onto the stack. A coroutine call instruction is sometimes called **resume**. It does, in fact, exist on some level 2 machines in the form described here. Figure 5-48 illustrates RESUME.

```
TOWERS:     PUSH    IX              ; BEGIN PROLOG. SAVE OLD LB (IX) ON STACK
            LD      (TEMP),SP       ; START COPYING SP TO LB
            LD      IX,(TEMP)       ; FINISH COPYING SP TO LB
            PUSH    HL              ; ADVANCE SP TO ALLOCATE LOCALS; END PROLOG
            LD      A,(IX+8)        ; FETCH N INTO A TO COMPARE TO 1
            CP      1               ; IF N = 1 THEN . . .
            JP      NZ,RECUR        ; IF N IS NOT 1, GO TO ELSE PART
            LD      HL,FORMAT       ; HL = ADDRESS OF FORMAT STRING
            PUSH    HL              ; PUSH FORMAT
            LD      L,(IX+6)        ; L = I
            PUSH    HL              ; PUSH I
            LD      L,(IX+4)        ; L = J
            PUSH    HL              ; PUSH J
            CALL    WRITELN         ; PRINT THE "MOVE A DISK . . . " MESSAGE
            POP     DE              ; 3 POPS IS FASTEST WAY TO REMOVE THE PARAMS
            POP     DE              ; REMOVE SECOND PARAMETER
            POP     DE              ; REMOVE LAST PARAMETER
            JP      DONE            ; EXIT PROCEDURE
RECUR:      LD      A,6             ; START COMPUTING K = 6 − I − J
            SUB     (IX+6)          ; A = 6 − I
            SUB     (IX+4)          ; A = 6 − I − J
            LD      (IX−2),A        ; K = 6 − I − J
            LD      L,(IX+8)        ; STARTING WORKING ON TOWERS(N−1, I, K)
            DEC     L               ; L = N − 1
            PUSH    HL              ; PUSH FIRST PARAMETER = N − 1
            LD      L,(IX+6)        ; L = I
            PUSH    HL              ; PUSH SECOND PARAMETER = I
            LD      L,(IX−2)        ; L = K
            PUSH    HL              ; PUSH THIRD PARAMETER = K
            CALL    TOWERS          ; CALL TOWERS(N − 1, I, K)
            POP     DE              ; REMOVE THE PARAMETERS ONE
            POP     DE              ; BY
            POP     DE              ; ONE
            LD      HL,1            ; START WORKING ON TOWERS(1, I, J)
            PUSH    HL              ; PUSH FIRST PARAMETER = 1
            LD      L,(IX+6)        ; L = I
            PUSH    HL              ; PUSH SECOND PARAMETER = I
            LD      L,(IX+4)        ; L = J
            PUSH    HL              ; PUSH THIRD PARAMETER = J
            CALL    TOWERS          ; CALL TOWERS (1, I, J)
            POP     DE              ; REMOVE THE PARAMETERS
            POP     DE              ; BY
            POP     DE              ; ONE
            LD      L,(IX+8)        ; START WORKING ON TOWERS(N−1, K, J)
            DEC     L               ; L = N − 1
            PUSH    HL              ; PUSH FIRST PARAMETER = N − 1
            LD      L,(IX−2)        ; L = K
            PUSH    HL              ; PUSH SECOND PARAMETER = K
            LD      L,(IX+4)        ; L = J
            PUSH    HL              ; PUSH THIRD PARAMETER = J
            CALL    TOWERS          ; CALL TOWERS(N−1, K, J)
            POP     DE              ; REMOVE THE PARAMETERS
            POP     DE              ; BY
            POP     DE              ; ONE
DONE:       POP     DE              ; REMOVE THE LOCAL VARIABLES
            POP     IX              ; RESTORE LB AS IT WAS PRIOR TO CALL
            RET                     ; RETURN
```

Fig. 5-45(a). Towers of Hanoi in Z80 assembly language.

TOWERS	S	14,=F'12'	BEGIN PROLOG. ADVANCE SP
	ST	15,8(14)	STORE RETURN ADDRESS ON THE STACK
	ST	13,4(14)	STORE OLD LB
	LR	13,14	END PROLOG. LB = SP
	L	0,20(13)	FETCH N
	C	0,=F'1'	COMPARE N TO 1
	BNE	RECUR	IF N IS NOT 1, GO TO ELSE PART
	L	0,16(13)	REG 0 = I
	L	1,12(13)	REG 1 = J
	L	2=A(FORMAT)	REG 2 = ADDRESS OF FORMAT
	S	14,=F'12'	ADVANCE SP BY 3 WORDS
	ST	0.8(14)	PUSH I
	ST	1,4(14)	PUSH J
	ST	2,0(14)	PUSH ADDRESS OF FORMAT
	L	12=A(WRITELN)	REG 12 = ADDRESS OF WRITELN
	BALR	15,12	JUMP INDIRECT TO 12, PUT RETURN ADDR IN 15
	A	14,=F'12'	REMOVE THE PARAMETERS FROM THE STACK
	B	DONE	EXIT PROCEDURE
RECUR	L	0,=F'6'	START COMPUTING 6 − I − J
	S	0,16(13)	REG 0 = 6 − I
	S	0,12(13)	REG 0 = 6 − I − J
	ST	0,0(13)	K = 6 − I − J
	L	0,20(13)	START WORKING ON TOWERS(N−1, I, K)
	S	0,=F'1'	REG 0 = N − 1
	L	1,16(13)	REG 1 = I
	L	2,0(13)	REG 2 = K
	S	14,=F'12'	ADVANCE SP BY 3 WORDS
	ST	0,8(14)	PUSH N−1
	ST	1,4(14)	PUSH I
	ST	2,0(14)	PUSH K
	L	12,=A(TOWERS)	REG 12 = ADDRESS OF TOWERS
	BALR	15,12	JUMP INDIRECT TO 12, PUT RETURN ADDR IN 15
	A	14,=F'12'	REMOVE THE PARAMETERS FROM THE STACK
	L	0,=F'1'	START WORKING ON TOWERS(1, I, J)
	L	1,16(13)	REG 1 = I
	L	2,12(13)	REG 2 = J
	S	14,=F'12'	ADVANCE SP BY 3 WORDS
	ST	0,8(14)	PUSH 1
	ST	1,4(14)	PUSH I
	ST	2,0(14)	PUSH J
	L	12,=A(TOWERS)	REG 12 = ADDRESS OF TOWERS
	BALR	15,12	CALL TOWERS(1, I, J)
	A	14,=F'12'	REMOVE THE PARAMETERS FROM THE STACK
	L	0,20(13)	START WORKING ON TOWERS(N − 1, K, J)
	S	-,=F'1'	REG 0 = N − 1
	L	1,0(13)	REG 1 = K
	L	2,12(13)	REG 2 = J
	S	14,=F'12'	ADVANCE SP BY 3 WORDS
	ST	0,8(14)	PUSH N−1
	ST	1,4(14)	PUSH K
	ST	2,0(14)	PUSH J
	L	12,=A(TOWERS)	REG 12 = ADDRESS OF TOWERS
	BALR	15,12	CALL TOWERS(N−1, K, J)
	A	14,=F'12'	REMOVE THE PARAMETERS FROM THE STACK
DONE	L	15,8(13)	REG 15 = RETURN ADDRESS
	L	13,4(13)	RESTORE OLD LB
	A	14,=F'12'	RESTORE SP TO PREVIOUS VALUE
	BR	15	RETURN

Fig. 5-45(b). Towers of Hanoi in 370 assembly language.

```
TOWERS:    MOV    R0,-(SP)          / BEGIN PROLOG. SAVE LB (IN R0) ON STACK
           MOV    SP,R0             / CURRENT SP BECOMES NEW LB
           SUB    $2,SP             / END PROLOG. ALLOCATE STORAGE FOR LOCALS
           CMP    8(R0),$1          / IF N = 1 THEN . . .
           BNE    RECUR             / N IS NOT 1; GO TO ELSE PART
           MOV    $FORMAT,-(SP)     / PASS FORMAT STRING TO PRINT ROUTINE
           MOV    6(R0),-(SP)       / PASS I TO THE PRINT ROUTINE
           MOV    4(R0),-(SP)       / PASS J TO THE PRINT ROUTINE
           JSR    PC,WRITELN        / PRINT THE ''MOVE A DISK . . . '' MESSAGE
           ADD    $6,SP             / REMOVE THE PARAMETERS FROM THE STACK
           BR     DONE              / EXIT FROM PROCEDURE
RECUR:     MOV    $6,R1             / START COMPUTING K = 6 - I - J
           SUB    6(R0),R1          / R1 = 6 - I
           SUB    4(R0),R1          / R1 = 6 - I - J
           MOV    R1,-2(R0)         / K = 6 - I - J
           MOV    8(R0),R1          / START WORKING ON TOWERS(N-1, I, K)
           DEC    R1                / R1 = N - 1
           MOV    R1,-(SP)          / PUSH FIRST PARAMETER = N - 1
           MOV    (R0),-(SP)        / PUSH SECOND PARAMETER = I
           MOV    -2(R0),-(SP)      / PUSH THIRD PARAMETER = K
           JSR    PC,TOWERS         / CALL TOWERS(N-1, I, K)
           ADD    $6,SP             / REMOVE THE PARAMETERS FROM THE STACK
           MOV    $1,-(SP)          / START WORKING ON TOWERS(1, I, J)
           MOV    6(R0),-SP         / PUSH SECOND PARAMETER = I
           MOV    4(R0),-(SP)       / PUSH THIRD PARAMETER = J
           JSR    PC,TOWERS         / CALL TOWERS(1, I, J)
           ADD    $6,SP             / REMOVE THE PARAMETERS FROM THE STACK
           MOV    8(R0),R1          / START WORKING ON TOWERS(N-1, K, J)
           DEC    R1                / R1 = N - 1
           MOV    R1,-(SP)          / PUSH FIRST PARAMETER = N - 1
           MOV    -2(R0),-(SP)      / PUSH SECOND PARAMETER = K
           MOV    4(R0),-(SP)       / PUSH THIRD PARAMETER = J
           JSR    PC,TOWERS         / CALL TOWERS(N-1, K, J)
           ADD    $6,SP             / REMOVE THE PARAMETERS FROM THE STACK
DONE:      ADD    $2,SP             / REMOVE THE LOCAL VARIABLES FROM THE STACK
           MOV    (SP)+,R0          / RESTORE LB AS IT WAS PRIOR TO THIS CALL
           RTS    PC                / RETURN TO CALLER
```

Fig. 5-45(c). Towers of Hanoi in PDP-11 assembly language.

TOWERS:	LINK	A0,#-4	; PROLOG. STACK LB (A0), COPY SP TO LB, DECR SP
	MOVEQ	#1,D0	; IF N = 1 THEN . . .
	CMP.L	16(A0),D0	; COMPARE N TO 1. THE SUFFIX .L MEANS LONG
	BNE	RECUR	; IF N IS NOT 1, GO TO ELSE PART
	MOVE.L	#FORMAT,-(SP)	; FORMAT STRING
	MOVE.L	12(A0),-(SP)	; PUSH I ONTO THE STACK
	MOVE.L	8(A0),-(SP)	; PUSH J ONTO THE STACK
	JSR	WRITELN	; PRINT THE ''MOVE A DISK . . . '' MESSAGE
	ADDI.L	#12,SP	; REMOVE THE PARAMETERS FROM THE STACK
	BRA	DONE	; EXIT PROCEDURE
RECUR:	MOVEQ	#6,D0	; START COMPUTING K = $-$ I $-$ J
	SUB.L	12(A0),D0	; D0 = 6 $-$ I
	SUB.L	8(A0),D0	; D0 = 6 $-$ I $-$ J
	MOVE.L	D0,-4(A0)	; K = 6 $-$ I $-$ J
	MOVE.L	16(A0),D0	; START WORKING ON TOWERS(N$-$1, I, K)
	SUBQ.L	#1,D0	; D0 = N $-$ 1
	MOVE.L	D0,-(SP)	; PUSH FIRST PARAMETER = N $-$ 1
	MOVE.L	12(A0),-(SP)	; PUSH SECOND PARAMETER = I
	MOVE.L	-4(A0),-(SP)	; PUSH THIRD PARAMETER = K
	JSR	TOWERS	; CALL TOWERS(N$-$1, I, K)
	ADDI.L	#12,SP	; REMOVE THE PARAMETERS FROM THE STACK
	MOVE.L	#1,-(SP)	; START WORKING ON TOWERS(1, I, J)
	MOVE.L	12(A0),-(SP)	; PUSH SECOND PARAMETER = I
	MOVE.L	8(A0),-(SP)	; PUSH THIRD PARAMETER = J
	JSR	TOWERS	; CALL TOWERS(1, I, J)
	ADDI.L	#12,SP	; REMOVE THE PARAMETERS FROM THE STACK
	MOVE.L	16(A0),D0	; START WORKING ON TOWERS(N$-$1, K, J)
	SUBQ.L	#1,D0	; D0 = N $-$ 1
	MOVE.L	D0,-(SP)	; PUSH FIRST PARAMETER = N $-$ 1
	MOVE.L	-4(A0),-(SP)	; PUSH SECOND PARAMETER = K
	MOVE.L	8(A0),-(SP)	; PUSH THIRD PARAMETER = J
	JSR	TOWERS	; CALL TOWERS(N$-$1, K, J)
	ADDI.L	#12,SP	; REMOVE THE PARAMETERS FROM THE STACK
DONE:	UNLK	A0	; COPY A0 TO SP, THEN POP NEW A0
	RTS		

Fig. 5-45(d).   Towers of Hanoi in 68000 assembly language.

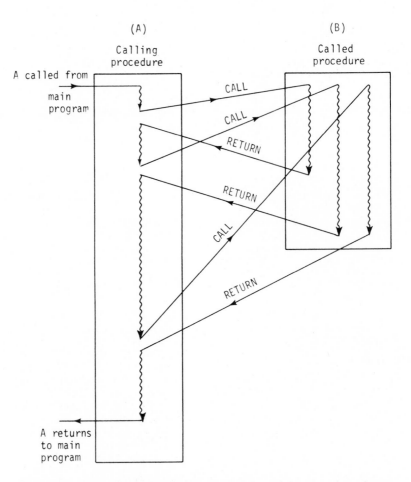

Fig. 5-46. When a procedure is called, execution of the procedure always begins at the first statement of the procedure.

The PDP-11 instruction

$$\text{JSR PC, *(SP)+}$$

performs a swap of the program counter and top of the stack. First, the mode 3, register 6 destination is evaluated. This evaluation specifies the jump address indirectly from the top of the stack and then pops the address off the stack. Next the instruction executes, pushing the program counter onto the stack.

Coroutine calls can be achieved on the 370 using the BALR I,J instruction, which calls the routine whose address is in register I and leaves the return address in register J. The called routine should return using BALR J,I. The 68000 and Z80 cannot call coroutines in a single instruction.

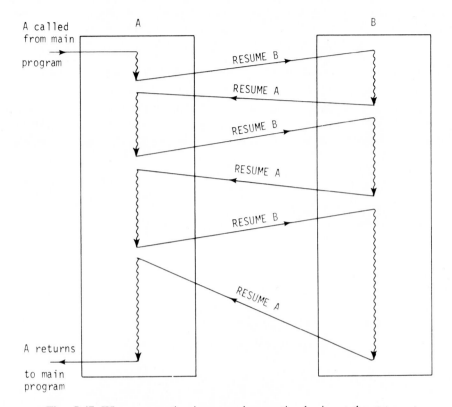

Fig. 5-47. When a coroutine is resumed, execution begins at the statement where it left off the previous time, not at the beginning.

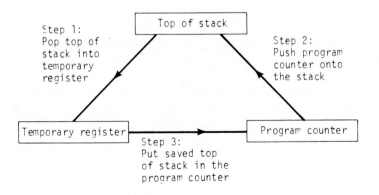

Fig. 5-48. Operation of the RESUME instruction.

As an example of the use of coroutines, consider a very advanced programming package that provides automatic program documentation. At any place in the program, the programmer may insert a comment preceded and followed by #. The program is used by the compiler to produce the object program. The comments are used by the documentation system to produce the manual. The compiler ignores the comments and the documentation system ignores the program. To make the problem interesting we will assume that the documentation part is very clever and parses all the comments to make sure that there are no grammatical errors, because programming manual writers seem to have great difficulties with the English language. A sample input is shown below.

  .
  .
  .

if *seats* = 350 # if the plane is full#
  then
    begin
      full = 1; #set a flag#
      NewPlane #request another aircraft#
    end
  else *reserve(passenger);* #otherwise give this person a seat#

  .
  .
  .

The package described can be written as two coroutines—one for parsing the program and one for parsing the English. The coroutine for the program, the compiler, begins reading the input, parsing as it goes. Eventually, it comes to the first comment symbol, #. At this point it wants to get rid of the comment so that it can continue parsing. To get rid of the comment, the compiler calls the documentation coroutine to skip the comment.

The documentation package begins running and parses the comment. Eventually, it runs across the comment symbol. From its point of view, the program text is to be ignored, so it resumes the compiler to skip the program text. The compiler will be restarted with all its variables and internal pointers intact, from the point it left off, not the beginning. The English parser may be in a complicated state at this point; it is essential that when the compiler has eaten the next piece of program text, the English parser is restarted in the state it was in when it resumed the compiler.

It is worth noting that to implement coroutines, multiple stacks are needed, because each coroutine can also call procedures in the usual way, in addition to making coroutine calls.

5.5.4. Traps

A **trap** is a kind of automatic procedure call initiated by some condition caused by the program, usually an important but rarely occurring condition. A good example is overflow. On many computers, if the result of an arithmetic operation exceeds the largest number that can be represented, a trap occurs, meaning that the flow of control is switched to some fixed memory location instead of continuing in sequence. At that fixed location is a jump to a procedure called the overflow trap handler, which performs some appropriate action, such as printing an error message. If the result of an operation is within range, no trap occurs.

The essential point about a trap is that it is initiated by some exceptional condition caused by the program itself and detected by the hardware or microprogram. An alternative method of handling overflow is to have a 1-bit register that is set to 1 whenever an overflow occurs. A programmer who wants to check for overflow must include an explicit "jump if overflow bit is set" instruction after every arithmetic instruction. Doing so would be both slow and wasteful of space. Traps save both time and memory compared with explicit programmer controlled checking.

The trap may be implemented by an explicit test performed by the interpreter at level 1. If an overflow is detected, the trap address is loaded into the program counter. What is a trap at one level may be under program control at a lower level. Having the microprogram make the test still saves time compared to a programmer test, because it can be easily overlapped with something else. It also saves memory, because it need only occur in a few level 1 procedures, independent of how many arithmetic instructions occur in the main program.

A few common conditions that can cause traps are floating-point overflow, floating-point underflow, integer overflow, protection violation, undefined opcode, stack overflow, attempt to start nonexistent I/O device, attempt to fetch a word from an odd-numbered address and division by zero.

5.5.5. Interrupts

Interrupts are changes in the flow of control caused not by the running program but by something else, usually related to I/O. For example, a program may instruct the disk to start transferring information, and set the disk up to provide an interrupt as soon as the transfer is finished. Like the trap, the interrupt stops the running program and transfers control to an interrupt handler, which performs some appropriate action. When finished, the interrupt handler returns control to the interrupted program. It must restart the interrupted process in exactly the same state it was in when the interrupt occurred, which means restoring all the internal registers to their preinterrupt state.

The essential difference between traps and interrupts is this: *traps* are synchronous with the program and *interrupts* are asynchronous. If the program is rerun a million times with the same input, the traps will reoccur in the same place each time but the interrupts may vary, depending, for example, on precisely when a person at a terminal pushes the carriage return key. The reason for the reproducibility of traps and irreproducibility of interrupts is that traps are caused directly by the program and interrupts are, at best, indirectly caused by the program.

The need for interrupts arises when input or output can proceed in parallel with CPU execution. On computers where the CPU issues an I/O instruction and then stops to wait for the I/O to be completed, there is no need for an interrupt. When the I/O is finished, the CPU is automatically restarted at the instruction following the I/O instruction. Because the CPU can generally execute many thousands of instructions during the time required to complete a single I/O instruction, it is wasteful to force the CPU to be idle during this time. Interrupt schemes allow the CPU to compute concurrently with the I/O and be signaled as soon as the I/O is completed.

A large computer may have many I/O devices running at the same time. For example, it might be reading data from cards, printing results on the line printer, writing output on a disk for future use, and plotting a graph of results on the plotter. All this activity can lead to complicated situations. When the card reader has finished reading a card, the CPU is interrupted and the card reader service procedure is begun. The card reader service procedure must move the card just read to the main memory location where the CPU expects it (if it is not already there), check to see if any reading errors occurred, possibly check to see if each card column contains a valid character, and issue an instruction to start reading the next card.

A nonzero probability exists that another I/O device—for example, the disk—will complete its I/O instruction before the reader service procedure has completed its task. This situation can be handled in one of two ways. First, the disk can cause a CPU interrupt, halting execution of the card reader service procedure and starting execution of the disk service procedure. Second, the disk can be forced to wait until the reader service procedure is finished and can then cause an interrupt. We will now examine these possibilities in detail.

If we allow the disk to interrupt the card reader service procedure, we must also be prepared for the printer to interrupt the disk service procedure and for the plotter to interrupt the printer service procedure. If this interrupt sequence actually occurs, it is necessary to decide what to do when the plotter service procedure finishes. Possibilities are to continue the printer, disk, or card reader service procedures or to continue the CPU program that was running when the card reader interrupt occurred. It is clear that the administration involved in keeping track of which procedure to run when can get complicated.

One method for simplifying this administration is to require that all interrupts be **transparent**, which means that whenever an interrupt occurs, the state of the interrupted process is saved, including the program counter, registers, and condition codes. The interrupt service procedure is then run. Finally, the state of the interrupted process is restored to exactly the same condition it was in when the interrupt occurred and the process restarted.

The interrupted process neither requires any special precautions nor needs to be concerned with the interrupt handling. It is not even aware of its existence (unless it is timing something). Because the program running at the time of the interrupt is not aware of the fact that it has been interrupted, stopped, and later restarted, the interrupt is said to be transparent (or invisible). If all interrupts are transparent, an interrupt procedure will not even notice if it, itself, is interrupted.

Turning again to our earlier example, it is clear that the card reader interrupt must be transparent to the main program, the disk interrupt must be transparent to the card reader service procedure, and so on. When the plotter service procedure finally finishes its task, the printer service procedure must be restarted, not one of the other service procedures.

Similarly, for the printer service procedure to be transparent to the disk service procedure, the latter must be restarted (when the printer service procedure is through) from the point where it was interrupted. In other words, the interrupt service procedures must be restarted in the reverse order in which they occurred, as shown in Fig. 5-49. Whenever an interrupt service procedure completes its task, the most recently interrupted procedure must be restarted.

From Fig. 5-49 we see that interrupts are nested in time, meaning that a program will not be restarted until all the interrupts subsequent to it have been completely processed. Situations involving nesting are common in computer science. All nesting situations have one property in common: an inner nest is always completed before the surrounding nest is completed. A stack can often be used to implement a nesting situation. Whenever a new nest is entered, the state of the computation just before the entry is saved on the stack. Whenever a nest is exited, the state of the computation just previous to entering that nest is popped off the stack and restored.

Figure 5-50 illustrates the use of a stack for processing interrupts. The numbers 1 to 9 represent the time intervals shown in Fig. 5-49. During interval 1, no preceding state need be remembered, and the stack is empty. After the card reader interrupt has occurred, the state of the main program at the time of the interrupt must be remembered so that it can be restarted in the correct place later. This situation is shown as 2. When the disk interrupts the card reader service procedure, the state of the card reader service procedure must also be stacked, shown as 3.

Each of the nine stack configurations refers to some sequence of as yet uncompleted interrupt procedures. If another interrupt occurs at 7, while the disk service procedure is running, the state of that procedure will be saved again. If the computer possesses many I/O devices, a given interrupt service procedure may be stopped and resumed several times before it completes.

The model we have just given for interrupt processing is, however, not complete because we have ignored the critical timing aspects of I/O devices. Some I/O devices must be serviced within a specific time interval or information will be lost. For example, if data are being transmitted over a communication line at 960 characters/sec, a character arrives in the receiver buffer every 1042 μsec. If the interrupt service procedure fails to fetch the character within 1042 μsec, it may be overwritten by the next one and lost. An interrupt system needs a provision for handling this kind of problem. In other words, once the service procedure for a highly critical interrupt has begun, it must not be interrupted by a less critical interrupt.

When an I/O processor on the 370 finishes executing its program, it can interrupt

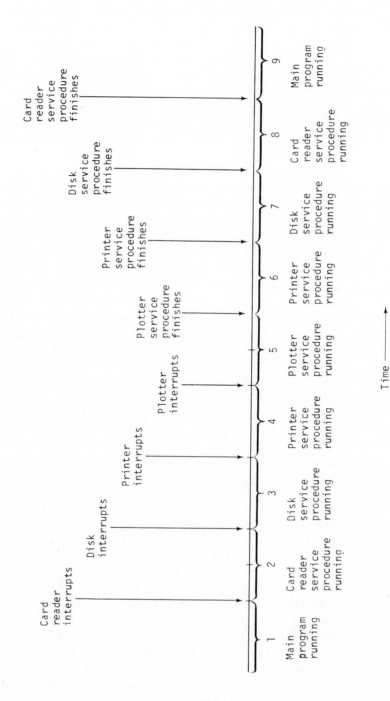

Fig. 5-49. Time sequence of interrupts from the card reader, disk, printer, and plotter.

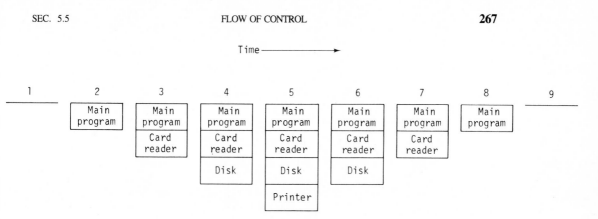

Fig. 5-50. Use of a stack for interrupt handling. Each box is the saved state of the indicated process. The numbers correspond to Fig. 5-49. The stack grows downward.

the CPU. It does so in the following steps. The CPU has a 64-bit register called a **program status word** (PSW) that contains the program counter, condition code, interrupt code, and other pieces of status information, as illustrated in Fig. 5-51. When an interrupt occurs, the PSW's interrupt code is set to the number of the interrupting device. Then the PSW is stored in location 56 and a new PSW is loaded from location 120. As soon as the new PSW has been loaded, the CPU begins execution at the start of a general interrupt service procedure. The interrupt service procedure must first determine which I/O device finished by examining the interrupt code in the old PSW at location 56. Then it can call the appropriate service procedure.

If a second interrupt occurred while the first one was being processed, the current PSW would be stored at location 56, thereby erasing the one already there. The situation is similar to a procedure call instruction that always puts the return address in a fixed place in memory. To prevent having a PSW overwritten before the interrupt procedure has had a chance to save it, the 370 has a bit associated with each I/O processor called a **mask bit**. When this bit is a 0, interrupts from that I/O processor are forced to wait until it becomes a 1. Setting mask bits to zero is called **disabling** interrupts. The mask bits are located in an internal processor register. If the I bit in Fig. 5-51 is 0, all interrupts are disabled, no matter what values the mask bits have.

When the PDP-11 is interrupted by an I/O device, the PSW (see Fig. 5-51) and program counter are pushed onto the stack, and a new PSW and program counter are loaded from the memory address associated with the I/O device. These memory addresses are called **interrupt vectors** and each device has a unique one. During the hardware interrupt sequence, the device specifies an interrupt vector by putting the vector's address on the UNIBUS. Each interrupt vector contains the starting address of the service procedure for the corresponding device, thus eliminating the need to test which device caused the interrupt. The 370 has only one interrupt vector for all I/O devices, so the interrupt handler must first determine which device wants attention. Only then can it call the proper service procedure.

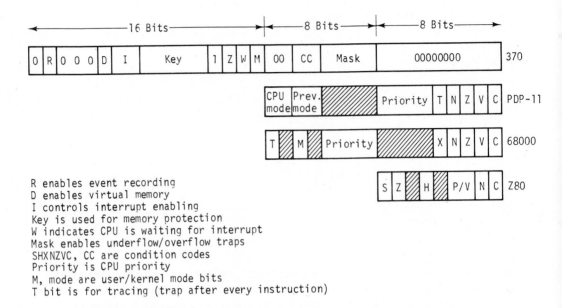

R enables event recording
D enables virtual memory
I controls interrupt enabling
Key is used for memory protection
W indicates CPU is waiting for interrupt
Mask enables underflow/overflow traps
SHXNZVC, CC are condition codes
Priority is CPU priority
M, mode are user/kernel mode bits
T bit is for tracing (trap after every instruction)

Fig. 5-51. The PSW on four computers. The 370 PSW is the EC format and only the upper 32 bits are shown. The lower 32 bits contain eight zeros and the program counter.

The PDP-11 has a system of priority interrupts. Each I/O device has a priority number associated with it. The CPU also has a priority (from 0 to 7), which can be set by the program, and which is part of the PSW. If the priority of the I/O device is higher than the current CPU priority, the interrupt takes place; otherwise, it is forced to wait until the CPU priority is reduced. This feature can be used to ensure that time-critical interrupt service procedures can be interrupted only by still more critical ones, not by less critical ones. For example, if the disk interrupt service procedure runs at priority 5, an interrupt from magnetic tape at priority 6 can interrupt it but an interrupt from the paper tape reader at priority 4 will be forced to wait until the CPU priority is set to 3 or less, which will not occur until the critical disk service procedure is finished. The priority of an I/O device is determined by a switch on the device itself. The devices that need the fastest service are naturally given the highest priorities. Traps use interrupt vectors, the same as true interrupts.

The 68000's interrupt system is similar to the PDP-11's, including the eight priority levels. When an external device whose priority is higher than the CPU's signals an interrupt, the PSW and program counter are stacked and a new program counter is fetched from the interrupt vector. A new PSW is not fetched from memory as on the PDP-11 but the CPU priority is set to that of the interrupting device. This approach saves space in the interrupt vectors because no PSWs need be stored but means that a priority n device service routine can be interrupted by a priority $n + 1$ device before the routine has been able to execute even one instruction. On the PDP-11, the new PSW may contain priority 7 to prevent all other interrupts for a few instructions to allow the routine to do some initial work without being disturbed. Afterward the routine can lower the priority if it wants to.

On the 370, PDP-11, and 68000 but not the Z80, the CPU is always in one of two (on some PDP-11 models, three) modes or states. The more powerful of the two is called **kernel mode** or **supervisor state**. The less powerful is called **user mode** or something similar. In user mode, some instructions, principally those that do I/O or affect the current mode, are forbidden and cause traps to kernel mode. In kernel mode, everything is allowed. When these machines are used for multiprogramming (time sharing), the user programs are forced to run in user mode to prevent them from interfering with each other. The operating system, in contrast, runs in kernel mode so that it can control the whole machine. A bit or field in the PSW determines the current mode. When an interrupt occurs on the 370 or PDP-11, the new PSW fetched determines which mode the interrupt routine will run in. In practice it is always kernel mode. On the 68000, no new PSW is loaded on interrupt, so the hardware always switches directly into kernel mode.

The PDP-11 and 68000 have different hardware stack pointers for user mode and kernel mode. The kernel stack pointer points to the kernel stack, which is in an area of memory protected from user programs. When the interrupt hardware switches the CPU into kernel mode, it simultaneously switches stack pointers, so the program counter and PSW are saved on the (protected) kernel stack rather than on the user stack.

The Z80 interrupt system is more primitive than that of the PDP-11 and 68000. Two (rather than eight) interrupt levels are present: maskable and nonmaskable. The maskable interrupts can be disabled by the DI instructions; the nonmaskable interrupts cannot be disabled. The latter are frequently used for emergencies such as shutting down industrial process control equipment in the few milliseconds available after an impending power failure has been detected.

The interrupt sequence consists of storing the program counter on the stack and disabling maskable interrupts. The accumulator and flags must be saved in software with the PUSH AF instruction. Nonmaskable interrupts always force control to address 102. Three different (software selected) modes are available for maskable interrupts. In mode 0, the interrupting device provides the next instruction to be executed on the data bus. Normally, it is RST. In mode 1, control is forced to address 56. In mode 2, the high-order 8 bits of the interrupt service routine come from the I register; the device provides the low-order 8 bits on the data bus. This somewhat peculiar scheme is intimately related to the issue of 8080 compatibility.

5.6. SUMMARY

The conventional machine level is what most people think of as "machine language." At this level the machine has a byte- or word-oriented memory ranging from tens of kilobytes to tens of megabytes, and instructions such as MOVE, ADD, and JUMP. Most instructions have one or two operands, which are addressed using immediate, direct, indirect, indexed, base register, or other addressing modes. Instructions are generally available for moving data, dyadic and monadic operations, including arithmetic and Boolean operations, jumps, procedure calls, and loops, and sometimes for I/O.

Control flow at level 2 is achieved using a variety of primitives, including jumps, procedure calls, coroutine calls, traps, and interrupts. Each of these is used for a different purpose.

PROBLEMS

1. Design an expanding opcode to allow all the following to be encoded in a 36-bit instruction:

    7 instructions with two 15-bit addresses and one 3-bit register number
    500 instructions with one 15-bit address and one 3-bit register number
    50 instructions with no addresses or registers

2. Is it possible to design an expanding opcode to allow the following to be encoded in a 12-bit instruction? A register is 3 bits.

    4 instructions with 3 registers
    255 instructions with one register
    16 instructions with zero registers

3. A certain machine has 16-bit instructions and 6-bit addresses. Some instructions have one address and others have two. If there are n two-address instructions, what is the maximum number of one-address instructions?

4. Given the memory values below and a one-address machine with an accumulator, what values do the following instructions load into the accumulator?

    word 20 contains 40
    word 30 contains 50
    word 40 contains 60
    word 50 contains 70

    a. LOAD IMMEDIATE 20
    b. LOAD DIRECT 20
    c. LOAD INDIRECT 20
    d. LOAD IMMEDIATE 30
    e. LOAD DIRECT 30
    f. LOAD INDIRECT 30

5. Compare 0-, 1-, 2-, and 3-address machines by writing programs to compute

    $X = (A + B \times C)/(D - E \times F)$

for each of the four machines. The instructions available for use are as follows:

0 Address	1 Address	2 Address	3 Address
PUSH M	LOAD M	MOV (X := Y)	MOV(X := Y)
POP M	STORE M	ADD (X := X+Y)	ADD(X := Y+Z)
ADD	ADD M	SUB (X := X−Y)	SUB(X := Y−Z)
SUB	SUB M	MUL (X := X∗Y)	MUL(X := Y∗Z)
MUL	MUL M	DIV (X := X/Y)	DIV(X := Y/Z)
DIV	DIV M		

M is a 16-bit memory address, and X, Y, and Z are either 16-bit addresses or 4-bit registers. The 0-address machine uses a stack, the 1-address machine uses an accumulator, and the other two have 16 registers and instructions operating on all combinations of memory locations and registers. SUB X,Y subtracts Y from X and SUB X,Y,Z subtracts Z from Y and puts the result in X. Assuming 8-bit opcodes and instruction lengths that are multiples of 4 bits, how many bits does each machine need to compute X?

6. Base register addressing involves four lengths:

L1 = number of bits in the field specifying a base register
L2 = number of bits in the field specifying a displacement
L3 = number of bits in a base register
L4 = number of bits in a memory address

For any given set of base register values:

a. How many distinct memory addresses can be referenced?
b. What fraction of memory can be addressed?

7. Devise an addressing mechanism that allows an arbitrary set of 64 addresses, not necessarily contiguous, in a large address space to be specifiable in a 6-bit field.

8. An alternative design for base-register machines like the 370 is to provide 24 bits in each instruction to directly address the entire memory. Compare this proposal to the 370 for the following cases:

a. The data consist of a few clumps.
b. The data are uniformly distributed throughout the address space.

Which one did the 370 designers think was more probable?

9. Convert the following formulas from infix to reverse Polish.

a. $A + B + C + D + E$
b. $(A + B) \times (C + D) + E$
c. $(A \times B) + (C \times D) + E$
d. $(A - B) \times ((((C - D \times E)/F)/G) \times H$

10. Convert the following reverse Polish formulas to infix.

a. $A B + C + D \times$
b. $A B / C D / +$
c. $A B C D E + \times \times /$
d. $A B C D E \times F / + G - H / \times +$

11. Which of the following pairs of reverse Polish formulas are mathematically equivalent?

    a. A B + C + and A B C + +
    b. A B − C − and A B C − −
    c. A B × C + and A B C + ×

12. Write three reverse Polish formulas that cannot be converted to infix.

13. Convert the following infix Boolean formulas to reverse Polish.

    a. (A AND B) OR C
    b. (A OR B) AND (A OR B)
    c. (A AND B) OR (C AND D)

14. Convert the following infix formula to reverse Polish and evaluate it using a stack as shown in the text.

    $(2 \times 3 + 4) − (4/2 + 1)$

15. Your company, like many before it, is planning to launch a line of computers compatible with the IBM 370. To help sales, it has been decided that your machine must be more powerful than the 370 in some way but it must also be able to run existing 370 programs. One of your machine architects has suggested allowing both positive and negative displacements from a base register, so compilers can set LB to point just after the return address as is usually done on the PDP-11 and 68000. Parameters would then be accessed using positive displacements, and local variables would be accessed using negative displacements. What do you think of this idea?

16. The company of the preceding problem went bankrupt and you found a new job with a company that wants to produce a machine very much like the PDP-11, only with a 32-bit word instead of a 16-bit word. Is such a design possible without greatly altering the PDP-11's addressing structure? The new machine need not run existing programs. Discuss the design.

17. It is common in programming for a program to need to determine where a variable X is with respect to the interval A to B. If a three-address instruction were available with operands A, B, and X, how many condition code bits would have to be set by this instruction?

18. One of your friends has just come bursting into your room at 2 A.M., out of breath, to tell you about his brilliant new idea: an instruction with two opcodes. Should you send your friend off to the patent office or back to the drawing board?

19. Tests of the form

    if $n = 0$ **then** ...
    if $i > j$ **then** ...
    if $k <= 4$ **then** ...

    are common in programming. Devise an instruction to perform these tests efficiently. What fields are present in your instruction?

20. For the 16-bit binary number 1001 0101 1100 0011, show the effect of:

    a. A right shift of 4 bits with zero fill.
    b. A right shift of 4 bits with sign extension.

   c. A left shift of 4 bits.
   d. A left rotate of 4 bits.
   e. A right rotate of 4 bits.

21. How can you clear a memory word on a machine with no CLEAR instruction?

22. Compute the Boolean expression (A AND B) OR C for

   A = 1101 0000 1010 1101
   B = 1111 1111 0000 1111
   C = 0000 0000 0010 0000

23. Devise a way to interchange two variables *A* and *B* without using a third variable or register. *Hint:* Think about the EXCLUSIVE OR instruction.

24. On a certain computer it is possible to move a number from one register to another, shift each of them left by different amounts, and add the results in less time than a multiplication takes. Under what condition is this instruction sequence useful for computing "constant × variable?"

25. On a machine using base registers, it is necessary for an interrupt handler to save one base register for use by the interrupt handler itself. However, the instruction to store a base register itself requires a base register to address the memory location where the register is to be stored. Because an interrupt can happen at an arbitrary time, the values of the base registers are all unknown at the start of the interrupt handler. This means that it has no base register available to use for the store base register instruction. Devise a solution to this problem.

26. Both the PDP-11 and 68000 switch to the kernel stack when saving the program counter and PSW for interrupts. Why is the user stack not used instead?

27. Write an assembly language subroutine to convert an infix formula to reverse Polish.

28. Write two assembly language subroutines for N!. The first one should be iterative and the second should be recursive.

29. If you are not convinced that recursion is at times indispensable, try programming the Towers of Hanoi without using recursion and without simulating the recursive solution by maintaining a stack in an array. Be warned, however, that you will probably not be able to find the solution.

30. Write an assembly language subroutine to convert a signed binary integer to ASCII.

6

THE OPERATING SYSTEM MACHINE LEVEL

In the preceding chapter it was shown how an interpreter running at the microprogramming level (level 1) could execute programs written for the conventional machine level (level 2). On a microprogrammed computer, the conventional machine level instructions such as procedure call, multiplication, and loop, are not carried out directly by the hardware. Instead, they are fetched, examined, and executed as a series of small steps by the microprogram. The level 2 machine can be programmed by people who know nothing at all about the level 1 machine and its interpreter. As far as they are concerned, the level 2 machine can be used as though it were the real hardware.

Just as an interpreter running on the level 1 machine can interpret programs written in level 2 machine language, an interpreter running on the level 2 machine can interpret programs written in level 3 machine language. For historical reasons (see Sec. 1.3) the interpreter running on the level 2 machine that supports the level 3 machine is called an **operating system**, as shown in Fig. 6-1. Therefore, we will call level 3 the "operating system machine level," for lack of a generally accepted term.

6.1. IMPLEMENTATION OF THE OPERATING SYSTEM MACHINE LEVEL

There is an important difference between the way the operating system machine level is supported and the way the conventional machine level is supported. This difference is due to the fact that the operating system machine level has gradually

274

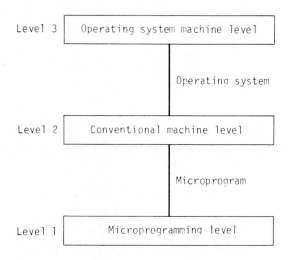

Fig. 6-1. Levels 2 and 3 are both supported by software.

evolved out of the conventional machine level. Most of the operating system machine level's instructions are also present at the conventional machine level. We will call these instructions the "ordinary" level 3 instructions, because they include such ordinary operations as arithmetic, Boolean operations, shifting, and so on. We will call the other level 3 instructions (those that are not present at level 2) the OSML instructions, to emphasize their existence only at the Operating System Machine Level.

Although it would be possible to have the operating system interpret all level 3 instructions, doing so is neither efficient nor necessary. The ordinary level 3 instructions can be interpreted directly by the microprogram. This situation is illustrated in Fig. 6-2(a) for the case of a computer with a single memory used to store all programs. As long as only ordinary instructions are being executed, the microprogram fetches instructions directly from the user program, examines them, and executes them.

However, as soon as an OSML instruction is encountered, the situation changes. The microprogram stops interpreting the user program and begins interpreting the operating system instead. The operating system then examines the OSML instruction in the user program and carries it out. When the OSML instruction has been executed, the operating system executes a certain instruction that causes the microprogram to continue fetching and executing user program instructions. Of course, if the next user program instruction is also an OSML instruction, the operating system will be started up again.

This method of executing level 3 programs means that part of the time the computer is functioning as a three-level machine and part of the time as a two-level machine. During the execution of an OSML instruction, three programs are running, one on each (virtual) machine. Each process has its own state, including its own

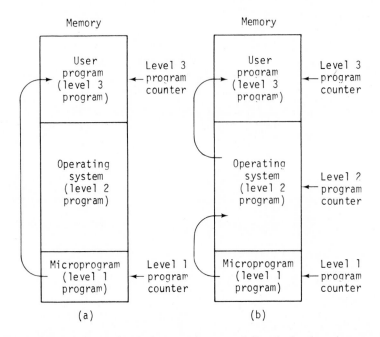

Fig. 6-2. (a) Ordinary instructions are interpreted directly by the micropro-gram. (b) OSML instructions are interpreted by the operating system, which is interpreted by the microprogram.

program counter. Conceptually, the level 3 program counter points to the OSML instruction (or its successor, depending on when the program counter is advanced), the level 2 program counter points to that operating system instruction currently execut-ing, and the level 1 program counter tells the actual hardware which microinstruction is to be executed.

In this chapter the operating system will be treated as a single level, for simplicity—which does not mean that all operating systems are organized as one level. On the contrary, some advanced operating systems are constructed as a series of several levels. However, the subject of how to design an operating system is beyond the scope of this book.

It should be mentioned that most operating systems for large computers are **mul-tiprogramming systems**, which means that rather than supporting only one level 3 virtual machine, the operating system supports several level 3 virtual machines in parallel. If each of these virtual machines is connected to a remote terminal, it is called a time-sharing system. If there are no remote terminals, it is called a batch multiprogramming system. Hybrid forms in which some virtual machines are being used on line and others are not, are common. A substantial part of the operating sys-tem is concerned with managing all the virtual machines rather than with interpreting OSML instructions.

6.2. VIRTUAL I/O INSTRUCTIONS

Normally, the level 2 instruction set is completely different from the level 1 instruction set. Both the operations that can be performed and the formats for the instructions are quite different at the two levels. The existence of a few instructions that are the same at both levels is essentially accidental.

In contrast, the level 3 instruction set contains most of the level 2 instructions, with a few new, but important, instructions added and a few potentially damaging instructions removed. Input/output is one of the areas where level 2 and level 3 machines differ considerably. The reason for this difference is simple: a user who could execute the real level 2 instructions could read confidential data stored in the system, write on other users' terminals, and, in general, be a big nuisance. Second, normal, sane programmers do not want to write their own level 2 I/O programs themselves. Device registers for disks typically have error bits for the following:

1. An I/O operation overflowed out of the last cylinder.

2. An attempt to write on a protected cylinder was aborted.

3. Disk arm failed to seek properly.

4. Error in previous command format.

5. Nonexistent memory specified as buffer.

6. Disk I/O started before previous one finished.

7. Read timing error.

8. Nonexistent disk addressed.

9. Nonexistent cylinder addressed.

10. Nonexistent sector addressed.

11. Checksum error on read.

12. Write check error after write operation.

When one of these errors occurs, the corresponding bit in a device register is set. Few users want to be bothered keeping track of all these error bits and the other status information.

6.2.1. Sequential Files

One way of organizing the virtual I/O is to conceive of data that is to be read or written as a sequence of logical records, where a **logical record** is some unit of information meaningful to the programmer. In the simplest case, a logical record might be a single character or an integer. For another application, a logical record might be a 10×10 matrix. For still another application, it might be a data structure consisting of five items: two character strings, "name," and "supervisor"; two integers, "depart-ment" and "office"; and a 1-bit string, "sex." A sequence of logical records is called a **file**. The records of a file need not all be the same length, in which case they are called **variable-length records**.

The basic virtual input instruction reads the next record from the specified file and puts it into consecutive cells in main memory beginning at a specified address, as illustrated in Fig. 6-3. To perform this operation, the virtual instruction must directly or indirectly specify (at least) two items of information:

1. The file to be read.

2. The main memory address into which the record is to be put.

No address within the file is specified. Consecutive sequential READ instructions get consecutive logical records from the file. This situation will be contrasted with ran-dom access files in the next section, in which the virtual instruction also specifies which logical record is to be read.

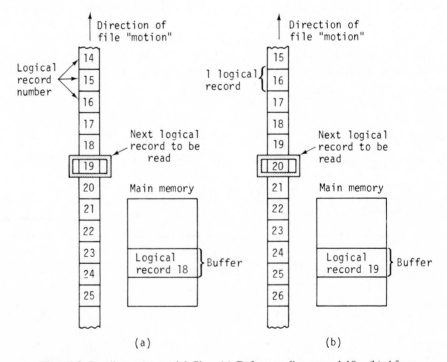

Fig. 6-3. Reading a sequential file. (a) Before reading record 19. (b) After reading record 19.

The basic virtual output instruction writes a logical record from memory onto a file. Consecutive sequential WRITE instructions produce consecutive logical records on the file. There is also a virtual REWIND instruction that repositions the file at the beginning so that the next logical record read or written will be the first one. The usual sequence is for a program first to create a file by writing a series of logical records onto it. The file is then rewound and read back one record at a time. In this manner, a file can be used to store large quantities of information that are too big for the main memory. In addition, if the file is stored on a magnetic tape or removable disk pack, it can be transported to another computer and read there.

Many operating systems require a file to be opened before it can be used, in which case an instruction OPEN is provided. The OPEN checks to see if the user is allowed to access the file, and if so, fetches information about the file into main memory. Then the file can be read or written. When the program is finished with a file it must close the file; an instruction is also provided for this operation.

Certain files can be permanently assigned to particular I/O devices. For example, there might be a file called OUTPUT, which consists of a series of 132 character strings and is associated with the printer. To print a line, the level 3 program writes a 132-character string onto the file OUTPUT, and somehow or other that string later appears on the printed output. The details of how that happens and how the printer actually works are of no concern to the level 3 programmer, although they are, of course, of great concern to the level 2 programmers who must write the software that carries out the virtual instructions (i.e., the operating system writers).

Another example might be a file called "INPUT", which consists of 80 character strings. Whenever a read from INPUT is performed, the contents of the next card are copied to memory. As far as the level 3 programmer is concerned, every instruction to read from input causes the next card in the deck to be read. In fact, the entire card deck may have been read all at once a while back and kept on the disk until needed, at which point one card at a time is copied to the user's buffer in main memory.

6.2.2. Random Access Files

The sequential files discussed previously are not addressable. A virtual READ instruction simply reads the next logical record. The program need not supply the logical record number. Many I/O devices, such as card readers, are by nature sequential. The level 3 instruction to read from the file associated with the card reader reads the next card. The program cannot say "Now read the 427th card" unless, by accident, it happens to have already read the first 426 cards. A sequential file is therefore a good model of such a device.

For some applications the program needs to access the records of a file in a different order from the order in which they have been written. As an example, consider an airline reservation system in which the passenger list for each flight forms a logical record and all the flights for one day form a file. A person may call up the airline's ticket agent and inquire about the availability of a seat on a flight to White Plains next Wednesday. The ticket agent enters the question into an on-line terminal. If the passenger list for that flight is record 26 of a certain file, the program needs only record 26. It clearly should not have to read sequentially starting at record 1 until it gets to record 26. The program needs to be able to access a specific record from the middle of a file by giving its record number.

Similarly, it is sometimes necessary to rewrite a particular logical record on a file without rewriting any logical records before or after it. In the preceding example, the person might want to make a reservation on the flight he inquired about. In order for this action to be performed, the program must rewrite the logical record containing the reservation list, adding the caller's name to the passenger list. It is neither necessary nor desirable to change any other logical records, however.

Most operating systems provide a virtual instruction to read the nth logical record of a file. These virtual instructions must provide (at least) three items of information:

1. The file to be read.

2. The main memory address into which the record is to be put.

3. The position of the logical record within the file.

The corresponding WRITE instructions must also provide this information as well.

Another form of file organization is one in which logical records are addressed not by their position in the file but by the contents of some field within each logical record, called the **key**. For example, a file containing a company's personnel data will have one field in each record containing the employee's name. A virtual instruction might be provided that allowed the program to give the name of an employee and have his logical record read in. It is the responsibility of the operating system to search the file for the needed logical record, saving the programmer the effort necessary to write the search procedure personally. This situation is analogous to a level 2 multiplication instruction, which spares the programmer the effort of (micro)programming his own multiplication procedure.

On some computers, a distinction is made between files that may be addressed by record number or key and files on which only the next record may be read. The former are called **random access** files, to distinguish them from the latter, the **sequential** files. On other computers, no such distinction is made, and both kinds of virtual instructions (with and without addressing) are allowed on all files.

6.2.3. Implementation of Virtual I/O Instructions

To understand how virtual I/O instructions are implemented on the level 2 machine, it is necessary to examine how files are organized and stored. In the following discussion we will assume that a disk is being used to hold the files but similar considerations apply to other media.

A basic issue that must be dealt with by all file systems is allocation of storage. A disk consists of a series of arm positions or cylinders, each of which has one or more tracks, equal to the number of surfaces (typically from 2 to 20). Tracks are divided into sectors, each of which holds a certain number of words. On some disks, the sector size is adjustable. For example, the programmer may choose to format a track as 10 sectors of 600 bytes, 12 sectors of 500 bytes, or 15 sectors of 400 bytes. On other disks, the sector size is fixed.

A fundamental property of a file system implementation is the size of the unit in which space is allocated. A disk has three reasonable candidates: the sector, the track, or the cylinder. Allocating space in units of 2.93 tracks is absurd. The difference can be most clearly seen in the case of a file consisting initially of only a single character. If the sector is the allocation unit, only one sector will be reserved for the file, and the other sectors on the same track will be available for use by other files. If the track is the allocation unit, one entire track will be reserved for the file but the other tracks in the same cylinder will be available for other files. If disk space is allocated by the cylinder, an entire cylinder will be reserved even for a file of only one character.

Another fundamental property of a file system implementation is whether a file is stored in consecutive allocation units or not. Figure 6-4 depicts a simple disk with one surface consisting of five tracks of 12 sectors each. Figure 6-4(a) shows an allocation scheme in which the sector is the basic unit of space allocation and in which a file consists of consecutive sectors. Figure 6-4(b) shows an allocation scheme in which the sector is the basic allocation unit but in which a file need not occupy consecutive sectors.

If the track is the allocation unit, a consecutively allocated file will occupy consecutive tracks. As a rule, all the tracks in a cylinder will be allocated before the next cylinder is allocated. If a file is allocated in units of tracks but is not consecutively allocated, the tracks may be chosen anywhere on the disk, without regard to proximity to one another.

There is an important distinction between the level 3 view of a file and the operating system's view of a file. The level 3 program sees the file as a linear sequence of logical records, card images, print lines, arrays, and so on. The operating system sees the file as an ordered, although not necessarily consecutive, collection of allocation units.

In general the logical record size will be different from the allocation unit size, possibly being smaller and possibly being larger. A file may consist of a sequence of 80-byte strings stored on a disk on which space is allocated in units of 16384-byte tracks. Bytes 0 to 79 of track 0 will contain the first logical record, bytes 80 to 159 will contain the second logical record, and so on. The tracks are regarded as logically contiguous, even if they are not physically contiguous, and a logical record may be split over two tracks. It is the task of the operating system to make the physical allocation unit size transparent to the level 3 program. When the level 3 program asks for logical record n, it gets logical record n, without regard to which track or tracks that record may occupy.

In order for the operating system to deliver logical record n of some file on request, it must have some method for locating the record. If the file is allocated consecutively, the operating system need only know the location of the start of the file and the sizes of the logical and physical records in order to calculate the position of the logical record. For example, if a logical record consists of eight words and a

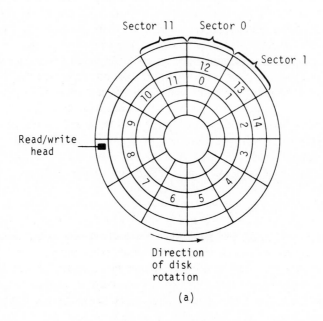

(a)

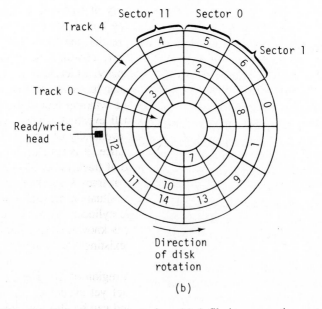

(b)

Fig. 6-4. Disk allocation strategies. (a) A file in consecutive sectors. (b) A file not in consecutive sectors.

track consists of 100 sectors of 64 words apiece, logical record 5000 will be in sector 25 of track 6. From its knowledge of the location of the first track, the level 2 software can calculate the exact disk address of the needed sector and issue a disk command to read it.

If the file is not allocated consecutively, it is not possible to calculate the position of an arbitrary logical record from the position of the start of the file alone. In order to locate any arbitrary logical record, a table called a **file index** giving the allocation units and their actual disk addresses is needed. The file index can be organized either in terms of the logical records, giving the disk address of each one, or simply as a list of the allocation units and their disk addresses. To illustrate how the file index is used, consider a disk allocated in sectors as in Fig. 6-4(b), with 512 bytes per sector. The file consists of 132-byte logical records (print lines) with bytes 0 to 131 constituting logical record 0, bytes 132 to 263 logical record 1, and so forth. Logical record 21 occupies bytes 2772 to 2903, which are in sector 5. By using the file index, the operating system can look up the address of the required sector, no matter which file index organization is used.

An alternative method of locating the allocation units of a file is to organize the file as a linked list. Each allocation unit contains the address of its successor. This can be done most efficiently if the hardware provides an extra word in each allocation unit for storing this address. This method is equivalent to dispersing the file index throughout the file. On a disk file allocated by sectors, each sector would contain the address of the succeeding sector. Such a file can only be read sequentially and cannot be accessed randomly.

Up until now we have discussed both consecutively allocated files and nonconsecutively allocated files but we have not specified why both kinds are used. A user who creates a file sometimes knows the maximum size that the file will later attain and sometimes does not. As an example of the latter, consider the computerized accounting system of the Ecology Manufacturing Company, which has just announced its latest product, a wind-up toothbrush. Their computer has a file listing the names and addresses of all their customers but at the time the wind-up toothbrush is put on sale, they have no idea how many customers they will eventually have, and consequently, do not know how large the customer file will eventually become.

When the maximum file size is not known in advance, it is usually impossible to use a consecutively allocated file. If the file is started at track j and allowed to grow into consecutive tracks, it may bump into another file at track k and have no room to expand. If the file is not allocated consecutively, this situation presents no problem, because succeeding tracks can be put in any available cylinder. If a disk contains a number of "growing" files, none of whose final sizes is known, storing each of them as a consecutive file will be impossible. Moving an existing file is sometimes possible but always expensive.

If the maximum file size is known in advance, a region of the disk can be allocated when the file is created, even if the data are not yet available. For example, daily weather data for 1991 will require 365 records and can be allocated on or before December 31, 1990, even though none of the data are known at file-creation time.

Consecutively allocated files are less flexible than nonconsecutively allocated files, because their maximum sizes must be known in advance. On the other hand, they are simpler to implement because no file index is needed. Note that both consecutively and nonconsecutively allocated files can be used as sequential access and as random access files.

In order to allocate space on the disk for a file, the operating system must keep track of which allocation units are available, and which are already in use storing other files. One method consists of maintaining a list of all the holes, a hole being any number of contiguous allocation units. This list is called the **free list**. Figure 6-5(a) illustrates the free list for the disk of Fig. 6-4(b).

Track	Sector	Number of sectors in hole
0	0	5
0	6	6
1	0	10
1	11	1
2	1	1
2	3	3
2	7	5
3	0	3
3	9	3
4	3	8

(a)

Sector											
0	1	2	3	4	5	6	7	8	9	10	11

Track

Track	0	1	2	3	4	5	6	7	8	9	10	11
0	0	0	0	0	0	1	0	0	0	0	0	0
1	0	0	0	0	0	0	0	0	0	0	1	0
2	1	0	1	0	0	0	1	0	0	0	0	0
3	0	0	0	1	1	1	1	1	1	0	0	0
4	1	1	1	0	0	0	0	0	0	0	0	1

(b)

Fig. 6-5. Two ways of keeping track of available sectors. (a) A free list. (b) A bit map.

An alternative method is to maintain a bit map, with one bit per allocation unit, as shown in Fig. 6-5(b). A 1 bit indicates that the allocation unit is already occupied and a 0 bit indicates that it is available.

The first method has the advantage of making it easy to find a hole of a particular length but it has the disadvantage of being variable sized. As files are created and destroyed the length of the list will fluctuate, an undesirable characteristic. The bit table has the advantage of being constant in size. In addition, changing the status of an allocation unit from available to occupied is just a matter of changing one bit. However, finding a block of a given size is difficult. Both methods require that when any file on the disk is allocated or returned, the allocation list or table be updated.

Before leaving the subject of file system implementation, it is worth commenting about the size of the allocation unit. Few files will occupy exactly an integral number of allocation units. Therefore, some space will be wasted in the last allocation unit of nearly every file. If the file is much larger than the allocation unit, the average space wasted will be half of an allocation unit. The larger the allocation unit, the larger the amount of wasted space.

If the expected file size is short, it is inefficient to allocate disk space in large units. For example, if most users of a proposed file system will be students with short programs averaging about 3000 characters, and a disk track contains 100 sectors of 640 characters apiece (i.e., 64000 characters), it would be foolish to allocate space in units of a track or, worse yet, a cylinder.

A disadvantage of allocating space in small chunks is that the file index and bit map (if used) will be large. Furthermore, if the file is nonconsecutively allocated, it will, in general, be necessary to do one disk seek per allocation unit. Disk seeks are slow; having to seek every 640 characters is less desirable than having to seek every 64000 characters. Of course, the strategy used to allocate new space to growing files can take this into consideration and try to assign allocation units close to the existing ones.

6.2.4. Directory Management Instructions

In the early days of computing, people kept their programs and data on punched cards in their offices. As the programs and data grew in size and number, this situation became less and less desirable. It eventually led to the idea of using the computer's secondary memory (e.g., disk) as a storage place for programs and data as an alternative to people's offices. Information that is directly accessible to the computer without the need for human intervention is said to be **on-line**, as contrasted with **off-line** information, which requires human intervention (e.g., reading in a card deck) before the computer can access it.

On-line information is stored in files, making it accessible to programs via the file I/O instructions discussed in Secs. 6.2.1 and 6.2.2. However, additional instructions are needed to keep track of the information stored on line and to protect it from unauthorized use.

The usual way for an operating system to organize on-line files is to group them into **directories** or **catalogs**. Figure 6-6 shows an example directory organization. Level 3 instructions are provided for at least the following functions:

1. Create a file and enter it in the owner's directory.

2. Delete a file from the directory.

3. Rename a file.

4. Change the protection status of a file.

Various protection schemes are in use. The simplest one is for the owner of each file to specify a secret password for each file. When attempting to access a file, a program must supply the password, which the operating system then checks to see if it is correct before permitting the access. Another protection method is for the owner of each file to provide an explicit list of people whose programs may access that file.

Some operating systems allow users to maintain more than one file directory. Each directory is typically itself a file and, as such, may be listed in an other

| File 0 |
| File 1 |
| File 2 |
| File 3 |
| File 4 |
| File 5 |
| File 6 |
| File 7 |
| File 8 |
| File 9 |
| File 10 |

File name:	Rubber-ducky
Length:	1840
Type:	Pascal program
Creation date:	March 16, 1066
Last access:	September 1, 1492
Last change:	July 4, 1776
Total accesses:	144
Block 0:	Track 4 Sector 6
Block 1:	Track 19 Sector 9
Block 2:	Track 11 Sector 2
Block 3:	Track 77 Sector 0

Fig. 6-6. (a) A user file directory. (b) The contents of a typical entry in a file directory.

directory, thus giving a tree of directories. Multiple directories are particularly useful for programmers working on several projects. They can then group all the files related to one project together in one directory. While working on that project, they will not be distracted by unrelated files.

Few computers have virtual I/O instructions as simple and straightforward as the conceptual I/O instructions discussed so far. In the following sections we will examine how the concept of virtual I/O instructions have been implemented on our four example machines. A slight complication is that each of these machines has a variety of operating systems—and hence a variety of virtual I/O instructions—available. As examples we have chosen to look at OS/MVS for the 370, the UNIX operating system for the PDP-11 and 68000, and CP/M for the Z80. These three cover a broad spectrum philosophically and technically and two of them (the CP/M and UNIX systems) are available for a large number of CPU types, which makes them especially good examples. Our treatment will be brief and will just touch on some of the interesting features. Readers intending to use any of them should consult the appropriate reference manuals.

6.2.5. IBM 370 Virtual I/O

The 370 has many operating systems, each of which implements a different set of level 3 instructions. They are all far too complicated even to summarize in a few pages, so we will just restrict ourselves to a few general remarks about files and file types. Files are distinguished by the method in which the data are accessed. Four of the major kinds are: sequential files, partitioned files, indexed sequential files, and direct access files. A **sequential file** is one in which the logical records will be read in order, one after another. This is the only kind allowed for files stored on sequential devices such as magnetic tapes. A **partitioned file** consists of several parts, each of which is a sequential file. In a partitioned file, each of the parts has a name, and the program may use the name to access a part. Within a part, all accesses are sequential. This file type is often used for program libraries.

Files in which the logical records are requested on the basis of a key are often useful. As an example, consider a hypothetical automated zoo with a terminal in front of each cage on which visitors can ask questions about the habits of the animals. The information could be organized as a single file, with one logical record per species. When a visitor asked for information about giant pandas, the program would have to find the logical record containing the information about pandas. An **indexed sequential file** could be used here.

Associated with each indexed sequential file is an index containing one entry for each logical record in the file. Each entry contains a character string identifying the record, along with the record's location in secondary memory (e.g., disk address). Such an index is illustrated in Fig. 6-7. In this example the animal species would be the keys. A virtual I/O instruction for accessing indexed sequential files provides a key, which the operating system looks up in the index to find the logical record. Because a search must be performed, this access method can be slow if a large number of records exist.

Record key	Cylinder	Track	Sector
California condor	4	0	10
European bison	16	1	3
Giant panda	9	1	4
Monkey-eating eagle	34	0	11
Orangutang	84	1	3
Pelican	19	1	7
Whooping crane	16	0	2
Wild yak	5	1	5

Fig. 6-7. An index for an indexed sequential file.

Figure 6-7 is a conceptual representation of an index rather than an attempt to depict an actual 370 index. In reality, three different kinds of indices—track indices, cylinder indices, and master indices—exist. They form an index hierarchy. Furthermore, a distinction is made between data in the "prime" tracks and data in the "overflow" tracks. When a file is created, all the data are put in the prime area. If new records are added later, there may be insufficient room in the appropriate prime tracks, so they are put in the overflow tracks. Moreover, Fig. 6-7 assumes that the logical records are unblocked (not packed together into larger units for reading and writing efficiency), although files on the 370 may be blocked or unblocked.

A **direct access file** is one in which the virtual I/O instruction explicitly specifies the actual disk address where the logical record is to be found. This method is the fastest method but it requires the most work from the programmer, because he must maintain an index himself. A variation of this file access method allows a logical record to be specified by its position within the file—that is, by its logical record number.

Associated with each file is a table, which on the 370 is called a **data control block** or DCB. In order for a file to be read or written, it must have a DCB in main memory. Figure 6-8 shows a few of the many fields in a DCB.

```
Specification of the file name
Maximum logical record length
Buffer size
Number of buffers required
Access method
Record type (variable length/fixed length)
Key length
Key position within logical record
Address of end-of-file procedure
Address of error handling procedure
Number of overflow tracks per cylinder
Other information
```

Fig. 6-8. Some of the fields required for the DCB of an indexed sequential file on the 370.

When a file is being read sequentially, the operating system knows which logical record will be needed next—namely, the one following the logical record most recently read. To speed up I/O, the operating system can read one or more logical records in advance, so that when the program executes a virtual READ instruction, the next record will already be in main memory and no time will be lost waiting for it. This technique is called **queueing** (or anticipatory buffering) and is shown in Fig. 6-9. For files accessed randomly, queueing is not possible because the operating system cannot predict which logical record will be needed next.

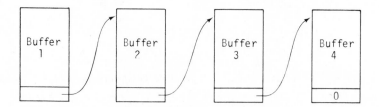

Fig. 6-9. Anticipatory buffering automatically prefills buffers before they are needed. While the program is using buffer 1, the operating system can be busy filling buffers 2, 3, and 4.

Anticipatory buffering on sequential files is called Queued Sequential Access Method or QSAM. Indexed sequential files may also be read sequentially instead of randomly. When an indexed sequential file is being read sequentially, queueing is possible and is called Queued Indexed Sequential Access Method or QISAM. Queueing is not permitted on partitioned or direct files. The names of some access methods are given in Fig. 6-10.

File type	With anticipatory buffering	Without anticipatory buffering
Sequential	QSAM—Queued sequential access method	BSAM—Basic sequential access method
Indexed sequential	QISAM—Queued indexed sequential access method	BISAM—Basic indexed sequential access method
Partitioned	Not allowed	BPAM—Basic partitioned access method
Direct	Not allowed	BDAM—Basic direct access method

Fig. 6-10. Some of the access methods available on the 370.

Separate virtual I/O instructions are provided for the queued and basic (non-queued) access methods. Queued access is performed by the virtual instruction

GET dcbname, buffer

where dcbname is the name of a DCB and buffer is the address where the logical record is to be put. If the logical record has already been read, it is copied into the buffer. If it has not been read, the program will have to wait until it has been read. The farther ahead the system reads in advance, the less likely it is that the program will have to wait for a GET to be completed. Of course, if the operating system tries to keep 10 records ahead of the program, a lot more memory will be needed for buffer space than if it tries to keep only one record ahead. The programmer specifies how far ahead the system should read by a field in the DCB.

Similarly, output can be queued. With queued output, the program can fill up a new buffer (or buffers) even though the previous one has not yet been output. With basic output (e.g., BSAM) the program must wait until the output of a buffer is complete before continuing. The virtual instruction for queued output is

PUT dcbname, buffer

For unqueued input and output (i.e., BSAM, BISAM, BPAM, or BDAM), the virtual instructions are READ and WRITE instead of GET and PUT.

The GET, PUT, READ, and WRITE virtual instructions, as well as all other virtual instructions on the 370, are mnemonics for **supervisor calls**, also known as

system calls. They are implemented using the SVC instruction, which tells the microprogram to stop interpreting the user program and start interpreting the operating system. The operating system then examines and interprets the virtual instruction. (We tend to use the term "level 3 instruction" when referring to computers in the abstract and the term "system call" when referring to specific operating systems but they mean the same thing.)

6.2.6. UNIX Virtual I/O

The UNIX† operating system was developed at Bell Laboratories in the early 1970s. Although the first versions were for the PDP-7 and PDP-9 computers, the PDP-11 version quickly gained a worldwide reputation as a powerful and elegant system. Subsequently, it was moved to the VAX, 68000, and many other machines. By the early 1980s it was available on more machines than any other operating system and was still gaining adherents in universities, industry, and government.

Much of the popularity of the UNIX system can be traced directly to its simplicity, which, in turn, is a direct result of the organization of the file system. An ordinary file is a linear sequence of 8-bit bytes starting at 0 and going up to a maximum of over 1000 megabytes. The operating system itself imposes no record structure on files, although many user programs regard ASCII text files as sequences of lines, each line terminated by a line feed.

Associated with every file currently in use (i.e., every open file) is a pointer that points to the next byte to be read or written. The READ and WRITE calls read and write data starting at the file position indicated by the pointer. Both calls advance the pointer after the operation by an amount equal to the number of bytes transferred. The LSEEK call moves the pointer to an arbitrary byte number, either absolute, relative to the current position, or relative to the end of the file. By first moving the pointer and then calling READ or WRITE, any byte in the file can be accessed randomly.

Figure 6-11 is a fragment of a Pascal program that illustrates how the major file I/O calls work. Before entering the loop, the program opens an existing file, *data*, and creates a new file, *newf*. The second parameters to the two calls specify that the files are to be read and written, respectively. Both calls return a small positive integer called a **file descriptor** that is used to identify the file in subsequent calls. If either OPEN or CREAT fails, a negative file descriptor is returned, telling that the call failed.

The call to READ has three parameters: a file descriptor, a buffer, and a byte count. The call tries to read the desired number of bytes from the indicated file into the buffer. The number of bytes actually read is returned in *count*, which will be smaller than *bytes* if the file was too short. The WRITE call deposits the newly read bytes on the output file. The loop continues until the input file has been completely read, at which time the loop terminates and both files are closed.

---

† UNIX is a trademark of Bell Laboratories.

```
infd:=open ("data", 0);                              {open existing file data}
outfd:=creat ("newf", ProtectionBits);               {create new file newf}

repeat
    count := read(infd, buffer, bytes);              {read buffer}
    if count > 0 then write (outfd, buffer, count)   {write buffer}
until count <= 0;

close (infd);                                        {close input file}
close (outfd);                                       {close output file}
```

Fig. 6-11. A fragment of a Pascal program for copying a file using the UNIX system calls.

In addition to ordinary files, the UNIX system also has special files, which are used to access I/O devices. Each I/O device typically has one or more special files assigned to it. By reading and writing from the associated special file, a program can read or write from the I/O device. Magnetic tapes, paper tapes, terminals, and many other devices are handled this way.

Closely related to the file system is the directory system. Each user may have multiple directories, with each directory containing both files and subdirectories. UNIX systems normally are configured with a main directory, called the **root directory**, containing subdirectories *bin* (for frequently executed programs), *dev* (for the special I/O device files), *lib* (for libraries), and *usr* (for user directories), as shown in Fig. 6-12. In this example, the *usr* directory contains subdirectories for *ast* and *jim*. The *ast* directory contains two files, *data* and *foo.p*, and a subdirectory, *bin*, containing four games.

Files can be named by giving their **path** from the root directory. A path contains a list of all the directories traversed from the root to the file, with directory names separated by slashes. For example, the absolute path name of *game2* is */usr/ast/bin/game2*.

At every instant, each running program has a **working directory**. Path names may also be relative to the working directory, in which case they do not begin with a slash, to distinguish them from absolute path names. When */usr/ast* is the working directory, *game3* can be accessed using the path *bin/game3*. A user may create a **link** to someone else's file using the LINK system call. In the above example, */usr/ast/bin/game3* and */usr/jim/jotto* both access the same file. To prevent cycles in the directory system, links are not permitted to directories. The calls OPEN and CREAT take either absolute or relative path names as arguments.

Associated with every file (including directories, because they are also files) is a bit map telling who may access the file. The map contains three RWX fields, the first controlling the Read, Write, eXecute permissions for the owner, the second for others in the owner's group, and the third for everybody else. Thus RWX R-X --X means that the owner can read the file, write the file, and execute the file (obviously, it is an executable program, or execute would be off), whereas others in his group can

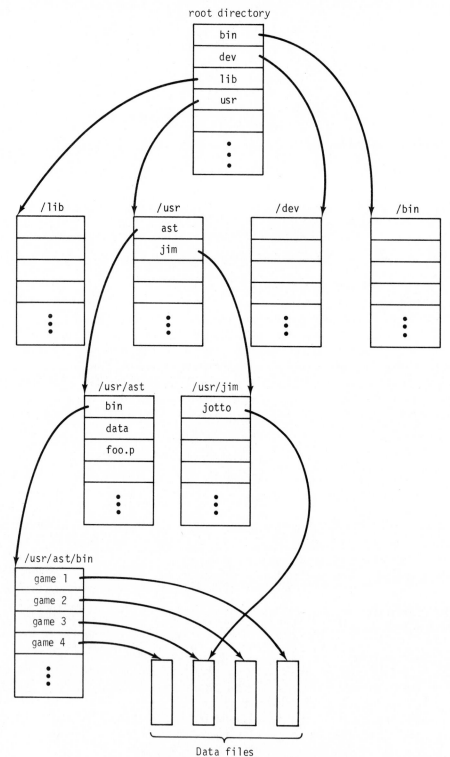

Fig. 6-12. Part of a typical UNIX directory system.

read or execute it and strangers can only execute it. With these permissions, strangers can use the program but not steal (copy) it because they do not have read permission. The assignment of users to groups is done by the system administrator, usually called the **superuser**. The superuser also has the power to override the protection mechanism and read, write, or execute any file.

The major file and directory calls in the UNIX system are listed in Fig. 6-13. ACCESS determines if a potential read, write, or execute on a file is permitted. CHDIR switches to a new working directory, the name of which can be specified either absolutely or relative to the current one. CHMOD allows the owner of a file to change all the RWX protection bits. STAT deposits information about a file in a buffer so the program can inspect it. The information comes from the i-node (see below). LINK makes a new directory entry with the new entry pointing to an existing file. For example, the entry */usr/jim/jotto* might have been created by the call

LINK("/usr/ast/bin/game3/", "/usr/jim/jotto")

or an equivalent call using relative path names, depending on the working directory of the program making the call. UNLINK removes a file. If the file has only one link, the file is deleted. The call

UNLINK("/usr/ast/bin/game3")

makes *game3* only accessible via the path */usr/jim/jotto* henceforth. LINK and UNLINK can be used in this way to "move" files from one directory to another.

Implementation of the UNIX File System

Now we will briefly describe how files and directories are implemented in the UNIX system. For a more complete treatment, see Thompson (1978). Associated with each file (and each directory, because a directory is also a file) is a 64-byte block of information called an **i-node**. The i-node tells who owns the file, what the permissions are, where to find the data, and similar things. The i-nodes for the files on each disk are located in numerical sequence at the beginning of the disk. Thus given an i-node number, the UNIX system can locate the i-node by simply calculating its disk address.

A directory entry consists of 16 bytes: 14 bytes for the file (or subdirectory) name and a 2-byte i-node number. When a program executes

OPEN("foobar",0)

the system searches the working directory for the file name, "foobar," in order to locate the i-node number for that file. Having found the i-node number, it can then read in the i-node, which tells it all about the file.

When a longer path name is specified, the basic step outlined above is repeated several times. For example, to locate the i-node number for */usr/ast/data*, the system first searches the root directory for an entry *usr*. Having found the i-node for *usr*, it can read the file (remember that a directory is a file, and as such, can be read the

File calls

creat (name, mode)	Create a File; mode gives protection
open (name mode)	Open a File; return file descripter
close (fd)	Close a file
read (fd, buffer, count)	Read count bytes into buffer
write (fd, buffer, count)	Write count bytes from buffer
lseek (fd, offset, w)	Move the file pointer according to offset, w

Directory calls

access (name, mode)	Check access permission; mode = read/write/execute
chdir (dirname)	Change working directory
chmod (name, mode)	Change protection mode
stat (name, buffer)	Put file status in buffer
link (name 1, name 2)	Create directory entry name 2 pointing to name 1
unlink (name)	Remove a directory entry

Fig. 6-13. Some of the UNIX file and directory system calls.

usual way). In this file it looks for an entry *ast*, thus locating the i-node number for the file */usr/ast*. By reading */usr/ast*, the system can then find the entry for *data*, and thus the i-node number for */usr/ast/data*. Given the i-node number for the file, it can then find out everything about the file from the i-node.

An i-node contains the following information:

1. The file type, the 9 RWX protection bits, and a few other bits.

2. The number of links to the file (number of directory entries for it).

3. The owner's identity.

4. The owner's group.

5. The file length in bytes.

6. Thirteen disk addresses.

7. The time the file was last read.

8. The time the file was last written.

9. The time the i-node was last changed.

The file type distinguishes ordinary files, directories, and two kinds of special files, for block-structured and unstructured I/O devices, respectively. The number of links and the owner identification have already been discussed. The file length is a 32-bit integer giving the highest byte that has a value. It is perfectly legal to create a file, do an LSEEK to position 1,000,000 and write one byte, which yields a file of length 1,000,001. The file would *not,* however, require storage for all the ''missing'' bytes.

The first 10 disk addresses point to data blocks. With the usual block size of 512 bytes, files up to 5120 bytes can be handled this way. Address 11 points to a disk block, called an **indirect block**, which contains 128 disk addresses. Files up to 5120 + 128 × 512 = 70656 bytes are handled this way. For still larger files, address 12 points to a block containing the addresses of 128 indirect blocks, which takes care of files up to 70656 + 128 × 128 × 512 = 8,459,264 bytes. If this **double indirect block** scheme is still too small, disk address 13 is used to point to a **triple indirect block** containing the addresses of 128 double indirect blocks. The largest file that can be handled is 1,082,201,088 bytes. Free disk blocks are kept on a linked list. When a new block is needed, the next block is plucked from the list. As a result, the blocks of each file are scattered randomly around the disk.

To make disk I/O more efficient, when a file is opened, its i-node is copied to a table in main memory and is kept there for handy reference as long as the file remains open. In addition, a pool of recently referenced disk blocks is maintained in memory. Because most files are read sequentially, it often happens that a file reference requires the same disk block as the previous reference. To strengthen this effect, the system also tries to read the *next* block in a file, before it is referenced, in order to speed up processing. All this optimization is hidden from the user; when a user issues a READ call, the program is suspended until the requested data are available in the buffer.

With this background information, we can now see how file I/O works. OPEN causes the system to search the directories for the specified path. If the search is successful, the i-node is read into an internal table. READs and WRITEs require the system to compute the block number from the current file position. The disk addresses of the first 10 blocks are always in main memory (in the i-node); higher-numbered blocks require one or more indirect blocks to be read first. LSEEK just changes the current position pointer without doing any I/O.

LINK and UNLINK are also simple to understand now. LINK looks up its first argument to find the i-node number. Then it creates a directory entry for the second argument, putting the i-node number of the first file in that entry. Finally, it increases the link count in the i-node by one. UNLINK removes a directory entry and decrements the link count in the i-node. If it is zero, the file is removed and all the blocks are put back on the free list.

6.2.7. CP/M Virtual I/O

CP/M* (Control Program/Microcomputers) is a popular operating system used on the Z80 and some other microcomputers. It was written by a California company,

---

*CP/M is a trademark of Digital Research, Inc.

Digital Research, Inc. One of its principal design requirements was that it be compact, which obviously means that it can do less than operating systems designed for larger machines. The original version was intended for a single user, in the sense that CP/M did not keep track of who "owned" which file. Subsequent versions support multiple file owners, although only one user may be logged in at any moment. Portions of the CP/M Operating System file structure described below are proprietary to Digital Research, and are described in this book with the express written permission of Digital Research, Inc.

CP/M makes a basic distinction between I/O devices and files. First, we will look at how it treats I/O devices and then we will examine how it deals with files. Four logical I/O devices, called CONSOLE, READER, LIST, and PUNCH, exist. These are intended as abstractions of real I/O devices to make it possible to write device-independent programs. For example, programs can be written to put their output on LIST, with LIST assigned to a line printer, a terminal, or some other device just before the program is run. The program itself need not be modified just to change the output destination. The principal device I/O system calls are shown in Fig. 6-14. They each read a character from, or write a character to, a logical I/O device. A few other calls are also available.

CP/M has a completely different set of system calls for manipulating files. A file is conceptually a linear sequence of up to 65536 128-byte records, giving a maximum file size of 8 megabytes. File operations always read or write exactly one record from a 128-byte buffer called the DMA area. The program can tell CP/M where the DMA area is by means of a system call. Both sequential and random file I/O are allowed, although different system calls are provided for each.

CP/M maintains a separate directory for each disk drive. A file has a one- to eight-character name and a one- to three-character type that tells what the file is: for example, ASM for assembler, BAS for BASIC, COB for COBOL, and DAT for data. The name and type are written separated by a period, as in INPUT.DAT, although the period is not stored. As mentioned above, the later versions of CP/M keep track of which files belong to which user, which is a convenience but does not provide any protection against unauthorized use. On the other hand, because most CP/M systems use floppy disks, you can easily protect your files by locking the disks in your office.

All the file system calls require the calling program to supply the address of a 36-byte data structure called a **File Control Block** (FCB), as shown in Fig. 6-15. The FCB contains information taken from the directory when the file is opened, including the name and type of the file, the current record number (for sequential access), a record number for random access, and some information about where on the disk the data are located.

Before a file can be read or written, it must be opened; when it is no longer needed it should be closed. Reads and writes are done by system calls with two parameters: the system call number and the FCB address. Sequential reads and writes automatically read or write the next record in sequence. Random reads and writes affect the record whose number appears in the last three bytes of the FCB.

System calls are also provided for some directory operations, including creating,

Device I/O

Read 1 character from CONSOLE
Write 1 character to CONSOLE
Read 1 character from READER
Write 1 character to PUNCH
Write 1 character to LIST

Directory Operations

Make File
Delete file
Rename file
Search directory for file
Set file attributes

File I/O

Open file
Close file
Read record sequentially
Write record sequentially
Random access read
Random access write
Set DMA address
Compute file size
Set random record

Miscellaneous

System reset
Reset disk system
Get console status
Get I/O byte
Set I/O byte
Return CP/M version number
Return disk status vector
Select disk
Return current disk

Fig. 6-14. Some of the CP/M system calls.

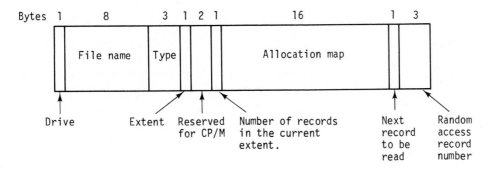

Fig. 6-15. The 36-byte CP/M File Control Block (FCB).

deleting and renaming files, directory searching, and setting file attributes (e.g., read only). Some miscellaneous operations are listed in Fig. 6-14.

Internally, CP/M regards a disk as a sequence of allocation units, typically 1K, 2K, or 4K bytes. A standard floppy disk has 77 tracks of twenty-six 128-byte sectors, so there are 250.25 allocation units per disk and an 8-bit byte is sufficient to represent a "disk address," that is, an allocation unit. With these disks, a 1K allocation unit can be used, allowing up to 256K of disk space to be addressed.

A CP/M directory consists of 32-byte slots, with each slot having almost the same layout as an FCB (see Fig. 6-15). When the allocation unit is 1K and the file is smaller than 16K, the allocation map in the directory entry (and FCB) simply contains all the disk addresses used by the file. When a file is opened, the user-supplied FCB (which has zeros everywhere except the first three fields) is loaded from the directory entry. Once a file is opened, CP/M can directly locate each of its $8 \times 16 = 128$ records from the information in the FCB.

When the allocation unit is 1K and a file is larger than 16K, it is split up into chunks or **physical extents** of 16K each. Each extent occupies a directory entry. When one of these large files is opened, only the allocation map for the first extent is brought into memory. When a sequential read or write crosses the 16K boundary, the next piece of the allocation map is fetched from the directory on the disk. The fourth FCB field tells which extent is current. For random access I/O, the record number in the last field is used to determine which extent is needed, and the allocation information for that extent is read in if it is not already present.

When disks larger than 256K came into use, the combination of 1K allocation units and 8-bit numbers to indicate allocation units was no longer enough to address the whole disk. More recent releases of CP/M have therefore allowed the 16-byte allocation map to be split up into eight 2-byte disk addresses as well as sixteen 1-byte addresses. To prevent the size of a physical extent from shrinking, allocation units larger than 1K were also introduced. With an allocation unit of, say, 4K, a directory entry is sufficient for $8 \times 4K = 32$ Kbytes.

6.3. VIRTUAL INSTRUCTIONS USED IN PARALLEL PROCESSING

Some computations can be most conveniently programmed for two or more cooperating processes, running in parallel (i.e., simultaneously, on different processors) rather than for a single process. Other computations can be divided into pieces, which can then be carried out in parallel to decrease the time required for the total computation. In order for several processes to work together in parallel, certain virtual instructions are needed. These instructions will be discussed in the following sections.

The laws of physics provide yet another reason for the current interest in parallel processing. According to Einstein's special theory of relativity, it is impossible to transmit electrical signals faster than the speed of light, which is nearly 1 ft/nsec. This limit has important implications for computer organization. For example, if a

CPU needs data from the main memory 1 ft away, it will take at least 1 nsec for the request to arrive at the memory and another nanosecond for the reply to get back to the CPU. Consequently, subnanosecond computers will need to be extremely tiny. An alternative approach to speeding up computers is to build machines with many CPUs. A computer with a thousand 1-nsec CPUs may have the same computing power as one CPU with a cycle time of 0.001 nsec, but the former may be much easier and cheaper to construct.

On a computer with more than one physical processor, each of several cooperating processes can be assigned to its own processor, to allow the processes to progress simultaneously. If only one physical processor is available, the effect of parallel processing can be simulated by having the processor run each process in turn for a short time. In other words, the processor can be shared among several processes.

Figure 6-16 shows the difference between true parallel processing, with more than one physical processor, and simulated parallel processing, with only one physical processor. Even when parallel processing is simulated, it is useful to regard each process as having its own dedicated virtual processor. The same communication problems that arise when there is true parallel processing also arise in the simulated case.

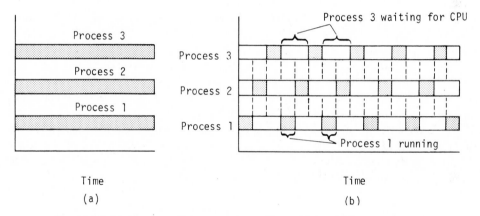

Fig. 6-16. (a) True parallel processing with multiple CPUs. (b) Parallel processing simulated by switching one CPU among three processes.

6.3.1. Process Creation

When a program is to be executed, it must run as part of some process. This process, like all other processes, is characterized by a state and an address space through which the program and data can be accessed. The state includes the program counter and possibly, a program status word, a stack pointer, and general registers.

Simple operating systems usually support a fixed number of processes, all of which are created when the computer is started up in the morning and all of which remain in existence until the computer is stopped at night. On these computers a program must wait in the input queue until a process becomes available before it can be loaded into the process's address space and executed.

More sophisticated operating systems allow processes to be created and terminated without stopping the computer. A computer with this kind of operating system can support a variable number of level 3 machines, each process corresponding to one virtual machine. To take full advantage of parallel processing, a level 3 program needs a virtual instruction to create new processes, to which it can delegate work. Some operating systems provide a level 3 instruction for creating a new process, allowing the creating process to specify the initial state of the new process, including its program, data and starting address. With some IBM 370 programming systems, for example, a procedure can call another procedure in a special way so as to have the caller and callee run in parallel as separate processes.

In some cases, the creating (parent) process maintains complete control over the created (child) process. To this end, virtual instructions exist for a parent to stop, restart, examine, and terminate its children. In other cases, a parent has less control over its children: once a process has been created, there is no way for the parent to forcibly stop, restart, examine or terminate it. The two processes then run independently of one another.

The UNIX system provides a different mechanism for process creation. A system call FORK is available which creates a duplicate of the forking process. Conceptually, the newly created child process is given its own private copy of the parent's registers, program, data, and stack. So the two processes can tell which is which, the FORK returns a 0 to the child and a nonzero number, the child's process number, to the parent. A parent can send a termination signal to its children but, other than that, has no control over them.

Another system call, EXEC, allows either process to overlay its program with a new one. Typically, the code following a FORK checks to see if the value returned is zero, and if so an EXEC is done to load a new program into the address space. In this way, parent and child can end up running different programs.

After a FORK, parent and child each have file descriptors for all the open files. The files themselves are not duplicated, so if both processes start reading from a file simultaneously, each one will get some of the data at random. Normally, one process closes all its files to avoid conflict. However, if the parent and child wish to communicate, a mechanism is provided to permit that. Before making the FORK call, the parent makes a PIPE system call, which creates a first-in, first-out queue called a **pipe**. PIPE returns two file descriptors, one for reading and one for writing. After the FORK, one process can write to the pipe and the other can read from it. As far as both processes are concerned, reading or writing from a pipe is identical to reading or writing from a file. Thus file I/O, device I/O (using special files), and interprocess communication are all the same. Programs can be written to take their input from a file, an I/O device, or another process, with the program not even aware of where the input comes from.

CP/M systems support only one process and thus have no primitives creating new processes or doing interprocess communication.

6.3.2. Race Conditions

In this section the difficulties involved in synchronizing parallel processes will be explained by means of a detailed example. A solution to these difficulties will be given in the following section. Consider a situation consisting of two independent processes, process 1 and process 2, which communicate via a shared buffer in main memory. For simplicity we will call process 1 the **producer** and process 2 the **consumer**. The producer computes prime numbers and puts them into the buffer one at a time. The consumer removes them from the buffer one at a time and prints them.

These two processes run in parallel at different rates. If the producer discovers that the buffer is full, it goes to sleep, that is, it temporarily suspends its operation awaiting a signal from the consumer. Later, when the consumer has removed a number from the buffer it sends the signal to the producer to wake it up—that is, restart it. Similarly, if the consumer discovers that the buffer is empty, it goes to sleep. When the producer has put a number into the empty buffer, it wakes up the sleeping consumer.

In this example we will use a circular buffer for interprocess communication. The pointers *in* and *out* will be used as follows: *in* points to the next free word (where the producer will put the next prime) and *out* points to the next number to be removed by the consumer. When *in* = *out*, the buffer is empty, as shown in Fig. 6-17(a). After the producer has generated some primes, the situation is as shown in Fig. 6-17(b). Figure 6-17(c) illustrates the buffer after the consumer has removed some of these primes for printing. Figure 6-17(d)-(f) depict the effect of continued buffer activity. The top of the buffer is logically contiguous with the bottom; that is, the buffer wraps around. When there has been a sudden burst of input and *in* has wrapped around and is only one word behind *out* (e.g., *in* = 52, and *out* = 53), the buffer is full. The last word is not used; if it were, there would be no way to tell if *in* = *out* meant a full buffer or an empty one.

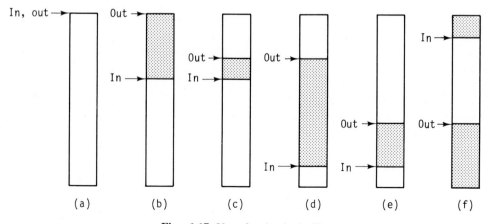

Fig. 6-17. Use of a circular buffer.

Figure 6-18 shows some declarations and the procedures used by the producer and the consumer in pseudo Pascal. Pascal does not allow parallel processing, so we have invented two "library" procedures: *sleep*, which puts a process to sleep, and *wakeup*, which wakes up the process named by its parameter (if it was asleep). After appropriate initialization ($in = 1$ and $out = 1$), the producer and consumer should be started in parallel.

After the producer has found the next prime number in statement P1, it checks (in P2) to see if *in* is one behind *out*. If it is (e.g., $in = 62$ and $out = 63$), the buffer is full and the producer goes to sleep. If the buffer is not full, the new prime is inserted into the buffer (P3) and *in* is incremented (P4). If the new value of *in* is 1 ahead of *out* (P5) (e.g., $in = 17$ and $out = 16$), *in* and *out* must have been equal before *in* was incremented. The producer concludes that the buffer was empty and that the consumer was, and still is, sleeping. Therefore, the producer sends a signal to wake the consumer up. Finally, the producer begins looking for the next prime.

The consumer's program is structurally similar. First, a test is made (C1) to see if the buffer is empty. If it is, there is no work for the consumer to do, so it goes to sleep. If the buffer is not empty, it removes the next number to be printed (C2) and increments *out* ($C3$). If *out* is two positions ahead of *in* at this point (C4), it must have been one position ahead of *in* before it was just incremented. Because $in = out - 1$ is the "buffer full" condition, the producer must have been sleeping, and thus the consumer sends a signal to wake up the producer. Finally, the number is printed (C5) and the cycle repeats.

Unfortunately, this design contains a fatal flaw, as shown in Fig. 6-19. Remember that the two processes run asynchronously and at different, possibly varying, speeds. Consider the case where only one number is left in the buffer, in word 21, and $in = 22$ and $out = 21$, as shown in Fig. 6-19(a). The producer is at statement P1 looking for a prime and the consumer is busy at C5 printing out the number in position 20. The consumer finishes printing the number, makes the test at C1, and takes the last number out of the buffer at C2. It then increments *out*. At this instant, both *in* and *out* have the value 22. The consumer prints the number and then goes to C1, where it fetches *in* and *out* from memory in order to compare them, as shown in Fig. 6-19(b).

At this very moment, after the consumer has fetched *in* and *out* but before it has compared them, the producer finds the next prime. It puts the prime into the buffer at P3 and increments *in* at P4. Now $in = 23$ and $out = 22$. At P5 the producer discovers that $in = next(out)$. In other words, *in* is one higher than *out*, signifying that there is now one item in the buffer. The producer therefore (incorrectly) concludes that the consumer must be sleeping, so it sends a wakeup signal, as shown in Fig. 6-19(c). Of course, the consumer is still awake, so the wakeup signal is lost. The producer begins looking for the next prime.

At this point in time the consumer continues. It has already fetched *in* and *out* from memory before the producer put the last number in the buffer. Because they both have the value 22 the consumer goes to sleep. Now the producer finds another prime. It checks the pointers and finds $in = 24$ and $out = 22$, therefore it assumes that

const *MaxPrime* = ...;   {largest prime to look for}
    BufSize = 100;   {number of buffer slots}

type *index* = 1 .. *BufSize*;   {buffer slots numbered from 1 to *BufSize*}

var *in* : *index*;   {next free slot for a prime to go into}
   out : *index*;   {next prime to be fetched and printed}
   buffer : **array**[index] **of** *integer*;   {shared buffer}

function *next* (*k* : *index*): index ;
{ Compute the successor to *k* taking wraparound into account.}
begin
  if *k* < *BufSize* **then** *next* := *k* + 1 **else** *next* := 1
end; {next}

procedure *producer* ;
{ The producer computes prime numbers and puts them in a shared buffer for
  subsequent printing . When the buffer is full , the producer goes to sleep .
  When the consumer sends a wakeup signal , the producer continues at P3.}

var *prime* : *integer* ;
begin
  prime := 2;
  while *prime* < *MaxPrime* **do**
    begin
      {P1} *ComputeNextPrime*(*prime*);
      {P2} **if** *next*(*in*) = *out* **then** *sleep;*
      {P3} *buffer*[*in*] : = *prime;*
      {P4} *in* : = *next*(*in*);
      {P5} **if** *next*(*out*) = *in* **then** *wakeup*(*consumer*)
    end
end; {producer}

procedure *consumer* ;
{ The consumer takes numbers out of the buffer and prints them. If the buffer
  becomes empty , the consumer goes to sleep . When the producer sends a wakeup
  signal , the consumer continues at C2.}
var *emirp* : *integer* ;
begin
  emirp := 2;
  while *emirp* < *MaxPrime* **do**
    begin
      {C1} **if** *in* = *out* **then** *sleep;*
      {C2} *emirp* : = *buffer*[*out*];
      {C3} *out* : = *next*(*out*);
      {C4} **if** *out* = *next*(*next*(*in*)) **then** *wakeup*(*producer*);
      {C5} *writeln*(*emirp*)
    end
end; {consumer}

Fig. 6-18. Parallel processing with a fatal race condition.

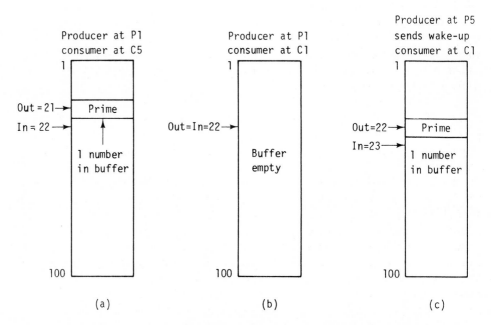

Fig. 6-19. Failure of the producer-consumer communication mechanism.

there are two numbers in the buffer (correct) and that the consumer is awake (incorrect). The producer continues looping and eventually it fills the buffer up and goes to sleep. Now both processes are sleeping and will remain so forever.

The difficulty here is that between the time when consumer fetched *in* and *out* and the time it went to sleep, the producer snuck in, discovered that $in = out+1$, assumed that the consumer was sleeping (which it was not yet), and sent a wakeup signal that was lost because the consumer was still awake. This difficulty is known as a **race condition,** because the method's success depends on who wins the race to test *in* and *out* after *out* is incremented.

6.3.3. Process Synchronization Using Semaphores

The race condition can be solved in at least two ways. One solution consists of equipping each process with a "wakeup waiting bit." Whenever a wakeup is sent to a process that is still running, its wakeup waiting bit is set. Whenever the process goes to sleep when the wakeup waiting bit is set, it is immediately restarted and the wakeup waiting bit is cleared. The wakeup waiting bit stores the superfluous wakeup signal for future use.

Although this method solves the race condition when there are only two processes, it fails in the general case of *n* communicating processes because as many as $n - 1$ wakeups may have to be saved. Of course, each process could be equipped with $n - 1$ wakeup waiting bits to allow it to count to $n - 1$ in the unary system, but this solution is rather clumsy.

Dijkstra (1968c) proposed a more general solution to the problem of synchronizing parallel processes. Somewhere in the memory are two nonnegative integer variables called **semaphores**. Two level 3 instructions that operate on semaphores, UP and DOWN, are provided by the operating system. UP adds 1 to a semaphore and DOWN subtracts 1 from a semaphore.

If a DOWN instruction is performed on a semaphore that is greater than 0, the semaphore is decremented by 1 and the process doing the DOWN continues. If, however, the semaphore is 0, the DOWN cannot complete; the process doing the DOWN is put to sleep and remains asleep until the other process performs an UP on that semaphore.

The UP instruction checks to see if the semaphore is 0. If it is and the other process is sleeping on it, the semaphore is increased by 1. The sleeping process can then complete the DOWN operation that suspended it, resetting the semaphore to 0 and allowing both processes to continue computing. An UP instruction on a nonzero semaphore simply increases it by 1. In essence, a semaphore provides a counter to store wakeups for future use, so that they will not be lost. An essential property of semaphore instructions is that once a process has initiated an instruction on a semaphore, no other process may access the semaphore until the first process has either completed its instruction, or been suspended trying to perform a DOWN on a 0. Figure 6-20 summarizes the properties of the UP and DOWN instructions.

	Value of the semaphore before the instruction	
Instruction	Semaphore = 0	Semaphore > 0
UP	Semaphore = semaphore + 1 If the other process was halted attempting to complete a DOWN instruction on this semaphore, it may now complete the DOWN and continue running	Semaphore = semaphore + 1
DOWN	Process halts until the other process UPs this semaphore	Semaphore = semaphore - 1

Fig. 6-20. The effect of a semaphore instruction.

Figure 6-21 shows how the race condition can be eliminated through the use of semaphores. Two semaphores are used, *available*, which is initially 100 (the buffer size), and *filled*, which is initially 0.

The producer starts executing at P1 in Fig. 6-21 and the consumer starts executing at C1. The DOWN instruction on *filled* halts the consumer processor immediately. When

```
const MaxPrime = ...;                      {largest prime to look for}
      BufSize = 100;                       {number of buffer slots}

type index = 1 .. BufSize ;                {buffer slots numbered from 1 to BufSize}

var in : index ;                           {next free slot for a prime to go into}
    out : index ;                          {next prime to be fetched and printed}
    buffer : array[index ] of integer ;    {shared buffer}

function next (k : index ): index ;
{ Compute the successor to k taking wraparound into account.}
begin
  if k < BufSize then next := k + 1 else next := 1
end; {next}


procedure producer ;
{ In this improved version, the producer puts the primes in the buffer for
  subsequent printing .  When the buffer is full , the producer goes to sleep
  by doing a DOWN on available.  When the consumer does an UP on available,
  the producer continues at P3.  DOWN and UP are level 3 instructions that
  are invoked by the library procedures down and up, respectively .}

var prime : integer ;
begin
  prime := 2;
  while prime < MaxPrime do
    begin
      {P1}  ComputeNextPrime(prime);
      {P2}  down(available);
      {P3}  buffer[in] := prime;
      {P4}  in := next(in);
      {P5}  up(filled)
    end
end; {producer}


procedure consumer ;
{ The consumer takes numbers out of the buffer and prints them.  If the buffer
  becomes empty , the consumer goes to sleep .  When the producer sends a wakeup
  signal , the consumer continues at C2.}
var emirp : integer ;
begin
  emirp := 2;
  while emirp < MaxPrime do
    begin
      {C1}  down(filled);
      {C2}  emirp := buffer[out];
      {C3}  out := next(out);
      {C4}  up(available);
      {C5}  writeln(emirp)
    end
end; {consumer}
```

Fig. 6-21. Parallel processing using semaphores.

the producer has found the first prime, it executes a DOWN instruction on *available*, setting it to 99. At P5 it does an UP on *filled*, making it 1. This action releases the consumer, which is now able to complete its DOWN instruction. At this point, *filled* is 0 and both processes are running.

Let us now reexamine the race condition. At a certain point in time, $in = 22$, $out = 21$, the producer is at P1, and the consumer is at C5. The consumer finishes what it was doing and gets to C1 where it DOWNs the semaphore, which had the value 1 before the DOWN instruction and 0 after it. The consumer then takes the last number out of the buffer and UPs *available*, making it 100. The consumer prints the number and goes to C1. Just before the consumer can perform the DOWN instruction, the producer finds the next prime and in quick succession executes statements P2, P3, and P4.

At this point, *filled* is 0. The producer is about to UP it and the consumer is about to DOWN it. If the consumer executes its instruction first, it will be suspended until the producer releases it (by performing an UP). On the other hand if the producer executes its instruction first, the semaphore will be set to 1 and the consumer will not be suspended at all. In both cases, no wakeup is lost.

The essential property of the semaphore operations is that they are indivisible. Once a semaphore operation has been initiated, no other process can use the semaphore until the first process has either completed the operation or been suspended trying. Furthermore, with semaphores, no wakeups are lost. In contrast, the **if** statements of Fig. 6-18 are not indivisible. Between the evaluation of the condition and the execution of the selected statement, another process can send a wakeup signal.

In effect the problem of process synchronization has been eliminated by declaring the UP and DOWN instructions to be indivisible. In order for these level 3 instructions to be indivisible, the operating system must prohibit two or more processes from using the same semaphore at the same time.

Synchronization using semaphores is a technique that works for arbitrarily many processes. Several processes may be sleeping, attempting to complete a DOWN instruction on the same semaphore. When some other process finally performs an UP on that semaphore, one of the waiting processes is allowed to complete its DOWN instruction and continue running. The semaphore value remains 0 and the other processes continue waiting.

An analogy may make the nature of semaphores clearer. Imagine a picnic with 20 volleyball teams divided into 10 games (processes) each playing on its own court, and a large basket (the semaphore) for the volleyballs. Unfortunately, only seven volleyballs are available. At any instant, there are between zero and seven volleyballs in the basket (the semaphore has a value between 0 and 7). Putting a ball in the basket is an UP instruction because it increases the value of the semaphore. Taking a ball out of the basket is a DOWN instruction, because it decreases the value of the semaphore.

At the start of the picnic, each court sends a player to the basket to get a volleyball. Seven of them successfully manage to get a volleyball (complete the DOWN instruction); three are forced to wait for a volleyball (i.e., fail to complete the DOWN instruction). Their games are suspended temporarily. Eventually, one of the other games finishes and puts a ball into the basket (executes an UP instruction). This operation allows one of the three players waiting around the basket to get a ball (complete an unfinished DOWN instruction), allowing one game to continue. The other two games remain suspended until two more balls are put into the basket.

6.4. VIRTUAL MEMORY

In the early days of computers, memories were expensive and small. The IBM 650, the leading scientific computer of its day (late 1950s) had only 2000 words of memory. One of the first ALGOL 60 compilers was written for a computer with only 1024 words of memory. In those days the programmer spent a lot of time trying to squeeze programs into the tiny memory. Often it was necessary to use an algorithm that ran a great deal slower than another, better algorithm simply because the better algorithm was too big—that is, a program using the better algorithm could not be fitted into the computer's memory.

The traditional solution to this problem was the use of secondary memory, such as tape, drum, and disk. The programmer. divided the program up into a number of pieces, called **overlays**, each of which could fit in the memory. To run the program, the first overlay was brought in and it ran for a while. When it finished, it read in the next overlay and called it, and so on. The programmer was responsible for breaking the program into overlays, deciding where in the secondary memory each overlay was to be kept, arranging for the transport of overlays between main memory and secondary memory, and in general managing the whole overlay process without any help from the computer.

Although widely used for many years, this technique involved much work in connection with overlay management. In 1961 a group of people at Manchester, England, proposed a method for performing the overlay process automatically, without the programmer even knowing that it was happening (Fotheringham, 1961). This method, now called **virtual memory**, had the obvious advantage of freeing the programmer from a lot of annoying bookkeeping. It was first used on a number of computers during the 1960s, mostly associated with research projects in computer systems design. By the early 1970s virtual memory had become available on most computers, including the 370 and PDP-11.

6.4.1. Paging

The idea put forth by the Manchester group was to separate the concepts of address space and memory locations. Consider an example of a computer with a 16-bit address field in its instructions and 4096 words of memory. A program on this computer can address 65536 words of memory. The reason is that 65536 (2^{16}) 16-bit addresses exist. The number of addressable words depends only on the number of bits in an address and is in no way related to the number of memory words actually available. The **address space** for this computer consists of the numbers 0, 1, 2 . . . , 65535, because that is the set of possible addresses.

Before virtual memory was invented, people would have made a distinction between the addresses below 4096 and those equal to or above 4096. Although rarely stated in so many words, these two parts were regarded as the useful address space and the useless address space, respectively (the addresses above 4095 being useless because they did not correspond to actual memory addresses). People did not make much of a distinction between address space and actual memory addresses, because the hardware enforced a one-to-one correspondence between them.

The idea of separating the address space and the memory addresses is as follows. At any instant of time, 4096 words of memory can be directly accessed but they need not correspond to addresses 0 to 4095. We could, for example, "tell" the computer that henceforth whenever address 4096 is referenced, memory word 0 is to be used. Whenever address 4097 is referenced, memory word 1 is to be used; whenever address 8191 is referenced, memory word 4095 is to be used, and so forth. In other words, we have defined a mapping from the address space onto the actual memory addresses, as shown in Fig. 6-22.

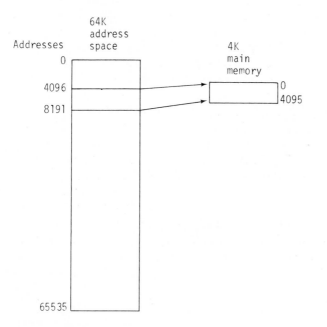

Fig. 6-22. A mapping in which addresses 4096 to 8191 are mapped onto main memory addresses 0 to 4095.

In terms of this picture of mapping addresses from the address space onto the actual memory locations, a 4K machine without virtual memory simply has a fixed mapping between the addresses 0 to 4095 and the 4096 words of memory. An interesting question is: What happens if a program jumps to an address between 8192 and 12287? On a machine without virtual memory, the program would cause an error trap that would print a suitably rude message, such as "Nonexistent memory referenced" and terminate the program. On a machine with virtual memory, the following sequence of steps would occur:

1. The contents of main memory would be saved in the secondary memory.

2. Words 8192 to 12287 would be located in the secondary memory.

3. Words 8192 to 12287 would be loaded into main memory.

4. The address map would be changed to map addresses 8192 to 12287 onto memory locations 0 to 4095.

5. Execution would continue as though nothing unusual had happened.

This technique for automatic overlaying is called **paging** and the chunks of program read in from secondary memory are called **pages**.

A more sophisticated way of mapping addresses from the address space onto the actual memory addresses is also possible. For emphasis, we will call the addresses that the program can refer to the **virtual address space**, and the actual, hardwired memory addresses the **physical address space**. A **memory map** relates virtual addresses to physical addresses. We presume that there is enough room in the secondary memory—for example, a drum or a disk—to store the whole program and its data.

Programs are written just as though there were enough main memory for the whole virtual address space, even though such is not the case. Programs may load from, or store into, any word in the virtual address space, or jump to any instruction located anywhere within the virtual address space, without regard to the fact that there really is not enough physical memory. In fact, the programmer can write programs without even being aware that virtual memory exists. The computer just looks like it has a big memory.

This point is crucial and will be contrasted later with segmentation, where the programmer must be aware of the existence of segments. To emphasize it once more, paging gives the programmer the illusion of a large, continuous, linear main memory, the same size as the address space, when, in fact, the main memory available may be smaller (or larger) than the address space. The simulation of this large main memory by paging cannot be detected by the program (except by running timing tests); whenever an address is referenced, the proper instruction or data word appears to be present. Because the programmer can program as though paging did not exist, the paging mechanism is said to be **transparent**.

The idea that a programmer may use some nonexistent feature without being concerned with how it works is not new to us, after all. The instruction set of a level 2 computer is nonexistent in the sense that none of the instructions are hardware primitives, but all of them are, in fact, carried out by software at level 1. Similarly, the level 3 programmer can use the virtual memory without worrying about how it works. The level 2 programmers who write the operating system must, of course, know exactly how it works.

6.4.2. Implementation of Paging

One essential requirement for a virtual memory is a secondary memory in which to keep the complete program. It is conceptually simpler if one thinks of the copy of the program in the secondary memory as the original one and the pieces brought into main memory every now and then as copies rather than the other way around. Naturally, it is important to keep the original up to date. When changes are made to the copy in main memory, they should also be reflected in the original (eventually).

The virtual address space is broken up into a number of equal-sized pages. Page sizes ranging from 512 to 4096 addresses per page are common at present. The page size is always a power of 2. The physical address space is broken up into pieces in a similar way, each piece being the same size as a page, so that each piece of main memory is capable of holding exactly one page. These pieces of main memory into which the pages go are called **page frames**. In Fig. 6-22 the main memory only contains one page frame. In practical designs it will contain tens, hundreds, or even thousands in a large machine.

Figure 6-23 illustrates a possible way to divide up a 64K address space. The virtual memory of Fig. 6-23 would be implemented at level 2 by means of a 16-word table called the **page table**. When the program tried to reference its memory, whether to fetch data, store data, fetch instructions or jump, it would first generate a 16-bit address corresponding to a virtual address between 0 and 65535. Indexing, indirect addressing, and all the usual techniques may be used to generate this address.

In this example, the 16-bit address is taken as a 4-bit virtual page number and a 12-bit address within the selected page, as shown in Fig. 6-24(a). In this figure the 16-bit address is 12310, which is regarded as address 22 of page 3. The relation between pages and virtual addresses for this example is shown in Fig. 6-24(b). If virtual address 0 of page 3 is at physical address 12288, virtual address 22 must be at physical address 12310.

Having discovered that virtual page 3 is needed, the operating system must find out where virtual page 3 is located. There are nine possibilities: eight page frames in main memory, or somewhere in secondary memory, because not all the virtual pages can be in main memory at once. To find out which of these nine possibilities is true, the operating system looks in the page table, which has one entry for each of the 16 virtual pages.

The example page table of Fig. 6-25 has three fields. The first is a bit which is 0 if the page is not in main memory and 1 if it is. The second gives the address where the virtual page is kept in secondary memory (e.g., a drum track and sector) when not in main memory. This address is needed so that the page can be found and brought in when necessary and later returned to its original place in secondary memory when no longer needed in main memory. The third is a 3-bit field giving the page frame

64K virtual address space   32K main memory

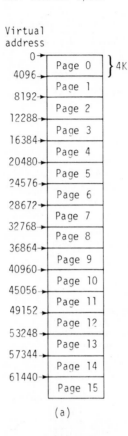

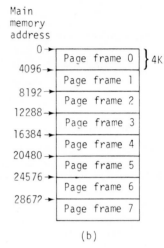

(a)

Fig. 6-23. (a) A 64K address space divided into 16 pages of 4K each. (b) A 32K main memory divided up into eight page frames of 4K each.

where the page is located if it is in main memory. If the page is not in main memory, field 3 is ignored.

Assuming that the virtual page is in main memory, the 3-bit page frame specifies where the page is. The page frame number is then gated into the leftmost 3 bits of the MAR, and the address within the virtual page—that is, the rightmost 12 bits of the original address—are gated into the rightmost 12 bits of the MAR. In this way a main memory address can be formed, as shown in Fig. 6-26. The 3-bit page frame plus the 12-bit offset give a 15-bit address, which is precisely what is needed for the 32K main memory of Fig. 6-23 which we are considering. The hardware can now use this address and fetch the desired word into the MBR or it can store the MBR into the desired word.

Figure 6-27 shows a possible mapping between virtual pages and physical page

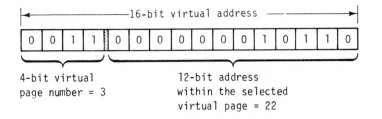

4-bit virtual
page number = 3

12-bit address
within the selected
virtual page = 22

(a)

Page	Virtual address
0	0 - 4095
1	4096 - 8191
2	8192 - 12287
3	12288 - 16383
4	16384 - 20479
5	20480 - 24575
6	24576 - 28671
7	28672 - 32767
8	32768 - 36863
9	36864 - 40959
10	40960 - 45055
11	45056 - 49151
12	49152 - 53247
13	53248 - 57343
14	57344 - 61439
15	61440 - 65535

(b)

Fig. 6-24. (a) A virtual address consisting of a 4-bit virtual page number and a 12-bit offset. (b) Page numbers and
their virtual addresses.

frames. Virtual page 0 is in page frame 1. Virtual page 1 is in page frame 0. Virtual page 2 is not in main memory. Virtual page 3 is in page frame 2. Virtual page 4
is not in main memory, and so on.

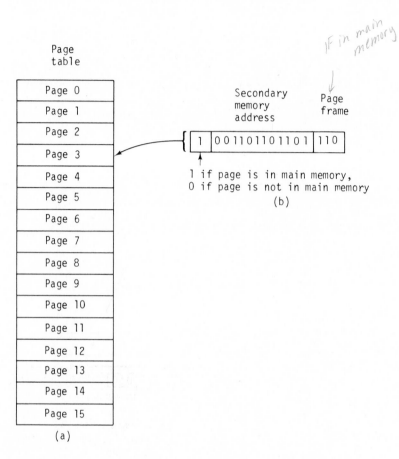

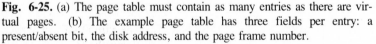

Fig. 6-25. (a) The page table must contain as many entries as there are virtual pages. (b) The example page table has three fields per entry: a present/absent bit, the disk address, and the page frame number.

If the operating system had to convert every level 3 machine instruction's virtual address into an actual address, a level 3 machine with virtual memory would run many times slower than one without virtual memory, and the whole idea would be impractical. To speed up the virtual-to-physical address translation, the page table is usually maintained in special hardware registers, and the transformation from virtual address to actual address is done directly in hardware. Another way of doing it is to maintain the map in fast registers and let the microprogram do the transformation by explicit programming. Depending on the architecture of the microprogramming level, having the microprogram perform the transformation might be almost as fast as doing it directly in the hardware, and would require no special circuits or hardware modifications.

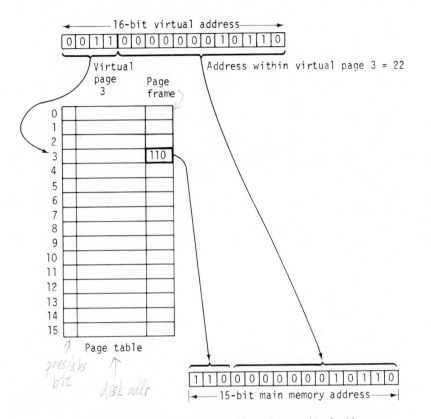

Fig. 6-26. Formation of a main memory address from a virtual address.

6.4.3. Demand Paging and the Working Set Model

In the preceding discussion it was assumed that the virtual page referenced was in main memory. However, that assumption will not always be true because there is not enough room in main memory for all the virtual pages. When a reference is made to an address on a page not present in main memory, it is called a **page fault**. After a page fault has occurred, it is necessary for the operating system to read in the required page from the secondary memory, enter its new physical memory location in the page table, and then repeat the instruction that caused the fault.

It is possible to start a program running on a machine with virtual memory even though none of the program is in main memory. The page table merely has to be set to indicate that each and every virtual page is in the secondary memory and not in main memory. When the CPU tries to fetch the first instruction, it immediately gets a page fault, which causes the page containing the first instruction to be loaded and entered in the page table. Then the first instruction can begin. If the first instruction has two addresses, with the two addresses on different pages, both different from the

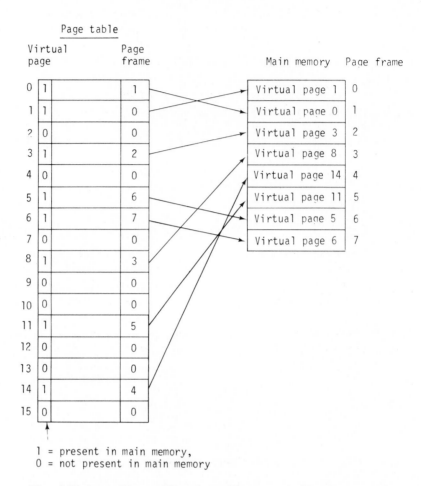

1 = present in main memory,
0 = not present in main memory

Fig. 6-27. A possible mapping of an address space with 16 pages onto a main memory with eight page frames.

instruction page, two more page faults will occur, and two more pages will be brought in before the instruction can finally execute. The next instruction may possibly cause some more page faults, and so forth.

This method of operating a virtual memory is called **demand paging**, in analogy to the well-known demand feeding algorithm for babies: when the baby cries, you feed it (as opposed to feeding it at regular times of day). In demand paging, pages are brought in only when an actual request for a page occurs, not in advance.

The question of whether demand paging should be used or not is only relevant when a program first starts up. Once it has been running for a while, the needed pages will already have been collected in main memory. If the computer is time-shared and users are swapped out after running 100 msec or so, each program will be restarted many times during the course of its run. Because the memory map is unique to each process and is changed when processes are switched, the question repeatedly becomes a critical one.

The alternative approach is based on the observation that most programs do not reference their address space uniformly but that the references tend to cluster on a small number of pages. A memory reference may fetch an instruction, it may fetch data, or it may store data. At any instant in time, t, there exists a set consisting of all the pages used by the k most recent memory references. Denning (1968) has called this the **working set**, $w(k, t)$. Because the $k + 1$ most recent references must have used all the pages used by the k most recent references, and possibly others, $w(k, t)$ is a monotonically nondecreasing function of k. The limit of $w(k, t)$ as k becomes large is finite, because the program cannot reference more pages than its address space contains, and few programs will use every single page.

Figure 6-28 depicts the size of the working set as a function of k. The fact that most programs randomly access a small number of pages but that this set changes slowly in time explains the initial rapid rise of the curve and then the slow rise for large k. For example, a program that is executing a loop occupying two pages, using data occupying four pages, may reference all six pages every 1000 instructions, but the most recent reference to some other page may be a million references earlier, during the initialization phase. Because of this asymptotic behavior, the contents of the working set is not sensitive to the value of k chosen, or to put it differently, there exists a wide range of k values for which the working set is unchanged.

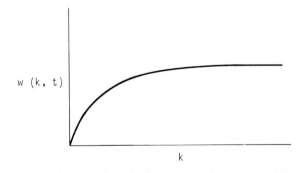

Fig. 6-28. The working set is the set of pages used by the k most recent memory references. The function $w(k, t)$ is the size of the working set at time t.

Because the working set varies slowly with time, it is possible to make a reasonable guess as to which pages will be needed when the program is restarted, on the basis of its working set when it was last stopped. These pages could then be loaded in advance before starting the program up (assuming they fit).

The argument in favor of bringing the working set into main memory in advance is that it can be brought in while some other program is running. When a program is started, it will not immediately generate a large number of time-consuming page faults, an event that may cause the CPU to be idle while the needed pages are being brought in. Remember that the time needed to read in a page from a drum is typically 20000 instruction times or more.

The argument against bringing the working set into main memory in advance is that if the program is in transition between one working set and another, and has not yet settled down, a lot of work will have been done bringing in pages that are not going to be referenced. With demand paging that situation cannot occur. The only pages that are loaded are those that are actually needed. The relative merits of these two strategies are still being debated.

6.4.4. Page Replacement Policy

Up to now, we have tacitly assumed that there is always a vacant page frame in which to put the newly loaded page. In general, this will not be true, and it will be necessary to remove some page (i.e., copy it back to the secondary memory) to make room. Thus an algorithm that decides which page to remove is needed.

Choosing a page to remove at random certainly is not a good idea. If the page containing the instruction should happen to be the one picked, another page fault will occur as soon as an attempt is made to fetch the next instruction. Most operating systems try to predict which of the pages in memory is the least useful in the sense that its absence would have the smallest adverse effect on the running program. One way of doing so is to make a prediction when the next reference to each page will occur and remove the page whose next reference lies furthest in the future. In other words, rather than evict a page that will be needed shortly, try to select one that will not be needed for a long time.

One popular algorithm evicts the page least recently used because the a priori probability of its not being in the current working set is high. It is called the **least recently used** or LRU algorithm. Although it usually performs well, there are pathological situations, such as the one described below, where LRU fails miserably.

Imagine a program executing a large loop that extends over nine virtual pages on a machine with room for only eight pages in memory. After the program gets to page 7 the main memory will be as shown in Fig. 6-29(a). An attempt is eventually made to fetch an instruction from virtual page 8, which causes a page fault. A decision has to be made about which page to evict. The LRU algorithm will choose virtual page 0, because it has been used least recently. Virtual page 0 is removed and virtual page 8 is brought in to replace it, giving the situation in Fig. 6-29(b).

After executing the instructions on virtual page 8, the program jumps back to the top of the loop, to virtual page 0. This step causes another page fault. Virtual page 0, which was just thrown out, has to be brought back in. The LRU algorithm chooses page 1 to be thrown out, producing the situation in Fig. 6-29(c). The program continues on page 0 for a little while. Then it tries to fetch an instruction from virtual page 1, causing a page fault. Page 1 has to be brought back in again and page 2 will be thrown out.

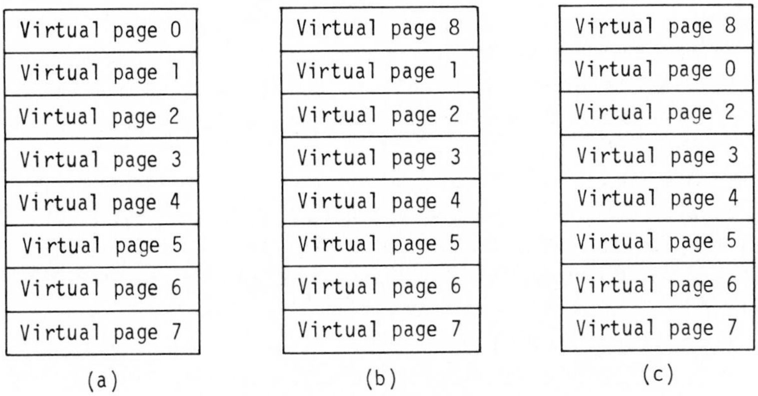

Virtual page 0
Virtual page 1
Virtual page 2
Virtual page 3
Virtual page 4
Virtual page 5
Virtual page 6
Virtual page 7

(a)

Virtual page 8
Virtual page 1
Virtual page 2
Virtual page 3
Virtual page 4
Virtual page 5
Virtual page 6
Virtual page 7

(b)

Virtual page 8
Virtual page 0
Virtual page 2
Virtual page 3
Virtual page 4
Virtual page 5
Virtual page 6
Virtual page 7

(c)

Fig. 6-29. Failure of the LRU algorithm.

It should be apparent by now that here the LRU algorithm is consistently making the worst choice every time. If, however, the available main memory exceeds the size of the working set, LRU tends to minimize the number of page faults.

Another algorithm is **First-In, First-Out,** or FIFO. FIFO removes the least recently loaded page, independent of when this page was last referenced. Associated with each virtual page is a counter, possibly kept in the page table. Initially, all the counters are set to 0. After each page fault has been handled, the counter for each page presently in memory is increased by one, and the counter for the page just brought in is set to 0. When it becomes necessary to choose a page to remove, the page whose counter is highest is chosen. Since its counter is the highest, it has witnessed the largest number of page faults. This means that it was loaded prior to the loading of any of the other pages in memory and therefore (hopefully) has a large a priori chance of no longer being needed.

If the working set is larger than the number of available page frames, no algorithm that is not an oracle will give good results, and page faults will be frequent. A program that generates page faults frequently and continuously is said to be **thrashing**. Needless to say, thrashing is an undesirable characteristic to have in your system. If a program uses a large amount of virtual address space but has a small, slowly changing working set that fits in available main memory, it will give little trouble, even if, over its lifetime, it uses hundreds of times as many words of virtual memory as the machine has words of main memory.

If a page about to be evicted has not been modified since it was read in (a likely occurrence if the page contains program rather than data), then it is not necessary to write it back into secondary memory, because an accurate copy already exists there. If it has been modified because it was read in, the copy in the secondary memory is no longer accurate, and the page must be rewritten.

If there is a way to tell whether a page has remained unchanged because it was read in (page is clean) or whether it, in fact, has been stored into (page is dirty), all the rewriting of clean pages can be avoided, thus saving a lot of time. Some computers have 1 bit per page, in the page table, which is set to 0 when a page is loaded and set to 1 by the microprogram or hardware whenever it is stored into. By examining this bit, the operating system can find out if the page is clean or dirty, and hence whether it need be rewritten or not. Such a bit is sometimes referred to as a **dirty bit**.

It is obviously desirable to maintain a high ratio of clean pages to dirty pages to minimize the chance that a rewrite will be required at the next page fault. On nearly all computers, pages can be copied from main memory to secondary memory, particularly drums and disks, while the CPU is computing. The CPU need only start the transfer and then it can return to its computation. If the secondary memory is a drum and no transfers are waiting to be done, the CPU could choose a dirty page, preferably one likely to be written out shortly (due to its age), and issue a drum command to copy it to the drum. Copying it to the drum does not alter or destroy the copy in main memory, of course.

If the page is made dirty again immediately after the copying process or even during it, the copying has been done in vain but because the drum was idle anyway, and the CPU was free to compute again as soon as it issued the drum command, the cost of performing the copy was not high. Writes to secondary memory made with the intention of making dirty pages clean have been called **sneaky writes**. It is still an open issue whether the amount of time saved swapping is enough to counterbalance the administration involved in setting up the sneaky writes.

6.4.5. Page Size and Fragmentation

If the user's program and data accidentally happen to fill an integral number of pages exactly, there will be no wasted space when they are in memory. If, on the other hand, they do not fill an integral number of pages exactly, there will be some unused space on the last page. For example, if the program and data need 26000 words on a machine with 4096 words per page, the first six pages will be full, totaling $6 \times 4096 = 24576$ words, and the last page will contain 26000 - 24576 = 1424 words. Since there is room for 4096 words per page, 2672 words will be wasted. Whenever the seventh page is present in memory, those words will take up precious main memory but will serve no useful function. The problem of these wasted words is called **fragmentation**.

If the page size is n words, the average amount of space wasted in the last page of a program by fragmentation will be $n/2$ words—a situation that suggests a small page size to minimize waste. On the other hand, a small page size means many pages, as well as a large page table. If the page table is maintained in hardware, a large page table means that more registers are needed to store it, which increases the cost of the computer. In addition, more time will be required to load and save these registers whenever a process is started or stopped.

Furthermore, small pages make inefficient use of secondary memories with long rotational delays, such as drums and disks. Given that one is going to wait 10 msec or more before the transfer can begin, one would like to transfer a large block of information, because the transfer time is usually shorter than the rotational delay time. Generally, it costs little extra time to read 1024 words as compared to 256 words. If a secondary memory with no rotational delay is being used, such as low-speed core or solid-state memory, the total transfer time is proportional to the block size.

Small pages do have the advantage that if the working set consists of a large number of small, separated regions in the virtual address space, there may be less thrashing with a small page size than with a big one. For example, consider a program that is randomly accessing 20 widely separated regions of 100 words each. If a 1000×20 matrix A is stored with $A[1, 1]$, $A[2, 1]$, $A[3, 1]$, and so on, in consecutive words, then $A[1, 1]$, $A[1, 2]$, $A[1, 3]$, and so on, will be 1000 words apart. A program performing some calculation on all the elements of the first 20 rows would use 20 regions of 20 words with 980 words separating these regions. If the page size were 2048 words, at least 10 pages, totaling 20480 words, would be in the working set. If the page size were 128 words, then even if each region occupied parts of two pages, only 40 pages, totaling 5120 words, would be needed to run the program. If the main memory available was more than 5120 words but less than 20480 words, the large page size would prohibit the complete working set from being in main memory, thereby causing thrashing, whereas the small page size would cause no problems.

6.4.6. Cache Memory

The principle behind a paged virtual memory can be generalized to a hierarchical memory. Some computers have a small, high-speed memory called a **cache memory** (or simply a cache) in addition to the usual main memory and secondary memory. The cache holds those parts of the program and data that are most heavily used, the main memory holds those parts that are less heavily used, and the secondary memory holds those parts that are least heavily used.

The cache works as follows. Main memory is divided up into blocks. These blocks may be the same size as, or smaller than, the page size. Copies of the most heavily used blocks are kept in the cache, as well as in main memory. When a program tries to reference its address space, it presents a virtual address to the hardware (or microprogram). If the page containing that address is in main memory, the virtual address is translated into a main memory address; otherwise a page fault occurs and the page is brought into main memory.

The cache hardware then checks to see if the block referenced happens to be in the cache memory. If it is there, the contents of the addressed location are fetched from the cache, or the result is stored into the cache. If it is not there, a cache block fault, analogous to a page fault, occurs and the needed block is copied from main memory into the cache. After the block has been loaded into the cache, the instruction is executed again.

This arrangement is essentially a two-level paging system, with the cache treating physical main memory addresses as virtual addresses and cache addresses as real addresses. However, there are two significant differences between paging from secondary memory into main memory and paging from main memory into the cache:

1. Main memory has no latency, as a disk does, so the block can be copied from main memory to the cache immediately. Because the transfer will be completed within microseconds instead of milliseconds, the CPU can afford to stop and wait for it. When paging from a disk, the delay is so long that the CPU will usually find another process to run while waiting for the page.

2. Due to the very short time involved and the simplicity of the transfer, the cache-main memory paging system is handled completely by the microprogram without any assistance from the operating system. Typically, the operating system does not even know a cache exists.

The comments made earlier about replacement algorithms, dirty bits, and fragmentation apply equally well to the cache-main memory system as to the main memory-secondary memory system to which they were originally applied. Furthermore, there is no reason a memory hierarchy must be limited to only three levels. Figure 6-30 illustrates a six-level memory hierarchy. From the cache to the top level, the speed steadily decreases and the storage capacity steadily increases. The access-time ratio between the top and the bottom can be a factor of 10^9 (50 nsec to randomly access the cache, 50 sec to randomly access a magnetic tape). Similarly, a large tape library may contain tens of millions of times as many bits as the cache. The cost per bit of storage also varies from level to level, being most expensive for the cache and cheapest for the archival storage.

The advantage of a memory hierarchy is that a huge virtual address space can be provided at an effective access time only slightly worse than that of the fastest level. If the **hit ratio** (fraction of main memory references that can be satisfied out of the cache) is high, the program will run fast. In other words, if the cache working set changes slowly, the program will, in effect, be running out of the cache and not out of main memory.

6.4.7. Segmentation

The virtual memory discussed above is one-dimensional because the virtual addresses go from 0 to some maximum address, one address after another. For many problems, having two or more separate virtual address spaces may be much better than having only one. For example, a compiler has many tables that are built up as compilation proceeds, including

1. The source text being saved for the printed listing.

2. The symbol table, containing the names and attributes of declared variables.

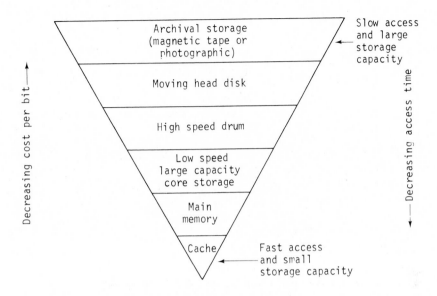

Fig. 6-30. A six-level memory hierarchy.

3. The numeric constant table, containing all the integer and floating-point constants used.

4. The parse tree, containing the syntactic analysis of the program.

5. The stack used for procedure calls within the compiler.

Each of the first four tables grows continuously as compilation proceeds. The last one grows and shrinks in unpredictable ways during compilation. In a one-dimensional memory, these five tables would have to be allocated contiguous chunks of virtual address space, as in Fig. 6-31.

Consider what happens if a program has an exceptionally large number of variables. The chunk of address space allocated for the symbol table may fill up, but there may be lots of room in the other tables. The compiler could, of course, simply issue a message saying that the compilation cannot continue due to too many variables, but doing so does not seem very sporting when unused space is left in the other tables.

Another possibility is to play Robin Hood, taking space from the tables with much room and giving it to the tables with little room. This shuffling can be done but it is analogous to managing one's own overlays—a nuisance at best and a great deal of work at worst.

What is really needed is a way of freeing the programmer from having to manage the expanding and contracting tables, in the same way that virtual memory eliminates the worry of organizing the program into overlays.

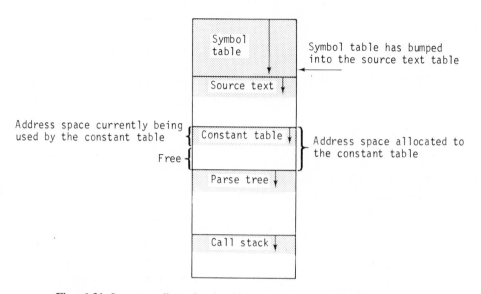

Fig. 6-31. In a one-dimensional address space with growing tables, one table may bump into another.

A straightforward and extremely general solution is to provide the level 3 machine with many, completely independent address spaces, called **segments**. Each segment consists of a linear sequence of addresses, from 0 to some maximum. The length of each segment may be anything from 0 to the maximum allowed. Different segments may, and usually do, have different lengths. Moreover, segment lengths may change during execution. The length of a stack segment may be increased whenever something is pushed onto the stack and decreased whenever something is popped off the stack.

Because each segment constitutes a separate address space, different segments can grow or shrink independently, without affecting each other. If a stack in a certain segment needs more address space to grow, it can have it, because there is nothing else in its address space to bump into. Of course, a segment can fill up but segments are usually very large, so this occurrence is rare. To specify an address in this segmented or two-dimensional memory, the program must supply a two-part address, a segment number, and an address within the segment. Figure 6-32 illustrates a segmented memory being used for the compiler tables discussed earlier.

We emphasize that a segment is a logical entity, which the programmer is aware of and uses as a single logical entity. A segment might contain a procedure, or an array, or a stack, or a collection of scalar variables, but usually it does not contain a mixture of different types.

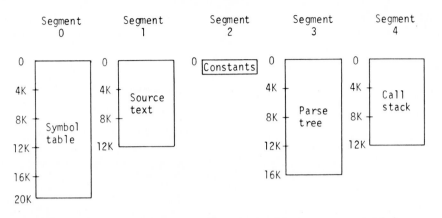

Fig. 6-32. A segmented memory allows each table to grow or shrink independently of the other tables.

A segmented memory has other advantages besides simplifying the handling of data structures that are growing or shrinking. If each procedure occupies a separate segment, with address 0 as its starting address, the linking up of procedures compiled separately is greatly simplified. After all the procedures that constitute a program have been compiled and linked up, a procedure call to the procedure in segment n will use the two-part address $(n, 0)$ to address word 0 (the entry point).

If the procedure in segment n is subsequently modified and recompiled, no other procedures need be changed (because no starting addresses have been modified), even if the new version is larger than the old one. With a one-dimensional memory, the procedures are packed tightly next to each other, with no address space between them. Consequently, changing one procedure's size can affect the starting address of other, unrelated procedures. This, in turn, requires modifying all procedures that call any of the moved procedures, in order to incorporate their new starting addresses. If a program contains hundreds of procedures, this process can be costly.

Segmentation also facilitates sharing procedures or data between several processes. If a computer has several level 3 machines running in parallel (either true or simulated parallel processing), all of which use certain library procedures, it is wasteful of main memory to provide each one with its own private copy. By making each procedure a separate segment, they can be shared easily, thus eliminating the need for more than one physical copy of any shared procedure to be in main memory.

Because each segment forms a logical entity of which the programmer is aware, such as a procedure, or an array, or a stack, different segments can have different kinds of protection. A procedure segment could be specified as execute only, prohibiting attempts to read from it or store into it. A floating-point array could be specified as read/write but not execute, and attempts to jump to it would be caught. Such protection is helpful in catching programming errors.

You should try to understand why protection makes sense in a segmented memory but not in a one-dimensional paged memory. In a segmented memory the user is aware of what is in each segment. Normally, a segment would not contain a procedure and a stack, for example but one or the other. Since each segment contains only one type of object, the segment can have the protection appropriate for that particular type.

The contents of a page are, in a sense, accidental. The programmer is unaware of the fact that paging is even occurring. Although putting a few bits in each entry of the page table to specify the access allowed would be possible, to utilize this feature the programmer would have to keep track of where in his address space the page boundaries were, and that is precisely the sort of administration that paging was invented to eliminate. Because the user of a segmented memory has the illusion that all segments are in main memory all the time—that is, he can address them as though they were—he can protect each segment separately, without having to be concerned with the administration of overlaying them.

Before going on to the sections on implementation of segmented memories, you should be sure to understand the differences between paging and segmentation. They are summarized in Fig. 6-33.

Consideration	Paging	Segmentation
Need the programmer be aware that this technique is being used?	No	Yes
How many linear address spaces are there?	1	Many
Can the total address space exceed the size of physical memory?	Yes	Yes
Can procedures and data be distinguished and separately protected?	No	Yes
Can tables whose size fluctuates be accomodated easily?	No	Yes
Is sharing of procedures between users facilitated?	No	Yes
Why was this technique invented?	To get a large linear address space without having to buy more physical memory	To allow programs and data to be broken up into logically independent address spaces and to aid sharing and protection

Fig. 6-33. Comparison of paging and segmentation.

6.4.8. The MULTICS Virtual Memory

The ideal virtual memory consists of a large number of large segments. The MULTICS operating system (Corbató and Vyssotsky, 1965; Daley and Neumann, 1965; Organick, 1972) for the Honeywell 6000 series provides each program with a virtual memory of up to 2^{18} segments (more than 250,000), each of which can be up to 65536 (36-bit) words long. To implement this, the MULTICS designers choose to treat each segment as a virtual memory and to page it, combining the advantages of paging (uniform page size and not having to keep the whole segment in memory if only part of it is being used) with the advantages of segmentation (ease of programming, modularity, protection, and sharing).

Each MULTICS process has a segment table, with one descriptor per segment. Since there are potentially more than a quarter of a million entries in the table, the segment table is itself a segment and is paged. A segment descriptor contains an indication of whether the segment is in main memory or not. If any part of the segment is in memory, the segment is considered to be in memory, and its page table will be in memory. If the segment is in memory, its descriptor contains a pointer to its page table [see Fig. 6-34(a)]. Because physical memory addresses are 24 bits, the low-order 6 bits of the address are assumed to be 0. The descriptor also contains the segment size, the protection bits, and a few other items. Figure 6-34(b) illustrates the MULTICS segment descriptor. The address of the segment in secondary memory is not in the segment descriptor but in another table used by the segment fault handler.

Each segment is an ordinary virtual address space and is paged in the same way as the nonsegmented paged memory described in Sec. 6.4.2. The normal page size is 1024 words (although a few small segments used by MULTICS itself are not paged or are paged in units of 64 words).

An address in MULTICS consists of two parts: the segment and the address within the segment. The address within the segment is further divided into a page number and a word within the page, as shown in Fig. 6-35. When a memory reference occurs, the following algorithm is carried out.

1. The segment number is used to find the segment descriptor.

2. A check is made to see if the segment's page table is in memory. If it is not, a segment fault occurs. If there is a protection violation, a fault (trap) occurs. If the page table is in memory and the access allowed, the page table is located.

3. The page table entry for the requested virtual page is examined. If the page is not in memory, a page fault occurs. If it is in memory, the main memory address of the start of the page is extracted from the page table entry.

4. The offset is added to the page origin to give the main memory address where the word is located.

5. The read or store finally takes place.

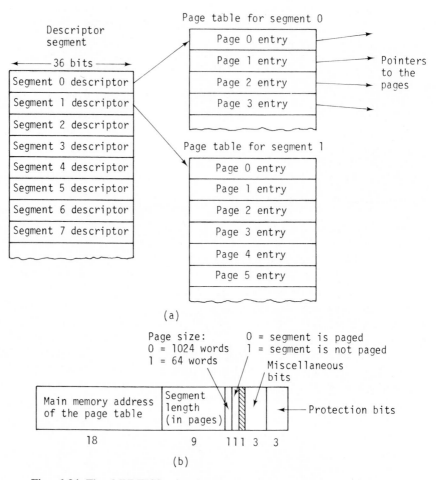

(a)

(b)

Fig. 6-34. The MULTICS virtual memory. (a) The descriptor segment points to the page tables. (b) A segment descriptor. The numbers are the field lengths.

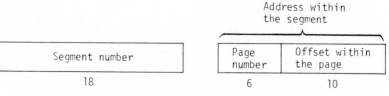

Fig. 6-35. A 34-bit MULTICS virtual address.

This process is illustrated in Fig. 6-36. For simplicity, the fact that the descriptor segment is itself paged has been omitted. What really happens is that a register, called the descriptor base register, is used to locate the descriptor segment's page table, which, in turn, points to the pages of the descriptor segment. Once the descriptor for the needed segment has been found, the addressing proceeds as shown in Fig. 6-36.

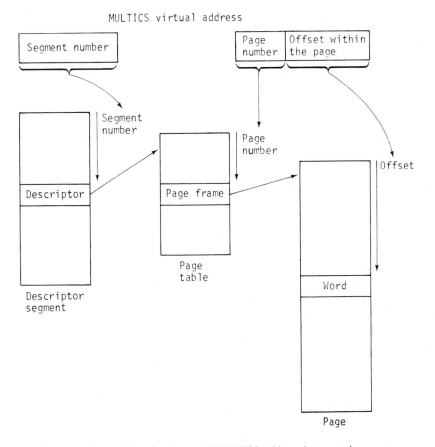

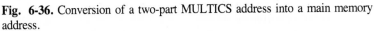

Fig. 6-36. Conversion of a two-part MULTICS address into a main memory address.

As you have no doubt guessed by now, if the preceding algorithm were actually carried out by the operating system on every instruction, programs would not run very fast. In reality, the MULTICS hardware contains a 16-word high-speed **associative memory** that can search all its entries in parallel for a given key. It is illustrated in Fig. 6-37. When an address is presented to the computer, the addressing hardware first checks to see if the virtual address is in the associative memory. If so, it gets the page frame number directly from the associative memory and forms the actual address of the referenced word without having to look in the descriptor segment or page table.

Segment number	Virtual page	Page frame	Protection	Age	Is this entry used?
4	1	7	Read/write	13	1
6	0	2	Read only	10	1
12	3	1	Read/write	2	1
					0
2	1	0	Execute only	7	1
2	2	12	Execute only	9	1

Fig. 6-37. A simplified version of the MULTICS associative memory. The existence of two page sizes makes the actual associative memory more complicated.

The addresses of the 16 most recently referenced pages are kept in the associative memory. Programs whose working set is smaller than the size of the associative memory will come to equilibrium with the addresses of the entire working set in the associative memory and therefore will run efficiently. If the page is not in the associative memory, the descriptor and page tables are actually referenced to find the page frame address, and the associative memory is updated to include this page, the least recently used page being thrown out. The age field keeps track of which entry has been least recently used. The reason that an associative memory is used is that segment and page number of all the entries can be compared simultaneously, for speed.

Segmented Virtual Memory and File I/O

The availability of a large segmented address space has important implications for file I/O. By making each file into a segment, a program can directly reference any part of any file without the need for special virtual I/O instructions. For example, a program could directly add an integer in a file to a register, using the ordinary ADD instruction, without first having to "read in" the integer. If the logical record referenced were not in main memory, a page fault would occur, and the page fault handler would bring it in.

In a sense, virtual I/O instructions on files and virtual memory are competing mechanisms for transferring information from secondary memory to main memory. Virtual memory is by far the more convenient of the two from the programmer's point of view, because it does not require the programmer to issue any special instructions to access the data, or even be aware of whether the data are in main memory or not. Furthermore, it is wasteful to have two distinct mechanisms in the operating system both of which perform the same function (transferring information from secondary memory to main memory).

The MULTICS system carries the correspondence between files and segments to its logical extreme: no distinction is made between files and segments. When a process is started up, all the files it initially needs (both procedures and data) are given segment numbers in order to make them directly addressable without the need for any I/O instructions. If it is discovered later that other files from one of the user's directories (or someone else's directories, if permitted) are needed, they will automatically be added to the virtual address space by simply indirectly addressing their symbolic names. This technique is called **dynamic linking** and is described in Sec. 7.4.4. Because all the parts of all the files that a program needs can be accessed directly simply by using the proper virtual address, a typical MULTICS program never does any explicit I/O, even if it is processing large amounts of data.

Although files and segments are not identical on the 370, it is possible to make a file addressable as a segment by using the Virtual Storage Access Method (VSAM). If accessing a number of large files by mapping them onto segments is desired, the total amount of virtual address space available becomes important. The total virtual address space on the 370 is approximately enough to access the data contained on one small magnetic tape. In contrast, the MULTICS virtual address space is sufficient to access all the data on over 1000 large magnetic tapes.

6.4.9. Virtual Memory on the IBM 370

Like MULTICS, the 370 has a sophisticated virtual memory with paged segments. IBM calls its virtual memory **dynamic address translation**. The 370s total virtual address is smaller then that of MULTICS (2^{24} 8-bit bytes versus 2^{34} 36-bit words). Due to the comparatively small address space, the division of the 24 bits into segment number and address within the segment is much more critical than in MULTICS. A decision to have 2^{18} segments like MULTICS would have meant a maximum segment size of 64 bytes, hardly a realistic possibility.

To provide additional flexibility within the limitations of a 24-bit virtual address, the designers of the 370 provided two possibilities:

16 segments of 2^{20} bytes (262,144 words)

256 segments of 2^{16} bytes (16384 words)

The MULTICS goal of making each procedure and each large array a separate segment will be difficult to realize on the 370 if there are more than 16 procedures and data segments, some of which exceed 16K words.

All segments on the 370 are paged. Two page sizes are provided: 2K bytes and 4K bytes. The 370 uses a descriptor segment and page tables, similar to those used in

MULTICS. Figure 6-38 shows the formats of the segment descriptors and page table entries. The segment length is in units of 1/16 of the maximum number of pages, using 0-origin counting. The page table address is concatenated to three low-order zeros to give a 24-bit main memory address. Similarly, the page addresses are only the high-order bits of a 24-bit address.

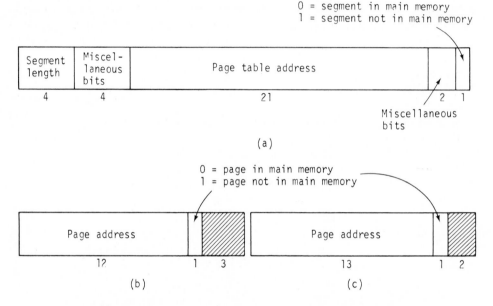

Fig. 6-38. (a) A 370 segment descriptor. (b) A page table entry for a segment with 4K byte pages. (c) A page table entry for a segment with 2K byte pages.

The addressing mechanism on the 370 is the same one used by MULTICS, including the use of a small, high-speed associative memory. The size of the associative memory is different for models of the 370 series, being larger in the larger machines. Associated with each page are bits to record whether or not the page has been used or modified. These bits, along with the protection bits, are stored not in the page or segment tables but in special seven bit registers, called **storage keys**.

Segmentation on the 370 differs from that of MULTICS in one important way. If a 370 base register contains the highest address of a segment and 1 is added to it, it will then point to address 0 of the following segment. Because each segment is a logical entity, unrelated to the segments with segment numbers above and below its own, the property of incrementing a register and having it suddenly point to a new and unrelated segment is highly undesirable. On MULTICS, no operation on the page and offset part of the virtual address can change the segment part (i.e., there is no "carry" from it into the segment part). The PDP-11 suffers from the same unfortunate "carry" problem as the 370.

6.4.10. Virtual Memory on the PDP-11

In this section we will examine the virtual memory on the PDP-11/44, a member of the PDP-11 series. The PDP-11/44 uses a simple form of segmentation. The virtual address space consists of 16 segments, each of which can have a maximum size of 2^{13} bytes. This situation is depicted in Fig. 6-39. Eight of the segments are for procedures and eight for data, with the "hardware" automatically using procedure segments to fetch instructions and data segments to fetch and store data. In this manner, 2^{17} addresses can be specified in 16 bits. User mode and kernel mode each have their own set of 16 segments. In addition, a third mode, supervisor mode, also has two address spaces, like the other two modes.

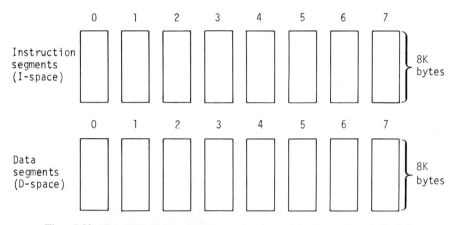

Fig. 6-39. The PDP-11/44 virtual memory has eight instruction and eight data segments in each of its three modes: user, supervisor, and kernel.

At first, this observation may appear to violate what we said earlier about only having 2^{16} addresses accessible with 16 bits. Note, however, that it is impossible to jump to the data. The instruction

jmp 200 (segment 0, address 200)

will always jump to the instruction space and not to the data space. Similarly, the instruction

clr 200 (segment 0, address 200)

will always clear (set to zero) the word at address 200 of the data space and not the instruction space. The instructions "jump to segment 0 address 200 of the data space" and "clear the word at address 200 of segment 0 of the instruction space" cannot be expressed. Half the addressing power has been traded for twice as much addressable memory. In addition to allowing 2^{17} bytes of memory to be addressed in 16 bits, programs are prevented from changing themselves, which reduces errors, aids recursion, and reduces disk transfers by increasing the number of clean segments.

Furthermore, programs are prevented from accidentally jumping into the data, which helps debugging, because wild jumps are notoriously difficult to track down.

The PDP-11/44 virtual address is broken up into two fields—a 3-bit segment field and a 13-bit offset within the segment (see Fig. 6-40). Sixteen segment descriptors are kept in high-speed hardware registers, one describing each segment. When an instruction is being fetched, the 3-bit segment field selects one of the eight instruction space descriptors. Similarly, when a data word is being referenced, one of the eight data space descriptors is selected.

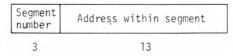

Fig. 6-40. PDP-11/44 virtual addresses are divided into a 3-bit segment number and a 13-bit address within the segment.

A segment descriptor is 32 bits long, as shown in Fig. 6-41. Because the PDP-11/44 has three operating modes, each with two eight-segment address spaces, the virtual memory map contains a total of 48 descriptors. When a particular segment is not currently resident in main memory, it contains a 0 in the protection field. When a segment is resident, this field specifies which kinds of accesses are allowed (e.g., read only, or read and write). For instruction space segments, execute only is the only possibility. The protection field can be set to trap every access, in order to keep statistics on usage.

Stacks on the PDP-11 grow from high addresses to low addresses. Words pushed onto the stack by consecutive instructions will be moved into consecutively lower-numbered word addresses (e.g., addresses 1006, 1004, 1002, 1000). Consequently, if segment 0 contains a 256-word (512-byte) stack, it will be located in virtual addresses 7680 to 8191 rather than virtual addresses 0 to 511. The *stack* field of the segment descriptor indicates whether the segment is a stack or not.

The *dirty* bit is automatically set whenever a segment is modified. This bit can be used by the operating system to determine which segments must be written back to the disk later. The *segment length* field tells how long the segment is. Because a segment can be as long as 2^{13} bytes, 13 bits are needed. To save space in the descriptor, the low-order 6 bits are not stored but are assumed to be 0 instead. Thus segment length is restricted to integral multiples of 64 bytes. The descriptor also has a bit that is used to bypass the cache memory.

The address field specifies the location of the segment in main memory. To save space in the segment descriptor again, the low-order 6 bits are not stored here either but are also assumed to be 0. This means that a segment must be positioned at an address that is an integral multiple of 64 bytes. With 16 explicit bits and 6 implicit ones, physical memory addresses are 22 bits long, allowing up to 4 megabytes of memory on a PDP-11/44. The segment's secondary memory address is kept in a table in main memory.

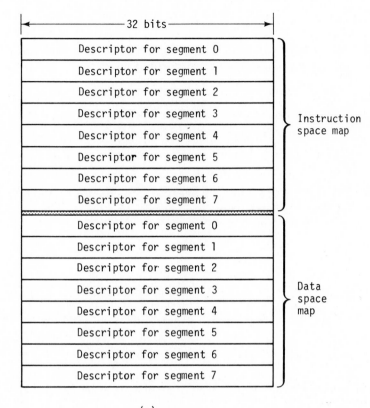

(a)

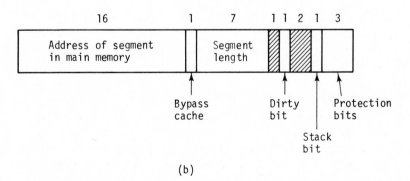

(b)

Fig. 6-41. (a) The PDP-11/44 virtual memory map for user, supervisor, or kernel mode. (b) The fields within a descriptor. The numbers give the field lengths.

A PDP-11/44 virtual address is converted to a physical memory address in the following steps:

1. The segment descriptor is fetched, using the 3-bit segment number to select a descriptor from the appropriate map.

2. A check is made to see if the segment is in main memory.

3. A check is made to see if there is a protection violation (e.g., an attempt to write into a read-only segment).

4. A check is made to see if the offset is within the segment by comparing it to the segment length field.

5. The offset is added to the implicit 22-bit segment origin to give a physical main memory address.

Three different faults can occur during the conversion of a virtual address to a physical address:

1. Segment fault - the segment is not in main memory (or is nonexistent).

2. Length fault - an address beyond the end of the segment has been referenced.

3. Protection fault - the attempted access is not permitted.

If a segment fault occurs, there is a trap to the segment fault handler, whose function is to bring the segment in. The algorithms for deciding which segment to throw out are similar to those used in paged memories, except that each segment has its own length. Consequently, if memory is full of segments smaller than the one referenced, it may be necessary to evict not one but several segments. Furthermore, if a segment grows, it may be necessary to move the other segments in memory around in order to provide it with enough room.

Checkerboarding

Consider what happens to the memory of Fig. 6-42(a) if segment 1 is evicted and segment 7, which is smaller, is put in its place. We arrive at the memory configuration of Fig. 6-42(b). Between segment 7 and segment 2 is an unused area—that is, a hole. Then segment 4 is replaced by segment 5, as in Fig. 6-42(c), and segment 3 is replaced by segment 6, as in Fig. 6-42(d). After the system has been running for a while, memory will be divided up into a number of chunks, some containing segments and some containing holes. This phenomenon is called **checkerboarding**, and, as a result, memory is wasted in the holes.

Consider what would happen if the program referenced segment 3 at the time

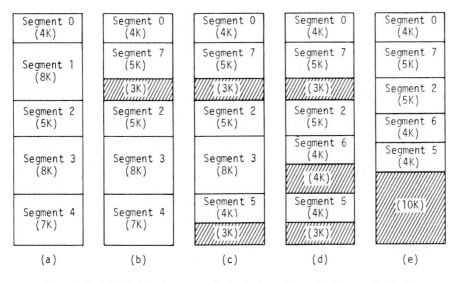

Fig. 6-42. (a)-(d) Development of checkerboarding. (e) Removal of the checkerboarding by compaction.

memory was checkerboarded, as in Fig. 6-42(d). The total space in the holes is 10K, more than enough for segment 3 but because the space is distributed in small, useless pieces, segment 3 cannot simply be loaded. Instead, another segment must be removed first.

One way to avoid checkerboarding is as follows: every time a hole appears, move the segments following the hole closer to memory location 0, thereby eliminating that hole but leaving a big hole at the end. Alternatively, one could wait until the checkerboarding became quite serious (e.g., more than a certain percentage of the total memory wasted in holes) before performing the compaction. Figure 6-42(e) shows how the memory of Fig. 6-42(d) would look after compaction. The intention of compacting memory is to collect all the small useless holes into one big hole, into which one or more segments can be put. Compacting has the obvious drawback that some time is wasted doing the compacting. Compacting after every hole is created is usually too time consuming.

If the time required for compacting memory is unacceptably large, an algorithm is needed to determine which hole to use for a particular segment. Hole management requires maintaining a list of the addresses and sizes of all holes. One popular algorithm, called **best fit**, chooses the smallest hole into which the needed segment will fit. The idea is to match holes and segments so as to avoid breaking off a piece of a big hole, which may be needed later for a big segment.

Another popular algorithm, called **first fit**, circularly scans the hole list and chooses the first hole big enough for the segment to fit into. Doing so obviously takes less time than checking the entire list to find the best fit. Surprisingly, first fit is also a better algorithm in terms of overall performance than best fit, because the latter tends to generate a great many small, totally useless holes (Knuth, 1974).

Both first fit and best fit have a tendency to decrease hole size. Whenever a segment is placed in a hole bigger than itself, which happens almost every time a segment is read in (exact fits are rare), the hole is divided in two parts. One part is occupied by the segment and the other part is the new hole. The new hole is always smaller than the old hole. Unless there is a compensating process recreating big holes out of small ones, both first fit and best fit will eventually fill memory with small useless holes.

One such compensating process is the following one. Whenever a segment is removed from memory and one or both of its nearest neighbors are holes rather than segments, the adjacent holes can be coalesced into one big hole. If segment 5 were removed from Fig. 6-42(d), the two surrounding holes and the 4K used by the segment would be merged into a single 11K hole.

With segments as small as the PDP-11s, the full power of segmentation is not really used. In fact, one could legitimately regard the PDP-11/44 as having two paged address spaces (I-space and D-space) with a page size of 8K bytes rather than a segmented address space. The fact that the units of address space are variable sized and can be individually protected makes them more like segments than pages, however.

If you are confused about this point, you may take comfort in the fact that you are not alone. Prior to 1973, DEC publications described the PDP-11 virtual memory in terms of segments; starting in 1973 it was described in terms of pages, although the pre-1973 hardware was identical to the post-1973 hardware.

6.4.11. Virtual Memory on the 68000

The 68000 memory management unit (MMU) consists of a chip that is logically positioned between the CPU and the memory. The memory addresses generated by the CPU and output on the 23 address pins are virtual addresses. The MMU translates these to physical addresses and sends them to the memory. Since the 68000 can output 24-bit addresses (using 23 pins and an implied zero for bit 0), it has a virtual address space of 24 bits. Other versions of the CPU chip having more pins have a correspondingly larger address space. A chip with 31 address pins would have an address space of 2^{32} bytes, corresponding to the full 32-bit A registers.

On every memory reference, the 68000 outputs three signals, FC0 to FC2, that tell which of the address spaces the address belongs to. The CPU has instruction space and data space, like the PDP-11. It also has user mode and supervisor (kernel) mode, each of which has its own instruction space and its own data space. Interrupt acknowledgments use another address space, making five in all, hence the need for three function code pins.

The MMU contains a table, called the **address space table**, which has 16 entries of 1 byte each [see Fig. 6-43(a)]. The three function code signals select one of the entries in this table, yielding an 8-bit address space number. (Sixteen entries are provided rather than just eight to allow for DMA address spaces or a second CPU.)

Address
space
table

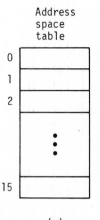

(a)

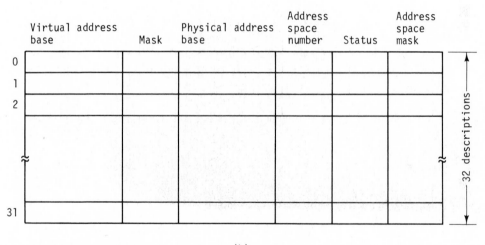

(b)

Fig. 6-43. Two of the tables internal to the 68000's memory management unit.

The main table in the MMU is shown in Fig. 6-43(b). Given a 24-bit virtual address and an address space number, the table provides the MMU with the information it needs to map the virtual address onto a physical one. The virtual address is simultaneously compared to each of the 32 entries in the column labeled *Virtual address base*. In general, only a few of the high-order bits should participate in the match, so the *Mask* field is provided to tell which bits. Only bit positions containing a 1 in the mask are compared. Thus, for example, if all the *Mask* fields contain

70000000 (octal), the selected address space is divided up into eight segments of 2^{21} bytes each. If, however, the *Mask* fields contain 74000000 (octal), there are 16 segments of 2^{20} bytes each per address space. Clearly, this scheme is much more flexible than, say, the PDP-11's, with a fixed division of each address space into eight segments. Furthermore, unlike the PDP-11's mapping, different segments on the 68000 may have different sizes. We will give an example with unequal-sized segments shortly.

When an incoming (address space, virtual address) pair is matched to a descriptor, the bits corresponding to one bits in the mask are replaced by the corresponding bits in the *Physical address base*. Under normal conditions, this rule means that the high-order bits in the virtual address are replaced by bits from the *Physical address base* field. With equal-sized segments, this situation is just like that of Fig. 6-26: the virtual page number is replaced by a page frame number from the map. With unequal-sized segments, it is more complicated.

The *Status* field in the descriptor contains various control bits for enabling the descriptor, recording the fact that the segment has been read or written, write protecting it, and so on. The *Address space mask* is used to enable partial matching on address space numbers in order to allow two or more address spaces to share descriptors. Although we have described the first three fields of the descriptor as having 24 bits, to save space in the table, only the high-order 16 bits are stored. The rest are implicitly zero.

As mentioned above, the MMU can also be used with segments of different sizes. As an example of such use, consider Fig. 6-44. In part (a) of the figure, a typical 16-megabyte address is shown. Three segments are defined in it: a 32K program segment, a 16K data segment contiguous with the program, and an 8K stack segment at the top of the address space. The machine has 256K of main memory. The segments are to be positioned as shown in Fig. 6-44(b). The 32K operating system is part of another address space and will not be dealt with further here. It is shown simply to avoid a one-to-one mapping of virtual-to-real for program and data, thus making the example more general.

One MMU descriptor is needed for each segment, as illustrated in Fig. 6-44(c). The two columns labeled *Virtual address range* are not part of the descriptor, of course, but are included to make it clearer which virtual addresses are to be mapped for each segment. For the 32K program, the 24-bit address is split up into the high-order 9 bits, which must be zero, and the low-order 15 bits, which give an address within the 32K segment. Consequently, the *Virtual address base* and *Mask* fields have been set up to match only when the top 9 bits are zero. If a match occurs, the top 9 bits are replaced by 001 (octal), which maps the program onto addresses 00100000 to 00177777 (octal). The data segment's virtual address is split up into the high-order 10 bits and the low-order 14 bits because 14 bits are needed to specify a byte with a 16K segment. If virtual address 00123456 is presented to the MMU, it will be mapped onto 00223456 (octal). Finally, the descriptor for the stack uses 11 bits for matching and only 13 bits for the offset within the segment. Address 77770124 maps onto 00770124.

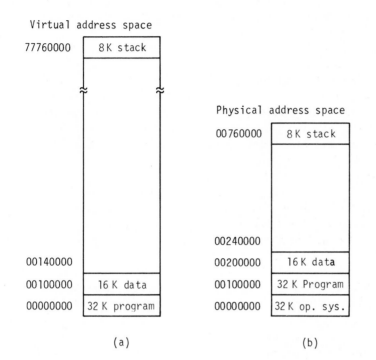

Fig. 6-44. An example of memory mapping on the 68000 in octal.

Segment	Virtual address range Low	High	Virtual address base	Mask	Physical address base
Program	00000000	00077777	00000000	77700000	00100000
Data	00100000	00137777	00100000	77740000	00200000
Stack	77760000	77777777	77760000	77760000	00760000

Descriptor fields
(low-order 8 bits are not stored)

(c)

6.5. JOB CONTROL LANGUAGES

Besides implementing a wide variety of virtual instructions for the level 3 programmer to use, many operating systems also provide a **job control language** that allows the user to call programs, manipulate files, and so on from a terminal instead of from inside a running program. Although the practice of having the job control language processor be integrated with the operating system is widespread, it is technically a poor idea. It is far better to have the job command processor simply be a user program that reads commands from the terminal and issues the appropriate system calls to carry these commands out. This way, any user who objects to the standard job control processor is free to write his own.

From this point of view, the job control processor is not part of the operating system at all, hence should not be discussed in this chapter. Nevertheless, the concepts "operating system" and "job control language" have historically been so closely associated, we will briefly look at the subject here. The IBM 370 job control language is so complex that entire books have been written about it (e.g., Cadow, 1970). The CP/M job control language is so simple there is really nothing to say. Instead, we will focus on the UNIX system's job control language, called the **shell**, which is powerful yet extremely elegant. The shell is described in more detail by Kernighan and Mashey (1981).

The simplest form of a shell command is just a program name:

date

tells the shell to find a file named *date* for which the user has execute permission (remember the RWX bits) and run it. A slightly more complicated example is

cp oldfile newfile

which executes the *cp* program, passing two file names to it in essentially the same way parameters are passed to procedures. The *cp* program makes a copy of *oldfile* and calls the copy *newfile*.

An extremely useful facility provided by the shell is **I/O redirection**. Earlier we mentioned that file, device, and interprocess I/O in the UNIX system all use the same mechanism. To achieve this goal, programs are started up with file descriptor 0 already set up for **standard input** and file descriptor 1 for **standard output**. Thus if a program calls *write* (1, *buffer*, *n*), the contents of the buffer will be written to standard output. By default, both standard input and standard output are the user's terminal. Thus a program that reads using file descriptor 0 and writes using file descriptor 1 will read its input from the terminal and write its output to the terminal.

However, a program can be started up with either input or output redirected. For example.

date >x

writes the time and date on the file *x* instead of the terminal. Similarly,

sort <a >b

reads a sequence of input lines from *a*, sorts them, and writes the output to *b*. It is important to realize that the program *sort* is not aware of whether its input is coming from the terminal or a file.

I/O redirection provides a way to link programs together. It is possible to run two programs, say, *sort* and *uniq*, so that the output of *sort* becomes the input of *uniq*. (The program *uniq* looks for consecutive lines that are identical and deletes all but·the first one.) The syntax is illustrated by the command

sort <a | uniq >b

which runs *sort* with standard input taken from *a*, connects the output of *sort* to the input of *uniq*, and puts the output of *uniq* on the file *b*. Had ">b" been missing, the output would have appeared on the terminal.

Arbitrarily many programs can be hooked together this way. For example,

prep <book | sort | uniq | wc

feeds the file *book* through four programs, with the final output going to the terminal (default standard output). The program *prep* strips off all punctuation and places each word of the input file (assumed to consist of lines of ASCII text) on a separate line. The output of *prep* is then run through *sort* and *uniq*, resulting in a sorted file containing every word in the original file exactly once. The program *wc* (word count) outputs one line telling how many lines, words, and characters its input contains. The command above thus tells how many unique words are contained in *book*.

A program that reads standard input, does some processing, and writes standard output is called a **filter**. A sequence of filters strung together as above is called a **pipeline**. Many small filters such as *prep*, *sort*, *uniq*, and *wc* exist, allowing powerful commands to be built up from small programs. It is probably fair to say that the concept of a filter is to job control languages as Eli Whitney's invention of interchangeable parts was to assembly line manufacturing.

The implementation of redirection and pipelines is straightforward. To run a single program (i.e., not a pipeline), the shell forks off a child process. Since the child's memory is a copy of the parent's, it has access to the command line read in by the parent (shell). When confronted with redirected input, the child process just does a CLOSE on file descriptor 0 and then an OPEN on the input file. Since the system always returns the lowest available file descriptor for OPEN and CREAT, the new file will get file descriptor 0, replacing the original file descriptor 0 (the terminal). Then the child does an EXEC to overlay itself with the needed program. Since EXEC does not affect the file descriptors, only the memory, the new program automatically has the redirected input file as its standard input. Output works the same way.

When the shell sees a pipeline, it just forks off one child process for each component program. The child first performs any necessary I/O redirection and then does an EXEC to overlay itself with the desired program. To make pipelines such as

sort | uniq

work, the shell calls PIPE to get a pipe to connect *sort* to *uniq*. By manipulating file descriptors, the shell arranges that *sort* gets the write file descriptor for the pipe as its standard output (1), and *uniq* gets the read file descriptor for the pipe as its standard input (0). Thus when *sort* writes, the data are read by *uniq*. Again, neither child is aware that the input is coming from a process rather than a file or terminal.

Normally, the shell waits for the current command to finish before asking for more input. However, when the user types an ampersand in the command line, the shell asks for new input immediately, so the user need not wait for long pipelines to complete. The implementation of this feature is trivial: the shell just refrains from executing the WAIT system call that suspends the caller until one of its children terminates.

The shell has many more interesting features, including high-level language control structures such as if statements, case statements, for loops, and while loops, but these are beyond the scope of this book.

6.6. SUMMARY

The operating system can be regarded as an interpreter for certain architectural features not found at level 2. Chief among these are virtual I/O instructions, facilities for parallel processing, and virtual memory.

The most important I/O abstraction present at level 3 is the file. It consists of a sequence of logical records that can be read and written without knowledge of how the disks, tapes, and other secondary memory and I/O devices work. Files can be accessed sequentially, randomly by record number, or randomly by key. Various implementation issues were discussed and illustrated by MVS, UNIX, and CP/M.

Parallel processing is often present at level 3 and is implemented by simulating multiple processors by time sharing a single CPU. Uncontrolled interaction between processes can lead to race conditions. To solve this problem, synchronization primitives are introduced, of which semaphores are a simple example. Using semaphores producer-consumer problems can be solved in a simple and elegant way.

Virtual memory is an architectural feature whose purpose is to allow programs to use more address space than the machine has physical memory, or to provide a consistent and flexible memory protection mechanism. It can be implemented as pure paging, pure segmentation, or a combination of the two. Page replacement algorithms and semiconductor caches also play an important role in memory management. Several examples of virtual memory were given.

PROBLEMS

1. Why does an operating system only interpret some of the level 3 instructions, whereas a microprogram interprets all the level 2 instructions?

2. Why do many file systems require that a file be explicitly opened with an OPEN instruction before being read?

3. Compare the bit map and hole list methods for keeping track of free space on a disk with 800 cylinders, each one having 5 tracks of 32 sectors. How many holes would it take before the hole list would be larger than the bit map? Assume that the allocation unit is the sector and that a hole requires a 32-bit word.

4. To be able to make some predictions of disk performance, it is useful to have a model of storage allocation. Suppose that the disk is viewed as a linear address space of $N \gg 1$ sectors, consisting of a run of data blocks, then a hole, then another run of data blocks, and so on. If empirical measurements show that the probability distribution for data and hole lengths are the same, with the chance of either being i sectors as 2^{-i}, what is the expected number of holes on the disk?

5. On a certain computer, a level 3 program can create as many files as it needs, and all files may grow dynamically during execution without giving the operating system any advance information about their ultimate size. Do you think that files are stored in consecutive sectors? Explain.

6. Although disk addresses in UNIX are 3-byte numbers, only 128 of them are put in the indirect blocks. If all the indirect blocks were changed to hold $512/3 = 170$ disk addresses instead of 128, what would the maximum file size become?

7. Normally, UNIX uses 512-byte disk blocks and CP/M uses 1024-byte disk blocks. Suppose that were reversed, with UNIX now using 1024-byte blocks and CP/M 512-byte blocks. Could this change affect the number of directory slots used for a given collection of files in either system?

8. Suppose that the UNIX system call

UNLINK(''/usr/ast/bin/game3'')

were executed in the context of Fig. 6-12. Describe carefully what changes are made in the directory system.

9. Consider the following method by which an operating system might implement semaphore instructions. Whenever the CPU was about to do an UP or DOWN on a semaphore (an integer variable in memory), it first sets the CPU priority or mask bits in such a way as to disable all interrupts. Then it fetches the semaphore, modifies it, and branches accordingly. Finally, it enables interrupts again. Does this method work if:

a. There is a single CPU that switches between processes every 100 msec?
b. Two CPUs share a common memory in which the semaphore is located?

10. Make a table showing which of the processes P1, P2, and P3 are running and which are blocked as a function of time from 0 to 1000 msec. All three processes perform UP and DOWN instructions on the same semaphore. When two processes are blocked and an UP is done, the process with the lower number is restarted, that is, P1 gets preference over P2 and P3, and so on. Initially, all three are running and the semaphore is 1.

At $t = 100$ P1 does a DOWN
At $t = 200$ P1 does a DOWN
At $t = 300$ P2 does an UP
At $t = 400$ P3 does a DOWN
At $t = 500$ P1 does a DOWN
At $t = 600$ P2 does an UP
At $t = 700$ P2 does a DOWN
At $t = 800$ P1 does an UP
At $t = 900$ P1 does an UP

11. The Nevercrash Operating System Company has been receiving complaints from some of its customers about its latest release, which includes semaphore operations. They feel it is immoral for processes to block (they call it "sleeping on the job"). Since it is company policy to give the customers what they want, it has been proposed to add a third operation, PEEK, to supplement UP and DOWN. PEEK simply examines the semaphore without changing it or blocking the process. In this way, programs that feel it is immoral to block can first inspect the semaphore to see if it is safe to do a DOWN. Will this idea work if three or more processes use the semaphore? If two processes use the semaphore?

12. In an airline reservation system, it is necessary to ensure that while one process is busy using a file, no other process can also use it. Otherwise, two different processes, working for two different ticket agents, might each inadvertently sell the last seat on some flight. Devise a synchronization method using semaphores that makes sure that only one process at a time accesses each file (assuming that the processes obey the rules).

13. To make it possible to implement semaphores on a computer with multiple CPUs that share a common memory, computer architects often provide a Test and Set Lock instruction. TSL X tests the location X. If the contents are zero, they is set to 1 in a single, indivisible memory cycle, and the next instruction is skipped. If it is nonzero, the TSL acts like a no-op. Using TSL it is possible to write procedures LOCK and UNLOCK with the following properties. LOCK(X) checks to see if X is locked. If not, it locks X and returns control. If X is already locked, it just waits until it becomes unlocked, then it locks X and returns control. UNLOCK releases an existing lock. If all processes lock the semaphore table before using it, only one process at a time can fiddle with the variables and pointers, thus preventing races. Write LOCK and UNLOCK in assembly language. (Make any reasonable assumptions you need.)

14. Show the values of *in* and *out* for a circular buffer of length 65 words after each of the following operations. Both start at 0.

    a. 22 words are put in.
    b. 9 words are removed.
    c. 40 words are put in
    d. 17 words are removed.
    e. 12 words are put in.
    f. 45 words are removed.
    g. 8 words are put in.
    h. 11 words are removed.

15. Discuss some possible algorithms for removing segments in an unpaged, segmented memory such as the PDP-11/44's.

16. Compare fragmentation to checkerboarding. What can be done to alleviate each?

17. Supermarkets are constantly faced with a problem similar to page replacement in virtual memory systems. They have a fixed amount of shelf space to display an ever increasing number of products. If an important new product comes along, say, 100% efficient dog food, some existing product must be dropped from the inventory to make room for it. The obvious replacement algorithms are LRU and FIFO. Which of these would you prefer?

18. A virtual memory has a page size of 1024 words, eight virtual pages and four physical page frames. The page table is as follows:

Virtual Page	Page Frame
0	3
1	1
2	not in main memory
3	not in main memory
4	2
5	not in main memory
6	0
7	not in main memory

a. Make a list of all virtual addresses that will cause page faults.
b. What are the physical addresses for 0, 3728, 1023, 1024, 1025, 7800, and 4096?

19. In Sec. 6.4.4 an algorithm was presented for implementing a FIFO page replacement strategy. Devise a more efficient one. *Hint:* It is possible to update the counter in the newly loaded page, leaving all the others alone.

20. A segmented memory has paged segments. Each virtual address has a 2-bit segment number, a 2-bit page number, and an 11-bit offset within the page. The main memory contains 32768 words. Each segment is either read only, read/execute, read/write, or read/write/execute. The page tables and protection are as follows.

Segment 0		Segment 1		Segment 2	Segment 3	
Read only		Read/execute		Read/write/execute	Read/write	
Virtual page	Page frame	Virtual page	Page frame		Virtual page	Page frame
0	9	0	On drum		0	14
1	3	1	0	Page table not in main memory	1	1
2	On drum	2	15		2	6
3	12	3	8		3	On drum

For each of the following accesses to virtual memory, tell what physical address is computed. If a fault occurs, tell which kind.

Access	Segment	Page	Offset within page
1. Fetch data	0	1	1
2. Fetch data	1	1	10
3. Fetch data	3	3	2047
4. Store data	0	1	4
5. Store data	3	1	2
6. Store data	3	0	14
7. Jump to it	1	3	100
8. Fetch data	0	2	50
9. Fetch data	2	0	5
10. Jump to it	3	0	60

21. A computer system uses segmentation and paging. The mean segment size is s words and the page size is p words. When a segment is in memory, some words are wasted in the last page. In addition, s/p words are "wasted" because they comprise the page table (one word per entry). The smaller the page size, the less waste in the last page of the segment, but the larger the page table. What page size minimizes the total waste?

22. In the paged systems discussed in the text, the page fault handler was part of the level 2 machine and thus was not present in any level 3 programs address space. In reality, the page fault handler also occupies pages, and might, under some circumstances (e.g., FIFO page replacement policy), itself be removed. What would happen if the page fault handler was not present when a page fault occurred? How could this be prevented?

23. You are trying to decide which drum to use for paging a virtual memory on a microcomputer. The Big Eight Drum Company has a drum with 64 tracks of 8K words around the circumference. The Kilodrum company sells a drum with 512 tracks of 1K. Both drums can switch tracks instantaneously. The Big Eight drum has a 32-msec rotation time; the Kilodrum has an 8-msec rotation time. Compute the average time to read a block of n words for each. Under what circumstances would you recommend the Big Eight drum?

24. On a computer with a three-level memory hierarchy, cache, main memory, and disk, the hope is that most accesses can be satisfied from the cache. If a memory word is in the cache, A nanoseconds is required to access it. If the word is not in the cache, B nanoseconds is first needed to load it into the cache, then the reference is started again. If the word is not in the main memory, C nanoseconds of CPU time is used to initiate the disk access to fetch it, followed by B nanoseconds to get it into the cache. If one out of every n references is not in the cache and one out of every m main memory references initiates a disk transfer, what is the main memory reference time?

25. Minicomputer caches frequently use a different principle from the one described in the text. Consider, for example, a cache of 4K 16-bit words for a machine with 22-bit physical addresses, such as the PDP-11/44. Each of the 4K cache entries contains a 22-bit physical address field, a 16-bit value field, and a 1-bit field marking the entry as in use or not in use. When a 22-bit physical address is to be read, the low-order 13 bits are used to index into the cache. (Address bit 0 is always zero on word references, so the index is bits 1 through 12.) If the 22-bit address field matches the physical address and the "in use" bit is set, the value field is read. If the 22-bit address does not match, which it may well be because the words at 0, 8192, 16384, 24576, 32768, and so on, all use slot 0 in the cache, the needed word is loaded into the cache. Describe a modified cache that needs fewer than $(22 + 16 + 1) \times 4K$ bits, but works essentially the same way.

26. Suppose that the program of Fig. 6-44(a) had a fourth segment of 4K, just above the data segment. The new segment is to be located just above the data segment in physical memory. Show the new entry needed for Fig. 6-44(c).

27. Imagine that you had to implement the UNIX system on a microcomputer where main memory was in short supply. After a considerable amount of shoehorning, it still did not quite fit, so you picked a system call at random to sacrifice for the general good. PIPE lost. Is it still possible to implement I/O redirection somehow? What about pipelines? Discuss the problems and possible solutions.

28. The Committee for Fairness to File Descriptors is organizing a protest again the UNIX system because whenever the latter returns a file descriptor, it always returns the lowest number not currently in use. Consequently, higher-numbered file descriptors are hardly ever used. Their plan is to return the lowest number not yet used by the program rather than the lowest number currently not in use. They claim that it is trivial to implement, will not affect existing programs, and is fairer. What do you think?

29. Implement the CP/M file system.

30. Implement the UNIX file system.

31. Write an assembly language function to map a segmented, paged virtual memory address to a physical address. The parameters are: the descriptor segment, the page tables, the access type (read, write, execute), the segment number, the page number, and the offset within the page. Choose sizes and formats appropriate to your favorite computer. If the translation fails, return an error message.

7

THE ASSEMBLY LANGUAGE LEVEL

In Chapters 4, 5, and 6 we discussed three different levels present on most contemporary computers. This chapter is concerned primarily with another level that is also present on nearly all modern computers: the assembly language level. The assembly language level differs in a significant respect from the microprogramming, conventional machine, and operating system machine levels—it is implemented by translation rather than by interpretation.

Programs that convert a user's program written in some language to another language are called **translators**. The language in which the original program is written is called the **source language** and the language to which it is converted is called the **target language**. Both the source language and the target language define levels. If a processor that can directly execute programs written in the source language is available, there is no need to translate the source program into the target language.

Translation is used when a processor (either hardware or an interpreter) is available for the target language but not for the source language. If the translation has been performed correctly, the execution of the translated program on its processor will give precisely the same results as the execution of the source program would have given had a processor for it been available. Consequently, it is possible to implement a new level for which there is no processor by first translating programs written for that level to a target level and then executing the resulting target-level programs.

It is important to note the difference between translation on the one hand, and interpretation, on the other. In translation, the original program in the source language is not directly executed. Instead, it is converted to an equivalent program called an **object program** or **object module** whose execution is carried out only after the translation has been completed. In translation, there are two distinct steps:

1. Generation of an equivalent program in the target language.

2. Execution of the newly generated program.

These two steps do not occur simultaneously. The second step does not begin until the first has been completed. In interpretation, there is only one step: executing the original source program. No equivalent program need be generated first. Interpretation has the advantage of smaller program size and more flexibility, but translation has the advantage of faster execution.

While the object program is being executed, only three levels are in evidence: the microprogramming level, the conventional machine level, and the operating system machine level. Consequently, three programs—the user's object program, the operating system, and the microprogram—can be found in the computer's memory at run time. All traces of the original source program have vanished. Thus the number of levels present at execution time may differ from the number of levels present before translation. It should be noted, however, that although we define a level by the instructions and linguistic constructs available to its programmers (and not by the implementation method), other authors sometimes make a greater distinction between levels implemented by execution-time interpreters and levels implemented by translation.

7.1. INTRODUCTION TO ASSEMBLY LANGUAGE

Translators can be roughly divided into two groups, depending on the relation between the source language and the target language. When the source language is essentially a symbolic representation for a numerical machine language, the translator is called an **assembler** and the source language is called an **assembly language**. When the source language is a problem-oriented language such as ALGOL 68, COBOL, FORTRAN, or Pascal and the target language is either a numerical machine language or a symbolic representation for one, the translator is called a **compiler**.

7.1.1. What Is an Assembly Language?

A pure assembly language is a language in which each statement produces exactly one machine instruction. In other words, there is a one-to-one correspondence between machine instructions and statements in the assembly program. If each line in the assembly program contains one assembly statement and each machine word contains one machine instruction, then an n-line assembly program will produce an n-word machine language program.

The reason that people use assembly language, as opposed to programming in machine language (octal or hex), is that it is much easier to program in assembly language. The use of symbolic names and symbolic addresses instead of binary or octal ones makes an enormous difference. Most people can remember that the abbreviations for add, subtract, multiply, and divide are ADD, SUB, MUL, and DIV, but few can remember that the machine instructions (for the PDP-11) are 24576, 57344, 28672, and 29184. The assembly language programmer need only remember the symbolic names ADD, SUB, MUL, DIV, because the assembler translates them to the machine instructions, but the machine language programmer must remember, or constantly look up, the numerical values.

The same remarks apply to addresses. The assembly language programmer can give symbolic names to memory locations and have the assembler worry about supplying the correct numerical values. The machine language programmer must always work with the numerical values of the addresses. As a consequence, no one programs in machine language today, although people did so years ago, before assemblers had been invented.

Assembly languages have another property, besides the one-to-one mapping of assembly language statements onto machine instructions, that distinguishes them from problem-oriented languages. The assembly programmer has access to all the features and instructions available on the target machine. The problem-oriented language programmer does not. For example, if the target machine has an overflow bit, an assembly language program can test it, but a FORTRAN program cannot directly test it. If there are switches on the operator console, an assembly language program can read their status. Such a program can execute every instruction in the instruction set of the target machine, but the problem-oriented language program cannot. In short, everything that can be done in machine language can be done in assembly language, but many instructions, registers, and similar features are not available for the problem-oriented language programmer to use. Languages for system programming are often a cross between these types, with the syntax of a problem-oriented language but access to the machine of an assembly language.

7.1.2. Format of an Assembly Language Statement

Although the structure of an assembly language statement closely mirrors the structure of the machine instruction that it represents, assembly languages for different machines and different levels have sufficient resemblance to one another to allow a discussion of assembly language in general. Figure 7-1 shows fragments of assembly language programs for the 370, PDP-11 (UNIX), and Z80 (CP/M), all of which perform the computation $N = I + J + K$ (UNIX uses lowercase). In all three examples the statements above the dots perform the calculation. The statements below the dots are commands to the assembler to reserve memory for the variables I, J, K, and N and are not symbolic representations of machine instructions. Statements that are commands to the assembler are called **pseudoinstructions**.

Assembly language statements have four parts: label field, operation field, operands field, and comments field. Labels, which are used to provide symbolic names for memory addresses, are needed on executable statements so that the

Label field	Operation field	Operands field	Comments field
FORMUL	L	1,I	LOAD I INTO REGISTER 1
	A	1,J	ADD J TO REGISTER 1
	A	1,K	ADD K TO REGISTER 1
	ST	1,N	STORE SUM IN N
	.		
	.		
	.		
I	DC	F'2'	RESERVE A WORD INITIALIZED TO 2
J	DC	F'3'	RESERVE A WORD INITIALIZED TO 3
K	DC	F'4'	RESERVE A WORD INITIALIZED TO 4
N	DC	F'0'	RESERVE A WORD INITIALIZED TO 0

(a)

formul:	mov	i,r1	/load i into register 1
	add	j,r1	/add j to register 1
	add	k,r1	/add k to register 1
	mov	r1,n	/store register 1 in n
	.		
	.		
	.		
i:	2		/reserve a word initialized to 2
j:	3		/reserve a word initialized to 3
k:	4		/reserve a word initialized to 4
n:	0		/reserve a word initialized to 0

(b)

FORMUL:	LD	A,(I)	;LOAD I INTO A
	LD	HL,J	;LOAD ADDRESS OF J INTO HL
	ADD	(HL)	;ADD J TO A
	LD	HL,K	;LOAD ADDRESS OF K INTO HL
	ADD	(HL)	;ADD K TO A
	LD	(N),A	;STORE A IN N
	.		
	.		
	.		
I:	DB	2	;RESERVE A BYTE INITIALIZED TO 2
J:	DB	3	;RESERVE A BYTE INITIALIZED TO 3
K:	DB	4	;RESERVE A BYTE INITIALIZED TO 4
N:	DB	0	;RESERVE A BYTE INITIALIZED TO 0

(c)

Fig. 7-1. Computation of the formula N = I + J + K.
(a) IBM 370. (b) PDP-11. (c)Z80.

statements can be jumped to. They are also needed on memory allocation pseudoinstructions (e.g., DC and DB), to permit the data stored there to be accessible by symbolic name. If a statement is labeled, the label (usually) begins in column 1. Figure 7-1(a) shows five labels: *FORMUL, I, J, K,* and *N.*

It is an unfortunate characteristic of some assemblers that labels are restricted to six or eight characters. In contrast, most problem-oriented languages allow the use of arbitrarily long names. Long, well-chosen names make programs much more readable and understandable by other people (see Fig. 2-2 for an example of this point).

The operation field contains either a symbolic abbreviation for the opcode—if the statement is a symbolic representation for a machine instruction—or a pseudoinstruction if the statement is a command to the assembler. The choice of an appropriate abbreviation is often a matter of taste, and different assembly language designers often choose different abbreviations. The 370 assembler uses "L" for loading a register, whereas the PDP-11 assembler uses "mov" and the Z80 assembler uses "LD." The choice for the instruction name is determined by the person who wrote the assembler and need not be the same as that used in the manufacturer's reference manual. In fact, IEEE has developed a standard, machine-independent assembly language (Fischer, 1979) to try to bring some order to the chaos created by every manufacturer using different names for the same instruction.

Similarly, the three assemblers have different ways to reserve memory for variables. IBM's assembler has a pseudoinstruction "DC" for Define Constant, the UNIX assembler does not have a pseudoinstruction at all—you just give the value—and the CP/M assembler has pseudoinstructions DB and DW to define bytes and words, respectively.

The operands field of an assembly language statement is used to specify the addresses and registers used as operands by the machine instruction. The operand field of an integer addition instruction tells what is to be added to what. The operands field of a jump instruction tells where to jump to. The operands field of a pseudoinstruction depends on the pseudoinstruction, for example, how much memory space to reserve.

The comments field provides a place for programmers to put helpful explanations of how the program works for the benefit of other programmers who may subsequently use or modify the program. An assembly language program without such documentation is nearly incomprehensible to all programmers except perhaps its author. If a long time has passed because it was written, an assembly language program with no comments may be incomprehensible to its author as well. The comments field is solely for the benefit of human beings and has no effect on the assembly process or on the generated program.

7.1.3. Comparison of Assembly Language and Problem-Oriented Languages

A popular myth is that programs that will be used a great deal, especially large ones, should, for efficiency, be written entirely in assembly language. Although true at one time, it is no longer. It is instructive to compare the MULTICS system with the IBM time-sharing system for the 360/67, TSS/67. Both operating systems were started around the same time and are roughly the same size (huge). MULTICS was written, for the most part (95%), in a problem-oriented language, PL/1, whereas TSS/67 was written entirely in assembly language.

A large operating system such as MULTICS is a stringent test for a problem-oriented language. Because an operating system must control all the I/O devices, deal with critical timing situations, handle large data bases, and do many other tasks, good performance is crucial. If problem-oriented languages can pass this critical test, there are few large applications indeed where one could demonstrate the advantages to be gained by using assembly language. (Programming the microprocessor inside a washing machine is a different story, however, due to the large number sold.)

The results of these two projects can be summed up nicely by pointing out that each took about the same length of time to get running. However, MULTICS was written by 50 people at an estimated cost of 10 million dollars whereas TSS/67 needed 300 people at an estimated cost of 50 million dollars (Graham, 1970). The conclusion that the use of PL/1 saved the MULTICS project millions of dollars is inescapable.

Studies have shown that the number of lines of debugged code a programmer can produce per month on a project over a period of several years is approximately 100 to 200 lines, independent of the programming language used (Corbató, 1969). Only on small programs can higher productivity be expected. Since one PL/1 statement is equivalent to 5 or 10 assembly language statements, the productivity of a PL/1 programmer will be 5 or 10 times that of an assembly language programmer.

Another strong argument against programming in assembly language is that understanding someone else's assembly language program is nearly impossible. A complete listing of MULTICS in PL/1 is about 3000 pages, hardly something one digests in an evening. Nevertheless, absorbing that amount is trivial compared to reading 30,000 pages of assembly code. Although no one ever tries to read the entire MULTICS listing, people do try to understand particular procedures, about four pages of PL/1 on the average. Personnel turnover on large projects often averages 15% per year; consequently, after 5 years few of the original programmers are still around. If the new programmers cannot understand their predecessors' programs, the project will be in big trouble.

7.1.4. Program Tuning

Studies have shown that, in most programs, a small percentage of the total code is responsible for a large percentage of the execution time (Darden and Heller, 1970). It is common to have 1% of the program be responsible for 50% of the execution time and 10% of the program be responsible for 90% of the execution time. A common situation is in a compiler, where searching the symbol table can eat up more time than the rest of the compiler combined.

Assume, for example, that it requires 10 person-years to write some big compiler in a problem-oriented language and that the resulting compiler requires 100 sec to compile a certain test program. Writing the whole compiler in assembly language would require about 50 to 100 person-years, due to the lower productivity of assembler language programmers; the final program would, however, perform the test in about 33 sec, because a clever programmer can outdo a clever compiler by a factor of 3. This situation is illustrated in Fig. 7-2.

	Man-years needed to produce program	Program execution time in seconds
Assembly language	50	33
Problem oriented language	10	100
Mixed approach before tuning		
Critical 10%	1	90
Other 90%	9	10
Total	10	100
Mixed approach after tuning		
Critical 10%	6	30
Other 90%	9	10
Total	15	40

Fig. 7-2. Comparison of assembly language and problem-oriented language programming, with and without tuning.

Another approach to producing software is based on the empirical observation that, for most programs, a small percentage of the total program is responsible for nearly all the execution time. Using this approach, the entire program is first written in a problem-oriented language. Then a series of measurements is performed to determine which parts of the program account for most of the execution time. Such measurements would normally include using the system clock to compute the amount of time spent in each procedure, keeping track of the number of times each loop is executed, and similar steps.

As an example, let us assume that 10% of the total program accounts for 90% of the execution time. This means that for a 100-sec job, 90 sec is spent in this critical 10% and 10 sec is spent in the remaining 90% of the program. The critical 10% can now be improved by rewriting it in assembly language. This process is called **tuning** and is illustrated in Fig. 7-2. Here an additional 5 person-years are needed to rewrite the critical procedures but their execution time is reduced from 90 sec to 30 sec.

It is instructive to compare the mixed problem-oriented language/assembly language approach with the pure assembly language version (see Fig. 7-2). The latter is about 20% faster but at more than triple the price. Furthermore, the advantage of the mixed approach is really more than indicated, because recoding an already debugged problem-oriented language procedure in assembly code is, in fact, much easier than writing the same assembly code procedure from scratch. In other words, the estimate of 5 person-years to rewrite the critical procedures is exceedingly conservative. If this recoding actually took only 1 person-year, the cost ratio between the mixed approach and the pure assembly language approach would be more than 4 to 1 in favor of the mixed approach.

A programmer who uses a problem-oriented language is not immersed in moving bits around, and sometimes obtains insights into the problem that allow *real* improvements in performance. This situation occurs much less often with assembly language programmers, who are usually trying to juggle instructions to save a few microseconds. Graham (1970) reports a PL/1 procedure in MULTICS that was rewritten in 3 months with the new version 26 times smaller and 50 times faster than the original, as well as another that became 20 times smaller and 40 times faster with 2 months of work.

Corbató (1969) describes a PL/1 drum management procedure that was reduced from 50,000 to 10,000 words of compiled code in less than a month and an I/O controller that shrank from 65,000 to 30,000 words of compiled code, with an improvement in speed of a factor of 8 in 4 months. The point here is that because problem-oriented language programmers have a more global view of what they are doing, they are far more likely to obtain insights leading to totally different and vastly better algorithms.

Despite all these disadvantages, with almost no compensating advantages, some people still program in assembly language. The reason is essentially a hangover from the days when machine time was so expensive that wasting months or even years of programmer time to save a few hours or days of machine time was understandable. It has been estimated that 80% of total computer costs at present are people costs and 20% are machine costs, so having a team of 40,000 dollar a year programmers work for 6 months to save 10 hours of machine time that costs 100 dollars per hour simply does not make sense.

After this introduction, you may be wondering: "Why bother studying assembly language programming at all, when it is so awful?" At least three good reasons exist. First, because the success or failure of a large project may depend on being able to squeeze a factor of 5 or 10 improvement in performance out of some critical procedure, it is important to be able to write good assembly language code when it is really necessary. Second, on microprocessors, assembly code is sometimes the only alternative due to lack of compilers or tight memory requirements. Third, a compiler must either produce output used by an assembler or perform the assembly process itself.

7.2. THE ASSEMBLY PROCESS

In the following sections we will briefly describe how an assembler works. Although each machine has a different assembly language, the assembly process is sufficiently similar on different machines that it is possible to describe it in general terms.

7.2.1. Two-Pass Assemblers

Because an assembly language program consists of a series of one-line statements, it might seem natural to have an assembler that read one statement, translated it to machine language, and then output the generated machine language onto a file, along with the corresponding piece of the listing, if any, onto another file. This process would then be repeated until the whole program had been translated. Unfortunately, this method does not work.

Consider the situation where the first statement is a jump to L. The assembler cannot assemble this statement until it knows the address of statement L. Statement L may be near the end of the program, making it impossible for the assembler to find the address without first reading almost the entire program. This difficulty is called the **forward reference problem**, because a symbol, L, has been used before it has been defined, that is, a reference has been made to a symbol whose definition will only occur later.

Forward references can be handled in two ways. First, the assembler may in fact read the source program two times. Each reading of the source program is called a **pass**; any translator which reads the input program two times is called a **two-pass translator**. On pass one of a two-pass assembler, the definitions of symbols, including statement labels, are collected and stored in a table. By the time the second pass begins, the values of all symbols are known; thus no forward reference remains and each statement can be read, assembled, and output. Although this method requires an extra pass over the input, it is conceptually straightforward.

The second method consists of trying to do the assembly in one pass anyway. Whenever a statement is encountered that cannot be assembled because it contains a forward reference, no output is generated; instead, an entry is made in a table indicating that the statement with the forward reference has not yet been assembled. At the end of the assembly, all symbols will have been defined, so all statements in the not-yet-assembled table can be assembled.

The latter method generates output in a different order than the two-pass method. If the assembly is followed by loading, the loader can put the pieces of output back in the right order. Hence this objection is not a serious one. The one-pass assembler does have the problem that if many statements contain forward references, the table containing the statements not yet assembled may become too large to fit in memory. The assembler could write the table out into secondary memory and then read it back later, however.

One-pass assemblers tend to be more complicated than two-pass assemblers. For example, assembly language programmers often expect a program listing that contains the source statements listed in the order they appear in the program, along with the machine language translation of each. The one-pass assembler cannot print the machine translation until it has actually done it. Consequently, it must have either a second pass to print the listing or another internal table where pieces of the listing are kept until they can be printed. Most assemblers are two pass.

7.2.2. Pass One

The principal function of pass one is to build up a table called the **symbol table**, containing the values of all symbols. A symbol is either a label or a value that is assigned a symbolic name by means of an explicit pseudoinstruction such as

BUFSIZE EQU 100

In assigning a value to a symbol in the label field of an instruction, the assembler must know what address that instruction will have during execution of the program. To keep track of the execution-time address of the instruction being assembled, the assembler maintains a variable during assembly, known as the **instruction location counter** or ILC. This variable is set to 0 at the beginning of pass one and incremented by the instruction length for each instruction processed, as shown in Fig. 7-3. The instruction length is determined by looking up the opcode in a table and, on some computers, such as the PDP-11, making a preliminary analysis of the operands as well.

Label field	Operation field	Operands field	Comments	Instruction length in bytes	ILC value (decimal) just before the statement is read
	⋮				
SUZANNE	L	2,I	R2 = I	4	100
	L	4,J	R4 = J	4	104
	L	6,K	R6 = K	4	108
MARIA	MR	2,2	R2 = I * I	2	112
	MR	4,4	R4 = J * J	2	114
	MR	6,6	R6 = K * K	2	116
MARILYN	AR	2,4	R2 = I * I + J * J	2	118
	AR	2,6	R2 = I * I + J * J + K * K	2	120
CAROL	ST	2,N	N = I * I + J * J + K * K	4	122
	B	DONE	EXIT TO DONE	4	126
	⋮				

Fig. 7-3. The instruction location counter (ILC) keeps track of the address where the instructions will be loaded in memory. In this example, the statements prior to SUZANNE occupy 100 bytes.

Some assemblers allow programmers to write instructions using immediate addressing even though no corresponding target language instruction exists. Such "pseudo-immediate" instructions are handled as follows. The assembler allocates memory for the immediate operand at the end of the program and generates an instruction that references it. For instance, in 370 assembly language, a programmer can write

L 1,=F'2'

to load register 1 with a Full word constant 2. In this way, the programmer avoids explicitly writing a DC pseudoinstruction to allocate a word initialized to 2. Constants for which the assembler automatically reserves memory are called **literals**. In addition to saving the programmer a little writing, literals improve the readability of a program by making the value of the constant apparent in the source statement. Pass one of the assembler must build a table of all literals used in the program.

Pass one uses at least three tables: the symbol table, the opcode table, and the literal table. The symbol table has one entry for each symbol, as shown in Fig. 7-4. Symbols are defined either by using them as labels or by explicit definition (e.g., EQU on the 370). Each symbol table entry contains the symbol itself (or a pointer to it), its numerical value, and sometimes other information. This additional information may include:

1. The length of data field associated with symbol.

2. The relocation bits. (Does the symbol change value if the program is loaded at a different address than the assembler assumed?)

3. Whether or not the symbol is to be accessible outside the procedure.

Symbol	Value	Other information
SUZANNE	100	
MARIA	112	
MARILYN	118	
CAROL	122	

Fig. 7-4. A symbol table for the program of Fig. 7-3.

The opcode table contains one entry for each symbolic opcode (mnemonic) in the assembly language. Figure 7-5 shows part of an opcode table. Each entry contains the symbolic opcode, its numerical value, the instruction length, and a class number that separates the opcodes into groups depending on the number and type of operands. For example, the 370 RR, RX, RS, SI, and SS instructions have different formats for their operands, requiring a different procedure for analyzing each one. On some machines, such as the 370, the length of the instruction is uniquely determined by the opcode, but on others, such as the PDP-11, it is not. The PDP-11 MOV instruction takes two operands, either of which can be a register or memory location, yielding three different lengths:

MOV R0,R1	register to register	(2 bytes)
MOV R0,X	register to memory	(4 bytes)
MOV X,R0	memory to register	(4 bytes)
MOV X,Y	memory to memory	(6 bytes)

Symbolic opcode	Opcode in hexadecimal	Instruction length in bytes	Instruction class
A	5A	4	1
AH	4A	4	1
MR	1C	2	7
CR	19	?	7
MVC	D2	6	4
L	58	4	1
B	47	4	9

Fig. 7-5. Part of the opcode table for an assembler for the 370.

The third table is the literal table. For each literal, one entry is made in the table. An entry contains the value of the literal in binary and the address where the literal is stored. The literals will eventually be stored in memory in locations following the object program. This means that the address where a particular literal is to be stored will only be known when the program length is known—that is, after pass one is finished.

If a literal is used several times in the program, it is desirable, nevertheless to allocate only one copy of it in the object program. This goal can be achieved in two ways. If the literal table is searched before a literal is entered—to see if it is already there—duplicate entries can be prevented. Alternatively, all literals are entered, and after pass one the literal table is sorted and duplicates removed.

Figure 7-6 shows a procedure that could serve as a basis for pass one of an assembler. The style of programming is noteworthy in itself. The procedure names have been chosen to give a good indication of what the procedures do. Most important, Fig. 7-6 represents an outline of pass one which, although not complete, forms a good starting point. It is short enough to be easily understood and it makes clear what the next step must be—namely, to write the procedures used in it.

Some of these procedures will be quite short, such as *CheckForLabel*, which returns the label as a character string if there is one and a blank string if there is not. Other procedures, such as *type1* and *type2*, may be longer and may call other procedures. In general, the number of classes will not be two, of course but will depend on the language being assembled.

Structuring programs in this way has other advantages in addition to ease of programming. If the assembler is being written by a group of people, the various procedures can be parceled out among the programmers. All the (nasty) details of the getting input are hidden away in *ReadNextStatement*. If they should change—for example, due to an operating system change—only one subsidiary procedure is affected, and no changes are needed to the *PassOne* procedure itself.

```
procedure PassOne ;
{This procedure is an outline of pass one of a simple assembler}

const size = 8;  EndStatement = 99;

var LocationCounter, class, length, value : integer ;
    MoreInput : boolean ;
    literal, symbol , opcode : array[1..size ] of char ;
    line : array[1..80] of char ;

begin
    LocationCounter := 0;                           {init instruction location counter}
    MoreInput := true ;                             {set to false at END statement}
    InitializeTables ;                              {call a procedure to set up tables}

    while MoreInput do
    begin                                           {loop executed once per line}
        ReadNextStatement (line );                  {go get some input}
        SaveLineForPassTwo(line );                  {save the line}

        if LineIsNotComment (line ) then            {is it a comment?}
            begin
                CheckForSymbol (line , symbol );    {is there a symbol?}
                if symbol [1] <> ' ' then           {if column 1 blank, no symbol}
                    EnterNewSymbol (symbol , LocationCounter );
                LookForLiteral (line , literal );   {literal present?}
                if literal [1] <> ' ' then          {blank means no literal present}
                    EnterLiteral (literal );

                {Now determine the opcode class.  −1 used to signal illegal opcode.}
                ExtractOpcode (line , opcode );
                SearchOpcodeTable (opcode , class , value );
                if class < 0 then TryPseudoInstr (opcode , class , value );
                length := 0;                        {compute instruction length}
                if class < 0 then IllegalOpcode ;
                case class of
                    0: length := type0(line );      {compute instruction length}
                    1: length := type1(line );      {ditto}

                    {Other cases here}

                end;

                LocationCounter := LocationCounter + length ;
                if class = EndStatement then
                    begin
                        MoreInput := false ;
                        RewindPassTwoInput ;
                        SortLiteralTable ;
                        RemoveRedundantLiterals
                    end
            end
    end
end; {PassOne}
```

Fig. 7-6. Pass one of a simple assembler.

In some assemblers, after a statement has been read in, it is stored in a table. If the table should fill up, it must be written out into secondary memory. It may fill up several times and be written out several times. If the program being assembled is short enough to fit in the table, pass two can get its input directly from the table, thus saving the time needed to write it out and read it back in again.

When the END pseudoinstruction is read, pass one is over. The symbol table and literal tables can be sorted at this point if needed. The sorted literal table can be checked for duplicate entries, which can be removed. The literal table is then compacted and an address is assigned to each literal, beginning at the first word following the program being assembled.

7.2.3. Pass Two

The function of pass two is to generate the object program and possibly print the assembly listing. In addition, pass two must output certain information needed by the linker for linking up procedures assembled at different times. Figure 7-7 shows a procedure for pass two.

The procedure for each class knows how many operands that class may have and calls the *EvaluateExpression* procedure (not shown) the appropriate number of times. The *EvaluateExpression* procedure must convert the symbolic expression to a binary number. It must first find the values of the symbols and the addresses of the literals from the respective tables. Once the numerical values are known, the expression can be evaluated. Numerous techniques for evaluating arithmetic expressions are known. One method (described in Sec. 5.3.7) is to convert the expression to reverse Polish and evaluate it by using a stack.

Once the numerical value of the opcode and the values of the operands are all known, the complete instruction can be assembled. The assembled instruction is then placed in an output buffer that is written to secondary memory when the buffer becomes full.

The original source statement and the object code generated from it (in octal or hexadecimal) are either printed or put into a buffer for later printing. After the ILC has been adjusted, the next statement is fetched.

Up until now it has been assumed that the source program does not contain any errors. Anyone who has ever written a program, in any language, knows how realistic that assumption is. Some of the common errors are as follows:

1. A symbol has been used but not defined.

2. A symbol has been defined more than once.

3. The name in the opcode field is not a legal opcode.

4. An opcode is not supplied with enough operands.

5. An opcode is supplied with too many operands.

6. An octal number contains an 8 or a 9.

```
procedure PassTwo ;
{This procedure is an outline of pass two of a simple assembler}

const size = 8; EndStatement = 99;

var code, class, value, LocationCounter, length : integer ;
    MoreInput : boolean ;
    opcode : array[1..size ] of char ;
    line : array[1 .. 80] of char ;
    operands : array[1 .. 3] of integer ;

begin
    MoreInput := true ;                                  {set to false at end statement}
    LocationCounter := 0;

    while MoreInput do
      begin
        GetNextStatement (line );                        {get input saved by pass one}
        if LineIsNotComment (line ) then
          begin
            ExtractOpcode (line, opcode );
            SearchOpcodeTable (opcode, class, value );
            if class < 0 then TryPseudoInstr (opcode, class, value );
            length := 0;                                 {compute instruction length}
            if class < 0 then BadOpcode ;
            case class of
              0: length := eval0(line, operands );
              1: length := eval1(line, operands );

              {Other cases here}

            end;

            AssemblePieces (code, class, value, operands );
            OutputCode (code );
            LocationCounter := LocationCounter + length ;
            if class = EndStatement then
              begin
                MoreInput := false ;
                FinishUp
              end
          end
      end
end; {PassTwo}
```

Fig. 7-7. Pass two of a simple assembler.

7. A register expression has been used where that is not allowed (e.g., a jump to a register).

8. The END statement is missing.

Programmers are most ingenious at thinking up new kinds of errors to make.

Undefined symbol errors are frequently caused by typing errors, so a clever assembler could try to figure out which of the defined symbols most resembles the undefined one and use that instead. Little can be done about correcting most other errors. The best thing for the assembler to do with an errant statement is to print an error message and try to continue assembly.

7.2.4. Symbol Table

During pass one of the assembly process, the assembler accumulates information about symbols and their values that must be stored in the symbol table for lookup during pass two. Several different methods are available for organizing the symbol table. In this section we will briefly describe some of them. All the methods attempt to simulate an **associative memory**, which conceptually is a set of (symbol, value) pairs. Given the symbol, the associative memory must produce the value.

The simplest implementation method is indeed to implement the symbol table as an array of pairs, the first element of which is (or points to) the symbol and the second of which is (or points to) the value. Given a symbol to look up, the symbol table routine just searches the table linearly until it finds a match. This method is easy to program but is slow, because on the average half the table will have to be searched on each lookup.

Another way to organize the symbol table is to sort it on the symbols and use the **binary search** algorithm to look up a symbol. This algorithm works by comparing the middle entry in the table to the symbol. If the symbol comes before the middle entry alphabetically, the symbol must be located in the first half of the table. If the symbol comes after the middle entry, the symbol must be located in the second half of the table. If the symbol is equal to the middle entry, the search terminates.

Assuming that the middle entry is not equal to the symbol sought, we at least know which half of the table to look for it in. Binary search can now be applied to the correct half, which yields either a match, or the correct quarter of the table. Applying the algorithm recursively, a table of size n entries can be searched in about $\log_2 n$ attempts. Obviously, this method is much faster than searching linearly, but it requires first sorting the table.

A completely different way of simulating an associative memory is a technique known as **hash coding**. This method requires having a "hash" function that maps symbols onto integers in the range 0 to $k - 1$. One possible function is to multiply the ASCII codes of the characters in the symbols together, ignoring overflow, and taking the result modulo k. In fact, almost any function of the input that gives a uniform distribution of the hash values will do. Symbols can be stored by having a table consisting of k "buckets" numbered 0 to $k - 1$. All the (symbol, value) pairs whose symbol hashes to i are stored on a linked list pointed to by slot i in the hash table. With n symbols and k slots in the hash table, the average list will have length n/k. By choosing k approximately equal to n, symbols can be located with only about one lookup on the average. By adjusting k we can reduce table size at the expense of slower lookups. Hash coding is illustrated in Fig. 7-8.

Symbol	Value	Hash code
andy	14025	0
ceriel	45012	5
ed	34004	2
hans	45019	2
henri	45009	7
jaco	15015	0
jim	14013	2
john	25014	1
marja	34101	3
martin	25014	3
peter	25018	1
reind	14004	4
ruud	34004	6
sape	24005	6
wiebren	24014	1

(a)

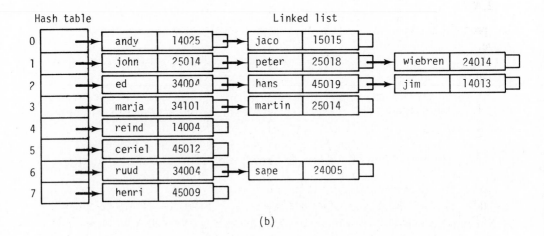

(b)

Fig. 7-8. Hash coding. (a) Symbols, values, and hash codes derived from symbols. (b) Eight entry hash table with linked lists of symbols and values.

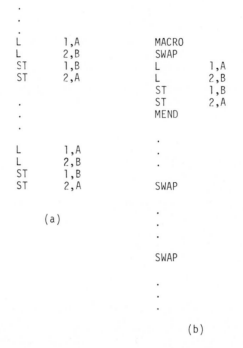

7.3. MACROS

Assembly language programmers frequently need to repeat sequences of instructions several times within a program. The most obvious way to do so is simply to write the required instructions wherever they are needed. If a sequence is long, however, or must be used a large number of times, writing it repeatedly becomes tedious.

An alternative method is to make the sequence into a procedure and call it wherever it is needed. This strategy has the disadvantage of requiring a procedure call instruction and a return instruction to be executed every time a sequence is needed. If the sequences are short—for example, two instructions—but are used frequently, the procedure call overhead may significantly slow the program down. Macros provide an easy and efficient solution to the problem of repeatedly needing the same or nearly the same sequences of instructions.

7.3.1. Macro Definition, Call, and Expansion

A **macro definition** is a method for giving a name to a piece of text. After a macro has been defined, the programmer can write the macro name instead of the piece of program. A macro is, in effect, an abbreviation for a piece of text. Figure 7-9(a) shows an assembly language program for the 370 that exchanges the contents of the variables *A* and *B* twice. These sequences could be defined as macros, as shown in Fig. 7-9(b). After its definition, every occurrence of SWAP causes it to be replaced by the four lines:

```
L 1,A
L 2,B
ST 1,B
ST 2,A
```

The programmer has defined SWAP as an abbreviation for the four statements shown above.

Although different assemblers have slightly different notations for defining macros, all require the same basic parts in a macro definition:

1. A macro header giving the name of the macro being defined.

2. The text comprising the body of the macro.

3. A pseudoinstruction marking the end of the definition (e.g., MEND).

When the assembler encounters a macro definition, it saves it in a macro definition table for subsequent use. From that point on, whenever the name of the macro (SWAP in the example of Fig. 7-9) appears as an opcode, the assembler replaces it by the macro body. The use of a macro name as an opcode is known as a **macro call** and its replacement by the macro body is called **macro expansion**.

Macro expansion occurs during the assembly process and not during execution of

```
  .
  .
  .
  L        1,A              MACRO
  L        2,B              SWAP
  ST       1,B              L           1,A
  ST       2,A              L           2,B
                            ST          1,B
  .                         ST          2,A
  .                         MEND
  .

  L        1,A              .
  L        2,B              .
  ST       1,B              .
  ST       2,A              SWAP

                            .
          (a)               .
                            .

                            SWAP

                            .
                            .
                            .

                          (b)
```

Fig. 7-9. IBM 370 assembly language code for interchanging *A* and *B* twice. (a) Without a macro. (b) With a macro.

the program. This point is important. The program of Fig. 7-9(a) and that of Fig. 7-9(b) will produce precisely the same machine language code. Looking only at the machine language program, it is impossible to tell whether or not any macros were involved in its generation, because the macro expansion has been completed and the macro definitions discarded by the time the program has been completely assembled.

Macro calls should not be confused with procedure calls. The basic difference is that a macro call is a signal to the assembler to replace the macro name with the macro body. A procedure call is a machine instruction that is inserted into the object program and that will later be executed to call the procedure. Figure 7-10 compares macro calls with procedure calls.

Although macros are generally expanded on pass one of the assembly process, it may be conceptually simpler to think of the assembler as having an extra pass before pass one during which macro definitions are saved and macros are expanded. In this view, the source program is read in and is then transformed into another program from which all macro definitions have been removed, and in which all macro calls have been replaced by their bodies. The resulting output, an assembly language program containing no macros at all, is then fed into the assembler.

It is important to keep in mind that a program is a string of characters including

Item	Macro call	Procedure call
When is the call made?	During assembly	During execution of the object program
Is the body inserted into the object program every place the name appeared?	Yes	No
Is a procedure call instruction inserted into the object program and later executed?	No	Yes
Must a return instruction be used to return control to the statement following the call?	No	Yes
How many copies of the body appear in the object program?	One for each macro call	1

Fig. 7-10. Comparison of macro calls with procedure calls.

letters, digits, spaces, punctuation marks, and "carriage returns" (change to a new line). Macro expansion consists of replacing certain substrings of this string with other character strings. A macro facility is a method of manipulating character strings, without regard to their meaning.

7.3.2. Macros with Parameters

The macro facility first described can be used to shorten programs in which precisely the same sequence of instructions occurs repeatedly. Frequently, however, a program contains several sequences of instructions that are almost but not quite identical, as illustrated in Fig. 7-11(a). Here the first sequence exchanges A and B, and the second sequence exchanges C and D.

Macro assemblers handle the case of nearly identical sequences by allowing macro definitions to provide **formal parameters** and by allowing macro calls to supply **actual parameters**. When a macro is expanded, each formal parameter appearing in the macro body is replaced by the corresponding actual parameters. The actual parameters are placed in the operand field of the macro call. Figure 7-11(b) shows the program of Fig. 7-11(a) rewritten using a macro with parameters. The symbols P and Q are the formal parameters. Each occurrence of P within a macro body is replaced by the first actual parameter when the macro is expanded. Similarly, Q is replaced by the second actual parameter. In the macro call

CHANGE A,B

```
        .                    .
        .                    .
        .                    .
    L       1,A          MACRO
    L       2,B          CHANGE      &P,&Q
    ST      1,B          L           1,&P
    ST      2,A          L           2,&Q
                         ST          1,&Q
                         ST          2,&P
        .                MEND
        .
        .

                             .
    L       1,C              .
    L       2,D              .
    L       1,D
    L       2,C          CHANGE A,B


        .                    .
        .                    .
        .                    .

       (a)               CHANGE C,D

                            (b)
```

Fig. 7-11. Nearly identical sequences of statements. (a) Without a macro. (b) With a macro.

A is the first actual parameter and B is the second actual parameter. The 370 assembler requires an ampersand to indicate the start of each formal parameter.

7.3.3. Implementation of a Macro Facility in an Assembler

To implement a macro facility, an assembler must be able to perform two functions: save macro definitions and expand macro calls. We will examine these functions in turn.

The assembler must maintain a table of all macro names and, along with each name, a pointer to its stored definition so that it can be retrieved when needed. Some assemblers have a separate table for macro names and some have a combined opcode table in which all machine instructions, pseudoinstructions, and macro names are kept.

When a macro definition is encountered, a table entry is made giving the name of the macro, the number of formal parameters, and a pointer to another table—the macro definition table—where the macro body will be kept. A list of the formal parameters is also constructed at this time for use in processing the definition. The macro body is then read and stored in the macro definition table. Formal parameters occurring within the body are indicated by some special marker, in this case, ampersand. As an example, the internal representation of the macro definition of CHANGE with semicolon as "carriage return" is as follows:

L 1,&P;L 2,&Q;ST 1,&Q;ST 2,&P

Within the macro definition table the macro body is simply a character string.

During pass one of the assembly, opcodes are looked up and macros expanded. Whenever a macro definition is encountered, it is stored in the macro table. When a macro is called, the assembler temporarily stops reading input from the input device, and starts reading from the stored macro body instead. Formal parameters extracted from the stored macro body are replaced by the actual parameters provided in the call. The presence of an ampersand in front of the formal parameters makes it easy for the assembler to recognize them.

7.4. LINKING AND LOADING

Most programs consist of more than one procedure. Compilers and assemblers generally translate one procedure at a time and put the translated output in secondary memory. Before the program can be run, all the translated procedures must be found and linked together properly. If virtual memory is not available, the linked program must be explicitly loaded into main memory as well. Programs that perform these functions are called by various names, including **linker**, **loader**, **linking loader**, and **linkage editor**. The complete translation of a source program requires two steps, as shown in Fig. 7-12:

1. Compilation or assembly of the source procedures.

2. Linking of the object modules.

The first step is performed by the compiler or assembler and the second one is performed by the linker.

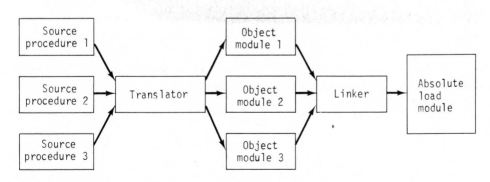

Fig. 7-12. Generation of an absolute load module from a collection of independently translated source procedures requires using a linker.

The translation from source procedure to object module represents a change of level because the source language and target language have different instructions and notation. The linking process, however, does not represent a change of level, since both the linker's input and the linker's output are programs for the same virtual machine. The linker's function is to collect procedures translated separately and link them together to be run as a unit, usually called an **absolute load module**. The loader's function is to load the absolute load module into main memory. These functions are often combined.

Compilers and assemblers translate each source procedure as a separate entity for a good reason. If a compiler or assembler read a series of source procedures and directly produced a ready-to-run machine language program, changing one statement in one source procedure would require that all the source procedures be retranslated.

If the separate-object-module method of Fig. 7-12 is used, it is only necessary to retranslate the modified procedure and not the unchanged ones, although it is necessary to relink all the object modules again. Linking is usually much faster than translating, however; thus the two-step process of translating and linking can save a great deal of time during the development of a large program. Short student jobs do not need the flexibility of separate translation. As a result, compilers have been written for certain languages (e.g., WATFOR and PL/C) that produce ready-to-run machine language programs.

7.4.1. Tasks Performed by the Linker

At the start of pass one of the assembly process, the instruction location counter is set to 0. This step is equivalent to assuming that the object module will be located at (virtual) address 0 during execution. Figure 7-13 shows four object modules. In this example, each module begins with a JUMP instruction to a MOV instruction within the module.

In order to run the program, the loader brings the object modules into main memory, as shown in Fig. 7-14(a). Typically, a small section of memory starting at address zero is used for interrupt vectors, communication with the operating system, or other purposes, so programs must start above 0. In this figure we have (arbitrarily) started programs at address 100.

The program of Fig. 7-14(a), although loaded into main memory, is not yet ready for execution. Consider what would happen if execution began with the instruction at the beginning of module A. The program would not jump to the MOVE instruction as it should, because that instruction is now at 300. In fact, all memory reference instructions will fail to operate properly for the same reason.

This problem, called the **relocation problem**, occurs because each object module in Fig. 7-13 represents a separate address space. On a machine with a segmented address space, such as that provided by MULTICS, each object module can have its own address space by being placed in its own segment. On a machine with a linear, one-dimensional memory, the object modules must be merged into a single address space. The two-dimensional nature of the MULTICS virtual memory eliminates the need for merging object modules and greatly simplifies the task of the linker. The

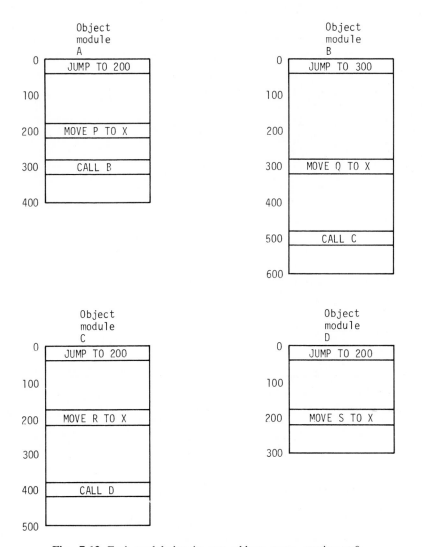

Fig. 7-13. Each module has its own address space, starting at 0.

separate address spaces of the object modules must also be merged on a machine with a paged, one-dimensional virtual memory.

Furthermore, the procedure call instructions in Fig. 7-14(a) will not work either. At address 400, the programmer had intended to call object module B, but because each procedure is translated by itself, the assembler has no way of knowing what address to insert into the CALL instruction. The address of object module B is not known until linking time. This problem is called the **external reference** problem. Both of these problems can be solved by the linker.

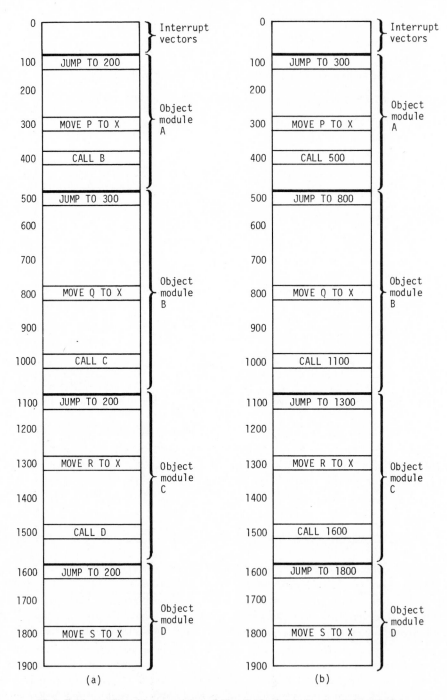

Fig. 7-14. (a) The object modules of Fig. 7-13 after being loaded but before being linked. (b) The same object modules after linking. Together they form an absolute load module, ready to run.

The linker merges the separate address spaces of the object modules into a single linear address in the following steps:

1. It constructs a table of all the object modules and their lengths.

2. Based on this table, it assigns a load address to each object module.

3. It finds all the instructions that contain a memory address and to each one adds a **relocation constant** equal to the starting address of the module in which it is contained.

4. It finds all the instructions that reference other procedures and inserts the address of these procedures in place.

The object module table constructed in step 1 is as follows for the modules of Fig. 7-14.

Module	Length	Starting Address
A	400	100
B	600	500
C	500	1100
D	300	1600

Figure 7-14(b) shows how the address space of Fig. 7-14(a) looks after the linker has performed these steps.

Base-register addressing speeds up linking by reducing the number of instructions that must be relocated. Because the calling sequence loads a base register with the origin of the procedure being called, that procedure can reference its instructions and data by specifying the displacement from the start of the procedure, which is independent of where the procedure is loaded. Self-relative addressing on the PDP-11 and 68000 also eliminates the need for the linker to add relocation constants to instructions.

7.4.2. Structure of an Object Module

Object modules contain six parts, as shown in Fig. 7-15. The first part contains the name of the module, certain information needed by the linker, such as the lengths of the various parts of the object module, and sometimes the date of assembly.

The second part of the object module is a list of the symbols defined in the module that other modules may reference, together with their values. For example, if the module consists of a procedure named BIGBUG, the entry point table will contain the character string "BIGBUG" followed by the address to which it corresponds. The assembly language programmer indicates which symbols are to be declared as **entry points** or **internal symbols** by using a pseudoinstruction.

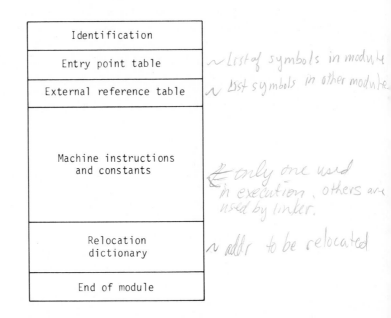

Handwritten annotations:
- ~ List of symbols in module
- ~ List symbols in other module.
- ≠ only one used in execution, others are used by linker.
- ~ addr to be relocated

Fig. 7-15. The internal structure of an object module produced by a translator.

    The third part of the object module consists of a list of the symbols used in the module but defined in other modules, along with a list of which machine instructions use which symbols. The linker needs the latter list in order to be able to insert the correct addresses into the instructions that use external symbols. A procedure can call other independently translated procedures by declaring the names of the called procedures to be external. The assembly language programmer indicates which symbols are to be declared as external by using a pseudoinstruction. On some computers the entry point table and the external reference table are combined into a single table.

    The fourth part of the object module is the assembled code and constants. This part of the object module is the only one that will be loaded into memory to be executed. The other five parts will be used by the linker and then discarded before execution begins.

    The fifth part of the object module is the relocation dictionary. As shown in Fig. 7-14, instructions that contain memory addresses must have a relocation constant added. Since the linker has no way of telling by inspection which of the data words in part 4 contain machine instructions and which contain constants, information about which addresses are to be relocated is provided in this table. The information may take the form of a bit table, with 1 bit per potentially relocatable address, or an explicit list of addresses to be relocated.

    The sixth part is an end-of-module indication, sometimes a checksum to catch errors made while reading the module, and the address at which to begin execution.

Most linkers require two passes. On pass one the linker reads all the object modules and builds up a table of module names and lengths and a global symbol table consisting of all entry points and external references. On pass two the object modules are read, relocated, and linked one module at a time. Some linkers assemble the absolute load module directly in main memory so that it can be executed, whereas others write it into secondary memory along with the tables so that it can be merged with other object modules later.

7.4.3. Binding Time and Dynamic Relocation

In a time-sharing system, a program can be read into main memory, run for a little while, written back into secondary memory, and then read back into main memory to be run again. In a large system, with many programs, it is difficult to ensure that a program is read back into the same locations every time.

Figure 7-16 shows what would happen if the already relocated program of Fig. 7-14(b) were reloaded at address 400 instead of address 100, where the linker put it originally. All the memory addresses are incorrect; moreover, the relocation information has long since been discarded. Even if the relocation information were still available, the cost of having to relocate all the addresses every time the program was swapped would be orders of magnitude too high.

The problem of moving programs that have already been linked and relocated is intimately related to the time at which the final binding of symbolic names onto absolute physical memory addresses is completed. When a program is written it contains symbolic names for memory addresses, typically in the form JUMP L. The time at which the actual main memory address corresponding to L is determined is called the **binding time**. At least six possibilities for the binding time exist:

1. When the program is written.

2. When the program is translated.

3. When the program is linked but before it is loaded.

4. When the program is loaded.

5. When a base register used for addressing is loaded.

6. When the instruction containing the address is executed.

If an instruction containing a memory address is moved after binding, it will be incorrect (assuming that the object referred to has also been moved). If the translator produces an absolute load module as output, the binding has occurred at translation time, and the program must be run at the address the translator expected it to be run at. The linking method described in the preceding section binds symbolic names to absolute addresses during linking, which is why moving programs after linking fails, as shown in Fig. 7-16.

Two related issues are involved here. First, there is the question of when

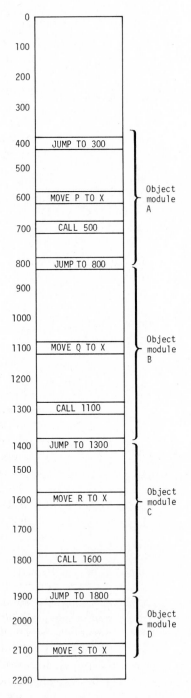

Fig. 7-16. The absolute load module of Fig. 7-14(b) moved up 300 addresses.

symbolic names are bound to virtual addresses. Second, there is a question of when virtual addresses are bound to physical addresses. Only when both operations have taken place is binding complete. When the linker merges the separate address spaces of the object modules into a single linear address space, it is, in fact, creating a virtual address space. The relocation and linking serve to bind symbolic names onto specific virtual addresses. This observation is true whether or not virtual memory is being used.

Assume for the moment that the address space of Fig. 7-14(b) were paged. It is clear that the virtual addresses corresponding to the symbolic names A, B, C, and D have already been determined, even though their physical main memory addresses will depend on the contents of the page table at the time they are used. An absolute load module is really a binding of symbolic names onto virtual addresses.

Any mechanism that allows the mapping of virtual addresses onto physical main memory addresses to be changed easily will facilitate moving programs around in main memory, even after they have been bound to a virtual address space. One such mechanism is paging. After a program has been moved in main memory, only its page table need be changed, not the program itself.

A second mechanism is the use of a run-time relocation register. On machines using this relocation method, the register always points to the physical memory address of the start of the current program. All memory addresses have the relocation register added to them by the hardware before being sent to the memory. The entire relocation process is transparent to the user programs. They do not even know that it is occurring and have no way of interfering with it. When a program is moved, the operating system must update the relocation register. This mechanism is less general than paging because the entire program must be moved as a unit.

A third mechanism is possible on machines that can use the program counter as a base register, such as the PDP-11. Whenever a program is moved in main memory only the program counter need be updated. Furthermore, if virtual memory is being used, a program can be "slid up" from one virtual address to another and still work correctly provided that the program counter is updated and provided that the procedure call stack does not contain any absolute addresses. In contrast, a program on a machine that uses paging or a relocation register but that does not use the program counter as a base register can be moved in physical memory but it cannot be moved to a different virtual address after linking. The ability to load a procedure anywhere within the virtual address space without having to modify it is particularly useful for library procedures. A module having the property that it can be loaded at any address without the need for relocation, is said to consist of **position-independent code.**

At first, you might think that base register addressing also solves the dynamic relocation problem, but in fact it does not. The procedure call sequence on a base register machine loads a base register with the address of the procedure called. This register is then used as a base register for addresses within the procedure. As long as the procedure is not moved subsequent to being called, everything works fine. However, if the procedure is moved during its execution (a normal situation in a time-sharing system), the base register will no longer contain the correct origin.

Furthermore, it is not possible for the operating system to move a program and update its base register because a program may use several base registers. The operating system has no way of knowing which of the general registers are being used as base registers and which are being used for holding data. This problem is solved on the 370 by using virtual memory. However, on the earlier 360 machines, which did not have virtual memory (except the 360/67), there was no solution and programs could not be moved after being loaded.

7.4.4. Dynamic Linking

The linking method discussed in Sec. 7.4.1 has the property that all procedures that a program might call are linked before the program can begin execution. On a computer with virtual memory, completing all linking before beginning execution does not take advantage of the full capabilities of the virtual memory. Many programs have procedures that are only called under unusual circumstances. For example, compilers have procedures for compiling rarely used statements, plus procedures for handling error conditions that seldom occur.

A more flexible method for linking separately compiled procedures is to link each procedure at the time it is first called. This process is known as **dynamic linking** and it is used by MULTICS. The location of each compiled procedure in secondary memory is recorded somewhere (e.g., the owner's file directory) so that the linker can find it when needed. Associated with each program is a segment, called the **linkage segment**, which contains one block of information for each procedure that might be called. This block of information starts with a word reserved for the virtual address of the procedure and it is followed by the procedure name, which is stored as a character string.

When dynamic linking is being used, procedure calls in the source language are translated into instructions that indirectly address the first word of the corresponding linkage block, as shown in Fig. 7-17(a). The translator fills this word with either an invalid address or a special bit pattern that forces a trap.

When a procedure in a different segment is called, the attempt to address the invalid word indirectly causes a trap to the dynamic linker. The linker then finds the character string in the word following the invalid address and searches the user's file directory for a compiled procedure with this name. That procedure is then assigned a virtual address, usually in its own private segment, and this virtual address overwrites the invalid address in the linkage segment, as indicated in Fig. 7-17(b). Next, the instruction causing the linkage fault is reexecuted, allowing the program to continue from the place it was before the trap.

All subsequent references to that procedure will be executed without causing a linkage fault, for the indirect word now contains a valid virtual address. Consequently, the dynamic linker is invoked only the first time a procedure is called and not thereafter.

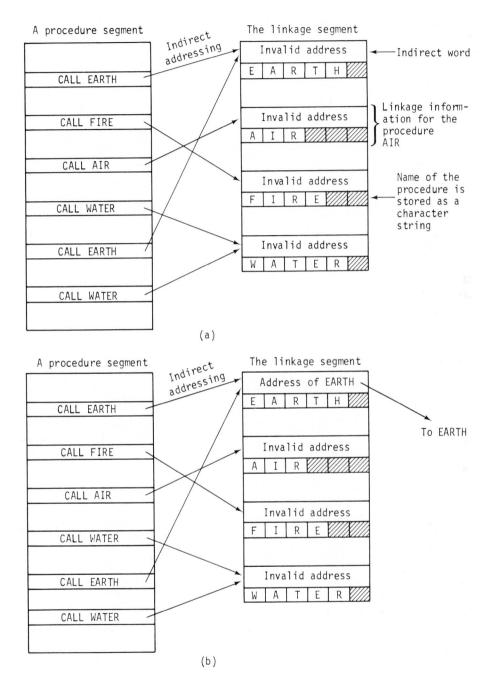

Fig. 7-17. Dynamic linking. (a) Before EARTH is called. (b) After EARTH has been called and linked.

7.5. SUMMARY

Although most programs can and should be written in a high-level language, occasional situations exist in which assembly language is needed, at least in part. An assembly language program is a symbolic representation for some underlying machine language program. It is translated to the machine language by a program called an assembler.

Various studies have shown that even when fast execution is needed, a better approach than writing everything in assembly language is to first write the whole program in a high-level language, then measure where it is spending its time, and finally rewrite only those portions of the program that are heavily used. In practice, a small fraction of the code is usually responsible for a large fraction of the execution time.

Most assemblers are two pass. Pass one is devoted to building up a symbol table for labels, literals, and explicitly declared identifiers. The symbols can either be kept unsorted and then searched linearly, first sorted and then searched using binary search, or hashed. If symbols do not need to be deleted during pass one, hashing is usually the best method. Pass two does the code generation. Some pseudoinstructions are carried out on pass one and some on pass two.

Many assemblers have a macro facility that allows the programmer to give commonly used code sequences symbolic names for subsequent inclusion. Usually, these macros can be parameterized in a straightforward way. Macros are implemented by a kind of literal string processing algorithm.

Independently assembled programs can be linked together to form an absolute load module. This work is done by the linker. Its primary tasks are relocation and binding of names.

PROBLEMS

1. For a certain program, 1% of the code accounts for 50% of the execution time. Compare the following three strategies with respect to programming time and execution time. Assume that it would take 100 person-months to write it in Pascal, and that assembly code is 10 times harder to write and four times more efficient.

   a. Entire program in Pascal.
   b. Entire program in assembler.
   c. First all in Pascal, then the key 1% rewritten in assembler.

2. Do the considerations that hold for two-pass assemblers also hold for compilers?

   a. Assume that the compilers produce object modules, not assembly code.
   b. Assume that the compilers produce symbolic assembly language.

3. Suggest a method for allowing assembly language programmers to define synonyms for opcodes. How could this be implemented?

4. Can the following program be assembled in two passes? EQU is a pseudoinstruction that equates the label to the expression in the operand field.

A EQU B
B EQU C
C EQU D
D EQU 4

5. The Dirtcheap Software Company is planning to produce an assembler for a computer with a 48-bit word. To keep costs down, the project manager, Dr. Scrooge, has decided to limit the length of allowed symbols so that each symbol can be stored in a single word. Scrooge has declared that symbols may consist only of letters, except the letter Q, which is forbidden (to demonstrate their concern for efficiency to the customers). What is the maximum length of a symbol? Describe your encoding method.

6. What is the difference between an instruction and a pseudoinstruction?

7. What is the difference between the instruction location counter and the program counter, if any? After all, both keep track of the next instruction in a program.

8. Show the symbol table after the following statements have been encountered. The first statement is assigned to address 1000.

EVEREST	L	1,X	(4 bytes)
K2	L	2,Y	(4 bytes)
WHITNEY	MR	1,1	(2 bytes)
MCKINLEY	MR	2,2	(2 bytes)
FUJI	AR	1,2	(2 bytes)
KIBO	ST	1,Z	(4 bytes)

9. Show the steps needed to look up Berkeley using binary search on the following list: Ann Arbor, Berkeley, Cambridge, Eugene, Madison, New Haven, Palo Alto, Pasadena, Santa Cruz, Stony Brook, Westwood, and Yellow Springs. When computing the middle element of a list with an even number of elements, use the element just below the middle index.

10. Is it possible to use binary search on a table whose size is prime?

11. Compute the hash code for each of the following symbols by adding up the letters (A = 1, B = 2, etc.) and taking the result modulo the hash table size. The hash table has 19 slots, numbered 0 to 18.

ELS, JAN, JELLE, MAAIKE

Does each symbol generate a unique hash value? If not, how can the collision problem be dealt with?

12. The hash coding method described in the text links all the entries having the same hash code together on a linked list. An alternative method is to have only a single n-slot table, with each table slot having room for one key and its value (or pointers to them). If the hashing algorithm generates a slot that is already full, a second hashing algorithm is used to try again. If that one is also full, another is used, and so on, until an empty is found. If the fraction of the slots that are full is r, how many probes will be needed, on the average, to enter a new symbol?

13. As VLSI technology progresses, it may one day be possible to put thousands of identical CPUs on a chip, each CPU having a few words of local memory. If all the CPUs can read and write three shared registers, how can an associative memory be implemented?

14. Some assemblers have pseudoinstructions DATA and TEXT that allow the programmer to intermix data and machine instructions in the source program. After a DATA pseudoinstruction, it is permitted to assemble constants until the next TEXT pseudoinstruction and vice versa. At the end of the assembly all the data are collected together in a contiguous block. All the instructions are collected in another contiguous block. In other words, despite the fact that the data and text were mixed in the source program, they are separated in the object program. What implications does this scheme have for the instruction location counter?

15. If a macro definition contains a label, that label will be generated every time the macro is called, leading to multiply defined labels. Because macros may contain loops, labels are sometimes needed. Devise a solution to this problem.

16. You are to implement a macro assembler. For esthetic reasons, your boss has decided that macro definitions need not precede their calls. What implications does this decision have on the implementation?

17. Think of a way to put a macro assembler into an infinite loop.

18. A linker reads five modules, whose lengths are 200, 800, 600, 500, and 700 words, respectively. If they are loaded in that order, what are the relocation constants?

19. Prof. Martin Metabit has suggested solving the dynamic relocation problem for base-register machines by adding a special bit to each base register, and providing new instructions to set, clear, and test the bit. The bit could be used to indicate that the register contained a relocatable memory address, so the operating system would know which register to relocate when the program was moved. What do you think?

20. Write a symbol table package consisting of two routines: ENTER(SYMBOL, VALUE) and LOOKUP(SYMBOL, VALUE). The former enters new symbols in the table and the latter looks them up. Use some form of hash coding.

21. Write a simple assembler for the Mac-1 computer of Chap. 4. In addition to handling the machine instructions, provide a facility for assigning constants to symbols at assembly time, and a way to assemble a constant into a machine word. See Fig. 4-11(b) for an example program.

22. Add a simple macro facility to the assembler of the preceding problem.

8

MULTILEVEL MACHINES

The preceding five chapters each covered one specific level found on many modern computers. In this chapter we will take a more global view and examine some of the techniques and problems associated with organizing a computer in a structured way, as a hierarchy of levels. The topics to be covered include methods for implementing new levels, the order of the design decisions, the use of multilevel machines for producing portable software, self-virtualizing machines (machines in which the same level occurs more than once), and the nature of the principal interface level.

8.1. METHODS OF IMPLEMENTING NEW LEVELS

Three different methods for implementing new levels will be summarized in the following sections—interpretation, translation, and procedural extension. Interpretation and translation are the most important methods, with procedural extension being used only for certain specialized applications.

8.1.1. Interpretation

The essence of interpretation is that a process fetches, examines, and carries out the instructions contained in some program. The program being interpreted is really the data used by the interpreter, just as a file of employee names and salaries is the data for a payroll program. The process carrying out the interpretation acts exactly like a "hardware" processor, so the program being interpreted cannot tell whether it is being interpreted by a lower-level process or whether it is running on a real hardware processor of equivalent speed. In both cases, the process whose program is being interpreted passes through exactly the same sequence of states.

It is possible to have a hierarchy of interpreters, each one interpreting the level above it. As an example, consider a Pascal program that interprets PDP-11 conventional machine level instructions. This program can be used on an IBM 370 by first compiling the Pascal program to 370 level 3 language. The resulting program consists of load register, store register, and other "ordinary" instructions, as well as the 370's file I/O OSML instructions for performing I/O (see Sec. 6.2). The file I/O instructions are needed to simulate the PDP-11 when it reads from its disk, for example. The number of interpreters active depends on whether an "ordinary" or an OSML instruction is being executed by the level 3 program. For an ordinary instruction, there are two interpreters, the microprogram and the PDP-11 simulator. For an OSML instruction, such as reading a record from a file, these interpreters are at work: the microprogram, the operating system, and the PDP-11 interpreter.

Figure 8-1 shows this six-level machine. After compilation has been completed (i.e., during execution), four processes will be running, corresponding to the execution of the microprogram, the operating system, the PDP-11 simulator, and the PDP-11 program running on the simulator. Each process has its own program, its own state vector, and its own program counter. When the PDP-11 simulator executes an ordinary instruction, the operating system becomes inactive, however.

When all four levels are active, each microinstruction contributes to the progress of all four processes. Every microinstruction carries out part of a conventional machine level instruction, which in turn carries out part of a PDP-11 I/O instruction, which in turn advances the PDP-11 user program. In other words, every microinstruction contributes to the progress of not just one but four processes, all running simultaneously on different virtual machines.

Although in this example we have chosen to simulate the PDP-11's conventional machine level, we could equally well have chosen to simulate its microprogramming level or even its digital logic level. The choice depends on why the simulator is needed. If the intention is to develop PDP-11 compilers, a simulated conventional machine level is sufficient. However, if the goal is to experiment with new microprograms, at least one and possibly both of the underlying levels will also be needed.

8.1.2. Translation

A language, L, implicitly defines a virtual machine—namely, the virtual machine whose machine language is L. This fact is equally true for problem-oriented languages, such as Pascal, as for the conventional machine level type. In principle, there is no reason a computer could not be provided with a Pascal virtual machine, a level whose machine language is Pascal. Such a machine could directly execute Pascal programs, just as the 370 conventional machine level can directly execute

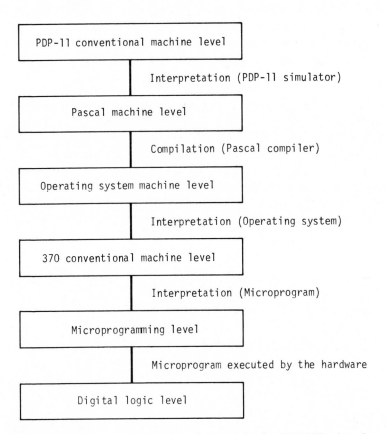

Fig. 8-1. A PDP-11 simulator written in Pascal for the IBM 370, viewed as a six-level machine.

programs written using the instructions of Fig. 5-4. All that is required is a Pascal interpreter. Such an interpreter could be written for the level 3 machine, for example, thus making the Pascal machine level 4.

Although a Pascal machine is certainly conceivable, it is rarely implemented as such for a very good reason. The syntaxes of the microprogramming level and conventional machine levels are simple: an opcode field and a few address fields. On the 370 conventional machine level, for example, the leftmost 8 bits form the opcode. As a result, decoding the instructions is easy for the microprogram. A 256-entry table, with one entry per opcode, can provide the address of the part of the interpreter to be used.

Instruction decoding for a Pascal machine is far more difficult. Determining what operations are needed to execute even a simple Pascal statement like

if *andy* = *hungry* **then** *CookieCount* := *CookieCount* − 1;

will require considerably more time than simply using an 8-bit number as an index into a table, because manipulating variable-length character strings is inherently more complicated than performing one indexing operation. Worse yet, each time a Pascal statement is to be executed, its syntax must be analyzed again, even though it was already analyzed when previously used. If a statement in a loop is executed 1000 times, its syntax will be analyzed 1000 times, which is obviously inefficient.

Translation provides a method for efficiently implementing a level with an elaborate syntax. The translator first reads and analyzes the program to be executed. Then it produces as output a new program (the object program) in a different language (the target language) that is equivalent to the original. Because one of the main reasons for translation is to avoid having to perform long and time-consuming syntax analysis repeatedly, languages used as target languages normally have instructions with a simple syntax, such as an opcode field and a few address fields.

The most important kinds of translators are assemblers, compilers and macro processors. Assemblers translate languages that are, in fact, symbolic representations of the target languages. The assembler's principal task is replacing the symbolic names of the variables and the symbolic opcodes by binary numbers, to spare the interpreter the need for time-consuming character handling.

Compilers translate problem-oriented languages to a form suitable for interpretation, or, sometimes, to an assembly language for subsequent translation by an assembler. The distinction between a compiler and an assembler is more a matter of degree than anything else. If a great deal of syntax analysis must be performed, the translator is called a compiler; otherwise, it is called an assembler.

General-Purpose Macro Processors

Macro processors represent a third type of translator. The assembly language macros of Sec. 7.3 represent a simple form of macro. Far more general and powerful macro processors are available, however, than those provided by most assemblers. Basically, a general-purpose macro processor first reads and stores a series of macro definitions. Then it reads the program to be translated, looking for macro calls and replacing them by the previously defined bodies.

The resulting text, which may be in any language, is written onto a file rather than being fed directly into an assembler. This output file can later be used as input to any assembler or compiler. Macro processors simply recognize certain character strings (the macro calls) and replace them by other character strings (the macro bodies).

ML/I (Brown, 1967) is an example of a general-purpose macro processor. ML/I allows the programmer to define his own syntax by defining patterns that ML/I is to recognize and replace by other patterns. As an example of a user-defined macro, we will show how statements of the form

IF PROGRAM = PERFECT THEN STUDENT = HAPPY;
IF TIME = NOON THEN STOMACH = EMPTY;
IF MONTH = AUGUST THEN BEACH = FULL;

can be handled by ML/I and converted into PDP-11 assembly language, for subsequent use by the PDP-11 assembler.

These statements all have the form

IF * = * THEN * = *;

where * indicates that an actual parameter is expected at that position. An ML/I macro to convert this kind of statement to PDP-11 assembly language is

```
MCDEF IF = THEN = ;
AS<    CMP %A1.,%A2.
       BNE .+8
       MOV %A4.,%A3.
>
```

The MCDEF statement is a MaCro DEFinition for a macro with five delimiters:

1. IF
2. =
3. THEN
4. =
5. ;

A call of this macro must supply an actual parameter between each of the four pairs of delimiters. In the call

IF NAME = FRODO THEN TYPE = HOBBIT

the actual parameters are

actual parameter 1 = NAME
actual parameter 2 = FRODO
actual parameter 3 = TYPE
actual parameter 4 = HOBBIT

The macro body is enclosed between < and >. The marker %A1. is replaced during expansion by actual parameter 1, the marker %A2. is replaced during expansion by actual parameter 2, and so on. ML/I numbers its formal parameters rather than naming them because it is possible to define macros with a variable number of parameters. For example, a single CALL macro could be defined so that it could be used with zero, one, two, or arbitrarily many actual parameters. The preceding macro call is replaced by

```
CMP NAME,FRODO    (compare NAME to FRODO)
BNE .+8           (if unequal, skip one statement)
MOV HOBBIT,TYPE   (move HOBBIT to TYPE)
```

ML/I allows macros far more complicated than shown in this example. A macro may have arbitrarily many alternative sets of delimiters, a feature that could be exploited to allow the IF macro above to handle "<", ">", and so on, as well as "=". The programmer can write conditional macros whose expansion depends on both the actual parameters and the delimiters, for example, checking for "=" or "<". The pattern to be recognized as a macro call may be arbitrarily long and may have an arbitrary number of parameters. Furthermore, the actual parameters themselves may be arbitrarily long and may even contain nested macro calls.

A general IF macro could be written to handle THEN clauses several pages long, including other calls of the IF macro. Macros are fully recursive and a macro may be called from within its body as well as from within one of its actual parameters. Macros may be redefined or deleted. Provision is made for performing both arithmetic tests and string comparisons during the macro expansion process, the results of which can direct the course of the expansion. In short, ML/I can be used to translate a fairly sophisticated programming language (Tanenbaum, 1976).

8.1.3. Procedural Extension

It is common for applications packages in statistics, computer graphics, and other areas to be implemented as a collection of procedures in Pascal, FORTRAN, or another language. As an illustration of this approach, consider the following representative procedures from a statistics package.

ReadData(*x*);	{ read a data deck into the vector *x* }
ReadData(*y*);	{ read a data deck into the vector *y* }
correlate(*x*,*y*,*r*);	{ correlation coefficient }
print(*r*);	{ print *r* }
LeastSquares(*x*,*y*,*a*,*b*);	{ fit a straight line to the data }
plot(*x*,*y*);	{ plot the data }
DrawLine(*a*,*b*);	{ plot the best fit line }
NextFrame;	{ prepare to make another plot }

Although this language is technically Pascal, an unsophisticated user who knew nothing about Pascal might think of it as a programming language with instructions *ReadData*, *correlate*, *print*, and so forth. The user can combine these one-line "instructions" to form programs, just as an assembly language programmer can combine other one-line instructions to form programs.

In one sense, these instructions define a virtual machine. This virtual machine can also be implemented by translation or interpretation, of course. In another sense, this level is no different than the Pascal level. Construction of a level using procedures is not as widely used as the other two methods.

8.2. DESIGN STRATEGIES FOR MULTILEVEL MACHINES

Conceptually, three different methods can be used to design a multilevel system. Method 1, the **top-down** design technique, consists of first designing the topmost level, the one that the end user ultimately sees. Next, the level below it is designed, then the level below that, and so forth, until a level is reached that can be interpreted by an interpreter running on the bare hardware. In the top-down method, the levels are designed starting at the top and working downward.

Method 2, the **bottom-up** design technique, is precisely the opposite of the top-down approach. When designing bottom-up, the level closest to the hardware is designed first, then the level above it, and so on, until the top level is reached.

Method 3, the **middle-out** design technique, consists of first designing one of the intermediate levels and then working upward and downward simultaneously. This approach has the advantage that once one of the middle levels has been completely specified, one design group can get to work designing upward starting at that level, while another design group can get to work designing downward from that level, toward the hardware.

8.2.1. Top-Down Design

The top-down design philosophy is intuitively appealing, because a designer using it starts out by carefully specifying the virtual machine (and language) that the customer will ultimately use. He must specify the data types to be provided and the instructions available for manipulating them.

Sometimes, this step is done even before the project begins. For example, if the goal of the project is to design and implement a Pascal or an ALGOL 68 level, the designer need not first design Pascal or ALGOL 68, for they have already been carefully specified. If, on the other hand, the project is to design a level (machine and language) to be used for research in artificial intelligence, the choice of features to include at the top level is an open question that must be first resolved.

After the top level has been completely and precisely specified, the designers try to think of another level from which the implementation of the top level would be convenient. In other words, they must ask themselves: "If we were to write an interpreter for the top level, in what language would we like to write the interpreter?" Or they might ask: "If we were to write a compiler to compile programs written for the top level into some other language, into what language would we like to compile them?"

As an example of the top-down approach, consider the design of a computer system to be used as a base for an automated library. The first step is to decide what kind of features and services the library will have. Will it simply have the books and magazines and an automated subject, title, and author catalog? Will it be able to accept and provide responses to such requests as: "Give me a list of all journal articles in 1929 about the mating habits of lemmings?" This level can be thought of as a virtual library machine, as shown in Fig. 8-2(a).

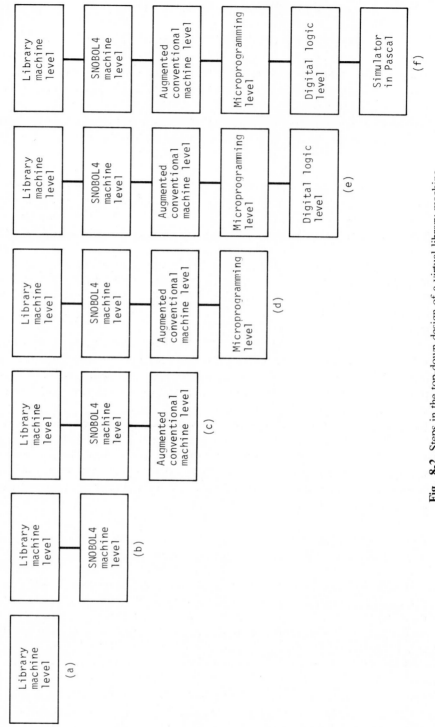

Fig. 8-2. Steps in the top-down design of a virtual library machine.

392

Once the virtual library machine has been specified, the designers must devise a method for implementing it. One technique would be to invent a programming language that is particularly suited to string and character manipulation. Alternatively, they may decide that an existing-string processing language, such as SNO-BOL4, is adequate. The system designed so far is shown in Fig. 8-2(b).

The designers must now face the problem of implementing the virtual machine defined by the string-processing language SNOBOL4. One method would be to invent a more or less conventional computer that had, in addition to the usual kinds of instructions, special instructions for processing strings. Such instructions might include instructions for moving a string, comparing two strings, concatenating two strings, searching a string for a substring, and appropriate string I/O. Programs written in the string processing language would first be compiled to this augmented conventional machine level and then run at that level. Figure 8-2(c) illustrates the design up to this point.

The next step in the design is to find a method for supporting the augmented conventional machine level. One way is to construct a microprogrammable CPU to interpret it. The microprogramming level of the machine chosen should have good character-handling facilities. Figure 8-2(d) shows this step. Figure 8-2(e) depicts the complete system.

Before investing time, energy, and money in the construction of the CPU, it would be useful to be able to measure the performance of the complete system. Otherwise, when faced with the choice of using the low-cost Turtle-brand chips or the expensive Jackrabbit-brand ones, there will be no basis for making intelligent decisions. The way to handle this situation is to write a simulator (interpreter) for the digital logic level before actually building or buying anything. Figure 8-2(f) shows the implementation of the system simulated in Pascal. Although not shown, quite a few levels may be beneath the Pascal level, supporting it. Using the simulator, the system can be constructed and partially tested to see how well it performs. If it performs badly, the design can be changed before any irreversible commitments to particular hardware are made.

8.2.2. Bottom-Up Design

The opposite approach to the top-down design is to begin with the existing hardware and construct a level above it whose properties are more attractive (or perhaps less obnoxious) than those of the hardware. This new level is then used as a base for creating a still more convenient virtual machine. As many new levels as necessary are added until the desired virtual machine is achieved.

Many advanced operating systems are constructed not as a single level, as suggested in Chap. 6 but as a hierarchy of levels. Dijkstra's (1968b) "THE" system is the spiritual progenitor of this type of operating system.

These designs usually begin at the conventional machine level rather than at the microprogramming or digital logic levels. Most conventional machine levels have an interrupt system, which means that any instruction may be followed in time either by its normal successor, or by the first instruction of some interrupt procedure, should an interrupt occur.

Consequently, the precise sequence of states that occurs depends on the exact time that the interrupts happen. Since the physical motion of an I/O device is rarely reproducible to milliseconds, let alone microseconds or nanoseconds, if a program is rerun several times, it is highly unlikely that exactly the same sequence of states will occur on each run. A process whose behavior is not uniquely determined by its program, data, and initial state is said to be **nondeterministic**, to distinguish it from the normal deterministic or sequential process.

Since programming for a deterministic machine is much easier than programming for one that is not, the level above the conventional machine level is chosen to be deterministic. Instead of having a single nondeterministic process, this level has several cooperating deterministic processes running in "parallel," such as the producer-consumer example of Chap. 6. The only process running on the conventional machine level is the interrupt handler.

When an interrupt occurs, the interrupt handler stops the process currently running and starts the appropriate interrupt process. After the interrupt process has done its job, it signals that it is finished, and the other process continues. Each of these processes is completely deterministic. The only peculiarity is that sometimes the interval between two instructions is unusually long, because another process ran for a while. However, in order for a process to be deterministic, the only feature that need be guaranteed is that the sequence of states be fully reproducible. No one guarantees how much or how little time may elapse between instructions. The level on which all processes are deterministic will be called the deterministic virtual machine level, as shown in Fig. 8-3(b).

Programs running on the deterministic machine level reference physical memory locations. Because virtual memories provide programmers with the convenience of a large and, in some cases, segmented address space, most modern computers have a virtual memory. The process or processes for supporting the virtual memory can run on the deterministic machine. This situation is shown in Fig. 8-3(c). The level above the deterministic machine level has the following two properties:

1. All processes are strictly deterministic.

2. Processes may use the virtual memory without worrying about its implementation.

Note that not every instruction executed by a process running on the virtual memory machine is interpreted by a process on the level below. On the contrary, most instructions are interpreted directly by the microprogram, and only those instructions that cause page, segment, or protection faults cause processes at the deterministic machine level to become active.

Programs running on the virtual memory machine must directly access each I/O

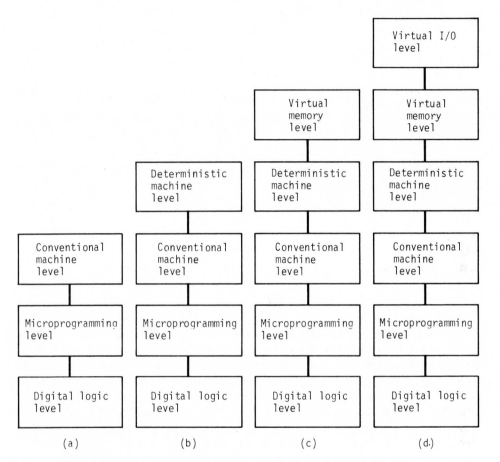

Fig. 8-3. Steps in the bottom-up design of a multilevel operating system.

device by giving its hardware device number. It is more convenient for the programmer to have an instruction TYPE LINE that simply types a line on the terminal. Accordingly, the next level provides virtual I/O instructions, as shown in Fig. 8-3(d). When a process on the virtual I/O machine executes a TYPE LINE instruction, a process on the machine below it carries it out.

8.2.3. Middle-Out Design

In practice, designs are rarely pure top-down or bottom-up. A pure top-down design has the inherent danger that some attractive features built into the uppermost virtual machine may be difficult, if not impossible, to implement on the available hardware. A pure bottom-up design may proceed through many levels before the designer discovers that the resulting machine is not what the customer requested.

Good designers generally have some idea of what the ultimate top and bottom levels will be like, and they (consciously or unconsciously) use this information during the design process. An experienced designer doing a top-down design is not going to include any features in the top level unless he is confident that the level can be implemented somehow, even if he does not have the details worked out yet. As a result, the design is not really pure top-down, because information about the bottom level has influenced the design of the top level.

Some designers start in the middle and then work outward in both directions. Many computers (e.g., 370, PDP-11) have been designed middle-out, with the conventional machine level being specified first. After that level was specified, it was possible to begin the detailed specification of the microgramming levels and microprograms, on the one hand, and the operating systems and compilers, on the other. Middle-out design allows the upward and downward designs to proceed simultaneously, with two design groups working in parallel.

8.3. PROGRAM PORTABILITY

Ever since the appearance of the *second* computer, several decades ago, people have been trying to devise ways to allow programs written for one computer to be run on another computer. When a university or corporate computer center replaces its old computer with a shiny new one, the users want to run their old programs on the new machine without having to rewrite them. When a student graduates and goes to work, he may want to bring some programs with him. When a research worker discovers that a colleague elsewhere has written a useful program, he would like to use it, even if the program was written for a brand X computer and his computer is a brand Y. A program that can be moved from one computer to another with relatively little effort is said to be **portable**.

Many proposals have been made over the years to increase program portability. In the following sections we will briefly examine six of these methods:

1. Universal programming language.

2. Brute-force approach.

3. UNCOL.

4. Abstract machine language.

5. Portable compilers.

6. Emulation.

Most of these techniques involve multilevel machines in one way or another.

8.3.1. A Universal Programming Language

The first approach to achieving portability is to design a general-purpose programming language and then request or require all programmers to use it exclusively. By implementing the virtual machine defined by this language on a large number of computers (by providing compilers or interpreters for all of them) programs can be moved easily from computer to computer. This approach is shown in Fig. 8-4.

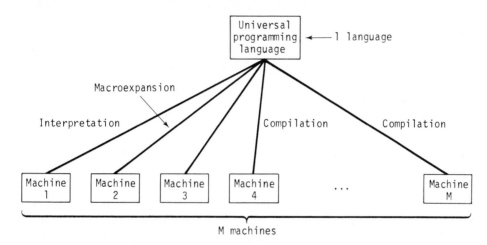

Fig. 8-4. A universal programming language available on all computers.

All attempts to produce such a universal programming language have failed miserably with respect to their goal of universal acceptance and use. On the contrary, dozens of programming languages are already in use, and their numbers are increasing like rabbits.

The basic reason for the lack of success of a universal programming language is that each programmer wants a language particularly suited to the application at hand and does not want to pay (in terms of a large, inefficient compiler and difficult-to-learn language) for facilities that are not needed or wanted. Systems programmers use binary trees heavily, physicists need real matrices, librarians require character strings, and administrators want to be able to handle large data bases. Each group naturally prefers a language that emphasizes the data types and operations needed for its application rather than a general-purpose language.

Although no universal programming language is used by everybody for everything, two languages are widely used: COBOL and FORTRAN. You might think that a FORTRAN program written for one computer will run the first time it is tried on another but such is rarely the case. Some of the difficulties are listed below.

1. Few manufacturers's compilers adhere exactly to the official ANSI Standard. Most have "new, improved" (and incompatible) extra features.

2. Word lengths vary from machine to machine, which means that the larg-
    est integer available also varies.

3. The smallest positive floating-point number is machine dependent. This
    dependence has drastic effects on programs that iterate until something is
    "less than epsilon."

4. The number and type of I/O devices available differ from machine to
    machine. An eight-tape sort will have trouble on a computer with only
    five tape drives.

5. Subroutine libraries differ.

6. The level 3 virtual instructions depend on the operating system. If a
    program creates a file of 136-character records, it will not work on a
    computer whose operating system insists that all records be less than or
    equal to 132 characters.

7. The program may not fit in the new machine's memory.

8. The character sets may be incompatible. A certain bit pattern may be a
    printable character on one computer and illegal or an end-of-record mark
    on another.

9. One's complement computers may give different results than two's com-
    plement computers. The biggest source of problems is tests on -0.

10. If the program contains any assembly language subroutines, they will
    have to be rewritten.

11. Most of these problems have the same cause: the virtual machine defined by the
    programming language is not completely specified. Details like word lengths,
    I/O, and libraries are not part of the definition.

8.3.2. The Brute Force Approach

Once the goal of a universal programming language has been abandoned as hopeless, a second approach is to provide an implementation of every language on every
computer. In this way, no matter what language a programmer chooses to use, the
virtual machine defined by it will be implemented on whatever real computer he has
available.

If there are L programming languages and M machines, the number of implementations (compilers and interpreters) needed is the product L $\times$ M, as shown in Fig. 8-
5. Hundreds of different computers have been built and even more languages have
been developed, so the number of implementations needed probably exceeds 100,000.
Producing that many compilers and interpreters would create lots of jobs for computer

scientists, but it would be prohibitively expensive. Moreover, it would be a never-ending task, because new languages and computers are constantly appearing.

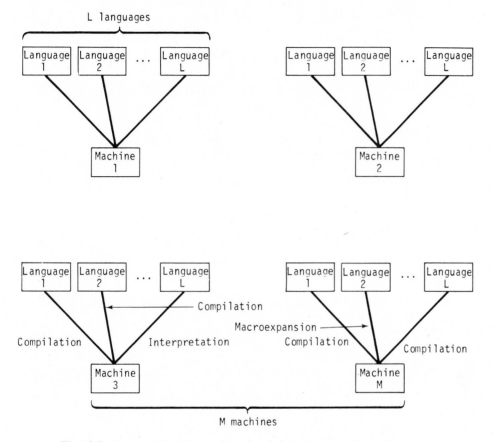

Fig. 8-5. A separate implementation of each language on each machine.

8.3.3. UNCOL

A third attempt at solving the portability problem is to design a virtual machine to be used as a base for implementing various language levels. To achieve the goal of portability, this virtual machine, called an **UNCOL** (UNiversal Computer Oriented Language), should be implemented on as many computers as possible. The idea of an UNCOL is illustrated in Fig. 8-6. The UNCOL level defines a language in which it is possible to write interpreters for FORTRAN, PL/1, COBOL, BASIC, Pascal, and so on, or in which to write compilers that translate programs in these languages into UNCOL programs. The UNCOL approach is an application of multilevel machines.

In order to use these compilers and interpreters, it is necessary to support the

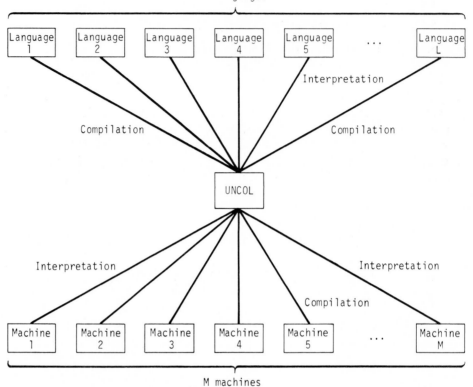

Fig. 8-6. Implementation of L languages on M machines using an UNCOL.

UNCOL level on each existing computer. The UNCOL level can be implemented by equipping each computer with either an UNCOL interpreter or an UNCOL-to-machine language translator. The UNCOL strategy requires only L + M compilers and interpreters, as shown in Fig. 8-6 compared to the L × M compilers and interpreters needed by the brute force approach of Fig. 8-5.

The UNCOL approach to portability has been adopted by IBM, DEC, and other manufacturers. IBM, for example, manufactures a whole series of different computers, which we have blithely lumped together under the name "370." Each of these computers is microprogrammed. Each one has a microprogramming level that is completely and totally different from all the others. Some of the ways in which computers can differ are:

1. Instruction length.

2. Bus widths (e.g., ALU output width).

3. Number and size of the memories.

4. Instruction set.

5. Number and function of processor registers.

6. Number and organization of the I/O processors.

In terms of these measures, no two models of the 360 or 370 series are even similar. Figure 8-7 shows the ALU width and microinstruction length for a few models of the 360 and 370 series as examples. Obviously, the 3125 with a 19-bit microinstruction and 16-bit ALU width has little, if any, relation to the 3168 with its 108-bit microinstructions and 64-bit ALU width. The other aspects of the 370 CPUs are as different as these. The various models of the 370 series are simply different computers, just as the 370/125 and PDP-11/44 are different computers.

Model	CPU	ALU width	Microinstruction length
360/30	2030	8	50
360/40	2040	8	56
360/50	2050	32	88
370/115	3115	8	20
370/125	3125	16	19
370/135	3135	16	16
370/145	3145	32	32
370/158	3158	32	72
370/168	3168	64	108

Fig. 8-7. Comparison of some models of the 360 and 370 series.

IBM is faced with the problem of customers whose work load has gradually increased over the years and who want to trade in their current 370 model for one of the larger and more powerful ones. If a 370/125 customer did all his programming in 3125 level 1 language, he would be stuck. There would be no way of moving him up to a 370/135, short of rewriting everything.

IBM's solution to this problem is to use the 370 conventional machine level as an UNCOL. Each model of the 370 series has an interpreter for interpreting 370 conventional machine level programs. Because each interpreter supports exactly the same virtual machine, programs can be easily moved from one model to another despite the enormous differences in the hardware.

To complete the UNCOL picture, IBM has written compilers that translate PL/1, FORTRAN, COBOL, and the other languages to the UNCOL, as shown in Fig. 8-8. Since the UNCOL is available on all models, only one PL/1 compiler is needed for all of them despite their lack of similarity. Strictly speaking, the compilers produce level 3 and not level 2 programs as output but because the operating systems are also portable (they all run on the same level 2 machine) the level 3 machine is also an UNCOL.

The UNCOL approach has enormous benefits to IBM compared with the brute-

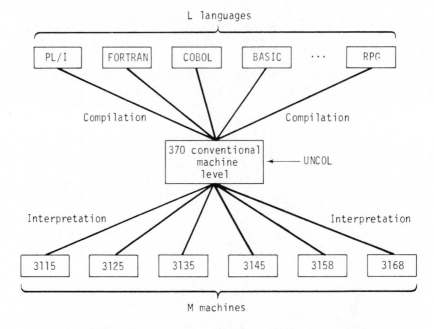

Fig. 8-8. The 370 conventional machine language as an UNCOL.

force approach. When IBM wants to introduce a new computer, it need only provide one program for it: an interpreter for the 370 conventional machine level. Writing one interpreter is obviously less work than writing compilers for Pascal, FORTRAN, COBOL, and the rest. Because only one program is needed, it is economically feasible to have a team of the best programmers spend months carefully optimizing every instruction in the interpreter.

Nevertheless, the strategy of using an UNCOL to achieve portability is not without its price. Siewiorek et al. (1981) estimate that a given algorithm programmed in the 360 conventional machine language and interpreted by a microprogram running on the 2025 (used by the 360/25) could be speeded up by a factor of 45 if the conventional machine level were skipped and the algorithm programmed directly in 2025 machine language. They also state that a 2025 microprogram interpreting a FORTRAN virtual machine might easily approach the speed of FORTRAN running on the 360/50 conventional machine level. They give the average cost of the 360/50 CPU and memory as roughly a factor of 6 more than that of a 360/25, so the cost of portability to the user is not negligible.

8.3.4. Abstract Machine Language

In the preceding section we saw how the IBM 370 conventional machine language functions as an UNCOL. Now we will see how exactly the same idea can be applied one level higher to allow programs to be moved trivially from one (micro)computer to another. The key idea is to invent an abstract machine language—the UNCOL—that is implemented on top of the conventional machine level of each microcomputer by writing an interpreter for it in the conventional machine language. It is not essential that the machines be microcomputers, but in practice the technique is rarely used on larger machines due to the loss of performance. A typical system is P-code (Pemberton and Daniels, 1982). Figure 8-9 illustrates a common abstract machine language implemented on three dissimilar microcomputers.

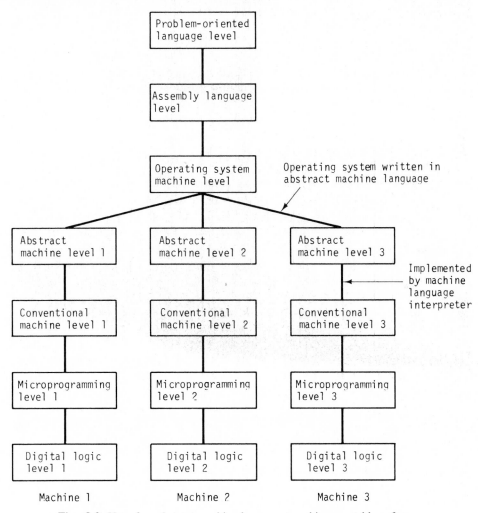

Fig. 8-9. Use of an abstract machine language to achieve portable software.

Once the same abstract machine level has been implemented, all the machines are effectively identical, and can all run the same software. To take advantage of this uniformity, an operating system is prepared and then translated to the abstract machine language. Because an operating system is just a program, after all, it can be easily installed on all the machines. (Actually, it is not entirely trivial, because a little bit of the operating system such as device drivers must be written in conventional machine language for each machine separately.) Once the operating system has been made operational on all the machines, the rest of the system software can be moved over as well. The result is a collection of identical abstract machines all running the same operating system and all having the same assembler, compilers, and other system programs.

Clearly, under these conditions the object code of user programs can be moved from machine to machine at will without even needing to be recompiled. The embedded system calls give no trouble because the same operating system is running on all the machines as well. The whole idea is simple and attractive if one is willing to give up a factor of 10 in performance due to the extra level of interpretation. For microcomputer programs that are mostly limited by the speed of the (floppy) disk anyway, the effective loss in performance may actually be much less.

8.3.5. Portable Compilers

As we saw in the preceding section, the UNCOL concept can be used to achieve portability via interpretation. Interestingly enough, the same concept can also be applied to make it easy to produce portable compilers. As an example, consider the Amsterdam Compiler Kit (Tanenbaum et al., 1983), which is outlined in Fig. 8-10. The kit consists of several programs, called **front ends**, that translate source language programs into the UNCOL (known as EM), optimizers that improve the quality of the UNCOL programs, a back end that translates them into various assembly languages, and a table-driven assembler that assembles these programs.

The task of each front end is to convert source programs in some language to EM. To make this job easier, EM has been designed to be straightforward, without a lot of the idiosyncrasies that plague most real machines. It is a simple stack machine, with no general registers. Instead, it has instructions to push operands onto the stack, perform operations on the top one or two stack items, and push results back into memory.

The next phase of the compilation process is the EM-to-EM optimization. Because all source programs are translated to EM, no matter what the original source language or ultimate target machine, this optimization is both language and machine independent. Although it is not possible to perform every conceivable optimization on the EM code, those optimizations that are possible should be performed to avoid repeating them later in various machine-dependent optimizers. Tanenbaum et al. (1982) describe peephole optimization on EM code. Global optimization is also possible.

The back end is a program parametrized by a machine-dependent driving table. The table tells how to translate EM to the assembly language of some target machine. During the translation process the back end maintains a simulated stack that is used to

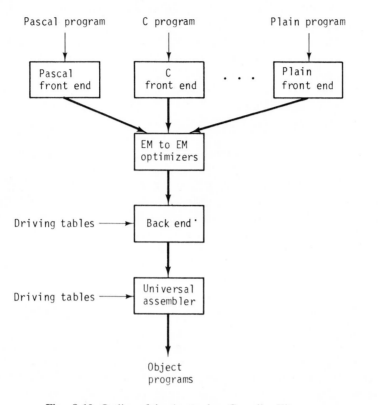

Fig. 8-10. Outline of the Amsterdam Compiler Kit.

eliminate most run-time stack action when compiling code for register machines. At most points during the translation, several different code sequences are possible. They are all evaluated and the best one is chosen.

Although it may seem surprising at first, the basic structure of an assembler is remarkably machine independent. This fact gave rise to the universal assembler, which is also parametrized by a machine-dependent table. The table gives the machine mnemonics and their binary values. Adding a new assembler to the kit is a matter of a week's work. The assembler also searches libraries and acts as a linker as well.

8.3.6. Emulation

When a computer center mothballs its old computer and gets a new one, the problem of portability becomes acute. Some of the users may have foreseen this transition and written all their programs with portability in mind. They will have few problems. Other users will have programmed only in problem-oriented languages, without thought of portability. These users will have some problems, as outlined in Sec.

8.3.1, but as long as their languages are available on the new machine, they will generally manage somehow.

For the programs written in the machine language of the old machine or for compilers that translate special-purpose languages to the old machine language, the new machine spells disaster. These programs can be moved to the new machine provided that the old machine language is available as one of the new machine's levels. The most convenient way to accomplish this transition is to provide the new microprogramming level with an interpreter for executing programs in the old machine language.

If this strategy is adopted, the new machine will have (at least) two microprograms: one for its own conventional machine level and one for the old machine's. The interpreter for the old machine is usually called an **emulator**, to distinguish it from the **native** conventional machine level interpreter. Typical examples are the DEC VAX emulating the PDP-11 and the IBM 370 emulating the 1401.

The most difficult part of an emulator's job is emulation of the old I/O instructions and devices. I/O instructions are normally carried out in parallel with CPU instructions and, unlike CPU instructions, I/O is strongly timing dependent. If the program being run in emulation mode makes assumptions about relative speeds, ensuring that it works properly on the new computer can be difficult.

To illustrate the kind of problems that can arise, consider a program that sequentially read records from a disk file into a buffer the same size as one record and processed them. To gain speed and save space, the program initiated reading the next record into the buffer before it had finished processing the old record, knowing that the new data would not actually begin overwriting the old data for X milliseconds, due to the seek time of the old disk. It then used these X milliseconds to finish up its processing just in time. If the new disk seeks relatively faster (compared to the speed of the emulated CPU) than the old one, the old data may be erased before they have been processed. Mallach (1975) gives an excellent introduction to emulation techniques, particularly emphasizing I/O emulation.

8.4. SELF-VIRTUALIZING MACHINES

In a time-sharing or multiprogramming system, a single level 2 machine supports a number of level 3 machines by running each one in turn for a little while. Figure 8-11 depicts this situation. Machine 1 will be interpreted by the microprogram and operating system (depending on the instruction) for a short time interval, then machine 2 will be run, and so forth.

Usually the level 3 machines supported in this way have a major subset of the conventional machine level instructions (the "ordinary" ones but not the I/O instructions, HALT, and so on) as well as new virtual instructions for reading and writing files, managing directories, and communicating with other processes.

The instructions available at either level 2 or level 3 can be categorized as follows:

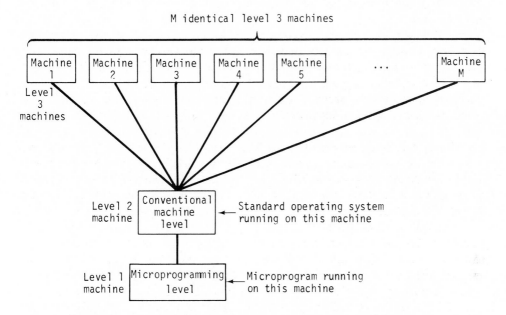

Fig. 8-11. A multiprogramming operating system supporting M level 3 machines in parallel.

1. Available only at level 2 (e.g., command the disk to seek).

2. Available at both level 2 and level 3 (e.g., load register).

3. Available only at level 3 (e.g., read a record from a file).

Although the level 2 and level 3 machines have many instructions in common, the two machines are by no means identical.

The picture of similar, but not identical, level 2 and level 3 machines outlined above is not the only possibility, however. Another kind of operating system exists whose level 3 machines are not just similar to the level 2 machine but are *exactly* identical to it. On these level 3 machines, every single instruction available on the level 2 machine is also available on the level 3 machine, with no exceptions whatsoever. Each of the level 3 machines has the complete repertoire of instructions in categories 1 and 2 above. A program running on one of these level 3 machines has no way of telling that it is not running on the bare level 2 machine, except possibly by timing itself.

A multilevel machine in which two or more levels are identical is called a **self-virtualizing** machine. Such machines exist in practice as well as in theory and have some interesting properties and applications, both of which will be briefly examined in the following sections.

8.4.1. IBM VM/370 System

An example of an operating system producing a self-virtualizing machine is the IBM VM/370 operating system, which is based on an earlier system for the 360/67, called CP-67. Figure 8-12 illustrates how VM/370 might be used.

The microprogramming level supports a single 370 level 2 machine (conventional machine level). This machine runs the VM/370 operating system, resulting in five (or any other number of) virtual 370s at the level above it. These virtual 370s are identical to the level 2 machine, even though they are running at level 3. To avoid confusion, we will call the conventional machine level 370s running at level 3 "virtual 370s." However, it should be kept in mind that the level 2 370 is also "virtual" in that it is interpreted by the microprogram. Each of the virtual 370s has the same instruction set as a "real" 370—that is, a level 2 370. The virtual 370's ordinary (category 2) instructions are interpreted directly by the microprogram. The I/O and other category 1 instructions are interpreted by VM/370. An operating system that supports virtual copies of the machine it, itself, runs on is called a **virtual machine monitor**. VM/370 is an example of a virtual machine monitor.

The virtual 370s are run in parallel, just as the level 3 machines of Fig. 8-11. A simple scheduling algorithm might run the first machine for 100 msec, then the second for 100 msec, then the third, fourth, and fifth, each for 100 msec, and then the first again, and so on indefinitely. It is important to remember that each of the virtual 370s supported by VM/370 is a normal 370 just as described by the "IBM System/370 Principles of Operation" manual, except its timing. Peculiarities in the timing are due partly to the multiprogramming and partly to the special handling given to the category 1 instructions, as described later.

8.4.2. Goals of Self-Virtualizing Machines

Since each of the virtual machines supported by VM/370 can run any 370 conventional machine level program, there is no reason it cannot run any of the standard 370 operating systems. Nor is there any reason why different virtual 370s cannot run different operating systems. Figure 8-12 shows how three different operating systems can be used simultaneously.

IBM has produced a number of standard operating systems that support multiprogramming (and, in some cases, time sharing). These systems include DOS (for the smaller models), OS (for the larger models), VS1 (a simple operating system with virtual memory), and MVS (a sophisticated multiprogramming system with virtual memory), among others. The original intention was probably that they all be compatible with one another, but it has not quite worked out that way. Furthermore, each one has passed through many (sometimes incompatible) versions.

As a consequence of the plethora of operating systems, the following situation often happens. A computer center has been using a certain operating system for a while and all its users have programs that run on the (level 3) virtual machines it provides. A new operating system whose level 3 machines offer some attractive features

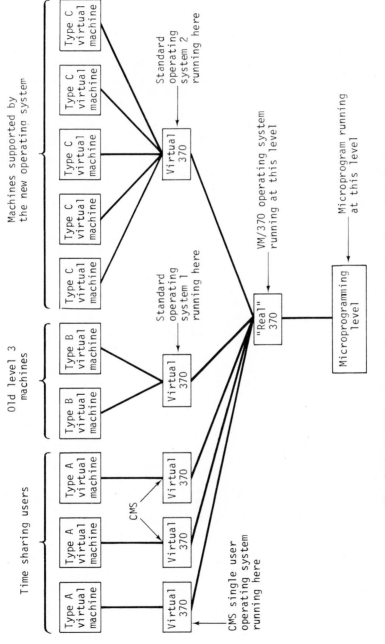

Fig. 8-12. VM/370 supporting five virtual machines in parallel, all of them identical to the 370 conventional machine level.

409

becomes available. The users would like to use the new operating system but are not enthusiastic about converting all their old level 3 programs.

What is needed is a multiprogramming system that provides some virtual machines identical to the old level 3 machines and some virtual machines identical to the new level 3 machines. These machines are called type B and type C in Fig. 8-12. The standard operating systems referred to are multiprogramming systems such as OS and MVS, which support virtual machines with file I/O and all the other OSML instructions discussed in Chap. 5. The machines at level 4 in Fig. 8-12 are usually found at level 3 instead.

It is interesting to note the similarity between emulation and the use of self-virtualizing machines to support two operating systems in parallel. The purpose of emulation is to allow two different level 2 machines to be run in parallel by multiprogramming a single processor. VM/370 allows running two or more different level 3 machines in parallel, by creating multiple virtual 370s and running different operating systems on them. In both cases two or more different machines can coexist. In one case, they are level 2 machines, and in the other they are level 3 machines.

Self-Virtualizing Machines and Time Sharing

One of the major goals of having self-virtualizing machines is to allow simultaneous operation of several different operating systems, but it is not the only one. A time-sharing system based on a standard operating system is a very complicated beast because it must perform two different functions:

1. Handle multiprogramming.

2. Interpret OSML virtual I/O and other instructions.

Multiprogramming management deals with activities like deciding which process (virtual machine) is to be run next, preparing it to be run (e.g., loading its registers into the hardware registers), running it, saving it, and deciding which process to run next). Interrupt handling is also part of multiprogramming. Interpreting the OSML instructions is unrelated to multiprogramming activities.

The VM/370 operating system allows these functions to be completely separated. VM/370 can be used to produce a large number of bare virtual 370s. Each of these virtual 370s can run a single-user operating system that need only interpret OSML instructions and need not worry about multiprogramming. IBM's CMS (Cambridge Monitor System or Conversational Monitor System) is a single-user system that is used in conjunction with VM/370. The virtual machine supported by CMS is labeled as type A in Fig. 8-12.

A complete time-sharing system can be constructed using VM/370 to support many bare virtual 370s, each of which runs CMS. By dividing a standard operating system's functions into two parts—the VM/370 part to handle multiprogramming and the CMS part to handle OSML interpretation—each of the two parts becomes smaller and simpler. Considering the enormous complexity of a standard operating system such as MVS, any simplification is enormously useful.

Operating System Testing

A third goal of self-virtualizing machines follows from the ability to run multiple operating systems simultaneously. One or more of the virtual 370s can be used to test a new version of an operating system while other virtual 370s are running production jobs and providing time-sharing service using CMS. Should the new version crash to a halt, there will be no effect on the production jobs or time-sharing service. What will happen is that VM/370 will continue to run each virtual 370, in turn, for a certain length of time.

Whether a particular virtual 370 actually does any useful work during its time quantum or simply sits there halted is of no concern to VM/370. When the time quantum is up, VM/370 moves on to the next virtual 370. A virtual 370 coming to a halt under VM/370 is analogous to a user program coming to a halt under an ordinary time-sharing system. In neither case are any of the other virtual machines running in parallel affected.

The virtual 370s supported by VM/370 can run any 370 operating system, including VM/370 itself. This ability can be exploited for testing new versions of VM/370 without disturbing production jobs. Figure 8-13 shows VM/370 running itself. This situation is sometimes called a **recursive virtual machine**.

Protection of Confidential Data

Because each of the virtual 370s is functionally equivalent to a real 370, there is no way for a process running on one virtual 370 to even know about the existence of, let alone be able to spy on, another virtual 370. Consequently, VM/370 can provide a highly secure environment for handling confidential data, such as that possessed by banks, hospitals, law enforcement agencies, credit bureaus, and other institutions that maintain personal data about people. Standard operating systems are usually much less secure.

8.4.3. Implementation of a Self-Virtualizing Machine

A typical third-generation computer such as a 370 or a PDP-11 has two (or three) modes of operation at the conventional machine level. On the 370 these modes are called **supervisor state** and **problem state**; on the PDP-11, they are called **kernel mode** and **user mode**, as discussed in Chap. 5. In supervisor state, all instructions are allowed. In problem state only those instructions regarded as category 2 in Sec. 8.4 are allowed (i.e., the ordinary instructions). Supervisor state was intended for running the operating system at level 2. Problem state was intended for making sure that level 3 user programs were prevented from executing I/O and other instructions that might interfere with other users.

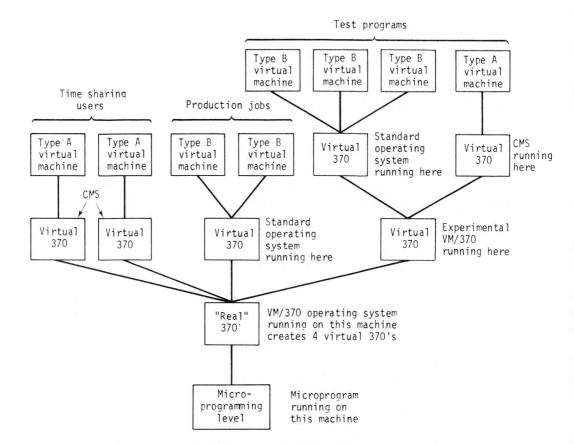

Fig. 8-13. VM/370 running VM/370 in one of the virtual 370s.

The instructions that are prohibited in problem state are called **privileged instruc-tions**. They are the category 1 instructions of Sec. 8.4 and typically include

1. I/O instructions.

2. Instructions that affect the virtual address mapping.

3. Instructions affecting memory protection.

4. Instructions that load, store, or test the program status word.

5. Instructions that read or set clocks or timers.

All operating systems, including VM/370, run their level 3 programs in problem state and protect any privileged addresses that the machine may have. If a level 3 program (in problem state) tries to execute a privileged instruction, the microprogram refuses to interpret it and instead starts up the operating system so that it can handle the situation. On a standard operating system, a message like

ATTEMPT TO EXECUTE PRIVILEGED INSTRUCTION AT LOCATION 3B6D

is printed and the job is aborted.

Exceptions and Virtual Machine Faults

For a virtual 370 being supported by VM/370, this situation is inadequate. A virtual 370 always runs with the real (level 2) machine in problem state, in order to trap any attempts to actually perform I/O. However, logically, the virtual 370 may be in either problem state or supervisor state, just as a real 370 may be in either problem state or supervisor state. If a virtual 370 executes a privileged instruction when it is logically in problem state, it must act *exactly* like a real 370—namely, trap to the operating system in its machine. When it executes a privileged instruction while logically in supervisor state, VM/370 must simulate the privileged instruction.

These two situations are illustrated in Fig. 8-14 for the case of VM/370 supporting two virtual 370s, both running CMS. When the user program is running, the virtual 370 is logically in problem state, because a real 370 is in problem state while running user programs. When the virtual 370 is running the operating system (in this case, CMS), it is logically in supervisor state, because a real 370 is in supervisor state while running the operating system.

At the time the privileged instruction actually occurs, the real hardware 370 will be in problem state (in order to catch all privileged instructions). The microprogram does what it always does when a privileged instruction is executed in problem state. It stores the PSW in location 40 and loads a new PSW from location 104. This action starts VM/370 running. VM/370 must then look at its tables to determine which virtual 370 was running and which state it was in. In other words, it must update its tables whenever a virtual 370 switches states, in order to keep an accurate record of which virtual 370s are logically in problem state and which are logically in supervisor state. If the virtual 370 was logically in problem state, VM/370 must reflect the trap back to the virtual machine and start CMS running with the virtual 370's PSW taken from the virtual machine's location 104. Goldberg (1973) called this situation an **exception**. It is illustrated in Fig. 8-14(a).

If, however, the virtual 370 was logically in supervisor state at the time of the trap, as shown in Fig. 8-14(b), then VM/370 must simulate the instruction. After all, the operating system in the virtual 370 will need to perform I/O occasionally, just like any other operating system. Goldberg (1973) calls this situation a **virtual machine fault**, to distinguish it from an exception. Note that their causes and treatments are different. Ideally, the 370 microprogram should give control to the operating system in the virtual machine when an exception occurs, and not to VM/370. In fact, an optional modification to the microprogram for handling virtual machine faults and exceptions more efficiently is available.

From the above discussion, it should be clear that an architecture is suited to the

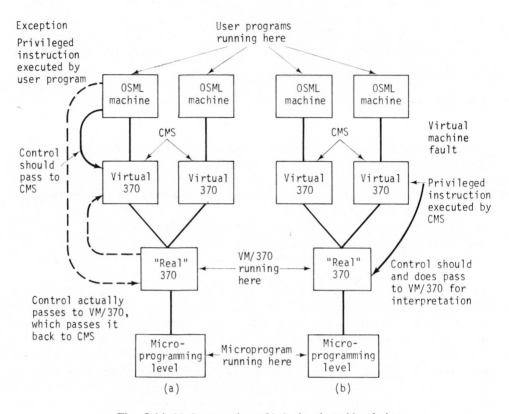

Fig. 8-14. (a) An exception. (b) A virtual machine fault.

virtual machine idea only if all the privileged instructions cause traps when executed in problem state. On some machines, among them the PDP-11, privileged instructions such as SPL and RTT are ignored, rather than trapped. Thus these machines cannot run virtual machine operating systems.

Simulation of Virtual Machine I/O

Most of the privileged instructions can be carried out in a straightforward way. Virtual I/O devices are mapped onto physical I/O devices because VM/370 may support n virtual 370s, each of which thinks it has a complete disk. Of course, if each actually fills up its entire disk, VM/370 really needs n disks to handle the data. Normally, a virtual 370 uses only a small portion of its virtual disk, in which case VM/370 can allocate the available real disk space among the virtual disks. When virtual machine 4 writes onto cylinder 25 of its virtual disk, VM/370 can keep these data wherever it wants, provided that it can find the data again when virtual machine 4 tries to read cylinder 25 back in again.

This mapping of virtual disk addresses is similar to the operation of a segmented virtual memory, with the virtual disk number being the segment and the cylinder being the page. VM/370 must keep tables specifying the mapping. Similarly, virtual printers can be mapped onto real printers or, if there are insufficient real printers, onto disk files for subsequent printing.

Self-Modifying Channel Programs

One aspect of the 370's I/O method causes considerable difficulty for VM/370. On a real 370, the CPU normally prepares an I/O channel program and then executes a START I/O instruction to cause one of the channels to begin executing it. When a virtual 370 executes a START I/O instruction, a virtual machine fault occurs and VM/370 must carry out the I/O.

The I/O channels on the 370 use real addresses, not virtual addresses. As a rule, this fact poses no problems. VM/370 examines the I/O channel program instruction by instruction, replacing the virtual disk addresses by the actual disk addresses and the virtual machine's memory addresses by the corresponding real addresses. Then VM/370 starts one of the real I/O channels executing the modified I/O channel program.

One minor problem can arise if a single channel instruction reads in a block of data that crosses a page boundary. Because consecutive virtual pages need not be adjacent in real memory, the data may have to be read into two or more widely separated areas of real memory. Unfortunately, the I/O channel hardware cannot switch buffers in the middle of a channel instruction. VM/370 must check for this possibility and break up any instructions that cross page boundaries into several I/O instructions, each of which is for one contiguous block.

The real trouble comes from the fact that an I/O transfer may overwrite part of the channel program, thereby changing the channel program before it is finished running. An even bigger problem is that most of the IBM operating systems make heavy use of this feature for performing virtual I/O on files. VM/370 has no way of properly modifying those parts of a channel program that are read in by the execution of the channel program itself. It can only fix up those parts of the channel program that are in memory at the time that the START I/O instruction is executed. However, with certain restrictions (self-modifying channel programs must be arranged so that the virtual disk addresses are the same as the actual disk addresses), VM/370 struggles through.

Shadow Page Tables

Self-modifying channel programs are not the only problem caused by peculiarities of the 370 organization. Because real 370s have virtual memory, virtual 370s must also have virtual memory. To illustrate the difficulties that can arise when supporting a virtual 370 with virtual memory, consider the use of VM/370 to run MVS on a virtual 370. A change has been made to the page-replacement algorithms used by MVS, and a test run is being made to see if it works. Keep in mind the fact that MVS thinks it is running on a real 370.

Just before MVS gives control to one of the user programs in its machine, it sets up the user program's page tables to map the user program's virtual addresses onto what it considers to be real memory. The box in Fig. 8-15(a) shows a four-page user program mapped onto the virtual 370's memory. The virtual 370's memory is mapped onto a portion of the real 370's memory as shown.

The hardware of a 370, real or virtual, has an internal register that points to the segment table for the current program. The segment table points to the page tables. For simplicity, only the page tables are shown in Fig. 8-15. When an operating system is about to run a user program, it must set this register to point to the segment table of that program.

When VM/370 needs to run a user program on one of the virtual 370s, which page tables should it set this register to? Not the page tables in the virtual 370, because they map the user's program onto the virtual machine's memory, not onto real memory. [These two are the same only if VM/370 keeps the virtual 370's memory in one contiguous block starting at real address 0, which is not the case in Fig. 8-15(a).]

To solve this problem, VM/370 maintains a **shadow page table** that maps the user program's virtual addresses onto the real memory addresses where the pages are located. This mapping is shown in Fig. 8-15(b). VM/370 constructs the shadow page table from the page table in the virtual 370, plus its knowledge of where it is keeping the virtual 370's memory in real memory.

Because MVS thinks it is running on a real 370, it carries out all the memory management functions associated with paging. These functions include reading and writing pages, as well as making the corresponding changes to the page tables in its memory. Changes to the page tables are accomplished by using ordinary load and store register instructions, which do not cause virtual machine faults. Consequently, any change to a page table invalidates at least one of VM/370's shadow page tables, without VM/370 being aware that this has happened. MVS can hardly be expected to inform VM/370 that it has changed its page tables, because it thinks it is running on a real 370 and may, in fact, do so later.

Fortunately, there is a solution to this problem. Like MULTICS, the 370 has a high-speed associative memory (see Fig. 6-37) that keeps track of the locations of the most heavily used pages. Whenever the page tables are changed, the operating system must erase the associative memory so as to force the hardware to reload it dynamically from the modified page tables. The instruction to erase the associative memory is privileged and causes a virtual machine fault. When the virtual machine fault occurs, VM/370 constructs new shadow page tables. As long as MVS is properly programmed and always erases the associative memory after modifying the page tables, everything will work fine. If MVS fails to erase the associative memory, it will not work on either a virtual 370 or a real one.

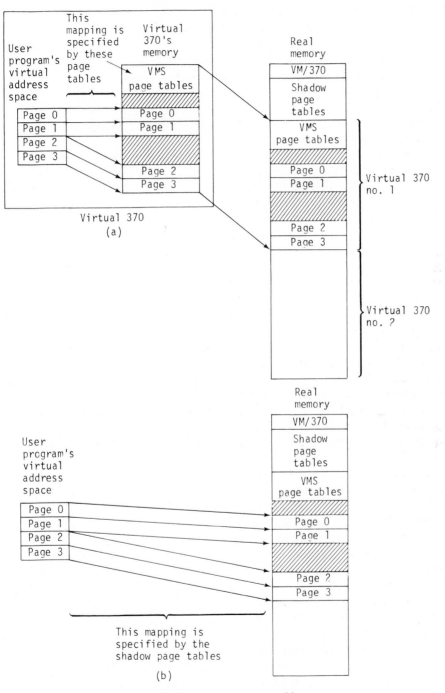

Fig. 8-15. The shadow page tables.

8.5. THE COMPILER-INTERPRETER INTERFACE

When a programmer wants to run a program written in Pascal or some other problem-oriented language on a typical multilevel computer, the following steps occur. First, the program is read and analyzed by the compiler. Then the compiler generates an object program to be run on the level 3 machine. Finally, the object program is interpreted by the microprogram and the operating system, the former handling the ordinary instructions and the latter handling the file I/O and other OSML instructions.

In effect, the level 3 machine defines an interface between the compiler and the interpreters. This situation is illustrated in Fig. 8-16. The compiler translates source programs to this interface level and then these programs are interpreted. The architecture and instructions of this interface level are not determined by the hardware but by the compiler and interpreters. If a new interface level were defined, the compilers would have to be modified to produce object programs for it, and a new interpreter (microprogram) would be needed to interpret it, but in principle the old CPU could still be used.

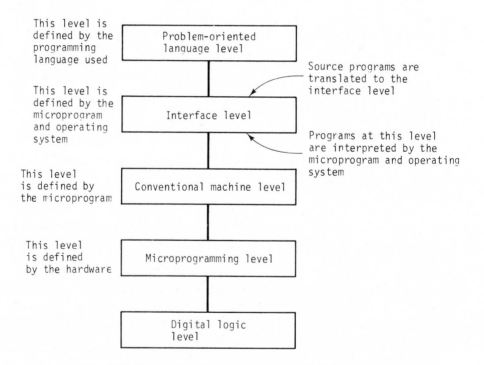

Fig. 8-16. The interface between the compiler and the interpreter.

In a sense, the design of the compiler-interpreter interface level is arbitrary. Of course, a particular CPU may be most efficient at interpreting a certain class of virtual machines, so the designer is not completely free if efficiency is the dominant consideration, which it often is. Nevertheless, the microprogramming level of many computers is flexible enough to be able to support virtual machines that differ appreciably from the conventional machine level described throughout this book.

Once one has realized that the design of the compiler-interpreter interface level is not uniquely determined by the hardware, certain questions naturally arise:

1. What is the best interface level?

2. Should different programming languages use different interface levels?

3. If the level 2 and 3 machines currently in use are not optimal, why are they used?

This subject is examined in some detail by Wulf (1981).

8.5.1. High-Level Interfaces

At the moment no one really knows what kind of interface is optimal. However, it seems unlikely a priori that the ideal compiler-interpreter interface for COBOL and Pascal are identical, given the great disparity in the source languages. The logical consequence of this conclusion is that different languages should have different interface levels. Pascal programs should compile to a "Pascal machine level" to be interpreted by one microprogram, whereas COBOL programs should compile to a different machine level and be interpreted by a different microprogram. By having different interfaces for different languages it is possible to have a much "higher" (i.e., closer to the source language) machine language than with a level that must of necessity be a compromise between various conflicting demands. Figure 8-17 illustrates the idea of replacing the conventional machine level by a set of levels, one per language. The Burroughs B1700 uses this principle.

As an example of what the interface level for Pascal might conceivably look like, consider the proposal of Fig. 8-18. Each program variable has an entry in the **descriptor** table of part (a). The entry gives the variable's type, size, and location. The purpose of having descriptors is twofold: (1) to provide type and size information about variables at run time, and (2) to make it possible to address variables with relatively few bits. The former makes it possible to have, for example, a single ADD instruction, with the microprogram determining whether an integer or floating-point addition is needed and on what size number. The latter means that a program with, say, 256 variables only needs 8 bits in variable addresses, no matter how big the variables are.

In Fig. 8-18(b) five instructions are shown that might be useful for Pascal. The first one is intended for assignments of the form

$$a := b + c$$

The *Op* field indicates that the operator is an addition and the other three fields give

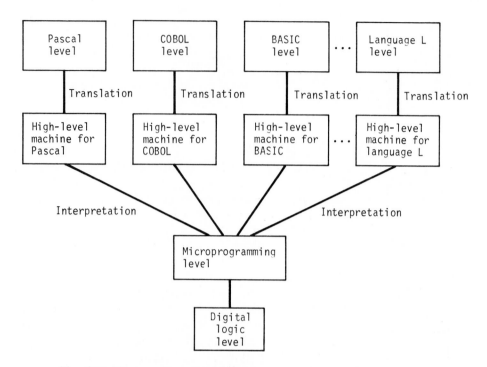

Fig. 8-17. The use of several microprograms on the same hardware, each one supporting a different high-level language.

the descriptor numbers of the variables. Conceivably, the first bit or two of these fields could be used to distinguish between variables and constants, and perhaps provide escapes to longer formats.

The next instruction handles statements of the form

if $a < b$ **then** ...

telling which variables to test, what relation to test them for, and where to jump if the test fails. The third instruction is for **while** loops, giving a variable to test and an address to jump to if it is false. The fourth instruction does **for** loops, incrementing the index, testing it against the limit, and jumping if necessary. The last instruction calls a procedure, passing it parameters if need be.

8.5.2. Discussion of High-Level Interfaces

One of the major advantages of using a high-level interface is the resulting simplification in the compiler. Since the target language has essentially the same semantics as the source language, the compiler has considerably less work to do. Consequently, it can be smaller, faster, easier to write, easier to understand, and more

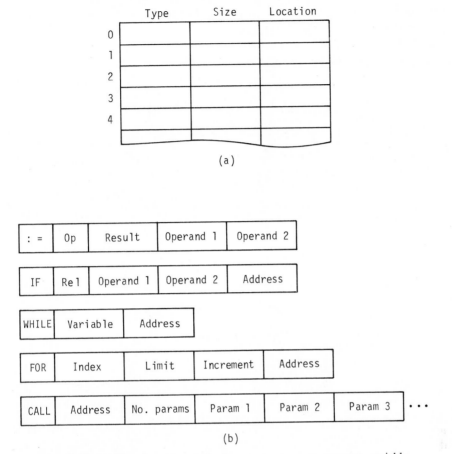

Fig. 8-18. (a) The descriptor table has one entry per program variable.
(b) Five typical Pascal instructions.

reliable. Some researchers (e.g., Chu and Abrams, 1981) have even proposed doing away with the compiler altogether, and directly executing the source text. For a dissenting view, see Kavi et al. (1982).

At many computer centers, more than half the computer time is "wasted" doing compilations. A user who submits a program is interested in its execution, not in its translation to another language. Because the high-level interface matches the programming language much better, much of this waste can be reduced.

The large gap between the semantics of the programming language and the instructions and idiosyncrasies of present level 3 machines often causes traditional compilers to produce highly inefficient programs. The very existence of 8 or 16 general registers is practically a mandate for the compiler writer to attempt to optimize their use, whereas there is almost certainly nothing in either the program or the programming language about 8 or 16 registers, much less optimal usage thereof. The result of this mismatch is that the compiler spends a great deal of time trying to solve problems created by the underlying machine architecture, problems that are irrelevant to the user's program.

The worst part is that compilers rarely succeed at bridging this gap, despite their time-consuming efforts. A good assembly language programmer can usually write code that outperforms that of even an optimizing compiler by a factor of 2 or 3. Abolishing the conventional machine level also abolishes the gap between it and the program.

It is an unfortunate but all too common occurrence that compilers contain errors years after they are pronounced finished. Greatly simplifying a compiler tends to reduce the number of errors it contains.

A compiler for a high-level machine (i.e., interface) is really more like an assembler than a true compiler. Its primary tasks are as follows:

1. Removing comments.

2. Syntax analysis.

3. Converting symbolic names to binary addresses.

4. Allocating storage for data.

5. Converting constants to the internal representation.

6. Generating object code.

Simplifying the compiler is not the only advantage of a high-level machine. The execution time of a program may also be reduced if the interpreter can directly carry out those combinations of primitive actions required by the programming language. For example, in many programming languages, entire arrays can be assigned in a single statement of the form $a = b$. A single high-level machine instruction MOVE ARRAY can easily be made to outperform an explicitly programmed loop for the conventional machine level. The saving in instruction fetching and decoding alone can be substantial.

Another advantage of high-level machines over conventional machines is in program debugging. When a program fails to behave as expected, the only help the programmer generally gets is a message like

ILLEGAL INSTRUCTION DETECTED AT ADDRESS 7A4F

and a hexadecimal dump of memory. Unless he understands all the details of how the compiler stores its programs and data, the dump is nearly useless. On a high-level machine, it is possible for the post-mortem program to relate the error much more closely to the source program, a big help to the programmer.

Still other potential advantages of high-level machines are compiler portability and arithmetic of the required precision. If a compiler produces 370 assembly language code as output, it is of little use on machines other than a 370. If it produces output for a high-level machine, the compiler can be used on any computer where this high-level machine has been implemented. Also, a high-level machine may offer the possibility of setting the number of bits in an integer to whatever the programmer needs rather than forcing him to use 32-bit integers.

The principal disadvantage of a high-level machine is the greater complexity required in the interpreter. However, because interpreters are usually much simpler than compilers, the decrease in compiler complexity can be expected to more than offset the increase in interpreter complexity.

You may be wondering why the conventional machine level is still so widely used despite its many disadvantages. There are several reasons. For one, the subject of high-level machines is still a research topic, and any new idea takes a number of years of development to move from the research laboratories to the stage of being a commercial product.

Another reason is the inertia generated by years of doing things in a certain way. Back in the 1940s, when the conventional machine level was first designed, it was an excellent idea. It provided machines that were both possible to understand and feasible to build. When the correct operation of the computer depended on the simultaneous functioning of 20,000 unreliable, power-hungry vacuum tubes, designers were understandably hesitant to shift any complexity from software to hardware.

A powerful force working against change has been the desire to build machines that are compatible with earlier ones. If a computer design group is told that the new machine it is to produce must be functionally identical to one that the company has been selling for the past 10 years, it is extremely difficult to incorporate any of the new ideas about computer architecture that have been discovered because the original machine was designed. Consequently, compatibility is also a recipe for stagnation. However, the current state of hardware technology (such as inexpensive single-chip CPUs) and microprogramming technology, coupled with the widespread use of problem-oriented languages, has created a situation favorable to the development of high-level machines. The result, in turn, has generated commercial interest in microprogrammable CPUs specifically designed to support high-level machines.

8.6. SUMMARY

Multilevel machines can be designed top down, bottom up, or middle out. Implementation techniques include compilation, macro expansion, and procedural extension.

An important application of multilevel machines is program portability. The UNCOL idea, abstract machine language, and portable compilers all illustrate this concept. In the UNCOL approach, a common intermediate language is first designed. Source programs are translated to the common code for subsequent translation to target machine language or possible interpretation on the target machine. The idea of the UNCOL is to reduce the number of programs needed from $m \times n$ to $m + n$. Abstract machine language is basically similar. Emulation is another technique for achieving portability, usually with an obsolete machine for which the user has a substantial investment in software.

Self-virtualizing machines are an interesting concept that can lead to simplifying operating systems design by disentangling the multiprogramming functions of an operating system from the interpretation of level 3 instructions. On a self-virtualizing machine, the virtual machine monitor creates several copies of the bare machine, each of which can run its own operating system. This technique allows multiple, incompatible operating systems to run simultaneously without interfering with each other. VM/370 is the best known example of such a system.

Looking at machines as a series of levels brings up the question of where the compiler and interpreter should meet. The traditional interface is quite low-level. Some thoughts about alternatives were presented at the end of the chapter.

PROBLEMS

1. Imagine that you are to write a complex numerical analysis package on a computer with only a macro assembler and no floating-point instructions. Describe how you might go about this task.

2. What are the advantages and disadvantages of top-down versus bottom-up design?

3. In point 11 in the list of Sec. 8.3.1, we said that incomplete specification is the root of all evil. Do you think that more complete specification is a good way to attack the problem?

4. A number of computer manufacturers use the UNCOL principle to provide compatibility on fundamentally different computes. To ensure this compatibility, they prevent users from doing their own microprogramming. What benefits do the customers get from this policy? What costs are associated with it?

5. DEC manufactures several different machines (e.g., PDP-8, PDP-11, DEC-20) all of which have FORTRAN available. Programs written for one machine can run on the others. Is this an example of an UNCOL?

6. As a homework problem, Prof. Slavedriver assigns her students the task of writing a complete 370 interpreter for the PDP-11 level 3 machine. The interpreter is to be written in PDP-11 assembly language and use the UNIX system calls. This virtual 370 is then used to compile and execute a PDP-11 level 2 simulator written in Pascal. To measure the efficiency of their work, the students are to run the Towers of Hanoi for 64 disks on the simulated PDP-11. The results are due in tomorrow at 9 A.M. How many levels are present during *execution?* Do not count levels that disappear after translation. *Note:* Because nobody is going to finish anyway, it is not required to implement an operating system machine level on the simulated PDP-11.

7. When the abstract machine language idea is used to implement a common interface on a collection of machines, it is often the case that the people writing the interpreters on the microcomputers are different from the people who designed the abstract machine and who wrote the software for it. How can the latter aid the former in making sure their implementation is accurate?

8. Compare a time-sharing system based on a self-virtualizing machine with a conventional time-sharing system.

9. How can the advantage of an UNCOL (portability) be combined with the advantages of high-level machines (simple compilers, efficient execution)? If four programming languages are to be implemented on each model of a computer family with 10 members, how many compilers and interpreters must be implemented in your proposal?

10. In the design of Fig. 8-18(b), only 8 bits are allocated for addressing an operand. What could be done if a program had twenty 256-byte arrays?

11. Work out the details of the Pascal machine of Fig. 8-18 and write an interpreter for it.

9

READING LIST AND BIBLIOGRAPHY

In the preceding eight chapters, a large number of topics were discussed in various degrees of detail. This chapter is meant to assist readers interested in pursuing further their study of computer organization. Section 9.1 contains a list of suggested readings arranged by chapter. Section 9.2 is an alphabetical bibliography of all books and articles cited in this book.

9.1. SUGGESTIONS FOR FURTHER READING

9.1.1. Introduction and General Works

Baer, *Computer Systems Architecture*
   A potpourri of ideas about advanced computer architecture. Among the topics treated are arithmetic algorithms, memory hierarchies, microprogramming, I/O, microcomputers, minicomputers, and supercomputers. The book goes into each of these subjects in considerable technical detail.

Gear, *Computer Organization and Programming*
   An introductory text covering the CPU, memory, I/O, microprogramming, assembly language and numerous other related topics. The IBM 370, PDP-11, CDC Cyber, and Intel 8080 are used as running examples. The informal style, together with the

use of the 370, PDP-11, and 8080 (on which the Z80 was based), make this a good reference.

Sloan, *Introduction to Minicomputers and Microcomputers*
A general introduction to computer architecture and programming. Deals with binary numbers, conventional machine level programming, assemblers, macros, linkers, arithmetic, I/O, and other topics.

9.1.2. Computer Systems Organization

Chen, "Overlap and Pipeline Processing"
A tutorial on pipelined instruction execution in computer systems. Numerous examples are discussed in detail.

Hamming, *Coding and Information Theory*
An extremely readable introduction to coding theory, including error-detecting codes, error-correcting codes, frequency-dependent codes, entropy, channel capacity, and related topics.

Kuck, "A Survey of Parallel Machine Organization and Programming"
An introduction to both parallel machines and the algorithms used on these machines. Methods for solving recurrence relations are examined in some detail as an example.

Peterson, *Error Correcting Codes*
Probably the most complete work on error correcting codes to date. It is by no means easy reading, requiring a knowledge of Galois field theory in places. Among other topics, it covers linear codes, cyclic codes, Bose-Chaudhuri codes, and burst-correcting codes.

Siewiorek et al., *Computer Structures: Principles and Examples*
A vast compendium (more than 900 pages) of information covering just about every kind of computer organization ever devised by mind of man. The authors use a notation called PMS to describe the interaction of processors, memories, switches, and other computer components, and another notation, called ISP, to describe instruction sets. Many of the 52 chapters are reprints of key papers in the development of computer organization. In addition to conventional machines, array processors, list processors, multiprocessors, and desk calculators are also covered. A comprehensive bibliography is included.

Tanenbaum, *Computer Networks*
A general textbook on various aspects of networking, both long-haul and local. It follows the ISO reference model, one layer per chapter, more or less. Many examples are given from SNA, DECNET, ARPANET, and X.25.

Tanenbaum, "Network Protocols"
A shortened version of the above for readers who are interested in networks, but not *so* interested.

Weitzman, *Distributed Micro/Minicomputer Systems*
Chapter 2 is a 77 page introduction to local networks and multiprocessors. It covers shared memory, buses, loops, stars, and other interconnection systems. Chapter 3 looks at the software issues for local networks.

9.1.3. The Digital Logic Level

Artwick, *Microcomputer Interfacing*
The title says it all. There are chapters on memory, I/O, interface components, interface circuits, and bus interfaces, among other topics.

Borrill, "Microprocessor Bus Structures and Standards"
A nice introduction to component, backplane, system, parallel, and serial buses. In addition to discussing the various kinds of buses, the paper treats bus termination, software visibility, DMA, interrupts, and data representation.

Blakeslee, *Digital Design with Standard MSI and LSI*
Most books on logic design focus primarily on simple SSI circuits. This one is different. It deals largely with MSI chips, microprocessors, I/O, and interfacing. The style is sometimes amusing, with sections entitled "The Rat Race" and "The Engineer as Dope Pusher."

McKay, *Digital Circuits*
A book on traditional logic design. Much of it is concerned with minimizing gates in SSI circuits. Both combinational and sequential circuits are covered.

Myers, *Digital System Design with LSI Bit-Slice Logic*
Although the information in this book is derived largely from manufacturers' data sheets, it does collect a lot of it together in one convenient source. The bit-slice chip series discussed include the AMD 2900, Intel 3000, Motorola 10800, Texas Instruments 74LS481, Fairchild 9400, and others.

Oleksy and Rutkowski, *Microprocessors and Digital Computer Technology*
For readers with a hardware bent, Chaps. 4 to 6 of this book discuss the digital logic level and the underlying device level in some detail.

Pooch and Chattergy, *Designing Microcomputer Systems*
After a short introduction to the basic hardware components, the authors look at three microprocessors (Intel 8080, Zilog Z80, Motorola 6800) and how to make

interfaces for them. The book has a nutsy-boltsy flavor, and is oriented toward the reader who actually intends to build a small system based on one of these three CPU chips.

Tomek, *Introduction to Computer Organization*
Chapters 2 to 4 describe the digital logic level in some detail. The remaining chapters deal with a variety of topics in computer architecture.

9.1.4. The Microprogramming Level

Andrews, *Principles of Firmware Engineering in Microprogram Control*
A thorough treatment of many aspects of microprogramming, including microinstruction organization, sequencing, and control. Optimization and engineering techniques are discussed in detail and the relevant theory is covered.

Landskov et al., "Local Microcode Compaction Techniques"
Horizontal microprogrammable machines have the potential for performing a substantial number of microoperations in parallel. The trick is to exploit this parallelism subject to the machine's constraints. This article provides a good introduction to the problems and solutions involved in packing microoperations into microinstructions.

Rosin, "Contemporary Concepts of Microprogramming and Emulation"
An excellent tutorial on microprogramming. The basic concepts are introduced by means of an example. This is followed by sections on the virtues of microprogramming, the properties of some existing microprogrammable computers, and current research topics and problems.

Salisbury, *Microprogrammable Computer Architectures*
A highly readable introductory text on microprogramming. The first three chapters cover general principles. Each of the next four chapters treats a commercially available microprogrammable machine in detail. The final chapter summarizes six other machines.

9.1.5. The Conventional Machine Level

Garside, *The Architecture of Digital Computers*
An introductory text on the conventional machine level. It has chapters on data types, the instruction set, addressing, memory, and I/O.

Gear, *Computer Organization and Programming*
A textbook for a second course in computer science. The coverage and level are similar to this book, which makes it a good reference. There are chapters on the CPU and memory, assembly language, I/O devices and programming, microprogramming, multiprocessors, and other subjects.

Wakerly, *Microcomputer Architecture and Programming*

An introductory text on Pascal, computer architecture, assembly language, and microcomputers. Part 1 covers Pascal and number systems, Part 2 deals with the conventional machine level, and Part 3 gives a synopsis of the conventional machine level for the PDP-11, Motorola 6809 and 68000, Intel MCS-48 and 8086, Zilog Z8000, and Texas Instruments 9900.

9.1.6. The Operating System Machine Level

Anderson, "Operating Systems"

Our way of looking at an operating system as just another level in the machine hierarchy is somewhat unconventional. Anderson's paper is a nice review of the traditional view of an operating system as a resource manager.

Calingaert, *Operating System Elements*

A modern, nonmathematical introductory text on operating systems. It contains chapters on the storage, processor, process, device, file, and system management.

Corbató and Vyssotsky, "Introduction and Overview of the MULTICS System"

A general introduction to the design goals of MULTICS. This article introducing MULTICS to the world was written by two of its chief designers long before the system was completed. One of their intentions was to put their ideas into print before carrying them out, to be able to see later how far the system drifted from its original plans.

Daley and Neumann, "A General Purpose File System for Secondary Storage"

The first published description of the MULTICS file system, written by its designers. It discusses the relation between files and segments, directories, links and branches, and many other aspects of the file system.

Denning, "Virtual Memory"

An excellent tutorial on virtual memory. Topics covered include segmentation, paging, storage utilization, replacement algorithms, page size, fragmentation, demand paging, and the working set model. The bibliography contains 84 entries.

Ritchie and Thompson, *The UNIX Time-Sharing System*

This is the original published paper on UNIX. It is still well worth reading. From this small seed has grown a great operating system.

Shaw, *The Logical Design of Operating Systems*

An introductory text on operating systems, emphasizing process management, resource management, and file systems. The treatment is not tied to any specific system. System organization, batch systems, processors, multiprogramming, memory management, sharing, resource control, deadlocks, and file systems are each the subject of separate chapters. Many algorithms are illustrated by short programs in ALGOL 60.

9.1.7. The Assembly Language Level

Darden and Heller, "Streamline Your Software Development"
This paper discusses measurements of program performance showing that in many programs a very large fraction of the execution time is accounted for by a very small fraction of the program. This strongly suggests writing programs in a higher-level language, testing them, and rewriting only the critical parts in assembly language, instead of writing everything in assembly language.

Donovan, *Systems Programming*
Pages 59 to 110 contain a highly detailed discussion of how an assembler works, with emphasis on algorithms and data bases used. The book also contains a detailed but clearly written chapter on linkers and loaders. Compile and go loaders, general loaders, absolute loaders, relocating loaders, direct linking loaders, and dynamic linking loaders are all mentioned. Read this before writing your next assembler or linking loader.

Heath and Patel, "How to Write a Universal Cross-Assembler"
The "why" and the "how" of writing a modern assembler, complete with numerous flowcharts of the assembler and the source listing in Basic Plus.

Knuth, *Sorting and Searching*
The definitive work on the subject of sorting and searching. Anything not said here is probably not worth saying. Particularly noteworthy is Knuth's analysis of algorithms, giving best- and worst-case analyses for all algorithms, as well as averages.

Morris, "Scatter Storage Techniques"
A good survey of hash-coding techniques applicable to symbol tables. Several methods for handling collisions are analyzed, and the expected performance for each is derived. The article also considers the implications of virtual memory on hash tables. Several sample programs for entering and retrieving data in hash tables are given.

Presser and White, "Linkers and Loaders"
A tutorial on absolute loaders, relocating loaders, and linking loaders, with emphasis on the latter. The article is highly readable, despite its use of IBM jargon.

9.1.8. Multilevel Machines

Brown, *Software Portability*
    The lecture notes of a course on software portability given by seven experts in the field, with subsequent contributions by several others as well. Macro processors, portable compilers, portable operating systems and portable libraries are among the numerous subjects covered.

Buzen and Gagliardi, "The Evolution of Virtual Machine Architecture"
    An excellent introduction to the concept of a self-virtualizing machine (which the authors call a virtual machine) and how it has evolved. The paper covers virtual machines and emulators, process state mapping, I/O mapping, memory mapping, dual- and single-state architectures, virtual machine faults, and dynamic map composition.

Flynn, "Directions and Issues in Architecture and Language"
    An interesting discussion of where the interface between the compiler and interpreter should be. The arguments are backed up with numerous statistics and examples. The conclusion is that the current interface is too low.

Goldberg, "Architecture of Virtual Machines"
    Third-generation computer systems are all to a greater or lesser degree unsuited for supporting virtual copies of themselves. Their microprograms make no distinction between exceptions and virtual machine faults, and there are problems keeping the shadow page tables accurate, among other difficulties. This article proposes a machine architecture that solves these and other problems in hardware (or in the microprogram).

Myers, *Advances in Computer Architecture*
    In contrast to virtually all other books on computer architecture, this one quickly dispenses with essentially all existing machines as being hopelessly obsolete. It then focuses on experimental high-level machines, most of which were language driven, that is, designed to implement a specific high-level language or group of high-level languages.

Tsichritzis and Bernstein, *Operating Systems*
    A chapter on design methods for multilevel machines. Both the top-down and bottom-up approaches are discussed.

Wilner, "Design of the Burroughs B1700"
    An introduction to the Burroughs B1700, an advanced machine intended as the basis of multilevel hierarchical machines.

Wulf, "Compilers and Computer Architecture"
An experienced compiler writer tells what is wrong with the conventional machine level as an interface between the compiler and the interpreter. He makes a plea for architectures that are regular and orthogonal above all else.

9.1.9. Binary Numbers and Arithmetic

Cody, "Analysis of Proposals for the Floating-Point Standard"
Some time ago, IEEE designed a floating-point architecture that is becoming widespread on smaller machines. Cody discusses the various issues, proposals, and controversies that came up during the standardization process.

Garner, "Number Systems and Arithmetic"
A tutorial on advanced binary arithmetic concepts, including carry propagation, redundant number systems, residue number systems, and nonstandard multiplication and division. Strongly recommended for anyone who thinks he learned everything there is to know about arithmetic in sixth grade.

Knuth, *Seminumerical Algorithms*
A wealth of material about positional number systems, floating-point arithmetic and multiple-precision arithmetic. All algorithms are specified carefully, both in English and in the assembly language of a hypothetical computer called MIX. This material requires and deserves careful study.

Stein and Munro, *Introduction to Machine Arithmetic*
A thorough treatment of computer arithmetic in a general radix. Although the emphasis is primarily on the theory of machine arithmetic, there are also a large number of carefully worked problems and examples illustrating the algorithms covered.

9.2. ALPHABETICAL BIBLIOGRAPHY

ANDERSON, D. A.: "Operating Systems," *Computer*, vol. 14, pp. 69-82, June 1981.

ANDREWS, M.: *Principles of Firmware Engineering in Microprogram Control*. Rockville, Md.: Computer Science Press, 1980.

ARTWICK, B. A.: *Microcomputer Interfacing*. Englewood Cliffs, N.J.: Prentice-Hall, 1980.

BAER, J.-L.: *Computer Systems Architecture*. London: Pitman, 1980.

BIRRELL, A. D., LEVIN, R., NEEDHAM, R. M., and SCHROEDER, M. D.: "Grapevine: An Exercise in Distributed Computing," *Commun. ACM*, vol. 25, pp. 260-274, Apr. 1982.

BLAAUW, G.: *Digital System Implementation*. Englewood Cliffs, N.J.: Prentice-Hall, 1976.

BLAKESLEE, T. R.: *Digital Design with Standard MSI and LSI*. New York: John Wiley, 1979.

BOBERG, R. W.: "Proposed Microcomputer System 796 Bus Standard," *Computer*, vol. 13, pp. 89-105, Oct. 1980.

BORRILL, P. L.: "Microprocessor Bus Structures and Standards," *IEEE Micro*, vol. 1, pp. 84-95, Feb. 1981.

BROWN, P. J.: "The ML/I Macro Processor," *Commun. ACM*, vol. 10, pp. 618-623, Oct. 1967.

BROWN, P. J. (ed.): *Software Portability*. Cambridge: Cambridge University Press, 1977.

BURR, W. E., PARKER, A. C., ALLISON, D. R., COOPER, A. B.,III, and SILIO, C. B., JR.: "A Bus System for the Military Computer Family," *Computer*, vol. 12, pp. 11-25, Apr. 1979.

BUZEN, J. P., and GAGLIARDI, U. O.: "The Evolution of Virtual Machine Architecture," *Proc. NCC*, pp. 291-299, 1973.

CADOW, H.: *OS/360 Job Control Language*. Englewood Cliffs, N.J.: Prentice-Hall, 1970.

CALINGAERT, P.: *Operating System Elements*. Englewood Cliffs, N.J.: Prentice-Hall, 1982.

CHEN, T. C.: "Overlap and Pipeline Processing," in *Introduction to Computer Architecture,* 2nd ed. Chicago: Science Research Associates, 1980.

CHU, Y., and ABRAMS, M.: "Programming Languages and Direct-Execution Computer Architecture," *Computer*, vol. 14, pp. 22-32, July 1981.

CLARK, D. D., POGRAN, K. T., and REED, D. P.: "An Introduction to Local Area Networks," *Proc. IEEE*, vol. 66, pp. 1497-1517, Nov. 1978.

CODY, W. J.: "Analysis of Proposals for the Floating-Point Standard," *Computer*, vol. 14, pp. 63-68, Mar. 1981.

COHEN, D.: "On Holy Wars and a Plea for Peace," *Computer*, vol. 14, pp. 48-54, Oct. 1981.

CORBATO, F. J.: "PL/1 as a Tool for System Programming," *Datamation*, vol. 15, pp. 68-76, May 1969.

CORBATO, F. J., and VYSSOTSKY, V. A.: "Introduction and Overview of the MULTICS System," *Proc. FJCC*, pp. 185-196, 1965.

DALEY, R. C., and NEUMANN, P. G.: "A General Purpose File System for Secondary Storage," *Proc. FJCC*, pp. 213-229, 1965.

DARDEN, S. C., and HELLER, S. B.: "Streamline Your Software Development," *Computer Decisions*, vol. 2, pp. 29-33, Oct. 1970.

DASGUPTA, S.: "The Organization of Microprogram Stores," *Computing Surveys*, vol. 11, pp. 39-65, Mar. 1979.

DENNING, P. J.: "The Working Set Model for Program Behavior," *Commun. ACM*, vol. 11, pp. 323-333, May 1968.

DENNING, P. J.: "Virtual Memory," *Computing Surveys*, vol. 2, pp. 153-189, Sept. 1970.

DIJKSTRA, E. W.: "GOTO Statement Considered Harmful," *Commun. ACM*, vol. 11, pp. 147-148, Mar. 1968a.

DIJKSTRA, E. W.: "The Structure of the 'THE' Multiprogramming System," *Commun. ACM*, vol. 11, pp. 341-346, May 1968b.

DIJKSTRA, E. W.: "Co-operating Sequential Processes," in *Programming Languages*, F. Genuys (ed.). New York: Academic Press, 1968c.

DONOVAN, J. J.: *Systems Programming*. New York: McGraw-Hill, 1972.

ELMQUIST, K. A., FULLMER, H., GUSTAVSON, D. B., and MORROW, G.: "Standard Specification for S-100 Bus Interface Devices," *Computer*, vol. 12, pp. 28-52, July 1979.

FAIRCLOUGH, D. A.: "A Unique Microprocessor Instruction Set," *IEEE Micro*, vol. 2, pp. 8-18, May 1982.

FARBER, D. J., and LARSON, K. C.: "The System Architecture of the Distributed Computer System—The Communications System," *Symp. Computer Networks*, Polytechnic Institute of Brooklyn, Apr. 1972.

FISCHER, W. P.: "Microprocessor Assembly Language Draft Standard," *Computer*, vol. 12, pp. 96-109, Dec. 1979.

FLYNN, M. J.: "Directions and Issues in Architecture and Language," *Computer*, vol. 13, pp. 5-22, Oct. 1980.

FOTHERINGHAM, J.: "Dynamic Storage Allocation in the Atlas Computer Including an Automatic Use of a Backing Store," *Commun. ACM*, vol. 4, pp. 435-436, Oct. 1961.

GARNER, H. L.: ''Number Systems and Arithmetic,'' in *Advances in Computers*. Vol. 6., F. Alt and M. Rubinoff (eds.). New York: Academic Press, 1965, pp. 131-194.

GARSIDE, R. G.: *The Architecture of Digital Computers*. Oxford: Clarendon Press, 1980.

GEAR, C. W.: *Computer Organization and Programming,* 3rd ed. New York: McGraw-Hill, 1980.

GILBERT, R.: "The General-Purpose Interface Bus," *IEEE Micro*, vol. 2, pp. 41-51, Feb. 1982.

GOLDBERG, R. P.: "Architecture of Virtual Machines," *Proc. NCC*, pp. 309-318, 1973.

GRAHAM, R.: "Use of High Level Languages for System Programming," Project MAC Report TM-13, Project MAC, MIT, Sept. 1970.

HAMMING, R. W.: "Error Detecting and Error Correcting Codes," *Bell Syst. Tech. J.*, vol. 29, pp. 147-160, Apr. 1950.

HAMMING, R. W.: *Coding and Information Theory*. Englewood Cliffs, N.J.: Prentice-Hall, 1980.

HEATH, J. R., and PATEL, S. M.: "How to Write a Universal Cross-Assembler," *IEEE Micro*, vol. 1, pp. 45-66, Aug. 1981.

HUFFMAN, D.: "A Method for the Construction of Minimum Redundancy Codes," *Proc. IRE*, vol. 40, pp. 1098-1101, Sept. 1952.

JONES, A. K., CHANSLER, R. J., JR., DURHAM, I., FEILER, P., and SCHWANS, K.: "Software Management of CM*—A Distributed Multiprocessor," *Proc. NCC*, pp. 657-663, 1977.

KAVI, K., BELKHOUCHE, B., BULLARD, E., DELCAMBRE, L., and NEMECEK, S.: "HLL Architectures: Pitfalls and Predilections," *9th Annu. Symp. Computer Arch.*, ACM and IEEE, 1982.

KERNIGHAN, B. W., and MASHEY, J. R.: "The Unix Programming Environment," *Computer*, vol. 14, pp. 12-24, Apr. 1981.

KNUTH, D. E.: "An Empirical Study of FORTRAN Programs," *Software—Practice & Experience*, vol. 1, pp. 105-133, 1971.

KNUTH, D. E.: *The Art of Computer Programming: Sorting and Searching.* Reading, Mass.: Addison-Wesley, 1973.

KNUTH, D. E.: *The Art of Computer Programming: Seminumerical Algorithms,* 2nd ed. Reading, Mass.: Addison-Wesley, 1974.

KNUTH, D. E.: *The Art of Computer Programming: Seminumerical Algorithms,* 2nd ed. Reading, Mass.: Addison-Wesley, 1981.

KUCK, D. J.: "A Survey of Parallel Machine Organization and Programming," *Computing Surveys*, vol. 9, pp. 29-59, Mar. 1977.

LANDSKOV, D., DAVIDSON, S., SHRIVER, B., and MALLET, P. W.: "Local Microcode Compaction Techniques," *Computing Surveys*, vol. 12., pp. 261-294, Sept. 1980.

LIU, M. T.: "Distributed Loop Computer Networks," in *Advances in Computers*, M. C. Yovits (ed.). New York: Academic Press, 1978, pp. 163-221.

LUKASIEWICZ, J.: *Aristotle's Syllogistic,* 2nd ed. Oxford: Oxford University Press, 1958.

MALLACH, E. G.: "Emulator Architecture," *Computer*, vol. 8, pp. 24-32, Aug. 1975.

MCKAY, C. W.: *Digital Circuits.* Englewood Cliffs, N.J.: Prentice-Hall, 1978.

METCALFE, R. M., and BOGGS, D. R.: "Ethernet: Distributed Packet Switching for Local Computer Networks," *Commun. ACM*, vol. 19, pp. 395-404, July 1976.

MORRIS, R.: "Scatter Storage Techniques," *Commun. ACM*, vol. 11, pp. 38-44, Jan. 1968.

MYERS, G. J.: *Advances in Computer Architecture.* New York: John Wiley, 1978.

MYERS, G. J.: *Digital System Design with LSI Bit-Slice Logic.* New York: John Wiley, 1980.

NEEDHAM, R. M.: "System Aspects of the Cambridge Ring," *Proc. Seventh Symp. Oper. Syst. Prin.*, ACM, pp. 82-85, 1979.

NORI, V. AMMANN, U., JENSEN, K., and NAGELI, H.: "The Pascal (P) Compiler Implementation Notes," Institut für Informatik, Eidgen. Tech. Hochschole, Zurich, 1975.

OLESKSY, J. E., and RUTKOWSKI, G. B.: *Microprocessors and Digital Computer Technology.* Englewood Cliffs, N.J.: Prentice-Hall, 1981.

ORGANICK, E.: *The MULTICS System.* Cambridge, Mass.: MIT Press, 1972.

PATTERSON, D. A., and SÉQUIN, C. H.: "RISC I: A Reduced Instruction Set VLSI Computer," *Proc. 8th Annu. Symp. Computer Arch.*, ACM and IEEE, pp. 443–457, 1981.

PATTERSON, D. A., and SEQUIN, C. H.: "RISC I: A Reduced Instruction Set VLSI Computer," *Proc. 8th Annu. Symp. Computer Arch.*, ACM and IEEE, pp. 443-457, 1981.

PEMBERTON, S., and DANIELS, M. C.: *Pascal Implementation: The P4 Compiler*, Chichester, U.K.: Ellis Horwood, 1982.

PETERSON, W. W.: *Error Correcting Codes.* Cambridge., Mass.: MIT Press, 1961.

POOCH, U. W., and CHATTERGY, R.: *Designing Microcomputer Systems*. Rochelle Park, N.J.: Hayden, 1979.

PRESSER, L., and WHITE, J.: "Linkers and Loaders," *Computing Surveys*, vol. 4, pp. 150–167, Sept. 1972.

RITCHIE, D. M., and THOMPSON, K.: "The UNIX Time-Sharing System," *Commun. ACM*, vol. 17, pp. 365-375, July 1974.

ROSIN, R. F.: "Contemporary Concepts of Microprogramming and Emulation," *Computing Surveys*, vol. 1, pp. 197-212, Dec. 1969.

ROSIN, R. F.: "The Significance of Microprogramming," *SIGMICRO Newsletter*, vol. 4, pp. 24-39, Jan. 1974.

SALISBURY, A. B.: *Microprogrammable Computer Architectures*. New York: American Elsevier, 1976.

SHAW, A.: *The Logical Design of Operating Systems*. Englewood Cliffs, N.J.: Prentice-Hall, 1974.

SIEWIOREK, D. P., BELL, C. G., and NEWELL, A.: *Computer Structures: Principles and Examples*. New York: McGraw-Hill, 1981.

SLOAN, M. E.: *Introduction to Minicomputers and Microcomputers*. Reading, Mass.: Addison-Wesley, 1980.

STEIN, M. L., and MUNRO, W. D.: *Introduction to Machine Arithmetic*. Reading, Mass.: Addison-Wesley, 1971.

STRITTER, E., and GUNTER, T.: "A Microprocessor Architecture for a Changing World: The Motorola 68000," *Computer*, vol. 12, pp. 43-52, Feb. 1979.

STRITTER, S., and TREDENNICK, N.: "Microprogrammed Implementation of a Single Chip Microprocessor," *Proc. 11th Annu. Microprogr. Workshop*, ACM and IEEE, pp. 8-16, 1978.

TANENBAUM, A. S.: "A General Purpose Macro Processor as a Poor Man's Compiler-Compiler," *IEEE Trans. Software Eng.*, vol. SE-2, pp. 121-125, June 1976.

TANENBAUM, A. S.: "Implications of Structured Programming for Machine Architecture," *Commun. ACM*, vol. 21, pp. 237-246, Mar. 1978.

TANENBAUM, A. S.: *Computer Networks*. Englewood Cliffs, N.J.: Prentice-Hall, 1981.

TANENBAUM, A. S.: "Network Protocols," *Computing Surveys*, vol. 13, pp. 453-489, Dec. 1981.

TANENBAUM, A. S., VAN STAVEREN, H., KEIZER, E. G., and STEVENSON, J. W.: "A Practical Toolkit for Making Portable Compilers," *Commun. ACM,* vol. 26, 1983.

TANENBAUM, A. S., VAN STAVEREN, H., and STEVENSON, J. W.: "Using Peephole Optimization on Intermediate Code," *ACM Trans. Prog. Lang. Syst.*, vol. 4, pp. 21-26, Jan. 1982.

THOMPSON, K.: "UNIX Implementation," *Bell Syst. Tech. J.*, vol. 57, pp. 1931-1946, July-Aug. 1978.

TOMEK, I.: *Introduction to Computer Organization*. Rockville, Md.: Computer Science Press, 1981.

TSICHRITZIS, D., and BERNSTEIN, P.: *Operating Systems*. New York: Academic Press, 1974.

VAN DER POEL, W. L.: "The Software Crisis, Some Thoughts and Outlooks," *Proc. IFIP Congr. 68*, pp. 334-339, 1968.

WAKERLY, J. F.: *Microcomputer Architecture and Programming.* New York: John Wiley, 1981.

WEITZMAN, C.: *Distributed Micro/Minicomputer Systems.* Englewood Cliffs, N.J.: Prentice-Hall, 1980.

WILNER, W.: "Design of the Burroughs B1700," *Proc. FJCC*, pp. 489-497, 1972.

WITTIE, L. D.: "A Distributed Operating System for a Reconfigurable Network Computer," *Proc. First Int. Conf. Distrib. Computer Syst.*, IEEE, pp. 669-677, 1979.

WORTMAN, D. B.: "A Study of Language Directed Computer Design," Report CSRG-20, University of Toronto, 1972.

WULF, W. A.: "Compilers and Computer Architecture," *Computer*, vol. 14, pp. 41-47, July 1981.

A

BINARY NUMBERS

The arithmetic used by computers differs in some ways from the arithmetic used by people. The most important difference is that computers perform operations on numbers whose precision is finite and fixed. Another difference is that most computers use the binary rather than the decimal system for representing numbers. These topics are the subject of this appendix.

A.1. FINITE PRECISION NUMBERS

While doing arithmetic, one usually gives little thought to the question of how many decimal digits it takes to represent a number. Physicists can calculate that there are 10^{78} electrons in the universe without being bothered by the fact that it requires 79 decimal digits to write that number out in full. Someone calculating the value of a function with pencil and paper who needs the answer to six significant digits simply keeps intermediate results to seven, or eight, or however many are needed. The problem of the paper not being wide enough for seven-digit numbers never arises.

With computers, matters are quite different. On most computers, the amount of memory available for storing a number is fixed at the time that the computer is designed. With a certain amount of effort, the programmer can represent numbers two, or three, or even many times larger than this fixed amount, but doing so does not change the nature of this difficulty. The finite nature of the computer forces us to deal only with numbers that can be represented in a fixed number of digits. We call such numbers **finite-precision numbers**.

In order to study properties of finite-precision numbers, let us examine the set of positive integers representable by three decimal digits, with no decimal point and no sign. This set has exactly 1000 members: 000, 001, 002, 003, ..., 999. With this restriction, it is impossible to express several important sets of numbers, such as:

1. Numbers larger than 999.

2. Negative numbers.

3. Fractions.

4. Irrational numbers.

5. Complex numbers.

One important property of arithmetic on the set of all integers is **closure** with respect to the operations of addition, subtraction, and multiplication. In other words, for every pair of integers i and j, $i + j$, $i - j$, and $i \times j$ are also integers. The set of integers is not closed with respect to division, because there exist values of i and j for which i/j is not expressible as an integer—for example 7/2 and 1/0.

Finite-precision numbers unfortunately are not closed with respect to any of these four basic operations, as shown below, using three-digit decimal numbers as an example:

600 + 600 = 1200	(too large)
003 − 005 = −2	(negative)
050 × 050 = 2500	(too large)
007 / 002 = 3.5	(not an integer)

The violations can be divided into two mutually exclusive classes: operations whose result is larger than the largest number in the set (overflow error) or smaller than the smallest number in the set (underflow error), and operations whose result is neither too large nor too small but is simply not a member of the set. Of the four violations above, the first three are examples of the former, and the fourth is an example of the latter.

Because computers have finite memories and therefore must of necessity perform arithmetic on finite-precision numbers, the results of certain calculations will be, from the point of classical mathematics, just plain wrong. A calculating device that gives the wrong answer even though it is in perfect working condition may appear strange at first but is a logical consequence of its finite nature. Some computers have special hardware that detects overflow errors.

The algebra of finite-precision numbers is different from normal algebra. As an example, consider the associative law:

$$a + (b - c) = (a + b) - c$$

Let us evaluate both sides for $a = 700$, $b = 400$, $c = 300$. To compute the left-hand side, first calculate $(b - c)$, which is 100, and then add this amount to a, yielding 800. To compute the right-hand side first calculate $(a + b)$, which gives an overflow in the finite arithmetic of three-digit integers. The result may depend on the machine being used but it will not be 1100. Subtracting 300 from some number other than 1100 will not yield 800. The associative law does not hold. The order of operations is important.

As another example, consider the distributive law:

$$a \times (b - c) = a \times b - a \times c$$

Let us evaluate both sides for $a = 5$, $b = 210$, $c = 195$. The left-hand side is 5×15, which yields 75. The right-hand side is not 75 because $a \times b$ overflows.

Judging from these examples, one might conclude that although computers are general-purpose devices, their finite nature renders them especially unsuitable for doing arithmetic. This conclusion is, of course, not true but it does serve to illustrate the importance of understanding how computers work and what limitations they have.

A.2. RADIX NUMBER SYSTEMS

An ordinary decimal number with which everyone is familiar consists of a string of decimal digits and, possibly, a decimal point. The general form and its usual interpretation are shown in Fig. A-1. The choice of 10 as the base for exponentiation, called the **radix**, is made because we are using decimal, or base 10, numbers. When dealing with computers, it is frequently convenient to use radices other than 10. The most important radices are 2, 8, and 16. The number systems based on these radices are called **binary**, **octal**, and **hexadecimal** respectively.

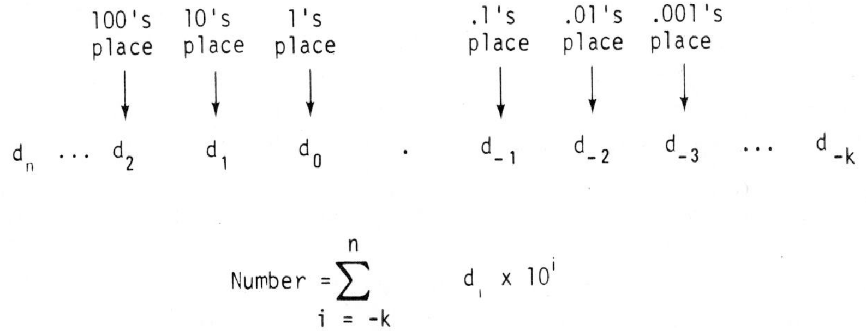

Fig. A-1. The general form of a decimal number.

A radix k number system requires k different symbols to represent the digits 0 to $k - 1$. Decimal numbers are built up from the 10 decimal digits

0 1 2 3 4 5 6 7 8 9

Binary numbers are built up from the two binary digits

0 1

Octal numbers are built up from the eight octal digits

0 1 2 3 4 5 6 7

For hexadecimal numbers, 16 digits are needed. Thus six new symbols are required.
It is conventional to use the uppercase letters A through F for the six digits following
9. Hexadecimal numbers are then built up from the digits

0 1 2 3 4 5 6 7 8 9 A B C D E F

   The expression "binary digit" meaning a 1 or a 0 is usually referred to as a **bit**.
Figure A-2 shows the decimal number 2001 expressed in binary, octal, and hexadecimal form. The number 7B9 is obviously hexadecimal, because the symbol B can
only occur in hexadecimal numbers. However, the number 111 might be in any of
the four number systems discussed. To avoid ambiguity, people use a subscript of 2,
8, 10, or 16 to indicate the radix when it is not obvious from the context.

Binary   1   1   1   1   1   0   1   0   0   0   1

$1{\times}2^{10} + 1{\times}2^9 + 1{\times}2^8 + 1{\times}2^7 + 1{\times}2^6 + 0{\times}2^5 + 1{\times}2^4 + 0{\times}2^3 + 0{\times}2^2 + 0{\times}2^1 + 1{\times}2^0$
1024 + 512 + 256 + 128 + 64 + 0 + 16 + 0 + 0 + 0 + 1

Octal   3   7   2   1

$3{\times}8^3 + 7{\times}8^2 + 2{\times}8^1 + 1{\times}8^0$
1536 + 448 + 16 + 1

Decimal   2   0   0   1

$2{\times}10^3 + 0{\times}10^2 + 0{\times}10^1 + 1{\times}10^0$
2000 + 0 + 0 + 1

Hexadecimal   7   D   1

$7{\times}16^2 + 13{\times}16^1 + 1{\times}16^0$
1792 + 208 + 1

Fig. A-2. The number 2001 in binary, octal, and hexadecimal.

Figure A-3 shows some numbers expressed in all four systems.

A.3. CONVERSION FROM ONE RADIX TO ANOTHER

   Conversion between octal or hexadecimal numbers and binary numbers is easy.
To convert a binary number to octal, divide it into groups of 3 bits, with the 3 bits
immediately to the left (or right) of the decimal point (often called a binary point)

Decimal	Binary	Octal	Hexadecimal
0	0	0	0
1	1	1	1
2	10	2	2
3	11	3	3
4	100	4	4
5	101	5	5
6	110	6	6
7	111	7	7
8	1000	10	8
9	1001	11	9
10	1010	12	A
11	1011	13	B
12	1100	14	C
13	1101	15	D
14	1110	16	E
15	1111	17	F
16	10000	20	10
17	10001	21	11
18	10010	22	12
19	10011	23	13
20	10100	24	14
30	11110	36	1E
40	101000	50	28
50	110010	62	32
60	111100	74	3C
70	1000110	106	46
80	1010000	120	50
90	1011010	132	5A
100	1100100	144	64
200	11001000	310	C8
300	100101100	454	12C
400	110010000	620	190
500	111110100	764	1F4
600	1001011000	1130	258
700	1010111100	1274	2BC
800	1100100000	1440	320
900	1110000100	1604	384
1000	1111101000	1750	3E8
2989	101110101101	5655	BAD

Fig. A-3. Decimal numbers and their binary, octal, and hexadecimal equivalents.

forming one group, the 3 bits immediately to their left, another group, and so on. Each group of 3 bits can be directly converted to a single octal digit, 0 to 7, according to the conversion given in the first lines of Fig. A-3. It may be necessary to add one or two leading or trailing zeros to fill out a group to 3 bits. Conversion from octal to binary is equally easy. Each octal digit is simply replaced by the equivalent three-bit binary number. Hexadecimal to binary conversion is essentially the same as octal to binary except that each hexadecimal digit corresponds to a group of 4 bits instead of 3 bits. Figure A-4 gives some examples of conversions.

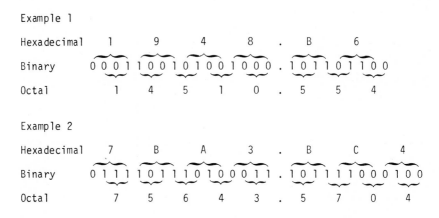

Fig. A-4. Examples of octal to binary and hexadecimal to binary conversion.

Conversion of decimal numbers to binary can be done in two different ways. The first method follows directly from the definition of binary numbers. The largest power of 2 smaller than the number is subtracted from the number. The process is then repeated on the difference. Once the number has been decomposed into powers of 2, the binary number can be assembled with 1s in the bit positions corresponding to powers of 2 used in the decomposition, and 0s elsewhere.

The other method (for integers only) consists of dividing the number by 2. The quotient is written directly beneath the original number and the remainder, 0 or 1, is written next to the quotient. The quotient is then considered and the process repeated until the number 0 has been reached. The result of this process will be two columns of numbers, the quotients and the remainders. The binary number can now be read directly from the remainder column starting at the bottom. Figure A-5 gives an example of decimal-to-binary conversion.

Binary integers can also be converted to decimal in two ways. One method consists of summing up the powers of 2 corresponding to the 1 bits in the number. For example,

$$10110 \text{ is } 2^4 + 2^2 + 2^1 = 16 + 4 + 2 = 22$$

In the other method, the binary number is written vertically, one bit per line, with the leftmost bit on the bottom. The bottom line is called line 1, the one above it line 2, and so on. The decimal number will be built up in a parallel column next to the binary number. Begin by writing a 1 on line 1. The entry on line n consists of two times the entry on line $n - 1$ plus the bit on line n (either 0 or 1). The entry on the top line is the answer. Figure A-6 gives an example of this method of binary-to-decimal conversion.

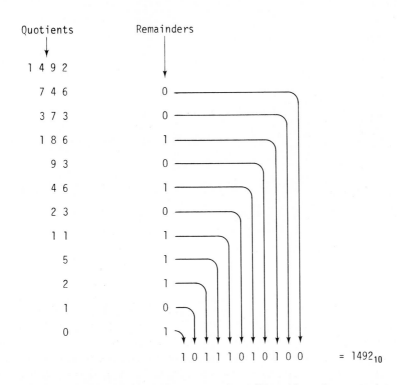

Fig. A-5. Conversion of the decimal number 1492 to binary by successive halving, starting at the top and working downward. For example, 93 divided by 2 yields a quotient of 46 and a remainder of 1, written on the line below it.

Decimal-to-octal and decimal-to-hexadecimal conversion can be accomplished either by first converting to binary and then to the desired system or by subtracting off powers of octal or hexadecimal numbers.

A.4. NEGATIVE BINARY NUMBERS

Four systems for representing negative numbers have been used in digital computers. The first one is called **signed magnitude**. In this system the leftmost bit is the sign bit (0 is + and 1 is −) and the remaining bits hold the absolute magnitude of the number.

The second system, called **one's complement**, also has a sign bit with 0 used for plus and 1 for minus. To negate a number, replace each 1 by a 0 and each 0 by a 1. This holds for the sign bit as well.

The third system, called **two's complement**, also has a sign bit that is 0 for plus and 1 for minus. Negating a number is a two step process. First, each 1 is replaced

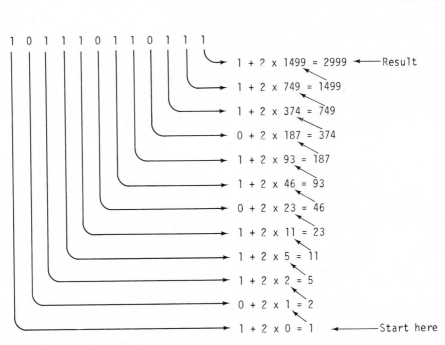

Fig. A-6. Conversion of the binary number 101110110111 to decimal by successive doubling, starting at the bottom. Each line is formed by doubling the one below it and adding the corresponding bit. For example, 749 is twice 374 plus the 1 bit on the same line as 749.

by a 0 and each 0 by a 1, just as in one's complement. Second, 1 is added to the result. Binary addition is the same as decimal addition except that a carry is generated if the sum is greater than 1 rather than greater than 9. For example, converting 6 to two's complement is done in two steps:

```
00000110  (+6)
11111001  (−6 in one's complement)
       1  (add 1)
────────
11111010  (−6 in two's complement)
```

If a carry occurs from the leftmost bit, it is thrown away.

The fourth system, which for m-bit numbers is called **excess** 2^{m-1}, represents a number by storing it as the sum of itself and 2^{m-1}. For example, for 8-bit numbers, $m = 8$, the system is called excess 128 and a number is stored as its true value plus 128. Therefore, -3 becomes $-3 + 128 = 125$, and -3 is represented by the 8-bit binary number for 125 (01111101). The numbers from -128 to $+127$ map onto 0 to 255, all of which are expressible as an 8-bit positive integer. Interestingly enough, this system is identical to two's complement with the sign bit reversed. Figure A-7 gives examples of all four systems.

N (decimal)	N (binary)	-N (signed mag.)	-N (1's compl.)	-N (2's compl.)	-N (excess 128)
0	00000000	10000000	11111111	00000000	10000000
1	00000001	10000001	11111110	11111111	01111111
2	00000010	10000010	11111101	11111110	01111110
3	00000011	10000011	11111100	11111101	01111101
4	00000100	10000100	11111011	11111100	01111100
5	00000101	10000101	11111010	11111011	01111011
6	00000110	10000110	11111001	11111010	01111010
7	00000111	10000111	11111000	11111001	01111001
8	00001000	10001000	11110111	11111000	01111000
9	00001001	10001001	11110110	11110111	01110111
10	00001010	10001010	11110101	11110110	01110110
11	00001011	10001011	11110100	11110101	01110101
12	00001100	10001100	11110011	11110100	01110100
13	00001101	10001101	11110010	11110011	01110011
14	00001110	10001110	11110001	11110010	01110010
15	00001111	10001111	11110000	11110001	01110001
16	00010000	10010000	11101111	11110000	01110000
17	00010001	10010001	11101110	11101111	01101111
18	00010010	10010010	11101101	11101110	01101110
19	00010011	10010011	11101100	11101101	01101101
20	00010100	10010100	11101011	11101100	01101100
30	00011110	10011110	11100001	11100010	01100010
40	00101000	10101000	11010111	11011000	01011000
50	00110010	10110010	11001101	11001110	01001110
60	00111100	10111100	11000011	11000100	01000100
70	01000110	11000110	10111001	10111010	00111010
80	01010000	11010000	10101111	10110000	00110000
90	01011010	11011010	10100101	10100110	00100110
100	01100100	11100100	10011011	10011100	00011100
127	01111111	11111111	10000000	10000001	00000001
128	--------	--------	--------	10000000	00000000

Fig. A-7. Negative 8-bit numbers in four systems.

Both signed magnitude and one's complement have two representations for zero: a plus zero, and a minus zero. This situation is highly undesirable. The two's complement system does not have this problem because the two's complement of plus zero is also plus zero. The two's complement system does, however, have a different singularity. The bit pattern consisting of a 1 followed by all 0s is its own complement. The result is to make the range of positive and negative numbers unsymmetric; there is one negative number with no positive counterpart. The excess notation has the same idiosyncracy.

The reason for these problems is not hard to find: we want an encoding system with two properties:

1. Only one representation for zero.

2. Exactly as many positive numbers as negative numbers.

The problem is that any set of numbers with as many positive as negative numbers and only one zero has an odd number of members, whereas m bits allow an even number of bit patterns. There will always be either one bit pattern too many or one bit pattern too few, no matter what representation is chosen. This extra bit pattern can be used for -0 or a large negative number, or something else but it will always be a nuisance.

A.5. BINARY ARITHMETIC

The addition table for binary numbers is given in Fig. A-8.

Addend	0	0	1	1
Augend	+0	+1	+0	+1
Sum	0	1	1	0
Carry	0	0	0	1

Fig. A-8. The addition table in binary.

Two binary numbers can be added, starting at the rightmost bit and adding the corresponding bits in the addend and the augend. If a carry is generated, it is carried one position to the left, just as in decimal arithmetic. In one's complement arithmetic, a carry generated by the addition of the leftmost bits is added to the rightmost bit. This process is called an end-around carry. In two's complement arithmetic, a carry generated by the addition of the leftmost bits is merely thrown away. Examples of binary arithmetic are shown in Fig. A-9.

Decimal	1's complement	2's complement
10	00001010	00001010
+ (-3)	11111100	11111101
+7	1 00000110	1 00000111
	carry 1	discarded
	00000111	

Fig. A-9. Addition in one's complement and two's complement.

If the addend and the augend are of opposite signs, overflow error cannot occur. If they are of the same sign and the result is of the opposite sign overflow error has occurred and the answer is wrong. In both one's and two's complement arithmetic, overflow occurs if and only if the carry into the sign bit differs from the carry out of the sign bit. Most computers preserve the carry out of the sign bit, but the carry into the sign bit is not visible from the answer. For this reason, a special overflow bit is usually provided.

PROBLEMS

1. Convert the following numbers to binary: 1984, 4000, 8192.

2. What is 1001101001 (binary) in decimal? In octal? In hexadecimal?

3. Which of the following are valid hexadecimal numbers? BED, CAB, DEAD, DECADE, ACCEDED, BAG, DAD.

4. Express the decimal number 100 in all radices from 2 to 9.

5. How many different positive integers can be expressed in k digits using radix r numbers?

6. Most people can only count to 10 on their fingers; however, computer scientists can do better. If you regard each finger as one binary bit, with finger extended as 1 and finger touching palm as 0, how high can you count using both hands? With both hands and both feet? Now use both hands and both feet, with the big toe on your left foot as a sign bit for two's complement numbers. What is the range of expressible numbers?

7. Perform the following calculations on 8-bit two's complement numbers.

00101101	11111111	00000000	11110111
+ 01101111	+ 11111111	- 11111111	- 11110111

8. Repeat the calculation of the preceding problem but now in one's complement.

9. Consider the following addition problems for 3-bit binary numbers in two's complement. For each sum, state:
a. Whether the sign bit of the result is 1.
b. Whether the low-order three bits are 0.
c. Whether an overflow occurred.

000	000	111	100	100
001	111	110	111	100

10. Signed decimal numbers consisting of n digits can be represented in $n + 1$ digits without a sign. Positive numbers have 0 as the leftmost digit. Negative numbers are formed by subtracting each digit from 9. Thus the negative of 014725 is 985274. Such numbers are called nine's complement numbers and are analogous to one's complement binary numbers. Express the following as three-digit nine's complement numbers: 6, -2, 100, -14, -1, 0.

11. Determine the rule for addition of nine's complement numbers and then perform the following additions.

```
   0001        0001        9997        9241
 + 9999      + 9998      + 9996      + 0802
```

12. Ten's complement is analogous to two's complement. A ten's complement negative number is formed by adding 1 to the corresponding nine's complement number, ignoring the carry. What is the rule for ten's complement addition?

13. Construct the multiplication tables for radix 3 numbers.

14. Multiply 0111 and 0011 in binary.

B

FLOATING-POINT NUMBERS

In many calculations the range of numbers used is very large. For example, a calculation in astronomy might involve the mass of the electron, 9×10^{-28} grams, and the mass of the sun, 2×10^{33} grams, a range exceeding 10^{60}. These numbers could be represented by

00000000000000000000000000000000000.00000000000000000000000000009
20000000000000000000000000000000000.00000000000000000000000000000

and all calculations could be carried out keeping 34 digits to the left of the decimal point and 28 places to the right of it. Doing so would allow 62 significant digits in the results. On a binary computer, multiple-precision arithmetic could be used to provide enough significance. However, the mass of the sun is not even known accurately to five significant digits, let alone 62. In fact few measurements of any kind can (or need) be made accurately to 62 significant digits. Although it would be possible to keep all intermediate results to 62 significant digits and then throw away 50 or 60 of them before printing the final results, doing this is wasteful of both CPU time and memory. What is needed is a system for representing numbers in which the range of expressible numbers is independent of the number of significant digits.

One way of separating the range from the precision is to express numbers in the familiar scientific notation

$$n = f \times 10^e$$

where f is called the **fraction**, or **mantissa**, and e is a positive or negative integer called the **exponent**. The computer version of this notation is called **floating point**. Some examples of numbers expressed in this form are

3.14 $\quad$ =0.314 $\times 10^1$ $\quad$ =3.14 $\times 10^0$
0.000001 $\quad$ =0.1 $\quad \times 10^{-5}$ $\quad$ =1.0 $\quad \times 10^{-6}$
1941 $\quad$ =0.1941 $\times 10^4$ $\quad$ =1.941 $\times 10^3$

The range is effectively determined by the number of digits in the exponent and the precision is determined by the number of digits in the fraction. Because there is more than one way to represent a given number, one form is usually chosen as the standard. In order to investigate the properties of this method of representing numbers, consider a representation, R, with a signed three-digit fraction in the range $0.1 \leqslant |f| < 1$ or zero and a signed two-digit exponent. These numbers range in magnitude from $+0.100 \times 10^{-99}$ to $+0.999 \times 10^{+99}$, a span of nearly 199 orders of magnitude, yet only five digits and two signs are needed to store a number.

Floating-point numbers can be used to model the real number system of mathematics, although there are some important differences. Figure B-1 gives a grossly exaggerated schematic of the real number line. The real line is divided up into seven regions:

1. Large negative numbers less than -0.999×10^{99}.

2. Negative numbers between -0.999×10^{99} and -0.100×10^{-99}.

3. Small negative numbers with magnitudes less than 0.100×10^{-99}.

4. Zero.

5. Small positive numbers with magnitudes less than 0.100×10^{-99}.

6. Positive numbers between 0.100×10^{-99} and 0.999×10^{99}.

7. Large positive numbers greater than 0.999×10^{99}.

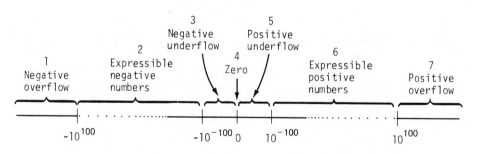

Fig. B-1. The real number line can be divided into seven regions.

One major difference between the set of numbers representable with three fraction and two exponent digits and the real numbers is that the former cannot be used to express any numbers in region 1, 3, 5, or 7. If the result of an arithmetic operation yields a number in regions 1 or 7—for example, $10^{60} \times 10^{60} = 10^{120}$, overflow error will occur and the answer will be incorrect. The reason is due to the finite nature of the representation for numbers and is unavoidable. Similarly, a result in region 3 or 5 cannot be expressed either. This situation is called underflow error. Underflow error is less serious than overflow error, because 0 is often a satisfactory approximation to numbers in regions 3 and 5. A bank balance of 10^{-102} dollars is hardly better than a bank balance of 0.

Another important difference between floating-point numbers and the real numbers is their density. Between any two real numbers, x and y, is another real number, no matter how close x is to y. This property comes from the fact that for any distinct real numbers, x and y, $z = (x + y)/2$ is a real number between them. The real numbers form a continuum.

Floating-point numbers, in contrast, do not form a continuum. Exactly 179,100 positive numbers can be expressed in the five-digit, two-sign system used above, 179,100 negative numbers and 0 (which can be expressed in many ways), for a total of 358,201 numbers. Of the infinite number of real numbers between -10^{+100} and $+0.999 \times 10^{99}$, only 358,201 of them can be specified by this notation. They are symbolized by the dots in Fig. B-1. It is quite possible for the result of a calculation to be one of the other numbers, even though it is in region 2 or 6. For example, $+0.100 \times 10^{3}$ divided by 3 cannot be expressed *exactly* in our system of representation. If the result of a calculation cannot be expressed, in the number representation being used, the obvious thing to do is to use the nearest number that can be expressed. This process is called **rounding**.

The spacing between adjacent expressible numbers is not constant throughout region 2 or 6. The separation between $+0.998 \times 10^{99}$ and $+0.999 \times 10^{99}$ is vastly more than the separation between $+0.998 \times 10^{0}$ and $+0.999 \times 10^{0}$. However, when the separation between a number and its successor is expressed as a percentage of that number, there is no systematic variation throughout region 2 or 6. In other words, the **relative error** introduced by rounding is approximately the same for small numbers as large numbers.

Although the preceding discussion was in terms of a representation system with a three-digit fraction and a two-digit exponent, the conclusions drawn are valid for other representation systems as well. Changing the number of digits in the fraction or exponent merely shifts the boundaries of regions 2 and 6 and changes the number of expressible points in them. Increasing the number of digits in the fraction increases the density of points and therefore improves the accuracy of approximations. Increasing the number of digits in the exponent increases the size of regions 2 and 6 by shrinking regions 1, 3, 5, and 7. Figure B-2 shows the approximate boundaries of region 6 for floating-point decimal numbers for various sizes of fraction and exponent.

A variation of this representation is used in computers. For efficiency, exponentiation is usually to base 2, 4, 8, or 16 rather than 10, in which case the fraction consists of a string of binary, base 4, octal, or hexadecimal digits. If the leftmost of these digits is zero, all the digits can be shifted one place to the left and the exponent

Digits in fraction	Digits in exponent	Lower	Upper
3	1	10^{-12}	10^9
3	2	10^{-102}	10^{99}
3	3	10^{-1002}	10^{999}
3	4	10^{-10002}	10^{9999}
4	1	10^{-13}	10^9
4	2	10^{-103}	10^{99}
4	3	10^{-1003}	10^{999}
4	4	10^{-10003}	10^{9999}
5	1	10^{-14}	10^9
5	2	10^{-104}	10^{99}
5	3	10^{-1004}	10^{999}
5	4	10^{-10004}	10^{9999}
10	3	10^{-1009}	10^{999}
20	3	10^{-1019}	10^{999}

Fig. B-2. The approximate lower and upper bounds of expressible (unnormalized) floating-point decimal numbers.

decreased by 1, without changing the value of the number (barring underflow). A fraction with a nonzero leftmost digit is said to be **normalized**.

Normalized numbers are generally preferable to unnormalized numbers, because there is only one normalized form, whereas there are many unnormalized forms. Examples of normalized floating-point numbers are given in Fig. B-3 for two bases of exponentiation. In these examples a 16-bit fraction (including sign bit) and a 7-bit exponent using excess 64 notation are shown. The radix point is to the left of the leftmost fraction bit—that is, to the right of the sign bit.

PROBLEMS

1. On a PDP-11, single-precision floating-point numbers have a sign bit, excess 128 exponent, and 24 bit fraction. Exponentiation is to the radix 2. The binary point is at the left end of the fraction. Because normalized numbers always have a 1 bit at the left end, this bit is not stored; instead, just the low-order 23 bits of the fraction are stored. Express the number 7/64 in this format.

Example 1: Exponentiation to the base 2

Unnormalized: 0   1010100   0000000000011011

Sign + Excess 64 exponent is 84 − 64 = 20

2^{-1} 2^{-2} 2^{-3} 2^{-4} 2^{-5} 2^{-6} 2^{-7} 2^{-8} 2^{-9} 2^{-10} 2^{-11} 2^{-12} 2^{-13} 2^{-14} 2^{-15} 2^{-16}

Fraction is $1 \times 2^{-12} + 1 \times 2^{-13} + 1 \times 2^{-15} + 1 \times 2^{-16}$

$$= 2^{20}(1 \times 2^{-12} + 1 \times 2^{-13} + 1 \times 2^{-15} + 1 \times 2^{-16}) = 432$$

To normalize, shift the fraction left 11 bits and subtract 11 from the exponent.

Normalized: 0   1001001   1101100000000000

Sign + Excess 64 exponent is 73 − 64 = 9

Fraction is $1 \times 2^{-1} + 1 \times 2^{-2} + 1 \times 2^{-4} + 1 \times 2^{-5}$

$$= 2^{9}(1 \times 2^{-1} + 1 \times 2^{-2} + 1 \times 2^{-4} + 1 \times 2^{-5}) = 432$$

Example 2: Exponentiation to the base 16

Unnormalized: 0   1000101   0000 0000 0001 1011

16^{-1} 0000 16^{-2} 0000 16^{-3} 0001 16^{-4} 1011

Sign + Excess 64 exponent is 69 − 64 = 5

Fraction is $1 \times 16^{-3} + B \times 16^{-4}$

$$= 16^{5}(1 \times 16^{-3} + B \times 16^{-4}) = 432$$

To normalize, shift the fraction left 2 hexadecimal digits, and subtract 2 from the exponent.

Normalized: 0   1000011   0001 1011 0000 0000

16^{-1} 0001 16^{-2} 1011   0000   0000

Sign + Excess 64 exponent is 67 − 64 = 3

Fraction is $1 \times 16^{-1} + B \times 16^{-2}$

$$= 16^{3}(1 \times 16^{-1} + B \times 16^{-2}) = 432$$

Fig. B-3. Examples of normalized floating-point numbers.

2. The format of single-precision floating-point numbers on the 370 has a 7-bit exponent in the excess 64 system, and a fraction containing 24 bits plus a sign bit, with the binary point at the left end of the fraction. The radix for exponentiation is 16. The order of the fields is: sign bit, exponent, fraction. Express the number 7/64 as a normalized number in this system.

3. Express the 32-bit PDP-11 floating-point number 3FE00000 (hexadecimal) as a decimal fraction (see Prob. 1 for format).

4. The following binary floating-point numbers consist of a sign bit, an excess 64 exponent, and a 16 bit fraction. Normalize them:

0 1000000 0001010100000001
0 0111111 0000001111111111
0 1000011 1000000000000000

5. To add two floating-point numbers, you must adjust the exponents (by shifting the fraction) to make them the same. Then you can add the fractions and normalize the result, if need be. Add the IBM 370 floating-point numbers (see Prob. 2): 41C80000 and 3FF00000 (both in hexadecimal) and express the result in hexadecimal.

6. What is the smallest positive single-precision floating-point number on the PDP-11?

7. The Tightwad Computer Company has decided to come out with a machine having 16-bit floating-point numbers. The Model 0.001 has a floating-point format with a sign bit, 7-bit, excess 64 exponent, and 8-bit fraction. The Model 0.002 has a sign bit, 5-bit, excess 16 exponent, and 10-bit fraction. Both use radix 2 exponentiation. What are the smallest and largest positive normalized numbers on both models? About how many decimal digits of precision does each have? Would you buy either one?

8. Write a procedure to add two PDP-11 floating-point numbers. Each number is represented by a 32-element Boolean array.

9. Repeat the preceding problem but now for the 370. Remember to use radix 16 for exponentiation.

INDEX